**OXFORD TEXTBOOKS IN LINGUIS**

*Series editors*
Keith Brown, Eve V. Clark, April McMahon, Jim Miller, and Lesley Milroy

# A Semantic Approach to English Grammar

*Second Edition*

# OXFORD TEXTBOOKS IN LINGUISTICS

General editors: **Keith Brown**, University of Cambridge; **Eve V. Clark**, Stanford University; **April McMahon**, University of Sheffield; **Jim Miller**, University of Auckland; **Lesley Milroy**, University of Michigan

This series provides lively and authoritative introductions to the approaches, methods, and theories associated with the main subfields of linguistics.

# A Semantic Approach to English Grammar

*Second Edition*

## R. M. W. Dixon

OXFORD

UNIVERSITY PRESS

# OXFORD
### UNIVERSITY PRESS

Great Clarendon Street, Oxford OX2 6DP

Oxford University Press is a department of the University of Oxford.
It furthers the University's objective of excellence in research, scholarship,
and education by publishing worldwide in

Oxford New York

Auckland Cape Town Dar es Salaam Hong Kong Karachi
Kuala Lumpur Madrid Melbourne Mexico City Nairobi
New Delhi Shanghai Taipei Toronto

With offices in

Argentina Austria Brazil Chile Czech Republic France Greece
Guatemala Hungary Italy Japan Poland Portugal Singapore
South Korea Switzerland Thailand Turkey Ukraine Vietnam

Oxford is a registered trade mark of Oxford University Press
in the UK and in certain other countries

Published in the United States
by Oxford University Press Inc., New York

First edition published 1991 by Oxford University Press as
*A New Approach to English Grammar on Semantic Principles*
(reprinted five times)

Revised and enlarged second edition first published 2005

British Library Cataloguing in Publication Data
Data available

Library of Congress Cataloging in Publication Data
Data available

Typeset by SPI Publisher Services, Pondicherry, India
Printed in Great Britain on acid-free paper by
Biddles Ltd., King's Lynn, Norfolk

ISBN   978–0–19–928307–1
ISBN   978–0–19–924740–0 (Pbk.)

3 5 7 9 10 8 6 4

# Contents

# List of tables

# How to read this book

This book is, of course, designed to be read from first to last page. But other strategies are possible.

Some of Part A (at least Chapter 1) should be read before Part B. Some of Part B (at least §3.3 and §3.4) should be read before Part C. Within Part B, Chapter 3 should be read first but Chapters 4, 5 and 6 could be covered in any order. Within Part C, the chapters can be read in any order.

A reader familiar with the details of English grammar may prefer to skim over Chapter 2. Note though that §2.7, on complement clauses (which contains some original analysis), should be read before Chapter 7, on complement clauses.

Chapters 4–6 go through every semantic type associated with the class Verb. It is not necessary to study these in detail before looking at some of the discussions of grammatical topics in Part III.

# Preface

When I first became interested in linguistics, in 1961, it was with the idea that it should be possible to put forward the kind of description and explanation which is attempted in this book.

I was thinking about the meanings of words and how their grammatical properties should be a function of those meanings. I thought: there really ought to be a discipline, perhaps called linguistics, which deals with such things. Then I found that there actually was a subject called linguistics. It was not immediately obvious that linguists at the time were interested in the interrelation between meaning and grammar. Nevertheless, I settled down—in a state of some excitement—to study the principles of linguistics. This was at the University of Edinburgh, under the fine tutelage of Michael Halliday and Angus McIntosh.

It seemed to me that if I wished properly to understand the methodology and theory of linguistics, I should try applying it to description of a previously undescribed language. So I went on my first year of fieldwork in North Queensland (in 1963–4) studying Dyirbal. After that I struggled for a while to find a framework in which to present the description of Dyirbal. I decided that the facts of the language were difficult enough to explain without the added impediment of an opaque jargon, and settled for a straightforward description in terms of the categories that linguists have evolved over two thousand years. After publishing long grammars of Dyirbal (1972) and Yidiɲ (1977b)—plus shorter grammars of three other Australian languages that were on the brink of extinction—I wrote a grammar of Boumaa Fijian (1988) and, most recently, a comprehensive description of Jarawara, a language of the Arawá family, spoken deep in the Amazonian jungle of Brazil (2004a). For all of these endeavours—and for typological enquiries on topics including ergativity (1979, 1994) and adjectives (1977a, 2004b)—I followed the time-tested framework of what has recently come to be called basic linguistic theory.

Occasionally during the 1970s and intensively since the 1980s, I have also worked on my native language, English, leading to the first edition of this book (1991) and now this enlarged and revised edition. There are three new chapters: 7, on Tense and Aspect, 10, on Nominalisation and Possession, and 12, on Adverbs and Negation. Also added are §1.5, on Clitics, and §3.2.1, on Comparison of Adjectives. Chapter 2 has been revised and expanded in a number of places; in §2.1, I mention the new 3rd person singular human (non-sex-differentiated) pronoun *they*, and its reflexive *themself*.

This is not a full grammar of English, or even an exhaustive account of certain topics in the grammar of English. It attempts to put forward a semantically oriented framework for grammatical analysis, and to indicate how this framework can be applied. Many detailed studies could be undertaken, building up from the groundwork I have tried to provide.

Over the past thirty or forty years I have read many descriptions of English and of other languages and have learnt something from all of them. I have studied many accounts of bits of English in terms of 'formal theories'—which, like all fashions, bloom and fade with such regularity—and have learnt, in different ways, from that. Formal theories impose a straitjacket on a language: the formal theory states that every language has X, where is X in this language? In contrast, basic linguistic theory seeks to describe a language in its own terms, within a general typological framework. Language is not neat and symmetrical; it is neither necessary nor desirable to pretend that it is, or to insist that everything should be accounted for at every level.

I have benefited from contact with many scholars—through reading their works, correspondence and discussion; the list is too long to include here. This book was greatly helped by the four semesters during which I taught the 'Advanced Syntax' course at the Australian National University, in 1980, 1983, 1986 and 1988. I owe a debt to the students taking these courses—for the ideas they shared, for their scepticism and criticism, and for their opinions about what they would and wouldn't say, and why.

A number of people provided most helpful comments on a draft of the first edition of this book. Thanks are due to Bernard Comrie, Lysbeth Ford, Rodney Huddleston, Timothy Shopen, Anna Wierzbicka and the late James McCawley. A number of scholars sent in helpful comments on the first edition. These include Kim Yun Kyung, who translated the first eight chapters for a Korean edition (Kim 1995). Kate Burridge, Stig Johansson, Gerhard Leitner and Per Lysvåg provided most useful comments on some or all of the three new chapters. Alexandra Aikhenvald read through the whole draft (old and new chapters) and made the most pertinent and helpful comments.

Of all the people I have read and talked to, the late Dwight Bolinger stands out, as someone who has approached the sorts of questions which I consider interesting, in ways that are stimulating and provocative. He found time in a busy schedule (in 1989) to read parts of this book and, of course, provided the most pertinent counter-examples and further generalisations. He also offered a comment that encouraged me more than anything anyone else said: 'After going through Part B (Chapters 3–6) I can appreciate the heroic proportions of your undertaking. It is a conquest of the linguistic wilderness, backpacking your way through—the only way to do what other descriptions, conducted at 20,000 feet using a camera without a focus, have failed to do. The job will take a while, but this is a fine beginning.'

*Research Centre for Linguistic Typology,*
*La Trobe University, Melbourne*
*October 2004*

# List of abbreviations

## For grammatical functions

| | |
|---|---|
| A | transitive subject |
| S | intransitive subject |
| O | transitive object |
| CS | copula subject |
| CC | copula complement |

## Other

| | |
|---|---|
| NP | noun phrase |
| VP | verb phrase |

## In Chapter 12, for adverb positioning

### For sentential adverbs

| | |
|---|---|
| A | After the first word of the auxiliary. If there is no auxiliary then immediately before the verb unless the verb is copula *be*, in which case it follows the copula. |
| F | As final element in the clause. |
| I | As initial element in the clause. |

### For manner adverbs

| | |
|---|---|
| V | Immediately before the verb. |
| O | Immediately after the verb, or verb-plus-object if there is an object. |

# Part A

## Introduction

# 1

# Orientation

This book provides a fresh look at parts of the grammar of English. It pays particular attention to meaning, considering the different sorts of meanings words have, and showing how the varying grammatical behaviours of words are a consequence of their meaning differences.

My 'meaning orientation' stance is a little novel. In addition, some of the topics discussed here (especially in Chapters 13 and 14) are scarcely mentioned in regular grammars of English. It could be said that the present book takes off from the point where most other grammars end.

The reader will not find here any detailed discussion of the irregular inflections of verbs or plural forms of nouns, topics which are covered in standard grammars. A basic knowledge of certain aspects of English grammar is needed for understanding the later part of the book, and these are presented in Chapter 2 (which does include some original analysis).

There are two approaches to the study of language. That followed here considers linguistics to be a kind of natural science. Just as there is a single chemical theory and a single geological theory, so there is a single linguistic theory, which has gradually evolved over more than two thousand years, from the great Sanskrit grammar of Pāṇini and the Greek grammars of Dionysius Thrax and Apollonius Dyscolus to recent grammars by Edward

Sapir and Mary Haas, and contemporary ones by James Matisoff, Nora England, William Foley, Nicholas Evans, and Alexandra Aikhenvald.

The cumulative theory of linguistics as a natural science has recently been called 'basic linguistic theory', simply to distinguish it from the ever-shifting panoply of 'formal theories' (mentioned below). It provides an inclusive framework—covering word classes, main and subordinate clauses, underlying and derived forms, structures, systems, and so on—in terms of which the descriptions of individual languages are cast. There is constant interplay between theory and description. Some unusual aspect of the grammar of a previously undescribed language may lead to a revision or extension of the theory. And theoretical parameters (worked out inductively from examination of the structures of a range of languages) will provide insight into the underlying structure of a newly considered language. In the present volume, theoretical ideas are brought in as they assist the central task, of describing the syntactic and semantic organisation of English.

An alternative approach to language study—not followed here—has come into fashion during the past few decades. This imitates disciplines such as politics, economics, philosophy and literary study in having a number of competing 'theories' (many, but not all, emanating from Chomsky and his former students) each with its own sets of axioms and limited focus of interest; there is typically a rather exotic 'formalism'. In contrast to the cumulative nature of the theory of linguistics as a kind of natural science, 'formal theories' are eclipsing; each is held to be superior to its predecessors and competitors. 'Formal theories' tend to come and go, at the fancy of their practitioners.

A primary dictum of linguistics as a science is due to Ferdinand de Saussure: each language must be studied as a whole system, not individual bits in isolation. Each part has meaning and function and life only with respect to the whole. 'Formal theorists' eschew this most basic principle. They simply select and examine bits of language data (out of the context of the full language to which they belong) in connection with some hypothesis of detail within their 'formal theory'. People working with a 'formal theory' do not attempt to write a complete grammar of a language in terms of their theory. They say that this is not their aim, and in any case each 'formal theory' is so restricted—and so convoluted—that it would not be possible to accomplish it.

In the present volume, the use of jargon and symbolisation has been kept to a minimum on the principle that, in a subject such as scientific linguistics, if something can be explained it should be explainable in simple, everyday language, which any intelligent person can understand. That is not to say that this book can be read through quickly, like a novel. It is a serious, scientific attempt to explain the interrelations of grammar and meaning; the reader is advised to proceed slowly and deliberately, thinking carefully about what is said and often referring back to an earlier discussion (following the cross-references given).

Many modern books on linguistics build up to a grand generalisation, something which attracts attention at the time but is found, on reflection, to be a little over glib, to which many exceptions can be given. Language, as a pattern of human behaviour, does not yield 'laws' like those of Newton or Einstein. It is a complex phenomenon, whose parts intersect in complex ways. But it does have a principled basis and it is the purpose of this book to explore this, demonstrating that a large part of the basis concerns the meanings of words, and of grammatical constructions, and how these interrelate.

## 1.1. Grammar and semantics

A language consists of words and grammar. Grammar itself has two parts:

**Morphology** deals with the structure of words, e.g. the fact that *un-friend-li-ness* consists of four parts (called 'morphemes'), each of which has a meaning, and *laugh-ing* of two morphemes.

If a morpheme is added to a word and yields a word of a different kind this is called a **derivation**, e.g. the formation of adjective *beautiful* from noun *beauty*, noun *decision* from verb *decide*, verb *widen* from adjective *wide*, and verb *untie* from verb *tie*.

If a morpheme just adds some extra element of meaning to a word which is required by the grammar of the language, then it is called an **inflection**, e.g. the verb *kill* inflects for past tense, becoming *killed*, and the noun *horse* inflects for plural number, becoming *horses*.

The second component of grammar, **syntax**, deals with the way in which words are combined together. In English an adjective must come before a noun and an article before the adjective—we can get *the old lion*, which is a noun phrase (or NP). A verb (or a verb phrase, such as *was sleeping*) must in English be preceded by a noun phrase—we get *The old lion was sleeping*, which is a clause.

A sentence may consist of just one clause (it is then called a simple sentence) or it can be a complex sentence, involving several clauses. There may be a main clause and a subordinate clause, joined to it by a conjunction, which can indicate reason (*The old lion was sleeping because he was exhausted*) or temporal sequence (*The old lion was sleeping after eating the hunter*) and so on.

Underlying both words and grammar there is **semantics**, the organisation of meaning. A word can have two sorts of meaning. First, it may have 'reference' to the world: *red* describes the colour of blood; *chair* refers to a piece of furniture, with legs and a back, on which a human being may comfortably sit. Secondly, a word has 'sense', which determines its semantic relation to other words, e.g. *narrow* is the opposite (more specifically: the antonym) of *wide*, and *crimson* refers to a colour that is a special sort of red (we say that *crimson* is a hyponym of *red*).

Every morpheme has a meaning. The ending *-er*, added to a verb, may derive a noun which refers either to the agent (e.g. *baker*) or else to an instrument intended for the activity (e.g. *mower*). Some morphemes have different meanings with different kinds of word: *un-* indicates an opposite quality with an adjective (e.g. *kind*, *unkind*), but a reverse action with a verb (*tie*, *untie*).

Meaning is also associated with the way in which words are combined to make phrases, clauses and sentences. Compare *The dog bit the postman* and *The postman bit the dog*, which involve the same word meanings but quite different sentence meanings because of the different syntactic arrangements.

As language is used, meaning is both the beginning and the end point. A speaker has some message in mind, and then chooses words with suitable meanings and puts them together in appropriate grammatical constructions; all these have established phonetic forms, which motivate how one speaks. A listener will receive the sound waves, decode them, and—if the act of communication is successful—understand the speaker's message.

The study of language must surely pay close attention to meaning. We consider the meanings of words, and their grammatical properties, and see how these interrelate. When a speaker of a language encounters a new word they may first of all learn its meaning, and will then have a fair idea of the morphological and syntactic possibilities. Or they may first of all learn something of how to use the word grammatically, and this will help them to work out its meaning.

If a child or adult learner hears the word *boulder* for the first time and discovers that it refers to a large rock, they will know (from analogy with *pebble, rock, stone*) that it must be able to take the plural ending -*s*, and that it will probably not take the ending -*en* (which occurs in *widen, blacken*).

Suppose that the verb *begin* is first encountered in a sentence like *He'll soon begin to understand grammar*; that is, the verb is followed by a clause introduced by *to*. Other verbs have this grammatical property, e.g. *He started to read my book, He hopes to finish it*. But the meaning of *begin* is similar to that of *start*, which is why it is scarcely surprising that it can be followed by a clause whose verb ends in -*ing* (*I began cooking dinner an hour ago*) just as *start* can (*I started writing my thesis yesterday*). And the meaning of *begin* is different from that of *hope*, which is why it should not be surprising that *begin* cannot be followed by a clause introduced by *that*, in the way that *hope* can (e.g. *He hopes that he will finish it*).

There is, as we have said, a principled interaction between the meaning of a word and its grammatical properties. Once a learner knows the meaning and grammatical behaviour of most of the words in a language, then from the meaning of a new word they can infer its likely grammatical possibilities; or, from observing the grammatical use of a new word, they may be able to infer a good deal about what it means.

## 1.2. Semantic types and grammatical word classes

There are many thousands of words in a language, each with a meaning; some meaning differences are large, others small. The words can be grouped together in a natural way into large classes that have a common meaning component. I will refer to these as **semantic types**. Verbs *begin, start, commence, finish, cease, stop, continue* and a few others all make up one type. (Rather than manufacture some high-sounding label for a type, I generally name it after one of its more important members—calling this the BEGINNING type.) Adjectives such as *big, broad, short, shallow* comprise the DIMENSION type. And so on, for forty to fifty more types, which between them cover the whole of the vocabulary of a language.

At the level of semantics words can be arranged in semantic types, with a common meaning element. At the level of grammar, they can be arranged in **word classes** (traditionally called 'parts of speech'), with common morphological and syntactic properties.

Languages differ in the weightings they assign to different parts of grammar. Some languages have a simple morphology but make up for this by having complex rules for the ways in which words are combined. Other languages have long words, typically consisting of many morphemes, but a fairly straightforward syntax. For every language we can recognise word classes, sets of words that have the same grammatical properties, although the nature of these properties will vary, depending on the grammatical profile of the language.

There are two sorts of word classes—major and minor. The minor classes have limited membership and cannot readily be added to. For instance, there are just seven Personal Pronouns in English (*me, us, you, him, her, it, them*—see §2.1); new pronouns do not get coined in a hurry. (As a language evolves some pronouns do disappear and others evolve, but this is a slow and natural process. Old English had *thou* for second person singular; its context of use became more and more restricted and it was finally replaced by *you*, which was originally used just for second person plural.) Most minor classes do not have any independent referential meaning (they do not correspond to any object or quality or activity) but serve just to modify words from the major classes, and link them together into phrases, clauses and sentences. Articles (*a, the,* etc.) and Linkers (*and, because, after,* and so on) are minor classes in English, whose functions and meanings should be fully covered within a comprehensive grammar of the language.

Then there are major word classes—such as Noun, Verb and Adjective— which have a large and potentially unlimited membership. It is impossible to give an exhaustive list of the many thousands of nouns, since new ones are being coined all the time (and others will gradually be dropping out of use). Two words that belong to the same class may have almost exactly the same grammatical properties (*monkey* and *baboon,* for instance, or *black* and *red*) and will only be distinguishable through definitions in a dictionary.

For every language a number of major word classes can be recognised, on internal grammatical criteria. Latin has one class (which we can call A) each member of which inflects for case and number, another (B) showing inflection for case, number and gender, and a third (C) whose members inflect for tense, aspect, mood, person and number. Note that it is possible to give entirely morphological criteria for the major word classes in Latin. But English is much less rich morphologically and here the criteria must mingle morphological and syntactic properties. One major word class in English (which we can call X) can have the inflection -*ed* (or some variant) on virtually every member. A word belonging to a second class (Y) may be immediately preceded by an article and does not need to be followed by any other word. Members of a third open class (Z) may be immediately preceded by an article and must then normally be followed by a word from class Y.

We can make cross-language identification between classes A and Y, calling these Noun, between B and Z, calling them Adjective, and between C and X, calling them Verb. The identification is not because of any detailed grammatical similarity (the criteria employed for recognising word classes in the two languages being rather different) but because the classes show semantic congruence. That is, most nouns in Latin would be translated by a noun in English, and vice versa. (There are just a few exceptions—where English has a noun *hunger* there is a verb in Latin, *ēsurio* 'to be hungry'. Interestingly, English has a derived adjective *hungry*, formed from the noun, and Latin also has an adjective *ēsuriens* 'hungry', derived from the verb.)

There is a relationship between semantic types and grammatical word classes. Each major word class is essentially a grouping together of semantic types. The types are related to classes in similar (but not identical) ways in different languages. The Noun class always includes words with CONCRETE reference (*house*, *foot*, *grass*, *star*, *fire*, *hill*, *boy*, *city*, etc.). It usually also includes KIN terms, but in some languages these words belong to the Verb class (after all, *John is Tom's father* indicates a relationship between John and Tom, comparable to *John employs Tom*).

Verbs have different grammatical properties from language to language but there is always a major class Verb, which includes words referring to MOTION (*run*, *carry*, etc.), REST (*sit*, *put*), AFFECT (*hit*, *cut*, *burn*), ATTENTION (*see*, *hear*), GIVING and SPEAKING.

Many semantic types belong to the same word class in every language. But for others there is quite a bit of variation. Words to do with LIKING (*love*, *loathe*, *prefer*, etc.), for instance, belong to the Verb class in some languages, to the Adjective class in other languages, and even to the Noun class in a few languages.

## 1.3. Semantic roles and syntactic relations

A verb is the centre of a clause. A verb may refer to some activity and there must be a number of participants who have roles in that activity (e.g.

*Sinbad carried the old man*); or a verb may refer to a state, and there must be a participant to experience the state (e.g. *My leg aches*).

A set of verbs is grouped together as one semantic type partly because they require the same set of participant roles. All GIVING verbs require a Donor, a Gift and a Recipient, as in *John gave a bouquet to Mary, Jane lent the Saab to Bill*, or *The Women's Institutes supplied the soldiers with socks*. All ATTENTION verbs take a Perceiver and an Impression (that which is seen or heard), as in *I heard the crash, I witnessed the accident, I recognised the driver's face*. AFFECT verbs are likely to involve an Agent, a Target, and something that is manipulated by the Agent to come into contact with the Target (which I call the Manip). A Manip can always be stated, although it often does not have to be, e.g. *John rubbed the glass* (*with a soft cloth*), *Mary sliced the tomato* (*with her new knife*), *Tom punched Bill* (*with his left fist*).

We are here working at the semantic level, and it should be stressed that each type has a quite distinct set of roles. There is nothing in common between Gift (that which is transferred from one owner to another) and Impression (an object or activity that is seen or heard), or Perceiver (a person who receives visual or auditory sense impressions) and Agent (a person who wields a Manip to come into contact with a Target), and so on.

There are about thirty semantic types associated with the Verb class. Some verbs, such as those in the GIVING and AFFECT types, have three semantic roles. Some, like ATTENTION, have just two. And some have just one (CORPOREAL verbs like *breathe*, and MOTION verbs like *fall*). Altogether, it is necessary to recognise forty or fifty semantic roles.

Turning now to syntax, we find that every language has a limited number of syntactic relations. Subject and Object are probably universal relations, which apply to every language. But just as the criteria for the major word classes Noun and Verb differ from language to language, so do the ways in which syntactic relations are marked. In Latin, for instance, the Subject occurs in nominative case (e.g. *domin-us* 'master-NOMINATIVE') and the object in accusative case (e.g. *serv-um* 'slave-ACCUSATIVE'). Words can occur in many different orders in a clause in Latin, so that *Dominus servum videt, Servum videt dominus, Videt dominus servum*, etc. all mean 'The master sees the slave'. In English, nouns have no case inflection and grammatical relations are shown primarily by word order, Subject before the verb and Object after it.

The roles of each type, at the semantic level, are mapped onto syntactic relations, at the grammatical level. For ATTENTION verbs, for instance, the Perceiver is grammatical Subject and the Impression is marked as Object.

There are quite often several different ways in which semantic roles may be associated with grammatical relations. With the GIVING type either the Gift may be Object, as in *Jane lent the Saab to Bill*, or the Recipient may be, as in *Jane lent Bill the Saab*; for both of these clauses the Donor is Subject. It is also possible to have Recipient as Subject, and then a different verb is used: *Bill borrowed the Saab from Jane*. *Borrow* is the semantic converse of *lend*; both verbs belong to the GIVING type and involve the same three semantic roles.

For AFFECT verbs the Agent is usually the Subject and the Target the Object, with the Manip marked by a preposition such as *with*—*John hit the pig with his stick*. But we can have the Manip in Object slot (this often carries an implication that the Manip is less strong than the Target, and likely to be more affected by the impact)—*John hit his stick against the lamp post*. Or, as a third alternative, the Manip can be placed in Subject relation—*John's stick hit Mary* (*when he was swinging it as she walked by, unnoticed by him*); use of this construction type may be intended to imply that John was not responsible for any injury inflicted.

Verbs fall into two broad subclasses—those that require only one role (intransitive verbs) and those which require two or more roles (transitive verbs). There is considerable difference between intransitive subject and transitive subject. We will need to refer a good deal to these relations, so it will be useful to employ abbreviatory letters for them, and for object:

S—intransitive subject
A—transitive subject
O—transitive object

If a verb has only one role, at the semantic level, then it must be mapped onto S relation, at the syntactic level. Some of the roles in S slot can control the activity in which they are involved (e.g. *walk*, *speak*) but other S roles exercise no control (e.g. *break*, *die*, *grow*).

If a verb has two or more roles, one will be mapped onto A and another onto O. It is the role which is most relevant for the success of the activity which is put in A relation; compare *Bill tried to borrow the Saab from Jane* with *Jane tried to lend the Saab to Bill*. And it is the non-A role which is regarded as most salient for the activity (often, the role which is most affected by the activity) which is put into O relation—compare *Mary cut the cake into slices* with *Mary cut slices off the cake.* (There is further discussion of these points beginning in §3.3.1.)

There is a subset of transitive verbs which require a further argument (sometimes called E, for extension to the core). The extended transitive (or ditransitive) verbs in English include *give*, *show* and also *put*. (One cannot say just *\*I put the teapot*, it is necessary to specify where it was put, e.g. *on the table* or *here*.)

A number of verbs have dual transitivity; that is, they can be used both transitively and intransitively. These 'ambitransitive' (or 'labile') verbs fall into two types. Some ambitransitives identify O in transitive with S in intransitive use, as in *John* (A) *broke the glass* (O) and *The glass* (S) *broke*. Others identify A with S, as in *Mary* (A) *has eaten lunch* (O) and *Mary* (S) *has eaten*. Verbs with dual transitivity are discussed in some detail in §9.3.

Besides the major intransitive and transitive clause types, there is a minor but important type, copula clause. This involves two further grammatical relations:

CS—copula subject
CC—copula complement

In English, the CS has similar properties to S and A; however, in some languages CS is like S and unlike A, and in at least one language it is like A and unlike S. What follows the copula verb (generally *be* or *become*) is the CC; for example, the CC is enclosed in brackets in *My son is* [*a doctor*], *You are* [*generous*], *The dog is* [*in the garden*]; this is further discussed in §2.4. It is important to note that the CC is a type of noun phrase in grammatical relation with the (copula) predicate, similar to S, A, O and CS. A Copula Complement has sometimes been described as a 'nominal predicate'; this is not a useful designation, and can be highly confusing.

The core syntactic relations are Subject, Object and Copula Complement. Other, peripheral relations are in English marked by a preposition—these can refer to a place or time setting (*in the morning*, *at the races*) or to some additional participant (*for Mary*, *with a hammer*).

## 1.4. The approach followed

Having established the theoretical framework for this study—in terms of semantic types, semantic roles, their mapping onto syntactic relations, and so on—I worked inductively, examining the semantic and syntactic properties of a large number of individual verbs, and gradually inducing generalisations from these.

I began with a list of the 2,000 most commonly used words in English (in West 1953) and looked in detail at all those which can function as verbs (about 900 in all). Each verb was taken separately, and its semantic and syntactic characteristics investigated. The verbs were grouped into types—on the basis of semantic and syntactic similarities—and the semantic and syntactic profiles of each type were then studied. In this way—proceeding from the particular to the general—I worked out a pan-language classification of complement clauses, in Chapter 8; of transitivity, in Chapter 9; and so on.

The present volume should be regarded as the first attempt to follow through a new approach to grammatical description and explanation. It is essentially programmatic, providing a broad outline of the semantic types, and the ways in which their meanings condition their syntactic properties.

The reader will not find, in the chapters that follow, a fully articulated grammar of English from a semantic viewpoint, with the meaning of every important verb discussed in appropriate detail, and each syntactic construction dealt with exhaustively. Such a study would fill a dozen or more volumes of this size. Rather, I try to provide the parameters in terms of which more detailed studies—of individual semantic types, and of individual constructions—may be carried out. This book aims to lay a foundation, upon which elegant edifices of semantico-syntactic description and explanation may be constructed.

Studying syntax in close conjunction with semantics, and in an inductive manner, differs from the approach followed by many modern linguists. It is most common to begin with syntax (looking for 'semantic interpretation' at a late stage, if at all) and also to begin with putative generalisations, later looking to see if there might be any counter-examples to them.

I noted above that there is a many-to-one mapping between semantic types and grammatical word classes, and also between semantic roles and syntactic relations. Textbooks of grammar will typically note that both *hope* and *believe* accept a THAT complement in the O slot (*Susan hopes that she will win the race, Susan believes that she will win the race*) and then express surprise that only *hope* takes a TO complement clause in which the subject is not stated but is understood to be the same as the subject of the main verb (*Susan hopes to win the race*, but not *\*Susan believes to win the* *race*). They appear to begin with the premiss that if two words share some grammatical properties then they might well be expected to share them all. Linguists who argue in this way generally pay only perfunctory attention to meaning.

A more rewarding approach is to commence with consideration of semantic types. *Believe* belongs to the THINKING type, together with *think*, *reflect*, *wonder*, *doubt*, all of which take THAT complements, but not TO complements of the type illustrated here. *Hope* can be semantically grouped (in the WANTING type) with *dread*, *desire* and *wish*, all of which take both THAT complements and also TO complements (with omission of a subject that is identical to the subject of the main verb).

Although there are important differences—as just illustrated—my approach does of course have many points of similarity with the work of other linguists. I have tried to build on all previous work (and add to it) rather than to ignore the insights of other scholars and strike off in some idiosyncratic direction of my own.

One idea that has been taken from the Greek tradition (being also used in the early 'transformational theory' of Chomsky), and adapted to the needs of the present study, is the usefulness of recognising 'underlying forms', and then general conventions for omitting or rearranging parts of them in specifiable circumstances—see §§2.13–14. (In fact, I go a good deal further than many linguists along this path, and am consequently able to explain things that others have dismissed as perverse irregularities.)

To mention one example, there are a number of verbs in English which must take a preposition and a following NP, e.g. *decide on*, *rely on*, *hope for*, *refer to*, *object to*. This NP behaves like a direct object (e.g. it may become passive subject). I suggest that *decide on*, *hope for*, and the like are each a transitive verb, involving an inherent preposition. There then appears to be a general rule of English syntax stating that a preposition must be omitted when it is immediately followed by one of the complementisers *that*, *to* and *for*. Compare (1)–(2) with (3)–(4):

(1)   *Everyone in the office hoped for an English victory*
(2)   *They decided on the order of precedence*

Here there is an NP in O slot, and the prepositions *for* and *on* are retained.

(3)   *Everyone in the office hoped that England would win*
(4)   *They decided that Mary should lead the parade*

Here the O slot is filled by a THAT complement clause, before which *for* and *on* are omitted. The fact that there *is* an underlying preposition in (3) and (4) is shown under passivisation. The THAT clause, as object, is moved to the front of the sentence to become passive subject and the preposition again appears as the last part of the verb:

(5)   *That England would win was hoped for*
(6)   *That Mary should lead the parade was decided (on)*

But note that a THAT complement clause in subject position is typically extraposed to the end of the sentence, with *it* then occupying the subject slot. When this happens the THAT clause again follows the inherent preposition of the verb, which is omitted:

(7)   *It was hoped that England would win*
(8)   *It was decided that Mary should lead the parade*

There are fashions and fads in linguistic explanation. At one time it was all the rage to talk of underlying forms and deep structures and ways in which surface forms and structures could be derived from these. Nowadays some scholars are reluctant to work in such terms. My explanations in terms of underlying forms and structures could perfectly well be restated as alternations between two possibilities—saying that *hope for* is used in certain environments and *hope* in other, complementary environments, for instance, without suggesting that *hope* is derived by prepositional omission from *hope for*; and similarly in other cases. This is essentially a matter of 'terminology', carrying no differences in descriptive or explanatory power. The approach I adopt involves shorter statements and seems pedagogically more effective; but nothing else hangs on it.

There is one respect in which I differ from the early practitioners of Chomsky's 'transformational grammar'. They might say that *I believed him to be mad* has a 'deep structure' something like [*I believed* [*it* [*he is mad*]]] with the third person singular (3sg) pronoun as subject of *be mad*, but after a 'raising' transformation has been applied the 3sg pronoun is now the object of *believe*. I suggest that the 3sg pronoun bears two simultaneous syntactic relations, as object of *believe* and as subject of *be mad* (even though it is morphologically encoded as the unmarked and object form *him*—see §2.1).

I have tried to make this book consistent and self-sufficient. In particular, I have *not* ventured to recapitulate every previous attempt to deal with the syntactic questions I consider, and to criticise aspects of these before presenting my own solution (which is, in most cases, partly based on earlier work and partly original). To have done this would have made the book two or three times as long and much less easy to read. There are references to the relevant literature at the end of most chapters.

Finally, let it be stressed that I am describing educated British English—essentially my own dialect of it (which is based on what I learnt as a child in Nottingham, slightly modified by several decades of residence in Australia). I am fully aware that other dialects, such as American English, differ markedly—more so concerning the topics discussed here (e.g. the HAVE A construction in Chapter 14) than concerning the topics dealt with in traditional grammars. These differences should not affect the broad sweep of conclusions reached in this book, only their detailed articulation. It would be an interesting and rewarding task to investigate dialect differences in terms of the framework adopted here; this remains a job for the future.

## 1.5. Words and clitics

A difficulty associated with describing English is that the orthography relates not to the present-day language, but to what it was like some centuries ago; for example, *knee* used to be pronounced with an initial *k*. One way in which how the language is written may mislead concerns word spaces. Sometimes, what is written as a word is not pronounced with separate stress (as a word must be), but is rather a clitic. This is a syllable, generally with a reduced vowel, which is attached to a preceding word (it is then an enclitic) or to a following word (a proclitic).

About sixty of the most common grammatical elements have two forms. They can carry stress and then function as an independent word; for example, *and* can be pronounced /ǽnd/, as in /kǽts ǽnd dɔ́gz/, *cats AND dogs* (with stress on the *and*). But *and* typically reduces to /ən=/, which is then a proclitic to the following word, as in /kǽts ən=dɔ́gz/, *cats and dogs* ('=' indicates a clitic boundary). Indeed, in some places (New Zealand is a prime example) people may write this as *cats 'n' dogs*. But generally, the conjunction is written *and*, whether pronounced as /ǽnd/or as /ən=/.

Most clitics include the central vowel ə, called schwa. For example, preposition *to* has stressed form /túː/ but reduces to proclitic /tə=/ before a consonant, as in /tə=pǽris/, *to Paris*; definite article *the* has stressed form / ðíː/ but reduces to proclitic /ðə=/ before a consonant, as in /ðə=mǽn/, *the man*; modal verb *would* has stressed form /wúd/ but can reduce to enclitic /=wəd/, as in /híː=wəd góu/, *He would go*.

The grammatical elements which can be clitics are as follows:

(1)  Nominal determiners *a*, *an*, *the* and *some* can be proclitics.

(2)  Eight monosyllabic prepositions are generally proclitics—*for*, *of*, *to*, *at*, *from*, *till*, *than* and *as* (and *by* is sometimes a proclitic). Note that other monosyllabic prepositions are never clitics; these include, *in*, *on*, *up*, *through*.

(3)  Conjunctions *and*, *but*, *or* and *nor* are typically proclitics, as is relator *that* when it introduces a relative clause or a complement clause (but not *that* when it is a demonstrative).

(4)  Possessor modifying pronouns are often proclitics—*your*, *his*, *her*, *its*, *our*, *their* and *my*. (Pronouns are listed in Table 2.1.)

(5)  Some series II (subject) pronouns may be proclitics—*she*, *he*, *we*, *it*, and *you*.

(6)  Series I pronouns can be enclitics when following a verb or preposition (in stressed form)—*me*, *you*, *him*, *her*, *it*, *us* and *them*. For instance /wǽtʃ=im/, *Watch him!*

(7)  A number of auxiliary and copula verb forms can be enclitics—*is*, *am*, *was*, *were*, *has*, *have*, *had*, *will*, *would*, *shall*, *should*, *can*, *could* and *must*.

A few auxiliaries can be proclitics—*be*, *been* and (just in interrogative use) *do*. For example /də=wíː góu nóu/, *Do we go now?*

The behaviour of the verb *are*, /áː(r)/ is fascinating. It becomes an enclitic /=ə(r)/ after a pronoun as subject, as in /ðéi=ə kʌ́miŋ/, *They're coming*. And it becomes a proclitic /ə(r)=/ to the following word when the subject is not a pronoun, as in /ðə=bɔ́iz ə=klévə/, *The boys are clever*.

(8)  *There*, /ðέə(r)/, can become a proclitic /ðə(r)=/ when in subject function before a copula in stressed form, as in /ðər=íz ən=ǽnt ðέə/, *There IS an ant there*.

(9)  The negator *not*, /nɔ́t/, can take on enclitic form /=nt/, or be reduced further to /=n/. This is discussed in §12.11.

There are portions of the grammar which appear to be without explanation when considered in terms of the conventional orthography. But, once the role of clitics is acknowledged, there is a simple and natural explanation. One example of this concerns phrasal verbs. One can say either *The police brought the criminal in* or *The police brought in the criminal*, with *in* either following or preceding the O NP *the criminal*. However, when the O is a pronoun, the preposition can only follow it; one can say *The police brought him in*, but not *\*The police brought in him*. §9.2.2 provides an explanation for this, in terms of the clitic nature of series I pronouns and of some prepositions.

## Notes to Chapter 1

The grammars referred to at the beginning of this chapter are Sapir (1922, 1930), Haas (1940), Matisoff (1973), England (1983), Foley (1991), Evans (1995) and Aikhenvald (2003). I have also attempted to apply basic linguistic theory in my own grammars—Dixon (1972, 1977b, 1988, 2004a).

The 'semantic orientation' approach followed here has a close affinity with the work of Apollonius Dyscolus (see Householder 1981).

§1.2. An example of a language in which KIN terms belong to the Verb class is Yuma (e.g. Halpern 1942).

§1.3. There is an important difference between my semantic roles and the 'cases' of Fillmore (1968) or the 'theta-roles' of some recent formal theories (see chapter 7 of Radford 1988 and references therein). A single set of 'theta-roles' or 'cases' is set up for a given language (or for all languages) to cover all semantic types within that language. In contrast, I recognise a *separate* set of semantic roles for *each* semantic type in a language; semantic roles belonging to different types are related together *only* through being mapped onto the same syntactic relation.

Discussion of the basic syntactic relations S, A and O is in Dixon (1994). The discussion is extended to copula clauses, and the relations CS and CC, in the first part of Dixon (2002).

§1.4. The *hope/believe* example is from Perlmutter and Soames (1979: 111), which is an excellent textbook of its kind.

Generative grammarians have pointed out that *hope* takes a THAT object complement clause (*They hope that a solution will be found*) but this does not have a passive (i.e. *\*That a solution will be found is hoped* is not grammatical) although it does have a passive when the complement is extraposed (*It is hoped that a solution will be found*)—Jacobson (1982: 65–6). I suggest, instead, that the underlying form is *hope for* (including an inherent preposition) and that this transitive verb does have a normal passive (as in *That a better solution would be found was earnestly hoped for*). It is just that *for* drops when it would be immediately followed by *that*, in consequence of a general syntactic rule for English, given in §1.4 (see also Bolinger 1975).

Kiparsky and Kiparsky (1970: 160) say that 'after prepositions infinitives are automatically converted to gerunds, e.g. *I decided to go* vs. *decided on going*'. I prefer to take the basic form of the verb as *decide on* and say that it can take a TO or an ING complement clause, with a difference in meaning; and to further say that the preposition *on* drops before *to* by an automatic rule of English syntax.

§1.5. There is full discussion of clitics in English in Dixon (forthcoming).

# 2

# Grammatical sketch

This chapter outlines some of the main points of English syntax which are necessary for an understanding of later chapters (it does not go into exhaustive detail on any issue).

On a fair number of analytical issues there is currently disagreement between grammarians; only some of the disagreements are mentioned here. In a book of this size it would be impracticable to discuss all alternative proposals. What I have tried to do is provide a single, internally consistent view of the syntax of English.

## 2.1. Pronouns

The pronoun system of English, at the beginning of the twenty-first century, is shown in Table 2.1. As mentioned in §1.5, pronouns in series I are likely to reduce to enclitics, while series II and possessor modifier forms are likely to reduce to proclitics.

**Table 2.1.** *Pronoun system*

|  |  | SERIES I | SERIES II | POSSESSOR AS MODIFIER | POSSESSOR AS NP HEAD | REFLEXIVE |
|---|---|---|---|---|---|---|
| 1sg |  | *me* | *I* | *my* | *mine* | *myself* |
| 2sg |  | *you* | *you* | *your* | *yours* | *yourself* |
| 3sg | masculine | *him* | *he* | *his* | *his* | *himself* |
|  | feminine | *her* | *she* | *her* | *hers* | *herself* |
|  | human | *them* | *they* | *their* | *theirs* | *themself* |
|  | neuter | *it* | *it* | *it* | *its* | *itself* |
| 1pl |  | *us* | *we* | *our* | *ours* | *ourselves* |
| 2pl |  | *you* | *you* | *yours* | *yours* | *yourselves* |
| 3pl |  | *them* | *they* | *their* | *theirs* | *themselves* |

In an earlier stage of English the function of an NP in a clause was shown by its case ending—nominative for subject, and accusative for object; there was then considerable freedom of word order. The case endings on nouns and adjectives have been lost and in modern English the function of an NP is generally shown by its place in order—subject before and object after the predicate in a simple clause. However, the pronouns—except for *you* and *it*—still retain two case forms, series I and II.

Series I are the 'unmarked' forms. Series II occurs only in subject function (as in *I went*), except following a preposition; in *John brought the applicants in for me to interview them, me* is subject of *interview* but also follows the preposition *for*, and here takes a series I form. Series I occurs in all other positions—when object of a clause (for example, *watch me*), following a preposition (as in *after me*) and when making up a whole clause. If someone asks *Who wants to go?*, one could reply either *I do* (here using a series II form as subject of the verb *do*) or else just the series I form *Me* (but not just the series II form *\*I*).

When a pronoun is conjoined with a noun, in subject position, then the pronoun has series II form only when it immediately precedes the verb, as in *John and I went*. If the pronoun occurs first in the conjunction, then a series I form is required; one can only say *Me and John went*, not *\*I and John went*. (In object position, series I is always used: *He saw me and John* and *He saw John and me*.) A pronoun will not usually be modified by an adjective, but when this does happen it is the series I form that must be used; one says *Lucky me won the lottery*, not *\*Lucky I won the lottery*.

There is a fair degree of variation in pronominal use. Some people still say *It was I who did it, She is younger than I*, and *It is I*, where most speakers would prefer *me* in place of *I* in all three sentences. There appears to be a long-term trend towards the replacement of series II by series I (this has gone all the way with the second person pronoun where *you*, the original object form, has entirely replaced the old subject form *ye*).

In some complex constructions an NP may come between two verbs, e.g. *I know John took the ball* and *I saw John take the ball*. We may ask whether, in these sentences, *John* is object of the verb it follows, or subject of the verb it precedes, or both of these simultaneously. On substituting a pronoun for *John* we get different results: *I know he took the ball* and *I saw him take the ball*.

This information from pronominal forms is one important factor in deciding on the function of an NP in a complex sentence. We can infer that *John* is the subject of *took* in the first example, and the object of *saw* in the second. *John* may well also be object of *know* and/or subject of *take* (respectively), with other grammatical factors deciding which of two simultaneous functions determines surface form. (This question is considered in §2.7, §2.11.5 and Chapter 8.) Data on pronominal form do not provide an immediate and total answer to the question we posed in the last paragraph, but they are a most useful element in the formulation of a full answer.

During the past couple of decades, a new row has been added to the pronoun paradigm. For hundreds of years, *he* had been used for 3sg masculine and also for general human, where the sex of the referent was not relevant. There then arose a campaign against this—but what to do instead? One suggestion was a new pronoun *per* (from the noun *person*), but this did not catch on. Some people use the awkward *he or she* (or *she or he*) or the ugly *(s)he*.

What has evolved, quite naturally, is an internal shift within the pronoun system. In earlier times, *you* was used just for 2pl but then was extended to also cover 2sg. The 3pl pronoun *they* has long been used with an indefinite singular sense, as in *Anyone can be courteous if they try hard enough*, and *Whoever calls, tell them I'm not available*. It was natural for *they* to be also used for 3sg human, when the sex (now called gender) of the referent is not specified; for example, *When a linguist goes into the field, they must have a good quality recorder*.

It will be seen, in Table 2.1, that 2sg and 2pl are distinguished only in the final column, reflexive form—*You hide yourself!* and *You hide yourselves!* In similar fashion, 3sg human and 3pl are only distinguished in their reflexive form. Compare *When a linguist goes into the field, they must ask themself what their first priority is,* and *When linguists go into the field, they must ask themselves what their first priorities are.*

## 2.2. Verb and verb phrase

We first examine the forms of the verb, and the elements which can make up a verb phrase, before setting out the systems of mood, reality status, modality, tense and aspect which underlie the English predicate, and the way in which the terms in these systems are marked.

### *2.2.1. Forms of the verb*

It is important to distinguish between the base form of a verb, the three tense forms, and the two non-tense suffixed forms. Illustrating for one regular and three sample irregular verbs:

|  |  | REGULAR | IRREGULAR | | |
|---|---|---|---|---|---|
|  | base | *discover* | *swim* | *give* | *hit* |
| TENSE FORMS | 'present', 3sg subject | *discover-s* | *swim-s* | *give-s* | *hit-s* |
|  | present, other subject | *discover* | *swim* | *give* | *hit* |
|  | 'past' | *discover-ed* | *swam* | *gave* | *hit* |
| NON-TENSE | -ing | *discover-ing* | *swimm-ing* | *giv-ing* | *hitt-ing* |
|  | -en | *discover-ed* | *swum* | *giv-en* | *hit* |

*Be* (base form) is the most irregular verb, with *am* for 1sg subject, *is* for 3sg m, f and n and *are* elsewhere in present; *was* for 1sg and 3sg m, f and n and *were* elsewhere in the past; plus *being* and *been*. All other verbs are regular for present and the *-ing* form; irregularities are found for irregular verbs in past tense and in the *-en* form.

The tense forms are used in main clauses and must be preceded by a subject (at the least, the impersonal subject, *it*); the only circumstance in which a subject can be omitted is when two clauses with identical subject are coordinated, e.g. *John came in and sat down* (see §2.12). The base form is used in the imperative, and after *to* (the misnamed 'infinitive').

Non-tense forms are used after auxiliary verbs: *-ing* after 'imperfective' *be*; *-en* after 'previous' *have* and after passive *be* (e.g. *was giving*; *had given*, *was given*). In addition, *-ing* is used in varieties of complement clause, one often with *'s* on the subject (if it is stated), e.g. *I like Mary('s) playing the piano*; the other with *from* between subject and verb, e.g. *I discouraged John from going*. It can also mark the predicate of a circumstantial clause, e.g. *Having made his will, he shot himself*, and *Being absorbed in her task, she didn't notice the tiger approach*. Both *-ing* and *-en* forms may also function as adjectival modifiers within an NP, although only some verbs have (one or both of) their non-tense forms used in this way, e.g. *worrying news*, *worried expression, helping hand, informed reply, swum distance*. (§2.9 lists the types of clauses marked by *-ing*.)

Unlike tense forms, the non-tense forms do not have to be preceded by a stated subject within that clause, e.g. *I like playing the piano*, and the two circumstantial clauses given in the last paragraph.

(As described in Chapter 10, nouns can be derived from some verbs and this sometimes involves the addition of *-ing*, e.g. *the singing of the birds, the rocking of the boat*. But with many verbs a different derivational form is used, e.g. *the departure of the army*, rather than \**departing*, and *decision* not \**deciding, belief* not \**believing*, etc. Or the same form can be used for verb base and noun, e.g. *laugh, bite, witness*.)

It is informative to compare the past tense form, which must have a preceding subject, with the *-en* form, which may lack a stated subject. Compare:

(1)   *All students* [(*who were*) *seen in the bar last night*] *should report to the principal's office at noon*

(2)   *All teachers* [*who saw students in the bar last night*] *should report to the principal's office at noon*

The relative clause in (1) can be shortened by the omission of *who* (a relative pronoun filling subject slot) and *were*; the non-tense form *seen* then becomes clause-initial. *Who* cannot be omitted from (2); this is because the past tense form *saw* must be preceded by a subject (see §2.6).

For all regular (and some irregular) verbs the *-en* and past tense forms fall together—both *seen* in (1) and *saw* in (2) could be replaced by *discovered*. For these verbs it is important to enquire whether a form like *discovered* is, in a particular clause, realising the past tense category (since it will then require a subject) or the *-en* category (when it will have different syntactic possibilities); if *discovered* is substituted for *seen* in (1) and for *saw* in (2), then we can still omit *who were* from (1) but not *who* from (2). This is parallel to the situation concerning those few nouns that have a single form for both singular and plural—there *is* still an operative category of number, which is realised in the form of accompanying demonstrative and verb; compare *this sheep is bleating* with *these sheep are bleating* (*this* versus *these* and *is* versus *are* showing that *sheep* once realises singular and once plural number).

All verbs (except *be*) have a present non-3sg form that is identical to the base form. Once again, we must know what category a plain verb form is representing in a given clause. Compare *I know all about your children; they eat ice cream* and *I said to your children: '(you) eat this ice cream!'* The pronoun *they* cannot be omitted from the first sentence since the tensed verb *eat* must be preceded by a subject; but the subject pronoun *you* can be omitted from the second sentence since the base form *eat* (here, in imperative function) does not require a preceding subject.

## 2.2.2. Verb phrase

The predicate of a clause in English is filled by what can usefully be called a 'verb phrase' (VP); this is a string of verbs. (An alternative use, which is not followed here, is to say that the VP also includes an object NP.) A VP must include a main verb as head. This may optionally be preceded by auxiliary verbs: either *do*, or any or all of:

(i)   a modal—one of *will, can, must*, etc. (see §6.1.1);
(ii)  the 'previous' aspect marker *have*, which requires the following verb to be in *-en* form, e.g. *had beaten*;
(iii) the 'imperfective' aspect marker *be*, which requires the following verb to be in *-ing* form, e.g. *was beating*;
(iv)  the passive marker *be*, which requires the following verb to be in *-en* form, e.g. *was beaten*.

It is, then, at least theoretically possible to say *might* (i) *have* (ii) *been* (iii) *being* (iv) *beaten* (head).

The first word in a VP inflects for tense, e.g. *has/had broken, is/was breaking, is/was broken*. Negation is shown by *not* or *-n't*, which must follow the first auxiliary verb, e.g. *can't break, isn't breaking, hadn't broken*. If none of the auxiliary elements (i)–(iv) are present then *do* must be included with a negative, e.g. *broke, didn't break*. If a VP does not include a negation or any of (i)–(iv) then *do* may be included to carry emphasis, e.g. *He did go*. (Note that *do* is incompatible with any or all of (i)–(iv), except in an imperative, where one could say, for instance, *Do be sitting down when they arrive!*) Negation is discussed further in §12.11.

### 2.2.3. Verbal systems

The basic distinctions of mood, reality status, modality, tense and aspect in English are set out in Table 2.2, together with illustrative examples involving the verb *swim*. Modal and semi-modal verbs, which express modalities within irrealis, are discussed in §6.1.1. The tense and aspect systems are the subject of Chapter 7. Note that *is -ing*, often called 'progressive' or 'continuous', is here termed 'imperfective' (as opposed to *-s*, the 'perfect-

**Table 2.2.** *Mood, reality, modality, tense and aspect*

**imperative** mood, used in commands; base form of the verb: *Swim!*
**non-imperative** mood, used in statements and questions: *He has swum*; *Has he swum?*

    **irrealis** status, something which is uncertain in the future, or was unrealised in the past

        nine **modalities**, expressed by modal and/or semi-modal verbs, listed and discussed in §6.1.1; for example, Prediction *She will swim*, Imminent activity *She is about to swim*

            each may be further specified by perfective/imperfective and actual/ previous aspects; for example *She will have been swimming*

    **realis** status, something which has reality in past, present or future time

        **generic** tense: *Ducks swim*

        **future** tense

            **established** aspect: *We swim in the race tomorrow*

            **particular** aspect: *We're swimming in the river tomorrow*

        **present** tense

            **actual perfective** aspect: *She swims*

            **actual imperfective** aspect: *She is swimming*

            **previous perfective** aspect: *She has swum*

            **previous imperfective** aspect: *She has been swimming*

        **past** tense

            **actual perfective** aspect: *She swam*

            **actual imperfective** aspect: *She was swimming*

            **previous perfective** aspect: *She had swum*

            **previous imperfective** aspect: *She had been swimming*

ive'). The term 'perfect' has traditionally been used for *has -en*, but this does not accord with the general linguistic meaning of 'perfect'—to describe 'an action, etc. considered as a completed whole'. *Has -en* is here termed 'previous' aspect, as opposed to 'actual' aspect *-s*. The terms are justified—and the aspectual systems explained and illustrated—in Chapter 7.

## 2.3. Noun phrase

A noun phrase (NP) can be just a pronoun (e.g. *she*) or a proper name (e.g. *Shirley*). Or it can have a common noun (e.g. *mountain, boy*) as head. It is not ordinarily permissible in English to omit the noun head; if no specific head is stated the form *one* may be used (e.g. *the big one* rather than just *\*the big*).

A multitude of elements may precede the head of an NP:

(*a*)   an adverb which modifies a complete NP, e.g. *even, simply, really* (see Table 12.3 in §12.4); or *what*, as in *what a scandal, what the devil*; or *such* as in *such a nice boy, such delicious oysters*;

(*b*)   a predeterminer, e.g. *all (of), some (of), both (of), one (of), any (of), one-quarter (of)*;

(*c*)   a determiner, which can be an article (*the, a*), a demonstrative (e.g. *this, those*) or a possessive word or NP (*my, John's, the old man's*);

(*d*)   a superlative (*tallest, most beautiful*), a comparative (*taller, more beautiful*); or an ordering word (*next, last*) and/or a cardinal number (*three*) or a quantifier (*many, few*) or a qualifier (*some, any*);

(*e*)   an ordinal number, e.g. *fourth*;

(*f*)   one or more adjectival modifiers (see §3.2 for the ordering among adjectives); an adjective here may be modified by an adverb (such as *simply, really* or *very*; see Chapter 12);

(*g*)   a modifier describing composition (*wooden, vegetable, electrical*);

(*h*)   a modifier describing origin or style (*British, outside* in *outside toilet*),

(*i*)   a modifier describing purpose/beneficiary (*rabbit* in *rabbit food, medical* in *medical building*).

Note that the two choices under (*d*) can occur in either order, and may carry a meaning difference, e.g. *the two cleverest girls* (the cleverest and the second cleverest) versus *the cleverest two girls* (can refer to the cleverest pair, when they were already grouped into pairs). All of possibilities (*a*)–(*i*) are unlikely all to be taken up in a single NP, although it is theoretically possible to say something like: *only* (*a*) *some of* (*b*) *the* (*c*) *best* (*d*) *fifteen* (*d*) *very new* (*f*), *shiny* (*f*), *plastic* (*g*) *German* (*h*) *cat* (*i*) *baskets* (HEAD).

Following the head there can be any or all of:

(*j*)   *of* followed by an NP which refers to something in syntactic relation to the head; the relation may vary, as illustrated by *the arrival of the chief*—corresponding to *The chief arrived*—*the destruction of the city*—corresponding to *Someone/thing destroyed the city*—and *the leaves of the tree*—corresponding to the possessive construction *the tree's leaves*;

(*k*)   one of a limited selection of time and spatial adverbs, e.g. *tomorrow, now, last week*; *here, there, upstairs*; *outside* (see §§12.5.1–2);

(*l*)   any preposition plus an NP, e.g. *for Mary*; can refer to time or space, e.g. *after lunch, in the sky*;

(*m*)   a relative clause (see §2.6);

(*n*)   an adverb modifying the whole NP—*even, only* or *alone* (see Table 12.3 in §12.4).

An NP including all of (*j*)–(*n*) is (*he wouldn't buy*) *the* (*c*) *engine* (HEAD) *of Fred's old car* (*j*) *outside* (*k*) *in the back garden* (*l*) *which John tried to mend* (*m*) *even* (*n*). Note that (*j*) is generally incompatible with the choice of a possessor under (*c*): we may say *this old car's engine* or *John's engine* or *the engine of John's old car* but not *\*John's engine of the old car*. But *of* may introduce a non-possessor NP, under (*j*), which can co-occur with a choice under (*c*), e.g. *the President's promise of peace*.

## 2.4. Main clauses

Each main clause has an 'argument governor' (which is the predicate) and one or more 'arguments', which are in grammatical relationship to the governor. English has three varieties of main clause, as shown in Table 2.3.

In each clause type, the predicate is a verb phrase and each argument is a noun phrase. As the term 'predicate' is used here, it does not include an NP. For example, in *John will be interviewing Mary*, the predicate is *will be*

**Table 2.3.** *Varieties of main clauses*

|  | GOVERNOR | CORE ARGUMENTS | CLAUSE TYPE |
|---|---|---|---|
| GOVERNOR IS REFERENTIAL | transitive predicate | A  (transitive subject relation) and<br>O  (transitive object relation) | transitive clause |
|  | intransitive predicate | S  (intransitive subject relation) | intransitive clause |
| GOVERNOR IS RELATIONAL | copula verb (copula predicate) | CS (copula subject relation) and<br>CC (copula complement relation) | copula clause |

**Table 2.4.** *Relations and copula complement possibilities for* be

| RELATION SHOWN BY *be* | POSSIBILITIES FOR CC | EXAMPLES |
|---|---|---|
| IDENTITY | NP | *John is the President* |
|  | THAT complement clause | *The point is that it is unsafe* |
| EQUATION | NP | *Susan is an evil woman* |
| ATTRIBUTION | adjective | *He is happy* |
| POSSESSION | NP which includes possessive NP | *Mary is the President's daughter* |
|  |  | *That is my car* |
|  | Possessor pronoun as NP | *That is mine* |
| BENEFACTIVE | *for* + NP | *This bouquet is for the President* |
| SPATIAL/TIME | spatial/time adverb | *The meeting is here/outside/tomorrow* |
|  | preposition + NP | *The meeting is in the garden/at noon* |
|  | adverbial clause | *The meeting is where we had it last time/after we have finished eating* |

*interviewing* (not *will be interviewing Mary*); and in *Mary was a good dancer* the predicate is simply *was* (not *was a good dancer*).

All NPs have reference to a concrete or abstract entity (for example, *the tall woman* or *sincerity*), and all transitive and intransitive VCs have reference to a concrete or abstract activity or state (for example, *fall* or *kick* or *like*). In contrast, a copula expresses a relation between the CS and CC arguments. And whereas A, O, S and CS are realised by NPs with essentially the same structure, the possibilities for CC are somewhat different. By far the most common copula in English is *be*; the possibilities for its CC are set out in Table 2.4.

Many languages require a verb of rest or motion to be included with a locational expression, saying something like *She is staying in Prague* or *She is going to Vienna*. English can use just the copula to describe a position of rest, e.g. *She is in Prague*; but a verb of motion must normally be included with any specification of motion 'to' or 'from'—that is, *going* cannot be omitted from *She is going to Prague*. There is an interesting exception: the 'previous' auxiliary *have* plus copula *be* can be used with a *to* phrase, without a verb of motion, e.g. *She has been to Prague* (with the meaning 'she went to Prague at least once').

The other copula verbs in English include *become*, which can be followed by (i) an NP, or (ii) an adjective (*She became a doctor/my wife/sick*) and *get, come, go, grow, turn, feel*, each of which may only be followed by a restricted set of adjectives, e.g. *get dirty, come true, go bad, grow stupid, turn green*. Whereas *become* only functions as a copula and *be* only as copula and in the imperfective and passive auxiliaries, the other five also have non-copula uses; indeed, their lexical and copula uses can merge—compare *He turned/grew sad* with *He turned/grew into a sad man*. (§11.1 includes a list of the varied uses of *get*. §6.4.1 discusses verbs of the SEEM type, which also have copula-like properties.)

A main clause in English generally includes a subject, which precedes the predicate. Intransitive verbs have a single core role and this must be intransitive subject (referred to as 'S' relation). Transitive verbs have two or more core roles, and that role which is most likely to be relevant for the success of the activity is in transitive subject relation (referred to as 'A').

A transitive verb must also have a role in object (O) relation, and this will immediately follow the predicate. After an intransitive predicate, or a transitive-predicate-plus-object or a copula-predicate-plus-copula complement, a clause may include one or more peripheral NPs (each introduced by a preposition), referring to recipient (*give the book to Mary*), or beneficiary (*take the book for Mary*), or instrument (*shave with a razor*), or reason (*do it for money/kicks*) etc.; and also one or more spatial or time or frequency or manner expressions (see §2.5).

## 2.4.1. Imperative clauses

In a prototypical imperative clause in English:

(a)  The subject is 2nd person and is generally omitted. Other languages distinguish 2sg and 2pl with the convention that a 2sg imperative subject may be omitted but a 2pl subject should be retained. English makes no distinction between 2sg and 2pl (save in reflexives).

(b)  The verb is in base form. Since imperative is incompatible with irrealis, an imperative VP will not normally include a modal. It is generally actual perfective, but imperfective (e.g. *Be working when the boss comes in!*) and previous (*Have the work finished by the time the boss arrives!*) are possible. An imperative can involve a copula verb with limited possibilities for the CC argument; it may be a VALUE, HUMAN PROPENSITY or SPEED adjective (*Be good!, Don't be jealous!, Be quick!*) but scarcely a PHYSICAL PROPERTY term (not *Be thin!*).

(c)  In the negative, *do* must be included with *not*, giving clause-initial *Don't*; e.g. *Don't (you) do that!*

An imperative can have different degrees of intensity, shown by varying loudness and abruptness of voice quality. A mild imperative will often be preceded or followed by *please*. Often, the person being ordered is identified by name, in apposition to the main clause and either preceding or following it; for example *John, come here!* or *Come here John!* The pronoun *you* can be included, either in apposition to the imperative clause, like a personal name (*You, come here!* or *Come here, you!*) or in subject slot (*You come here!*). These are distinguished by intonation, shown by a comma in writing.

There are also particular construction types which can be identified as imperative with 3rd person subject. Imperatives with indefinite subject include *Someone find that file for me!* and *Everybody shut their eyes!* (the command is here directed at an addressee, but without using a second person pronoun). One can employ a command to entreat a deity, as in *God bless our house!* And there may be an unstated subject which could not be 2nd person, as in *Damn these mosquitoes!* There are also idiomatic expressions including *Long may she live!* (a rearrangement of *May she live long!*, with the modal *may*), *Far be it from me to complain!* and *Heaven help you if you are late!*

A variety of imperative is introduced by *let*; for example, *Let John do it!* This could be regarded as a prototypical imperative with understood 2nd person subject, (*You*) *let John do it!* However, subject reference is often more general, so that *let* is best regarded as an imperative with 3rd person subject (here, *John*). *Let* imperatives are also encountered with 1st person subject, either 1sg, as in *Let me do it!* or 1pl, as in *Let's go home!* (this could hardly be regarded as having underlying structure (*You*) *let us go home!*). Note that the *us* in *Let's go home* must be inclusive, referring to 'you and me' (rather than exclusive, referring to 'you and someone else').

## 2.5. Adverbial elements

Adverbial elements can refer to (i) space; (ii) time; (iii) frequency or degree; or (iv) manner of an activity or state. They can comprise a word (e.g. *there, inside; today, already; often, always; slowly, craftily*), a phrase (*in the garden, (during) last night, at infrequent intervals, with sincerity*) or a clause (*where we had built the house, before she arrived, whenever he felt like it, as his mother had always told him*). Adverbial phrases are generally introduced by a preposition, although there are exceptions, e.g. *last week, many times, this way*. Adverbial clauses generally have the structure of a main clause with a preposed subordinator, e.g. *where, after*. There is an additional type of adverbial clause of time whose VP begins with the *-ing* form of a verb, e.g. *His mother having gone out for the day, John invited his friends in to play poker*. The subject of an *-ing* time clause will be omitted if it is the same as the main clause subject, e.g. *(After) having failed his final exam, John threw a tantrum*. (See also (c) in §2.8, (d) in §2.9 and §2.12.)

There are basically five syntactic functions for an adverb (which is underlined):

(a)  Modifying a complete clause or sentence (sentence function), as in *She had deliberately broken the vase*.

(b)  Modifying a verb, plus object if it has one (manner function), as in *She had [gathered up the pieces carefully]*.

(c)  Modifying a complete noun phrase, as in *She had gathered up [almost all the pieces]*.

(d)  Modifying an adjective, as in *She had gathered up [the really big pieces]*.

(e)  Modifying another adverb, as in *She had [gathered up the pieces [terribly carefully]]*.

Each of the functions has a set of possible positions, chosen from final, initial, after the first word of the auxiliary, immediately before the verb etc. These are discussed in detail in Chapter 12. Note that an adverb may not intervene between a verb and its direct object.

Spatial adverbials behave in two rather different ways, depending on the semantic type of the predicate head. With verbs from the REST and MOTION types and from the LOOK subtype of ATTENTION we get a spatial adverbial (an 'inner adverbial') that is semantically linked to the reference of the verb—*He sat on a chair, She carried the pig to market, She stared at the picture*. Indeed, some of these verbs demand a spatial adverbial, e.g. *He put the box down/there/on the table* (*He put the box* is incomplete and thus unacceptable). Such 'inner adverbials' generally occur after the predicate; they can exceptionally occur initially, and may then take a marked intonation pattern, e.g. *On top of the hill(,) he put his boundary marker*. Spatial adverbs occurring with verbs of other semantic types do not have the same sort of semantic link to the verb (they can be called 'outer adverbials') and are often moved to initial position, e.g. *In the garden Mary kissed John* is as acceptable as *John kissed Mary in the garden*. (See also §12.5.2.)

A time or spatial adverbial element—which may be a word, a phrase or a clause—can also occur as part of an NP (in slot (*l*) of §2.3), as in *[The noises in the night] upset Father*; although the noises occurred in the night, Father might not have been upset until he was told about them at breakfast, on his return from the night shift. Compare with *The noises upset Father in the night*, which has *in the night* as a clause constituent, and implies that Father was actually upset in the night by the noises. A sentence like *We are expecting my uncle from the city* is ambiguous between the NP-modifier parsing (my uncle lives in the city, but he might be arriving today from some other direction) and the clause-adverbial reading (he is coming from the city today, although he might live somewhere entirely different). It will be disambiguated when further material is added, e.g. *We are expecting [my uncle from the city] to come here today*, and *We are expecting my uncle [to come here from the city] today*.

## 2.6. Relative clauses

A relative clause is a constituent of an NP and provides a description of the referent of the head noun, parallel to an adjectival or adverbial modifier— compare *the tall man, the man [in the corner]* and *the man [the man kicked John]*.

A relative clause has the same basic structure as a main clause, with subject, tensed verb as head of the predicate, etc. It must contain an NP that has the same reference as the head of the superordinate NP in whose structure the relative clause functions, i.e. *the man [who kicked John]*. A relative pronoun is placed at the beginning of the clause and the occurrence of the coreferential NP is omitted. The relative pronoun is *which* if the coreferential NP was a non-human in subject or object function or following a preposition, *who* if a human (or, for some speakers, a higher animal) in subject function, *whom* if a human in object function or following a preposition (*whom* is now being replaced by *who* in object function), *whose* if a human or non-human in possessive function, *where* if a locational, and *when* if a temporal element. Thus *I saw the dog [which bit John]*, *I watched the man [who hit John]*, *I observed the tramp [who(m) John hit]*, *I discovered the man/dog [whose house John destroyed]*, *I saw the place [where you were born]*, *I remember the day [when you got married]*.

Where the coreferential NP was in subject function the relative pronoun both (*a*) marks the clause as a relative clause, and (*b*) fills the subject slot (recall that a tensed VP must normally be preceded by some sort of overt subject NP). Where the coreferential NP was in non-subject function then the relative pronoun only has property (*a*).

There are two major varieties of relative clauses, illustrated by:

**(3)** *The firemen who the managers sacked will meet in the engine shed*
**(4)** *The firemen, who the managers sacked, will meet in the engine shed*

Sentence (3) implies that only some firemen were sacked by the managers, and just those fireman will meet. This is called a 'restrictive relative clause' since it restricts the reference of the head noun *firemen* (to: just those firemen who were sacked). Sentence (4) implies that all the firemen are meeting, and that they were all sacked; it is called a 'non-restrictive relative clause' since it does not delimit the reference of the head noun.

A proper noun has unique reference and so any relative clause to it must be non-restrictive, e.g. *Amos, who I introduced you to last week, is coming to tea*. In a sentence like *My brother who lives in Athens won the lottery*, the relative clause must be non-restrictive if I have only one brother but may be restrictive if I have more than one, then indicating which of my brothers won the prize.

One can in fact usually infer from the intonation what type of relative clause is involved. A non-restrictive relative is like an inserted, parenthetical comment, and is set off by contrastive intonation (shown by commas in the written style). It could be considered as not really a part of the superordinate NP, but rather as an independent constituent in apposition with it. The relative pronoun in a non-restrictive clause is not likely to be replaced by *that*, and could not be omitted.

In a restrictive clause, a *wh-* relative pronoun (other than *whose*) may be replaced by *that* (which is here functioning as a kind of relative pronoun); or it can be omitted, so long as the coreferential NP was not in subject function in the relative clause. Thus, alternatives to (3) are *The firemen that the managers sacked . . .* and *The firemen the managers sacked . . .*(There are stylistic conditions operating—a relative pronoun is more likely to be replaced by *that* or omitted in informal talk, or when referring to some matter of little consequence, and a *wh-* form is more likely to be retained in a formal speech style, e.g. in a debate or a meeting, or when talking about some really significant happening.)

We mentioned that if the coreferential NP had been in subject slot then we can now think of this slot as being filled by the relative pronoun. This is why it cannot normally be omitted: a tensed verb must be preceded by a subject NP. Thus, if only some managers sacked firemen one could say, with a restrictive relative clause:

(5)   *The managers who/that sacked firemen have saved money for the company*

and *who/that* cannot be omitted.

Restrictive relative clauses that have a coreferential subject NP and refer to present time can have a reduced version; the relative pronoun is omitted and the verb is put in *-ing* form. Thus, corresponding to

(6)   *Those managers who/that are sacking firemen are saving money for the company*

we can have:

(7)   *Those managers sacking firemen are saving money for the company*

In the case of *sack*, and other verbs which refer to present time through the *be . . . -ing* imperfective auxiliary, it looks as if (7) is derived from (6) by omission of the relative pronoun and the tensed form of *be* (with the *-ing* on the retained verb being a residue of the *be . . . -ing* auxiliary).

However, reduced relatives like (7) also occur with those verbs that use perfective present, rather than the imperfective *be . . . -ing*, to refer to present time (see §2.2.3 and Chapter 7). That is, we get *Anyone owning a gun must register it* and *People knowing the whereabouts of the diamonds are asked to keep quiet*, which relate to *Anyone who owns a gun must register it* and *People who know the whereabouts of the diamonds are asked to keep quiet* rather than to the ungrammatical *\*Anyone who is owning a gun must register it* and *\*People who are knowing the whereabouts of the diamonds are asked to keep quiet*. A related example is *Anyone having seen the diamonds should keep quiet*, which relates to the previous present sentence *Anyone who has seen the diamonds should keep quiet* rather than to *\*Anyone who is having seen the diamonds should keep quiet* (the auxiliary *be . . . -ing* can follow but not precede *have . . . -en*).

These reduced present-time restrictive relatives are only found when the coreferential NP was in subject function. There is no reduced counterpart of *Those firemen (who/that) the managers are sacking will meet in the engine shed*; that is, we do not get *\*Those firemen the managers sacking will meet in the engine shed*, parallel to (7).

A restrictive relative clause may sometimes be moved out of its NP to the end of the main clause, usually being set off from the rest of the clause by appositional intonation; this is found in colloquial styles (*That man got sacked, who you were praising yesterday*) and also in legal English (*Those persons will be prosecuted who are found in possession of illegal firearms*). Such an extraposed clause must retain its relative pronoun. (This is an example of a general preference for a 'heavy' constituent to come at the end of a main clause—see §2.13A.)

There are a number of other constructions that may relate to relative clauses; but there are varying opinions among grammarians of English about their exact syntactic status. Some scholars talk in terms of a special subtype of restrictive relative clause in which the determiner (or determiner plus head) of the superordinate NP is fused with the relative pronoun, as in the (b) sentences of:

(**8a**)   *Those recipes which she used are marked in red*
(**8b**)   *What recipes she used are marked in red*
(**9a**)   *Any recipes which she used are marked in red*
(**9b**)   *Whatever recipes she used are marked in red*
(**10a**)  *That which he wrote was unbelievable*
(**10b**)  *What he wrote was unbelievable*
(**11a**)  *Our dog bites anyone who comes into the garden*
(**11b**)  *Our dog bites whoever comes into the garden*
(**12a**)  *He lives in the place where you'd like to live*
(**12b**)  *He lives where you'd like to live*

The subordinate clauses in the (b) sentences of (8)–(12) have some of the properties of relative clauses but also behave in some ways like interrogatives.

Let us now return to non-restrictive relative clauses. Suppose all managers are sacking firemen; we can say:

(**13**)   *The managers, who are sacking firemen, are saving money for the company*

We noted that the relative clause appears to be a parenthetical comment—almost an intrusion into the body of the main clause—and it is set off by contrastive intonation or commas. There are also constructions like:

(**14**)   *The managers are saving money for the company, sacking firemen*

Now in (14) the comment *sacking firemen* is plainly non-restrictive, suggesting that (14) might be taken as derived from (13), with a reduced relative clause (*who are* being omitted) that is moved to the end of the main clause. A comment such as *sacking firemen* in (14) may sometimes be retained in its original NP or else be placed at the beginning of the main clause. Compare:

(**15a**)  *John, who was wheezing noisily, came into the room*
(**15b**)  *John, wheezing noisily, came into the room*
(**15c**)  *John came into the room, wheezing noisily*

(**15d**)   *John came, wheezing noisily, into the room*
(**15e**)   *Wheezing noisily, John came into the room*

We also get constructions of this type where the 'host' NP, in the main clause, is a pronoun, e.g.

(**16a**)   *He came, wheezing noisily, into the room*
(**16b**)   *He came into the room, wheezing noisily*
(**16c**)   *Wheezing noisily, he came into the room*

However, English generally does not allow a relative clause to follow a pronoun; that is, one does not get:

(**16d**)   *\*He, who was wheezing noisily, came into the room*

This suggests that (16a–c) (and thus also (14) and (15b–e) ) should not be regarded as involving reduced relative clauses, but instead as being a distinct construction type—simultaneous appositional clauses; see (d) in §2.9.

There are similar appositional constructions where a 'comment clause' relates to the object of the main clause (although here it could not normally be moved to the beginning of the main clause):

(**17a**)   *We saw John in the garden, doing his weekly chores*

alongside the non-restrictive relative clause construction:

(**17b**)   *We saw John, who was doing his weekly chores, in the garden*

Note that sentences of this type may be ambiguous as to whether a final comment relates to subject or to object of the main clause, e.g. *John painted Mary naked* could correspond to *John, who was naked, painted Mary* or to *John painted Mary, who was naked* (and this is in turn ambiguous between a situation in which Mary posed naked and one where she was naked only on the canvas, with John having used his imagination as to what she looked like under her clothes).

## 2.7. Complement clauses

Every language has verbs which introduce direct speech, reporting the actual words which may have been uttered. Thus:

(**18**)   *'Roosevelt has won another election,' he announced*
(**19**)   *She told me: '(You) pick up the towel!'*

**(20)**   *'Put your bag in the top locker!' he instructed me*
**(21)**   *'Is the Saab back yet?' Mary asked*
**(22)**   *'Who left the window open?' John asked*
**(23)**   *'Mary shall lead the parade,' Captain Smee decided*
**(24)**   *'Jane was late again this morning,' the office boy mentioned on Tuesday*
**(25)**   *'John is a fool,' declared Mary*

Verbs such as *announce, tell, instruct, ask, mention* and *declare* always refer to some speech event. *Decide* does not have to, but it can be used in this way, as in (23).

Many languages, including English, have alternative 'indirect speech' constructions in which what was said is coded as a subordinate clause—called a 'complement clause'—in syntactic construction with the verb of speaking. (In fact the phenomenon of complement clauses covers a good deal more than indirect speech, as we shall show.)

English has a variety of complement clauses. The most straightforward involves placing *that* before the 'speech clause', as in:

**(18a)**   *He announced [that Roosevelt had won another election]*
**(19a)**   *She told me [that I should pick up the towel]*
**(20a)**   *He instructed me [that I should put my bag in the top locker]*
**(23a)**   *Captain Smee decided [that Mary should lead the parade]*
**(24a)**   *The office boy mentioned on Tuesday [that Jane had been/was late again that morning]*
**(25a)**   *Mary declared that [John was a fool]*

Examining these carefully we see that present tense in direct speech (*has won* in (18), *is* in (25)) becomes past in indirect speech (*had won* in (18a), *was* in (25a)) if the main clause is in past tense. Present tense would be retained if the verb of speaking were also in present—compare *'Mary is winning,' John says* and *John says that Mary is winning*. The actual past (*was late*) of direct speech in (24) may be either retained or replaced by previous past (*had been late*) in (24a). This tense replacement in indirect speech is called 'back-shifting'—see Quirk and Greenbaum (1973: 342ff.); it is discussed in §7.6.

Where the direct speech is an order or resolution, as in (19), (20) and (23), then the modal *should* is introduced in the THAT complement clause, as in (19a), (20a), (23a). Finally, deictic elements which were originally oriented to the pragmatic situation of the direct speech must be reoriented to the situation of the verb of saying: *your* in (20) becomes *my* in (20a); the optional—but always implicit—*you* in (19) becomes *I* in (19a); and *this morning* in (24) must be replaced by *that morning* in (24a).

Complement clauses which code questions begin with a *wh-* word in place of *that*, e.g.

**(21a)**   *Mary asked [whether/if the Saab was back yet]*
**(22a)**   *John asked [who had left the window open]*

If the direct question was of the polar variety (expecting 'yes' or 'no' as answer) then the complement clause will begin with *whether* or *if*; if the direct question began with *who, whom, whose, what, which, how, why, where* or *when* then this is retained at the front of the complement clause (see also §2.11.1). Once again, present in direct speech becomes past in indirect (*is* in (21) corresponding to *was* in (21a) ) and actual past becomes previous past (*left* in (22), *had left* in (22a) ) if the main verb is in past tense.

A third variety of indirect speech construction is exemplified by:

**(24b)**   *The office boy mentioned on Tuesday [Mary's having been late again that morning]*

Here the subject of the complement clause takes possessive ending *'s* and the first word of the VP is in *-ing* form (there is no tense inflection). Note that the previous imperfective auxiliary construction *having been late* in (24b) corresponds to actual perfective *was late* of (24).

A further construction type involves placing *for* at the beginning of the complement clause and *to* before the VP, which loses its tense inflection (the first word of the VP appearing in base form):

**(23b)**   *Captain Smee decided [for Mary to lead the parade]*

Note that although the direct speech in (23) includes a modal *shall*, no corresponding form (*shall* or *should*) can be included in the complement clause of (23b). We refer to (23b) as a 'Modal (FOR) TO complement construction'.

The same construction type is used when a direct speech order, as in (19) and (20), is coded into indirect speech. Here the *for* must be omitted, giving a complement clause marked just by *to*; the subject of the complement clause is now also object of the main clause (here, *me*):

**(19b)**   *She told me to pick up the towel*
**(20b)**   *He instructed me to put my bag in the top locker*

If the direct speech concerns a judgement (which generally involves the copula *be*), as in (25), then this may be coded into indirect speech through a second type of TO complement clause, which we call 'Judgement TO':

**(25b)**   *Mary declared John to be a fool*

There is one further type of complement clause that involves *to*; it has a *wh-* word before the *to*, e.g.

**(20c)**   *He instructed me where to put my bag*

This is not an exact correspondent of the direct speech sentence (20), but rather a description of it.

Many verbs of speaking can have an NP, giving the content of the speech act, in object function, e.g.

**(18c)**   *He announced [the election result]*
**(21c)**   *Mary asked [a tricky question]*
**(23c)**   *Captain Smee decided on [the order of procession]*
**(24c)**   *The office boy mentioned [Mary's latest misdemeanour]*

*Announce, ask, decide (on)* and *mention* are transitive verbs. They may occur in apposition to a statement of direct speech, which is in lieu of a constituent in object function. Or they can take a syntactic object, which may be either an NP (as in (18c), (21c), (23c), (24c) ) or a complement clause (as in (18a), (21a), (22a), (23a/b), (24a/b) ). The verbs *tell* and *instruct* (in (19) and (20) ) already have an NP object and this can be followed by direct speech or an indirect speech complement clause; it is also possible to have a further NP in place of the complement clause, e.g. *She told me my instructions, He instructed me in the proper procedure.*

Verbs from a number of other semantic types, in addition to the SPEAK-ING type, may have a complement clause as alternative to an NP, in object or subject function, etc., e.g.

**(26a)**   *I believed John/John's story*
**(26b)**   *I believed that John told the truth*
**(26c)**   *I believed John to have told the truth*

**(27a)**   *The exam results delighted Mr Smith*
**(27b)**   *His daughter's having gained first class honours delighted Mr Smith*
**(27c)**   *That his daughter had gained first class honours delighted Mr Smith*

**(28a)**   *Mary began her lunch at noon*
**(28b)**   *Mary began eating her lunch at noon*
**(28c)**   *Mary began to eat her lunch at noon*

It will be seen that some verbs allow several varieties of complement clause to fill a certain functional slot (sometimes with a substantial difference in meaning), e.g. *wish*, like *tell*, accepts both THAT and Modal (FOR) TO clauses;

*mention* and *delight* take THAT and ING; *begin* takes ING and TO; and *plan* and *remember* take all of THAT, ING and Modal (FOR) TO. Other verbs only accept a single variety of complement clause, e.g. *ensure* with THAT, *want* with TO, and *finish* with ING.

There are of course a number of semantic types all of whose verbs demand an NP (not a complement clause) for each functional slot, e.g. *hit, take, put, break, give*. Chapters 4, 5 and 6 provide a detailed semantic and syntactic description of each verb type, stating which may occur with complement clauses.

The types which take complement clauses in object, subject, or some other functional slot are BEGINNING, TRYING, HURRYING, DARING, WANTING, POSTPONING, MAKING, HELPING, SEEM, MATTER, ATTENTION, THINKING, DE-CIDING, LIKING, ANNOYING, ACTING, HAPPENING, COMPARING, RELATING and of course SPEAKING. Chapter 8 deals fairly thoroughly with this topic, describing the meaning of each variety of complement clause, their syntactic statuses and the possibilities for coreferential omission etc., and the semantic basis for which verb occurs with which complements. The remainder of this section gives a preliminary sketch of the syntax of the seven varieties of complement clause in English.

(A)   THAT complement clauses are exemplified in (18a), (19a), (20a), (23a), (24a), (25a), (26b) and (27c); and (B) WH- clauses in (21a) and (22a). Both of these have the full structure of a main clause, with obligatory subject, obligatory tense on the first word of the VP, and the full range of VP possibilities (modals, imperfective *be*, previous *have*, passive *be*). A THAT or WH- complement can have its subject coreferential with subject or object of the main clause, but it may never be omitted, e.g. *I promised you that I would go*; *I promised you that you could go*.

Besides introducing one variety of complement clause, *that* also functions as a deictic noun (*Did you see that?*), as a demonstrative determiner (*Did you see that car?*) and to introduce restrictive relative clauses, e.g.

(29)   *Everyone believed* [*the man* [*that had hired you*]]

Note that here the relative clause *that had hired you* is a constituent of the object NP *the man that had hired you*. When (29) is passivised the whole object NP becomes passive subject:

(29a)   [*The man* [*that had hired you*]] *was believed* (*by everyone*)

We mentioned in §2.6 that colloquial styles of English allow a restrictive relative clause to be moved from a subject NP to the end of the main clause, as in:

(**29b**)   *The man was believed* (*by everyone*), [*that had hired you*]

Compare the relative clause marked by *that* in (29) with a complement clause introduced by *that*, as in:

(**30**)   *Everyone believed* [*that the man had hired you*]

Here the clause *that the man had hired you* is object of *believe*, and can become passive subject:

(**30a**)   [*That the man had hired you*] *was believed* (*by everyone*)

A THAT clause in (underlying or derived passive) subject function can be extraposed to the end of the main clause, its subject slot before the predicate being then filled by the impersonal form *it*:

(**30b**)   *It was believed* (*by everyone*) [*that the man had hired you*]

Thus, although (29) and (30) have similar surface form, differing only in the order of *the man* and *that*, they do have entirely different syntactic structures and derivational possibilities.

*Whether, if* or a *wh-* word introducing a WH- complement clause can never be omitted. The complementiser *that* may often be omitted from a THAT clause which immediately follows the predicate, e.g. *I think* (*that*) *he's stupid*, *It was believed* (*that*) *the foreman had hired you*, or from a THAT clause which immediately follows the object NP of a verb like *promise* or *threaten* (a verb for which the main clause object is not expected to be coreferential with the complement clause subject), e.g. *I promised Mary* (*that*) *John could go*. That can never be omitted from a complement clause in subject relation (and so not from (27c) or (30a) ) and is seldom omitted from a complement clause which follows the object NP of a verb for which there is an expectation that main clause object will be coreferential with complement clause subject, e.g. not from *I instructed Mary that John should go*.

*That* is unlikely to be omitted from a post-predicate complement clause if an adverb, a linker or a peripheral NP intervenes between it and the predicate—thus, *that* is generally retained in *It was believed implicitly that the foreman had hired you* and in *It was believed, however, that the foreman had hired you*. And *that* would generally be retained in (30b) if the agentive phrase *by everyone* were included. The determining factors on omission of *that* from a complement clause which immediately follows a predicate are largely stylistic—it is more likely to be omitted in casual than in formal speech, and more likely to be omitted if the reference of the complement clause is to some minor item of information rather than an important piece of reportage. Compare *He announced* (*that*) *it was eggs for breakfast*, where *that* is quite dispensable, with (18a) *He announced that Roosevelt had won another election*, where it would be unusual not to include *that* (see also §2.14B). A few verbs will almost invariably include *that* in a following complement clause, and this is because they carry a formal aura of meaning, e.g. *require, propose, undertake, order, request* (note that these verbs are likely also to include *should* in their THAT clause and the *should* can be omitted—see below).

Of the verbs which take THAT complements, there are a number which typically include a modal in the complement clause. The identity of the modal depends partly on the semantics of the main verb and partly on the choice of subject for the complement clause, e.g. *I wish that I could . . .* but *I wish that you would . . .*

There is a group of verbs that commonly take *should*; indeed, the meaning of the verb implies obligation, requiring *should* in the complement clause. It is thus scarcely surprising that the *should* is generally omitted, producing what appears to be a tenseless, modal-less THAT clause (sometimes, unhelpfully, called 'subjunctive'), e.g. *order, command, suggest, propose, insist, require,* and:

(**31**)   *She demanded that he* (*should*) *empty the bin*
(**32**)   *He recommended that we* (*should*) *be told*

(Note that *should* is not omittable from THAT complements with other types of verbs, i.e. not from *She decided/knew/believed that he should do it*.) Partial justification for saying that *She demanded that he empty the bin* involves an underlying *should* comes from the fact that *empty* is here in base form, which would be expected after a modal. Compare this with *She says that he empties the bin*, where the verb *empties* is in tense form, and must be the initial element of its VP.

*Wh-* words in English may have a number of functions: (*a*) they may be used as interrogatives, e.g. *Who did you see?, What is that?*; (*b*) they can introduce a WH- complement clause, as in (21a), (22a); (*c*) they may introduce relative clauses, e.g. *I rather like the man who you married*; (*d*) they can be the fusion of part of an NP and the introducer to a relative clause within that NP, e.g. *she always takes what*(*ever*) *money I earn*.

All of *who*, *whom*, *whose*, *what*, *which*, *how*, *why*, *where* and *when* have functions (*a*) and (*b*). All except *how* and *what* occur in function (*c*) (*what* is in fact used with this function in some low-prestige dialects, e.g. *I like the car what you bought*; for other dialects *which* effectively replaces *what*, functioning as NP head whereas in (*a*), (*b*) and (*d*) it is generally modifier to an NP head). In function (*d*) we find all except *whose* and *why*; *-ever* can be added to those *wh-* words that occur in (*d*), usually carrying a difference in meaning (compare (8a/b) and (9a/b)). *Whether* and *if* only have function (*d*), introducing complement clauses. *If* also functions as a clause linker— see §2.12. *Whether* is the only form in English whose sole function is to mark a complement clause.

Complement clause constructions and 'fused' restrictive relative clause constructions can appear very similar, as with:

(**33**)  *He ate what they put on the plate* (relative clause construction)
(**34**)  *He knew what they put on the plate* (complement clause construction)

They can be distinguished on semantic grounds. *What* in (33) is a fusion of *that which*—he ate 'that', which is something concrete, and whose referent is further specified by the relative clause *which they put on the plate*. Thus, *ate* in (33) has an NP (which includes a restrictive relative clause) as object; *knew* in (34) has a complement clause *what they put on the plate* as object—the speaker knows a fact, referred to by this clause. Note that *know* could alternatively have a THAT clause as object, e.g. *He knew that they put apples on the plate*; but *eat* could not—*\*He ate that they put apples on the plate* is nonsensical.

(**C**)  ING complement clauses are exemplified by (24b), (27b), (28b). The VP does not show tense inflection; instead, its first word is in *-ing* form. It may not include a modal, but can include aspect markers *have* or *have* plus *be* (but not just *be*—see §2.13C) and/or passive *be*. The subject of an ING complement clause may be different from main clause subject and is then sometimes marked by possessive ending *'s* (or, if a pronoun, it is in possessive form). But the subject can be coreferential with main clause subject, and is then usually omitted from the complement clause (since the VP in an ING clause is not tensed, it does not have to be preceded by a subject), e.g.

(**35**)  *I remember John's/your winning the lottery*
(**36**)  *I remember (?\*my) winning the lottery*

A fair number of verbs form a derived noun by the suffixation of *-ing*. It is important to distinguish between an NP with such a deverbal noun as

head, as in (37), and an ING complement clause with the corresponding verb
as predicate head, as in (38):

(**37**)   *I admired Mary's singing of 'Salty Dog' in church*
(**38**)   *I admired Mary's singing 'Salty Dog' in church*

There is a meaning difference—(38) states that I admired the fact that she did
it (Mary's temerity in giving voice to a bawdy song in a sacred place); (37)
states that I admired the manner in which she sang (her syncopated style,
etc.).

There are concomitant syntactic differences:

- The object in (37) has the structure of an NP, with *Mary's* as determiner (*the*
  could be used instead) and with the preposition *of* introducing the post-head NP
  *'Salty Dog'*. In (38) *Mary* is the subject of the predicate *singing* (*Mary's* here
  could not be replaced by *the*), with the object *'Salty Dog'* immediately following
  the transitive verb.
- The noun *singing* in (37) could be modified by an adjective, e.g. *quiet singing*,
  whereas the verb *singing* in (38) would be modified by an adverb, e.g. *singing
  quietly*.

Of course a shorter version, *I admired Mary's singing*, is ambiguous—the
NP-as-object reading implies that I admired the way she sang, and the
complement-clause-as-object reading indicates that I admired the fact of
her singing. (There is further discussion of this in §10.2.1.)

The *'s* on the subject of an ING complement clause is often omitted,
especially in the most informal speech, and then the series I or unmarked
form of the pronoun is used (§2.1), i.e. *him, her*, etc., not *he, she*, etc. The *'s*
tends to be dropped most often from an inanimate subject, e.g. *I don't like
the washing machine(?\* 's) shuddering every time it hits 'spin' on the cycle*.
The *'s* can be dropped from (24b), (27b), (35), (38) and from:

(**39**)   *I hate that man ('s) watching Mary*

It was mentioned in §2.6 that there are constructions which appear to
involve a reduced version of a restricted relative clause. Thus, corresponding to *I hate that man who is watching Mary*, we can have:

(**40**)   *I hate that man watching Mary*

Examples (39) and (40) have quite different meanings: (39) states that I hate
the fact of that man's watching Mary, while (40) states that I hate a
particular man, whose identity is specified to the hearer by the fact that
he is watching Mary—the reason I hate him may be unconnected with his
watching Mary.

When the 's is omitted (39) coincides in form with (40) and *I hate that man watching Mary* is thus ambiguous between the readings 'NP with restrictive relative clause relating to object' and 'complement clause as object'.

There are two kinds of complement clause that are similar in form but quite different in meaning. The first is introduced by *for*, includes *to* immediately before the complement clause verb and has a 'Modal-type' meaning (e.g. *I intended for Mary to win*). The complement clause subject may be omitted when it is coreferential with an NP in the main clause, and *for* is then automatically dropped (e.g. *I intended to win*). But *for* may also be omitted, in certain semantic circumstances, when the complement clause subject is retained (e.g. *I intended Mary to win*). The second kind has *to* immediately before the complement clause verb, but no *for*, and carries a 'Judgement' meaning (e.g. *I consider Mary to be beautiful*). Like ING clauses, both of these kinds of TO complement may include *have* or *be* auxiliaries, but not a modal or tense inflection.

**(D)**   Modal (FOR) TO complement clauses are exemplified by (23b) and:

**(41)**   [*For John to have been so foolhardy*] *scares me*
**(42)**   *I would love it* [*for Mary to sing 'St Louis Blues'*]
**(43)**   *Everybody agreed* [*for John to give the funeral oration*]

The subject of a Modal (FOR) TO clause (together with the *for*) may be omitted when it is coreferential with a core NP of the main clause. The syntactic conditions for this omission are:

|  | FUNCTION OF COMPLEMENT CLAUSE IN MAIN CLAUSE | FUNCTION OF COREFERENTIAL NP IN MAIN CLAUSE |
|---|---|---|
| I | object | subject |
| II | subject | object |
| III | post-object constituent | object |

Scheme I is illustrated by *I longed for Mary to win, I longed to win*; II by *For John to have to work Sundays annoyed Mary, To have to work Sundays annoyed Mary*; III by *I urged all the teachers for their pupils to take care crossing the street, I urged all the teachers to take care crossing the street.* (There is a single addition to III, which only holds in some dialects of

English. *Promise* will omit the subject of a post-object complement clause when it is coreferential with main clause subject, not with main clause object, e.g. *I promised John for my charlady to clean his apartment*, and *I promised John to clean his apartment*, from underlying *I promised John for me to clean his apartment*.)

A Modal (FOR) TO clause may drop the *for* with the complement clause subject still being retained; this then becomes syntactic object of the main verb. Compare:

(44)   *I chose for Mary to lead the parade*
(45)   *I chose Mary to lead the parade*

In (45) *Mary* is object of the main clause verb *chose* (and can become passive subject, e.g. *Mary was chosen to lead the parade*). Note the difference in meaning between (44) and (45). It would be appropriate for me to say (44) if, as organiser of the parade, I communicated my decision to other people who would in turn inform Mary. But if I stood before the participants for the parade and pointed to Mary as I made the choice, then (45) would be the appropriate construction to use. (There is fuller discussion of the semantic role of *for* in §8.2.4.)

*For* may only be omitted (and the complement clause subject retained) when it immediately follows a transitive verb. This correlates with the syntactic shift we have just observed—that the complement clause subject then becomes surface syntactic object of the preceding main clause verb. That is, *for* may not be omitted in any of the following circumstances:

(i)   when the complement clause is in subject relation in the main clause, e.g. *For John to be out so late worries Mary*;
(ii)   when the complement clause follows a main clause object, e.g. *It worries Mary for John to be out so late*, *I told the captain for his men to clean the latrines*;
(iii)   when the complement clause follows an adjective, e.g. *It is usual for a man to open the door for a lady* (see also the discussion of Modal (FOR) TO complement clauses with adjectives in §3.2);
(iv)   when the complement clause follows *it*, e.g. *I hate it for John to pick his nose in public* (*for* may be omitted only when *it* is also dropped, e.g. *I hate John to pick his nose in public*, not *\*I hate it John to pick his nose in public*);
(v)   when the complement clause follows an adverb, e.g. *I chose quite deliberately for Mary to lead the parade*.

Some main verbs may not omit the *for* when complement clause subject is retained, e.g. *decide, offer, remember, know*. Some may optionally omit *for*, with a meaning difference, e.g. *choose* (as in (44/5) ) and *propose, intend, mean, desire, wish*. A third set generally omit *for* when the complement clause immediately follows the main verb, e.g. *want* in *I want you to go*, but will retain it when the verb and complement clause are separated, as when an adverb comes between them, e.g. *I want very much for you to go* or in constructions such as *What I want is for you to go*; other verbs behaving like this are *need, order* and *urge* (see also §6.2.1). A final set must always omit the *for* (and thus cannot include an adverb immediately after the main clause verb), e.g. *force, cause, allow, permit*.

There are also verbs that take what is essentially a Modal (FOR) TO complement clause but demand that the complement clause subject be identical to main clause subject and thus omitted (together with *for*), e.g. *begin* (as in (28c) ), *try, hasten*.

All of the four kinds of complement clause described so far—THAT, WH-, ING and Modal (FOR) TO—may fill object slot in the main clause and can then become passive subject, as in (30a) and:

(**46**)  [*Where he put it*] *is not known*
(**47**)  [*John('s) winning the lottery*] *is fondly remembered by all the office staff*
(**43a**)  [*For John to give the funeral oration*] *was agreed* (*on*)

(Many clauses with a Modal (FOR) TO clause as object, and some with complement clauses of other kinds as object, do not readily passivise. This is for semantic—and not syntactic—reasons; see §11.4.)

As already mentioned, once a Modal (FOR) TO complement drops the *for*, then its subject becomes main clause object and it is this that becomes passive subject, not the whole complement clause (see (45) ).

THAT, WH- and Modal (FOR) TO clauses in (underlying or derived passive) subject function may be extraposed to the end of the main clause, with *it* filling the subject slot. Thus (30b) and:

(**46a**)  *It is not known* [*where he put it*]
(**41a**)  *It scares me* [*for John to have been so foolhardy*]
(**43b**)  *It was agreed* [*for John to give the funeral oration*]

Extraposition is equally possible for a Modal (FOR) TO clause in subject relation that has its subject (and the preceding *for*) omitted under identity with the main clause object:

(**48**)  [*To have to give the welcoming speech*] *terrified me*
(**48a**)  *It terrified me* [*to have to give the welcoming speech*]

Note that a complement clause may not usually be extraposed over another complement clause. That is, a clause in subject relation is not open to extraposition if there is also a complement clause in object relation to the verb, e.g. corresponding to:

(49)   [*That Pegasus won the race*] *indicates* [*that Bellerophon is a fine rider*]

it is not possible to say:

(49a)   **It indicates* [*that Bellerophon is a fine rider*] [*that Pegasus won the race*]

ING clauses are generally not extraposable. However, we can get what is called 'right dislocation', in which the two clauses are set off by contrastive, appositional intonation (and *it* refers to 'Mary's singing in church'), as in:

(38a)   *It was admired, Mary's singing 'Salty Dog' in church*

But this is a different grammatical phenomenon from extraposition.

There are just a few verbs that omit *to* from a Modal (FOR) TO complement in post-predicate position. They are *make*, *let* and the causal sense of *have* from the MAKING type (compare *They made John go* with *They forced John to go*, which retains the *to*); a subset of ATTENTION verbs, which take a complement similar in form to Modal (FOR) TO (e.g. *They saw John swim*); and just *know* from the THINKING type (e.g. *I've never known him ask such a question before*). Note, however, that the *to* must be included in the corresponding passive, e.g. *John was made to go*, *John was seen to swim*. (See also §8.2.5.)

(E)   Judgement TO complement clauses are exemplified by (25b), (26c) and:

(50)   *I noticed John to be sleeping/incompetent/badly bitten*

All Judgement TO constructions involve a transitive verb, an object NP (which is simultaneously subject of the complement clause), and *to* followed by the complement clause predicate. This predicate most often includes *be*, which can be imperfective auxiliary, passive auxiliary, or copula, although other possibilities do occur (as in (26c) where the predicate begins with *have*).

Judgement TO constructions appear syntactically similar to a Modal (FOR) TO clause in object relation, with *for* omitted but complement clause subject retained, e.g. *I told John to sleep*. There is a critical semantic difference: if there is a THAT complement corresponding to a Modal (FOR)

TO clause then it will generally include a modal, e.g. *I told John that he should sleep*; but if there is a THAT complement clause corresponding to a Judgement TO complement then it cannot include a modal, e.g. *I noticed that John was sleeping*. There is further discussion of this in §8.2.3.

*To* does of course have other functions in the grammar of English—introducing a recipient NP (*give it to John*) or an NP referring to a destination (*go to Moscow*). It is also a (preferred) short form of the clause linker *in order to* (see §2.12), as in (51), which on the surface looks similar to the complement clause construction (52):

**(51)**   *He went to bathe*
**(52)**   *He likes to bathe*

There are profound syntactic differences. *Go* in (51) is an intransitive verb and its clause is linked by (*in order*) *to* with the clause *bathe*. *Like* in (52) is a transitive verb (e.g. *He likes the seaside*) and here *to bathe* is a complement clause; alternatives would be *He likes bathing*, *He likes Mary to bathe*, etc. The semantic type of the first verb in a construction like (51/2) enables one to infer the kind of construction that is involved.

**(F)**   WH- TO could perhaps be regarded as a subtype of Modal (FOR) TO complements. A *wh-* word (other than *why* or *if*) simply precedes the *to* (the VP has the same possibilities as in ING, Modal (FOR) TO and Judgement TO clauses). Thus (20c) and:

**(53)**   *I don't know who to blame*
**(54)**   *They remembered where to look*
**(55)**   *I'll choose when to go*

WH- TO clauses do not have any independent subject; their subject must be coreferential with the subject of the main clause or with its object (e.g. *I told John who to see*). A *wh-* element such as *who* (as in (53) ) or *what* can refer to any constituent of the main clause except its subject.

**(G)**   FROM ING complements are parallel to a variety of Modal (FOR) TO clause, in object relation, that omits *for* but retains the complement clause subject. Compare:

**(56)**   *John forced him to open the door*
**(57)**   *John prevented him (from) opening the door*
**(58)**   *John persuaded him to see the doctor*

**(59)**　*John dissuaded him from seeing the doctor*

*Him* has the same syntactic status in all of (56)–(59); it is underlying subject of the following verb, and is also object NP for the main verb, which may become passive subject, e.g.

**(56a)**　*He was forced to open the door*
**(57a)**　*He was prevented from opening the door*

The VP in a FROM ING clause has its first verb in *-ing* form. It may include previous *have*, imperfective *be*, and passive *be* but not a modal or any tense inflection (this is the same as for ING and the various kinds of TO complement). Interestingly, the *from* may optionally be omitted following a verb of negative causation (*prevent, stop, save*) when used in the active, but is retained in the passive—compare (57) and (57a). It can never be dropped after a verb from the SPEAKING type (*forbid, discourage, dissuade, prohibit*). The semantic conditioning of *from* omission is discussed in §8.2.9.

ING, FROM ING and all kinds of TO complement clause may not have tense inflection in their VP. How do they convey information about time reference, which is coded through tense in main clauses and in THAT and WH-complements? It appears that the auxiliary element *have*, which normally indicates previous aspect, here doubles for past tense and previous aspect; actual present is marked by the absence of *have*. Compare the THAT constructions in:

**(60)**　*I believe that Mary eats mangoes*
**(61)**　*I believe that Mary ate the mango (yesterday)*
**(62)**　*I believe that Mary has eaten the mango (that you brought)*
**(63)**　*I believe that Mary had eaten the mango (that you left there)*

with the corresponding TO constructions:

**(60a)**　*I believe Mary to eat mangoes*
**(61a/62a/63a)**　*I believe Mary to have eaten the mango*

Here *have* in the TO construction corresponds to all of actual past (in (61)), previous present (in (62)) and previous past (in (63)). (This is similar to the 'back-shifting' of indirect speech, mentioned at the beginning of this section; see §7.6.) An identical correspondence applies in ING clauses—all of *I mentioned that Mary ate/has eaten/had eaten the mango* correspond to *I mentioned Mary's having eaten the mango*; see also (24b).

The auxiliary *be* carries over its imperfective meaning into all varieties of complement clause, e.g. *I notice that Mary is eating mangoes* (*every time we go past*) and *I notice Mary to be eating mangoes* (*every time we go past*); see also §2.13C.

There are a number of instances in English where a verb base plus preposition effectively functions as a complete lexical verb, e.g. *decide on, hope for, complain about, rely on, agree on, object to* (§1.4). The preposition is retained before an NP object or an ING complement clause as object but must be omitted—by an automatic rule of English grammar—before complementisers *that, for* and *to* (no verb of this kind occurs with a FROM ING complement clause). The preposition may be omitted or retained before a complementiser beginning with *wh*-. Thus (see also (23a/b/c), (43a/b) and §2.13B):

(**64a**)   *He decided on John*
(**64b**)   *He decided that John would be captain*
(**64c**)   *He decided* (*on*) *who would be captain*

(**65a**)   *She complained about the interruption*
(**65b**)   *She complained about John's interrupting her recital*
(**65c**)   *She complained that John interrupted her recital*

(**66a**)   *I'm hoping for a promotion*
(**66b**)   *I'm hoping to get promoted*
(**66c**)   *I'm hoping that I'll get promoted*

A number of HUMAN PROPENSITY adjectives may take a preposition and then an NP or complement clause, e.g. *afraid of, sorry about, proud of, jealous of/about, careful about*. Once again, the preposition is retained before an NP or an ING complement, but dropped before *that, for* or *to*, e.g.

(**67a**)   *John is afraid of the dark*
(**67b**)   *John is afraid of going out in the dark*
(**67c**)   *John is afraid to go out in the dark*
(**67d**)   *John is afraid that it will be too dark*

(**68a**)   *Mary is sorry about her mistake*
(**68b**)   *Mary is sorry about making an error in the calculation*
(**68c**)   *Mary is sorry that she made an error in the calculation*

Table 2.5 summarises some of the more important syntactic features of complement clauses. It will be seen that (A) THAT and (B) WH- have almost identical syntax; they differ only in the minor detail, under 10, that a

**Table 2.5.** *Syntactic features of complement clauses*

| | THAT (A) | WH- (B) | ING (C) | Modal (FOR) TO (D) | Judgement TO (E) | WH- TO (F) | FROM ING (G) |
|---|---|---|---|---|---|---|---|
| 1. complement clause VP is tensed | x | x | — | — | — | — | — |
| 2. modal may be included in complement clause VP | x | x | — | — | — | — | — |
| 3. subject NP can be omitted from complement clause when coreferential with an NP in main clause | — | — | x | x | —¹ | x² | —¹ |
| 4. when complement clause is post-predicate, its subject can become main clause object | — | — | — | x | x¹ | — | x¹ |
| 5. complement clause may be in object relation, with potential to become passive subject | x | x | x | x | — | — | — |
| 6. adverbial element may come between main clause predicate and complement clause as object | x | x | — | x | — | — | — |
| 7. complement clause may follow object NP of main clause | x | x | — | x | —¹ | — | —¹ |
| 8. complement clause may be in subject relation | x | x | x | x | — | — | — |
| 9. complement clause may be extraposed from subject position | x | x | — | x | | | |
| 10. preposition is omitted before the complement clause | x | opt. | — | x | | opt. | |

*Key:* 'x' indicates 'yes', '—' indicates 'no', 'opt.' = optional; a blank shows that the question is not applicable.

¹Subject NP of complement clause always becomes surface syntactic object of main clause (but still functions as complement clause subject, as can be seen from reflexivisation).

²Subject NP must be coreferential with main clause subject or object, and omitted.

preposition may optionally be retained before *wh-*. Varieties (E) Judgement TO, (F) WH- TO and (G) FROM ING also show strong similarities.

ING clauses stand apart from the others. The fact that an ING clause is not readily extraposable from subject position, in 9, and that it does not easily take a preceding adverb, in 6, suggests that ING clauses function more like NPs than do other varieties of complement clause. Be that as it may, an ING clause is quite different in structure from an NP, as we saw when comparing (37) and (38).

## 2.8. Omission of *be*

Consider the following sentences:

(**69**)   *I consider John (to be) clever/a good doctor*
(**70a**)   *I want the house (to be) clean when I return*
(**70b**)   *I want the knave (to be) executed before lunch*
(**70c**)   *I want Mary (to be) doing her homework when her father comes home*
(**71**)   *I made Mary (be) interested in the project*
(**72a**)   *John retired (when he was) happy/a contented man*
(**72b**)   *Mary entered the room (when she was) angry/in tears*
(**73a**)   *I ate the fish (when it was) raw*
(**73b**)   *I like him (when he is) drunk*
(**74**)   *He licked the plate (so that it was) clean*

When the portions in parentheses are omitted, these sentences are superficially similar, in including an adjective after verb (plus object). Sentences like this have been grouped together and labelled 'secondary predicates', an unhelpful and misleading term. In fact (69)–(74) are reduced versions of four quite different construction types, which have little in common, save the tendency to omit copula *be* in a variety of circumstances.

(**a**)   Reduction of Judgement TO complement clause. Some, but not all, verbs which take a Judgement TO complement clause may drop the complementiser *to* plus a following copula *be*, as in (69). The complement clause then reduces to just its copula complement (here, *clever*, or *a good doctor*). This is discussed further in §8.2.6.

(**b**)   Reduction of Modal FOR TO complement clause. *To be* can never be omitted from the maximal form of a Modal (FOR) TO complement, e.g. not from *I hoped for the house to be clean when I returned* or from *I asked for him to be shot*. There is, however, a small set of verbs that can omit *to be* when *for* is also omitted. Whereas only the copula *be* may be omitted from a Judgement TO clause, here any of the three varieties of *be* can be omitted—copula *be* in (70a), passive *be* in (70b) and imperfective *be* in (70c). See §§8.2.5, 6.2.1, 6.3.1–2.

Verbs *make* and *let* take a FOR TO complement clause but always omit *for*, and omit *to* in an active (but retain it in a passive) clause. Example (71) shows that the copula *be* can also be omitted. This is discussed in §6.3.

**(c)**   Adverbial clauses of time. These undergo a variety of kinds of reduction, one of which is shown in (72)–(73). A *when* clause involving the copula *be* can omit the 'when-plus-pronominal-subject-plus-*be*-plus-tense'. This applies in (72a/b) when the understood pronominal subject of the time clause is identical to the subject (S) in the intransitive main clause, and in (73a/b) when it is identical to the object (O) in the transitive main clause. Other typical transitive main clause verbs include *drink* (*it undiluted*), *cook* (*it alive*), and *find* (*him in agony*).

There are a number of variants on this basic pattern. For example, *He started reading the letter* (*when he was*) *happy and finished it* (*when he was*) *sad*, where the unstated pronoun of the subordinate clause is identical to the transitive subject (A) of the main clause, the O here being inanimate.

**(d)**   Result construction. In (74) the main clause is linked by *so that* to a copula clause indicating something that is the result of what is described in the main clause; *so that it was* may be omitted. There are many instances of this, all fairly fixed expressions; they include *knock him unconscious*, *shoot him dead*, *shave it dry*, *squash it flat*, *sweep it clean*, *bury it deep*, and *paint it red*. This is further discussed in §4.2.

## 2.9. Types of *-ing* clause

The suffix *-ing* has a wide range of uses. It is part of the imperfective aspect marker, *be -ing* (§2.2). It is used to mark adjectives derived from verbs (such as *exhausting*) and also nouns derived from verbs (such as *happening*); see

§2.10 and §10.3. It is used to mark the verb in two kinds of complement clause, the ING and the FROM ING types (see §2.7). There are a number of other clause types marked just by -*ing* on the verb, which it will be useful to mention briefly here.

**(a)**   With *go* and *come* (see §4.1). Just these two verbs, which refer to motion to and away from the focus of attention, may be followed by a -*ing* verb, as in *We all went shopping*, and *Come swimming with me*. In this construction, *go* and *come* behave like secondary verbs.

**(b)**   With a SPEED adjective. When an adjective from this semantic type functions as copula complement, it can be followed by a preposition such as *at* plus an NP, as in *She is quick at arithmetic*. In place of the NP there can be an ING complement clause, and the preposition may then be omitted; for example, *She was quick (at) solving the problem, He was slow (at) asking for a rise*.

**(c)**   With a HUMAN PROPENSITY adjective. Items from this semantic type are typically followed by a preposition plus an ING complement clause. When the complement clause has the same subject as the main clause, the preposition can often be omitted. For example, *He was proud (of) winning the prize, She was generous (in) giving us her old car, She was lucky (in) finding the money, He was happy (at) working on the problem.* Note, however, that the preposition cannot be omitted if the two clauses have different subjects, as in *Mary was proud of her daughter winning the prize*.

**(d)**   Reduced time adverbial clauses. A time clause commencing with *after having* can omit the *after*; for example *(After) having made his will, John slashed his wrists*, and *Mary made an offer for the house (after) having inspected it*. Similarly, a time clause commencing with *while*, followed by a verb in -*ing* form, can omit the *while*, as in *(While) leaving the room, he tripped over the doormat*, and *She announced her wedding date, (while) blushing slightly*. This clause type is further discussed in §2.12.

The simultaneous appositional clauses in (14), (15b–e) and (16a–c) are also of this type.

Note that in all of (a)–(d), the -*ing* clause which apparently stands alone must have the same subject as the main clause.

**(e)** Appositional clauses of consequence and reason. Something which follows as a consequence from what is said in the main clause may be expressed by a following clause with the verb in *-ing* form, as in:

**(75)**   *The trains were on strike, (this) forcing us to travel by bus*

The unstated subject of the *-ing* clause refers to the preceding main clause. Another example is *The meeting finished early, (this) enabling us to have a drink together.*

Note that (75) can be restated with the subordinate clause as main clause:

**(75′)**   *The trains being on strike, we were forced to go by bus*

This is an appositional clause of reason. Whereas (75) has the structure '[Main clause] and as a consequence [*-ing* clause]', with the subject of the *-ing* clause effectively being the main clause, (75′) is '[*-ing* clause] and as a result main clause', where both clauses have a stated subject.

When an appositional clause of reason involves *being*, this may on occasion be omitted; for example, *The job (being) finished, we went off for a drink.*


## 2.10. Word derivations

English has a number of derivational affixes that change word-class membership, but each applies to a limited set of words. Nouns formed from verbs include *amusement, punishment; suggestion, conclusion; blessing, singing; resemblance; pleasure*; see §10.3. Among adjectives derived from verbs are *adorable, persuasive, contributory*. Verbs derived from adjectives and nouns include *purify, glorify; equalise, itemise; blacken, lighten, threaten.* Most of these derivational endings are of French or Latin origin (notable exceptions being *-en* and *-ing*).

Quite a number of English words appear to belong to more than one word class, e.g.

adjective and verb: *dirty, clean, tidy, narrow*
noun and verb: *stone, butter, bridge, cash*
verb and noun: *walk, punch, look, sleep, catch, laugh, roast*

In each case, speakers have a clear intuition that one word-class membership is primary and the other secondary. *Stone* is said to be firstly a noun, although it can also be used as a verb (e.g. *Stone the Christians!*). *Walk* is regarded as a verb, which can also be used as a noun (*That walk tired me out*). In the tabulation just given, the primary word-class membership is given first (as, indeed, it generally is in dictionary entries).

There are two ways of dealing with the facts reported in the last paragraph. One is to say that *stone, butter*, etc. are nouns pure and simple, while *walk, punch*, etc. are verbs, and then to state that all nouns may be head of an NP, but a subset of nouns (*stone, butter*, etc.) may also function as head of a VP (taking appropriate verbal endings); and that all verbs can be head of a VP but that a specified subset of verbs (*walk, punch*, etc.) can also be NP head (and will then take appropriate nominal endings). The other approach is to say that the head of a VP can only be a verb, etc., and that English has derivational processes, with zero marking, that derive verbs from some nouns (verb *stone* from noun *stone*), and so on.

Evidence for preferring the second (zero derivation) alternative in the case of English comes from considerations of pairs like:

(**76**)  adjective     *wide*         verb     *widen*
(**77**)  adjective     *narrow*       verb     *narrow*

(**78**)  verb          *converse*     noun     *conversation*
(**79**)  verb          *talk*         noun     *talk*

(**80**)  verb          *postpone*     noun     *postponement*
(**81**)  verb          *delay*        noun     *delay*

The words in each pair have related meanings. In each instance the first line shows an affix marking a derivational process. By analogy, it seems most satisfactory to say that the second line also involves a derivational process, with zero marking.

A further piece of evidence comes from examination of which words in a given semantic set may have double class membership. Consider:

| BOTH NOUN AND VERB | ONLY NOUN |
| --- | --- |
| *butter* | *margarine* |
| *stone* | *rock, pebble* |
| *house* | *cottage, bungalow* |
| *weather* | *climate* |

It will be seen that, in each row, the most generic and commonly used noun also undergoes zero derivation to function as a verb, while those with more specific meanings lack this derivation.

In summary, English lacks a full array of productive derivational affixes; the suffixes (mostly of foreign origin) that are used each occur with a restricted set of roots. As a result there is much use of 'zero derivation', i.e. use of a noun in verb function without any change in form, etc.

Some generalisations are possible. Many verbs referring to CORPOREAL function can also be used as nouns, e.g. *bite, swallow, drink, sniff, smell, taste, laugh, cry, sob, weep, wink, kiss, hug, pee*. And many nouns referring to implements can also be used as verbs, e.g. *spear, knife, saw, hammer, whip, nail, screw*.

Chapter 10 provides a full discussion of the eight types of nominalisations from verbs, and their markings—zero derivation, and also suffixes *-er, -ant, -ard, -ing, -ation, -ment, -ance*, etc. (Most suffixes mark several different kinds of nominalisation, with different verbs.)

## 2.11. Clause derivations

There are a number of ways in which the basic structure of a clause in English can be transformed. Only some of the more notable processes are outlined here.

### 2.11.1. Questions

To form a polar question (one expecting 'yes' or 'no' as answer), the first auxiliary verb (or copula *be*), which bears a tense inflection, is moved to the front of the clause. Corresponding to *John was eating the halva* we get *Was John eating the halva?* and alongside *John had been eating the halva* there is *Had John been eating the halva?* There must be at least one verb in the auxiliary for question formation—if the VP contains none of *have, be* or a modal then *do* must be included to take the tense inflection; thus, corresponding to the statement *John ate the halva*, we get the question *Did John eat the halva?* The possessor verb *have* can behave like an auxiliary or like a lexical verb; some people say *Have you any children?* while others prefer *Do you have any children?* Note that an auxiliary cannot be moved over a complement clause, in subject slot; to form a question the complement clause must be extraposed and replaced by *it*. That is, we must say *Is it surprising that we lost?*, rather than \**Is that we lost surprising?*, corresponding to *That we lost is surprising*.

There are two modes of behaviour for the negator *not* in a polar question. If it is reduced to be an enclitic *=nt* on an auxiliary, then the auxiliary-plus-*=nt* will be fronted in a question, as in *Shouldn't you go?* However, if *not* retains its stressed form, as an independent word, then it is not fronted; one says *Did he not go?* rather than? \**Did not he go?* and *Should you not go?* in preference to? \**Should not you go?* (See §12.11.)

A content question (expecting a phrase or clause as answer), often called a *wh-* question for English, involves the same fronting, and in addition a *wh-* word (*who, whom, whose, what, which, how, why, where* or *when*), which refers to some constituent of the main clause, must precede the preposed auxiliary word. Compare *John was hitting Mary* with *Who was hitting Mary?*; *Mary arrived yesterday* with *When did Mary arrive?*; and *John ate the halva* with *What did John eat?* If the constituent being questioned had a preposition associated with it, then this may either be moved to initial position, before the *wh-* word, or left in its underlying position in the clause. Thus, corresponding to *He owes his success to hard work* we can have either *What does he owe his success to?* or *To what does he owe his success?*

There is an important difference between a straightforward question and a WH- complement clause; the latter involves an initial *wh-* element, but no fronting of the first auxiliary word. Thus *Has he come?* and *She asked whether he had come*; and *Where did she hide the money?* alongside *He enquired where she had hidden the money*. Note also that WH- complement clauses occur with many verbs that do not introduce direct speech questions, e.g. *I know who did it, She remembered why he had built the boat* (see §8.2.1).

## 2.11.2. Causatives

Many languages have a special 'causative' affix, deriving a transitive from an intransitive verb (and a ditransitive verb from a transitive)—when *-dür* is added to *ölmek* 'to die' in Turkish, for instance, we get *öldürmek* 'to kill'. English, with its sparse morphology, lacks this, but does have two other means of coding causation. The first is the productive use of a verb from the secondary type MAKING (§6.3.1) with an intransitive or transitive verb in a TO complement clause, as in the (b) examples below. The other involves using some (but by no means all) basically intransitive verbs in a transitive construction, with the intransitive subject (S) becoming transitive object (O), and a new 'causer' NP being brought in for transitive subject (A) function; this is illustrated in the (c) examples below.

(**82a**)   *The child sat on the mat*
(**82b**)   *Mary made the child sit on the mat*
(**82c**)   *Mary sat the child on the mat*

(**83a**)   *The piece of metal bent*
(**83b**)   *Mary made the piece of metal bend*
(**83c**)   *Mary bent the piece of metal*

(**84a**)   *The pauper bled*
(**84b**)   *John made the pauper bleed*
(**84c**)   *John bled the pauper*

There is a difference in each case. Sentence (82c) implies that Mary picked up the child and put it sitting on the mat; for (82b) she could have got the child to sit by telling it to, or spanking it until it did. One could use (83c) when Mary changed the shape of the piece of metal with her hands, but (83b) when she heated it over a fire, so that it changed shape. Hearing (84c) one might presume that John was a doctor who drew blood from the pauper in a scientific manner to relieve some medical condition; for (84b) John might be a blackguard who bashed the pauper with a piece of lead pipe until he began to bleed.

The (c) sentences—a basically intransitive verb used transitively—imply careful and direct manipulation, whereas the periphrastic *make* constructions imply some more indirect means. (There are also of course semantic differences between the various verbs that can be used in (b) constructions—*make, cause, force*, etc. See §6.3.1.)

For most intransitive/transitive verb pairs with intransitive S = transitive O—such as *sit, bend* and *bleed*—native speakers pick the intransitive sense as primary. However, there are some S = O pairs for which the transitive sense is generally considered primary, e.g. *I broke the vase, The vase broke*. Further discussion of this is provided in §§9.3.2–3.

Other verbs can be used both transitively and intransitively but with S = A, rather than S = O, e.g. *He doesn't smoke* and *He doesn't smoke a pipe*; *I've eaten* and *I've eaten lunch*; *They are playing* and *They are playing hopscotch*. These could perhaps be regarded as transitive verbs that may omit an object NP under certain specific conditions. Note that some verbs (such as *take, hit, make, prefer*) can only omit an object NP under very special circumstances (e.g. when contrasted with another verb, as in *He takes more than he gives*), and others may do so only when the object can be inferred from the context or from the previous discourse, e.g. *You choose!* The general question of transitivity and object deletion is dealt with in §9.3.1.

## 2.11.3. Passives

In the passive derivation a direct object becomes subject of the derived intransitive construction; *be* is inserted immediately before the head of the VP, and the following head verb is in *-en* form. Thus, corresponding to *Fred stole the Saab*, there is *The Saab was stolen* (*by Fred*).

An underlying transitive subject may almost always be included in a passive construction, marked by the preposition *by*. This can indicate the role which was primarily responsible for the activity that has resulted in the state described by the passive verb. In fact, in most styles of English a *by* phrase is only included in a smallish minority of actual passive clauses.

Not all NPs that directly follow a verb can be passivised (i.e. become a passive subject)—not those in *possess an expensive house, resemble a famous film star*, or *stand fifteen minutes in the rain*, for instance. Some NPs that are introduced by a preposition may be passivisable, e.g. *This hat has been sat on* and *Has the new audition tape been listened to yet?* Chapter 11 discusses the syntax and semantics of passive constructions.

## 2.11.4. Promotion to subject

That role which is most likely to be relevant to the success of an activity is generally associated with the syntactic relation A (transitive subject) in a transitive clause. For *record*, this is the person doing the recording. If a VALUE adverb, such as *well*, is included, as in (85), it implies that the activity proceeded well owing to the efforts of John McDonald (the recording engineer) in A slot:

(85)  *John McDonald recorded the Hallé Orchestra well* (*with the Beyer microphone*) (*in studio B*)

But the success of a recording venture might be attributable to the qualities of the orchestra involved, or of the microphone used, or to the acoustic properties of the recording studio. To indicate these, any of the three non-A

NPs could be promoted to the A slot (displacing the original A, which cannot be included in the three sentences below). If a promoted NP was marked by a preposition, this is dropped.

**(86)**    *The Hallé orchestra recorded well* (*with the Beyer microphone*) (*in studio B*)

**(87)**    *The Beyer microphone recorded* (*the Hallé Orchestra*) *well* (*in studio B*)

**(88)**    *Studio B recorded* (*the Hallé Orchestra*) *well* (*with the Beyer microphone*)

Sentences (86)–(88) are still transitive. There can still be an O NP, *the Hallé Orchestra*, in (87)–(88); in (86) *the Hallé Orchestra* is in A slot, but is still understood to be the object of *record*.

There is a crucial semantic and syntactic difference between (86), a transitive clause with *the Hallé Orchestra* in A slot, and the passive of (85), which is intransitive and has *the Hallé Orchestra* in S relation:

**(89)**    *The Hallé Orchestra was recorded well* (*by John McDonald*) (*with the Beyer microphone*) (*in Studio B*)

In (86) the excellence of the recording venture is attributed to the qualities of the orchestra. In (89) (as in (85)) it is due to the skill of the underlying agent (and is so perceived even if the agentive phrase *by John McDonald* is omitted from (89)).

Non-A NPs can be promoted to A slot in the presence of a limited set of adverbs (*well, nicely, slowly, easily* and just a few more) or the negative marker, or a modal, or a combination of these. We can say *Studio C didn't record the Hallé Orchestra very well*, but plain *\*Studio C recorded the Hallé Orchestra* is not acceptable.

Chapter 13 discusses the conditions under which 'promotion to subject' is appropriate.


## 2.11.5. Reflexives


If an NP following the predicate (either an object or an NP introduced by a preposition) has the same reference as the subject NP within the same clause, then the post-predicate NP must be replaced by the appropriate reflexive pronoun, e.g. *Pablo cut himself, Agnes looked at herself in the mirror, Gonzales told a story about himself*. However, if two NPs are coreferential between different clauses in a single sentence then a reflexive pronoun is not applicable, e.g. *After John swore, Mary hit him*, not *\*After John swore, Mary hit himself*.

The occurrence of reflexive pronouns provides confirmation for our analysis of complement clauses (§2.7). In

**(90)**   *John imagined* [*that Mary was hitting him*]
**(91)**   *John imagined* [*that he was hitting Mary*]

the *he/him* are in a different clause from *John*, and are thus not in reflexive form. But in

**(92)**   *John imagined himself to be hitting Mary*
**(93)**   *John imagined Mary to be hitting herself*

we can see that the NP that follows *imagined* is both object of *imagine* and in the same clause as *John* (hence *himself* in (92)), and also subject of *hit* and in the same clause as *Mary* (hence *herself* in (93)). That it is both simultaneously is shown by:

**(94)**   *John imagined himself to be hitting himself*

The fact that *Mary* in (93) is simultaneously (*a*) object of *imagine*, and (*b*) subject of *hit*, leads to conflict of criteria over the form of a pronoun substituting for it. It should be series II (*she*) by (*b*) but series I (*her*) by (*a*). We can explain the occurrence of *her* (as in *John imagined her to be hitting Fred*) in terms of series I being the 'unmarked' form of the pronoun.

The occurrence of reflexive pronouns also confirms our analysis of relative clauses (§2.6). Consider [*the man* [*who cut himself*]] *bled to death*; the object of *cut* is in reflexive form since it is coreferential with *who*, the relative pronoun filling subject slot, and this is itself coreferential with determiner-plus-head of the superordinate NP, *the man*. We do not, however, get a reflexive pronoun for the object of *hit* in *Mary sacked* [*the man* [*who hit her*]] since this is in a different clause from *Mary*.

Whether or not a given verb may occur in a reflexive construction depends to a great extent on whether it is semantically plausible for the same referent to relate to both subject and some post-predicate slot. It seems a little more felicitous to say *John stopped himself from jumping in at the deep end* than ?*John prevented himself from jumping in at the deep end*. With some verbs reflexive reference is scarcely plausible, e.g. *fetch*. With others the opposite applies, e.g. for *think* the NP introduced by *to* must be coreferential with the subject, *I thought to myself*. The verb *pride* must be used with a reflexive object, as in *Mary prided herself on keeping the house tidy*.

*Self* pronouns can also be used with an 'intensive' or 'emphatic' or 'contrastive' function, in apposition to—and following—an NP (which is usually in subject function), e.g. *The President himself said so*, or *I myself told a story to Agnes*. An intensive pronoun from a subject NP can be moved to a later position in the clause—*The President (himself) said so (himself)*, and *I (myself) told the story (myself) to Agnes (myself)*.

The contrast between reflexive and intensive pronouns is well illustrated with *sit down*, an intransitive verb that can also be used causatively, e.g. *She sat the child down*. It can be seen that *John sat himself down* is a reflexivised causative, whereas *John himself sat down* and *John sat down himself* are intransitive, with an intensive pronoun that relates to the subject NP.

Intensive pronouns are generally not placed in structural positions that could be filled by a reflexive pronoun. *Watch* is a transitive verb which can omit its object—*John watched Mary*, *John watched himself (on the video)*, *John watched*. In this case an intensive pronoun from the subject NP (*John himself watched*) would not be likely to be moved to a position after the verb, since it could then be mistaken for a reflexive substitute for the object NP. However, an intensive pronoun could be moved after an explicit object NP (especially if there was a gender difference), e.g. *John watched Mary himself*.

There is a very small set of transitive verbs which may omit specification of an object with it being understood to be a reflexive pronoun (i.e. coreferential with the subject), e.g. *Mary hid* (sc. herself), *My daughter is dressing* (sc. herself), *John is shaving* (sc. himself), *The Queen is washing* (sc. herself). It appears that *hide* and *dress* may only omit an NP when it is reflexive. *Shave* and *wash* have wider possibilities of object omission; *Mary is washing* is thus ambiguous between a reflexive interpretation (she is washing herself) or simple transitive use with the object left unstated (she may be doing the weekly clothes wash for her family).

A number of verbs with a fairly concrete central meaning can take on a special metaphorical sense when used with a reflexive object NP, e.g. *put yourself in his place* 'imagine yourself to be him', *pull yourself together* 'stop behaving irrationally', *try and bring yourself to do it* 'force yourself to do it'.

Reflexives are often used to achieve a casual, informal style, e.g. the reflexive causative *Just sit yourself down here* is more chatty and friendly than the plain intransitive *Just sit down here*.

## 2.11.6. Reciprocals

Instead of saying *John punched Mary and Mary punched John* we would normally use a reciprocal construction, *John and Mary punched each other*. Here the two participants (each of whom is both Agent and Target in different instances of punching) are coordinated as subject, and the predicate is followed by *each other*. The subject of a reciprocal can refer to more than two participants, as in *Tom, Dick and Harry like one another*. We need not even know exactly how many it does refer to, e.g. *The boys hit one another*. This last sentence does not necessarily mean that each boy hit every other boy, just that each boy hit someone, and was hit by someone. (*Each other* tends to be preferred for two participants and *one another* for more than two, although there is a degree of substitutability.)

We mentioned in the last section that just a few verbs may omit a reflexive object, e.g. *John hid* (sc. himself). There is a slightly larger set of verbs which may omit the reciprocal marker *each other* or *one another*, e.g. *John and Mary hugged* (sc. each other), *All my aunts quarrelled* (sc. with one another). We will refer to verbs such as *hug* and *quarrel* (*with*), which can omit the reciprocal marker, as 'inherently reciprocal'. Note, though, that there are many verbs describing actions that are often reciprocal, which commonly occur with *each other* or *one another*, which cannot omit this reciprocal marker. If *each other* were dropped from *John and Mary watched each other*, giving *John and Mary watched*, there is an implication that they watched something (e.g. a game, or programme on TV) together, not that they watched each other.

The 'inherently reciprocal' verbs can be grouped into sets:

(I)   Verbs that only omit a post-predicate NP if it is *each other* or *one another*:
    (a)   simple transitive verbs—*adjoin, touch; hug, cuddle, kiss, fuck* (and synonyms); *match*;
    (b)   verbs that include a preposition plus NP, both of which can be omitted if the NP is *each other* or *one another*—*collide* (*with*), *quarrel* (*with*), *converse* (*with*), *differ* (*from*), *correspond* (*with*);
    (c)   copula *be* plus an adjective from the SIMILARITY type (§3.2) followed by a preposition plus NP, both being omitted under a reciprocal interpretation—*(be) similar (to), (be) different (from), (be) identical (with)*.

Note that when a verb from set (I) is used with no object (or no prepositional object) then it must have a subject with plural reference, e.g. *The cars collided*, not *\*The car collided*.

(II)   Verbs which may omit a non-reciprocal object NP (or preposition plus NP) but may also omit a reciprocal marker. If they occur with a plural subject and no stated object (or preposition plus NP) then the most natural interpretation is a reciprocal one:

    (a)   simple transitive verbs—*pass, meet, fight* (here *with* may optionally be inserted before the object), *marry* (this forms a causative; see §9.3.3);

    (b)   verbs that take preposition plus NP—*play, compete, struggle, speak, talk, chat, joke, argue, gossip, agree, disagree* (all taking *with*).

(III)   *Discuss* takes a direct object (the Message) and, optionally, *with* plus Addressee NP, which should be omitted if the NP is a reciprocal marker: *John discussed the accident* (*with Mary*), *John and Mary discussed the accident* (sc. with each other).

(IV)   *Exchange* and *trade* each take a direct object (the Gift), e.g. *John exchanged his knife for Mary's dagger.* If two tokens of the same gift are involved we can say *John exchanged knives with Mary* or *John and Mary exchanged knives* (sc. with each other).

The adverb *together* is often included when the reciprocal pronoun is omitted—with *play, struggle, speak, talk, chat, joke, argue* from (IIb), *fight* from (IIa) and *discuss* from (III), but not with the other verbs.

Some of these verbs must have a reciprocal meaning. If it is true that *This house differs from that one* then it must be true that *That house differs from this one* and also that *This house and that one differ* (sc. from each other). Similar verbs are *match, converse, marry, agree, disagree, discuss, exchange, trade.* Others of the verbs in (I)–(IV) refer to an activity that is normally entered into by both (or all, if more than two) participants, but need not necessarily be, e.g. *meet* (discussed in §11.2), *chat, hug, fuck* (there is a verb to describe this normally reciprocal activity being entered into freely by only one of the parties—*rape*).

There are odd anomalies. For instance, *resemble* has a symmetrical meaning just like *differ* (*from*) and yet it cannot omit *each other* or *one another*, e.g. *John's ideas and Mary's ideas resemble each other* but not *\*John's ideas and Mary's ideas resemble.* (*Be similar* (*to*) is very close in meaning to *resemble*, and here *each other/one another* can be omitted.)

## 2.11.7.   *HAVE A VERB, GIVE A VERB and TAKE A VERB*

As an alternative to *John ran* (*in the park before breakfast*) we can say *John had a run* (*in the park before breakfast*), with a slight difference in meaning. *Have* replaces an intransitive verb and this verb, preceded by the indefinite article *a*, becomes head of the NP that follows *have*. However, parallel to *John arrived (from town before breakfast)* it is not permissible to say *\*John had an arrive (from town before breakfast)*. Some verbs can occur in HAVE A VERB constructions but others, with similar meanings, cannot. Why can we say *have a cry* but not *\*have a die*; *have a yawn* but not *\*have a breathe*; *have a sit-down* but not *\*have a settle-down*; *have a think* but not *\*have a reflect?*

Similar to HAVE-A-plus-intransitive-VERB is GIVE-A-plus-transitive-VERB. *John kicked the door* could be rephrased, with a slight meaning difference, as *John gave the door a kick*. But it is not possible to say, alongside *John broke the door*, the sentence *\*John gave the door a break*. Similarly, *John gave the silver ornament a polish* is acceptable, but not *\*John gave the silver ornament a wrap*; and *Mary gave John a kiss* is fine, but not *\*Mary gave John a kill*.

HAVE A constructions occur primarily with intransitive and GIVE A constructions primarily with transitive verbs, but there are exceptions. *Laugh* is intransitive; one can *have a laugh* and also *give a laugh*, with a meaning difference. *Stroke* is transitive; one can *give the cat a stroke* or *have a stroke of the fur coat*. And, alongside *Mary looked at John* we can have both *Mary had a look at John* (with no implication that he knew he was being looked at) and *Mary gave John a look* (with the expectation that he did receive it, and that it was a meaningful gesture).

There are also TAKE A VERB constructions such as *take a stroll*, *take a look*, *take a kick*, which have a recurrent meaning difference from *have a stroll*, *have a look*, *have a kick*. It appears that in British English a subset of those verbs which occur with HAVE A also occur with TAKE A. (American English is significantly different, with *take a walk* etc. being used instead of *have a walk* etc. It is likely that the same general semantic principles hold, but are applied in a slightly different way.)

Chapter 14 considers the meanings of HAVE A VERB, GIVE A VERB and TAKE A VERB constructions, and the semantic motivation for which verbs may occur in these construction types and which may not.

## 2.12. Clause linking

There are a number of ways of linking clauses in English, including (*a*) by coordinate linkers such as *and*, *but*, *or*; (*b*) by temporal subordinate linkers such as *after*, *before*, *while*, *till*, *until*; (*c*) by logical subordinate linkers such as *since, because, if, although, even though, unless, in spite of*; (*d*) by contrastive linkers such as *however, moreover, nevertheless, therefore, accordingly, on the other hand, at all events, still*; (*e*) by the purposive linker *in order* (*to*/*that*).

English has a further, rather unusual, syntactic trick for clause linking. After *if*, some speakers use *were* (sometimes called a 'subjunctive' form) in place of the expected *was*. For example, *If Mary were to come, we'd ask her to propose the vote of thanks*. An alternative construction is to omit *if* and transpose the subject and *were*, giving *Were Mary to come, we'd ask her to propose the vote of thanks*. (Note that for speakers who use *was* in preference to *were*, this alternative is not possible; they can only say *If Mary was to come, . . .* , not *\*Was Mary to come, . . .*) See also §12.11.6.

Linked clauses often share a coreferential NP. It is infelicitous to repeat the same word several times in a sentence, and there are grammatical conventions in English for omitting a repeated NP, or replacing it by a pronoun.

A repeated NP can be omitted under two circumstances, one involving coordinate and the other involving temporal subordinate linkers. Firstly, if two coordinated clauses share an NP which is in subject (S or A) function in each clause, then it may be omitted from the second clause in sequence. From *Mary* (S) *came in* and *Mary* (A) *saw John* (O) can be formed the complex sentence *Mary came in and saw John*. But if the shared NP is in non-subject function in either clause then omission is not possible—from *John* (S) *came in* and *Mary* (A) *saw John* (O) it is not permissible to form *\*John came in and Mary saw*. (We do have available the passive construction, which puts an underlying O into derived S function. *John* (S) *came in* can be linked with *John* (S) *was seen by Mary* and the second *John* may now be omitted, giving *John came in and was seen by Mary*.)

A temporal subordinate clause may have the structure of a main clause, preceded by a subordinate marker such as *after* or *while*, e.g. *After he took off his hat, John sat down*; no omission of a coreferential NP is possible here. Alternatively, we may have a VP whose initial verb is in *-ing* form; the subject of such a clause must be omitted if it is coreferential with the subject of the main clause, e.g. *After taking off his hat, John sat down*. Note that such a temporal clause can come before, after, or in the middle of the main clause, e.g. *John was, while waiting for Mary, deciding what he would say to her* and *Fred always washes his hands before eating*. We find, in addition, that *after* and *while* (but never *before*) can be omitted under specific circumstances. As mentioned under (d) in §2.9, *after* can be dispensed with before a VP commencing with *having* (it appears that the previous aspect auxiliary *have* sufficiently conveys the idea of prior time, without requiring *after* as well), e.g. *(After) having taken off his hat, John sat down. While* may be—but perhaps less often is—omitted when the VP begins with a lexical verb in *-ing*, e.g. *(While) sitting in the garden, John studied the birds.* (As noted in §2.5, there are also temporal clauses, whose VP begins with an *-ing* form, that have a different subject from the main clause, e.g. *His mother having gone out for the day, John had a party.*)

Another important device—which is much used when a complex sentence includes two underlying occurrences of the same NP—is to replace one of them by the corresponding third person pronoun. This is possible whatever the syntactic functions involved, e.g. *Mary* (S) *came in and she* (A) *saw John*, or *Mary* (S) *came in and John saw her* (O). Pronominalisation can only apply 'forwards' within coordinate constructions, e.g. *She came in and Mary saw John* is not a possible paraphrase of *Mary came in and she saw John.* (If *She came in and Mary saw John* were heard, *she* would have to be taken to refer not to *Mary* but to someone else, previously mentioned in the discourse.)

Pronominalisation can apply forwards or backwards into a subordinate clause, whether introduced by a temporal connective such as *after* or *while*, or a logical connective such as *since* or *if*, e.g. *If he comes here, John will get a shock* and *After she lost her keys, Mary couldn't get into the house.* Backwards pronominalisation is not possible from subordinate clause to main clause; it is not acceptable to say *He will get a shock if John comes here* with the *he* referring to *John* (the *he* would have to be taken as referring to someone else).

Set (*d*), contrastive linkers, are typically placed at the beginning of the clause, as in *Jack is handsome; moreover his father has made a will leaving him a million pounds.* However, a contrastive linker may follow the subject, or the first word of the predicate, the word preceding it then being stressed (shown by ′); for example *Jack is handsome; his ′father, moreover, has made a will leaving him a million pounds* or *Jack is handsome, his father ′has, moreover, made a will leaving him a million pounds.* In §12.3.1, the placement and associated meanings of contrastive linkers are compared with those of sentential adverbs.

Two clauses linked by a coordinator such as *and*, or a logical subordinate linker such as *if*, or a contrastive linker such as *however*, each have the structure of a main clause. The fifth type of clause linker, *in order*, is quite different; it must occur with a main clause and be followed by a THAT, FOR-TO or TO complement clause (the main clause usually comes first although, as with *since* and *if* constructions, the order can be reversed), e.g. (51) and

**(95)**   *John told the children to keep quiet in order that he/Mary might work*

**(96)**   *John kept the children quiet (in order) for Mary to be able to work*

**(97a)**   *Mary went to her study (in order) to work/write a book*

**(97b)**   *John took Mary outside (in order) (for her) to relax/pick flowers*

A THAT clause, as in (95), may have the same subject as the main clause or a different one, while a FOR-TO complement, as in (96), will normally have a different subject. The TO complement after *in order*, as in (97a), has the same subject as the main clause, and this subject cannot be stated in the TO clause. In (97b), the O of the main clause is identical to the subject (S or A) of the TO clause; here *for her* can be omitted. *In order* may be—and usually is—omitted from *in order to* and from *in order for . . . to*; it is possible—but less usual—to omit *in order* from *in order that*.

When a complement clause occurs after *in order*, any verb may fill the predicate head slot in the accompanying main clause (subject to semantic plausibility of the complete sentence). The term 'complement clause' is perhaps not appropriate here, but it shows that a clause which follows *in order* does have the same structure as a complement clause that can fill a subject or object slot for semantically determined types of predicates, as described in §2.7 and Chapter 8.

There is a further convention in English grammar, concerning a VP that recurs in two clauses of a complex sentence. This is: if two coordinated clauses have the same predicate but different subjects, objects and other peripheral constituents, then the predicate can simply be omitted from the second clause (this is called 'gapping'), e.g. *John likes apples and Mary (likes) pears*; *Fred is sitting in the lounge and Jane (is sitting) in the garden*; *Peter has been looking at the Cézannes and Julius (has been looking) at the Renoirs.*

We mentioned that it is considered infelicitous in English to repeat the same word several times within a single sentence or, indeed, too closely together within a discourse. It is a feature of 'good style' to employ lexical substitution, using synonyms and near-synonyms rather than keep repeating a given word. This applies more in written than in spoken language, and more in literary than in scientific work—but it is to some extent a feature of every variety of English. Rather than employ the word 'use' several times in one paragraph a writer may alternate 'use' with 'utilise' and 'employ' (I first began this sentence with 'Rather than use the word "use"...' but then substituted 'employ' for the first 'use' since writing 'use' twice in four words seemed ugly). In the fourth paragraph of this section I alternated 'can', 'may', 'is possible' and 'is permissible' to save having too many occurrences of 'can'.

It was mentioned in §2.6 that restrictive relative clauses may be introduced by a *wh-* word or by *that*. These will often be alternated for stylistic effect, so as not to have too many occurrences of *that*, or too many of *which* or *who*, in close proximity. And in an NP beginning with *that* as demonstrative one would generally prefer *wh-* over *that* for introducing a relative clause—*that man who you saw* sounds much more felicitous than *that man that you saw*.

The topic of lexical substitution belongs to the domain of stylistics. It has an obvious semantic basis and is most deserving of systematic study. I have not attempted this here; it remains an important topic for future research.

## 2.13. Syntactic preferences and constraints

There are a number of general surface syntactic preferences and constraints in any language. Those in English include:

**A.** Placing a heavy (i.e. long) constituent at the end of its clause
There is a preference for stating the shorter constituents first, before a heavy constituent (whatever its syntactic function). This accounts for the frequency with which a complement clause in subject function is extraposed, and replaced by impersonal *it* in the subject slot, e.g. *It appears definite that the show has been postponed* and *It annoys Frances to have to say grace before meals* (see §2.7). There is also the tendency in some colloquial styles to extract a restrictive relative clause from a pre-predicate NP and move it to the end of the main clause, e.g. *The watch broke, which you gave me for Christmas* (see §2.6). And the prepositional element of a phrasal verb is likely to be moved leftward over a heavy object NP, so that this can occur clause-finally—compare *The doctor brought my father to*, where *to* follows the object NP, and *The doctor brought to [that thin man with grey hair who was brought in from that terrible smash-up ten miles down the Pacific Highway]*, where *to* precedes the bracketed object NP.

**B.**   Omission of a preposition before complementisers *that, for* or *to*

This has already been mentioned in §§1.4 and 2.7. It is a definite constraint. There are a number of verb-root-plus-preposition combinations which together function as a transitive verb; the preposition is retained before an NP or an ING complement clause, but must be omitted before a complement clause introduced by *that, for* or *to* (and may optionally be omitted before a complement clause beginning in *wh-*). Thus: *He boasted about his victory in the tournament, He boasted about winning the tournament* but *He boasted (\*about) that he had won the tournament.*

Note that if a THAT or Modal (FOR) TO object complement clause becomes passive subject, the underlying preposition may be stated, since it is not then immediately followed by *that* or *for*. Compare (cf. §§1.4, 2.7):

(98)   *They decided on John*
(99)   *They decided (\*on) that John would be captain*
(99a)   *That John would be captain was decided (on)*

But if the THAT clause is extraposed, it will again follow the (passive) predicate, and the preposition is normally suppressed:

(99b)   *It was decided (\*on) that John would be captain*

Note also *I was surprised by the fact that the plumber came*, where *by* is followed by two constituents in apposition, the NP *the fact* and the complement clause *that the plumber came. The fact* can be omitted, and the preposition *by* must then be dropped from its position before *that*, i.e. *I was surprised (\*by) that the plumber came.*


**C.**   Constraint against successive verbs in *-ing* form within a VP

There are two circumstances in which the general grammatical rules of English would be expected to generate a VP in which successive verbs were in *-ing* form. In both instances an ungrammatical string results, apparently because of a proscription on successive verbs being in *-ing* form *within* a VP. Both circumstances relate to the fact (reported in §2.7) that, unlike a main clause or a THAT or a WH- complement clause, an ING or TO complement cannot include a modal, or tense inflection.

(i) We describe in §6.1.1 the partial semantic equivalence between some semi-modals and some modals, e.g. *be able to* and *can, be going to* and *will*. The former may be used in place of the latter in functional possibilities where modals are not permitted, e.g. after another modal (if it is semantic-ally plausible to replace modal by semi-modal in this context), as in *He will be able to tell you*, rather than *\*He will can tell you*.

The semi-modal *be able to* may be used in a TO or ING clause correspond-ing to the modal *can* in a THAT clause:

**(100a)**  *I assume that John can climb the tree*
**(100b)**  *I assume John to be able to climb the tree*
**(100c)**  *I assume John's being able to climb the tree*

The same should apply to the semi-modal *be going to* vis-à-vis modal *will*. We do get *be going to* in a TO complement, as in (101b), but not in the ING complement at (101c); this is because of the constraint against two succes-sive *-ing* verbs within a VP:

**(101a)**  *I assume that John will climb the tree*
**(101b)**  *I assume John to be going to climb the tree*
**(101c)**  *\*I assume John's being going to climb the tree*

(ii) We mentioned in §2.7 that the VP of a TO complement clause can include auxiliary *have* (corresponding both to past tense inflection and to *have* in a main clause or a THAT clause) and/or auxiliary *be* (corresponding to *be* in a main or THAT clause), e.g. *I noticed John to have laughed/to be laughing/to have been laughing*. The VP of an ING complement can also include *have*, e.g. *I mentioned John's having laughed*. However, it cannot include *be* as the sole auxiliary element; if it did so there would be successive verbs in *-ing* form (the initial *be* taking the *-ing* which marks this variety of complement, and the following main verb taking the *-ing* specified by the imperfective auxiliary *be*), which is not permitted, e.g. *\*I mentioned John's being laughing*. We can, however, have *be* together with *have*, since there is then a verb (*be*, plus the *-en* ending demanded by *have*) between the two *-ing* forms, e.g. *I mentioned John's having been laughing*.

Note that it is perfectly permissible to have successive verbs in *-ing* form so long as they belong to the VPs of different clauses, e.g. *He is enjoying painting the garage* (where *enjoying* belongs to the main clause and *painting* to the object complement clause—§2.7) and *He's coming rubbing his eyes* (where *coming* belongs to the main clause and *rubbing* to a simultaneous appositional clause, as in (15) of §2.6).

There is a set of 'in-between' cases. Many languages code concepts like 'begin' and 'try' as affixes to a main verb. English uses lexical verbs that take an ING or TO complement clause; the complement must have the same subject as the BEGINNING or TRYING verb. There are some similarities between verbs of the BEGINNING and TRYING types and modals (in §§3.4 and 6.1 we group them all together as 'Secondary-A' verbs). Although *begin to walk* is best regarded syntactically as two VPs (main clause *begin* and complement clause *walk*) linked by *to*, it is semantically quite similar to *ought to walk* or *be going to walk*, each of which is syntactically a single VP.

Speakers vary in judgement as to whether a BEGINNING or TRYING verb preceded by the *be* imperfective auxiliary (which puts an *-ing* on the following main verb) may or may not be followed by an ING complement clause, i.e. as to whether *He is beginning walking*, *She is trying eating less*, *It is continuing raining* are grammatically acceptable. This reflects the Janus nature of such constructions—in some ways like two VPs and in others like a single VP.

## 2.14. Summary of omission conventions

The approach to grammatical description followed here involves relating together two constructions which differ only in that one includes and the other omits some minor element(s), and which appear to have essentially the same meaning. It generally seems appropriate to take the longer construction as more basic, and say that certain omissions are involved in the shorter.

It will be useful at this stage to summarise the major conventions for omission:

**A.**   Omission of subject NP

**A1.** Under coordination. If two coordinated clauses share an NP which is in subject function in each, then this NP can be omitted from the second clause in sequence.

**A2.** In subordinate time clauses. One variety of temporal clause has its VP beginning with an *-ing* verb; if the subject of this clause is coreferential with the main clause subject then it must be omitted, e.g. (*While*) *lying on the beach, Mary got sunstroke* (§2.12).

**A3.** From an ING complement clause. If the subject of an ING complement clause in object slot is coreferential with the main clause subject, or if the subject of an ING complement clause in subject slot is coreferential with the main clause object, then it is omitted, e.g. *Mary hates having to wash up* and *Having to wash up annoys Mary* (§2.7C). (An exception concerns ATTENTION verbs as head of the main clause predicate. Coreferentiality is rare, but if it is encountered then omission of the complement clause subject is not possible, e.g. *John watched his fighting the tiger on a video replay*.)

**A4.** From a Modal (FOR) TO complement clause. The subject of a Modal (FOR) TO clause, in post-predicate position, must be omitted if it is coreferential with main clause subject, following one class of verbs, e.g. *I need to mow the lawn*; or if it is coreferential with main clause object, following another class of main verbs, e.g. *I persuaded Mary to go*. If the subject of a Modal (FOR) TO complement, in subject function, is coreferential with the main clause object, then this subject (and the preceding *for*) may optionally be omitted, e.g. *(For her) to be expected to wash the car infuriated Mary* (§2.7D). A WH- TO clause must have its subject coreferential with the main clause subject or object, and omitted (§2.7F).

**B.**   Omission of complementiser *that*
The initial *that* may often be omitted from a complement clause when it immediately follows the main clause predicate (or predicate-plus-object-NP where the predicate head is *promise* or *threaten*). The *that* is more often omitted in casual speech (e.g. chatting between friends) than in formal communication (e.g. in court or parliament). And it is more often omitted if the complement clause refers to some minor item of information than if it describes something of significance; this can be inferred from the meaning of the main verb used, and the NPs, and the context of utterance. Thus, in the (a) sentences below it would sound infelicitous to omit the *that*; in the (b) sentences *that* could be included but might be more likely to be omitted (§2.7A):

(**102a**)   *He promised that he would lend me two million dollars*
(**102b**)   *He promised (that) he'd buy me an ice-cream*
(**103a**)   *He mentioned that the king had died*
(**103b**)   *He mentioned (that) Mary was coming to tea*

**C.**   Omission of relative pronoun *wh-/that*
A relative pronoun *that* or *who, which*, etc. may be omitted from a restrictive relative clause if the coreferential NP was not in subject function in the relative clause, e.g. *The chair (that/which) you bought is the one (that/which)*

*I sold last week*. Once again, omission is more likely in a casual speech style, and when referring to something that is not of huge importance (§2.6).

**D.   Omission of *to be* from complement clause**
Some verbs taking a Judgement TO complement clause, whose VP begins with *be*, may omit *to be*, e.g. *I thought him* (*to be*) *crazy*. In addition, just a few verbs taking a Modal (FOR) TO complement whose VP begins with *be* may omit *to be*, e.g. *I need my wound* (*to be*) *dressed* (§2.8 and see §8.2.6).

**E.   Omission of predicate**
If two coordinated clauses have the same predicate but different subject, object, etc. then the predicate may be omitted from the second clause (this is called 'gapping'), e.g. *John dug a long trench and Freddie* (*dug*) *a tiny hole* (§2.12).

**F.   Omission of modal *should* from a THAT complement**
There is a class of verbs which carry an implication of obligation, similar to that of *should*. This modal may be omitted from a THAT complement clause following such a verb, e.g. *He ordered that I* (*should*) *do it*, and *She suggested that John* (*should*) *propose the vote of thanks* (§2.7A).

**G.   Omission of preposition before complementisers *that*, *for* and *to***
Certain transitive verbs which have a preposition as the last element in their lexical form may take a complement clause in object function. The preposition is omitted before *that*, *for* or *to*, although it is retained before an ING complement clause or a plain NP as object (and may optionally be retained before a WH- clause), e.g. *He confessed to the crime*, *He confessed to strangling Mary*, but *He confessed* (*\*to*) *that he had strangled Mary* (§§2.7, 2.13B).

**H.   Omission of complementiser *to***
This must be omitted following a subtype of ATTENTION verbs, and following *make*, *have* or *let*; it can optionally be omitted following *help* or *know*. For example, *He let Mary* (*\*to*) *go*; *They heard John* (*\*to*) *sing in the bath*; *She helped John* (*to*) *wash up*. Note that *to* is not omitted from the corresponding passive, e.g. *John was heard to sing in the bath* (§§2.7D and 8.2.5).

**I.   Omission of *after/while***
A time clause whose VP begins with an *-ing* verb may omit the initial *after* if the first word of the VP is the previous aspect auxiliary *have*, e.g. (*After*)

*having dug the garden, John had a shower*. Similarly, an initial *while* may be—but less often is—omitted if the VP begins with a lexical verb, e.g. *John caught a bad cold* (*while*) *waiting for the bus* (§§2.9, 2.12).

**J.**   Omission of *in order*

The clause linker *in order* is usually omitted before *to* or *for*, e.g. *Fred rose early* (*in order*) *to get to work on time*, and it may occasionally be omitted before *that* (§2.12).

# Notes to Chapter 2

Further details on many of the points discussed here will be found in the standard grammars of English. These include Sweet (1891–8), Jespersen (1909–49), Poutsma (1914–29), Curme (1931, 1935, 1947), Quirk et al. (1985) (and the shorter versions, including Quirk and Greenbaum 1973), Huddleston (1984), Greenbaum and Quirk (1990), Declerck (1991), Huddleston and Pullum (2002).

§2.1.  Declerck (1991: 260–1) has a most useful discussion of the indefinite singular sense of *they*. The recently introduced use of *they* for 3sg human has not yet been accepted by some conservative authorities. For example, Oxford University Press does not generally allow *they* with singular reference (let alone *themself*); but it has been permitted in the present volume, which describes the usage.

§2.3.  An exemplary account of NP structure is in Declerck (1991: 27–31).

§2.6.  There are illuminating discussions on the alternations of *that*, *wh*- words and zero in relative clauses in Quirk (1957).

§2.7.  McDavid (1964) has a useful discussion of the omission of *that* from complement clauses; see also Borkin (1984).

§2.8.  Discussion of so-called 'secondary predicates' is in Nichols (1978) and Aarts (1995); see further references therein.

§2.10.  For a full account of word derivation in English see Adams (1973).

§2.13C.  The constraint against consecutive verbs ending in -*ing* is discussed in Ross (1972), Pullum (1974), Bolinger (1979) and Wierzbicka (1988: 89–93), among others.

# Part B

## The Semantic Types

# 3

# Noun, adjective and verb types

The lexical words of a language can be grouped into a number of semantic types, each of which has a common meaning component and a typical set of grammatical properties. One of the grammatical properties of a type is its association with a grammatical Word Class, or Part of Speech. (See §1.2.)

Chapters 4–6 contain brief sketches of the semantic and syntactic characters of those semantic types which are in English associated with the Verb class. Following chapters discuss the occurrence restrictions on specific syntactic constructions, providing explanations for these that link the meanings of the constructions with the meanings of semantic types. In this chapter, I provide a brief summary of the semantic types associated with the Noun and Adjective classes in English and introduce the division into Primary and Secondary verb types.

One preliminary point should be stressed: semantic types are not mutually exclusive. The central representatives of a type tend to be frequently used words with a simple, general meaning; these do have unequivocal membership. But words of more specialised meaning may combine the semantic properties of more than one type. *Offer*, for instance, relates both to GIVING (the most frequent kind of offer is an offer to give something) and to SPEAKING (the person offering will usually employ words, although gestures could be used instead). *Bite* is basically a CORPOREAL verb, alongside *eat*, *chew* and *swallow*, but it can also be used—like *cut*—as an AFFECT verb, e.g. *He bit/cut through the string*; it has slightly different grammatical properties in the two senses—a direct object when CORPOREAL and pre-position *through* when AFFECT. Generally, when a verb shares the semantic characteristics of two types, it will also blend their syntactic properties.

## 3.1. Types associated with the Noun class

There are five major types associated with the grammatical class Noun in English:

1. CONCRETE reference, e.g. *girl*, *horse*, *wrist*, *piece*, *grass*, *star*, *fire*, *hill*, *city*, *table*. This type can be divided into HUMAN; other ANIMATE; (body and other) PARTS; INANIMATE. INANIMATE may be further subdivided into: FLORA; CELESTIAL and WEATHER (e.g. *sun*, *wind*, *shade*); ENVIRONMENT (*air*, *water*, *stone*, *oil*, *gold*, *forest*); ARTEFACTS (*building*, *market*, *door*). One subgroup of HUMAN relates to RANK (*lady*, *lieutenant*, *chief*); another to SOCIAL GROUP (*nation*, *army*, *crowd*, *company*); and another to KIN terms (*father*, *daughter*, *uncle*, *wife*).

Members of this type are almost all basic noun roots, although there are a few which are derived from verbs (e.g. *building*); nominalisations are discussed in Chapter 10.

2. ABSTRACT reference. Subtypes here include: TIME (*time* itself, as well as words referring to position in time, e.g. *future*, *yesterday*, and units of time, e.g. *month*, *moment*, *night*, *summer*); PLACE (*place*, together with words referring to position or direction, e.g. *front*, *edge*, *north*, and to units of measurement, e.g. *mile*); QUANTITY (*number*, *amount*, *age*, *size*, *length*, etc.); VARIETY (e.g. *type*, *character*, *shape* and types of shape such as *circle*, *line*); LANGUAGE (*sound*, *word*, *sentence*, *noun*); and general abstract terms such as *idea*, *unit*, *problem*, *method*, *result*, *truth*.

Members of this type are also predominantly basic noun roots although there are some derived stems, e.g. *distance*, *height*, *truth*.

3. STATES (and PROPERTIES). This covers both the mental (*pleasure*, *joy*, *honour*; *ability*, *sagacity*) and the corporeal (e.g. *ache*; *strength*) domains.

Some are basic nouns (e.g. *anger, hunger*) but many are derived from adjectives (e.g. *jealousy*) and a few from verbs (e.g. *delight*).

4. ACTIVITIES. Some are basic nouns, e.g. *war, game*, but most are derived from verbs, e.g. *decision, speculation, whipping, sale*. For almost every activity noun there is a corresponding verb, even if it is not always cognate, e.g. *play* for *game*.

5. SPEECH ACTS, e.g. *question, order, report, description, talk, promise*. In each case there is a related verb; this is usually cognate, e.g. *answer, congratulat(ion)*, although there are some exceptions, e.g. *question/ask*.

Every language has words of these five types, but they do not always belong to the Noun class. In the Australian language Dyirbal, for instance, almost all nouns are CONCRETE. Dyirbal has an ample supply of words dealing with states, properties, activities and speech acts, but they all belong to the Verb and Adjective classes; For example, the English words *anger, game* and *question* must be translated into Dyirbal through adjectives ('angry') and verbs ('play', 'ask'). Dyirbal has only a few words with ABSTRACT reference, including some nouns like 'summer' and 'night'. Reference to size is through DIMENSION adjectives, and general reference to number through the interrogative 'how many?' There are in Dyirbal no words—of any word class—directly corresponding to English *time, past, idea* or *problem*. (There is also a distinct word class which includes specific TIME words such as 'long ago', 'yesterday', 'always', 'not yet'.)

In a fair number of languages it is appropriate to recognise KIN terms as making up a distinct type. Sometimes KIN is associated with the Verb class (e.g. 'X fathers Y'). In other languages KIN functions as a grammatically marked subset of Noun, in that a kin term must take an obligatory possessive affix (that is, one cannot just say 'mother', but must specify 'my mother', 'her mother', etc.).

In English almost all the CONCRETE, ABSTRACT and SPEECH ACT nouns have a plural form (exceptions include those referring to non-discrete material, e.g. *mud, milk*). ACTIVITY nouns that refer to a discrete act may form a plural, but others, referring to a mode of activity, sound infelicitous in the plural (compare *many mistakes* with *lots of ineptitude*, rather than *\*many ineptitudes*). STATE nouns seldom have a plural form—one does not hear *\*many hungers* or *\*three jealousies*. (*Pleasure* has a plural used in restricted contexts, e.g. *It is one of my few pleasures*, but note *It gave me much pleasure*, not *\*It gave me many pleasures*.)

The main significance of the five Noun types lies in the verbs with which they can occur. Thus, the object of *experience*, used in its literal sense, is generally a STATE noun, or an ACTIVITY noun derived from an AFFECT verb (*He experienced hunger/a whipping*). The object of *postpone* will normally be an ACTIVITY or SPEECH ACT noun (*They postponed the sale/the order*). *Punch* requires a CONCRETE object. But *discuss* can have any type of noun as head of its object NP.

## 3.2. Types associated with the Adjective class

The following semantic types are associated with the grammatical class Adjective in English:

1. DIMENSION, e.g. *big, great, short, thin, round, narrow, deep*.
2. PHYSICAL PROPERTY, e.g. *hard, strong, clean, cool, heavy, sweet, fresh, cheap, quiet, noisy*; this includes a CORPOREAL subtype, e.g. *well, sick, ill, dead; absent; beautiful, ugly*.
3. SPEED—*quick (at), fast (at), slow (at), rapid, sudden*.
4. AGE—*new, old, young, modern*.
5. COLOUR, e.g. *white, black, red, crimson, mottled, golden*.
6. VALUE, e.g. (*a*) *good, bad, lovely, atrocious, perfect*; (*b*) *odd, strange, curious; necessary, crucial; important; lucky*.
7. DIFFICULTY, e.g. *easy, difficult, tough, hard, simple*.
8. VOLITION, e.g. *deliberate, accidental, purposeful*.
9. QUALIFICATION, with a number of subtypes:
   (*a*) DEFINITE, a factual qualification regarding an event, e.g. *definite, probable, true, obvious*;
   (*b*) POSSIBLE, expressing the speaker's opinion about an event, which is often some potential happening, e.g. *possible, impossible*;
   (*c*) USUAL, the speaker's opinion about how predictable some happening is, e.g. *usual, normal, common*;
   (*d*) LIKELY, again an opinion, but tending to focus on the subject's potentiality to engineer some happening, e.g. *likely, certain*;
   (*e*) SURE, as for (*d*), but with a stronger focus on the subject's control, e.g. *sure*;
   (*f*) CORRECT, e.g. *correct, right, wrong, appropriate, sensible*. These have two distinct senses, commenting (i) on the correctness of a

fact, similar to (*a*) (e.g. *That the whale is not a fish is right*), and (ii) on the correctness of the subject's undertaking some activity (e.g. *John was right to resign*).

10. HUMAN PROPENSITY, again with a number of subtypes:

(*a*) FOND, with a similar meaning to LIKING verbs (§5.5), e.g. *fond* (taking preposition *of*);

(*b*) ANGRY, describing an emotional reaction to some definite happening, e.g. *angry* (*with/at/about*), *jealous* (*of*), *mad* (*about*), *sad* (*about*);

(*c*) HAPPY, an emotional response to some actual or potential happening, e.g. *anxious, keen, happy, thankful, careful, sorry, glad* (all taking *about*); *proud, ashamed, afraid* (all taking *of*);

(*d*) UNSURE, the speaker's assessment about some potential event, e.g. *certain, sure, unsure* (all taking *of* or *about*), *curious* (*about*);

(*e*) EAGER, with meanings similar to WANTING verbs (§6.2.1), e.g. *eager, ready, prepared* (all taking *for*), *willing*;

(*f*) CLEVER, referring to ability, or an attitude towards social relations with others, e.g. *clever, adept, stupid; lucky; kind, cruel; generous* (all taking *at*);

(*g*) HONEST, judgement of some person or statement as fair and just, e.g. *honest* (*about/in/at*), *frank* (*in*);

(*h*) BUSY, referring to involvement in activity, e.g. *busy* (*at/with*), *occupied* (*with*), *preoccupied* (*with*), *lazy* (*over*).

11. SIMILARITY, comparing two things, states or events, e.g. *like, unlike* (which are the only adjectives to be followed by an NP with no preposition); *similar* (*to*), *different* (*from*), *equal* (*to/with*), *identical* (*to*), *analogous* (*to*), *separate* (*from*), *independent* (*of*), *consistent* (*with*) (which introduce the second role—obligatory for an adjective from this type—with a preposition).

Almost all the members of DIMENSION, PHYSICAL PROPERTY, SPEED, AGE, DIFFICULTY and QUALIFICATION are basic adjectives (*dead*, derived from a verb, is an exception). Many of the less central COLOUR terms are derived from nouns, e.g. *violet, spotted*. There are a fair proportion of adjectives derived from verbs in the VALUE and VOLITION types (e.g. *interesting, amazing, desirable, accidental, purposeful*) and some in the HUMAN PROPENSITY and SIMILARITY types (e.g. *thankful, prepared, different*). A few words in VALUE and HUMAN PROPENSITY are derived from nouns (e.g. *angry, lucky*).

These eleven Adjective types do have rather different grammatical properties. The prefix *un-* occurs with a fair number of QUALIFICATION and
HUMAN PROPENSITY adjectives, with some from VALUE and a few from
PHYSICAL PROPERTY and SIMILARITY, but with none from DIMENSION,
SPEED, AGE, COLOUR, DIFFICULTY or VOLITION. The verbalising suffix *-en* is
used with many adjectives from types 1–5 but with none from 6–9 (*toughen*
and *harden* relate to the PHYSICAL PROPERTY sense of these lexemes) and
with none save *glad* and *like* from 10 and 11 respectively. Derived adverbs
may be formed from almost all adjectives in SPEED, VALUE, VOLITION,
DIFFICULTY, QUALIFICATION, HUMAN PROPENSITY and SIMILARITY and from
some in PHYSICAL PROPERTY but from none in AGE; adverbs based on
adjectives in DIMENSION and COLOUR tend to be restricted to a metaphorical
meaning (e.g. *warmly commend, dryly remark, darkly hint*); see §12.2.1.
When adjectives co-occur in an NP then the unmarked ordering is: 11–9–
8–7–6–1–2–3–10–4–5. (For a fuller discussion of these and related points
see Dixon 1977a, reprinted as Dixon 1982b: ch. 1.)

An adjective will typically modify the meaning of a noun, and can be
used either as modifier within an NP (*That clever man is coming*) or as
copula complement (*That man is clever*); only a few adjectives allow just
one of these syntactic possibilities (see Quirk and Greenbaum 1973: 121ff.;
Huddleston and Pullum 2002: 553–61). Notably, most adjectives commencing with *a-* (such as *asleep, aghast, afraid*) can only occur as copula
complement, not as modifier; this is because the *a-* goes back to a preposition *an* 'in, on' in Middle English.

DIMENSION, PHYSICAL PROPERTY, COLOUR and AGE adjectives typically
relate to a CONCRETE noun. SPEED can modify a CONCRETE or an ACTIVITY
noun. HUMAN PROPENSITY adjectives, as the label implies, generally relate to
a HUMAN noun. DIFFICULTY, VOLITION and QUALIFICATION adjectives tend to
refer to an event, and may have as subject an appropriate noun (e.g.
*Cyclones are common at this time of year*) or a complement clause. VALUE
adjectives may refer to anything; the subject can be any kind of noun, or a
complement clause. There is a tendency for a THAT or Modal (FOR) TO
complement clause in subject function (which is a 'heavy constituent') to be
extraposed to the end of the main clause, and replaced by *it*—compare *The
result was strange* with *It was strange that Scotland won*, which sounds a
little more felicitous than *That Scotland won was strange*. SIMILARITY adjectives relate together two things that can be CONCRETE, ABSTRACT or ACTIV-
ITIES (but should normally both come from the same category).

VALUE adjectives may take as subject an ING or THAT complement clause (a THAT clause will generally be extraposed), e.g. *Mary's baking a cake for us was really lovely, It is lucky that John came on time.* Subset (*b*) of the VALUE type may also take a Modal (FOR) TO subject complement, e.g. *It was necessary/odd for John to sign the document.* DIFFICULTY adjectives may take as subject a Modal (FOR) TO clause, again generally extraposed, e.g. *It is hard for Mary to operate our mower.* Both VALUE and DIFFICULTY types can also take in subject relation a complement clause which has no subject stated (it is understood to be 'everyone/anyone'). This applies to ING clauses for VALUE adjectives, e.g. *Helping blind people is good,* and to both Modal (FOR) TO and ING clauses for DIFFICULTY adjectives, e.g. *Operating our mower is hard, It is hard* (sc. *for anyone*) *to operate our mower.*

VALUE and DIFFICULTY adjectives occur in a further construction, one in which what could be object of a complement clause functions as subject of the adjective, with the rest of the complement clause following the adjective, introduced by *to,* e.g. *That picture is good to look at, Our mower is easy to start.* For the DIFFICULTY type it is tempting to derive *Our mower is easy to start* from *It is easy to start our mower,* by 'raising' the complement clause object to become main clause subject. However, this derivation is not available for some adjectives from the VALUE type which do not take a Modal (FOR) TO clause in subject slot. (See also §13.2.)

VOLITION adjectives typically have an ING complement clause as subject; for example, *John's spilling the milk was accidental.*

The various subtypes within QUALIFICATION differ in the kinds of complement clause they accept. The overall possibilities are:

(i) a THAT complement as subject, often extraposed, e.g. *That John will win is probable, It is probable that John will win;*

(ii) a Modal (FOR) TO complement as subject, normally extraposed, e.g. *It is unusual for a baby to be walking at twelve months;*

(iii) a variant of (ii), where the complement clause subject is raised to fill main clause subject slot, replacing *it* (and *for* is then dropped), e.g. *A baby is likely to walk by twenty-four months, John was wrong to resign;*

(iv) an ING complement clause (often with the subject omitted) in subject slot, e.g. *(Your) taking out accident insurance was sensible.*

The QUALIFICATION subtypes occur with subject complements as follows:

| | | | | |
|---|---|---|---|---|
| 9a DEFINITE | i | — | — | — |
| 9b POSSIBLE | i | ii | — | — |
| 9c USUAL | i | ii | — | — |
| 9d LIKELY | i | — | iii | — |
| 9e SURE | — | — | iii | — |
| 9f CORRECT | i | ii | iii | iv |

Some pairs of QUALIFICATION adjectives which might appear to have similar meanings do in fact belong to different subtypes, and show distinct syntactic properties. Compare *definite* (from 9a) and *certain* (from 9d):

(**1a**)   *It is certain that the King will visit us this month*
(**1b**)   *It is definite that the King will visit us this month*
(**2a**)   *It is certain that the monsoon will come this month*
(**2b**)   *\*It is definite that the monsoon will come this month*

Sentence (1b) implies that an announcement has been made; the speaker uses *definite* to report this. In contrast, (1a) presents an opinion (albeit a very strong one)—from all the signs of preparation, the King must be about to make this visit. One can say (2a), using *certain* to qualify an inference made from study of meteorological charts etc. But (2b) is an inappropriate sentence, simply because there is no ordinance that rains will come at a particular time.

Now compare *possible* (from 9b), *likely* (from 9d) and *sure* (9e):

(**3a**)   *That John will win the prize is possible*
(**3b**)   *That John will win the prize is likely*
(**3c**)   *\*That John will win the prize is sure*
(**4a**)   *\*John is possible to win*
(**4b**)   *John is likely to win*
(**4c**)   *John is sure to win*

Both *possible* and *likely* may comment on the chance of some event happening, as in (3a/b). *Likely* differs from *possible* in that it can focus on the outcome as due to the efforts of the subject—hence (4b) but not *(4a). When *sure* is used with a human subject it always focuses on the subject's effort, hence the unacceptability of *(3c).

   HUMAN PROPENSITY adjectives normally have a HUMAN noun as subject. They can be followed by a preposition introducing a constituent that states the reason for the emotional state; this may be an NP or a complement clause, e.g. *John was sorry about the delay*, *John was sorry about being late*,

*John was sorry that he was late, John was sorry to be late*. The preposition drops before *that* or *to* at the beginning of a complement clause, but is retained before an ING clause.

The various subtypes of HUMAN PROPENSITY have differing complement possibilities:

10*a*. FOND only accepts an NP or ING complement, e.g. *I'm fond of watching cricket*.

10*b*. ANGRY takes an NP or a THAT or ING clause, e.g. *She's angry about John('s) being officially rebuked, She's angry that John got the sack*.

10*c*. HAPPY takes an NP or ING or THAT or Modal (FOR) TO (complement clause subject, and *for*, is omitted when coreferential with main clause subject), e.g. *I'm happy about the decision, I'm happy about (Mary('s)) being chosen, I'm happy that Mary was chosen, I'm happy (for Mary) to be chosen*.

10*d*. UNSURE takes an NP or a THAT clause for its positive members *certain (of)* and *sure (of)*, e.g. *I'm sure of the result, She's certain that John will come*; but an NP or a WH- clause after those members that indicate uncertainty, *unsure (of)* and *curious (about)*, e.g. *I am unsure of the time of the meeting, She is curious (about) whether John will attend* (or after positive members when *not* is included, e.g. *I'm not certain whether he'll come*).

10*e*. EAGER takes an NP or a THAT or Modal (FOR) TO complement, e.g. *I'm eager for the fray, I'm eager that Mary should go, I'm eager (for Mary) to go*. *Ready* may only take an NP or a Modal (FOR) TO clause (not a THAT complement) while *willing* must take a THAT or Modal (FOR) TO clause, i.e. it cannot be followed by preposition plus NP.

10*f*. CLEVER shows wide syntactic possibilities. Firstly, like other HUMAN PROPENSITY adjectives, a member of the CLEVER subtype may have a HUMAN noun as subject, and a post-predicate prepositional constituent, e.g. *John was very stupid (about ignoring the rules/in the way he ignored the rules)*. Alternatively, there may be a complement clause as subject, with *of* introducing an NP that refers to the person to whom the propensity applies—either a THAT clause, e.g. *That John came in without knocking was very stupid (of him)*, or a Modal (FOR) TO clause, e.g. *For John to come in without knocking was very stupid (of him), To come in without knocking was very stupid of John, It was very stupid of John (for him) to come in without knocking, It was very stupid for John to come in without knocking*. (Note that *of John* and *for John* can both be included—with the second occurrence of John pronominalised—or either of these may be omitted.) As with some QUALIFICATION subtypes, the subject of an extraposed Modal (FOR) TO subject complement can be raised to become subject of the main clause, replacing impersonal *it*, e.g. *John was stupid to come in without knocking*.

10*g*. HONEST has very similar properties to *stupid*, shown in the last paragraph. For example, *That John declared his interest was honest (of him), For John to declare his interest was honest (of him), It was honest of John (for him) to declare his interest* and *John was honest to declare his interest*. The adjective *frank* has more limited possibilities; for example *John was frank in/about declaring his interest*.

10*h*. BUSY adjectives may take an NP or an ING complement clause; for example, *John was busy with the accounts, Mary was occupied with cooking jam, Fred was lazy at getting things done*.

SIMILARITY adjectives have similar meaning and syntax to COMPARING verbs (§5.7). There may be NPs or ING complement clauses, with comparable meanings, in subject slot and in post-predicate slot, e.g. *John is similar to his cousin, Applying for a visa to enter Albania is like hitting your head against a brick wall*.

Semantic explanation for the differing complement possibilities of the various adjectival types is given in §8.4.5.

Some adjectives have two distinct senses, which relate to distinct types. We have already mentioned *tough* and *hard*, which belong to both PHYSICAL PROPERTY (*This wood is hard*) and DIFFICULTY (*It was hard for John to bring himself to kiss Mary*). *Curious* is in one sense a VALUE adjective, taking a THAT complement in subject function, e.g. *The result of the race was rather curious, That Mary won the race was rather curious*. In another sense, *curious* (*about*) belongs to the UNSURE subtype of HUMAN PROPENSITY, e.g. *John was curious about the result of the race, John was curious* (*about*) *whether Mary won the race*. *Sure* and *certain* belong both to QUANTIFICA-TION (*That Mary will win is certain*) and also to the UNSURE subtype (*John is certain that he/Mary will win*).

As mentioned above, many adjectives from the DIMENSION, PHYSICAL PROPERTY, SPEED, AGE and COLOUR types form derived verbs by the addition of *-en*. These generally function both intransitively, with the meaning 'become', e.g. *The road widened after the state boundary* 'the road became wide(r) ...', and transitively, with the meaning 'make', e.g. *They widened the road* 'they made the road wide(r)'. The occurrence of *-en* is subject both to a semantic constraint—in terms of the types it can occur with—and also to a phonological constraint—only roots ending in $p, t, k, f, s, \int, \theta, d$ take *-en* (see Dixon 1982b: 22). Adjectives from the appropriate types which do not end in one of these permissible segments may have the root form used as a verb, e.g. *narrow* can function as an adjective, as an intransitive verb 'become narrow' and as a transitive verb 'make narrow'; *clean* and *dirty* may function both as adjectives and transitive verbs 'make clean/dirty'. The two main VALUE adjectives, *good* and *bad*, have suppletive verbal forms *improve* and *worsen*, which are used both intransitively 'become better/

worse' and also transitively, 'make better/worse'. (Further discussion of transitive verbs derived from adjectives is in §9.3.3.)

Whereas all (or almost all) languages have major word classes that can be labelled Noun and Verb, some do not have a major word class Adjective. A fair number of languages have a small, closed Adjective class, which generally comprises DIMENSION, AGE, VALUE and COLOUR. In such languages the PHYSICAL PROPERTY type tends to be associated with the Verb class ('be heavy', 'be wet', etc.) and the HUMAN PROPENSITY type with either the Noun class ('cleverness', 'pride', etc.) or the Verb class ('be clever', 'be proud', etc.). (See Dixon 1977a, 1982b: ch. 1, 2004b.) Many languages do not have words for QUALIFICATION as members of the Adjective class; they may be adverbs, or else grammatical particles.

## 3.2.1. Comparison of adjectives

Most adjectives are used in comparison; some take suffix *-er*, some take modifier *more*, and some take either of these. The typical comparative construction involves examining the similarity between two participants in terms of some property, as in *John is taller than Fred* and *Mary is more intelligent than Kate*. Whether a given adjective takes *-er* or *more* or either is determined by a combination of phonological and semantic factors. We will first state the phonological parameters, and then the semantically based exceptions to them.

   **(a)** A monosyllabic adjective (whether ending in a consonant or a vowel) will take *-er* and not *more*; for example, *longer, bigger, squarer, slower, newer, dryer*.

   **(b)** A disyllabic monomorphemic adjective ending in /i/ will also only take *-er*, not *more*; for example, *heavier, happier*.

   **(c)** Other disyllabic adjectives ending in a vowel take either *-er* or *more*; for example, *cleverer* or *more clever, narrower* or *more narrow, securer* or *more secure*. This set includes adjectives ending in derivational suffix *-y* or *-ly*; for example, *luckier* or *more lucky, friendlier* or *more friendly*.

   **(d)** Disyllabic adjectives ending in syllabic /l/ can also take either *-er* or *more*; for example, *simpler* or *more simple, nobler* or *more noble*.

   **(e)** All other adjectives take just *more*. These cover:

—Disyllabic or longer forms ending in a consonant; for example, *more famous,*
*more careful, more difficult.*
—Trisyllabic or longer forms ending in a vowel; for example, *more familiar, more*
*ordinary, more extraordinary.*

Turning now to the semantically-based exceptions:

(i)    There is a small set of disyllabic or longer forms ending in a consonant (none ending in a vowel) which would be expected from their phonological form not to take -*er* but in fact do so. The main exceptions are:

*stupid, solid, wicked*
*pleasant, polite*
*common, handsome*

There are a number of factors which go some way towards explaining these
exceptions. For instance, there appears to be a preference for antonymic
opposites to behave in the same way. One can say *ruder, cleverer,* and
*hollower*—sets (a) and (c)—and so also *politer, stupider* and *solider.* Another factor is that these are very common, everyday adjectives. A full
explanation (in the sense of something which could have been predicted) is
not possible. These are exceptions, although not totally surprising exceptions.

(ii)    There are adjectives which, by their meaning, should not really be
gradable; however, speakers do use them in comparative constructions.
Even though the phonological form relates to set (a) or set (b) or set (d),
they only occur with *more,* never with -*er*. These include:

*right, wrong, real, fake, dead, male, ready, single*

Basically, something should either be right or not, real or not, dead or
not, male or not, single or not, and so on. On logical grounds, one should
not compare two items in terms of such a property. But people do, although
only using *more,* never -*er* (despite the fact that the phonological form would
expect -*er*). If neither Mary nor Jane are married, then both are single.
However, one can say *Mary* [who lives alone] *is more single than Jane* [who
shares an apartment with her boyfriend]. Or *John was more right than Peter,*
if John got every detail correct but Peter only the outline. Or *He was more*
*dead than I had realised* (the body was starting to decompose).

This provides a fair outline of the comparative forms of adjectives. There
are, as would be expected, odd idiosyncrasies, since each lexeme has its own
individual character.

As mentioned at the beginning of this section, a comparative adjective is prototypically used to compare two participants in terms of a parameter, as in:

(5)   *Mary is kinder/more intelligent than Jane*

An alternative construction type is to compare two parameters in terms of one participant, as in:

(6)   *Mary is more kind than intelligent*

Note that in (6) the first adjective must take *more*. That is, *kind*—a mono-syllabic adjective from set (a)—must take *-er* (not *more*) in a prototypical comparative construction such as (5); but all adjectives are required to take *more* in the non-prototypical construction such as (6).

And then there are superlatives. Basically, every adjective which forms a comparative with *-er* has a corresponding superlative with *-est*, and those employing *more* for comparative use *most* for superlative. Whereas a comparative adjective typically makes up the whole of a complement clause complement, as in (5), the superlative form of an adjective typically mod-ifies a noun in an NP which is marked by the definite article *the*; for example, *Mary is the kindest/most intelligent girl in the class*. That is, whereas a comparative relates together two participants of equal status, a superlative effectively identifies a unique individual.

Chapter 12 describes which adjectives may form adverbs (by the addi-tion of *-ly*) and §12.9.1 discusses the comparatives and superlatives of adverbs.

## 3.3. Introduction to verb types

### 3.3.1. Subject and object

Each semantic type associated with the verb class takes a number of semantic roles. A GIVING verb involves Donor, Gift and Recipient; a SPEAKING verb can demand reference to Speaker, Addressee, Message and Medium. Not every verb from a type necessarily requires all of the roles—some MOTION verbs take just one role, the thing Moving (e.g. *John is running*), while others also take a second role, the Locus with respect to which motion takes place (e.g. *Mary passed the school*).

As described in §1.3, semantic roles are mapped onto syntactic relations. If a verb has only one core role this always corresponds to S (intransitive subject) at the level of syntax. S has a wide semantic range—compare *JOHN ran away, THE STONE rolled down the hill, FRED is winking, PETER is sleeping*.

If a verb has two or more semantic roles then one will be mapped onto A (transitive subject) and one onto O (transitive object) syntactic function. There is a semantic principle determining which role corresponds to which function. Basically, that role which is most likely to be relevant to the success of the activity will be identified as A—this is the Speaker for SPEAKING verbs, the Agent for AFFECT verbs like *hit*, and the Perceiver for ATTENTION verbs (e.g. *JOHN tried to watch Mary*).

Where there are just two core roles, then that which is not mapped onto A will become O, e.g. *John* in all of *The nurse sat John up, Fred kicked John, Mary watched John*. If there are more than two roles, that which is most saliently affected by the activity will be mapped onto O. A role that is not identified as A or O will be marked by an appropriate preposition; e.g. *John shot the deer with a rifle*.

Some semantic types include alternative lexemes which differ (only, or largely) in that one focuses on a particular non-A role as most salient (and in O function) while the other focuses on a different role (which is then O). *Mention* and *inform* both belong to the SPEAKING type, requiring Speaker, Addressee and Message. But *mention* focuses on the Message (and the consequences of telling it) whereas *inform* focuses on the Addressee (and the consequences of telling them the message). Compare:

(7)   *John* (A) *mentioned the decision* (O) *to Mary* (*and there was then no going back on it*)

(8)   *John* (A) *informed Mary* (O) *of the decision* (*with the result that she fainted away*)

Some verbs from semantic types that have three core roles appear in two kinds of construction, with alternative roles being mapped onto O, e.g. *John* (Donor: A) *gave all his money* (Gift: O) *to Mary* (Recipient) and *John gave Mary* (O) *all his money*. The two constructions have different semantic implications—the role identified as O is focused on, as particularly salient in this instance of the activity. Only an NP which has definite and specific reference is likely to be suitable to be O. Thus, one might say *John gave all his money* (O) *to good causes* but scarcely **John gave good causes* (O) *all his* *money*, simply because *good causes* is too vague and general to be a suitable candidate for the syntactic function O.

It is important to stress that there is nothing mechanical about 'alternative syntactic frames' such as those just illustrated for *give*; semantic conditions always apply. Compare (cf. §9.2.4):

**(9a)**   *Mary sent a present* (O) *to the doctor*
**(9b)**   *Mary sent the doctor* (O) *a present*

**(10a)**   *Mary sent John* (O) *to the doctor*
**(10b)**   \**Mary sent the doctor* (O) *John*

*Send* actually straddles the GIVING and MOTION types. *The doctor* in (9a/b) is in recipient role, and can be coded into O syntactic slot, as in (9b). But in (10a/b) *send* is being used as a MOTION verb, with *the doctor* simply a destination (parallel to *Mary sent John to Geneva*). Such a destination NP is not saliently affected by the activity, and is thus not a candidate for O slot. (Sentence (10b) could only be used if John were being sent to the doctor as something like a present, as in *Mary sent the doctor a slave/a new assistant*.)

## 3.3.2. Grammar versus lexicon

What is done by morphology in one language may be achieved through syntax in another. Latin (a language with fairly free word order) marks subject and object by nominative and accusative cases, respectively. English puts the subject before the verb and the object after it.

Some languages have derivational morphemes that correspond to separate lexemes in other languages. Consider the following:

(*a*) Warao, from Venezuela, has a verbal suffix *-puhu-* corresponding to the modal verb *can* in English. From *ruhu-* 'sit' is derived *ruhu-puhu-* 'can sit', which takes the full range of tense-aspect verbal inflections (Osborn 1967). To achieve the same semantic result, English must use the two verbs *can* and *sit* in syntactic construction within a VP.

(*b*) Dyirbal, from north-east Australia, has a verbal affix *-yarra-* 'start'. Thus *jangga-yarra-nyu* ('eat-START-PAST') is a single word, with the same meaning as *started eating* in English, a construction that has *started* as main verb and *eating* as a complement clause to it (Dixon 1972: 249).

(*c*) The Uto-Aztecan language Luiseño has derivational affixes *-viču-* 'want to' and *-ni-* 'make, force to'. From *ngée* 'leave' can be derived *ngée-viču* 'want to leave', *ngée-ni* 'make leave' and even *ngée-viču-ni-viču* 'want to make want to leave' (Langacker 1972: 76–7). Luiseño can achieve by a single verb what in English requires constructions involving one, two or three complement clauses.

Many other examples could be given of a concept that is expressed by a derivational process in one language but only as a separate lexical verb in another.

It is not, however, the case that *anything* which is a verb root in one language may be a derivational morpheme in another. Ideas like 'lean', 'stir', 'swallow', 'discuss' and 'remember' are always expressed by separate lexical verbs, in every language. This question will be taken further in the next section.

## 3.4. Primary and Secondary verbs

Verbal concepts naturally divide into two sorts:

PRIMARY—those directly referring to some activity or state, i.e. verbs which can make up a sentence by themselves with appropriate NPs filling the various semantic roles, e.g. *I HIT her, She SWAM across the river, He MUNCHED the apple, They WATCHED it*. These are lexical verbs in every language.

SECONDARY—those providing semantic modification of some other verb, with which they are in syntactic or morphological construction, e.g. the verbs printed in capitals in *I MAY hit her, She TRIED to swim across the river, We STOPPED him munching an apple, I LET them watch it*. Some or all of these may be realised as verbal affixes in languages that show a complex morphology (as exemplified in the last section). They are likely all to be realised as lexical verbs in languages, like English, which have a relatively sparse morphology.

Various subdivisions can be recognised within the two main divisions of Primary and Secondary verbs in English. We now list these, and the semantic types that correspond to them. The following three chapters consider the verb types one at a time, outlining their semantic and syntactic characteristics.

PRIMARY-A verbs must have NPs (not complement clauses) in subject and object slots. The semantic types with this property are:

MOTION, e.g. *run, return, take, pull, throw, fall, spill*
REST, e.g. *sit, stay, put, hang, surround, hold*
AFFECT, e.g. *hit, punch, cut, sweep, cover, twist, burn*
GIVING, e.g. *give, lend, pay, present, donate, exchange*
CORPOREAL, e.g. *eat, taste, kiss, laugh, sleep, bleed, die*
WEATHER, e.g. *rain, snow, thunder, hail*
COMPETITION, e.g. *beat, win, attack, lose, compete*
SOCIAL CONTRACT, e.g. *appoint, govern, manage, join, marry*
USING, e.g. *use, employ, operate, wear, waste*
OBEYING, e.g. *obey, process, deal with, grant, perform*

These verbs take CONCRETE nouns as heads of their subject and object NPs when used in a literal sense. There are some metaphorical uses of individual verbs that can involve nouns of other types, but these are in the nature of idiosyncratic extensions of meaning, e.g. *I hit on a good idea* (but not *\*I punched/cut on a good idea*, or even *\*I hit a good idea*), *She tasted the joys of victory* (but not *\*She ate/kissed the joys of victory*).

PRIMARY-B verbs may have NPs filling subject and object slots but they also allow—as an alternative—a complement clause to fill one of these slots, e.g. *I understand my father, I understand that he refused to sign the document*; and *My father surprised me, That he refused to sign surprised me.*

One semantic type may have a complement clause or an NP as subject:

ANNOYING, e.g. *please, satisfy, amuse, anger, disgust, surprise*

A number of types may have a complement clause as an alternative to an NP in object (or, sometimes, in a post-object) slot:

ATTENTION, e.g. *see, hear, notice, discover, watch*
THINKING, e.g. *think (of/about/over), imagine, assume; know, learn, understand, realise; believe, suspect*
DECIDING, e.g. *decide (on), choose, resolve, elect*
SPEAKING, e.g. *shout, state, remark, propose, inform, tell, order, ask, promise, describe*
LIKING, e.g. *like, love, hate, loathe, prefer, envy*
ACTING, e.g. *act, behave, copy, imitate; reproduce*
HAPPENING, e.g. *happen, take place, commit, experience, undergo*

There are also two types that may have complement clauses in both A and O slots:

COMPARING, e.g. *resemble, differ (from); compare, measure, cost*
RELATING, e.g. *depend on, relate to, imply, be due to*

Note that ATTENTION, ACTING, HAPPENING, COMPARING and RELATING strad-
dle Primary-A and Primary-B, each including some verbs that do—and
some that do not—take a complement clause.

The object of a verb from ANNOYING, and the subject of a verb from
ATTENTION, THINKING, DECIDING, SPEAKING, LIKING and ACTING (that is, the
function which cannot be realised by a complement clause for those types),
will generally be a HUMAN noun.

SECONDARY verbs all provide semantic modification of some other
verb. That is, in each of *Mary continued eating the pudding, Mary wants
to eat the pudding, John made Mary eat the pudding, It seems that Mary is
eating the pudding*, the underlying event is 'Mary eat the pudding'. *Eat* is the
central verb, from a semantic point of view. But at the level of syntax it is
*continue, want, make* and *seem* which are predicate head within the main
clause, with 'Mary eat the pudding' being a complement clause in syntactic
relation with this predicate.

There are four different kinds of semantic (and syntactic) link between a
secondary verb and the verb it semantically modifies:

SECONDARY-A verbs have the same subject as the verbs they modify,
and the same object too, if the verb is transitive. That is, modification by a
Secondary-A verb does not involve the addition of any semantic roles. The
semantic types with this property are:

MODALS, e.g. *will, can, should, might, ought to, must*
SEMI-MODALS, e.g. *be going to, be able to, have got to*
BEGINNING, e.g. *begin, start, finish, complete, continue (with)*
TRYING, e.g. *try, attempt, succeed, fail, practise*
HURRYING, e.g. *hurry (over/with), hasten (over/with), dawdle (over)*
DARING—*dare, venture*

For the MODALS, syntax is congruent with semantics, since they occur as
auxiliary in the same VP as the verb they modify.

A verb from BEGINNING, TRYING, HURRYING or DARING must occur as
syntactic main verb, with the verb that is semantic focus being predicate
head of a TO or ING complement clause, e.g. *She stopped hitting him, She
attempted to hit him.* The complement clause verb may, in certain circum-

stances, be omitted, yielding a sentence that has the superficial appearance of the BEGINNING, TRYING or HURRYING item being the only verb. Consider

**(11)**   *Mary began (cooking/to cook) the pudding at six o'clock*
**(12)**   *Mary began (eating/to eat) the pudding at six o'clock*

The bracketed portion from sentences like (11) and (12) could only be omitted if the addressee could be expected to infer it, on the basis of the contextual knowledge they share with the speaker. If Mary were known to be a cook then *Mary began the pudding at six o'clock* would be understood in terms of (11). If Mary were known to be a lady who employs a cook and never goes near a stove herself, then it would be understood in terms of (12). If the addressee could not be expected to have this sort of information about Mary, then no omission should be made from (11) or (12).

It is interesting to note that only certain verbs may be omitted after a BEGINNING or TRYING form. We can shorten the following, if the bracketed information—describing typical activities—could be expected to be inferred by the addressee: *John finished (making) the bricks before lunch, Mary started (learning) French at fifteen*. But we cannot normally omit the complement clause verb from: *John finished fetching/counting the bricks before lunch, Mary started liking/forgetting French at fifteen*. §§6.1.2–4 discuss the question of which verbs can be omitted after a BEGINNING or TRYING or HURRYING verb (there being a slightly different answer for each type).

Sentences such as *John has begun the potatoes* and *Fred has begun the carrots* are each at least five ways ambiguous. John could have begun planting, harvesting, peeling, cooking or eating, and Fred likewise. Now if *begin* in these two sentences was a simple transitive verb, we would expect the coordination *John has begun the potatoes and Fred (has begun) the carrots* to be $5 \times 5 = 25$ ways ambiguous. It is not—it is only five ways ambiguous. Whatever John is understood to have begun doing to the potatoes, Fred is understood to have begun doing a similar thing to the carrots.

This provides justification for our position that a sentence like *John has begun the potatoes* has an underlying complement clause verb, which can be omitted when certain linguistic and pragmatic conditions are satisfied. In a coordinate structure, such as *John has begun the potatoes and Fred (has begun) the carrots*, this omission applies in tandem in the two clauses, omitting verbs that have the same or similar meaning (e.g. *peeling* from before *the potatoes* and *scraping* from before *the carrots*, since these both refer to modes of preparation).

Further support for this syntactic treatment of BEGIN verbs is provided by evidence from passivisation, discussed in §11.3.

SECONDARY-B verbs introduce an extra role, the Principal or the Timer (which is subject of the main verb), in addition to the roles associated with the semantically central verb, which is predicate head within the complement clause, e.g. *Jane wants Jim to drive the Saab, Fred dreads Mary's seeing that photo*. However, the subject of the Secondary-B verb is often identical with the subject of the complement clause and the latter is then generally omitted, e.g. *Jane wants to drive the Saab, Fred dreads seeing that photo*. The semantic types with this property are:

WANTING (with a number of subdivisions; see §6.2.1), e.g. *want, wish (for); hope (for); need, require; expect; intend; pretend*
POSTPONING, e.g. *postpone, delay, defer, avoid*

(In some languages WANTING verbs must have the same subject as the verb they semantically modify; WANTING is then a Secondary-A type.)

The complement clause verb may be omitted after certain WANTING verbs if it has the general meaning 'get' (i.e. *get, receive, have*, etc.). Thus, *I want (to get) a rabbit for my birthday, He needs (to get/have) a haircut.* Some verbs from this type include a preposition in their basic form, e.g. *hope (for), wish (for)*; this is omitted before a TO complement but retained when immediately followed by an NP, e.g. *Fred hoped to receive a slice of your pudding, Fred hoped for a slice of your pudding.*

SECONDARY-C verbs must introduce a further role over and above the roles of the complement clause verb. This is subject of the main verb; it is the Causer or Helper role, and is generally HUMAN. Thus, *Harry forced Mary to eat the snail*. It is unlikely that main clause and complement clause subjects will be identical; if they are, neither can be omitted, e.g. *Harry forced himself to eat the snail* (not *\*Harry forced to eat the snail*). The types are:

MAKING, e.g. *make, force, cause, tempt; let, permit, allow, prevent, spare, ensure*
HELPING, e.g. *help, aid, assist*

SECONDARY-D verbs may optionally add a role (introduced by preposition *to*) to the roles required by the verbs they modify, e.g. *It seems likely* (*to Mary*) *that John voted for Roosevelt*, and *That Chris can't understand algebra doesn't matter* (*to Karen*). There are two semantic types with this property:

SEEM, e.g. *seem, appear, happen, look*
MATTER—*matter, count*

The *to* NP marks the person who makes the inference (for SEEM) or who attaches importance to the happening (for MATTER). If it is omitted, then, according to the pragmatic context, the statement of the complement clause will be taken to seem/matter 'to me', or 'to us' or 'to everyone'.

Secondary-D verbs take a complement clause in subject slot. Verbs from the SEEM type occur with one of those adjectives that may take a subject complement clause (VALUE, DIFFICULTY, QUALIFICATION and the CLEVER subtype of HUMAN PROPENSITY). There is further discussion of the semantics and syntax of Secondary-D verbs in §6.4.

Each Secondary verb modifies some other verb. The verb modified may be a Primary verb, or a further Secondary verb—in which case there must be a third verb which it in turn modifies. Thus:

**(13)**  *The invalid wants* (Sec-B) *to eat* (Prim-A)
**(14)**  *The nurse wants* (Sec-B) *to try* (Sec-A) *to force* (Sec-C) *the invalid to eat* (Prim-A)

A Primary-B verb may involve nothing but NPs as arguments, or it can take a complement clause, which can have any kind of Primary or Secondary verb as predicate head, e.g.

**(15)**  *John remembered* (Prim-B) *the swindle*
**(16)**  *John remembered* (Prim-B) *Mary's starting* (Sec-A) *to like* (Prim-B) *ordering* (Prim-B) *her jockey to appear* (Sec-D) *to try* (Sec-A) *to win* (Prim-A) *certain races*

Such a grammatical chain may carry on indefinitely; when it finishes, the final clause must contain a Primary-A verb, or a Primary-B verb with all argument slots filled by NPs.

# 4

# Primary-A verb types

This chapter deals with literal meanings of Primary-A verbs, with roles filled by NPs that have CONCRETE heads. As mentioned before, some Primary-A verbs do have secondary, metaphorical meanings, with other kinds of NP (or even a complement clause) as subject or object (e.g. *John's having got the job quite threw me*, i.e. 'discomfited me'); they are semantically and grammatically similar to the ANNOYING type, described in §5.6. However, these are almost all idiosyncratic to particular verbs so that no generalisations are possible across a type or subtype.

## 4.1. MOTION **and** REST

These two types have a number of subtypes which show pervasive semantic and syntactic parallels, so that they can usefully be considered together.

The role common to all MOTION verbs is (thing) Moving (e.g. *Mary ran*) and to all REST verbs (thing) Resting (e.g. *John knelt*). There may also be specification of Locus—the place of rest, or place with respect to which motion takes place. For some verbs specification of Locus is obligatory, e.g. *He resides in town*; for others it is optional, e.g. *John stood (on the stone)*.

An NP in Locus role is most often marked by the appropriate preposition. As noted in §2.5 such place adverbial NPs are semantically linked to the MOTION/REST verb and are typically placed after the predicate. Certain MOTION verbs may allow the preposition to be omitted, a slight semantic difference then resulting, e.g. *He jumped (over) the river, She climbed (up) the mountain.* It is also possible in certain circumstances to omit a preposition before a measure phrase, e.g. *He ran (for) a mile.* Conditions for omitting the preposition, and the status of the final NP in these constructions, are taken up in §§9.2.4–5.

A fair proportion of MOTION and REST verbs are intransitive. Quite a few of these may be used transitively in a causative sense (i.e. with S = O); thus, *The horse trotted around the ring, He trotted the horse around the ring,* and *The plant stood on the window-sill, He stood the plant on the window-sill.* (See §9.3.)

Others are basically transitive, e.g. *take*. Only some of these may omit an object NP if it can be inferred from context and/or surrounding dialogue, e.g. *We followed (him) as far as the minefield.* Transitivity is largely determined by the meaning of a verb; that is, by the subtype to which it belongs.

We can recognise seven subtypes of MOTION and six of REST. Taking these one or two at a time:

MOTION-a, the RUN subtype, refers to a mode of motion, e.g. *run, walk, crawl, slide, spin, roll, turn, wriggle, swing, wave, rock, shake, climb, dive, stroll, trot, gallop, jog, dance, march, jump, bounce, swim, fly* and one sense of *play* (as in *The child is playing in the sand*).

REST-a, the SIT subtype, refers to a stance of resting, e.g. *sit (down), stand (up), lie (down), kneel, crouch, squat, lean, hang (down), float.*

Verbs in these two subtypes are basically intransitive. Since they describe a mode of motion or stance of rest the only obligatory role is Moving/ Resting. A Locus can be included, but this is optional, e.g. *He loves strolling (in the park), Mary is sitting down at last (in her favourite armchair).*

There exists the potential for any verb from RUN or SIT to be used transitively, in a causative sense. The Moving or Resting role (which is S in an intransitive construction) becomes O, and an additional role—the Causer, normally HUMAN—is introduced in A syntactic function, e.g. *The dog walked, He walked the dog; The log slid down the icy track, He slid the log down the icy track; The child lay down on the couch, She laid the child down on the couch; The raft floated on the stream, He floated the raft on the stream.*

Some RUN and SIT verbs are commonly used in transitive constructions, e.g. *spin, roll, rock, trot, march, fly, sit, stand, lean, hang*. Others seldom or never are, e.g. *climb, dive, stroll, kneel, crouch*. This is simply because people do not often make someone or something climb or dive or kneel, as they do make them march or roll or sit (and this often relates to the activity, that it is something which is not easy for an outsider to control). But the potential exists for any verb from these types to be used causatively if the appropriate circumstances should arise. Suppose that someone chose to train a possum to climb high, for some marsupial Olympics; in such circumstances one could say, side by side with *The champion possum climbed to the top of a kauri pine*, the sentence *He climbed the champion possum to the top of a kauri pine*.

*Ride* and *drive* can be considered members of the RUN subtype which are only used in causative form, e.g. *John rode the mare*. Since there is no corresponding intransitive (e.g. *\*The mare rode*) it is permissible to omit specification of the object NP in appropriate circumstances, e.g. *John rides every morning* (cf. §9.3.1).

MOTION-b, the ARRIVE subtype, deals with motion with respect to a definite Locus, e.g. (i) *arrive, return, go, come*; (ii) *enter, exit, cross, depart, travel, pass, escape*; *come in, go out*; (iii) *reach, approach, visit* (which spans the MOTION and ATTENTION types).

REST-b, the STAY subtype, deals with rest at a definite Locus, e.g. *stay, settle (down), live, stop, remain, reside; attend*.

Since verbs from these two subtypes refer to motion or rest with respect to a Locus, the Locus must normally be stated, either through an NP or an adverbial, e.g. *He has remained outside/in the garage, She hasn't yet travelled to Spain/there*.

STAY verbs are almost all intransitive, and include a preposition before the Locus NP, e.g. *stay on the farm*. Some ARRIVE verbs have similar syntax, e.g. *arrive at the station, return to Sheffield, go to the cowshed, come into the kitchen. Go* and *come* include in their meanings a Locus specification 'to there' and 'to here' respectively; in view of this, *here* can be omitted from *come here* and *there* from *go there*, although these adverbs often are retained. *Arrive* and *return* may also be used without a Locus NP or adverb, and 'here' is then implied. (A Locus NP may also be omitted after these verbs when it could be inferred from the previous discourse, e.g. *He cycled all the way to town. Oh, what time did he arrive* (sc. in town)? and *She's driven over to Brighton. How long is she staying* (sc. in Brighton)?)

As mentioned under (a) in §2.9, just *come* and *go* may be followed by an *-ing* clause (then behaving like Secondary-A verbs), as in *We went hunting yesterday*. And, in American English, *go* and *come* (just in base form) may shorten an *in order to* construction, as in *Let's go (in order to) eat!*

Set (ii) of ARRIVE verbs could also be regarded as intransitive, with the Locus marked by a preposition; but this preposition may be omitted in appropriate circumstances. *Enter* and *exit* would generally omit the preposition, e.g. *enter (into) the room*. *Cross* can equally well retain or omit it, e.g. *cross (over) the road*. *Depart* may omit the preposition in some styles of speech, e.g. *depart (from) the city*. *Travel* can occur with a variety of prepositions; just *over* can be omitted, from a sentence like *He travelled ((all) over) Africa from coast to coast*. *Pass* can omit *by*, as in *pass (by) the church*, but not *through*, e.g. *pass through the tunnel/funfair*. In all of these instances omission of a preposition carries a semantic difference (see Chapter 9). This can clearly be seen with *escape*—a preposition is required with the meaning 'get away from a place, where one was confined', e.g. *escape from prison*, but not for the meaning 'avoid (confinement, or some other ill fortune)', e.g. *escape (being sent to) prison*, *escape punishment*.

A few ARRIVE verbs are basically transitive, e.g. *approach*, *visit* and *reach*, as in *They won't reach the lake tonight*. (There is also *reach (to)* 'extend to', as in *The road reaches to the coast*; this sense relates to the STRETCH subtype of AFFECT.) From the STAY subtype, *attend* is transitive and generally has a non-CONCRETE noun as object, e.g. *He attended the meeting/play/wedding*.

ARRIVE and STAY verbs generally cannot be used in a causative construction, but there are some exceptions. *Settle* may be used causatively and then the Causer will generally be in a position of authority, e.g. *Baby settled down for the night*, *Mother settled baby down for the night*; *Ex-servicemen settled on the plains*, *The government settled ex-servicemen on the plains*; see §9.3.2. *Return* would normally have an animate NP in S function, e.g. *Fred has returned to work*; it can be used causatively, generally with a non-human O NP, e.g. *John returned the book to the library*. If the Moving role for *pass* is a manipulable object the verb can then be used transitively, e.g. *They passed the port around the table* alongside *The port passed around the table*. (Compare *The procession passed around the front of the palace*, where the Moving role is non-manipulable, and a causative construction is implausible.)

MOTION-c, the TAKE subtype, refers to causing something to be in motion with respect to a Locus, e.g. (i) *take, bring, fetch*; (ii) *send*; (iii) *move, raise, lift, steal*.

These are all transitive verbs with a Causer (normally HUMAN) in A function. Set (i) involves double realisation of the Moving role—both A and O NPs normally refer to something in motion, e.g. *John* (Causer; Moving) *brought his dog* (Moving) *to the party*. For sets (ii) and (iii) the Causer need not be Moving but of course the O NP must be.

Most TAKE verbs are like ARRIVE in requiring specification of the Locus. However, *take* and *bring*, the transitive correspondents of *go* and *come*, have as part of their meaning the specifications 'to there' and 'to here' respectively, so that *there* can be omitted after *take* and *here* after *bring*. *Fetch* is a combination of *go* (to where something is) and *bring* (it back to the starting point); again 'here' is implied and can be omitted. *Send* involves a Causer arranging for a Moving thing to go, not normally accompanying it. Here a Locus should be specified, e.g. *I sent the cow to market* (unless it could be inferred from the preceding discourse, e.g. *Have you got in touch with Phoebe yet? Well, I sent a letter* (sc. to her) *yesterday*).

*Take, bring, fetch* and *send* may be used with the additional implication of 'giving'—compare *take the pig to market* (a destination) with *take the pig to/for Mary* (*for* is likely to imply a recipient, and *to* could mark recipient).

*Move* may be intransitive or transitive; the former use could be assigned to the ARRIVE subtype, the latter to TAKE. This verb does not denote a general mode of motion (like RUN) but rather motion with respect to various Locuses, e.g. *Mary moved from Seattle to Vancouver*. *Move* can be used with a general adverb, or with no overt specification of Locus, e.g. *He's always moving (about), She's continually moving the furniture (around)*, but the meaning of the verb still provides a clear implication of 'from this place to that place to another place . . .' *Raise* and *lift* behave similarly.

*Steal* is a more specific verb, relating to *take* and transitive *move* where the Moving role (in O function) refers to something that does not belong to the Causer and should not have been taken/moved by them. Here the focus is on the nature of the referent of the Moving role, and a Locus NP, while often included, is not obligatory, e.g. *He stole ten dollars (from Mary's purse)*.

REST-c, the PUT subtype, refers to causing something to be at rest at a Locus, e.g. (i) *put, place, set, arrange, install, put* NP *on, sow, plant, fill, load, pack; hide; beach, land, shelve, dump;* (ii) *leave, desert, abandon, ground, take* NP *off*.

These are also transitive verbs, with the Causer (normally HUMAN) in A and the thing Resting in O function. The Locus must be specified, by a prepositional NP or an adverb, e.g. *She put the box down/outside/there/on the table.* Some hyponyms of *put* have Locus specified as part of the meaning of the verb, e.g. *land* 'put on land', *beach* 'put on a beach', *shelve* 'put on a shelf'.

*Put* has an extended meaning in such expressions as *put the blame on, put trust in* and *put a question to*, alternatives to simple verbs *blame, trust* and *question.*

The transitive verbs *leave, desert* and *abandon* involve an intersection of MOTION and REST. They have two senses:

—(i)  the subject (Moving) goes away, and does not take a person or thing (Resting or conceivably Moving) which they might have been expected to take with them, or else expected to remain with, e.g. *John* (Moving) *abandoned his car* (Resting or Moving) *on the highway*, or *Mary* (Moving) *left her husband* (Resting);

—(ii)  the subject (Moving) goes away from a place (Locus) where they had been for some time and might have been expected to remain longer, e.g. *Trotsky left Russia in the twenties.*

In (i) the Moving participant has a kind of Causer role (i.e. did *not* take, did *not* stay with); this does not apply for (ii).


MOTION-d, the FOLLOW subtype, refers to motion with respect to something which is moving, e.g. (i) *follow, track, lead, guide, precede; accompany;* (ii) *meet.*

These are all transitive verbs with the Moving role in A and Locus (typically, also Moving) in O function, e.g. *Mbfira tracked the car/Mary, Fred met the train/Jane. Follow* has a further sense in which the O NP is a geographical feature extended in space, e.g. *They followed the river.* A further extension of meaning, applying to both *follow* and *meet*, has geographical features in both A and O slots, e.g. *That road follows the spur of the hill, Those two rivers meet at the foot of the mountain. Lead* may have a variety of non-human NPs in A function, in extensions from its central meaning, e.g. *The path/Those tell-tale noises/Her sense of direction led Mary to the robbers' lair.*

Verbs of set (i) are particularly susceptible to omission of the object NP if this is inferrable from the context or from previous dialogue, e.g. *You go and I'll follow (you); I'll lead (you) and you follow (me). Meet,* of set (ii), is typically reciprocal—see §§2.11.6 and 11.2.

An additional non-moving Locus is often specified, but is not obligatory, e.g. *John followed Mary (to the cave), John and Mary met (in town).*

REST-d, the CONTAIN subtype, describes relative position of two things, both at rest, e.g. *contain, enclose, encircle, adjoin; surround.*

These verbs are transitive. Both roles are Resting, and each is effectively a Locus with respect to the other; they typically have INANIMATE reference. *Adjoin*, like *meet*, is inherently reciprocal (§2.11.6). *Surround* straddles this subtype and also the WRAP subtype of AFFECT (§4.2).

MOTION-e, the CARRY subtype, refers to motion in juxtaposition with some moving object (prototypically, a person's hand), e.g. *carry, bear, transport, cart.*

REST-e, the HOLD subtype, refers to position of rest with respect to, prototypically, a person's hand, e.g. (i) *hold, handle*; (ii) *grab, grasp, clutch, catch, gather, pick up; capture, trap.*

These are all transitive verbs with the Moving/Resting role mapped onto O function. The subject maps a Causer role (normally HUMAN) and the Locus is likely to be some part of the human's body; the actual body part involved can be specified by a prepositional NP, e.g. *John carried/held the banana in/with his hand/teeth.* (If no body part is specified it is taken to be the unmarked one—hand for a human, mouth for a dog, etc.)

The CARRY subtype includes some more specialised verbs whose meaning involves specification of the Locus, e.g. *cart* 'carry on a cart' (cf. *land* 'put on land'). Here Causer and Locus are distinct although the Causer will move with the Locus (i.e. John goes with the cart in *John carted the potatoes (to market)*). (Nowadays, *cart* is also used to describe carrying something unwieldy or heavy, by any means.)

Whereas *hold* refers to being in a position of rest in juxtaposition with a person's body, the verbs in set (ii)—*grasp, grab, catch, pick up* and the like—refer to something being brought into such a position, e.g. *John grabbed/picked up the axe (and then held it tightly).*

As with FOLLOW, an additional non-moving Locus may be specified, but is entirely optional, e.g. *John held the baby (in the nursery); John carried the baby (to the bathroom). John held/carried the baby* are self-sufficient sentences, in the same way that *John ran/sat down* are.

MOTION-f, the THROW subtype, describes causing something to be in motion, e.g. *throw, chuck, fling, pour, spray, water; push, press; pull, jerk, drag, tug,* one sense of *draw* (e.g. *draw sword from scabbard*).

These are transitive verbs with the thing Moving as O and the Causer (which need not be moving) as A. The meanings of individual verbs describe both the mode of motion and the way in which it was caused.

As with RUN, a specification of Locus is possible, but quite optional, e.g. *Mary pushed the bed* (*out from the wall*) (*into the middle of the room*) and *John threw the javelin* (*towards the grandstand*). (Note that *throw* and *chuck* can take an adverb *away* or *out* and then have the additional sense of 'abandon', e.g. *Mary threw away all John's love letters to her*.)

REST-f, the OPEN subtype, refers to causing something to be in a particular position of rest, e.g. *open, close, shut* (the verb *lock* appears also to relate to this subtype).

These verbs are used transitively with the thing Resting in O and Causer (normally HUMAN or WEATHER) in A function, e.g. *John/the wind closed the door*. They also occur in what appears to be an intransitive construction, but most examples of this are in fact either copula plus a participial form of the verb (functioning as an adjective, and describing a state), e.g. *The door is closed*, or else a 'promotion to subject' construction, e.g. *This door opens easily* (see Chapter 13).

In the literal use of OPEN verbs the thing Resting is limited to a small set of PART nouns, e.g. *window, door, lid*. The Locus is inferrable from meanings of noun and verb and is unlikely to be stated (*The door was shut into the door-frame* sounds unbearably pedantic). These verbs, especially in their participial use, also have a metaphorical sense, e.g. *His mind is open/closed/ shut to new ideas*.

MOTION-g, the DROP subtype, refers to unwanted motion, e.g. *fall, drop, spill, tip* (*over*)*, upset, overturn, capsize, trip, slip*.

These verbs may be used intransitively, with the Moving thing in S function. The motion may be due to a combination of natural forces such as gravity (*The apple fell from the tree*) and weather (*The boat overturned in the storm*). All DROP verbs, with the sole exception of *fall*, are also used transitively, with the thing Moving as O. The A NP is Causer—either a natural force responsible for the movement (*The storm overturned the boat*) or some HUMAN who brought the movement about either through planned action (*John deliberately dropped the vase*) or—and this is the unmarked circumstance—through miscalculation (*John* (*accidentally*) *dropped the vase*). S = O intransitive pairs such as this are discussed further in §9.3.2.

It is interesting that *fall*, perhaps the most common verb of this subtype, is the only member that is exclusively intransitive. (There is the transitive *fell* but this is only used of trees—and, sometimes, people—and refers to deliberate action, whereas *fall* normally describes uncontrolled motion towards the ground.)

Locus NP(s) may be added, but are not obligatory, e.g. *The milk spilt* (*out of the jug*) (*onto the ground*).

## 4.2. AFFECT

AFFECT items are prototypical transitive verbs (according to the criteria set out by Hopper and Thompson 1980). They involve three basic semantic roles—an Agent moves or manipulates something (referred to as the Manip role) so that it comes into contact with some thing or person (the Target role). Either the Manip or the Target (or, occasionally, both) will be physically affected by the activity.

These roles can be mapped onto syntactic relations in three distinct ways:

| | | |
|---|---|---|
| I. *John* (Agent) | *hit the vase* (Target) | (*with the stick* (Manip)) |
| II. *John* (Agent) | *hit that stick* (Manip) | *on/upon/against the table* (Target) |
| III. *That stick* (Manip) | *hit the vase* (Target) | |

The most characteristic AFFECT verb construction is I, in which the Target is affected by the Manip being brought into contact with it—John swings that stick against the vase so that the vase breaks; the Manip is, in this instance of the activity, stronger than the Target. The Manip will either be an object held by the Agent (usually, in their hand) or else some body part of the Agent. The *with* instrumental phrase in construction I need not be stated, although it could always be supplied. (Neither A nor O can be omitted from any of the three construction types.)

Construction II is likely to be used when the Manip is less strong than the Target, so that it is the Manip which is physically affected by impact of Manip on Target—John swings that stick against the table and the stick breaks. That role which is physically affected is most salient in this instance of the activity and is coded onto O syntactic relation (§3.3.1)—this is the

Target in I and the Manip in II. In II the Target is marked by a preposition—*on, upon, against*, etc. It is noteworthy that this prepositional phrase cannot be omitted from II. (If it were, then *John hit that stick* would be taken to have *that stick* as Target, i.e. an instance of construction I where the *with* phrase has been omitted. This confirms I as the unmarked construction for AFFECT verbs.)

It is also possible to say, as an alternative to I, *John's stick hit the vase* (*when he was swinging it to test its weight, not aware that there was a vase nearby*) or just *That stick hit the vase* (*when John swung it*), as in III. To put the Manip into A (transitive subject) slot in this way may disclaim the Agent's responsibility for the result of the activity—true, they were swinging that stick, but they did not intend to hit the vase (and wouldn't have dreamt of swinging it if they'd known the vase was there). For III the Target must, as in I, be in O slot. The Agent has no obligatory syntactic coding in III, but it is usually hovering somewhere in the sentence, e.g. as possessor to Manip within the A NP (*John's stick*) or as A within a subordinate clause (*when John was swinging it*). Pattern III is, like II, a marked construction for AFFECT verbs; it is used to achieve a certain semantic effect.

(Sentences such as *The falling coconut hit Mary* (*as she sat under the palm tree*) can also be classified as III. The Manip role in this sentence, *the falling coconut*, is something moving due to a natural force—here, gravity.)

It will be seen that 'patient' and 'instrument' are not appropriate labels for the semantic roles associated with AFFECT verbs. That role which is affected by the hitting is the patient and is mapped onto O syntactic relation—this is the Target in I and the Manip in II. The role which engenders the affect on the patient is the instrument—this is the Manip in I; the Target could conceivably be called an instrument in II.

There are two other construction types applicable to some AFFECT verbs. The first is a variant of I, with a preposition inserted before the Target:

IV. *John* (Agent) *kicked at the door* (Target) (*with his hob-nailed boots* (Manip))

In Chapter 9 we discuss the syntactic status of *the door* in IV—whether or not it is still in O relation.

The other construction type is also a variant of I. An adverb may replace the O NP, indicating that the activity was indulged in rather wildly (rather than being directed, in a controlled fashion, at a specific Target):

V. *John* (Agent) *hit out* (*with that stick* (Manip))

It is not possible to include *the door* either before or after *out* in V. However, *at the door* is acceptable, yielding a blend of IV and V, where the Agent hits out wildly, but in the direction of a Target, i.e. *John hit out at the door* (*with that stick*).

Note that there is no necessary connection between IV and V. Some verbs can take a preposition before the Target, in IV, but cannot accept an adverb, in V, e.g. *He hammered at the door*, but not *\*He hammered out*. (*He hammered the message out* is different both syntactically—an O NP is included—and semantically.)

A number of AFFECT verbs may include an adjective after the Target NP (when this is in O function) in construction I or III describing the state in which the Target was put by the activity, e.g. *Mary knocked John unconscious, Mary's stick knocked John unconscious*. As mentioned under (a) in §2.8, these can be treated as reductions from underlying structures of the form *Mary knocked John so that he was unconscious*. Note that the peripheral NP indicating Manip comes after *John* in *Mary knocked John with her stick so that he was unconscious*. However, when *so that he was* is omitted, *knocked unconscious* functions like a single compound form, and a peripheral NP must follow it, as in *Mary knocked John unconscious with her stick*.

AFFECT, like MOTION and REST, is a large type, involving hundreds of verbs. It can usefully be divided into eight subtypes, each of which has its special semantic and syntactic characteristics. (Note that all AFFECT verbs are transitive; verbs in some subtypes (noted below) may also function intransitively.)

AFFECT-a, the TOUCH subtype, refers to Manip minimally coming into contact with Target, with no disturbance of the Target, e.g. *touch, stroke*.

These verbs occur in the first three constructions, e.g. I *She stroked the fur* (*with her left hand*), II *She stroked her left hand on/over the fur*, III *Her left hand stroked the fur* (*although she wasn't aware of it*). Note that *feel* only occurs in construction I; it is most appropriately regarded as a member of the ATTENTION type (§5.1).

AFFECT-b, the HIT subtype, refers to Manip being brought through the air to impact on Target, e.g. *hit, strike, punch, bump, kick, knock, tap, bash, slap, spank; whip, belt, stone, cane, hammer; shoot*.

All occur in constructions I, II and III. Those like *hit, strike, punch, kick*, which refer to some vigorous activity that can be done quite wildly (just moving the Manip without controlled focus on a particular Target), also occur in V and in IV. Verbs such as *knock*, *tap*, *bash*, *slap* and *spank* carry an implication that Manip should make contact with a specific Target—they occur in I, II and III, and also in IV, e.g. *He knocked on/at/against the door* (*with his stick*), but not in V. Then there are verbs derived from nouns—such as *whip*, *belt*, *stone*, *hammer*—which have more restricted syntactic possibilities (as verbs derived from nouns often do have). They may all occur in I, just *whip* in III (*The rope which John swung whipped my face*) and just *hammer* in IV. The meanings of these verbs include specification of an archetypical Manip (e.g. the central meaning of *hammer* is 'hit with a hammer') and because of this it would be implausible for the Manip to be in O slot in II. (Note, though, that these verbs may be used with a non-cognate Manip, which can be O in II, e.g. *He hammered his fists upon the door*.)

*Shoot* is an unusual verb in that there are effectively two Manips—the Agent operates a gun or bow (Manip$_1$) which sends on its way a projectile (Manip$_2$) that impacts on the Target. Either 'gun' or 'projectile' may fill the Manip slot in I/IV and III, with the 'other Manip' being introduced in I/IV by *using*; thus: I/IV *John shot* (*at*) *the pig with pellets using his shotgun/with his shotgun using pellets*, and III *John's shotgun/pellets accidentally shot the pig*. The 'gun', however, is unlikely to occur in O slot in II, simply because use of the verb *shoot* implies a gun as Manip—we may say *John shot pellets at the pig using his shotgun*, a II construction with the 'projectile' in O slot, but scarcely *\*John shot his shotgun at the pig using pellets*.

Some verbs from the HIT subtype may include an adjective after the Target role when it is in O function, describing a state engendered by the action, e.g. *kick/punch/knock unconscious*, *shoot dead*.

AFFECT-C, the STAB subtype, refers to a pointed or bladed Manip penetrating below the surface of the Target, e.g. *pierce*, *prick*, *stab*, *dig*, *sting*, *knife*, *spear*; *cut*, *prune*, *mow*, *saw*, *slice*, *chop*, *hack*.

All of these verbs occur in constructions I and III (although it is not terribly common for something to slice or chop or—especially—to saw or prune accidentally, in III). Construction II, with the Manip as O, is more marginal for most STAB verbs simply because their meanings focus on the affect on the Target, which should thus be in O slot (however, it is possible to say *He stabbed his dagger into the ground*, with focus on the dagger, since here the Target, the ground, is not critically affected by the activity). Construction II is least likely with *spear* and *knife*, verbs derived from nouns, since the meaning of the verb includes specification of an archetypical Manip; however, the Manip can be in O slot when it is not cognate with the verb, e.g. *She speared the garden fork through her foot.*

AFFECT-d, the RUB subtype, refers to the Manip being manipulated to affect the surface of the Target, e.g. *rub, wipe, scrape, scratch, mark; sweep, brush, shave, rake; polish; lick. Wash* has a slightly different meaning, referring to the effect on the Target ('make clean using liquid') but can be regarded as a divergent member of this subtype.

*Rub*, the prototypical member of the subtype, can occur in constructions I, e.g. *He rubbed the table with that cloth*, and II, e.g. *He rubbed that cloth over/on the table*. Construction III is just possible: *His trousers rubbed the table (as he squeezed by)*. Construction IV is also plausible (*He rubbed at the table with a clean cloth*) but not V.

We also get variants of I where the head of the O NP refers to something on a surface, whose relationship to the surface is affected by the activity:

Ia. *John rubbed [the polish into the table] (with that cloth)*
Ib. *John rubbed [the mark (off the table)] (with that cloth)*

It is interesting to note that, although prepositional NPs can usually occur in any order after a verb, *with that cloth* could not felicitously intrude between *the polish* and *into the table* in Ia, or between *the mark* and *off the table* in Ib.

Note that instead of *off* in Ib we could have *on*, describing just where the mark is, rather than where it should go. *On* must be used when *at* is inserted before the O NP, giving:

IVb. *John rubbed [at the mark on the table] with that cloth*

*Wipe, scrape* and *scratch* may—like *rub*—be used in I–IV and Ia, Ib, IVb. *Sweep, brush, shave* and *rake* all have meanings that focus on the Target— they occur in I, Ib, IV and IVb, less convincingly in III, and scarcely in II, where the Target is not in O function. *Polish* is even more limited, being effectively restricted to I and IV; since the meaning of the verb includes reference to the substance rubbed into a surface, the Target can only be the surface (i.e. *the table* in I, and not *the polish* in Ia). *Lick* occurs in I, Ib, IV and IVb but is scarcely plausible in II (?*The possum licked its tongue over the leaf*)—because the meaning of the verb includes specification of the Manip (a tongue), which is unlikely to be focused on and placed in O slot—or

III—because tongues do not lick things accidentally (although, in one metaphorical sense of the verb, flames do).

Verbs from the RUB subtype may typically take an adjective after the Target when it is in O slot, e.g. *rub/wipe/scrape/brush/lick clean.*

AFFECT-e, the WRAP subtype, refers to the Manip moving into juxtaposition with the Target, e.g. *wrap; cover; butter, roof, veil, clothe, dress, grease; plaster, paint, coat; surround, frame; put* NP *on.*

*Wrap*, the key member of this subtype, occurs in:

   I. *John* (Agent) *wrapped the box* (Target) *in/with the paper* (Manip)
   II. *John* (Agent) *wrapped the paper* (Manip) *around the box* (Target)

That role which is specifically focused upon is in O slot. Construction II talks about a piece of paper and what was done with it—the paper was wrapped around the box (no matter that perhaps it didn't cover all six sides). Construction I describes what was done to the box—it was well and truly wrapped in the paper (ready for mailing).

*Cover*, another verb from this subtype, occurs in I *John* (Agent) *covered the box* (Target) *with leaves* (Manip), and in III *Leaves* (Manip) *covered the box* (Target), but not in II (one would scarcely say \**John covered leaves over the box*). Interestingly, *wrap* is not used in a straightforward III construction, simply because it is not possible for 'the paper wrapped the box' to happen without an Agent intervening; there is, however, *That sheet of newspaper* (Manip), *blown by the wind, wrapped* (*itself*) *around my legs* (Target).

There are a number of hyponyms of *cover* and *wrap* (mostly derived from nouns) which occur only in construction I—*butter, roof, veil, clothe, dress, grease.* For these the Target is the focus of attention (in O slot) with the general nature of Manip being specified as part of the meaning of the verb. (Verbs derived from nouns typically have a rather specific meaning and, as a consequence, more restricted grammatical properties than non-derived verbs.)

*Paint* can be noun and verb but the Verb class membership is diachronically and synchronically prior; it may occur in I *He painted the door with emulsion*, and II *He painted emulsion onto the door. Plaster* and *coat* were historically verbs derived from nouns but in the present-day language they function as full members of the WRAP subtype, occurring in I *He plastered his bread with butter*, II *He plastered butter on his bread*, and even III *Mud plastered everything after the flood, Dust coated the window-sills.*

*Surround* involves intersection of the CONTAIN subtype of REST (*Those hills surround the waterhole*) and WRAP, appearing in I *The general* (Agent) *surrounded the city* (Target) *with his army* (Manip) and III *The army/flood-water* (Manip) *surrounded the city* (Target). *Frame* has a similar meaning with primary membership of WRAP, and perhaps a metaphorical extension to CONTAIN (*The clouds and hills frame the sunset tonight*).

Only *paint*, from this subtype, commonly takes an adjective after the Target in O slot, e.g. *paint the door red*.

There is a set of verbs describing an action which is the reverse of WRAP; this includes *un-* derivatives of some WRAP verbs, e.g. *unwrap, uncover, unroof, undress,* as well as *take* NP *off* and its hyponyms *peel* 'take peel off' and *shell* 'take shell off'. They are virtually restricted to a single construction, which is similar to Ib for RUB, e.g. *He took the lid off the pan with his left hand.*

AFFECT-f, the STRETCH subtype, refers to the Agent using a Manip to change the shape or state of a Target, e.g. *stretch, extend, compress, bend, curl, fold, coil; twist, pinch, squeeze; vaporise, liquefy, solidify, melt; dissolve; freeze, cool (down), warm (up), heat (up), burn, singe.*

The first set of verbs refer to changing the shape of a Target—in one dimension (*stretch, extend, compress*), in two dimensions (*bend, curl, fold, coil*), or in three dimensions (*twist, pinch, squeeze*). These focus on the change in the Target, which must be in O slot. Thus, construction II is not available, only I (III is implausible, since such changes are unlikely to be accidentally engendered). The Manip used to effect the change can be stated (e.g. *stretch it on a rack, curl them with a curling iron, squeeze it with pincers, twist it with his bare hands*) but need not be.

All these verbs are transitive. The one-dimensional and two-dimensional items (and perhaps *twist* of the three-dimensional) may also be used intransitively, with the Target as S, e.g. *Leaves curl in late summer, That patch of desert extends further each year.*

Related to change-of-shape verbs are those describing a change of state—*vaporise, liquefy, solidify* (all derived from nouns), *melt*—and a change of temperature—*freeze* (which may also involve change of state), *cool (down), warm (up), heat (up)*. These occur in constructions I and III (*She froze the mixture with solid carbon dioxide, John's bar heater/the hot weather melted the butter*), and may also be used intransitively, with O = S (*The butter melted*).

*Burn* and *singe* belong in this subtype. They can be used intransitively (*The fire/house is burning*) and transitively in I *Mary burned John with that hot poker*, III *That hot poker burned John*, and Ib *Mary burned the paint off the door with a blowtorch*.

Some STRETCH verbs may take a state adjective or an adverb after the Target role when in O relation, or after the verb used intransitively with Target in S relation, e.g. *John froze it solid, It froze solid*; and *bend double, fold over*.

AFFECT-g, the BUILD subtype, refers to manufacture and cooking. These verbs involve an Agent manipulating Manip so as to create something (called the Product role), e.g. *build, knit, tie, make, weave, sew, shape, form, stir, mix, knead; fry, bake, cook*.

The roles can be mapped onto syntactic relations in two ways:

|  | A | O | Peripheral |
|---|---|---|---|
| VI. | *Mary* (Agent) | *built those bricks* (Manip) | *into a wall* (Product) |
| VII. | *Mary* (Agent) | *built a wall* (Product) | *with those bricks* (Manip) |

That role out of Manip and Product which is the focus of attention is placed in O relation. Construction VI directs attention to 'those bricks', which may have been left over from another job so that Mary wondered what to do with them—then she hit upon the idea of building them into a wall. Construction VII is concerned with 'a wall', which was perhaps badly needed; it is likely that sufficient bricks were purchased to build it.

*Knit* behaves in a similar way: VI *Mary* (Agent) *knitted the wool* (Manip) *into a jumper* (Product); and VII *Mary knitted a jumper from/with the wool*. The verb *tie* combines the syntactic possibilities of *knit* and of the WRAP subtype—thus VI *Mary* (Agent) *tied the string* (Manip) *into a knot* (Product); VII *Mary tied a knot* (Product) *with the string* (Manip); and I *Mary tied the box* (Target) *with the string* (Manip); II *Mary tied the string* (Manip) *around the box* (Target).

Besides *make* (in the sense 'bake' or 'build', a different lexeme from the Secondary-C verb in *John made Mary eat it*), *weave, sew, shape* (with sculptor as Agent), *form*, and so on, this subtype also contains *stir* and *mix* (e.g. *She mixed the flour and water into a paste, She mixed a paste from the flour and water*).

Many cooking verbs have quite simple syntax, with Manip in O relation, e.g. *She fried a steak*; there is no special name for the product here, just *fried steak*. With *bake* it is possible to have a simple list of ingredients (the Manip) in O slot, as an alternative to the Product, e.g. *She baked the flour* (Manip) *into a damper* (Product), *She baked a damper with the flour*. But generally it is the Product role that is syntactic O, e.g. *She baked a chocolate cake (with/using flour, sugar, cocoa, milk, eggs, butter and vanilla essence)*. We mentioned that in *She built those bricks into a wall* the focus is on *those bricks*—what is to be done with them. It would be implausible to focus in the same way on a complex list of cake ingredients, which is why this is not found in O slot, i.e. *?She baked the flour, sugar, cocoa, milk, eggs, butter and vanilla essence into a chocolate cake* sounds very odd.

Two other sets of verbs can be assigned to the BUILD subtype—*mend, repair*; and *draw, write, sign, forge*. Both sets focus on the product and are confined to construction VII, e.g. *John mended the radio with some tape, Timmie drew a horse with the crayons you sent*.

AFFECT-h, the BREAK subtype, involves an Agent causing some object (the Breaking role) to lose its physical unity, e.g. *break, crush, squash, destroy, damage, wreck, collapse; tear, split, chip, crack, smash, crash; burst, explode, blow* NP *up, let* NP *off, erupt*.

It is useful to compare BREAK with HIT. *Hit* describes a type of action, a Manip being brought into contact with a Target; there often is, but need not be, damage to either Manip or Target—we can say *John hit the vase with that stick but it didn't even chip*, or *John hit that stick on the table but it didn't break*. In contrast, *break* describes the resultant effect of some action on an object (the Breaking).

BREAK verbs occur in constructions I, II and III (but not IV or V). The Breaking role is focused on (as part of the meaning of these verbs) and must be in O slot; it can be identified with either Target or Manip:

  I. *John* (Agent) *broke the vase* (Target = Breaking) (*with that stick* (Manip))
 II. *John* (Agent) *broke that stick* (Manip = Breaking) (*on the table* (Target))
III. *John's stick* (Manip) *broke the vase* (Target = Breaking)

Like such verbs as *bend* or *burn*, from the STRETCH subtype, *break* may also be used intransitively (with Breaking as S), either to describe something which appears to happen spontaneously (*It just broke*) or to describe the effect of a HIT activity. Sentences I, II and III above could be rephrased *John hit the vase* (Target) *with that stick and the vase* (Breaking) *broke; John hit that stick* (Manip) *on the table and that stick* (Breaking) *broke*; *John's stick hit the vase* (Target) *and the vase* (Breaking) *broke*.

Breaking may also be identified with roles from other types, e.g. with Moving from the THROW subtype of MOTION, as in *John* (Causer) *threw the vase* (Moving) *down and it* (Breaking) *broke*, which could be restated with *break* as transitive verb in the first clause, *John broke the vase* (Breaking) *by throwing it* (Moving) *down*.

*Crush*, *squash* and *destroy* all describe a massive disintegration of physical form, which can only be achieved if Breaking is Target (not Manip); they are not used intransitively and only in transitive constructions I and III. *Damage* and *wreck* occur in I, II and III but are not used intransitively, since there must be some identifiable agent for the effects referred to by these verbs. *Tear*, *split*, *chip*, *crack* and *smash* are like *break* in occurring in I, II and III and in an intransitive construction. *Burst* shows similar possibilities—*John burst the balloon with a pin* (i.e. he moved the pin to the balloon), *John burst the balloon on a nail* (he moved the balloon to the nail), *A nail burst the balloon* (when the balloon happened to touch it) or just *The balloon burst*. *Explode* and *blow up* occur in I and also intransitively; *let off* has a meaning similar to the transitive sense of *explode*, and is confined to I. *Erupt* only occurs intransitively, simply because people have not yet found a way of causing volcanoes to erupt.

*Chip* and *tear* also occur in construction IV (with *at* before the Target), indicating that something is done bit by bit until a result is achieved, e.g. *He kept tearing at the wrapping paper until it was all removed*.

Native speakers have clear intuitions that *break* and *smash* are primarily transitive verbs, which can also be used intransitively, but that *explode* and *burst* are basically intransitive, with the transitive constructions being causative (e.g. *The bomb exploded*, *The army disposal squad exploded the bomb*). We return to this question in §9.3.2.

Some BREAK verbs may have an adjective inserted after the Breaking role in O relation, or after the verb when used intransitively with Breaking in S slot, e.g. *He broke it open*, *It broke open*, *She squashed it flat*.

## 4.3. GIVING

Verbs of this type involve three semantic roles—a Donor transfers possession of some Gift to a Recipient. There are two basic construction types, both with Donor in A syntactic relation; one has the Gift and the other the Recipient as O:

| A | O | Peripheral |
|---|---|---|
| I. *John* (Donor) | *gave a book* (Gift) | *to Tom* (Recipient) |
| II. *John* (Donor) | *gave Tom* (Recipient) | *a book* (Gift) |

There is a variant of construction II in which the preposition *with* is inserted before the post-O Gift NP:

IIw. *John* (Donor) *supplied the army* (Recipient) *with bully beef* (Gift)

Some verbs occur in both I and II, others only in one of these constructions. Some verbs must take *with*, for some *with* is optional—shown as II(w)—and for a third set *with* is not permissible in construction II. Thus:

I and II—*give, hand* (*over*), *lend, sell, rent, hire, pay, owe, bequeath*
I and II(w)—*serve, feed, supply*
I and IIw—*present*
I only—*donate, contribute, deliver, let*
II only—*tip*
IIw only—*reward, bribe*

Construction I focuses on the Gift, which is then in O slot; these sentences centre on 'giving a book' (or other Gift). Constructions II and IIw focus on the Recipient, in O slot; they centre on 'giving Tom' (or some other Recipient). Suppose John wanted to sell his Caxton Bible to raise money; this would be described with the Gift as O, e.g. *John sold his Caxton Bible* (*to Tom, or whoever*). But suppose instead that Tom begs to be allowed to purchase the Bible; John doesn't need to sell it but he likes Tom and is prepared to oblige him—in this circumstance it would be appropriate to say *John sold Tom his Caxton Bible*, with the Recipient as O.

As mentioned in §3.3.1, an instance of a particular role should generally have specific reference in order to be a candidate for the O syntactic slot. One could say *John gave the Red Cross a hundred dollars* alongside *John gave a hundred dollars to the Red Cross*, but scarcely *\*John gave good causes a hundred dollars* (since *good causes* is too vague to be an acceptable O), only *John gave a hundred dollars to good causes*.

*Donate* and *contribute* focus on the Gift that the Donor makes available (others will also be giving to that Recipient). These verbs only occur in I, with the Gift as O. (*Bequeath* is most used in I, again with focus on the Gift, although for many speakers II is also possible.) *Reward* 'give in appreciation for some achievement', *bribe* 'give in recompense for doing something illegal' and *tip* 'give in return for some service' focus on the Recipient and are restricted to II or IIw; the important point is that this person is being rewarded, bribed or tipped, with the actual nature of the Gift being of secondary interest.

In §9.2.4 we suggest that construction II is derived from I by putting the Recipient role in O syntactic relation, with Gift being retained as 'second object' (many speakers can passivise on either Recipient or Gift in II, e.g. *Tom was given a book (by John), A book was given Tom (by John)* ). Besides *give*, verbs which occur in II include *hand* (*over*) 'give by hand', *lend* 'give for a limited period', *sell* 'give in exchange for a sum of money', *pay* 'give money in exchange for some service', *owe* 'have an obligation to give, according to social conventions', *bequeath* 'arrange to give on the Donor's death'.

*Rent* and *hire* have similar meanings, but there are differences. One can rent or hire a car, but only rent an apartment, not—in normal circumstances—hire an apartment. It appears that *rent* is 'give the use of for a limited period in exchange for a sum of money' whereas *hire* is 'give control of for a limited period in exchange for a sum of money'. *Let*, which has a meaning similar to *rent*, is essentially an abbreviation of *let have*, with the implication that monetary compensation is involved. It can occur only in frame I, i.e. *John let the house to Tim*, not *\*John let Tim the house* (although we find *let have* in a construction similar to II *John let Tom have the house (for a highish rental)*).

Construction II is used for the direct transfer of ownership of some specific Gift. Construction IIw tends to be used to describe a more general act, along the lines of 'make available'—compare *The ladies gave the soldiers warm socks* (each soldier might have been given a pair by one lady) with *The ladies supplied the soldiers with warm socks* (the ladies might here have delivered a large box, from which the soldiers could choose socks as they wished and needed). Some verbs occur in both II and IIw, enabling us to draw out a semantic contrast. Thus *They fed us with junk food at that camp (but most of us didn't eat it)* and *They fed us lots of vitamins*. The last sentence—without *with*—carries a definite expectation that the vitamins were transferred to (i.e. consumed by) the Recipients.

Construction IIw can be used with *supply* 'give as much as needed of some commodity', *feed* 'supply with food; make eat' and *serve* 'give food and/or drink, in a culturally acceptable manner'; IIw is also employed with *present* 'give in a formal manner', *reward* and *bribe* because here the focus is on the type of giving that the Recipient experiences, with the nature of the Gift being to some extent inferrable from the verb (something valuable with *present*, and either a sum of money or something that can easily be converted into money with *reward* and *bribe*).

Note that IIw may also be used with a verb like *pay*, where *with* highlights the special nature of the Gift, e.g. *Mary paid John with a kiss* (not \**Mary paid John a kiss* or \**Mary paid a kiss to John*). Or *Mary paid John with a silver dollar* (when he had expected to receive a dollar bill).

As mentioned in §4.1, some transitive MOTION verbs may, with appropriate NP referents, add a 'giving' sense to their basic meaning, e.g. *take/throw an apple to Mary*. The syntactic consequence of this is that these verbs may, just when they do carry an implication of giving, occur in construction II (which is not normally available to MOTION verbs), e.g. *take/throw Mary an apple*. (See §9.2.4.)

For *give*, all three roles must normally be stated—no constituent can be omitted from *John gave a book to Tom*, or from *John gave Tom a book*. However, an adverb such as *out* or *away* may be added—to *give* and to other verbs from this type—indicating a general giving activity, and the Recipient can then be omitted, e.g. *John gave out/away lots of books (to his pupils)*. Other, more specific verbs can allow one role (other than Donor) to be omitted. Thus, *lend, sell, rent, hire* and *supply* can all omit reference to a Recipient; the focus is on the commodity that the Donor sells, supplies, etc.—it is assumed that they will do this to any potential Recipient (e.g. *She sells stamps*). The Gift need not be stated for *pay, bribe, tip, reward, contribute, feed*. Here the verb indicates the nature of the giving activity; the unmarked Gift is a sum of money for all of these verbs save *feed*, for which it is food. *Serve* may, in different senses, omit either Gift (*We'll serve the Queen first*) or Recipient (*They serve a lovely quiche in the corner café*) but not both at once.

*Market* has the meaning 'put on sale', with no particular Recipient in mind; there are only two roles for this verb, e.g. *John* (Donor) *marketed his produce* (Gift). *Exchange* and *trade* describe reciprocal activities, where several people are both Donor and Recipient and are grouped together as referents of the A NP, e.g. *John and Mary* (Donors and Recipients) *exchanged hats* (Gifts).

A further set of GIVING verbs, including *borrow, buy, purchase, accept, receive, rent* and *hire*, occur in the construction:

III. *Tom* (Recipient) *bought a book* (Gift) *(from John* (Donor))

*Borrow* is the converse of *lend, buy* and *purchase* of *sell*, and *accept* and *receive* are close to being converses of *give*. *Rent* and *hire* function as converses of themselves—*John hired a boat to Mary* implies *Mary hired a boat from John*, and vice versa.

If the A relation is filled by Recipient, as in III, then the O relation must be Gift. The Donor role can be a peripheral constituent marked by *from*; but it can freely be omitted.

There is also the OWN subtype, related to GIVING, which includes *have, lack, get, obtain, come by, gain, own* and *possess*. These verbs require two roles—Owner and Possession. The Possession corresponds to Gift, while Owner can relate to both Donor and Recipient, e.g. *John* (Owner) *had a Saab* (Possession), *then he* (Donor) *gave it* (Gift) *to Mary* (Recipient) *so now she* (Owner) *has a Saab* (Possession).

*Have* refers not to an activity but to a general relationship between two roles; it has a very wide semantic range, e.g. *I have a stereo/a daughter/a headache/a wonderful idea/a good dentist. Lack*, the complement of *have*, is used to draw attention to someone's not having a thing that they might be expected to have. *Get, obtain* and *come by* carry a meaning of becoming, i.e. 'come to have'—compare *I have a Ford* and *I got a Ford yesterday. Gain* is often used for getting something in addition to what one had before, e.g. *gain weight, gain promotion, My shares gained fifteen pence. Own* implies legal or official right to a thing—*Now that the mortgage is paid off, I really own this house. Possess* indicates that there is a strong emotional or mental connection between Owner and Possession—*She possesses a good sense of humour/a fine brain*, or *He doesn't possess a single suit* (*possess* is used here partly to draw attention to what this lack tells us about his character). Compare the use of *own* and *possess* in *His father owns an old sedan but John possesses a fine new red sports car*—the verb *possess* implies that John is proud of his car, almost that it is an extension of his personality. (Note that the passive use of *possess*, as in *She is possessed by the devil*, seems to be a separate, homonymous lexeme.) In §11.2 we explain the different passivisation possibilities of OWN verbs in terms of these differences of meaning.

*Have* can substitute for most (perhaps all) instances of *possess*, but only for *own* in general statements (*John owns/has two cars*), not in deictically referring expressions (*John owns that car*, scarcely \**John has that car*). The general relationship indicated by *have* can alternatively be expressed by the clitic *'s* (which goes onto the last word of an NP), by the preposition *of*—see §10.1—or by the verb *belong to*. Whereas the other verbs of the OWN subtype have Owner as subject, *belong to* has Possession as subject, e.g. *John owns that car, That's John's car, That car belongs to John*.

(The verbs *have* and *get* also belong to the MAKING type; see §6.3.1—e.g. *She got him to run, She had him running*.)

The verb *lose* has a number of related senses—it can be the opposite of *gain*, e.g. *lose money*; or of *find* from ATTENTION (§5.1), e.g. *lost my wallet*; or of *win* from COMPETITION (§4.6), e.g. *lose the big game*.


## 4.4. CORPOREAL

This type covers verbs dealing with bodily gestures. All involve a Human role (which may be extended to animals), that is in Subject relation. There may be a second role, some Substance that is taken into or expelled out of the Human's body—thus *eat, dine* (*on*), *suck, smell, taste* on the one hand, and *spit, pee, vomit, fart* on the other. Other CORPOREAL verbs refer just to bodily postures and states—*dream, think* (both of which also belong to the THINKING type), *laugh, ache, die*, etc. There is no clear division between the subclasses—one can swallow a pill or some water or just swallow, much in the way that one blinks; and one can cough, or cough something up.

Some of these verbs may have the Substance in O relation, but this is always omissible—*She has eaten* (*lunch*), *She is vomiting* (*up*) (*her dinner*), *He is shitting* (*blood*).

A number of CORPOREAL verbs may be followed by an NP that has a head noun cognate with the verb, e.g. *He sneezed the most tremendous sneeze I have ever heard, I dreamt a really horrid dream, She died the most awful death*. It would not usually be felicitous to use a cognate NP that did not include some adjectival modification—*He sneezed a sneeze, I dreamt a dream* are only likely to occur in the most extreme rhetorical style; see §10.2.4. Sometimes the description of a bodily gesture can be achieved through an adverb, e.g. *He laughed raucously* (as alternative to *He laughed a raucous laugh*) but English grammar has much more restricted possibilities for adverbial modification of verbs than for adjectival modification of nouns—hence the usefulness of cognate NPs (one would not say *She died awfully* or *He sneezed (most) tremendously*, and even ?*She died most awfully* sounds a little odd). These cognate NPs have few of the properties of direct objects; for instance, they can only in fairly specific circumstances be the subject of a passive construction—one would scarcely say *The most awful death was died by her*, although *The same dream was dreamt by all of my brothers* is acceptable.

It is hard to draw boundaries within this type. There do appear to be a number of subsets but these tend to merge into each other:

(*a*)   verbs that can be followed by a direct object but not by a cognate NP: *eat, dine (on), chew, suck, drink, smoke*;

(*b*)   those that can be followed by a direct object or by a cognate NP: *bite* (e.g. *He bit off a piece of pie, He bit off a huge bite*), *nibble, sip; smell, feel, taste, sniff, swallow, breathe, smile, fart, burp, cough, spit, shit, pee, vomit* (and their synonyms); *live*;

(*c*)   those that can only be followed by a cognate NP: *yawn, sneeze, laugh, leer, wink, blink, sob, sleep, dream, think, die*;

(*d*)   those that cannot be followed by any NP: ($d_1$) verbs that are solely intransitive, e.g. *weep, cry, shiver, faint, pass out, wheeze, sweat, rest, ache, suffer, come to, recover, be born*; ($d_2$) those that also exist in causative form with the Human role (the original S) as transitive O, e.g. *wake, waken, grow, swell, hurt, bleed, heal, drown*.

A number of comments are in order about how individual verbs fit into this classification:

(i)   *Drink* and *smoke* exist as verbs and as independent nouns—*He drank a drink (of tea)* and *She smoked that whole packet of/some smokes* involve a Substance role in O slot, not a cognate NP.

(ii)   *Dine* is 'eat the principal meal of the day', with *dinner*, a noun (derived from the verb) describing that meal. One can specify the ingredients of the meal, after *on*, as in *John dined on sausages and mash*. (What one cannot say is *John dined on the dinner*.)

(iii)   We can *dream a horrid dream* or *dream a horrid nightmare*. *Nightmare* is not cognate with the verb *dream* but it is a hyponym of the cognate noun *dream*, and behaves like a cognate NP (e.g. *a horrid night-mare* can scarcely be passivised).

(iv)   *Laugh* and *cry* can take a reflexive pronoun, followed by *to*-plus-verb or a result adjective, e.g. *John cried himself to sleep, Mary laughed herself silly*. These constructions are similar to *John sang Timmie/himself to sleep, Mary talked Jane/herself into going*, where the object can be, but need not be, identical to the subject. Note that the natures of the activities referred to by *laugh* and *cry* are such that one could not laugh or cry anyone else into anything (as one can sing or talk them); these verbs may be used transitively, but are then obligatorily reflexivised. Both *laugh* and *cry* can be followed by a preposition plus an NP or ING complement clause describing the reason for the emotional reaction; e.g. *Mary laughed about the experience, John cried over breaking his leg*.

(v)   *Live* is mostly used intransitively, or else with a cognate NP (*He lived a full and happy life*). There are also limited possibilities for non-cognate NPs, e.g. *He lived a dream/an illusion of reality/a lie*. Jespersen (1909–49: part iii, p. 301) quotes *His whole life seemed to be lived in the past*, suggesting that for *live* (but perhaps not for other CORPOREAL verbs) the cognate NP should be considered a direct object (since it is passivisable), similar to non-cognate NPs such as *a lie*.

(vi)   *Blink* would not normally be followed by a cognate NP, as *wink* might be (*He winked a comradely wink at me across the room*), but it surely could be, if the circumstances were right (e.g. *She blinked a rapid series of staccato blinks, before dying*) and so is placed in set (*c*).

(vii)   In its literal sense *swell* is intransitive and should belong to ($d_1$), but it does have a causative when used metaphorically (*The new arrivals swelled the crowd*), indicating membership of ($d_2$).

Native speakers have intuitions that set (*a*), and *bite, smell, feel* and *taste* from set (*b*), are basically transitive, and that all the remainder are basically intransitive. As already mentioned, the subject is normally the Human role, except that for *ache* and *hurt* it is a body part of the Human (for *bleed* and *grow* the subject can be either a person or a body part). CORPOREAL verbs such as *grow* and *die* may be extended as appropriate to animals and plants.

There are a number of transitive verbs which have the Human role in O slot and a meaning something like 'make recover', e.g. *bring to* (the causative correspondent of *come to*), *comfort, console, cure, soothe, ease, nurse, doctor* (the last two derived from nouns). Related to them are *kill* 'make dead'—and its hyponyms such as *murder* 'kill with premeditation' and *assassinate* 'kill a political figure for political reasons'—*beat up, injure, wound, poison*. All of these can be classified with the causatives of set ($d_2$), as can *give birth to*, the transitive correspondent of *be born*.

Finally, there are a number of verbs which typically describe corporeal interaction between two people—*kiss, embrace, hug, cuddle, fuck* (and its many synonyms). These are basically symmetrical verbs: either Human can be in A with the other in O slot in a transitive construction, or else both may be covered by the subject NP of a reciprocal sentence, e.g. *John kissed Mary, Mary kissed John, John and Mary kissed* (*each other*); see §2.11.6.

*Smell, taste* and *feel*—referring to three of the human senses—involve intersection with two other types. They function in one way as ATTENTION verbs (e.g. *I tasted that it had gone off*), §5.1; and in another way like verbs of the SEEM type (*It tasted burnt*), §6.4.1.


## 4.5. WEATHER

A number of WEATHER verbs—notably *rain, snow, hail* and *thunder*—effectively have no semantic roles at all. The verb makes up a complete clause, but the impersonal subject *it* has to be added, to satisfy the requirement of English syntax that each clause have some constituent in the subject slot (see §2.4), e.g. *It is raining, It snowed in the night, Listen to it thundering out there*.

It is possible to include with a WEATHER verb an NP that contains a cognate noun, e.g. *It thundered the most ear-splitting cracks of thunder that I've ever heard*, or a noun that is a near synonym of the cognate noun, e.g. *It rained an absolutely tremendous storm while we were on holiday*. The 'cognate' NP is not properly either an object or an extraposed subject in such clauses—it is just an appositive mechanism for commenting on the nature of the weather event. As was noted above, when discussing cognate NPs with CORPOREAL verbs, there are much wider possibilities for modification of a noun in an NP (by adjectives, etc.) than there are for adverbial modification of a verb (e.g. we could not say *\*It thundered ear-splittingly*, or *\*It rained (absolutely) tremendously*).

## 4.6. Others

A number of other Primary-A types are surveyed here quite briefly, since they generally do not have critical properties in terms of the syntactic topics discussed in Chapters 7–14. The types listed below—unlike MOTION, REST, AFFECT, GIVING and CORPOREAL—do permit non-concrete nouns (mostly, ACTIVITY nouns) in core syntactic relations.

COMPETITION refers to some Competitor (who is invariably HUMAN) trying to establish their superiority, whether in fighting a battle or playing a game. These verbs are generally transitive, with the A relation filled by a Competitor role. With *conquer, beat, overcome* and *race (against)*, the O relation relates to another Competitor (and generally may not be omitted), e.g. *John beat Fred at Scrabble/in battle*. For *resist, fight* and *play* the O can be either another Competitor or else an ACTIVITY noun such as *attack*, e.g. *The French resisted the Germans/the attack/the attack of the Germans*. For *win* or *lose* the O will be either an ACTIVITY noun, or else a noun referring to some prize that is transferred as a result of the competition; an object of the first kind can be omitted but one of the second kind may not be. In addition, an NP referring to a second Competitor may be introduced by a preposition. Thus *Argentina lost (the battle of the Falkland Islands) (to Britain)*, and *John won the book (from Mary)*. With *win* and *lose* an NP that provides a general description of some kind of activity may be introduced by a preposition, whereas an NP referring to a specific instance of activity would be in O slot, e.g. *John won/lost that game of chess*, but *John wins/loses at chess* (see §9.2.3). For *attack, guard, shield* and *surrender* the O NP can refer to a place or to people, e.g. *They attacked the city/army, They surrendered the city/hostages/themselves (to the enemy)*, while for *defend* it must be a place or thing, e.g. *They defended the city (against enemy attack), They defended their company (against take-over bids)*. Finally, there are a number of 'symmetrical' verbs, as *John competed with Mary, John struggled against Mary* and *John and Mary competed (with each other), John and Mary struggled (against each other); fight* and *play* may be used in the same manner (see §2.11.6).

   *Race* can be used in a causative construction, e.g. *The tortoise raced against the hare, John raced the tortoise against the hare*. *Win* and *lose* form unusual causatives where the 'reason' for winning/losing (which may, in the plain construction, be introduced by *because*) becomes transitive subject and the original transitive subject is now introduced by *for*, e.g. *We lost/won the match because of that error* and *That error won/lost the match for us*. The NP governed by *for* can be moved into direct object slot (with the *for* dropping), e.g. *That error won/lost us the match*.

For greater pragmatic effect, sports commentators (in Australia, at least) often employ metaphorical senses of other verbs in place of plain *win* and *lose*. For example, an emphatic win can be described by *St Kilda crushed/thrashed/flogged/smashed Brisbane.*

SOCIAL CONTRACT refers to the ways in which some human societies are organised. Most of these verbs are transitive, and require a HUMAN in A relation. Some may have an O NP referring to one person or to a group of people, e.g. *appoint, employ, dismiss, sack, fire, promote, nominate, convert, arrest, prosecute, impeach, punish*. For others the O must refer to a group of people (often organised in units like a nation or company), e.g. *govern, rule, civilise, missionise* and *join*. *Manage* may have the O NP referring either to a group of people or to some activity, e.g. *manage the pupils/the school/the organisation of sports day*. There are also SOCIAL CONTRACT verbs that involve an inherent preposition introducing an NP that refers to some job or position, e.g. *apply for, qualify for, resign from*, one sense of *withdraw* (*from*) and one sense of *work* (*at*). A further kind of social contract is described by the inherently reciprocal verb *marry* (see §2.11.6).

USING verbs are all transitive. The verb *use* can take a wide range of O NPs; it means 'do with that thing whatever is most appropriately done with it, in the circumstances, doing this in a productive manner', thus *He used all the potatoes* might refer to cooking them; *She always uses flowers from the garden* could refer to picking them and putting them in vases through the house. *Use* will often be followed by a subordinate clause specifying the appropriate activity, e.g. *use the flour to make a cake, use the money to buy a dress, use the stick to hit Fred, use the bus to get to work, use those allegations of misconduct to get John to resign*. There are also hyponyms of *use* such as *operate, manipulate*, one sense of *work*, one sense of *employ, wear* (e.g. clothes); and there are *waste* 'use non-productively' and *fiddle with* 'play at using'.

OBEYING verbs are also transitive. The verb *obey* can have as referent of the O NP either a specific kind of SPEECH ACT (e.g. *order, instruction*) or else the person who issued such a speech act. For *execute* (in the 'obey' sense) the O must be a speech act. *Process*, *deal with*, *grant* and *refuse* (in one of its senses) take as head of the O NP another kind of SPEECH ACT noun (e.g. *request*, *application*). *Perform* requires an activity noun (e.g. *task*, *plan*). The O NP may be omitted after *obey* (e.g. *John always obeys*), but not after the other, more specific verbs.

## Notes to Chapter 4

The question of alternative syntactic frames (see especially §4.2) and their meaning differences was explored in a pioneering paper by S. R. Anderson (1971). Foley and Van Valin (1984: 57ff., 82ff.) provide useful discussion of this question; they also demonstrate—in terms of the possibilities of adverb placement—that both *Bill* and *the book* should be considered objects in *John gave Bill the book* (see §4.3 and also §11.2).

A number of recent studies have included some discussion of alternative syntactic frames (dealt with here and in Chapter 11); these include Pinker (1989) and Levin (1993). Although these quote useful examples, they do not work in terms of semantic types of verbs, and are not cast within a holistic account of English grammar.

# 5

# Primary-B verb types

Primary-B verbs can, like Primary-A, be the only verb in a sentence, with all their roles filled by NPs (e.g. *John saw Mary*). But they can also, unlike Primary-A, have a complement clause as alternative to an NP in one syntactic relation (e.g. *John saw that Mary had won*). Whereas most Primary-A verbs, when used in a literal sense, take CONCRETE NPs, many Primary-B verbs may take any type of NP in O relation, e.g. an ACTIVITY noun as in *John witnessed the incident*.

The sections below outline the variety of complement clauses that the various types and subtypes of Primary-B verbs take. We return to this topic in Chapter 8, there providing semantic explanation for the occurrences.

## 5.1. ATTENTION

Verbs of this type have two core roles. A Perceiver (which is HUMAN or higher animate) finds out something about an Impression through use of eyes, or ears, or nose, or the taste-buds in the tongue, or the tactile feelings in the skin. The Perceiver is always mapped onto A and the Impression

onto O syntactic relation (except for *show*—see below). Most subtypes of
ATTENTION are Primary-B, in that the Impression can be an NP or a
complement clause; one subtype must have the Impression realised through
an NP and is thus Primary-A.

People gather more kinds of information by their eyes than by other
sense organs, and many ATTENTION verbs imply vision, e.g. *see, watch, look*
(*at*), *stare* (*at*), *peep* (*at*), *inspect*. The only verbs specifically referring to
audition are *hear* and *listen* (*to*). The other human senses are each represented by a single verb—*feel, smell* and *taste* (these are also classified as
CORPOREAL—§4.4). There are, however, a number of general verbs of
ATTENTION which—while most frequently being used for something which
is seen—can be used to refer to any of the senses, e.g. *notice, recognise,
study*, as in *I noticed, on tasting it, that he'd put in too much salt; She
recognised John's voice; He is studying the various smells produced in a
Thai kitchen*.

The subtypes that can be recognised are:

(*a*)   The SEE subtype, involving straightforward description of an act of
perception (which can be involuntary)—*see, hear, smell, taste, feel*. Also in
this subtype are *observe*, which refers to seeing or hearing something
happening; *notice*, seeing or hearing something which stands out from its
background; and *perceive*, which implies picking out some particular thing
or state or event from its background (and is also used as a high-flown
alternative to other verbs from this subtype).

(*b*)   The SHOW subtype, describing how one person assists another to an
act of perception. The main verb in this subtype, *show*, is lexical causative
of *see/notice/observe*. There will be a Causer in A slot, and either Perceiver
or Impression will be in O relation, according to which is focused on in this
instance, e.g. *John picked up the book and showed it* (Impression: O) *to Mary*
(Perceiver), or *John brought Mary over and showed her* (Perceiver: O) *the
book* (Impression).

When *show* has NPs realising all roles it implies visual perception, e.g.
*John showed the parrot to Mary* implies that she saw it, not that she heard it.
But when the Impression is a complement clause, then *show* may imply use
of the eyes—*John showed Mary how to mend a fuse* can imply that he did it,
and she observed this—or of the ears—*John showed Mary how to make a
uvular trill* implies that he made the sound, and she heard it. (*Demonstrate*
is a near synonym of this sense of *show*.)

(*c*)   The RECOGNISE subtype, referring to perception of something (by any sense) and then knowing what it is, or what its significance is—*recognise, spot*.

(*d*)   The DISCOVER subtype, referring to perception of something that was not previously apparent, e.g. *discover* 'perceive something (which may be surprising) for the first time'; *find* 'perceive something that was either looked for, or which is familiar from the past'.

(*e*)   The WITNESS subtype, referring to observation of some definite unit of activity; *witness* may be the only member.

(*f*)   The LOOK subtype, referring to the Perceiver directing their attention in order to connect with some Impression, e.g. *look* (*at*), *listen* (*to*) and the more specific verbs *stare* (*at*), *glare* (*at*), *peep* (*at*), *peer* (*at*), *squint* (*at*); *eavesdrop* (*on*); also *search* (*for*), *look* (*for*), *hunt* (*for*); *inspect, study, investigate, scan, scrutinise, examine, check, view; explore, survey; visit* (which involves intersection of MOTION and ATTENTION).

(*g*)   The WATCH subtype, similar to (*f*) but referring to deliberate perception over a period of time. *Watch* may be the only verb uniquely belonging to this subtype; the contrast with *look* (*at*) can be seen in the acceptability of *I watched John eat his dinner* but not \**I looked at John eat his dinner*. *Listen* (*to*) has two senses, one parallel to *look* (*at*), belonging to subtype (*f*) (cf. *Look at this picture!*, *Listen to this noise behind the skirting!*), and the other parallel to *watch*, in subtype (*g*), e.g. *I listened to John say his prayers*.

The subtypes have differing grammatical properties:

(i)   Omission of object NP

All ATTENTION verbs are basically transitive. Some involve an inherent preposition but the following NP has the same syntactic properties as for those items where it immediately follows the verb root—compare *The repairman hasn't yet looked at our washing-machine* and *The foreman hasn't yet inspected that new switchboard*, and their passives, *Our washing-machine hasn't yet been looked at*, and *That new switchboard hasn't yet been inspected*.

An O NP, coding the Impression role, may be omitted after verbs in the LOOK and WATCH subtypes (a preceding preposition will then also drop). A sentence such as *He is listening/looking/staring/hunting/checking/ exploring/watching* simply focuses on the way in which the Perceiver is directing their attention, without noting any specific Impression to which it may be directed.

LOOK verbs, especially when the O NP is omitted, may take a spatial adverbial which is semantically linked to the verb, and thus must come after the predicate (§2.5), e.g. *He is exploring to the north, She is hunting in the forest*. An O NP could always be included, e.g. *He is exploring the country to the north, She is hunting (for) rabbits in the forest*.

*Look (at)* and *look (for)* are distinct lexemes—compare *She is looking at a millionaire* and *She is looking for a millionaire*. This contrast is neutralised when the O NPs (and preceding prepositions) are dropped, e.g. *She is looking under the table*. But, once again, an O NP could always be stated, e.g. *She is looking at the hole in the carpet under the table*, or *She is looking for spilt peanuts under the table* (in each sentence, the two prepositional NPs could occur in either order).

For three verbs in the SEE subtype—*see, hear* and *notice*—an O NP can be omitted if it could be inferred from the preceding discourse or context, e.g. *'Mary hit John on the temple!' 'Yes, I saw'* (sc. the blow), or *'John gave his pudding to the dog!' 'Yes, I noticed'* (sc. John('s) giving his pudding to the dog). An O NP cannot be omitted after *observe* or *perceive*; here one must include at least *it*, e.g. *'Did you know there was an eclipse of the sun today?' 'Yes, I observed it'*. *Smell, taste* and *feel*, in the senses corresponding to subtype (*a*), also require an O NP to be stated. These verbs are used less frequently than *see, hear* and *notice*, which may be why no convention for omitting an *it* NP has yet evolved.

*Show*, of subtype (*b*), must include either Perceiver or Impression in O slot, e.g. *Mary showed John her ring* or *Mary showed her ring to John*. It can freely omit a non-O Perceiver, e.g. *John and Mary showed their wedding presents (to the guests)*. And *show* can omit a non-O Impression NP where this is inferrable from previous discourse, e.g. *'Does Mary know where the key is?' 'She should, I showed her.'*

**(ii)   Realisation of Impression role**
All ATTENTION verbs can have a CONCRETE NP realising Impression, except for *witness*, which must relate to an activity, e.g. *He witnessed the battle, She witnessed John's signature on the document* (note that *signature* is an ACTIVITY noun—a paraphrase would be *She witnessed John's signing his name on the document*). All ATTENTION verbs can have an ACTIVITY noun as Impression (e.g. *They noticed/discovered/viewed the football match*) except

perhaps *explore* and *survey*, which in their central meanings relate to some geographical feature.

Most verbs in the LOOK subtype may only take an NP in O slot (and are thus Primary-A); some LOOK verbs can take a WH-clause, e.g. *examine, investigate, study*. All other subtypes allow complement clauses for the Impression role. We now discuss the various kinds of complement one at a time.

**(iii)**  THAT and WH- complements

These two varieties of complement clause can fill the O slot for subtypes (*a*)–(*e*) and (*g*). Thus, *I noticed/smelt/recognised/discovered that the meat was off/where the cheese was hidden*. A THAT clause with *see* can refer to an inference from direct observation (*I saw that his leg was broken*) or to a general mental assessment (*I saw that it was pointless to continue*). *Feel* has similar properties, e.g. *I felt that the dough was sufficiently kneaded* (tactile observation) and *I felt that she was the right person for the job* (intuition). A THAT clause with *hear* almost always refers to something the Perceiver has been told, e.g. *I heard that John had cursed*; for reporting direct observation a different variety of complement would be preferred, e.g. *I heard John curse, I heard John('s) cursing.*

Subtype (*g*), with *watch* and one sense of *listen* (*to*), may take THAT and WH- clauses which directly describe some activity, e.g. *I watched that he crossed the road safely*, and *She listened whether he locked all the doors before going to bed.*

**(iv)**  TO complements

A smallish number of ATTENTION verbs may take a special variety of Modal (FOR) TO complement clause: the *to* is obligatorily omitted in an active construction, but obligatorily included in the passive, e.g. *Everyone saw John kick Mary, John was seen to kick Mary.*

It is important to distinguish this TO complement construction, with the *to* omitted, from a THAT complement clause, which can omit the *that* when it comes directly after the predicate, e.g. *I noticed (that) John kicked Mary (every time he went past)*—here the verb *kicked* shows tense inflection, indicating that it is in a THAT clause—and *I noticed John kick Mary (when no one was looking)*—here the verb is in base form, as it always is in a TO clause. (For a verb like *hit*, which makes no distinction between the base and past tense forms, these would fall together, i.e. *I noticed John hit Mary* is ambiguous between THAT and TO readings.)

This variety of TO complement, where *to* is omitted in the active, occurs with *see*, *hear* and *notice* and, less readily, with *feel*, *smell*, *observe* and *perceive* from the SEE subtype (but not with *taste*). It is also attested with subtype (*g*), WATCH, but only in the active, e.g. *I watched John hit Mary*, *I listened to him sing* (here *to* comes from *listen to*, rather than being the complementiser); there are no acceptable passives of these sentences. (Van Ek (1966: 68) also mentions examples with *find*, from subtype (*d*), but these seem somewhat archaic; Bolinger (1974) quotes examples with *show* and *look at*, e.g. *Can you show it happen?* and *Look at him run!* The *look* example is only possible in the active.)

In addition, verbs in subtypes (*a*)–(*d*) may take a Judgement TO complement clause. As mentioned in §2.7, Judgement TO clauses most frequently have their VP beginning with *be* (although other possibilities do occur, e.g. *I noticed John to have lost some weight since last Christmas*). When *be* is the copula, then *to be* can be omitted only after verbs of the DISCOVER subtype, e.g. *I found John (to be) dead*, but *We noticed John to be dead*, where the *to be* must be retained. When *be* is the imperfective auxiliary, *to be* may be omitted after verbs from DISCOVER, SEE or SHOW, e.g. *I noticed/discovered John (to be) singing a hymn*.

**(v)   ING complement**
This occurs with verbs from the SEE, SHOW, WITNESS and WATCH subtypes, e.g. *We observed/watched/witnessed John('s) stealing those apples*; *I can't hear John('s) playing the trumpet*. The subject of the complement clause can take possessive marking, but this is most frequently omitted. (ATTENTION verbs seem particularly prone to loss of a complementiser; we just described a type of TO clause where *to* must be omitted in the active.)

A construction like *John noticed that tall man watching Mary*, with the complement clause subject followed by a verb in *-ing* form, can be derived in two ways: by omission of possessive marker from the subject of an ING clause, or by omission of *to be* from a Judgement TO complement whose VP begins with the imperfective auxiliary *be*. With some verbs there is no problem of ambiguity. *Watch* and *witness* may only take an ING, not a Judgement TO clause, and so *I watched/witnessed that tall man('s) saying his prayers in church (from two until four, so he couldn't have committed the burglary which took place at three o'clock)* must be an ING complement, describing some durative event. Similarly, *discover* only takes a TO, not an ING, complement, and so *I discovered that tall man (to be) saying his prayers (just when I'd decided he must be an atheist)* is also unambiguous, referring to the perception of some fact that was not previously known. But verbs from the SEE and SHOW subtypes can take both ING and TO complement clauses; an abbreviated sentence such as *I noticed that tall man saying his prayers* is thus ambiguous between the readings of the *watch/witness* and of the *discover* sentences just given.

There is still further room for ambiguity. In the discussion of relative clauses, in §2.6, we mentioned a reduced form of restrictive relative clause referring to present time which, for verbs that take the *be ... -ing* auxiliary, effectively involves omission of the relative pronoun and the form of *be*. Thus *I noticed that tall man (who was) watching Mary (he looks just like the picture on the 'Wanted' poster)*, where *(who was) watching Mary* helps restrict the reference of the O NP. This has a quite different meaning from the ING complement construction *I noticed that tall man('s) watching Mary (all afternoon, and took great offence at his ogling my wife for such a long time)*, where what I noticed was not the identity of the tall man, but the fact of his watching Mary. The abbreviated sentence *I noticed that tall man watching Mary* would thus be ambiguous between these two readings.

Table 5.1 summarises the more important syntactic properties of these ATTENTION verbs.

Complement clauses with ATTENTION verbs have one special property. The complement clause subject is generally distinct from the main clause subject, for the straightforward reason that one would not normally *see* or *hear* etc. oneself (or, perhaps more to the point, one would not normally report doing so). It is possible for the two subjects to have the same reference, but under no circumstances can the complement clause subject be omitted, e.g. *myself* cannot be dropped from *I saw myself on the video*, *I finally recognised myself to be middle-aged*. This contrasts with verbs from a number of other subtypes, where coreferential omission is normal, e.g. *I want (?myself/me) to eat an avocado.*

There are three further sets of ATTENTION verbs:

(i) *Ignore, disregard, overlook, pass* NP *over* refer to the Perceiver not making contact with a certain Impression (either accidentally or on

**Table 5.1.** *Syntactic properties of the main* ATTENTION *verbs*

| | Is O omittable? | Complement varieties allowed in O slot | | | | |
|---|---|---|---|---|---|---|
| | | THAT | WH- | Modal (FOR) TO[1] | Judgement TO | ING |
| (*a*) SEE subtype | | | | | | |
| *see, hear, notice* | yes | yes | yes | yes | yes | yes |
| *smell, taste, feel* | no | yes | yes | some | yes | yes |
| *observe, perceive* | no | yes | yes | yes | yes | yes |
| (*b*) SHOW subtype | | | | | | |
| *show* | no | yes | yes | yes | yes | yes |
| (*c*) RECOGNISE subtype | | | | | | |
| *recognise, spot* | no | yes | yes | no | yes | no |
| (*d*) DISCOVER subtype | | | | | | |
| *discover, find* | no | yes | yes | some | yes | no |
| (*e*) WITNESS subtype | | | | | | |
| *witness* | no | yes | yes | no | no | yes |
| (*f*) LOOK subtype | | | | | | |
| *look (at)* | yes | no | yes | yes[2] | no | no |
| *listen (to) etc.* | yes | no | some | no | no | no |
| (*g*) WATCH subtype | | | | | | |
| *watch, listen (to)* | yes | yes | yes | yes[2] | no | yes |

[1]  *To* omitted in active, retained in passive.
[2]  Only in the active.

purpose). These verbs are transitive, with either an NP or an ING complement clause in O slot, e.g. *She walked by and ignored me/ignored my waving at her.*

(ii)  *Appear, disappear* are intransitive and refer to an Impression (in S relation) being available or not available for the visual attention of a potential Perceiver. A Perceiver can be included with *appear*, marked by preposition *to*, e.g. *An angel appeared to Mary.* (With *disappear* we can say *The angel disappeared from the scene/from (Mary's) view*, but not \**The angel disappeared from Mary.*) *Appear* is also a member of the SEEM type—§6.4.1.

(iii)  *Look, sound, smell, taste* and *feel* are also intransitive verbs, with the Impression in S slot; the Perceiver may be included, marked by *to*, e.g. *This violin sounds good (to me) (now that it has been tuned), That chicken tasted really lovely (to all of us).* Note that there is one verb in this set corresponding to each of the five senses. *Smell, taste* and *feel* are identical in form to the corresponding transitive verb, e.g. *She felt the fur* (transitive), *It felt soft and silky* (*to her*) (intransitive). Intransitive *look* corresponds to transitive *see* and *look* (*at*), e.g. *He saw/looked at the painting* and *The painting looks good*. Only *sound* (derived from the noun) is not cognate with a corresponding transitive verb from the ATTENTION type. (There is of course a transitive verb *sound* with a meaning entirely different from *hear* and *listen* (*to*), and with quite restricted use, e.g. *sound the trumpet* 'make it sound out'.)

Both semantically and syntactically these five verbs behave like the SEEM type; they involve an intersection of this type with ATTENTION (and, for *smell, taste* and *feel*, also with CORPOREAL). They are normally followed by an adjective from the VALUE, DIFFICULTY or QUALIFICATION types, or the CLEVER subtype of HUMAN PROPENSITY, e.g. *It looks difficult, It sounds definite*—see §6.4.1. Interestingly, *bad* can be omitted after *smell*, i.e. *It smells* implies *It smells bad*. (Note that the derived adjective *smelly* refers to 'a bad smell' while *tasty* means 'a good taste'. One might expect, on a principle of analogy, that *good* should be omissible from *It tastes good*. It is not; languages seldom work on so symmetrical a pattern as this.)

## 5.2. THINKING

This type covers verbs of thinking, knowing, believing and the like. There are always two roles—a Cogitator (who is generally HUMAN) has in mind some Thought. THINKING verbs are basically transitive, with Cogitator in A and Thought in O syntactic relation. The Thought may be realised by an NP, or by one of a variety of complement clauses; the syntactic possibilities vary somewhat across subtypes.

The following subtypes can be distinguished:

(*a*)    The THINK subtype, referring to the Cogitator's mind just focusing on some person, thing, state or happening. The most general verb is *think* (*of/about/over*). Others include *consider* 'think about some actual or possible state of affairs (and its consequences)'; *imagine* 'think of something as if it were true, although the Cogitator is aware that it may not be true (and that it might be surprising if it were)'.

(*b*)    The ASSUME subtype, when there is some doubt as to whether the Thought is true, e.g. *assume* 'think of something as true when the Cogitator realises that it is only likely—not certain—that it is'; and *suppose* 'think of something as true when the Cogitator realises that there is insufficient evidence to be sure that it is'.

(*c*)    The PONDER subtype, referring to different modes of thinking, e.g. *ponder* (*on/ over*), *meditate* (*on/about*), *brood* (*on/over*), *speculate* (*on/about*), *wonder* (*at/about*), *reflect* (*on/about*), *dream* (*of/about*), *contemplate*.

(*d*)    The REMEMBER subtype, referring to the Cogitator having in mind, or trying to get in mind, something from the past, e.g. *remember* 'think about something from the past, or about something arranged in the past which is to take place in the present or future', and *forget* 'fail to think of something that one should have thought about, or that one should have been able to think about'.

(*e*)    The KNOW subtype, referring to the Cogitator being aware of some fact, or body of information, or method of doing something. The most general verb is *know*. There are also *sense* 'know some fact intuitively' (one meaning of *feel* may also belong here); *realise* 'suddenly think in an appropriate way, so as to know some fact'; *learn* 'come to know something by (often diligent) effort'; and *understand* 'know something, and also the reason for it'. *Teach*, a lexical causative related to *know/understand*, also belongs in this subtype; it has the meaning 'Causer tries to help Cogitator know/understand some Thought'. Causer must be in A relation. If Cogitator and Thought are both NPs then either may be focused on, and placed in O syntactic relation, e.g. *John taught geometry to Mary*, *John taught Mary geometry*. If the Thought is expressed by a complement clause then it will follow the Cogitator, which must be in O slot, e.g. *John taught Mary that the square on the hypotenuse is equal to the sum of the squares on the other two sides*.

(*f*)    The CONCLUDE subtype, referring to using the mind to think about the consequences of certain facts, observations, assumptions, suppositions, etc., e.g. *conclude, infer, reason*, one sense of *argue, prove*, one sense of *demonstrate*, one sense of *show, guess*.

(*g*)    The SOLVE subtype, referring to the mind thinking in such a way as to achieve some end, e.g. *solve, work* NP *out; devise, make* NP *up; analyse*.

(*h*)    The BELIEVE subtype, referring to thinking of something as true. The verb *believe* means 'think of something as true (when in fact it may not be, but the Cogitator will not accept that it may not be)'. There are also *suspect* 'think that something is likely to be true' and *doubt* 'think that something is unlikely to be true'.

Dealing now with the grammatical properties of THINKING verbs:

**(i)   NP as object, and object omission**
Verbs in all subtypes typically take a complement clause in O slot. An NP is a possible alternative, but for many verbs this must have non-CONCRETE reference, e.g. *She learnt weaving, We assumed his cooperation, He proved the truth of the theorem.* Some verbs may have a CONCRETE noun as head of the NP, but this leaves something unsaid about that thing, which the addressee may be assumed to be aware of, e.g. *We considered Mary (for promotion), She understands John* (i.e. the reason he acts as he does), *They speculated about the house* (what price it would fetch at the forthcoming auction). The most common verbs from the THINKING type may more frequently have a CONCRETE NP in Thought role, e.g. *think (of/about), remember, forget, believe,* but even here some amplification may be implicit, e.g. *I am thinking of Odette* (of how much I love her), *I forgot John* (i.e. forgot to invite him to my party). *Know* has a special sense, 'be acquainted with a person or place', e.g. *I know Paris/Peter Matthews well,* which is rather different from the 'be aware of something' meaning, which it shares with *sense, realise,* etc. *Believe* also has a special sense, marked by the preposition *in*—compare *I believed Mary* (i.e. what she said) with *I believe (in (the existence of) the Christian god),* and *I believe in (the wisdom and goodness of) my boss.*

Most verbs in the PONDER subtype take a preposition before a Thought NP (this does, of course, drop before *that,* e.g. *I reflected on John's deciding to withdraw, I reflected that John had decided to withdraw).* It is a difficult decision whether to regard these as transitive verbs with an inherent preposition, or as intransitive verbs which can take a peripheral NP referring to the Thought. In favour of the transitive alternative is the fact that these NPs passivise relatively easily, e.g. *That decision by the Vice-Chancellor has been wondered at in every committee room of the university.* But, as some support for the intransitive analysis, the preposition-plus-NP can be freely omitted after most PONDER verbs, e.g. *She is meditating/brooding/reflecting.*

Both *dream* and *think* have cross-membership of the CORPOREAL type. Like many other CORPOREAL verbs, they may be followed by a cognate NP, e.g. *I dreamt a perfectly lovely dream, She has a tendency to think really evil thoughts.* Note that these cognate NPs, which may not have the full syntactic status of 'object', immediately follow the verb. *Think (of/about)* and *dream (of/about),* as THINKING verbs, involve an inherent preposition before the O NP (which can readily be passivised, e.g. *That change in the plans has been thought about for an awfully long time*).

Some THINKING verbs, such as *think*, *dream* and *learn*, may omit an object NP only in the generic tense or imperfective aspect, e.g. *I dream every night*, *I'm learning (gradually)*. Others, such as *infer* and *prove*, are seldom used in the imperfective and must always have an O NP stated. Verbs from subtype (*d*) and some of those from (*e*)—*remember*, *forget*, *know* (in the 'be aware of something' sense) and *understand*—can omit an O NP if it can be inferred from the context, e.g. *'Mary won the prize'. 'I know'* (sc. that she did) and *'Fred won't come to the door'. 'Oh, I understand'* (sc. why he won't). (*Believe* can occur with no object only when used in a religious sense, e.g. *He believes (in the Christian god)*.)

Verbs from subtypes (*a*), (*b*) and (*g*) (excluding the negative verb *doubt*) may use *so* in place of the Thought role where this could be inferred, e.g. *'Does John know?' 'I assume so'* (sc. that he knows). For *guess* the *so* may optionally be omitted in some dialects, e.g. *'Will she win?' 'I guess (so).'*

**(ii)**   THAT, WH- and WH- TO complements

All THINKING verbs may take a THAT complement in O slot except perhaps for some from the PONDER subtype (e.g. *brood*, *meditate*). Only the ASSUME and BELIEVE subtypes, and certain members of SOLVE, do not accept some instance of WH- or WH- TO (*doubt* is an exception—it takes a WHETHER clause as a near-paraphrase of a THAT complement, e.g. *I doubt that/ whether John will win*—see §8.2.1).

**(iii)**   ING complements

Verbs from THINK, PONDER and REMEMBER may have an ING clause for the Thought role; the subject of the complement clause can be identical to the subject of the main clause and will then be omitted, e.g. *I thought of/imagined/speculated about/remember (Mary's) being attacked when on holiday in Nigeria*. *Understand*, from the KNOW subtype, may also have an ING clause in O slot. Here the complement clause subject is unlikely to be the same as the main clause subject; if it is, it would not normally be omitted, e.g. *I understood Mary's/my being denied promotion*.

**(iv)**   Judgement TO complements

All except the PONDER and SOLVE subtypes and *doubt* (and the causative *teach*) can take a Judgement TO complement, e.g. *I guessed/supposed/knew/*

*inferred/suspected John to be clever.* (*Forget* only takes Judgement TO in limited circumstances; some speakers accept *I'd forgotten him to be so fat.*) The *to be* can often be omitted, just after *think, consider* and *imagine*, e.g. *We considered him (to be) stupid, I think it (to be) very unlikely.* Other verbs allow the *to be* to drop only in certain circumstances, e.g. *I supposed him (to be) dead/sick* but only *I supposed him to be clever/tall/rich/alive*, with the *to be* retained. (See §8.2.6.)

*Show* and *prove* have the special property that, with a TO complement, the A and O NPs can be coreferential—compare the regular construction *John showed Fred to be stupid* (*by analysing his behaviour*) and the special one *Fred showed himself to be stupid* (*by the way he behaved*). *Prove*, but not *show*, has an even more abbreviated construction type, with the reflexive pronoun and *to be* omitted, e.g. *Our guide proved* (*himself*) (*to be*) *useless.*

**(v)** Modal (FOR) TO complements
*Remember, forget, know, learn* and *teach* may take a Modal (FOR) TO complement. This will often have its subject coreferential with the main clause subject, and then omitted, e.g. *I remembered/forgot/knew/learnt to stand up when the judge enters the room*; or, the subjects can be different (and then *for* must be retained), e.g. *I remembered for Mary to take her pill. Think* may also take a Modal (FOR) TO complement but only, it appears, in the past tense and in a negation or question, e.g. '*Did you think to lock the door?*', '*I didn't think to lock the door.*' (*Remember, know* and *learn*—and *think*, in restricted circumstances—are thus numbered among the very few verbs to accept both Modal and Judgement varieties of TO complement. See §8.2.3.)

Alone of THINKING verbs, *know* may take a Modal (FOR) TO complement with both *for* and *to* omitted, similar to a small set of ATTENTION verbs (§5.1). This usage appears always to involve past tense or previous aspect, and very often includes a negator such as *never* or *not*, e.g. *They'd never known him hit her.* As with ATTENTION (and MAKING) verbs, the suppressed *to* must be used in the passive, e.g. *He had never been known to hit her.*

The complement clause possibilities for THINKING verbs are summarised in Table 5.2.

## 5.3. DECIDING

This type involves two roles: a Decision-Maker (who is generally HUMAN) thinks to themself that they will follow a certain Course (of action).

**Table 5.2.** *Complement clause possibilities for* THINKING *verbs*

| | THAT | WH- and WH- TO | ING | Judgement TO | Modal (FOR) TO |
|---|---|---|---|---|---|
| (*a*) THINK subtype | | | | | |
| *think* (*of/about/over*) | yes | yes | yes | yes | yes |
| *consider, imagine* | yes | yes | yes | yes | no |
| (*b*) ASSUME subtype | | | | | |
| *assume, suppose* | yes | no | no | yes | no |
| (*c*) PONDER subtype | | | | | |
| *ponder* (*on/over*) *etc.* | some | yes | yes | no | no |
| (*d*) REMEMBER subtype | | | | | |
| *remember* | yes | yes | yes | yes | yes |
| *forget* | yes | yes | yes | limited | yes |
| (*e*) KNOW subtype | | | | | |
| *know, learn* | yes | yes | no | yes | yes[1] |
| *sense, realise* | yes | yes | no | yes | no |
| *understand* | yes | yes | yes | yes | no |
| *teach* | yes | yes | no | no | yes |
| (*f*) CONCLUDE subtype | | | | | |
| *conclude, infer, etc.* | yes | yes | no | yes | no |
| (*g*) SOLVE subtype | | | | | |
| *solve, work out, etc.* | yes | some | no | no | no |
| (*h*) BELIEVE subtype | | | | | |
| *believe, suspect* | yes | no | no | yes | no |
| *doubt* | yes | yes | no | no | no |

[1]  With *know*, the *to* may be omitted in the active, but must be retained in the passive.

DECIDING verbs are basically transitive; the Decision-Maker is always in A and the Course in O syntactic relation.

We can recognise two subtypes:

(*a*)  The RESOLVE subtype, focusing on one particular Course, e.g. *decide* (*on*), *determine* (*on*), *resolve*; *plan* (which intersects with WANTING).

(*b*)  The CHOOSE subtype, preferring one Course out of a number of alternatives—*choose* and its hyponyms such as *select, pick* NP (*out*); *appoint, elect*; *vote* (*for/on*).

Verbs of the RESOLVE subtype may have the Course role realised as a THAT, or WH-, or Modal (FOR) TO or WH- TO complement clause (the subject of a FOR TO complement is most often identical to the main clause subject, and is then omitted, together with the *for*), e.g. *Tom resolved that he would not be beaten, Father will decide whether we have lunch inside or out, The headmaster decided (for the girls) to go in front, John will determine where to erect the marquee. Decide (on)* and *determine (on)* may also take an ING complement, which normally has its subject identical to main clause subject, and then omitted, e.g. *He decided on (the gardener's) pruning the roses this weekend.*

There are two kinds of NP possible as Course. *Decide (on)* and *determine (on)*—but not, it seems, *resolve* or *plan*—may take a CONCRETE NP in O slot, e.g. *Fred decided on a red shirt, John decided on the theatre this evening.* But this NP is effectively the O (or other post-predicate constituent) of a complement clause, and is used as main clause O when the verb of the complement clause could be inferred by the addressee from the context—thus, Fred may have decided to wear, or to buy, a red shirt, and John may have decided to go to the theatre this evening.

*Decide, determine* and *resolve* have a further, related meaning (similar to one sense of *settle*), referring to someone indicating an appropriate Course where there had been some difficulty or doubt, e.g. *John decided the dispute, Mary determined the order of precedence, Einstein resolved the paradox* (see §9.2.1). Note that in this sense they take an ACTIVITY or other abstract NP in O slot, with no preposition *on*. (When used in this sense, verbs from the RESOLVE subtype may have a non-human NP in A slot, e.g. *That final speech determined the result of the debate, Fred's penalty kick decided the match.*)

*Choose* has similar syntactic properties to *decide (on)* (excluding that mentioned in the last paragraph), occurring with THAT, WH-, Modal (FOR) TO, WH- TO and ING complement clauses, e.g. *I chose that we should have Christmas dinner in the evening this year, I chose (for) Mary to give the vote of thanks, You choose who to give it to!* There can be a CONCRETE NP as O but this always does imply some suppressed complement clause, e.g. *Mary chose a teddy bear* could in appropriate contexts be understood by the addressee to state that she chose to buy one, or to make one in her soft toys evening class, or to receive one out of the list of possible presents her grandmother had offered.

The other verbs in the CHOOSE subtype are hyponyms of *choose* (that is, *choose* could almost always be substituted for an occurrence of any of them). *Select, pick (out), appoint* and *elect* must have a CONCRETE NP, not a complement clause, in O slot. (There will often be included in the sentence some specification of what the choice is related to, e.g. *Mary selected a teddy bear (as the Christmas gift from her grandmother), I appointed John (to be sales manager).) Vote (for/on)* may take a THAT, or a WH- or a Modal (FOR) TO or a WH- TO complement or a concrete NP, e.g. *I would have voted for Nixon to be impeached, I would have voted to impeach Nixon, I would have voted on whether to impeach Nixon, I would not have voted for Nixon (in any election).*

Only *decide* and *choose*, the two most general and most frequently used verbs from the DECIDING type, may omit specification of the Course when it could be inferred from the context, e.g. *'I don't think we should attack the enemy today, sir.' 'It's too late, Sergeant, I've already decided'* (sc. to attack them today) and *'Why don't you ask for that stereo set?' 'No, I've already chosen'* (sc. something else). *Vote* can occur without specification of Course, which is then taken to refer to the casting of a ballot, e.g. *Are you going to vote this time around?* (which might be said in an election year).


## 5.4. SPEAKING

English—like other languages—has many verbs in the SPEAKING type, reflecting the important role that language activity has in our lives. There are four semantic roles associated with SPEAKING verbs—the Speaker, the Addressee(s), the Message, and the Medium (language or speech-style used). Speaker, Addressee and Medium are realised as NPs; the Message can be an NP or complement clause or direct speech.

Speaker role is in every case mapped onto subject (A or S) syntactic relation. There is considerable variation in how the other three roles are associated with semantic relations—see the summary in Table 5.3. Many verbs have the Message as O, e.g. *She reported John's illness (to the chairman)*, while many others have Addressee as O, e.g. *She reminded the chairman of John's illness*. The verbs *speak* and *talk* may have the Medium in O slot, e.g. *They speak French here.*

If the Addressee is not in O slot it is generally introduced by the preposition *to*; if the Medium is not in O slot it is generally introduced by *in*. There are a variety of means for grammatical marking of the Message, which are discussed below.

Verbs in five of the eight SPEAKING subtypes may introduce direct speech, e.g. *'It's Christmas Day,' he shouted/said/informed Mary/told the children/ instructed the alien.* The other subtypes describe kinds of vocal activity (e.g. *speak, discuss, slander*) and generally do not occur in apposition to direct speech.

Thought is often considered internalised speech, and a verb like *think* may occur with an utterance in quotation marks (really referring to direct

**Table 5.3.** *Syntactic coding of semantic roles for* SPEAKING *verbs*

Speaker is always mapped onto subject (S or A) relation.

Medium is generally introduced by *in*; the *in* can be omitted, with Medium then appearing to be in object (O) relation, for some verbs from subtype (*a*).

The possibilities for coding Message and Addressee are:

| Subtype | Message | Addressee |
|---|---|---|
| (*a*) TALK | *about/concerning* | *with/to/at* |
| (*b*) DISCUSS | O | *with/to*[1] |
| (*c*) SHOUT | O | *to/at* |
| (*d*) REPORT | | |
| sets (i)–(vii) | O | *to* |
| set (viii) | post-O | O |
| (*e*) INFORM | *of/on/about* | O |
| (*f*) TELL | { *about/of* | O |
| | { O | *to/of/from* |
| (*g*) ORDER | post-O | O |
| (*h*) FORGIVE | Preposition | O[2] |

[1] Addressee not normally statable with *refer to*.

[2] Addressee introduced by *to* with *apologise*.

thought rather than direct speech), e.g. *'Maybe I'll win the lottery,' John thought*. People are sometimes represented as making decisions aloud, or thinking aloud in various ways, and a number of verbs from the DECIDING and THINKING types are sometimes used to introduce direct speech, as in (23) from §2.7 and *'I ought to spray the apple trees,' he reflected/remembered/concluded/decided/resolved*. (Note that the use of such verbs to introduce direct speech occurs much more often in written, literary English than in colloquial styles.)

The Message, if it is not shown by direct speech, may have two components, as in [*the news*] *about* [*the murder*], [*an announcement*] *concerning* [*the picnic*]. The first part, which we can call the Message-Label, is an NP whose head is a SPEECH ACT noun (e.g. *announcement*, *question*, *proposal*) or a noun referring to some language unit (e.g. *news*, *message*). The Message-Label is linked by a preposition to the second component, which we can call the Message-Content. This may be an NP, or an ING, WH- or THAT complement clause; thus *the news about the murder*, *the news about Mary's shooting John*, *the news about who Mary shot*, *the news that Mary had shot John* (as always, a preposition drops before *that*). (The Message-Content can alternatively be a full Message, consisting of Label, preposition and Content, e.g. *the news about* [[*the announcement*] *concerning* [*the election*]].)

A Message can consist of Label-preposition-Content or just Label or just Content. The possibilities are summarised in I–III. In each sentence the Message is in O slot. For Ia it consists just of a Label; in Ib–e it is Label followed by preposition plus Content, which is NP or ING, WH- or THAT clause. Constructions IIa–c show a Message that is just Content—NP, ING or WH- clause. Frame IIIa again shows just Content, here a THAT clause, while IIIb involves direct speech. (The possibilities are grouped in this way since some verbs show all I, some all II, some both of III, and some combinations of I, II and III.)

**Ia.**  *Fred reported the sad news*
**Ib.**  *Fred reported the sad news about the murder*
**Ic.**  *Fred reported the sad news about Mary('s) shooting John*
**Id.**  *Fred reported the sad news about who Mary shot*
**Ie.**  *Fred reported the sad news that Mary had shot John*
**IIa.**  *Fred reported the murder*
**IIb.**  *Fred reported Mary('s) shooting John*
**IIc.**  *Fred reported who Mary shot*
**IIIa.**  *Fred reported that Mary had shot John*
**IIIb.**  *Fred reported: 'Mary has shot John'*

We can now discuss the individual subtypes within the SPEAKING type; their occurrence in the various syntactic frames is summarised in Table 5.4.

(*a*)  The TALK subtype simply refers to an activity of vocal communication, e.g. *speak*, *talk*, *chat*, *gossip*, *converse*, *communicate*, *quarrel*, one sense of *argue* (that corresponding to 'have an argument'); *joke* involves intersection of the TALK and REPORT subtypes.

These verbs are basically intransitive and can occur with just the Speaker role filled. *In* may introduce a Medium NP and *about* or *concerning* a Message in frame I or II (that is, *speak about*, *talk about*, etc. can be substituted for *report* in I and II). Frame III is not possible—TALK verbs do not take a THAT complement or introduce direct speech.

*Chat, gossip, converse, communicate, quarrel* and *argue* generally refer to reciprocal activity—see §2.11.6; they should either have a plural Speaker NP or else an Addressee NP introduced by *with* (rather than *to*), e.g. *John and Mary chatted* or *John chatted with Mary*. *Talk* and *speak* may also be

**Table 5.4.** *Main grammatical frames for* SPEAKING *verbs*

| | I | II | III | IV | V | VI | VII | Used intransitively |
|---|---|---|---|---|---|---|---|---|
| (a) TALK subtype | | | | | | | | |
| e.g. *talk, speak* | prep[1] | prep[1] | no | | no | no | no | no | yes |
| (b) DISCUSS subtype | | | | | | | | |
| *discuss, refer to* | yes | yes | no | | no | no | no | no | no |
| *describe* | no | yes | no | no | no | no | no | no | no |
| (c) SHOUT subtype | | | | | | | | |
| e.g. *shout, call* | yes | no | yes | | no | no | no | no | yes |
| (d) REPORT subtype | | | | | | | | |
| (i) *say* set | limited | no | yes | some | no | no | no | no |
| (ii) *state* set | yes | no | yes | most | no | no | no | no |
| (iii) *announce* set | yes | yes | yes | most | no | no | no | no |
| (iv) *remark (on)* set | yes | yes | yes | | no | no | no | no | no |
| (v) *boast (about/of)* set | yes | yes | yes | | no | no | no | no | yes |
| (vi) *suggest* set | no | yes | yes | some | no | no | no | no |
| (vii) *undertake* set | no | yes | yes | | no | yes | no | no | no |
| (viii) *promise* set | no | yes | yes | | no | yes | no | no | no |
| (e) INFORM subtype | | | | | | | | |
| e.g. *inform, lecture* | prep[1] | prep[1] | yes | | no | no | no | no | no |
| (f) TELL subtype | yes/prep[2] | prep[2] | yes[2] | | no | no | no | no | no |
| (g) ORDER subtype | | | | | | | | |
| (i) *order* set | no | no | yes[3] | | no | no | yes | no | no |
| (ii) *forbid* | no | no | yes[4] | | no | no | yes | yes | no |
| *discourage, dissuade* | no | no | yes[4] | | no | no | no | yes | no |
| (h) FORGIVE subtype | | | | | | | | |
| e.g. *forgive, accuse* | no | no | some[4] | | no | no | no | no | some |

[1]   Preposition is required before Message.
[2]   There are two possibilities: (i) Addressee as O, with following Message introduced by a preposition (see text for details of preposition inclusion); or (ii) Message, which includes Message-Label, as O, in frame I only, followed by *to* plus Addressee.
[3]   Message as THAT clause following Addressee (which is in O relation).
[4]   Only direct speech (IIIb), not THAT complement clause (IIIa).

used reciprocally, taking *with*, but they may alternatively have an Addressee introduced by *to*; *speak* has, as a further alternative, *at*.

The meaning of *speak* focuses on the fact that the speaker is using a language (one asks *How many languages does he speak?* in preference to *How many languages does he talk?*) whereas *talk* refers to how the language is used, in what circumstances and on what topics (e.g. *Don't talk in church!*

and *What shall I talk about with your father?*). *Speak* tends to be used for one-way communication and may be employed where there is a difference of rank (*The King spoke to/with me!*) whereas *talk* carries an expectation of reciprocity and equality (*The King talked with the Queen*). We can say, focusing on the speaker's activity: *He spoke the truth, She spoke her mind*, but not \**He talked the truth*, \**She talked her mind*. (*Write* can be used in the same contexts as *speak*, referring just to a different medium, e.g. *She wrote the truth in that letter*, but it also has a wider range, e.g. *She wrote (to say) that she'd been ill*.)

Both *speak* and *talk* (but not other verbs from this subtype) may omit preposition *in* before the Medium NP, which then appears to be in O syntactic relation since it freely passivises, e.g. *They are talking Swahili, Spanish is spoken here* (see §9.2.4). Again, there is a difference between *talk* and *speak*—*Ken talked Navaho to Clyde* implies that Clyde can understand him; one could say *speak Navaho* with a similar interpretation but there is also *Ken spoke Navaho at Sally*, where the preposition *at* indicates that she probably didn't comprehend it.

There are examples of Message-Content (when it is a single noun) dropping its preposition and filling O slot, e.g. *The old men are talking politics and the young mothers are talking babies, A lot of linguistics was talked at that party last night* (*which made it extremely boring for the spouses*). This is possible with *talk*, which deals with what the language is used for, but not for *speak*, which centres more on what the speaker is doing. Some of the other verbs may also, in specially marked circumstances, drop the preposition before a Message-Content NP, e.g. *They are arguing (about) politics*. (One also hears *He is speaking/talking rubbish/double Dutch*, where the NP refers to the lack of comprehensibility of the Message; note that one could add specification of the Medium, e.g. *in Spanish*.)

(*Talk* also occurs in an idiomatic causative, e.g. *We talked Mary into going*, meaning 'We talked to Mary until we persuaded her to go'.)


(*b*)   The DISCUSS subtype refers to vocal activity that focuses on a specific message, e.g. *discuss, refer to, describe*.

These are strictly transitive verbs, with O slot filled by the Message role. *Discuss* and *refer to* may occur in frames I and II while *describe* is restricted to II, where the O NP is Message-Content, e.g. *John described the battle* (but scarcely frame I \**John described the news (about the battle)*). None of these verbs may be used in III, with a THAT clause or to introduce direct speech.

DISCUSS verbs could be regarded as transitive correspondents of TALK—in fact *talk about* may substitute for most occurrences of *discuss*, *refer to* and *describe*. *Discuss* has a reciprocal meaning; there should be either a plural Speaker NP or else an Addressee introduced by *with* (not *to*). *Describe* takes the normal *to* before the Addressee while *refer* would not generally include any mention of Addressee (at least partly because the appropriate preposition *to* is already present, as an inherent component of this transitive verb).

(*c*)   The SHOUT subtype refers to manner of vocal production, e.g. *shout*, *call*, *cry*, *roar*, *swear*, *pray*, *preach*, *narrate*, *recite*, *intone*, *read*, *sing*. Related to this subtype are *whistle* and *warble*. (*Shout*, *call*, *cry* and *read* often take the adverb *out*.)

These verbs may be used intransitively, or else transitively with the Message in O relation (see §9.3.1). They occur in frame III, with a THAT complement or with direct speech, e.g. *John called out that the pirates were approaching* or *'The pirates are approaching,' John called*; or in frame I, where the Message NP begins with a Label, e.g. *Fred read the message (about the murder)*. The Label can be omitted from the Message constituent, but the following preposition must be retained, so that we get a variant of frame I:

I'a.   *Fred read about the murder*
I'b.   *Fred read about Mary('s) shooting John*

Note that this is distinct from frame II, which is not possible with SHOUT verbs, i.e. \**Fred read the murder*.

All SHOUT verbs introduce the Addressee by *to* except *swear*, which takes *at* (*swear at the dog*), and *shout*, *roar*, *cry*, which can take *to* (when raising one's voice the better to communicate, e.g. *shout to the children that dinner is ready*) or *at* (when raising the voice in annoyance, e.g. *shout at the children (to go away)* ).

A number of other verbs are marginal members of this subtype. *Translate* shares all syntactic properties except that it does not take a THAT complement. *Pronounce*, *mispronounce* and *utter* take an O NP that begins with an appropriate label and may be followed by quotation of the sound or word or sentence which this label refers to, e.g. *pronounce the letter 's'*, *utter the name 'Jehovah'*.

*Name*, and one sense of *call*, have rather different syntax (and could perhaps be regarded as a separate small subtype). They have in O slot an NP referring to a person or thing or place, and this is followed by the name (which may be in direct or indirect speech), e.g. *She called him 'my little doll'*, *She called him her little doll*, and *They named the baby 'Imogene'*.

(*d*)   The REPORT subtype refers to the manner of presenting a message. We can distinguish a number of sets of verbs within this subtype, with sample members:

   (i)   *say, declare, assert*, one sense of *observe*, one sense of *joke*; *put* NP *about*, *give* NP *out, let* NP *out, put* NP *across, let on about* NP (see §9.2.2 for this method of citing phrasal verbs);
   (ii)   *state, affirm, rumour* (mostly used in the passive; cf. §11.4);
   (iii)   *announce, proclaim, mention, note, report; regret* (also in LIKING);
   (iv)   *remark* (*on*), *comment* (*on*); *explain*;
   (v)   *boast* (*about/of*), *brag* (*about/of*), *complain* (*about/of*), *grumble* (*about*);
   (vi)   *suggest, claim; acknowledge, admit, confess* (*to*); (*repute*, which is confined to the passive, may also belong here; cf. §11.4);
   (vii)   *undertake, offer, propose*; one sense of *agree* (*with*);
   (viii)   *promise, threaten*.

Sets (i)–(vii) are basically transitive, with the Message in O slot. *Promise* and *threaten* are ditransitive with Addressee as O (although this can freely be omitted), followed by the Message. For all REPORT verbs the Message may be a THAT clause or direct speech (frame III), e.g. *'New York is the finest city in the world,' she announced/remarked/boasted/suggested/proposed* and *She announced/remarked/boasted/suggested/proposed that New York is the finest city in the world*.

   All sets except (i) and (ii) may have the Message-Content as O (frame II), e.g. *He mentioned/complained about/suggested/offered/promised a dinner-party*. Sets (ii)–(v) occur in frame I, with Message-Label (optionally followed by preposition plus Content) as O, e.g. *They stated/announced/complained about/regretted the message* (*concerning our having to work on Sundays in future*). *Say* has somewhat unusual properties—if there is no direct speech or THAT complement it can take a Message whose first element is some qualification, e.g. *He said a lot/something/nothing* (*about the picnic*); there is also a very limited set of nouns that can occur in the label slot, e.g. *say a prayer* (*for/about* ... ), *say grace*.

   A Judgement TO complement may occur with most verbs from sets (ii) and (iii), as well as *declare, admit* and *claim* (and *say* only in the passive, §11.4). Thus:

**IV.**   *The Judge declared/reported/admitted him to be insane*

Sets (vii) and (viii) may take a Modal (FOR) TO complement, e.g.

**Va.**   *I offered/undertook/promised/threatened for my charlady to clean your house*

The subject of the complement clause will often be coreferential with main clause subject and then omitted (together with *for*):

**Vb.**   *I offered/undertook/promised/threatened to clean your house*

Speakers tend to accept the full FOR TO construction (in Va) with only some of these verbs; for the remainder they require coreferential subjects, as in Vb.

As already mentioned, *threaten* and *promise* have Addressee in O relation. This can be followed by Message-Content (introduced by *with* in the case of *threaten*) or by a THAT clause or by direct speech. Imagine a scenario in which I have the authority to transfer Mary and in which John has strong feelings about her; to taunt him I may either promise a transfer (if I want to please him) or threaten it (if I wish to annoy him):

(1)   *I promised John a transfer for Mary/I threatened John with a transfer for Mary*
(2)   *I promised/threatened (John) (that) I/Bill would transfer Mary*
(3)   *I promised/threatened (John): 'I/Bill will transfer Mary'*

When the Addressee is omitted these verbs may take a Modal (FOR) TO complement (with complement clause subject coreferential to main clause subject and thus omitted):

(4)   *I promised/threatened to transfer Mary*

In many dialects of English *promise* (but never *threaten*) may take a Modal (FOR) TO clause—with subject coreferential with main clause subject and thus omitted, together with *for*—even when the Addressee is retained:

(5)   *I promised John to transfer Mary*

However, speakers of other dialects (e.g. contemporary Australian English) do not accept (5) as grammatical, and must instead say (2), i.e. *I promised John that I would transfer Mary*. When confronted by (5) these speakers can only interpret it with the complement clause subject coreferential with main clause object (i.e. John arranges the transfer, the whole sentence then meaning perhaps that I let him transfer her); that is, they interpret (5) as having the syntax of a verb from the ORDER subtype.

Of this subtype only set (v)—*boast, brag, complain* and *grumble*—may be used intransitively; the meanings of these verbs indicate the Speaker's attitude towards some Message, which need not be specified, e.g. *She's complaining again*. *Confess* may omit the Message only when this could be inferred from the context, e.g. *'Did you steal the Saab?' 'Okay, I confess'* (sc. that I did steal it). All other verbs in sets (i)–(vii) must include a Message, which can be a THAT clause, or else introduce direct speech. Of set (viii), *threaten* should have either Message or Addressee stated, e.g. *He's threatening John, She's threatening to blow up the plane*; but *promise* is like *confess* in that it may omit both Addressee and Message when they could be inferred, e.g. *'Will you really mend the window?' 'Yes, I promise'* (sc. you that I will mend it).

*Offer* and *promise* are both very frequently used to convey a Message of giving (where the subject of *give* is coreferential with main clause subject); the verb *give* can then be omitted, with the Donor, Recipient and Gift roles being coded as surface constituents of the SPEAKING verb. Thus *She offered/ promised me an apple/an apple to me* are paraphrases of *She offered/promised to give me an apple/an apple to me*.

Note also that *offer* (especially in relation to giving) and *threaten*—and perhaps other REPORT verbs—need not necessarily involve language activity but could just refer to some gesture or mode of behaviour. The verbs can still be used in their full syntactic range to describe these gestures (except for the direct speech option), e.g. *The dumb giant threatened to hit her (but then she handed over the keys, and so he didn't)*.

(*e*)   The INFORM subtype refers to the way in which a Message (which is not an order or instruction) is conveyed to the Addressee, e.g. *inform, lecture, agree (with)*; *remind* has cross-membership of the INFORM and ORDER subtypes.

These verbs are transitive and have the Addressee role in O syntactic relation. This is followed by the Message introduced by a preposition—*of* (for *inform* and *remind*), *on* (for *lecture* and *agree*) or *about* (for all four verbs). The varieties of Message illustrated in frames I and II (with a preposition inserted) and III are all applicable, e.g. I *I informed John of the announcement (about the picnic)*; II *I informed John of the picnic*; IIIa *I informed John that there will be a picnic tomorrow*; IIIb *'There will be a picnic tomorrow,' I informed John*.

The Addressee NP is obligatory with *inform* and *remind* but can be omitted after *lecture* and *agree* when inferrable from the cotext, e.g. *Mary's father thought that she should resign and her mother agreed* (sc. with her father that she should resign). Statement of the Message may be omitted after any of the verbs when inferrable, e.g. '*Does Mary know about the picnic?*' '*She should, I did inform her*' (sc. about the picnic).

(*f*) The TELL subtype contains verbs which relate both to Message (particularly its Label component) and to Addressee; they may have either of these roles in O relation. The subtype includes *tell, ask, request* and *beg* (note that all these verbs also have cross-membership of the ORDER subtype).

*Tell* combines something of the syntactic properties of the last two subtypes. Compare:

| | | |
|---|---|---|
| *Message as O* | | |
| | (*d*) REPORT | *I reported the news (to John)* |
| | (*e*) INFORM | \**I informed the news to John* |
| | (*f*) TELL | *I told the news to John* |
| *Addressee as O* | | |
| | (*d*) REPORT | \**I reported John (of/about) the news* |
| | (*e*) INFORM | *I informed John of/about the news* |
| | (*f*) TELL | *I told John (of/about) the news* |

There are, however, important differences. The Message, as O of *report*, can be Label, Label-preposition-Content or just Content, e.g. *I reported the news/ the news about the accident/the accident (to John)*. For *tell* the Message, if in O slot, must include a Label—thus *I told the news (about the accident) to John* but not \**I told the accident to John*. In addition, a THAT complement or direct speech cannot be included with *tell* if the Addressee is marked by *to*.

The basic syntactic frame for *tell* appears to be with Addressee as O. The Message—which can be Label, Label-preposition-Content or Content—is then introduced by a preposition, e.g. *I told John about the news/about the news concerning the accident/about the accident*. The initial preposition may be dropped only if the Message begins with a Label, e.g. *I told John the news (concerning the accident)*, but not \**I told John the accident*. (There is, of course, a semantic difference between *tell John the news* and *tell John about the news*. And there can, in the Addressee-as-O frame, be a THAT clause or direct speech, e.g. *I told John that the bus had crashed*, and '*The bus has crashed,' I told John*.)

*Ask*, *request* and *beg* have similar syntactic properties, with some differences of detail. With Message as O the Addressee is introduced by *of* with *ask* and by *from* with *request* and *beg*, e.g. *She asked a question* (*about the accident*) (*of John*), *He requested information* (*about the accident*) (*from John*). When Addressee is O, *ask* does not include a preposition before a Message Label, e.g. *She asked John* (*a question*) (*about the accident*), whereas *request* and *beg* require *for*, e.g. *They begged John for information* (*about the accident*). *Enquire*, and one sense of *demand*, are semantically similar to *request* but may only have a Message (beginning with a Label) in O slot, e.g. *She enquired directions* (*about how to get to the station*) (*from John*).

*Ask* can omit specification of Message and/or Addressee if these could be inferred from the context, e.g. '*I'll ask Mary where the key is*'. '*No, don't, I've already asked*' (sc. her where it is). *Tell* can omit the Message in similar circumstances, e.g. '*Does Mary know where it is?*' '*She should, I've told her*' (sc. where it is), and it may omit the Addressee when the Message is being particularly focused on, e.g. *I don't want to tell that story again, I've already told it a hundred times*. But Message and Addressee may generally not both be omitted at once with *tell* (except perhaps in a style of children's English, where one child may sometimes be heard accusing another with: *Oh, you told!*).

*Answer* is an unusual verb in that there are effectively two Messages—the question which was asked, and the answer that may be given (*reply to* is similar, except that it can be used for the response to a question or as a comment on some statement). The question may be coded as an NP in O slot (sometimes with the Addressee as 'possessor' to the Label), e.g. *He answered the/Mary's question* (*about the accident*). Or the Addressee may be in O relation, e.g. *He answered Mary*. Or the answer may be shown by a THAT complement or by direct speech, e.g. *He answered that the accident was in Pall Mall*; '*The accident was in Pall Mall,*' *he answered*. Note, though, that question and answer may not both be coded in the same clause (e.g. one cannot say *\*He answered Mary's question that the accident was in Pall Mall*) simply because the conventions for interpreting apposition in English syntax would then imply that *Mary's question* and *that the accident was in Pall Mall* are coreferential, which they aren't. Instead, one might say *To Mary's question he answered that the accident was in Pall Mall* or *He answered Mary's question by saying that the accident was in Pall Mall*. *Answer* and *reply to* may, like *ask*, be used without any Addressee or Message where the relevant information is supplied by context, e.g. '*Have you asked him about the accident?*' '*Yes, but he won't answer*' (sc. my question about the accident).

(*g*)   The ORDER subtype refers to a Message (generally an order or instruction) directed at an Addressee, e.g. (i) *order, command, urge, instruct, encourage; warn, caution, persuade, invite, recommend* (*to*); senses of *tell, remind, ask, request, beg*; (ii) *forbid, discourage, dissuade, prohibit.*

All these verbs are transitive, with the Addressee in O slot. It is followed by the Message, which can only be direct speech (often, an imperative) or—for set (i)—a THAT complement (generally including a modal *should* or *would*) or a Modal (FOR) TO complement. The subject of the complement clause (or of the direct speech) may be different from the main clause subject:

**IIIb**.   *I instructed the lieutenant: 'Your platoon should be ready at dawn!'*
**IIIa**.   *I instructed the lieutenant that his platoon should be ready at dawn*
**VIa**.   *I instructed the lieutenant for his platoon to be ready at dawn*

Or the subject of the complement clause can be coreferential with the main clause object, and then omitted from a direct speech imperative or from a Modal (FOR) TO complementiser:

**IIIb′**.   *I instructed the lieutenant: 'Be ready at dawn!'*
**IIIa′**.   *I instructed the lieutenant that he should be ready at dawn*
**VIb**.   *I instructed the lieutenant to be ready at dawn*

(Speakers vary as to which verbs from this subtype may be used in frame VIa. For those that may not, we simply have to say that the subject of a Modal (FOR) TO clause *must* be coreferential with main clause object.)

The only verbs that may not omit the Addressee (in the presence of a THAT complement or direct speech) are *tell* and *remind*. As with their other senses—*remind* in subtype (*e*) and *tell* in (*f*)—these two verbs focus on the Addressee role, which must be stated. *Persuade* does not involve an order or instruction but refers to an attempt to get the Addressee to do something voluntarily; it is not used with direct speech (except perhaps if *try* is also included, e.g. *'You go there, and you'll really enjoy it,' we tried to persuade him*). *Warn* and *caution* may occur in IIIa/b and VIb (often, with the complement clause or direct speech including *not*), or with the negative preposition *against* plus an ING complement that lacks the negative particle (the ING clause will generally have its subject identical to the Addressee, and then omitted), e.g. *I warned him not to go, I warned him against going.*

We have already mentioned that, for all verbs in set (i), the subject of a reduced TO complement, in frame VIb, is understood to be identical to the O NP of the main verb (the Addressee role). All verbs except *ask, beg* and *request* must include an O NP in VIb; these three verbs can omit the

Addressee and the subject of the Modal (FOR) TO clause is then understood to be identical to main clause subject, i.e.

**VIa**.   *John asked Bill to watch Mary* (i.e. Bill will watch Mary)
**Va**.   *John asked to watch Mary* (i.e. John will watch Mary)

(The second sentence could perhaps be regarded as an abbreviation of *John asked to be allowed to watch Mary*.) *Ask*, *request* and *beg* appear to be the only verbs in English whose complement clause subject is taken to be coreferential with the main clause object if there is one, and with main clause subject otherwise.

*Recommend* has a meaning difference from the other verbs in set (i) in that it involves offering advice, not issuing an order, instruction or request. It has the regular syntactic possibilities of the subtype (except that *to* introduces the Addressee, but is dropped before a TO complement), e.g. *'Use brushbox for the steps,' he recommended (to me)*; *He recommended to me that I should use brushbox for the steps*, *He recommended me to use brushbox for the steps*. *Recommend* may also code the Message-Content through an ING complement clause, e.g. *He recommended (to me) (my) using brushbox for the steps*. And there is an abbreviated construction in which a concrete NP may fill the O slot, e.g. *He recommended brushbox (to me)*; a sentence like this could only be used where further necessary details could be inferred by the listeners (e.g. they know that I have been looking for a suitable timber to repair my steps).

The verbs in set (ii) involve negative instruction or advice (i.e. telling the Addressee not to do something that they may have intended to do). They can take direct speech, or a FROM ING complement, e.g.

**VII**.   *I discouraged John from going*

*Discourage* and *dissuade* only take a FROM ING, not a TO, clause. *Forbid* occurs in both frames with no difference in meaning (*John forbade Mary to go/from going*); speakers differ as to which frame they prefer.

(*h*)   The FORGIVE subtype refers to the Speaker saying something to the Addressee which reveals the Speaker's attitude, such as their approval or disapproval of the Addressee or of something the Addressee has done (or which the Addressee or some other person thinks reveals such an attitude), or saying something which satisfies a social convention (such as greeting), e.g. (i) *insult, slander, curse, abuse, scold, blame, rebuke, forgive, pardon, praise, thank, congratulate, compliment; tell* NP *off, pick on* NP; (ii) *accuse, excuse*; (iii) *greet, welcome, introduce*; (iv) *cheer, applaud, apologise.*

All the verbs in sets (i)–(iii) are strictly transitive, with Addressee as O. *Cheer* and *applaud* are also transitive, but may omit the O; *apologise* is intransitive, but *to*-plus-Addressee may optionally be included.

*Accuse* and *excuse* must have a Message following the Addressee (unless it could be inferred from the context); this will be an NP or ING clause, introduced by *of* after *accuse*, and by *for* or *from* (with very different meanings) after *excuse*, e.g. *He accused Mary of fiddling the books; She excused John for overlooking the mail/from dealing with the mail.*

Verbs from sets (i)–(ii) and (iv) may add specification of the way in which the attitude was revealed or the greeting effected, using *by* plus an NP or ING clause, e.g. *He insulted me by mispronouncing my name; She thanked me by making a very sweet speech.* Set (i) may also specify the reason for the Speaker's adopting this attitude, using *for* or *on* plus an NP or ING clause, e.g. *He thanked me for saving his life.* It follows from the meanings of these verbs that the subject of a clause introduced with *by* is taken to be coreferential with Speaker (main clause subject) while the subject of a clause introduced by *for* is taken to be coreferential with Addressee (main clause object), e.g. on hearing *John congratulated Tom by shaking his hand on/for winning the race*, a listener will infer that John did the shaking and Tom the winning.

Actually using one of these verbs may constitute an instance of the activity it refers to—that is, the verb is being used as a 'performative'—e.g. '*I greet you, stranger*', '*I forgive you, darling*'; this may be referred to in a *by* constituent, e.g. *He congratulated me just by saying 'I congratulate you, my boy' in that posh voice and didn't even shake my hand.* These verbs generally do not introduce direct speech in the ways that the SHOUT, REPORT, INFORM, TELL and ORDER subtypes do. But—like some THINKING and DECIDING verbs—they may be used with direct speech, especially in a popular literary style (and may then omit the Addressee), e.g. '*Oh, you are so wonderful,' she praised.*

Some FORGIVE verbs may of course refer to an activity that involves no speech at all, e.g. *The dumb giant greeted me by clutching my shoulders.* Or the subject may not even be human, e.g. *My cat greets me when I get home.* Syntactic possibilities remain unchanged.

SPEAKING is probably the most varied subtype, both semantically and syntactically. There are many more marginal properties, and differences of detail between verbs, than have been mentioned. But this abbreviated account has dealt with the major parameters which will be needed for the discussion in Chapters 7–14.

## 5.5. LIKING

Verbs of this type have two roles—an Experiencer (who must be HUMAN or a higher animal) gets a certain feeling about a Stimulus. The meaning of the verb expresses the nature of the feeling.

LIKING verbs can roughly be divided into the following sets: (i) *like, love, hate, prefer; fear; dread* (also in WANTING); (ii) *dislike, loathe, abhor, admire, value; regret* (also a member of the REPORT subtype of SPEAKING); *rejoice in/ at*; (*don't*) *mind* (*about*), (*don't*) *care* (*about*); (iii) *enjoy, favour, object to, approve of* (the adjective *fond*, in *be fond of*, patterns with set (iii); see §3.2); (iv) *worship, fall for*.

These verbs are transitive with the Experiencer in A relation and the Stimulus—which cannot be omitted—in O relation. The only exceptions are (*don't*) *care* (*about*) and (*don't*) *mind* (*about*), which may freely omit *about*-plus-Stimulus and are perhaps best regarded as basically intransitive. It used to be that *enjoy* was only used as a transitive verb, so that a waiter or waitress would urge a diner: *Enjoy it!* In recent years, this verb has taken on an intransitive sense, so that a waitperson now says just: *Enjoy!*

The Stimulus may be realised in a variety of ways. It can be a straight-forward concrete NP, as in I, or an ING complement, as in II. The subject of an ING clause will be omitted when it is coreferential with main clause subject, as in IIb.

    I.   *Fred likes horses/Mary/your uncle/the wet season*
**IIa**.  *Fred likes John's playing baseball*
**IIb**.  *Fred likes playing baseball*

Or the Stimulus can have two components (similar to those of the Message role for SPEAKING verbs)—a Stimulus-Label, generally a SPEECH ACT or other abstract noun—linked by a preposition to a Stimulus-Content, which can be an NP, or an ING, THAT, or Modal (FOR) TO complement. Thus:

**IIIa**.  *Fred likes the proposal*
**IIIb**.  *Fred likes the proposal about baseball*

**IIIc.**   *Fred likes the proposal about (our) playing baseball instead of cricket on Saturdays*

**IIId.**   *Fred likes the proposal that we should switch to baseball*

**IIIe.**   *Fred likes the proposal for us to switch to baseball*

**IIIf.**   *Fred likes the proposal to switch to baseball*

(Following a general rule of English, the preposition drops before *that, for* or *to* in IIId/e/f.)

As described in §5.4, a Message role may include just Label, or Label-preposition-Content, or—for some SPEAKING verbs—just Content. The Stimulus role allows different possibilities. It may just comprise a Label, as in IIIa. But it may not omit the Label from IIId. That is, one cannot say, in most dialects of English, *\*Fred likes that we now play baseball*.

It is possible, however, to substitute the impersonal pronoun *it* for the Label in frame IIId. The Label may be omitted from IIIf, with no substitution, and it may be omitted from IIIe with substitution of *it*. (Omitting the Label plus preposition from IIIc gives IIa.)

**IIId′.**   *Fred likes it that we now play baseball*

**IIIe′.**   *Fred would like (it for) us to switch to baseball*

**IIIf′.**   *Fred would like to switch to baseball*

We can first focus on the inclusion of the impersonal pronoun in IIId′/e′. It is clear that the substitution of *it* does engender a semantic difference. The Stimulus-Label may be one of a number of nouns, with different meanings, e.g. *proposal, idea, suggestion, fact*. When *it* replaces the Label the Stimulus has a meaning rather close to that with *fact*—*I like the fact that he stands up to the boss* is a near paraphrase of *I like it that he stands up to the boss*. A Stimulus with *it* certainly has a different sense from one with *the proposal* (which is why I changed the verb phrase of the complement clause in IIId′, in order to ensure a felicitous sentence). The sequence *it for* can be omitted from IIIe′, with a definite semantic effect—see §8.2.4.

Stimulus-Label and Stimulus-Content essentially make up one syntactic component, in O slot. An adverb may follow the complete statement of Stimulus, e.g. *I like the suggestion that we should disarm an awful lot, I'd like it for us to disarm very much*. But the Content component can be moved to the end of the clause, and an adverb may then come between the Label (which remains in O slot) and the Content, e.g. *I like the suggestion an awful lot that we should disarm, I'd like it very much for us to disarm*. (The longer the Content is, the more likely it is to be moved to the end of the clause; cf. §2.13A.) Extraposition of Content applies in almost exactly the same manner for ANNOYING verbs, described in the next section, and is then more visible. (See also the discussion of phrasal verbs, in §9.2.2, for further confirmatory data.)

No *it* can come before *to* in IIIf′ but an adverb may still come before or after the TO clause (as it may come before or after THAT and FOR TO complements in IIId′/e′), e.g. *I would like very much to switch to baseball, I would like to switch to baseball very much.* The question of why *it* should be obligatory in IIId′, optional in IIIe′ (speakers vary in their judgements here) and obligatorily absent in IIIf′ is an interesting one, to which no answer is at present known.

Turning now to the syntactic behaviour of different LIKING verbs, it appears that they can all occur with an NP or ING clause as Stimulus but may not all be equally happy with THAT and (FOR) TO complements. There are no hard and fast divisions (which is why we do not talk of subtypes), rather a scale of relative acceptability.

Set (i) is at home in all the frames discussed, with ING, THAT and (FOR) TO complements. Set (ii) is found with ING and THAT clauses but appears awkward with FOR and TO complements (IIIe/f and IIIe′/f′). One hears *I like/hate to go* but scarcely *\*I dislike/loathe to go*; they become more acceptable if *would* is included, e.g. *I would dislike/loathe to go.* (We do get *I don't care to go*, meaning 'don't want to', but this is a different meaning of *don't care (about)* from that in *I don't care about the proposal that we should go*, where the sense is 'be indifferent to'.) Set (iii) is almost restricted to NP and ING codings of Stimulus. It sounds most odd with (FOR) TO and TO complements, and the possibilities for THAT clauses (frames IIId/d′) are very limited—one might accept *I enjoy it that John cooks* and perhaps *?I favour the idea that Mary (should) organise the picnic*, but scarcely *??I enjoy the fact that John cooks* or *??I favour it that Mary should organise the picnic.* Set (iv) appears restricted to an NP Stimulus. (§8.4.5 attempts a semantic explanation for the varying syntactic possibilities of LIKING verbs.)

*Object to* and *approve of* each include an inherent preposition and *(don't) care (about)* includes a preposition before the Stimulus, if this is stated. These prepositions must be included in frames I, II, IIIa–f. In IIId′ *about it* is omitted after *don't care*, e.g. *I don't care (\*about it) that we may switch to baseball* and—to the extent that *object to* and *approve of* are used in frame IIId′—the *to it* and *of it* may either be omitted or retained, e.g. *I object (to it) that John wants to play cricket; I approve (of it) that John adores baseball.*

With (*don't*) *mind* the preposition may be included or omitted in all of I, II, IIIa–e. In fact it carries a semantic difference: *don't mind* implies that the speaker is stoical about something that may adversely affect them, whereas *don't mind about* indicates indifference, similar to *don't care about*. Compare *I don't mind Mary* (let her insult me all she wants, I've got a thick skin) with *I don't mind about Mary* (couldn't give a damn what happens to her); and *I don't mind the proposal that my salary should be cut* (sure it'll affect me, but I do have a private income) with *I don't mind about the proposal that my salary should be cut* (since I know it's just hot air, they wouldn't dare actually do it). The contrast should be neutralised in frame IIId′, since a preposition must drop before *that*; but in fact *I don't mind that my salary will/may be cut* has the clear sense of *don't mind* (not *don't mind about*).

*Rejoice in/at* appears to belong to set (ii), but is unusual in that it does not include *it* before a THAT complement (e.g. *I rejoiced that he had returned unharmed*).

*Fear* and *dread* have rather different meanings from the other LIKING verbs. They occur in frames I, II, IIIa–e and, typically, IIIf′, but not in IIIe′, where the Stimulus is realised as a FOR TO clause with no preceding Label. Both occur in IIId′ but here *dread* may omit the *it* and *fear* would generally omit *it*, e.g. *I dread (it) that she may return home, I fear (?it) that she may return home*. (It is interesting that *rejoice* and *fear*, two verbs which do not take *it* before a THAT clause, appear to be the only LIKING verbs to occur in parentheticals—see §8.1.)

Two further verbs may be regarded as divergent members of this type. *Envy*, but not *pity*, can occur in frames I and IIa, e.g. *I envy Mary's luck, I envy Mary's getting promoted*. But *envy* is more felicitously used—and *pity* must be used—in a quite different frame, where the verb is followed by an NP referring to a person (who is the object of the envy/pity), optionally followed by a constituent stating the reason for this emotional attitude— this can be an NP, or a Label followed by preposition and ING or THAT clause, or just an ING or THAT clause:

IVa.  *I envy Mary her promotion*
IVb.  *I envy Mary (the fact of) her husband('s) being such a good cook*
IVc.  *I envy Mary (the fact) that she got promoted*

Note that the subject of an ING complement (*her* in IVb) may optionally be omitted if it is coreferential with main clause object (e.g. *I envy Mary being so quick at figures*).

(The adjective *jealous* (*of*) has a very similar meaning to *envy* but different syntactic possibilities—we cannot say \**I was jealous of Mary her promotion*, only something like *I was jealous of Mary because of her promotion*.)

## 5.6. ANNOYING

This type has the same two roles as LIKING—an Experiencer gets a certain feeling about a Stimulus—but they are mapped differently onto syntactic relations, Stimulus becoming A and Experiencer O, e.g. *frighten, terrify, scare, shock, upset, surprise; offend; delight, please, satisfy, entertain, amuse, excite, inspire; impress, concern, trouble, worry, grieve, dismay, depress, sadden; madden, infuriate, annoy, anger, disappoint; confuse, bewilder, deceive, trick, perplex, puzzle; interest, distract, bore; attract; embarrass, disgust; tire, exhaust, bother*.

As mentioned earlier, some AFFECT verbs show a metaphorical sense and then have meaning and grammar similar to the ANNOYING type, taking an NP or a complement clause as A argument. For example, *The bad news broke my spirit*, *That he had not been promoted really cut John up*, *To have to help wash up stretched Mary's patience*, and *For John to get the job ahead of me stung me to the quick*.

All ANNOYING verbs are transitive. Some do have meanings similar to those of LIKING verbs (e.g. *please* and *delight* are almost converses of *like* and *love*—if *X pleases Y* it is likely that *Y likes X*, and vice versa) but most have meanings rather different from those of the LIKING type.

The syntactic frames we outlined for LIKING apply almost exactly to ANNOYING verbs, with A and O reversed, e.g.

    **I.**   *Horses/Mary/your uncle/the wet season annoy(s) Fred*
  **IIa.**  *John's playing baseball annoys Fred*
  **IIb.**  *Playing baseball annoys Fred*
 **IIIa.**  *The proposal annoys Fred*
 **IIIb.**  *The proposal about baseball annoys Fred*
 **IIIc.**  *The proposal about (our) playing baseball instead of cricket on Saturdays annoys Fred*
 **IIId.**  *The proposal that we should switch to baseball annoys Fred*
 **IIIe.**  *The proposal for us to switch to baseball annoys Fred*
 **IIIf.**  *The proposal to switch to baseball annoys Fred*

In §5.5 we presented evidence—from adverb placement—that a THAT, or Modal (FOR) TO clause, as the Content part of Stimulus, may be extraposed to the end of the clause, with the Label remaining in its original syntactic slot. This happens very plainly for ANNOYING verbs, where the extraposition is from A slot, i.e.

**III′d.**   *The proposal annoys Fred that we should switch to baseball*
**III′e.**   *The proposal annoys Fred for us to switch to baseball*
**III′f.**   *The proposal annoys Fred to switch to baseball*

(It should be noted that speakers differ over the acceptability of III′d–′f.)

LIKING verbs also occur in IIId′/e′/f′ where the Label is either omitted or replaced by *it*; the complement clause can again be transposed. These possibilities are once more clearly distinguished for verbs from the ANNOYING type:

**IIId′.**   *That we now play baseball annoys Fred*
**IIIe′.**   *For us to switch to baseball would annoy Fred*
**IIIf′.**   *To switch to baseball would annoy Fred*
**III′d′.**  *It annoys Fred that we now play baseball*
**III′e′.**  *It would annoy Fred for us to switch to baseball*
**III′f′.**  *It would annoy Fred to switch to baseball*

A minor syntactic difference is now revealed. Most LIKING verbs take *it* before a THAT clause and also have *it* before a full (FOR) TO complement (but omit *it* when the *for* is dropped). ANNOYING verbs retain *it* in subject slot for all three complement types when they are extraposed, but cannot include *it* when the complement clause stays in A slot. The inclusion of *it* when extraposition has taken place is necessary to satisfy the surface structure constraint that there be something in the subject slot for every main clause in English. The omission of *it* when there is no extraposition is also due to a surface syntactic constraint—no sentence in English may begin with *it that, it for* or *it to*.

(It is in keeping with the general syntactic structure of English (§2.7) that an ING complement generally cannot be extraposed; there can be what is called 'right dislocation', a quite different syntactic phenomenon, which is marked by contrastive intonation, shown in writing by a comma, e.g. II′a *It annoys Fred, John's playing baseball*.)

Not all verbs from this type occur equally freely with all kinds of complement; Modal (FOR) TO constructions may be especially rare for some. This relates to the meanings of the complement constructions and the meanings of the verbs (see Chapter 8). No hard and fast occurrence restrictions are evident as a basis for establishing subtypes.

Most verbs in this type do not allow an O NP to be omitted (even if it has a very general meaning, e.g. *He amuses everyone*). There are just two or three that occasionally occur with no Experiencer stated, in marked contexts, e.g. *He always offends, She does annoy, He can entertain, can't he!* A small subset of ANNOYING verbs may also be used intransitively, with S = O (i.e. the Experiencer is then in S relation). These include *worry, grieve* and *delight*, e.g. *The behaviour of his daughter worries/grieves John, John worries/grieves a lot (over the behaviour of his daughter); Playing golf delights John, John delights in playing golf.* (Note that there is semantic difference here: used transitively these verbs imply that it is the Stimulus which engenders the feeling in the Experiencer; used intransitively they imply an inherent propensity, on the part of the Experiencer, to the feeling.)

The passive participle—which is still a verbal form although it behaves in some ways like an adjective—and the past participle—which is a derived adjective—coincide in form (e.g. *broken* in *The window was broken by Mary* and in *the broken window*). With ANNOYING verbs it is not an easy matter to distinguish between a passive construction and a copula-plus-past-participle construction. Consider:

(1a)    *John's winning the race surprised me*
(2a)    *The result surprised me*
(1b)    *I was surprised at/by John's winning the race*
(2b)    *I was surprised at/by the result*

Sentences (1b) and (2b) have the syntactic appearance of passives except that the preposition may be *at* or *by* (carrying a slight meaning difference) whereas in a normal passive the underlying A can only be introduced with *by*. Note that we can have *at* or *by* after *surprised*, *about* or *with* or *by* after *pleased*, *in* or *by* after *interested*, *of* or *by* after *terrified*, etc. There is in each case a meaning difference, e.g. *terrified by a noise* (something specific), *terrified of strangers* (a general phenomenon). *By* is always one possibility, suggesting that this alternative could constitute a passive construction, with the other alternative (featuring *at* or *about* or *with* or *of* or *in*, etc.) marking an adjectival construction.

Adjectives from the ANGRY and HAPPY subtypes of HUMAN PROPENSITY have similar meanings to past participles of some ANNOYING verbs. These can introduce the Stimulus role by a preposition, e.g. *angry about, jealous of, sorry about, ashamed of.* It appears always to be a preposition other than *by*, lending support for the position that (1b) and (2b) with *surprised by* are passives, while (1b) and (2b) with *surprised at* are not passives but parallel to a construction with copula plus HUMAN PROPENSITY adjective.

One syntactic test for distinguishing between verbal and adjectival forms is that only the latter can be modified by *very*, e.g. we can say *This hat is very squashed*—where *squashed* is a derived adjective—but not *\*This hat was very squashed by Mary* or *\*Jane was very seen by her brother*—where *squashed* and *seen* are passive verbal forms. Most speakers accept *very* with *surprised at, pleased with, interested in* (supporting our contention that these are adjectival constructions) but are less happy when *very* is used with *surprised by, pleased by, interested by* (supporting our treatment of these as passive constructions).

There is one apparent counter-example. The prefix *un-* can be added to some verbs from the AFFECT type with a reversative meaning (e.g. *untie, uncover*), and to some adjectives from HUMAN PROPENSITY, QUALIFICATION, VALUE, SIMILARITY and PHYSICAL PROPERTY (see §3.2) forming an antonym (e.g. *unkind, impossible, unlike*). The antonymic sense of *un-* never occurs with a verb. Thus we get verb *impress*, derived adjective *impressed*, and negative adjective *unimpressed* (but not a negative verb *\*un-impress*). However, *unimpressed* can be followed with *by*, e.g. *I was (very) unimpressed by his excuses*. How can it be that *by* occurs with *unimpressed*, something that is not a verbal form?

This apparent counter-example can be explained. We have seen that a passive construction takes *by*, whereas a derived adjective (the past participle) may take one of an extensive set of prepositions; which preposition is chosen depends on the meaning of the past participle and of the preposition. This set of prepositions does include *by*, and it is this which is used with the adjectival forms *impressed* and *unimpressed*. Thus:

|  | In verbal passive construction | In adjectival past participle construction |
|---|---|---|
| *surprised* | *by* | *at* |
| *pleased* | *by* | *with* or *about* |
| *terrified* | *by* | *of* |
| *satisfied* | *by* | *with* |
| *dissatisfied* | — | *with* |

continues

| cont'd | | |
|---|---|---|
| *interested* | *by* | *in* |
| *uninterested* | — | *in* |
| *impressed* | *by* | *by* |
| *unimpressed* | — | *by* |

We see that *dissatisfied, uninterested* and *unimpressed* (which must be adjectival forms) take the same preposition, in the right-hand column, as *satisfied, interested* and *impressed* (which can be verbal or adjectival). It is just that *impressed* and *unimpressed* take *by* in the right-hand column, the same preposition that occurs with all verbs in a passive construction, as shown in the left-hand column. *Unimpressed* is an adjective, which takes *by* in the same way that *uninterested* takes *in*.

Since *impressed* has *by* in both columns, a sentence such as *John was impressed by the report* is ambiguous between passive and past participle interpretations. We also encounter ambiguity when a THAT or Modal (FOR) TO complement clause is involved. Compare:

(**3a**)   *That John won the race surprised me/It surprised me that John won the race*
(**3b**)   *I was surprised that John won the race*

Sentence (3a) is a normal active construction with an ANNOYING verb; (3b) could be either the passive of (3a) or a copula-plus-past-participle construction. Since, by a general rule of English, a preposition is automatically dropped before complementiser *that* (or *for* or *to*) we cannot tell, in the case of (3b), whether the underlying preposition is *by* or *at*.

Past participles of many ANNOYING verbs may—like adjectives—occur in construction with a verb of the MAKE type, e.g. *make confused, make depressed*. It is instructive to compare:

(**4a**)   *The pistol shot in the airport frightened me*
(**4b**)   *The stories I've heard about pistol shots in airports have made me frightened (of ever visiting an airport)*

The transitive verb *frighten*, in (4a), refers to the Stimulus putting the Experiencer directly in a fright. *Make*-plus-past-participle-*frightened*, in (4b), refers to the Stimulus causing the Experiencer, less directly, to get into a fright. (See also §9.3.3.)

Some verbs of the ANNOYING type are morphologically derived from adjectives, e.g. *madden* and *sadden*, from *mad* and *sad*, members of the ANGRY subtype of HUMAN PROPENSITY (here we would say *make mad/sad*, parallel to *make frightened* in (4b); we would not say *make maddened/sad-dened*). Quite a number of verbs from this type also function as nouns, with the same form, e.g. *scare, shock, upset, surprise, delight, concern, trouble, worry, puzzle, interest, bore, bother*. Some have nouns derived from them, e.g. *amusement, offence, satisfaction, confusion* (see Chapter 10); and a few are verbs derived from nouns, e.g. *frighten* from *fright*, *terrify* from *terror*.

## 5.7. OTHERS

A number of other Primary-B types are here surveyed quite briefly since— like those mentioned in §4.6—they do not have critical properties in terms of the syntactic topics discussed in Chapters 7–14. All of these types include some verbs which take complement clauses and some which do not.

The ACTING subtype refers to a manner of behaving. *Act* and *behave* are intransitive, generally with a HUMAN subject, and normally receive adverbial modification that expresses a value judgement about the activity, e.g. *He is acting like a fool, She is behaving well.* (If no adverbial element is included with *behave* then 'well' is implied, i.e. *She is behaving* is an abbreviation of *She is behaving well.* When *act* is used without adverbial modification it takes on a quite different sense, akin to 'behaving falsely'.)

Transitive verbs *adopt* (e.g. habits), *copy, imitate, mimic, mime* and *reproduce* have a similar, very general potential reference; their A NP is likely to be HUMAN and the O NP should refer either to a person or to some activity (either through an NP or—except for *adopt*—an ING complement clause), e.g. *She copied John, She adopted his manner of walking, They reproduced the fight, She imitated John's trying to button his shirt when he was drunk.*

HAPPENING verbs describe some event taking place and generally have an ACTIVITY noun in S or O slot. *Happen* and *take place* are intransitive, and carry no implication that an 'agent' was involved, e.g. *The fight just happened.* The transitive verbs *organise, arrange* and *bring* NP *about* will have a HUMAN as A and either an ACTIVITY noun or a THAT or ING clause as O, e.g. *He arranged the fight/that they should fight after school/their fighting after school.* There are transitive verbs with more specific meanings which are only likely to have an NP as O—*commit* (e.g. a crime), *attend to/neglect* (e.g. the arrangements), *put* NP *on* (e.g. the concert), *take* NP *on* (e.g. the responsibility of organising something), *do* (e.g. the organising), *tie* (e.g. the concert) *in with* (e.g. the prize-giving), one sense of *change* (e.g. the arrangements), *devise* (e.g. a new hierarchy).

*Experience* and *undergo* are transitive verbs with a different semantic profile—here the A NP is a HUMAN who is generally not in control of what happens. In O relation we can have an ACTIVITY or STATE noun or an ING complement clause (often in the passive, as befits the meanings of *experience* and *undergo*), always with the same subject as the main clause, e.g. *I experienced being shot at/a bloody battle/her jealousy.*

*Transpire* is an intransitive verb whose S can be the interrogative *what*—as in *What transpired at the meeting?*—or a THAT complement clause, generally with extraposition, as in *It transpired that John had forgotten his wallet.*

COMPARING verbs are all transitive (some having inherent prepositions). *Resemble* and *differ (from)* must have NPs or subjectless complement clauses with comparable meanings as fillers of A and O slots, e.g. *John differs a lot from his brother (in work habits)*, *Being kissed by Zelig resembles being licked by an elephant.* The phrasal verb *take after* NP is restricted to NPs in A and O relation, e.g. *He takes after his mother (in being deeply religious)*. Adjectives *like*, *unlike*, *similar (to)* and *different (from)* have similar semantics and syntax to *resemble* and *differ (from)*; see §3.2.

A second set—*distinguish (between)*, *compare*; *class*, *group*, *cost*, *grade* (the last four derived from nouns); *match*, *balance*, *measure*, *weigh*, *time* (e.g. a race) and *count*—describe the human activity of comparing and quantifying. They normally take a HUMAN noun as head of the A NP and an O that refers to several comparable things or activities (which can be described through NPs or ING complement clauses linked by a preposition), e.g. *He compared Headley and/with Hobbs*, *She found it hard to distinguish between John's nodding his head and his shaking his head.* *Fit* and *suit*, which can refer to natural connections between things, belong in the same type, e.g. *Yellow suits Mary*, *That dress fits you*, *Going in first wicket down suited Don Bradman.* *Equal* is most frequently used with numerical quantities, e.g. *The square on the hypotenuse equals the sum of the squares on the other two sides.*

The verbs *include, comprise, consist of/in* and *be made up of* may have NPs or complement clauses in A and O relations, e.g. *That book includes four maps, Mailing a letter consists of buying a stamp, sticking it on the top right corner of the envelope, and then dropping it into the mailbox. Comprise* is fascinating in that it has the same meaning as *be comprised of*, with the past participle as copula complement; for example, *The expeditionary force comprised/was comprised of four battalions.*

RELATING verbs are basically all transitive (again, some include an inherent preposition) and refer to a natural or logical relationship between two states or activities. A and O can each be a plain NP (generally, with an ACTIVITY or STATE noun as head) or a THAT or WH- or ING complement clause, e.g. *Whether John will agree to go depends on the weather/on who is appointed leader, Mary's refusing to eat dinner results from the fact that her dog just died, The fact that the dog died indicates that it wasn't properly cared for* (see the discussion in §8.4.6).

Verbs in this type, besides *depend* (*on*), *result* (*from*) and *indicate*, include *relate* (*to*), *imply*, *be due* (*to*) and particular senses of *show*, *demonstrate* and *suggest*. Note that these verbs, together with some from the COMPARING type (such as *resemble, differ from, include, comprise*) and some from MAKING (§6.3.1) and HELPING (§6.3.2), appear to be the only verbs in English which can take complement clauses in A and O slots simultaneously.

In an appropriate context one may hear someone say just *It depends*, but there is likely to be an expectation that the addressee is aware of what it depends on, in terms of knowledge shared with the speaker (this may relate to something which has just been discussed).

# 6

# Secondary verb types

## 6.1. Secondary-A types

None of the Secondary-A verbs have any independent semantic roles. Basically, they modify the meaning of a following verb, sharing its roles and syntactic relations.

### 6.1.1. MODALS and SEMI-MODALS

As stated in §2.2.3 (see Table 2.2) the basic choice for a non-imperative clause (a statement or a question) is between **realis**, referring to some action or state which has reality, and **irrealis**, something which is uncertain in the future or was unrealised in the past. There are nine modalities within irrealis, each realised by a secondary verb. There are two syntactically different but semantically related types, MODALS and what we can call SEMI-MODALS, which express the modalities. The main MODALS, and the SEMI-MODALS, are set out in Table 6.1. (As mentioned under (7) in §1.5, *will*, *would*, *shall*, *should*, *can*, *could* and *must* are typically pronounced as clitics.) Many tens of thousands of words have been written about the

Table **6.1**. *Modality expressed by modals and semi-modals*

| MODAL | SEMI-MODAL | MODALITY (central meaning) |
|---|---|---|
| *will/would* <br> *shall* | *be going to* | prediction |
| *should* <br> *ought to* | — | obligation |
| *must* | *have to* <br> *have got to* | necessity |
| *can/could* | *be able to* | ability |
| — | *be about to* | imminent activity |
| *be to* | — | scheduled activity |
| *may/might* | — | possibility |
| — | *get to* | achievement |
| — | *be bound to* | inevitability |

English modals. Only some of the main points of their grammatical and semantic behaviour are indicated here.

It was mentioned at the end of §3.4 that a clause may contain a chain of verbs, each in syntactic relation with its neighbours, e.g. *She will soon be able to begin telling John to think about starting to build the house.* A modal must occur initially in such a chain—that is, it cannot be preceded by any other verb. Semi-modals behave like other Secondary verbs in that they can occur at the beginning or in the middle of a chain, but not at the end. A VP can contain only one modal, but it may involve a sequence of semi-modals, e.g. *He has to be going to start writing soon.*

A semi-modal can occur in initial position; it does not then have exactly the same import as the corresponding modal. Semi-modals often carry an 'unconditional' sense, while modals may indicate prediction, ability, necessity, etc. subject to certain specifiable circumstances. Compare:

(1a)   *My sister will get married on Tuesday if I go home on that day*
(1b)   *My sister is going to get married on Tuesday, so I'm going home on that day*
(2a)   *John can do mathematics, when he puts his mind to it*
(2b)   *John is able to do mathematics, without even having to try*
(3a)   *The boat must call tomorrow, if there aren't any high seas*
(3b)   *The boat has to call tomorrow, even if there are high seas*

However, this is very much a tendency; there is a great deal of semantic overlap between the two sets of verbs.

As pointed out under C(i) in §2.13, a semi-modal may substitute for a corresponding modal in a syntactic context where a modal is not permitted—for example, *I assume John to be able to climb the tree*, alongside *I assume that John can climb the tree* (since a TO complement cannot include a modal).

The first word of the auxiliary component of a VP plays a crucial syntactic role in that it takes negator *not* ~ *n't* (§12.11), and is moved before the subject in a question (§2.11.1). Modals (the *ought* and *be* elements in the case of *ought to* and *be to*) fulfil this role, e.g. *Will he sing?*, *He shouldn't run today*, *Are we to go tomorrow?* When a semi-modal begins a VP then the *be* of *be going to, be able to, be about to*, and *be bound to* and the *have* of *have got to* will take the negator and front in a question, e.g. *Is he going to sing?*, *You haven't got to go*. The *have* of *have to* behaves in the same way in some dialects, e.g. *Has he to go? He hasn't to go*; but other dialects include *do* (effectively treating *have to* as a lexical verb in this respect, and not as an auxiliary), e.g. *Does he have to go?*, *He doesn't have to go*. The *get* of *get to* never takes the negator or fronts in a question—one must say *I didn't get to see the Queen*, not *\*I getn't to see the Queen*.

Each modal has a fair semantic range, extending far beyond the central meanings we have indicated (they differ in this from the semi-modals, which have a narrower semantic range). There is in fact considerable overlap between the modals (see the diagram in Coates 1983: 5). The central meaning of *can* refers to inherent ability, e.g. *John can lift 100 kilos (he's that strong)*, and of *may* to the possibility of some specific event happening, e.g. *We may get a Christmas bonus this year*. But both verbs can/may refer to a permitted activity, e.g. *John can/may stay out all night (his mother has said it's all right)* and to some general possibility, e.g. *The verb 'walk' can/may be used both transitively and intransitively*.

It is usually said, following what was an accurate analysis in older stages of the language, that four of the modals inflect for tense, as follows:

| present | *will* | *shall* | *can* | *may* |
|---------|--------|---------|-------|-------|
| past | *would* | *should* | *could* | *might* |

A main justification for retaining this analysis comes from back-shifting in indirect speech. Recall that a sentence uttered with present tense is placed in past tense when it becomes indirect speech to a SPEAKING verb in past tense (§2.7), e.g. *'I'm sweating,' John said* and *John said that he was sweating*.

We do get *would, could* and *might* functioning as the back-shift equivalents, in indirect speech, of *will, can* and *may*, e.g. *'I will/can/may go,'* he said and *He said that he would/could/might go*. *Shall* and *should* now have quite different meanings and the back-shift version of *shall*, referring to prediction, is normally *would* (as it is of *will* and *would*) while the back-shift version of *should*, referring to obligation, is again *should*. There is discussion of back-shifting for modals and semi-modals in §7.6.

*Would, could* and *might* nowadays have semantic functions that go far beyond 'past tense of *will, can* and *may*'. Whereas *will, can* and *may* tend to be used for unqualified prediction, ability and possibility, *would, could* and *might* are employed when there is some condition or other qualification. For example:

**(4a)**   *You will find it pleasant here when you come*
**(4b)**   *If you come, you would find it pleasant here*
**(5a)**   *You can borrow the car when you come*
**(5b)**   *If you come, you could borrow the car*
**(6a)**   *I may bake a cake*
**(6b)**   *I might bake a cake if you show me how*

In addition, *would* can mark a 'likely hypothesis', e.g. *'I saw John embrace a strange woman.' 'Oh, that would be his sister.'* *Could* is often a softer, more polite alternative to *can*—compare *Could you pass the salt?* and *Can you pass the salt?* (in both cases what is literally a question about ability is being used as a request). And only *may* (not *might*) can substitute for *can* in a statement of possibility.

There is a clear semantic difference between the 'necessity' forms *must/ has to/has got to* and the 'obligation' forms *should/ought to*:

**(7a)**   *I should/ought to finish this essay tonight (but I don't think I will)*
**(7b)**   *I must/have to/have got to finish this essay tonight (and I will, come what may)*

It is hard to discern any semantic difference between *should* and *ought to*, these two modals being in most contexts substitutable one for the other (see the discussion in Erades 1959/60, Coates 1983: 58–83). However, *ought to* is a little unwieldy in negative sentences—where the *ought* and the *to* get separated—so that *should* may be preferred in this environment; thus *You shouldn't dig there* seems a little more felicitous than *You oughtn't to dig there* (although the latter is still acceptable). The same argument should apply to questions, where *ought* and *to* would again be separated; interestingly, the *to* may optionally be dropped after *ought* in a question, e.g. *Ought I (to) go?*

A modal cannot be followed by another modal, although a semi-modal can be followed by a semi-modal, as in *is bound to be about to*. Generally, any modal may be followed by any semi-modal; for example, *will be able to* and *could be about to*. A notable exception is the modal *can*, which may not be followed by a semi-modal, *could* being used instead, as in *He could be about to win*, *She could be going to lose*. *Have to* and *have got to* are stylistic variants, but after a modal only *have to* is possible; for example, *He will have to go*, not *\*He will have got to go*. And, because of their meanings, the sequence *be to* followed by *be bound to* is unacceptable.

Parallel modals and semi-modals from the two columns can be combined—*will be going to* could refer to 'future in future', e.g. *He will be going to build the house when he gets planning permission (but even then I doubt if he'll do it in a hurry)*, while *could be able to* combines the 'possibility' sense of *could* (as in *That restaurant could be closed on a Sunday*) with the 'ability' meaning of *be able to*, e.g. *John could be able to solve this puzzle (let's ask him)*.

There are a few other verbs that have some of the characteristics of modals. *Used to* must be first in any chain of verbs but—unlike other modals—it generally requires *do* in questions and negation, e.g. *Did he use(d) to do that?*, *He didn't use(d) to do that* (although some speakers do say *Used he to do that?* and *He use(d)n't to do that*). It could be regarded as an aberrant member of the MODAL type.

Then there is *had better*, as in *He had better go*. Although the *had* is identical with the past tense of *have*, *had better* is used for any time reference, and without any inflection for person of subject (coinciding in this with all modals except *be to*); it can also be used where a past form would be expected in indirect speech, e.g. *I told him he had better go*. Sometimes the *had* is omitted—*You better (not) go!* This is perhaps another, rather unusual, modal.

*Need* (from the WANTING type) and *dare* (from DARING) have two patterns of syntactic behaviour. They may be used as lexical verbs, with a TO complement clause, taking the full set of inflections for tense, including 3sg subject present ending *-s*, and requiring *do* in questions and negatives if there is no other auxiliary element present, e.g. *Does he dare/need to go?*, *He doesn't dare/need to go*. But these may also be used as modals (with no *to*), fronting in questions and taking the negative directly, e.g. *Dare/Need he go?*, *He daren't/needn't go*. Note that in their modal use *dare* and *need* do not take the 3sg present inflection *-s* (behaving like all modals except *be to*) but they also lack a past tense form (like *must* but unlike *will, can, may*). There is a semantic contrast between the two uses of *need* and *dare*—see §§6.1.5, 6.2.1; because of this, the modal uses are almost restricted to questions and negatives.

As mentioned under (a) in §2.9—and in §4.1—there is a special use of *go* and *come*, followed by a lexical verb in *-ing* form, that is grammatically a little like a modal, as in *Let's go fossicking*.

### 6.1.2. BEGINNING

Semantically, the verbs of this type divide into three groups: (i) *begin, start, commence*; (ii) *continue* (*with*), *keep* (*on* (*with*)); *go on* (*with*); (iii) *finish, cease, stop, complete, discontinue*.

We suggested in §3.4 that a BEGINNING verb should be followed by another verb, which it modifies and which may in certain circumstances be omitted, e.g. *The choir started* (*singing*) *'Messiah' at two o'clock, Mary continued* (*with*) (*writing*) *her book after a short holiday, Tommy has finished* (*shelling*) *the peas, I've completed* (*grading*) *these assignments*. This statement of usage will be expanded and refined below.

There are two kinds of verbs that may readily be omitted after a member of the BEGINNING type:

(i)   Verbs concerned with making or preparing or performing something, such as *cook, knit* and *tell*, e.g. *He began* (*cooking*) *the supper, She began* (*knitting*) *a sweater, My uncle began* (*telling*) *another joke*. Other verbs of similar meaning that may be omitted include: *build, perform, write, copy, type, print, bind, weave, sew, mend, cook, boil, peel, scrape, shell, chop; clean, wash, polish, sweep*.

(ii)   Verbs concerned with consumption, such as *read, eat, drink* and *smoke*, e.g. *I started* (*reading*) *'Great Expectations' last night, John began* (*eating*) *the chocolate cake*.

Note that when a verb is omitted after a BEGINNING item its object NP is left behind. This NP should be something that is a typical object of the omitted verb, so that the nature of the verb can with a degree of probability be inferred from it. From *John began building Mary's house last February* it is permissible to omit *build*, since *house* is a prototypical object of that verb. However, from *Mary began liking her new house after she'd been living in it for six months* it is not possible to omit *liking* since this is a verb that can take any sort of object. As mentioned before, there may be more than one verb that is omissible before a given object NP, e.g. *John began (building/ painting) Mary's house, Hosanna began (reading/writing) a new detective novel, Junior began (shelling/cooking/eating) the peas*; a speaker will not normally omit a verb unless they think the addressee has enough background knowledge to be able to retrieve it, e.g. it might be known that John is a painter and not a builder, that Hosanna writes detective stories but seldom reads them.

The verbs which can be omitted after a BEGINNING item mostly come from the AFFECT, CORPOREAL and SPEAKING types (but are only a selection of verbs from these types, e.g. omission is quite impossible from *John began caning the children*). It would be highly unusual to omit a verb that belongs to MOTION, REST, GIVING, THINKING, DECIDING, LIKING or ANNOYING—that is, from sentences like *The old lady started fetching the firewood, Mary began choosing dresses, The army finished crossing the river.*

Verbs that are omitted normally have two stated NPs (in A and O syntactic relations) and both are retained. It is interesting that a verb for which three roles are stated is not open to omission, e.g. no GIVING items (not even from *She started giving alms to the beggars*). *Telling* may not be omitted from any sentence where all of Speaker, Addressee and Message are stated, e.g. not from *He began telling another joke to the delegates (although they hadn't laughed at the previous one)* nor from *He began telling the delegates another joke (...)*. But it may be omitted from *He began (telling) another joke (...)*, where just two roles are stated.

If the subject NP is a description of a person such that it indicates their habitual activity then it may be possible to omit an object NP together with a transitive verb, or to omit an intransitive verb. Parallel to *Mary started (cooking) the dinner at four o'clock*, we can have *The chef started (cooking) (the dinner) at four o'clock*. In the *Mary* sentence the NP *dinner* should be included to enable the listener to retrieve the verb *cook*; but if *the chef* is subject NP this is not necessary. Similarly, on hearing *The juggler finished two minutes before the conjuror appeared*, one would assume that the juggler had finished juggling; if the message to be conveyed were that he had finished eating then the verb should not be omitted and/or an object NP should be retained, e.g. *The juggler finished (eating/his dinner/eating his dinner) two minutes before the conjuror appeared*. (It goes without saying that more drastic omission is possible if relevant circumstances are known to all participants in the speech activity, e.g. *Mary has finished* may be said if everyone knows what Mary has been doing. My point is that *Mary has finished the jumper* or *The choir started five minutes ago* could be said in neutral circumstances, with the verbs *knitting* and *singing* being understood—as implied—by a stranger.)

When a BEGINNING verb modifies an intransitive verb, or a transitive verb that has no object stated, then this verb may often be replaced by an ACTIVITY or SPEECH ACT noun derived from the verb, e.g. *John began the apology before you arrived* corresponds to *John began apologising/to apologise before you arrived*, and *Mary started her swim at two o'clock* corresponds to *Mary started swimming/to swim at two o'clock*. There is a recurrent meaning difference—the noun may refer to some unit of activity (it might be a cross-Channel swim, for instance) and the verb just to the fact that the activity happens.

A BEGINNING verb may also appear in an intransitive construction where the subject is an ACTIVITY, STATE or SPEECH ACT noun, e.g. *The game continued after tea, John's jealousy first began when he saw Mary out with Tom, The offer finishes on Friday*. For each of these sentences there is a near-paraphrase that includes a related verb or adjective in a complement clause—*(Some) people continued playing the game after tea, John first began to be jealous when he saw Mary out with Tom, (Someone) finishes offering (something) on Friday* (the constituents introduced by *some* here could be replaced by more specific NPs, on the basis of information shared by speaker and hearer). There are some peripheral members of the BEGINNING type which can only be used intransitively, with an ACTIVITY noun in subject slot, e.g. *set in* and *break out* as in *The rains have set in for the monsoon season, Fighting broke out at midday*.

Some nouns with CONCRETE reference refer to things extended in space. A river moves in space, and it is appropriate to refer to the place where it begins moving, e.g. *The Murrumbidgee River rises on the Dividing Range*, or *The Murrumbidgee River starts on the Dividing Range*. A road does not move but, by analogy with a river, one can say *The Bruce Highway starts/ begins in Brisbane and finishes at Cairns* (or, depending on one's ethnocentric focus, *The Bruce Highway starts/begins at Cairns and finishes in Brisbane*). *Begin, start* and *finish* cannot here be related to any underlying verb, and such 'extended in space' usages of items from the BEGINNING type have to be considered additional senses of the verbs.

Turning now to semantic analysis, we can first note a clear contrast between *finish* on the one hand and *stop* and *cease* on the other:

**(1a)**  *John finished (painting) the wall on Tuesday*
**(1b)**  *John stopped/ceased painting the wall on Tuesday*

*Finish* has 'object orientation'; sentence (1a) implies that the activity terminated because the wall was fully painted. *Cease* and *stop* have 'subject orientation'; the activity terminates (perhaps only temporarily) because of something to do with the person doing it—it could be that on Tuesday John decided he'd had enough of painting, irrespective of the job not being completed. *Cease* and *stop* most often refer to the volition of the subject, but need not always do so, e.g. *His heart stopped beating, He ceased breathing*. It is because of their subject orientation that *cease* and *stop*—unlike other verbs in this type—scarcely allow a following verb to be omitted. These verbs mark the involvement of the subject in the activity referred to by the verb (here, *painting*) and because of this that verb should be retained.

The difference in meaning between these two verbs is that *stop* tends to refer to something happening suddenly (often, unexpectedly) while *cease* may describe a general winding down to nothing, e.g. *The clock stopped (going) at five past three* (it had been going perfectly until then) and *My starter motor finally ceased to work* (it had been in poor shape for months).

There is a meaning contrast of a different sort between *begin* and *start*. Consider

**(2a)**  *The marathon race begins at Santa Monica*
**(2b)**  *The marathon race starts at three o'clock*

*Start* tends to refer to a time and *begin* to a place—*He'll start the public reading from his new book after dinner, and I can assure you that he'll begin at page one, right at the beginning, and he won't stop until he's finished the whole book*. Another example combining several of these verbs is *The three o'clock race began at the 500-metre mark* (place); *it started ten minutes late* (time); *James Donohue finished first* (i.e. he finished the course—'object orientation') *and Tubby Arbuckle stopped racing* ('subject orientation') *a hundred yards from home because his horse lost a shoe*.

Wierzbicka (1988: 78ff.) has pointed out that the noun *start* refers to the first moment of some activity—which relates to my observation that the verb *start* tends to refer to a time—and the noun *beginning* to the first segment—see also Freed (1979: 77). Note that for a race we have both a *starting time* and a *starting point* (not a *\*beginning time* or *\*beginning point*).

In many sentences *start* and *begin* may be substituted one for the other with little or no change in meaning (as may *finish* and *stop* and *cease*). But there do appear to be semantic preferences for each verb, which motivate their use to an appreciable extent.

Both *commence* and *complete* tend to be used for some definite and significant piece of work, not just any everyday job, e.g. *He has commenced* (*writing*) *his new symphony, John should complete the wall tomorrow.* One would be less likely to say *They commenced breakfast at 8.30* or *John has completed the peas* (to say this implies that it was a fairly significant event!). *Commence* has orientation to time, similar to *start*—note that we can say *restart* or *recommence* (i.e. at a new time), but not \**rebegin*. *Complete* is like other verbs in the type (except *stop* and *cease*) in that it may omit a following verb referring to making, preparing or performing, but *complete* differs in that a verb referring to consumption would not normally be omitted, e.g. *They completed the meal* implies that they finished cooking it, not eating it.

*Continue* (*with*) is often used when someone has stopped doing something and then starts again; *keep on* (*with*) and *go on* (*with*) imply no cessation of activity. *Keep* (*on*)—without the *with*—can be used to describe relentless (and, often, unreasonable) repetition of some activity, e.g. *He kept on mowing the grass* could be used to refer to someone cutting his lawn twice a week, even though the grass had scarcely grown during that interval. All three verbs may optionally omit their preposition(s) before an ING complement but must include them before an NP, e.g. *John kept* (*on* (*with*)) *building the wall*, but *John kept on with the wall*. *Discontinue* implies a temporary or permanent cessation, e.g. *They discontinued* (*having*) *the daily paper* (*delivered*) (*while they were away on holiday*).

*Start, stop* and *keep* can all be used causatively (see §9.3.3)—*The official started the jockeys racing* implies *The jockeys started racing*; *The official started the race on time* implies *The race started on time*; *Peter stopped John chopping wood* implies *John stopped chopping wood*; *Mary kept her horse galloping at full pelt across the plain* implies *Her horse was galloping at full pelt across the plain*. *Begin* may also be used causatively, e.g. *The master began the boys racing as they passed the copse*; but it is used in a causative construction less often than the other three verbs.

The fact that *stop* has a causative use whereas *finish* does not is related to their semantic orientation. *Stop* generally refers to something done at the subject's instigation, and this can be transferred to a Causer, e.g. *John stopped chopping firewood* (he was tired) and *Fred stopped John chopping firewood* (Fred considered that John was tired). But *finish* refers to the referent of the O NP being fully satisfied, e.g. *Jack finished chopping firewood* (all the wood was chopped up); it would not be plausible to transfer this 'reason for termination' to a Causer; hence we do not get *\*Fred finished John chopping firewood*. It is mildly surprising that there is no causative use of *cease*; this may relate to its meaning of 'gradually falling away'; if a Causer makes someone halt in a task they are likely to do it reasonably abruptly, and *stop* is then the appropriate verb.

A sentence like *The parents started the game at three o'clock* is ambiguous between a non-causative use of *start* with the verb of the complement clause omitted, e.g. *The parents started (playing) the game at three o'clock*, and a causative sense, which could be an abbreviated version of *The parents started the children playing the game at three o'clock* (i.e. gave the signal to start). This ambiguity does not apply to *stop*, simply because that verb generally does not permit omission of a complement clause verb, i.e. *playing* cannot be dropped from *They stopped playing the game*, thus, *They stopped the game at three o'clock* has only a causative sense.

BEGINNING verbs are restricted to ING and Modal (FOR) TO complement clauses with subject omitted, e.g. *Mary began to like John, Mary began liking John. Mary* and *John* are in the same semantic roles and syntactic relations for *begin to like* and *begin liking* as they would be for *like*. *Begin to like* and *begin liking* are each, in one sense, a single syntactic unit. (But there is a difference—an adverb may intervene between a BEGINNING verb and *to*, e.g. *John began, after breakfast, to load the truck*, but not between a BEGINNING verb and a following verb in *-ing* form, e.g. we cannot say *\*John began, after breakfast, loading the truck*, only something like *John began loading the truck after breakfast*.)

All BEGINNING verbs may take an ING complement; just some of them also accept a Modal (FOR) TO clause:

ING and modal (FOR) TO complements—*begin, start, continue (with), go on (with), cease*
only ING complements—*commence, keep (on (with)), finish, stop, complete, discontinue*

§8.3.2 attempts a semantic explanation of these syntactic possibilities.

We should also note the verb *begin on*, which can be used in some circumstances where *begin* is appropriate. But *begin on*—unlike *begin*—

also has a special anaphoric sense, referring back to the verb of a previous clause. In *The compère described the new season's fur coats and then began on the new winter dresses*, the *began on* in the second clause is equivalent to *began describing* (that is, the *on* of *begin on* signals a kind of gapping—cf. §2.12). In contrast, a sentence like *He began the winter dresses* would be taken to have an underlying verb of making, etc., such as *design* or *produce* (but certainly not *describe*). *Begin on* can make anaphoric reference to any sort of verb, within the limits of discourse organisation and semantic plausibility.

There is one important point of similarity between some BEGINNING verbs and MODALS and SEMI-MODALS; this concerns passives. One can say both *Mary might victimise John* and *John might be victimised (by Mary)*, where the modal *might* precedes either active *victimised* or passive *be victimised*. In similar fashion, one can say either *Mary began to victimise John* or *John began to be victimised (by Mary)*. (Note that *begin* cannot itself be passivised when followed by a complement clause; that is, one cannot say *\*John was begun to be victimised (by Mary)* or *\*John was begun to victimise (by Mary)*.)

## 6.1.3. *TRYING*

Semantically, verbs of this type divide into four groups: (i) *try, attempt*; (ii) *succeed (in/at), manage*; (iii) *miss, fail*; (iv) *practise, repeat*. (We are here referring to the senses of *manage* and *succeed* in *He managed to solve the problem, She succeeded in solving the problem*, not those in *She manages the business, He succeeded his father*.)

Like the BEGINNING type, a TRYING verb is followed by another verb which it modifies semantically, but which is syntactically in a complement clause to it, e.g. *He attempted to open the safe, He succeeded in opening the safe*. Like BEGINNING, TRYING verbs are restricted to ING and Modal (FOR) TO complements with the subject omitted. The syntactic behaviour of individual verbs is:

ING and Modal (FOR) TO complements—*try*;
most used with Modal (FOR) TO, can also take ING—*attempt, manage*;
only Modal (FOR) TO—*fail*;
only ING—*succeed (in/at), miss, practise, repeat*.

*Try* has two distinct but related senses, as can be seen in:

(**1a**)   *John tried to eat the cake*
(**1b**)   *John tried eating the cake*
(**2a**)   *John tried to travel by train*
(**2b**)   *John tried travelling by train*

The (a) alternatives indicate that John wanted to engage in the activity, but may well not have been able to; the (b) alternatives indicate that he did engage in it for a sample period. Thus (2a) could be used if he went to the station but found that the train was full. Sentence (2b) implies that he did travel by train for a while (for long enough to decide whether he preferred it to the bus). Another pair is *John tried to catch the ball* (but missed) and *John tried catching the ball* (during the team's two-hour fielding practice).

Note that the first sense requires a Modal (FOR) TO and the second an ING complement clause. Chapter 8 provides an explanation for this, and for the other complement possibilities of TRYING verbs.

*Attempt* is basically a synonym of the (a) sense of *try*. Like *commence* and *complete*, it implies a fairly significant task, with a degree of difficulty involved—compare *He tried to climb to the top of that hill* with *He attempted to climb Mt Everest*. (For simple, everyday things, e.g. *She tried to eat all the pudding*, it is scarcely felicitous to substitute *attempt* for *try*.)

Both *manage* and *fail* are likely to imply that a certain result was obtained only after considerable perseverance, in contrast to *succeed* (*in/ at*) and *miss*, e.g.

(**3a**)   *Fred managed to solve the puzzle* (after weeks of trying)
(**3b**)   *Fred succeeded in solving the puzzle* (perhaps at once, perhaps after a little effort)
(**4a**)   *John failed to hit the target* (despite twenty attempts)
(**4b**)   *John missed hitting the target* (perhaps with the only bullet he had)

*Miss* (to a greater extent than *succeed*) can be used where there was no effort at all—something can be missed by chance. Compare *I failed to see Mary* (despite looking all over the place) and *I missed seeing Mary* (I didn't know she was calling in, and just happened to arrive after she'd left).

In §6.1.2 we mentioned that just verbs of making, preparing, performing and consuming can be omitted after a BEGINNING verb. No such simple categorisation can be given for verbs that may be omitted after a TRYING item. There is, however, a basic rule for omission after *try*, the central member of the type: a verb may be omitted when followed by a typical object, i.e. if its identity could be inferred from that object. Thus, on hearing *She tried a new book*, one would understand *She tried reading a new book* (since many more people read books than write or print or bind them); *He tried the chocolate cake* implies *He tried eating the chocolate cake* (not baking it). Some uses of *try* are semi-idiomatic—but do conform to the rule—e.g. *He tried (to open) the door*, *She tried (to solve) the problem*, and *She tried (putting on) the pink dress (to see how it looked on her)*. *Try out* is a little different; this generally has an implement as object and substitutes for *try using*, e.g. *He tried out the new axe*.

Virtually any verb (except one from the LIKING or ANNOYING types) may be omitted after *try* if it could be recovered by an addressee from the specific context and/or from previous dialogue, e.g. *'Where is the post office?' 'I don't know, you'd better try (asking) Mary'*. There is also *'I offered Mary an apple but she refused it' 'Well, why don't you try (offering her) a pear?'*, where verb-plus-NP (*offering her*) is omitted. Note in fact that only one NP may follow *try*—that is, one could not say *\*Well, why don't you try Mary an apple?*, with *offering* omitted.

Omission of a verb is much rarer after *attempt* or *manage*, but is possible with an appropriate object, e.g. *I'm going to attempt Everest next year* or *I managed the problem in the end* (there is only one verb that could plausibly be substituted in each case—*climb* and *solve* respectively). With *fail* we get only *He failed the exam/test*, where *to pass* is implied. *Miss* freely omits a wide range of verbs, e.g. *missed (seeing) Mary*, *missed (hitting) the target*, *missed (experiencing) that cyclone*. *Succeed (in/at)* may, like *fail*, omit *pass*, e.g. *I succeeded in (passing) the mathematics exam*, and just a few other verbs, as in *She succeeded at (playing) golf (well)*.

*Practise* refers to a continuous activity, typically described by the *-ing* form of a verb; deletion possibilities are virtually limited to *playing*, e.g. *He practised (playing) the clarinet*. *Repeat* describes a delimited activity being done more than once—it may take an ING complement and the verb is likely to be omitted if its identity could be inferred from the object, e.g. *Johnnie repeated (reciting) that poem all morning*, and *He repeated (making) the same old mistake*.

Like the BEGINNING type, a TRYING verb may take an ACTIVITY or SPEECH ACT noun as object; in most cases there is an equivalent construction with a complement clause whose verb is related to the noun, e.g. *Karen tried an apology (to Auntie Daphne) (but she ignored her)* and *Karen tried apologising (to Auntie Daphne) (but she ignored her)*.

One difference from the BEGINNING type is that TRYING verbs are not used intransitively, with an ACTIVITY, STATE or SPEECH ACT noun as subject (parallel to *The game continued, The offer finishes on Friday*). This is because TRYING verbs relate to volition on the part of a HUMAN, who must be referred to, whereas in the world-view of speakers of English things may begin, continue and finish spontaneously, e.g. *That fight just started* (i.e. no one was really responsible for starting it), and *My boring old life just continues on*.

### 6.1.4. HURRYING

This is a small type, consisting of verbs that describe the speed with which an activity is performed; *hesitate* falls naturally into the same type.

Complement possibilities are:

Modal (FOR) TO and ING complements—*hurry* (*over/with*), *hesitate* (*over/with*)
most used with Modal (FOR) TO, can also take ING—*hasten* (*over/with*)
ING complement only—*dawdle* (*over*)

The prepositions are, as usual, retained before an ING clause or an NP, but dropped before *to*, e.g. *He hurried over finishing the job, He hurried to finish the job*.

*Hurry* and *hasten* have a very similar meaning, 'do quickly', with *hurry* having stronger overtones of 'motion' than *hasten*. Thus both of *He hurried/hastened to change the lock on the door* can mean either (i) he moved quickly to the door, to change the lock when he got there, or (ii) he was quick about taking the old lock off and putting a new one on; but interpretation (i) is more likely with *hurry* and (ii) is more likely with *hasten*.

*Hurry* can freely take either a Modal (FOR) TO or an ING clause, e.g. *He hurried over* (*eating*) *his meal* (ate quickly the whole time), and *He hurried to finish his meal* (ate quickly towards the end). *Hasten* is found quite rarely with an ING clause. *Dawdle*, with the opposite meaning 'do slowly', only takes an ING complement.

*Hesitate* accepts both complement types. An ING clause implies that there was initial uncertainty but that the subject did it, in the end (unless the contrary is explicitly stated), e.g. *She hesitated about/over going*. A Modal (FOR) TO complement with *hesitate* indicates that the subject couldn't make up their mind whether or not to do it (and probably didn't do it, in the end), e.g. *She hesitated to go*. (There is further comment on the semantics of these complement choices in §8.3.2.)

As with *try*, a verb may be omitted after *hurry* or *dawdle* if its identity could be inferred from the nature of subject and object and shared socio-cultural knowledge of speaker and hearer, e.g. *She hurried/dawdled over (arranging) the flowers, The doctor hurried/dawdled over (examining) the last patient*. Verb omission is also possible with *hesitate*, e.g. *Auntie Daphne hesitated over (choosing) a present for Karen*, but is rare after *hasten*. Any of these four verbs may be used alone (i.e. just with a subject) in an appropriate context, e.g. *Hurry up!, Don't dawdle!*; and we get omission triggered by the surrounding text, e.g. *Mary hesitated (over going) before (in fact) going*.

*Hurry* and *hasten*, but not the other two verbs, form causatives, e.g. *John hurried/hastened Mary out of the house*, corresponding to *Mary hurried/ hastened (to go) out of the house*. (See §9.3.3.)

### 6.1.5. DARING

The verbs *dare* (and one sense of *venture*) indicate that the subject had enough courage to do something; they are often found in the negative *doesn't dare, doesn't venture. Dare* and *venture* take a Modal (FOR) TO complement and have no roles additional to those of the verb of the complement clause—compare *John didn't dare to enter the lion's cage, John didn't enter the lion's cage.*

*Dare* can be used causatively with a rather special meaning, 'say to someone that you think they haven't enough courage to do something', e.g. *Fred dared John to enter the lion's cage*. This use of *dare* is similar in meaning and syntax to *challenge*. (Note that the causative use of *dare* is not parallel to a Secondary-B verb like *want. Tom wants Bill to go* becomes *Tom wants to go* when the subjects of the two clauses coincide. However, *John didn't dare to go* ('lacked sufficient courage') has a quite different meaning from *John didn't dare himself to go* ('didn't challenge himself to go').)

Like *need* (§6.2.1), *dare* can be used as a lexical verb—taking tense and 3sg *-s* inflection, and complementiser *to*, and requiring *do* in questions and negatives when there is no other auxiliary element present—and it can also be used as a modal—with no inflections and no *to*, and itself acting as an auxiliary in questions and negatives. Compare: *John didn't dare to go, Did John dare to go?* and *John daren't go, Dare John go?*

The two syntactic uses of *dare* carry a semantic difference. The lexical-verb sense tends to refer to an inner state of the subject, as in (1a), and the modal use to some external circumstance, as in (1b).

**(1a)** *He doesn't dare to touch Mary* (he hasn't the courage, since she is so beautiful and he is too shy)

**(1b)** *He doesn't dare touch Mary* (for fear of catching AIDS)

Corresponding to its 'external' meaning, the MODAL sense of *dare* (as of *need*) is found almost exclusively in questions and negative sentences.

## 6.2. Secondary-B types

Secondary-B verbs introduce one role (the subject of the Secondary-B verb) in addition to the roles of the verb in the complement clause, e.g. *John* in *John wanted Fred to congratulate Mary*. However, the subject of the main clause often is identical to the subject of the complement clause, and the latter is then generally omitted, e.g. *John wanted to congratulate Mary*, although it can be retained for contrastive emphasis, e.g. *John wanted himself to congratulate Mary* (*not* (*for*) *Fred to congratulate her*). Note that *John wanted to congratulate Mary* has the same semantic roles, in the same syntactic relations, as *John congratulated Mary* (and is then similar to the Secondary-A construction *John began to congratulate Mary*).

### 6.2.1. WANTING

This type has one independent role, the Principal, who has a certain attitude (described by the WANTING verb) towards some event or state (described by the complement clause) that is not (yet) real. The Principal is always syntactic subject of the WANTING verb.

Verbs of this type divide into a number of semantic sets (some of which have special syntactic properties): (i) *want*, *wish* (*for*), *desire*, *crave*, *long* (*for*), *pine* (*for*); (ii) *hope* (*for*); (iii) *demand*; (iv) *need*, *require*, *deserve*; (v) *expect*, *wait* (*for*) and *dread* (which has cross-membership of LIKING); (vi) *intend*, *plan* (*for*) (which has cross-membership of DECIDING), *aim* (*for*), one sense of *mean*, *prepare* (*for*); (vii) *pretend*.

We mentioned in §3.4 that a verb with a meaning similar to *get, receive* or *have* can be omitted from a complement clause after *want*; the NP following the 'get' verb then becomes surface object to *want*. This applies to all verbs from sets (i)–(iv) and to *expect* (but probably not to *dread*), e.g. *I need (to get) a new pen, She deserves (to receive) a medal, I'm hoping to get/for a bit of peace this afternoon, She is expecting (to get/to be given) a horse for her birthday.* Note that this omission is only possible when main clause and complement clause share the same subject, which is then omitted from the complement clause—thus, *to get* can be omitted from *I want (to get) a new Honda*, but not from *I want Mary to get a new Honda*.

*Expect* and *dread* may take a surface object NP in two further ways. Firstly, if main and complement clauses have different subjects then a verb with the meaning 'come/arrive' can be omitted from the complement clause, e.g. *I expect John (to come) tomorrow, Mary always dreads the cyclone season (arriving)*. Secondly, there can be an ACTIVITY verb in O slot, e.g. *I expected a beating* (which corresponds to a passive complement clause with the same subject as *expect, I expected to be beaten*).

Some WANTING verbs, especially those from set (vi), may also have an activity verb in surface object slot, e.g. *We're planning a game (at the weekend), They're planning a surprise for Mary, She's preparing for the climb (up Everest)*. In most cases there is a corresponding complement clause construction, e.g. *We're planning to play a game (at the weekend), They're planning to surprise Mary, She's preparing to climb (up Everest)*.

The role of the preposition *for* with verbs from the WANTING type is particularly interesting. *Hope, long, pine, wait, plan, aim,* and *prepare* take *for* before an NP object (*I'm hoping/aiming for an invitation to her party*), and also retain *for* before the subject of a Modal (FOR) TO complement (*I'm longing/aiming for Mary to invite me to stay over Christmas*). There is a second group of verbs—*crave, demand, deserve* and *dread*—which do not include *for* before an NP object but do require it before the subject of a Modal (FOR) TO clause, e.g. *He demanded a drink, He demanded for Mary to bring him a drink.* (*Dread* may take *it* before a Modal (FOR) TO or before a THAT clause, by virtue of its cross-membership of the LIKING type—§5.5.) The third group consists just of *wish*, taking *for* before an object NP and allowing the *for* to be either omitted or retained (with a meaning difference—see Chapter 8) before the subject of a Modal (FOR) TO clause, e.g. *I wish Mary to go, I wish for Mary to go.* The fourth group—made up of *desire, intend, mean* and *pretend*—do not have *for* before an NP object but, like *wish*, may include or omit *for* before the subject of a Modal (FOR) TO complement, e.g. *I intended Mary to win, I intended for Mary to win*. The other verbs in the type (*want, need, require* and *expect*) do not include *for* before an O NP or a complement clause subject when this immediately follows the verb, e.g. *I want an apple, I want Mary to give me an apple*. But a *for* may become evident under other syntactic conditions, such as when an adverb is inserted between main clause predicate and complement clause, e.g. *I want very much for Mary to give me an apple* and *I need more than I can say for Mary to nurse me*. Another example involves optional inclusion of *for* when there has been anaphoric omission of the predicate, as in the sentence quoted in the first paragraph of §6.2, *John wanted himself to congratulate Mary, not (for) Fred to congratulate her*.

All WANTING verbs may take a Modal (FOR) TO complement clause. As just described, some retain the *for* before the complement clause subject, some may omit or retain it, and others normally omit it. When the subject is coreferential with main clause subject, this is generally omitted (together with *for*)—*I'm hoping for promotion, I'm hoping for Mary to promote me, I'm hoping to be promoted*.

There is a kind of syntactic abbreviation that applies with *order* from the SPEAKING type and with most verbs from sets (i) and (iv) of the WANTING type. If a Modal (FOR) TO complement has (*a*) an explicit subject, and (*b*) predicate consisting of copula plus the past participle of a verb or an adjective, then *to be* may be omitted, e.g. *I want her (to be) shot, I need the whole house (to be) cleaned thoroughly before the visitors arrive*. Note that the complement clause subject can be coreferential with main clause subject, but may not be omitted when there is no *to be*, e.g. *I wished myself (to be) invisible* but only *I wished to be invisible*, not *\* I wished invisible*. Only a limited set of participles and adjectives can occur in the complement clause of such a construction, e.g. *killed, cooked, taken away, put away, begun, finished, explained, dead, well, well-dressed, tidy*; see §8.2.6.

A TO clause after *want* or *wish* can be omitted when identical to what is stated in the preceding clause, as in *We can do it today if you want (to (do it today))*. Note that after *do it today* is omitted, the *to* can either be retained or omitted. However, when repetition goes over two utterances (rather than within one complex sentence), the *to* must be included; one may say *No, I don't want to* but not simply *\*No, I don't want*.

Most verbs from the WANTING type can also accept a THAT complement clause (preposition *for* is again omitted before *that*). Since WANTING verbs refer to a state or event that is not (yet) real, it is normal for a modal to be included in a THAT complement clause. Different verbs prefer different modals, relating to their meanings; e.g. *I wish that he would/I could sing, I dread that my children might leave home one day, I expect that I/he will die soon, She planned that he should stay the night, I hope that she will/may go* (*hope* is unusual in that it commonly also occurs without a modal, e.g. *I hope (that) she goes*).

A THAT complement does not appear possible for *want, need* or *prepare*, and is rather marginal with *crave, long, deserve* and *aim*. It might be thought surprising that *want* and *need*—which are among the most frequently used WANTING verbs—do not take a THAT complement; a semantic explanation for this lack is provided in §8.3.3.

An ING complement clause is only possible with some verbs from set (vi) (and then only if complement clause subject is coreferential with main clause subject, and omitted), e.g. *She intends qualifying within three years, He plans going abroad after he has finished his exams. Aim* must include *at* before an ING clause, e.g. *She aims at finishing her thesis before Easter*.

A quite different variety of *-ing* construction occurs just with a number of verbs that are frequently found with a passive complement clause—they comprise *need, require* and *deserve*, and also a sense of *want* that is almost synonymous with *need*. This *-ing* construction has similar meaning to a passive TO clause with coreferential subject omission, e.g. *That meat requires cooking* corresponds to *That meat requires to be cooked*; and *This brat needs/wants spanking* corresponds to *This brat needs/wants to be spanked*. The syntactic status of *cooking* in *That meat requires cooking* is hard to ascertain. It is not an NP since we cannot insert an article, e.g. *\*That meat requires a cooking*. (It is possible to say *This brat needs/wants a spanking*, with an NP object that refers to a unit of activity, e.g. going to the headmaster's study for an institutionalised punishment, but this has a different meaning from *This brat needs/wants spanking*.) And *cooking* might not be a clause since it sounds rather odd with an adverb as in *?That meat requires cooking well*—it is surely preferable to use a Modal (FOR) TO clause when an adverb is included, i.e. *That meat requires to be cooked well*.

A special syntactic property of some verbs from the WANTING type is that they occur with the modal *be to* only in the passive (and then only when no agent is stated), e.g. *It is to be hoped/expected that she will win*. This applies to *hope (for), expect* and *desire* and—with more marginal acceptability—to *wish* and *dread*. With verbs from other types *be to* may be used in the active or in the passive (with or without an agent stated), e.g. *The bishop is to crown him tomorrow*, *He is to be crowned (by the bishop) tomorrow*.

*Need* is basically a Secondary-B verb but has a further sense as a MODAL, and then shows quite different syntax. When used like a member of the WANTING type, *need* inflects for tense, takes *do* in negatives and questions if there is no preceding auxiliary element, and cannot omit the *to* complementiser, e.g. *He needs to go*, *Does he need to go?*, *He doesn't need to go*. When used as a MODAL it does not inflect for tense or show -*s* for 3sg subject, it acts like an auxiliary verb in questions and negatives, and it does not take complementiser *to*, e.g. *Need he go?*, *He needn't go*. There is a semantic difference—the Secondary-B sense relates to some inner state of the Principal (in subject relation), as in (1a), whereas the MODAL sense relates to some external circumstances as in (1b) (see also Leech 1971: 96):

(1a)   *I don't need to go to the toilet* (my bladder isn't full)
(1b)   *I needn't go to the toilet* (no one is telling me to go)

Corresponding to its 'external' meaning, the MODAL sense of *need* is found almost exclusively in questions and negative sentences. (*Dare* also has modal and non-modal senses, with the same syntactic contrast and a similar meaning difference—see §6.1.5.)

Most verbs from the WANTING type must have a following complement clause or NP. *Wish*, *hope* and *pretend* may be used without one in a suitable context, e.g. *She keeps on wishing*, *You can but hope*, *Stop pretending! Expect* and *hope* may, like some THINKING verbs (§5.2), replace a post-predicate constituent by *so*, e.g. *'Will John come tomorrow?' 'I expect/hope so'* (sc. that John will come tomorrow). Note the contrast between *hope so* and *hope*, with no following constituent in either case; the former is used for syntactic anaphoric reference to some definite constituent, e.g. *that John will come tomorrow* in the last example quoted, while the latter refers semantically to some general propensity of the Principal, e.g. *'You'll never get rich quick—win the lottery or receive a huge bequest'. 'Well, I can hope, can't I?'*

We will now discuss the meanings of verbs in each group (returning in Chapter 8 to explain their occurrences with complement types in terms of these meanings). *Want*—taking a Modal (FOR) TO complement—is directly pragmatic, referring to something which could be achieved, e.g. *I want to talk to my boss this afternoon*. *Wish*, in contrast, may have wistful overtones, relating—through a THAT complement—to something that could not possibly be realised, e.g. *I wish (that) I could ask a few questions of Winston Churchill about how he fought the war*. (Note that we can have *make a wish* but not \**make a want*.) *Wish* can be used with a Modal (FOR) TO complement and is then marked as particularly definite—compare the cold, forced demand *I wish you to leave*, with the more comradely (and possibly more emotional) *I want you to leave*. *Desire* is not used much as a verb in present-day English; when it is, there may be an overtone of hauteur (*I desire to be informed of any change*). Both *want* and *desire* are likely to have sexual implications when used with a human NP as surface object; compare the urgent and lustful *I want you* with the more polite and measured *Oh, how I desire you!* (which does invite a verbal response from the person desired). *Crave* describes an intense desire, often for some special foodstuff or other indulgence, which will be referred to by the O NP, e.g. *I crave fresh strawberries*. *Long (for)* has a similarly intense meaning, but covers a wider semantic range of 'things wanted', e.g. *I long for Mary to write*. *Pine (for)* carries the additional overtone that the well-being of the Principal is being adversely affected by their unrequited longing.

Whereas verbs of set (i) simply describe the Principal's eagerness that something acceptable (to them) will happen, *hope (for)* focuses on the Principal's thought that something acceptable may happen in the future. *Demand* involves the intersection of 'say' and 'want'; an Addressee can be included, introduced by *of*, e.g. *I demanded (of Mary) that she/John should clean my car*.

Set (iv) has similar meaning to necessity and obligation modals, *must*, *should*, etc. But whereas the modals tend to be used when the subject should/needs to do something, *need* and *require* are often used, with a passive complement clause, when something should/needs to be done to the subject, e.g. *You should encourage Mary; Mary needs to be encouraged*. Set (iv), unlike other WANTING verbs, may have an inanimate Principal, e.g. *The car needs to be cleaned*. (As already mentioned, there is one sense of *want*—more frequent in colloquial than in literary speech—that is close in meaning to *need*, e.g. *The car wants cleaning*.)

*Need* is similar to *want* (in its central sense) in often conveying a sense of emotional urgency, e.g. *I need my daughter to come home and look after me*, whereas *require* has a colder, more matter-of-fact sense, e.g. *I require three nurses, working in shifts, to look after me*. *Need* often relates to the Principal's physical and emotional state, and complement clause subject is most often the same as main clause subject, e.g. *I need to be loved* (compare with *?I require to be loved*, which sounds most odd, although *I require to be served* is fine). *Require* only rather seldom has complement clause subject coinciding with main clause subject, and is often used to specify the necessities of social interaction and employment obligations, e.g. *We require all our executives to join the superannuation fund* or the notice in a doctor's surgery, *We require payment at time of consultation*. Both semantically and syntactically, *require* shows similarities to the MAKING type and to the ORDER subtype of SPEAKING, e.g. *The Sultan required/ordered/forced John to wash his feet*. (Note that *need* can modify *require*, but not vice versa, e.g. *'Do you require the chancellor to call on you, sire?' 'No, I don't need to require him to call, for the simple reason that he is already here.'*) *Deserve* relates to something that should be done to someone as a payback for their (often, but not always, meritorious) behaviour; 'same subject' is normal, e.g. *Mary deserves to win the prize*, although 'different subject' is also possible, e.g. *Mary deserves for her dog to win the prize*.

Whereas *hope* refers to something acceptable that the Principal thinks may happen in the future, *expect* refers to something the Principal thinks will probably happen, and it needn't be acceptable to them. If the Principal thinks that this future happening is something they would greatly dislike then the appropriate verb to use is *dread*, which involves the intersection of 'expect' and 'hate' (and is a cross-member of the LIKING type).

Set (vi) describes the Principal's thought that they will do a certain thing in the future; the most general and neutral verb here is *intend*. *Aim (for)* implies a single-mindedness of purpose; it most often has the same subject as the complement clause (e.g. *I aim to win*). *Mean* is often used in the past tense, referring to an intention that was not in fact fulfilled, e.g. *I had meant (for John) to clean the bathroom, but then forgot about it*. *Plan* involves a set of intentions, plus detailed thought and scheming. (It also belongs to the DECIDING type and, as a member of that type, can take a WH-complement, e.g. *I planned who would fire the shot*.) The transitive verb *prepare* has the meaning 'do what needs to be done in advance for some expected future happening'; it only takes a Modal (FOR) TO, not a THAT, complement clause. The past participle of this verb has a rather different meaning, 'get oneself in the right frame of mind to accept some expected (and probably unpleasant) event or news', and should perhaps be regarded as a separate lexeme. *Be prepared* does take a THAT complement—compare *I am prepared for a long meeting*, and *I am prepared that the meeting will be a long one*, with *I have prepared for a long meeting* but not *\*I have prepared that the meeting* *will be a long one.* (In §3.2 we categorised *prepared* as a member of the EAGER subtype of HUMAN PROPENSITY adjectives.)

*Pretend* has all the syntactic properties of a WANTING verb—it can take a THAT complement (*I pretended that Mary/I was President*) or a Modal (FOR) TO complement (*I pretended (for) Mary to be President*). If the complement clause subject is the same as main clause subject then it is omitted (*I pretended to be President*). The main difference from other WANTING verbs is that *pretend* generally refers to present or past, not to the future (its THAT complement is not expected to include a modal, as it is for other verbs from the type). But it is semantically like other WANTING verbs in referring to something that is not (yet) real.


## 6.2.2. *POSTPONING*

This type again requires one role additional to those of the complement clause verb—a Timer, who adjusts the time at which it is planned to do something. Members of the type are *postpone, defer, put* NP *off, delay* and—standing a little apart semantically—*avoid*.

All five verbs take ING complement clauses. The subject may be different from the subject of the main clause but if it is the same it is normally omitted, e.g. *She postponed (John's) going on fieldwork until the wet season was over, We delayed starting dinner until you arrived, I avoided helping with the painting (by going out all afternoon).*

*Avoid* often omits the complement clause verb if it has a meaning similar to 'seeing' or 'attending/taking part in', e.g. *I walked home the long way round to avoid (seeing) the graveyard, He always manages to avoid (attending) formal dinners.* The object of any of these verbs may be an ACTIVITY or SPEECH ACT noun, which is often put into subject slot by passivisation, e.g. *The meeting was postponed, The question was avoided.*

*Postpone, defer* and *put off* have very similar meanings; they generally refer to a conscious decision, made in advance, e.g. *They postponed the wedding until August.* In contrast, *delay* often describes an ad hoc change of time, perhaps to accommodate some unforeseen circumstances, e.g. *They delayed the start of the meeting since the bus bringing delegates from the north had not arrived. Avoid* refers to evasive action taken so as not to be involved in some unwanted activity, often, not being in a certain place at a certain time, e.g. *I avoid visiting Mother on days Grandpa is likely to call.*

## 6.3. Secondary-C types

Secondary-C verbs are like Secondary-B in introducing just one role (the subject of the Secondary verb) in addition to the roles of the verb in the complement clause. They differ semantically in that Secondary-B verbs simply describe the subject's attitude towards some event or state (*John wants/expects Mary to propose the toast*) whereas the subject of a Secondary-C verb plays a role in bringing about the event or state (*John forced/ permitted/helped Mary to propose the toast*).

A Secondary-B verb often has complement clause subject identical to main clause subject and it is then normally omitted (*John wants (himself) to propose the toast*). A Secondary-C verb, in contrast, seldom has the two subjects identical, and if they do happen to be, then neither can be omitted (*John forced himself to propose the toast*, not *\*John forced to propose the toast*).

Another difference is that certain verbs may be omitted from the complement clause of a Secondary-B verb, e.g. *I want (to get) a new car*, *She expects John (to come) today*. This is possible after a Secondary-C verb only very occasionally, when the omitted verb could be inferred from the preceding discourse, e.g. *'Why did Mary resign?' 'Jane forced her to'* (sc. resign). Some Secondary-B verbs, but no Secondary-C items, can be used with nothing following the predicate, e.g. *I'm just wishing/hoping*, but not *\*I'm just forcing/allowing*.

The POSTPONING type has some semantic similarity with MAKING verbs, in that the subject has a role in controlling what happens, e.g. *I put off John's being examined by the doctor until tomorrow*, and *I forced John to be examined by the doctor*. However, the subject of a POSTPONING verb only organises the time of an event, they do not make or help it happen. POSTPONING is a Secondary-B type, with similar syntactic properties to WANTING, e.g. omission of complement clause subject (*I put off (my) being examined by the doctor until tomorrow*) and occasional omission of all post-predicate constituents (*She's always delaying*).

### 6.3.1. MAKING

This type has one independent role, the Causer, who does something to bring about an event or state, referred to by a complement clause. The subject of the main clause (the Causer) and the subject of the complement clause are most often human, but neither has to be, e.g. *These new shoes make my feet ache (by being too tight), She caused/allowed the flowers to die (by not watering them when we were away).* It is also possible, if not too common, for the Causer to be an ING complement clause, e.g. *Having been a failure in his first job made John try much harder in the second one.* There may also be an optional constituent stating how the Causer brought things about; it is often introduced with *by*, e.g. *John made Fred open the safe by threatening to tell about his indiscretions.*

Unlike other types, each MAKING verb takes just one variety of complement clause. There are four semantically defined sets; their more important members are:

(i)   *make, force, cause,* one sense of *drive,* causative senses of *get* and *have*; *tempt*—Modal (FOR) TO complement, with the *for* always omitted and the *to* sometimes omitted;

(ii)  *let, permit, allow*—Modal (FOR) TO complement, again with the *for* always and the *to* sometimes omitted;

(iii) *prevent, stop, spare, save,* specific senses of *check (oneself), rescue, release*— FROM ING complement, with the *from* sometimes omitted;

(iv)  *ensure*—THAT complement.

We first look briefly at the meanings of verbs in sets (i) and (ii). *Force* can imply coercion, e.g. *I forced the old lady to change her will in my favour by holding a gun at her head. Cause* is used of indirect action, often premeditated, e.g. *He caused Mary to crash by almost cutting through the brake cable and then sending her down the mountain road*; it may also be used of natural phenomena, e.g. *I believe that the underground nuclear tests caused that volcano to erupt. Make* has a wider meaning, referring to anything the Causer does to bring something about directly (including when the subject of the complement clause is not acting volitionally), e.g. *You made me burn the toast by distracting my attention, Lucy made Sandy wash up by saying he wouldn't get any pocket money unless he did.* (Note that *force* and *cause* are hyponyms of *make,* i.e. *make* could almost always be substituted for an occurrence of one of these verbs.) *Drive,* in its causative sense, implies continual pressure leading to some result, e.g. *Mary's nagging finally drove John to commit suicide. Tempt* combines 'make' and 'want', e.g. *The fact that gold bars were often left around the office tempted John to steal one* is a near paraphrase of *The fact that gold bars were often left around the office made John want to steal one.*

The causative senses of *get* and *have* refer to the Causer bringing something about, usually by indirect means, e.g. *She got Mary to wash up by saying how impressed John would be, She had Mary washing up when John arrived*. *Get* refers to arranging for something to happen and *have* for arranging that it be happening, e.g. *She had John and Mary talk about the crisis and then got Fred to join in*. This semantic difference parallels the contrast between *have* and *get* as members of the OWN subtype (§4.3), e.g. *She had two cars and then got a third*.

Turning now to set (ii), *permit* and *allow* may both be used impersonally; *permit* is often preferred where an official sanction is involved, e.g. *The law doesn't permit you to smoke in restaurants in Melbourne*. The meaning range of *allow* includes reference to some concession, e.g. *I was only allowed to drive the Mercedes on my birthday*, or oversight, e.g. *Those tenants allowed the garden to run to weed*. In contrast, *let* focuses on the identity of the Causer (which is why *let* is seldom found in the passive), e.g. *Mother doesn't let me stay out late*. *Let* also has a broad meaning, including 'didn't prevent/ forbid from doing', e.g. *She lets me do what I want, We let the cat go out at night if it wants to* (contrast with *We put the cat out at night*). *Permit* and *allow*—but not *let*—may omit a complement clause verb with the meaning 'get/receive/have', e.g. *Prisoners are only permitted* (*to receive*) *one visitor each month*; *She allowed John/herself* (*to have*) *just one chocolate*.

All verbs in sets (i) and (ii) take a Modal (FOR) TO complement clause. However, the *to* must be omitted after *make*, *let* and *have* when these verbs are used in the active. Compare:

(**1a**)    *Mary forced/allowed/got John to mow the lawn*
(**1b**)    *Mary made/had/let John mow the lawn*

*Make* may freely be used in the passive and then *to* is generally included, e.g. *John was made to mow the lawn*. *Let* is seldom used in the passive (except as part of the idiom *let go*, and there is then no *to*, e.g. *The rope was let go*). The causative sense of *have* can never be passivised. Note that *mow* in (1b) is in base form (not a tense form, which would be *mows* or *mowed*), which is what it would be in a TO complement. It is because of this that we describe (1b) as an instance of a TO clause with the *to* omitted; this omission does have semantic explanation and semantic consequences (see §§6.3.2 and 8.2.5).

A TO complement clause can have its predicate beginning with copula, imperfective or passive *be*. This *be* (and the preceding *to*, for verbs that take *to*) may optionally be omitted after *get* and *make* and must be omitted after *have*, e.g.

**(2a)**   *I got John to be interested in the puzzle*
**(2b)**   *I got John interested in the puzzle*
**(3a)**   *I made/\*had John be interested in the puzzle*
**(3b)**   *I made/had John interested in the puzzle*

There is a semantic difference. The (a) sentences, with *be*, imply that I exerted some influence over John so that he exercised his mind to be interested, whereas the (b) sentences imply that I did something as a result of which John became interested, quite spontaneously. That is why *have*, which refers just to 'something happening', is restricted to the (b) construction.

The three varieties of *be* show different possibilities for omission with these verbs. Both passive and imperfective *be* must be omitted after *have*, may be after *get*, but are seldom or never omitted after *make*. With passive *be* we can have *I got John to be examined by the doctor/I made John be examined by the doctor* (did something so that he agreed to undergo the examination) and *I got/had John examined by the doctor* (arranged for it to happen) but not *\*I made John examined by the doctor* since, when the predicate refers to an event, there would be a conflict between the meaning of *make* 'I did something so that John did something' and the semantic implication of *be* omission 'something happens fairly spontaneously'.

A similar argument applies for imperfective *be*. There are *I got John and Mary to be talking when Fred entered/I made John and Mary be talking when Fred entered* (did something so that they agreed to talk) and *I got/had John and Mary talking when Fred entered* (arranged for it to happen, without them really intending it), but not *\*I made John and Mary talking when Fred entered*, because of the same semantic conflict (when the predicate refers to an event).

With copula *be*—and a predicate referring to a state—all three verbs make the omission, e.g. *He made/got/had Mary angry* (*before Fred arrived*). The *be* can be retained, although it seldom is, with *make* and *get*. *He got Mary to be angry/He made Mary be angry* sound as if he persuaded her to pretend to be angry, whereas *He got/made Mary angry* implies that she entered that state quite spontaneously, as a natural reaction to whatever he did. A copula can of course also be followed by an NP. We get *The Board made John President of the Company* (it elected him), where *be* would not be appropriate since John is not exercising any volition; and *Mary got him to be President*, which does include *to be* since it describes Mary using some stratagem so that he would agree to accept the position.

*Force*—but not *cause, make, let*, etc.—occurs in another construction type, perhaps another kind of complement clause, with an *-ing* predicate preceded by *into*, e.g. *I forced John into resigning*. This implies a lengthy process before the result is achieved, as compared to *I forced John to resign*, which may describe a result achieved rather quickly. (The other verbs to take INTO ING all refer to some drawn-out activity, with negative overtones; e.g. *bully, coax, pester*.)

Verbs in set (iii) have meanings almost opposite to those of set (i). *Spare* and *save* indicate that the Causer obviates the need for someone to do a task that they should otherwise do, e.g. *John saved Mary from (having) to paint the porch by doing it himself*. *Prevent* and *stop* refer to the Causer making sure that someone does not do something that they may have wanted to do or tried to do; *prevent* often refers to indirect and *stop* to direct means, e.g. *He prevented her (from) going by hiding her passport*, and *He stopped her from going by standing in the doorway and barring the way*. (There is, however, a good deal of semantic overlap, and the two verbs are often used interchangeably.) There are also special senses of *check (oneself)*, *rescue* and *release* that belong in set (iii), e.g. *John checked himself from correcting Mary, Jane rescued Tony from having to give the speech by offering to do it herself*.

All of these verbs take a FROM ING complement, like *discourage, dissuade* and *forbid* from the ORDER subtype of SPEAKING (§5.4). Unlike the *discourage* group, *prevent, spare* and *save* may optionally omit the *from* in an active clause (it would seldom be omitted from a passive); there is a meaning difference, which is discussed in §8.2.9.

There is another, related sense of *stop* which belongs to the BEGINNING type, e.g. *She stopped swimming* (i.e. she was swimming and then decided not to any more). As mentioned in §6.1.2, this verb can be used causatively, and then shows some semantic and syntactic similarities to the Secondary-C verb *stop*. There are, however, crucial differences at both levels; compare

**(4a)**    *John stopped Mary swimming* (causative of Secondary-A verb *stop*)
**(4b)**    *John stopped Mary from swimming* (Secondary-C verb *stop*)

Sentence (4a) is the causative of *Mary stopped swimming*. This sentence implies that Mary was swimming and that John made her desist; note that *from* cannot be included in (4a). Sentence (4b) implies that John did not allow her to swim, i.e. she didn't enter the water. The *from*—which is optional after *prevent, spare* and *save*—would generally not be omitted from (4b), in order to distinguish the two constructions.

Set (iv), consisting just of *ensure*—which takes a THAT complement—may not refer to the Causer doing anything so that a certain state or event comes into being; the Causer might merely ascertain that something has been done (it does not matter by whom), e.g. *John ensured that all the doors were locked before going away on holiday.*

### 6.3.2. HELPING

This type has one independent role, the Helper (main clause subject), who joins in with someone (complement clause subject) to bring about some event. The main member of the type is *help*; there are also a number of hyponyms of *help* with specialised meanings, e.g. *aid, assist.*

Like MAKING verbs, *help* takes a Modal (FOR) TO complement. The subject of the complement clause must be different from the subject of the main clause. (There is an idiomatic usage, e.g. *He helped himself to the chocolates,* but the reflexive pronoun after *help* cannot here be followed by a verb.) *Help* differs from MAKING verbs in that either the subject or the post-subject portion of the complement clause can be omitted. One may say *John helped Mary* if one's listeners could be expected to know what he helped her do. And *John helped to paint the wall* is acceptable if one does not wish to specify who the other people painting were.

We noted that *force, allow,* etc. require the inclusion of *to* but that *make, have* and *let* require it to be omitted, at least in the active. With *help* the *to* may be either included or omitted, in both active and passive. There is a semantic difference. Compare:

(1a)   *John helped Mary to eat the pudding* (by guiding the spoon to her mouth, since she was still an invalid)
(1b)   *John helped Mary eat the pudding* (he ate half)

When *to* is omitted, as in (1b), the sentence is likely to mean that the Helper did part of the activity; when *to* is included, as in (1a), it is more likely to mean that the Helper made things easy for the complement clause subject so that she could do what needed to be done (see also §8.2.5).

The Helper is generally HUMAN, but can be an abstract noun or even a complement clause, e.g. *John's success helped him gain confidence*, *Believing in God helped me to get through that crisis.*

An alternative syntactic construction for *help* is for the 'person helped' to be followed by a preposition (usually *with*) and an *-ing* clause, e.g. *He helped Mary with writing the letter* (this is then more likely to have the sense of (1b) than that of (1a)). Of the more specialised HELPING verbs, *aid* usually refers to help given by some official body, rather than by an individual (*America aided Great Britain in fighting the Nazi terror*), while *assist* implies that the Helper fulfils a secondary role (*Fred assisted John in building the wall by handing him bricks*). There are also the inherently reciprocal verbs *cooperate* (*with*) and *collaborate* (*with*). All of these verbs can take a Modal (FOR) TO clause—the *to* may not be omitted—but are more frequently found with a preposition (often, *in*) plus an *-ing* clause, or else with an ACTIVITY noun in O slot, e.g. *America aided Great Britain in its war against the Nazi terror.*

*Hinder* is opposite in meaning to one sense of *help*, but does not freely occur with a complement clause; the preferred construction is with a simple NP in O slot (referring to the person who was hindered) and then a relative clause or an adverbial clause describing the activity that was affected, e.g. *John hindered the workman who was/while he was installing a new telephone (by continually hiding his tools). Support* has some semantic similarity with *help*. This verb, and its opposite, *oppose*, take ING complements, e.g. *She supported/opposed John's being nominated for president of the company.*

## 6.4. Secondary-D types

Secondary-D verbs are all intransitive and take a complement clause in subject slot. They may take one role additional to those of the complement clause; this is the Arbiter, which is marked by the preposition *to*, e.g. *That John should be promoted ahead of Dick seemed wrong (to Mary), That John should be promoted ahead of Dick didn't matter (to Mary).*

Statement of the Arbiter is often omitted and a Secondary-D construction then appears to have no roles beyond those of the complement clause verb. But some Arbiter is always implied and will be understood by listeners—according to pragmatic context—as being the speaker(s)—i.e. *to me, to us*—or else all rational or like-minded people—e.g. *to everyone*.

## 6.4.1. SEEM

Verbs from this type (*seem*, *appear*, *look*, *sound*, *feel* and *happen*) have two distinct modes of syntactic use. In the first they occur with an adjective—or adjectival phrase—as a kind of copula. In the second they may be used without any adjective.

When a SEEM verb is followed by an adjective this indicates that the Arbiter thinks—in a certain way (specified by the SEEM verb)—that the adjective is applicable to the event or state described by the complement clause, in subject slot.

SEEM verbs occur with just those adjectives that may take a complement clause in subject slot, i.e. VALUE, DIFFICULTY, QUALIFICATION and the CLEVER subtype of HUMAN PROPENSITY (§3.2). Instead of the copula *be* we can have either *seem to be* or else just *seem*. Thus, with the VALUE type, *John's having resigned was/seemed to be/seemed most odd*, *That John hit his grandmother is/seems to be/seems out of character*; with a DIFFICULTY adjective, *It is/ seems to be/seems hard for Mary to operate our mower*, *Our mower is/seems to be/seems hard to operate*; with QUALIFICATION adjectives, *It is/seems to be/ seems definite that the King will visit*, *It is/seems to be/seems normal for no one to work on Christmas Day*, *John is/seems to be/seems likely to win*; with a CLEVER adjective, *It was/seemed to be/seemed very stupid of John (for him) to enter without knocking*.

*Seem* (*to be*) can replace the copula in every construction open to an adjective that takes a complement clause in subject slot (except in frame (iii) with the CORRECT subtype of QUALIFICATION, in which the subject of an extraposed complement clause is raised to fill main clause subject slot, e.g. *John was correct to stand when the bishop entered*, but not *\*John seemed (to be) correct to stand when the bishop entered*); see §3.2.

The second syntactic usage of SEEM verbs is in what has the appearance of an extraposed THAT complement, and what could be a special variety of Judgement TO construction:

**(1a)** *It seems that Mary found the body*
**(1b)** *Mary seems to have found the body*

Sentence (1a) has a very similar meaning to a *seem*-plus-adjective construction like:

**(2)** *It seems (to be) true/(to be) correct/to be the case that Mary found the body*

Sentence (2) is a genuine example of a THAT complement clause extraposed from subject position—we can have, with no extraposition, *That Mary found the body seems (to be) true/(to be) correct/to be the case*.

The fact that (1a) is a construction distinct from (2) is shown by the non-acceptability of the THAT clause in subject slot, i.e. *That Mary found the body seems*.

The syntactic and semantic relations between (1a) and (1b) are parallel to those between the THAT complement construction in (3a) and the Judgement TO construction in (3b):

(**3a**)   *John knew that Mary was the murderer*
(**3b**)   *John knew Mary to be the murderer*

Sentence (1a) simply involves a THAT complement clause and the verb *seem*. A THAT clause must include a subject, and so *Mary* could not be moved out of the complement clause to replace the impersonal subject *it*. But a TO clause does not have to include an overt subject, and in (1b) we do, effectively, get *Mary* replacing the *it*.

After verbs like *think*, *consider* and *imagine*, the *to be* of a Judgement TO complement may be omitted, e.g. *John thought her (to be) stupid* (see (a) in §2.8 and also §8.2.6). Exactly the same omission is possible after *seem*, e.g. *Mary seemed (to be) stupid*. It appears that, following *seem*, *to be* can be omitted before an adjective or NP which makes a judgement, e.g. *He seems (to be) good, He seems (to be) a good doctor, He seems (to be) an idiot*; but *to be* cannot be omitted before an NP that does not involve a judgement—*He seems to be a doctor*, but not *\*He seems a doctor*.

There are two alternative constructions, one with *as if* and the other—occurring only in colloquial varieties of English—with *like* in place of *to be*, together with pronominal repetition of the main clause subject and a following copula, e.g. *John seems like/as if he's hitting Mary/hated by all his staff/stupid*.

*Seem* is used when the Arbiter is not fully certain whether the adjectival description is appropriate, or whether the statement of the complement clause in a construction like (1a) or (1b) is correct—perhaps when there is not quite enough evidence. *Appear* has the same syntactic possibilities and a very similar meaning, but may imply 'can be observed by me' in contrast to *seem* 'can be inferred by me'.

*Look*, *sound* and *feel* have similar grammar and meaning to *seem* and *appear*. *Look* is, like *appear*, often used when the Arbiter's evidence is visual observation, but it may also be employed whatever the nature of the evidence. *Feel* is most often used when the Arbiter has an intuition or other mental impression about something, and *sound* when the evidence is aural. Thus we get *It seems/sounds strange that John gave his car away*, *John looks/seems likely to be sacked, It feels/seems strange that we may never see him again*. These three verbs are seldom followed by *to be*; they are used a lot in *like/as if* constructions, e.g. *John looks/sounds like/as if he's seen a ghost*.

At the end of §5.1, we mentioned the intransitive use of some transitive ATTENTION verbs, e.g. *It sounds good, She looks pretty, It feels soft*. These could be treated as instances of the SEEM sense of the verbs, e.g. *That she is pretty looks (to be) true* is a fair if awkward paraphrase of *She looks pretty*. But note that *taste* and *smell* may also be used intransitively, and these are only very marginally found with meaning and syntax similar to *seem*.

*Happen* has a meaning something like 'it is, in fact, the case', and may carry the implication of it being somewhat surprising that this is so. It has a similar syntax to *seem* except that there must always be a following *to be*, and *happen* is not found in *as if/like* constructions. Thus, *That John is stupid happens to be true, John happens to be stupid. Happen* has a further sense, for which an ACTIVITY noun is subject, e.g. *The fight happened because John hit Mary*, or *The fight just happened* (no one started it). *Come about* has a similar meaning to this sense of *happen*, e.g. *The fight came about because John hit Mary*. (*Happen* also belongs to the HAPPENING type; see §5.7.)

### 6.4.2. MATTER

The main member of this type is *matter*, which is often used in the negative, *doesn't matter*. It carries the meaning that the event or state referred to by a complement clause (in subject relation to matter) is important to the Arbiter, e.g. *That John won doesn't matter (one little bit) (to Fred)*. Note that, unlike SEEM verbs, *matter* does not take a following adjective, but may be followed by something like *at all, one little bit* or *one iota*.

*Matter* takes THAT and WH- complement clauses, which are frequently extraposed, e.g. *It doesn't matter (to John) that Mary won the prize, Whether or not we are to be allowed to compete matters a hell of a lot to me*; ING complement clauses are also admissible, e.g. *John's voting Conservative doesn't matter. Matter* may also take an indefinite NP as subject and then the Arbiter may be introduced by *to* or by *for*, e.g. *Nothing/lots of things matter(s) to/for John.*

One sense of *count* may also belong to this type (and may have *to* or *for* before the Arbiter). It appears to be restricted to a THAT complement in subject slot, e.g. *That John was a churchgoer counted for a lot*, *That John was a churchgoer didn't count for anything (for Mary)* (he had still killed a man).

It is worth noting that very few languages have ideas such as 'happen' and 'matter' expressed through verbs. This kind of qualification is more often achieved by adverbs, verbal clitics or some other grammatical means.

## Notes to Chapter 6

§6.1.1. Coates (1983) is an insightful study of the syntax and semantics of MODALS in English; earlier useful books on MODALS include Leech (1971) and Palmer (1979). The contrast between *will* and *be going to* is revealingly discussed by Binnick (1971, 1972), Hall (1970) and McIntosh (1966).

Trudgill and Hannah (1982: 46–52) provide an instructive account of differences in modal use between American and British English.

Some dialects do permit a sequence of modals. To mention just one study, Brown (1991) describes how in Hawick Scots, some modals may be followed by *can*, *could* or *be to*, as in *He should can go tomorrow* (= *He ought to be able to go tomorrow*).

§6.1.2. *Begin* and related verbs are discussed by Perlmutter (1970), Newmeyer (1970, 1975) and Freed (1979) among others.

§6.2.1. McCawley (1979) has a useful account of what can be omitted from a complement clause after *want* (see also §3.4). Bolinger (1942) provides an illuminating account of *need*.

# Part C

## Some Grammatical Topics

# 7

## *She is departing for the jungle tomorrow, although the doctor has been advising against it*
## Tense and aspect

Within the English predicate, mood, reality status, modality, tense, and aspect are shown by a variety of formal means:

- MODAL and SEMI-MODAL verbs; these are Secondary-A semantic types;
- the auxiliary verbs *have* (taking *-en* on the following word) and *be* (with *-ing* on the following verb);
- verbal suffixes:
  —what is traditionally called 'past', which is *-ed* on regular verbs, with a variety of morphological processes applying for irregular (or 'strong') verbs; for example, *sing/sang*, *give/gave*, *cut/cut*;
  —what is traditionally called 'present', involving *-s* when the subject is 3rd person singular masculine, feminine or neuter, and zero suffix otherwise (verbs *be* and *have* show irregular forms).

In addition, the base form of the verb is used for imperative mood, and after *to*. The structure of the verb phrase is given in §2.2.2.

In this discussion, we begin with the grammatical systems involved, studying the contrastive meanings of the terms in these systems and their formal realisations (these were summarised in Table 2.2, §2.2.3).

## 7.1. Basic distinctions

The first distinctions are:

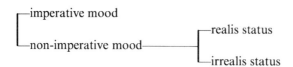

**Imperative mood**, employed in giving orders, uses the base form of the verb (see §2.2.1). The subject is generally 2nd person; it can then be (and usually is) omitted. In addition, the imperative generally has a distinctively loud and abrupt voice quality. This is further discussed in §2.4.1.

Statements and questions share the same reality status, modality, tense, and aspect categories and can be referred to as **non-imperative mood**. Questions are distinguished by a rising final intonation and usually also by word order rearrangement (and inclusion of *do* if there is no auxiliary or copula); see §2.11.1. For example:

| STATEMENT | QUESTION | | |
|---|---|---|---|
| *John is dead* | *Is John dead?* | or | *John is dead?* |
| *He must go* | *Must he go?* | or | *He must go?* |
| *She resigned* | *Did she resign?* | or | *She resigned?* |

The major distinction within non-imperative is between:

- **realis** status—something which has reality in past, present or future time (or, with negation added, which does not have reality);
- **irrealis** status—something which is uncertain in the future, or was unrealised in the past.

Compare:

| REALIS | IRREALIS |
|---|---|
| *John comes tomorrow* | *John will come tomorrow (if he can)* |
| *Mary had cooked dinner*  *by the time I got home got home* | *Mary would have cooked dinner by the time I*  *got home (but for the power failure)* |

Irrealis status is marked by modals or semi-modals. The nine main choices, which are listed and discussed in §6.1.1, include prediction (*will* and *is going to*), ability (*can* and *is able to*) and necessity (*must* and *has (got) to*). Irrealis also accepts the same aspectual distinctions as present tense—perfective/imperfective and actual/previous; see §7.5.

Within **realis**, there are four tense choices, all but generic with further aspect parameters; the realisation is given for each, for 3rd person singular masculine, feminine or neuter subject.

- 'generic': -*s*
- future 'established' aspect: -*s*
          'particular' aspect: *is -ing*
- present                      'ACTUAL' ASPECT        'PREVIOUS' ASPECT
          'perfective' aspect       -*s*                   *has -en*
          'imperfective' aspect   *is -ing*                *has been -ing*
- past                         'ACTUAL' ASPECT        'PREVIOUS' ASPECT
          'perfective' aspect       -*ed*                  *had -en*
          'imperfective' aspect   *was -ing*               *had been -ing*

It will be seen that the -*s* suffix marks three distinct tense-aspect specifications:

—generic
—established future
—actual perfective present

And *is -ing* is used for two:

—particular future
—actual imperfective present

We now discuss, in turn, generic, then future, then the present and past systems.

## 7.2. Generic

Generic (or habitual) is a timeless statement, whose core noun phrases generally have generic form. For example: *Crows are black, Dogs bark, Ducks like water, Italians eat lots of noodles, Mosquitoes spread malaria, Well-brought-up children know how to behave, Gods hate liars.*

A marginal type of generic may have as transitive subject a noun with singular reference (but the object noun phrase should be generic). For instance, a monotheistic speaker could opine: *God hates liars*. On a par with this is *My mother hates liars*.

The subject noun phrase may have singular form, but generic meaning, as in *Lead is heavy*. And an NP can have singular form but a generic sense, as in *The mosquito spreads malaria* and *Gods/God/My mother hate(s) a liar* (that is, they hate anyone who is a liar). Note that verbs from the LIKING and ANNOYING semantic types typically have a generic sense.

## 7.3. Future

There are two aspects within realis future:

- **established** (es), a regular occurrence: *-s*
- **particular** (pa), a non-regular or special occurrence: *is -ing*

Each will normally be accompanied by an adverb referring to future time. The difference in meaning can be seen in:

(**1es**)   *I get paid tomorrow*
(**1pa**)   *I'm getting paid tomorrow*

Sentence (1es) would be said if tomorrow is Friday and I get paid every Friday (this is an established part of my employment). Sentence (1pa) would be appropriate if I don't get a regular pay-cheque since I only do casual work but this week I did complete a time sheet and thus do expect to get paid this particular Friday.

Another example is:

(**2es**)   *We have a meeting this afternoon*
(**2pa**)   *We're having a meeting this afternoon*

Sentence (2es) could be said on Wednesday morning, as a reminder that there is each week a meeting on Wednesday afternoon; this is an established practice in the workplace. In contrast, (2pa) implies that a particular meeting has been organised, outside the normal schedule.

In essence, established future describes some event which is typically regular and expected. Particular future refers to a 'one-off' event, perhaps specially arranged. There are some instances where only the established future is possible. For example, one can say (3es) but not (3pa).

(3es)   *The sun rises at 7.06 tomorrow morning*
(3pa)   *\*The sun is rising at 7.06 tomorrow morning*

Sentence (3pa) sounds as if the sun can rise at whatever time it chooses, at its whim.

Suppose that at 9.50, someone inspects a cuckoo clock and expresses a desire to see the cuckoo pop out and sing. The clock's owner could reply with (4es) but scarcely with (4pa).

(4es)   *The cuckoo comes out at ten o'clock*
(4pa)   *\*The cuckoo is coming out at ten o'clock*

Sentence (4pa) sounds as if the cuckoo makes its own decision as to when it will emerge and has notified the owner that this will be ten o'clock.

An alternative to (4es) could be:

(4es′)   *The cuckoo comes out on the hour*

This is ambiguous between established future and a variety of generic.

We can now illustrate situations where only the particular future is allowed. For example, one could say (5pa) but scarcely (5es).

(5pa)   *She's having a baby in June*
(5es)   *\*She has a baby in June*

Sentence (5es) sounds as if it is an established event—she has a baby every June. (Note that it is possible to say *She's having her baby in June*. It must already have been established that she's having a baby, and this sentence then specifies the month.)

As a further example, one is more likely to hear (6pa) than (6es).

(6pa)   *We're having our own house next year* (our insurance policy matures next year, and we'll use the money as deposit against a mortgage for a new house)
(6es)   *\*We have our own house next year*

It would be possible to invent a situation for which (6es) would be appropriate. It might involve the unlikely scenario of an authoritative government allowing each family to have their own house every fifth year, and next year being our turn. But in a normal world, (6es) is infelicitous.

The contrast between irrealis prediction (pred), shown by *will* (see §6.1.1)—which is often called 'future'—and the realis futures can be seen in:

(7es)   *\*It rains tomorrow*

(**7pa**)   *\*It is raining tomorrow*
(**7pred**)   *It will rain tomorrow*

No reality can be attached to rain falling tomorrow, so that neither of the realis futures are possible. All one can do is make a prediction, which may or may not come true.

There are, of course, *will*-versions of the other examples just given. It sounds odd to say *She will have a baby in June*. However, the following is acceptable:

(**5pred**)   *She will have a baby quite soon* (when she got married, she said they planned to start a family right away)

This is a prediction, lacking in reality; it implies that she has yet to conceive (and may be unable to). If she has been confirmed as pregnant, then only *She's having a baby quite soon* is appropriate.

Sentences with *will* convey a prediction that something will happen; it is never a certainty and often bears qualification. For example:

(**4pred**)   *The cuckoo will come out at ten o'clock* (if the repairman who just left has done his job properly)
(**1pred**)   *I'll get paid tomorrow* (if the computer system doesn't break down again)
(**2pred**)   *We'll have a meeting this afternoon* (if enough people turn up to ensure a quorum)

Sometimes a prediction is as good as certain. But there is always some miniscule element of doubt. While listening to the ranting of a maniac I might well respond to a question about the time of sunrise with:

(**3pred**)   *The sun will rise at 7.06 tomorrow morning—if indeed, the world doesn't end before then, as this fellow is predicting it will*

There is an idiomatic particular future. When called to come, someone could reply:

(**8pa**)   *I'm coming in a couple of minutes*

Or the time adverb may be omitted, giving just:

(**8pa′**)   *I'm coming*

The person who says this may not actually be in the process of coming (as one would expect if *I'm coming* were interpreted—in the absence of a time adverb—as actual imperfective present). They may still have a couple of sentences to write in finishing a letter, before putting on shoes and coat and *then* coming. But by conventional usage, (8pa′) is used as and interpreted as particular future. A similar example is *He's moving to Lisbon in a few weeks*. The time adverb *in a few weeks* could be omitted and *He's moving to Lisbon* would be interpreted as a particular future relating to some time not far ahead.

There are rather few instances of time adverb being omissible from a realis future. Another relates to (5pa); one can say, just, *She's having a baby*. And the established future *Tomorrow is Wednesday* does not require a time adverb since the copula arguments *tomorrow* and *Wednesday* provide sufficient temporal specification.

## 7.4. Present and past systems

There are three binary systems underlying present and past realis:

- perfective aspect (pe)/imperfective aspect (im)
- actual aspect (ac)/previous aspect (pr)
- present tense/past tense

The combinations of these generate eight possibilities, which can be repeated from §7.1 (with realisations for 3rd person masculine, feminine or neuter singular subject):

|  | PRESENT | | PAST | |
| --- | --- | --- | --- | --- |
|  | ACTUAL | PREVIOUS | ACTUAL | PREVIOUS |
| PERFECTIVE | *-s* | *has -en* | *-ed* | *had -en* |
| IMPERFECTIVE | *is -ing* | *has been -ing* | *was -ing* | *had been -ing* |

These three parameters will be discussed one at a time. Then the difference in meaning between previous perfective present (*has -en*) and actual perfective past (*-ed*) will be explained and illustrated.

## 7.4.1. *Perfective versus imperfective*

Many statements can be phrased either with perfective *-s* or with imperfective *is -ing*. A commentary on a domestic scene could include any of:

(**9pe**)    *John washes up*
(**9im**)    *John is washing up*
(**10pe**)   *Mary does the ironing*
(**10im**)   *Mary is doing the ironing*

A perfective sentence treats an activity as a unit, without regard for its internal composition. It may have a duration in time but this is not taken into account in the perfective statement. In contrast, an imperfective statement refers to the activity as spanning a period of time.

A perfective can locate its event as included within the time span of an event described by an imperfective, as in both of (again from commentary on a domestic situation):

(**11**)   *John washes up while Mary is doing the ironing*
(**12**)   *Mary does the ironing while John is washing up*

In (11), the event of John washing up (here treated as a unit of activity by choice of perfective) is shown to be included within the time span of Mary's doing the ironing (marked as imperfective). This is reversed in (12).

However, the imperfective in English does not just focus on the time span and internal composition of an event. It also implies that the activity described is dynamic and evolving. Consider a perfective sentence with inanimate and animate subjects:

(**13pe**)   *The wall surrounds the city*
(**14pe**)   *The army surrounds the city*

These describe a continuing state, that the wall/army is all around the city. When imperfective is used the results are quite different:

(**13im**)   *\*The wall is surrounding the city*
(**14im**)   *The army is surrounding the city*

Sentence (14im) describes a continuous and evolving process whereby the army gradually extends itself until it is all around the city. Sentence (13im) is unacceptable since—although it describes something which is extended in time (maybe for several hundred years)—there is no activity involved.

Consider also:

(**15pe**)   *I think [that you should go]*
(**15im**)   *I'm thinking about [whether you should go]*

Sentence (15pe) describes a formed opinion, a unit. In contrast, (15im) describes a continuous and dynamic process, weighing up the pros and cons of whether you should go.

The contrast between a normally invariable state, and some unusual activity which interrupts it, can also be shown by using perfective for the former and imperfective for the latter, in order to stress the change. For example:

**(16)**  *He normally drives a Volvo but this week he's driving a Volkswagen* (his Volvo is being repaired and the garage has lent him a Volkswagen for the week)

Whether or not an imperfective can be used may depend not on subject or verb but on the nature of a non-subject argument. One can say:

**(17)**  *John is having a series of injections*

This is an extended dynamic process, with one injection after another. But it is infelicitous to say:

**(18)**  *John is having a lot of fruit in his orchard this year*

Such a non-dynamic statement is limited to the perfective: *John has a lot of fruit in his orchard this year*.

## 7.4.2. Actual versus previous

In general linguistic terminology, the label 'perfect' is 'used of an action, etc. considered as a completed whole' (Matthews 1997: 271). Although English *has -en* has traditionally been labelled 'perfect', this is not an appropriate label. Indeed, in the last sentence you read, *has ... been labelled* does not imply that this labelling is a thing of the past; it is, indeed, still very much in vogue.

*Has -en* is used of an event or state which commenced previous to the time of speaking. Depending on the verb used and accompanying adverb (if any), it may or may not be continuing up to the present. I employ the label 'previous' (pr) for *has -en*, as against 'actual' (ac) for *-s* (both are perfective present).

Consider the verb *live*, first with actual perfective and actual imperfective present:

**(19pe)**  *Roy lives in New York*
**(19im)**  *Roy is living in New York* (*now*)

Sentence (19pe) implies that Roy's living in New York is a long-standing situation. In contrast, the imperfective *is -ing* in (19im) indicates that he has recently relocated to the city, as a dynamic activity. Typically an adverb such as *now* will be included.

Now consider the corresponding sentences with actual and previous choices within perfective present:

(**20ac**)   *Roy lives in New York*
(**20pr**)   *Roy has lived in New York*
(**20pr′**)   *Roy has lived in New York since his wife died/for ten years*

Whereas (20ac) describes an actual present state, (20pr) states that he began to live in New York some time previous to the present. When there is no time adverb in the sentence, the implication is that he no longer lives there (this is a 'perfect' meaning). But with the addition of an adverb specifying a period of time, which indicates when his living in New York commenced (when his wife died, or ten years ago), the sentence states that he is still living there (this is not a 'perfect' meaning).

Even without a time adverb, a *has -en* sentence may refer to some activity which began at a previous time and continues up to (and quite likely beyond) the present. Suppose that I turn a street corner and come across two louts fighting, with a friend of mine standing close by. I could ask him *Did you see what happened?* and receive the reply, with my friend's eyes still on the battle:

(**21**)   *I've watched it all*

Suppose that a dramatist's mother is at the opening night of her son's new play. During the interval she remarks to him: *I have enjoyed it*; the *have -en* indicates that her enjoyment has extended from the beginning of the play up to that point.

With a sentence that refers to a completed process, *has -en* implies that it *just* happened. For example:

(**22**)   *The ice has melted*
(**23**)   *He has discovered gold*

These sentences carry the implication that the melting and the discovery took place in the very recent past. There is, however, no such implication with a verb which does not describe a completed process, as in:

(**24**)   *I have enjoyed Handel's 'Messiah'* (I saw it performed only once, ten years ago)

**(25)**   *I have believed in the Christian god* (I believed in this god for about six months when I was fourteen, over fifty years ago)

The perfective/imperfective and actual/previous parameters freely interact. Virtually any verb or copula type may take *has -en*. As noted in §7.4.1, there are restrictions as to whether a verb may occur with imperfective *is -ing*; it must be able to describe an evolving activity. A verb which permits *is -ing* may augment this with *has -en*. For example:

**(26)**   *I have been waiting for you* (for three hours/a long time/since three o'clock)

Even when the time adverb is omitted from (26), the stretch of time I have been waiting, which began at some previous time, is understood to extend up to the moment of speaking.

Examples (15)-(17) each describe a dynamic activity, extended in time. Adding *has -en* indicates that the activity began at a time previous to the present and in each example there is a clear implication that it continues to the present.

**(15pr-im)**   *I've been thinking about [whether you should go]* (ever since we got news of the civil unrest in your planned destination)
**(16′)**   *He normally drives a Volvo but this week he's been driving a Volkswagen* (ever since he crashed the Volvo)
**(17′)**   *John has been having a series of injections* (all this week)

As mentioned under (d) in §2.9 and in §2.12, a temporal clause commencing with *after having . . . -en* may omit the *after*, as in *(After) having brushed her teeth, Mary went to bed.*

## 7.4.3. Present versus past

Almost all the examples presented thus far—of perfective versus imperfective and of actual versus previous—have been in present tense. This is used for comment on what is happening now: for directions in a play (for example, *John enters from the right, and sits at the desk*) and for pragmatic speech acts (*I name this ship the Titanic*, or *I resign*). It can also be used, as a stylistic device, in a narrative about what happened in the past. For example, Miriam Makeba's (1988) life story uses present tense throughout. As a sample, it begins: *I kick my mother and cause her great pain. But she forgives me my tantrum this one time only. She is all alone in the house.*

Generally, descriptions of past events use past tense, which shows exactly the same aspectual parameters as the present. One simply uses -ed in place of -s, *was* for *is* and *had* for *has*. Sentence (11) becomes *John washed up while Mary was doing the ironing*. The time of reference is shifted to some point in the past, with respect to which the parameters operate. For example, *The wall surrounded the city* (*in 300* BCE, *before it fell into disrepair*) and *Your child was very stupid/rude/good* (*yesterday*). Note that the focus in the past may be specified with a time adverb (alternatively, it may be left vague and unspecified).

What is of particular interest is the contrast between previous perfective present, *has -en*, and actual perfective past, *-ed*. Compare:

**(21)**   *I've watched it all*
**(21′)**   *I watched it all*

The *-ed* sentence, (21′), implies that the fight is over, whereas use of *have -en*, in (21), implies that it may still be going on. Now compare:

**(27)**   *John tried* (and failed)
**(27′)**   *John has tried* (but not yet succeeded)

In (27), the try or tries and the failure(s) are in the past. But (27′) implies that although John has tried and failed up to now, he hasn't yet given up. The expectation is that he'll continue trying beyond the present time.

Whereas *-ed* describes something in the past, which is over and done with, *has -en* indicates an activity which either began in the past and continues up to the present, or took place in the past but has continuing reality and relevance in the present. This is exhibited in the following minimal pair of sentences:

**(28)**   *The police arrested the criminal* (but he later escaped from them)
**(28′)**   *The police have arrested the criminal*

In (28) the arrest was over and done with in the past; anything may have happened since then. But (28′) states that the criminal was arrested and remains in custody up to the present. Similarly, *The taxi has arrived* indicates that it is still here, waiting for its passenger. In contrast, *The taxi arrived* could be said if it came and then went away again, having got tired of waiting.

Now consider the pragmatic contexts for:

**(29)**   *Father brought home the fish*

(**29′**)    *Father has brought home the fish* (and now we can have dinner)

Sentence (29) simply states what happened at some time in the past. But (29′) would be used when this fish-bringing has particular relevance in present time. Similarly, one would say *John fell over* just to describe an event (perhaps in a detached kind of way). But *John has fallen over* carries a definite implication into the present—maybe his knees are bleeding and he needs some first-aid treatment.

If one heard

(**30**)    *The boss ordered them to go*

with nothing further being said, one would infer that they had gone. But if instead the report was:

(**30′**)    *The boss has ordered them to go*

one would want to ask what happened. Perhaps they refused to go and are still here. That is, the order was issued in the past but it has continuing relevance in the present.

Actual perfective past, *-ed*, generally describes a definite event at a definite time in the past. Compare:

(**31**)    *John told me yesterday*
(**31′**)    *John has told me already*

Sentence (31) recognises a definite time of telling, whereas with the previous perfective present, *has -en*, one can just use an adverb such as *already*, indicating that the activity took place at some unspecified time previous to the present. Now consider:

(**32**)    *John baked (*has baked) this cake*
(**32′**)    *John has baked (*baked) a cake*

Only *-ed* is possible in (32), describing the baking of a definite cake, and only *has -en* is permitted in (32′) describing the fact that, at some time in the past, John did bake a cake. Note that example (32′) is possible with *-ed* if some definite time frame is indicated; for example, *John baked a cake last week*. That is, in examples like this, *-ed* requires either a definite object or a definite time.

Further consequences of the use of *-ed* and *has -ing* become evident under negation. Winston Churchill is dead; he wrote many books (including one novel) but none of them a detective story. One says:

(33)    *Winston Churchill didn't write a detective story*

It is not felicitous to say *Winston Churchill hasn't written a detective story*; this would imply that he is still alive and still might.

Now suppose that one wanted to make a similar statement about Johnny Jones, who is still alive. One must say:

(33′)    *Johnny Jones hasn't written a detective story*

It would not be acceptable to say *Johnny Jones didn't write a detective story*; this would necessarily imply that he is dead. It may be that Johnny Jones is illiterate, senile, unconscious, with a terminal illness and a life expectancy of only three weeks. It could be utterly inconceivable that he should write a detective story. No matter, if the poor fellow is still alive then one must use *has -en* in (33′) rather than *-ed*.

We noted, in §7.3, that *-s* and *is -ing* are used not only for perfective and imperfective actual present, but also for established and particular future. Just as the imperfective present tense *is -ing* can be cast into past as *was -ing*, so particular future *is -ing* may become *was -ing*, this having the meaning 'particular future in past'. Consider (34), with particular future in its second clause:

(34)    *We've just arrived in Spain, and I'm meeting him in Toledo tomorrow*

When this is placed in the past, we get:

(34′)    *We'd just arrived in Spain, and I was meeting him in Toledo the following day*

Here the previous perfective present, *have -en*, in the first clause, becomes previous perfective past, *had -en*; and the particular future, *am -ing*, in the second clause, because particular future in past, *was -ing*.

This relocation into the past only applies to particular future, not to established future. (The established future, as in *I meet him tomorrow*, can only become a simple (actual perfective) past, as *I met him* (*yesterday*).)

## 7.5. Irrealis and aspect

The aspectual parameters perfective/imperfective and actual/previous—described above for present and past realis—also apply for irrealis status, marked by a modal (§6.1.1). For example (illustrating with verb *live*):

|  | PRESENT REALIS | | NECESSITY MODAL | |
|---|---|---|---|---|
|  | ACTUAL | PREVIOUS | ACTUAL | PREVIOUS |
| PERFECTIVE | *lives* | *has lived* | *must live* | *must have lived* |
| IMPERFECTIVE | *is living* | *has been living* | *must be living* | *must have been living* |

The exceptions appear to be that modal *can* and semi-modal *is able to* are not used with imperfective or with previous aspect. That is, one would not say, for example, *\*can be doing*, or *\*is able to have done*; *could* is used instead—*could be doing, could have done*.

However, past tense does not apply to irrealis when expressed by a modal (save for the scheduled activity modal, *be to*), except in the context of back-shifting, discussed in §7.6.

As pointed out in §6.1.1, modals and semi-modals differ in that a modal cannot follow another verb, whereas a semi-modal may occur anywhere within a sequence of verbs. A further difference is that semi-modals behave like regular verbs in showing present and past forms; thus, alongside *has to live, has to have lived*, etc., we get *had to live, had to have lived*, etc. Notwithstanding these grammatical differences, modals and semi-modals are linked to the same set of modal categories, within irrealis status (as described in §6.1.1).

## 7.6. Back-shifting

What is called 'back-shifting', mentioned in §2.7, relates to change of tense-aspect marking in a clause, when direct speech is converted to indirect speech. Compare:

(35)  *'John is hungry,' Fred told us*
(35')  *Fred told us that John was hungry*
(36)  *'Mary is having to leave,' Jane said*
(36')  *Jane said that Mary was having to leave*
(37)  *'Charlie ate the chocolate biscuits,' Kate announced*
(37')  *Kate announced that Charlie had eaten the chocolate biscuits*
(38)  *'Charlie has been eating the chocolate biscuits,' Kate announced*
(38')  *Kate announced that Charlie had been eating the chocolate biscuits*

The formula for back-shifting is:

| FORM IN DIRECT SPEECH | BACK-SHIFTED FORM IN INDIRECT SPEECH | FORM IN DIRECT SPEECH | BACK-SHIFTED FORM IN INDIRECT SPEECH |
|---|---|---|---|
| -s | -ed | is -ing | was -ing |
| -ed } has -en } had -en } | had -en | was -ing } has been -ing } had been -ing } | had been -ing |

That is, actual present becomes actual past, but all of actual past, previous present and previous past become previous past; this applies to perfective and to imperfective.

As noted in the discussion of (60)–(63) in §2.7, something similar to back-shifting occurs in the correspondence between THAT and TO complement clauses. For example, *I believe that Mary eats mangoes* corresponds to *I believe Mary to eat mangoes*, with *that . . . -s* corresponding to *to* plus the base form of the verb. Similarly, *-ed, has . . . -en* and *had . . . -en* all correspond to *to have* (base form). . . . *-en*.

It is instructive now to examine how back-shifting applies to modals and semi-modals. Semi-modals show present and past tense, and behave like other verbs under back-shifting; for example:

(39)  *'John isn't able to tie his shoelaces,' Mary remarked*
(39′)  *Mary remarked that John wasn't able to tie his shoelaces*

However, in modern English modals have no past tense forms. How then are they back-shifted? Here are some examples:

(40)  *'It will rain this afternoon,' she said*
(40′)  *She said that it would rain that afternoon*
(41)  *'I shan't go,' I said*
(41′)  *I said that I wouldn't go*
(42)  *'I ought to do it,' she said*
(42′)  *She said that she should do it*
(43)  *'I must go,' I said*
(43′)  *I said that I had to go*
(44)  *'I may get the job,' Mary speculated*
(44′)  *Mary speculated that she might get the job*

Examining each of the modals listed at the beginning of §6.1.1, we find:

| FORM IN DIRECT SPEECH | BACK-SHIFTED FORM IN INDIRECT SPEECH | FORM IN DIRECT SPEECH | BACK-SHIFTED FORM IN INDIRECT SPEECH |
|---|---|---|---|
| *will* *would* *shall* | *would* | *can* *could* | *could* |
| *should* *ought to* | *should* | *may* *might* | *might* |
| *must* | *had to* | *is to* | *was to* |

At an earlier stage of the language, four of what are now modals did exist in present and past forms:

| PRESENT | *will* | *shall* | *can* | *may* |
|---|---|---|---|---|
| PAST | *would* | *should* | *could* | *might* |

Nowadays, *would, should, could* and *might* function as modals in their own right. But the historical tense connection is echoed in back-shifting. *Would* is the back-shifted version of *will* (as it should be, were it the past form of *will*) and also of *would*; similarly for the other three. *Should* now indicates obligation, quite different from the prediction of *shall*, and the back-shift for *shall*—as for *will* and *would*—is *would*.

It was remarked in §6.1.1 that it is hard to discern any semantic difference between *should* and *ought to*. In keeping with this, *should* can be used as the back-shift equivalent of *should* and also *ought to* (although it is also possible for *ought to* to function as its own backshift). In §6.1.1, modal *must* and semi-modal *has to* were linked as alternative ways of expressing necessity modality. *Had to* functions as back-shifted version of both, demonstrating the close semantic link between modals and semi-modals, despite their differing grammatical properties. Finally, *is to*, being the only modal to mark tense, has a regular back-shifted form *was to*.

## 7.7. Occurrence

All verbs occur with modals and semi-modals—for marking irrealis status—and all occur in generic tense (*-s*), in actual and previous perfective present (*-s* and *has -en*), and in actual and previous perfective past (*-ed* and *had -en*). However, there are restrictions on which verbs can occur with:

- realis future (*-s* and *is -ing*);
- realis present and past imperfective (*is -ing*, *was -ing*; and also *has/had been -ing*);
- imperative (base form of verb).

The restrictions relate to the meanings of verbs, and of tense-aspect and mood categories. We now briefly survey these, by semantic types of verbs.

**Primary-A types.** Verbs from the REST-d subtype, CONTAIN, which describe the relative positions of things, are unlikely to be used in imperative, realis future or imperfective. They include *contain*, *enclose*, *adjoin*, and *surround* when it has an inanimate subject.

Verbs taking an inanimate subject which refers to some natural phenomenon are unlikely to be found in realis future, since this should involve volitional planning. But they can occur freely in imperfective; for example, *It is snowing*, *The ice is melting*, *The fire is burning brightly*, *The river is flowing strongly*. Their use in imperatives depends on the speaker's inclination to give orders to inanimates. One might hear *Burn, damn you!* to a fire, *Blow, wind, blow!*, and *Please rain on my dry and dusty paddocks!*

Verbs in the DROP subtype, MOTION-g, describe activities which are generally non-volitional and these verbs are unlikely to be used in realis future—*fall*, *slip*, *capsize*. They can occur in imperfective (*She's slipping on the ice*) and in a mean-spirited imperative (*Fall down!*, said under one's breath to a fellow competitor in a race). Intransitive verbs from AFFECT-h—*break*, *chip*, *crack* and so on—would not occur in realis future nor (save in a fairy story) in imperative but are fine in imperfective.

Some verbs from the OWN subtype of GIVING could not felicitously be used in imperatives—*own*, *lack*, *possess*, *belong to*. Only in an unusual context could they be used in realis future, and (except for *lack*) they sound distinctly odd in imperfective.

**Primary-B types.** Verbs in the ACTING, DECIDING and ATTENTION types are generally acceptable in imperative, realis future and imperfective. However, *see* and *hear* have restricted use in all of these, *look* and *listen* generally being preferred. There are limited possibilities for imperatives—*Hear this!* and *See with your own eyes!*

Most THINKING verbs can be used in imperative and imperfective. A few, including *consider* and *conclude*, are acceptable in realis future—*They consider the report tomorrow*—but most are not. Some THINKING verbs show severe limitations. *Believe* may be used in an imperative (*Believe me!*), but is very seldom found in realis future or in imperfective. It is just possible to invent a scenario in which *believe* takes imperfective:

(45)   *I was believing what he was saying until he mentioned he'd seen Elvis in the supermarket yesterday*

*Know* is scarcely used in imperative (perhaps *Know this!*, from an olden-days town crier, or *Know thy enemy!*) or in realis future. It is, though, generally possible, with a smidgeon of imagination, to contextualise a realis future with virtually any verb, however bizarre this might be. For example:

(45')   *He knows French today* (said of an actor who today will be playing a character envisaged by the playwright to be fluent in French)

However, it seems impossible to invent a plausible scenario in which one may use *know* with imperfective—*\*She is knowing*. This verb describes a state, which is *never* dynamic or evolving.

Verbs from the SPEAKING type are generally at home with imperative and imperfective but have limited possibilities for realis future. One can say *He writes his exam tomorrow*, *We pray at six o'clock*, or *We're discussing it at the get-together on Friday*. But for verbs such as *chat, shout, brag, threaten* and *argue*, realis future is unlikely in normal circumstances.

Quite a few verbs from the HAPPENING, COMPARING and RELATING types are unlikely to occur in imperative—*happen, resemble, differ from, result from/in, be due to*. Of these, only *happen* is readily used in imperfective. In addition, verbs such as *compare, measure* and *weigh* are typically used in the imperfective when transitive, as in:

(46)   *He is weighing the rubber*

However, when these verbs are used intransitively, only perfective is possible. One says:

(46')   *The rubber weighs thirty kilos*

rather than *\*The rubber is weighing thirty kilos*. Whereas (46) describes a dynamic activity, (46') does not. Most verbs in these three types are unlikely to be used in realis future.

Verbs from the LIKING and ANNOYING types are also excluded from realis future—*We like it tomorrow* and *He amuses me next week* are quite infelicitous. Imperative and imperfective are acceptable with ANNOYING verbs and with the LIKING-iii subtype (*enjoy, favour, object to*) but are not encountered much with LIKING-i/ii (*like, love, loathe*). However, it is possible with a stretch of the imagination to invent a context for *was liking*, as in:

(47)   *I was quite liking the performance until the first interval*

**Secondary types** (leaving aside MODALS and SEMI-MODALS). Secondary-D verbs (*seem, appear, matter*) are used with none of imperative, realis future and imperfective. Secondary-A and Secondary-C verbs generally take imperative and imperfective. Realis future is acceptable with the BEGINNING and TRYING types of Secondary-A and the HELPING type of Secondary-C but is scarcely plausible with HURRYING and DARING verbs or with most from the MAKING type. One can say *She bakes a cake tomorrow*, but realis future would be uncomfortable with *force, prevent* or *rescue*, for example; these are not activities which would in normal circumstances be planned for a definite future time.

Verbs of the Secondary-B WANTING type—such as *want, wish, hope, need, plan, intend*—have an implicit future reference and are not found in a realis future construction. Indeed, if one essays such a construction, with a time adverb included, this adverb is taken to refer to the verb of the complement clause rather than to the WANTING verb. For example, *He is hoping to go tomorrow* is taken to mean that *tomorrow* relates to the going rather than to the hoping. Almost all WANTING verbs may be used in the imperative and also in imperfective (although perfective is more common). The verb *want* stands out; it is seldom used in imperative (a rare example is *Only want what you can get!*) and not often in imperfective (although, in Old England, one might hear the butler saying to the footman *The duke is wanting his gin and tonic now, not in two hours' time*).

Verbs in the Secondary-B POSTPONING type—*postpone, defer, delay, avoid*—freely occur in imperative and imperfective but seldom in irrealis future. One would not normally plan to make a postponement at a later date; if this should happen, then *They're announcing the postponement of the egg-and-spoon race tomorrow* is preferred to *They're postponing the egg-and-spoon race tomorrow*.

**Copula clauses.** When the copula complement is an adjective, one would seldom encounter irrealis future. It takes a certain effort to imagine such a construction; one example of such an effort is:

(**48**)   *It's green tomorrow* (if by some edict we have to wear a different colour of clothing each day)

But in many circumstances irrealis future is not appropriate with adjective complements.

Only adjectives from the HUMAN PROPENSITY, SPEED and DIFFICULTY types, plus the main two VALUE adjectives, *good* and *bad*—which can all refer to some state achieved volitionally—may occur with imperative or with imperfective. For example:

(**49**)   *Your child is being stupid/rude/slow/difficult/good today*

It would take some effort to contextualise imperfective with adjectives from other semantic types; for example, *wide, heavy, young, red*.

Certain types of noun phrase in copula complement function may occur with realis established future. For instance:

(**50**)   *On the rotation principle, she's chair of the committee in March*

One can also use imperative or imperfective with noun phrase copula complements, especially in make-believe: *You be the doctor!* and *No, Mary's being the doctor today, I'm being the patient.*


## Notes to Chapter 7

The treatment of tense and aspect in this chapter is basically original. Many works have provided useful discussion of the topic, especially Leach and Svartvik (1975: 63–82), but also including Quirk et al. (1985: 93–239), Huddleston and Pullum (2002: 71–212), Prince (1982) and the multitude of further references therein.

# 8

## *I know that it seems that he'll make me want to describe her starting to say that she knows that it seems that . . .*
## Complement clauses

There are, as outlined in §2.7, seven kinds of complement clause, which can fill the object or subject (or, sometimes, a post-object) slot in a main clause. All Secondary and Primary-B verbs take complement clauses—but each one allows only some of the full range of complement clause possibilities. Which complement clauses a given verb may accept is determined by the meaning of the verb and the meanings of the complement clause constructions.

In §8.2 we outline the meanings of the different kinds of complement clause. §§8.3–4 then deal with Secondary and Primary-B types, one at a time, looking at the overall meaning of each type and the specific meanings of individual verbs within the type, thus providing a semantic explanation for the complement clauses that occur. §8.1 deals briefly with 'parentheticals', which are related to THAT complement constructions.

We can recapitulate here the kinds of complement clause (from the account in §2.7):

(i)   THAT. The initial *that* may often be omitted when it immediately follows the main clause predicate.

(ii)   WH-. This is introduced by *whether/if*, or by any other *wh-* word, e.g. *who, what, where, when, how, why*; this *wh-* introducer may not be omitted.

(iii)   ING. The complement clause subject, if included, may in some circumstances be marked by *'s*.

(iv)   Modal (FOR) TO. If the complement clause subject is omitted, then *for* is also dropped. *For* may (with some verbs) or must (with others) be omitted when the complement clause subject is retained, and this then becomes surface structure object of the main verb.

(v)   Judgement TO. Cannot undergo any NP omission. Complement clause predicate most often begins with *be*.

(vi)   WH- TO. Similar to a Modal (FOR) TO construction where the complement clause subject is omitted under coreferentiality with main clause subject or object, and the complement clause is introduced by *whether* (not *if*) or by any other *wh-* word except *why*.

(vii)   FROM ING. An ING clause with the subject (which is also surface object of the main clause) followed by *from*, the *from* being optionally omissible after one set of main verbs.

THAT and WH- complements have the full structure of a clause—they involve tense inflection, and may include a Modal. The other five kinds of complement clause cannot include either tense or a Modal. A subject must be stated for THAT, WH-, Judgement TO and FROM ING clauses, but can be omitted from ING and Modal (FOR) TO complements, and must be omitted from WH- TO clauses.

Some verbs that take an ING or Modal (FOR) TO complement must omit the complement clause subject (e.g. *begin*); others can optionally omit it (e.g. *like*); a further set must retain it (e.g. *see, allow*). A complement clause in object function, with no stated subject, is taken to have underlying subject coreferential with main clause subject; if the complement clause is in subject function, its underlying subject is taken to be coreferential with main clause object. Thus, *Mary didn't know where to put the box*, and *Where to put the box perplexed Mary*.

A THAT, WH- or Modal (FOR) TO (but, generally, not an ING) complement clause in subject function may be extraposed to the end of the main clause, provided there is not also a complement clause in object or other post-predicate position.

It is important to repeat here one of the most important rules of English grammar: a preposition must be omitted before complementisers *that*, *for* and *to*. (It may optionally be omitted before a *wh-* word introducing a complement clause.)

The theoretical stance of this study involves investigating how semantic categories are mapped onto syntactic categories. The mapping is generally many-to-one. Thus, a number of semantic types are associated with each grammatical word class. A number of semantic roles correspond to each syntactic relation, e.g. Perceiver (with ATTENTION verbs), Speaker (with SPEAKING verbs), Experiencer (with LIKING verbs), Agent (with AFFECT verbs) all relate to the A (transitive subject) syntactic relation.

In a similar way, semantically diverse expressions may be mapped onto the same syntactic construction. Compare *They began eating the chicken* with *They discussed eating the chicken*; these are syntactically identical, with main verbs *began* and *discussed*, and complement clause *eating the chicken*. But *They began eating the chicken* describes an activity of 'eating', with *begin* being a Secondary verb that provides aspectual-type modification (and would in some languages be realised through a derivational affix to 'eat'). In contrast, *They discussed eating the chicken* describes a discussion, and the topic of the discussion is eating the chicken.

The seven kinds of complement clause cover a wide semantic range. Consider:

- all BEGINNING verbs take ING complements, most also take a reduced Modal (FOR) TO;
- all WANTING verbs take Modal (FOR) TO complement, most also take THAT;
- all THINKING verbs take THAT or WH- complements, most also take Judgement TO, some ING, and a few Modal (FOR) TO;
- all LIKING verbs take ING, most also THAT, and some Modal (FOR) TO.

A given kind of complement clause may be applicable to all members of a certain type (because of the meaning of the type, and of the complement construction), but to just some members of another type (depending on the specific meanings of certain verbs within that type).

There are many examples in this chapter of a single syntactic construction being used to code a variety of diverse semantic configurations.

## 8.1. Parentheticals

There will usually be some SPEAKING verb introducing any segment of direct speech. This can come at the end of the direct speech, or it can interrupt it after the subject or after the first word (or a later word) of the auxiliary; or, less usually, it could come at the beginning. The word preceding a clause-internal parenthetical bears major stress (shown by '), and there is appositional intonation (shown in writing by commas) on the parenthetical. Thus:

**(1a)** *'John has been drinking absinthe again,' Mary remarked*
**(1b)** *''John', Mary remarked, 'has been drinking absinthe again'*
**(1c)** *'John 'has', Mary remarked, 'been drinking absinthe again'*
**(1d)** *Mary remarked: 'John has been drinking absinthe again'*

Direct speech can always be encoded as indirect speech, using a THAT complement clause, as in (2). And there are many THAT complement constructions which do not have any direct speech correspondents, as in (3).

**(2)** *Mary remarked (that) John had been drinking absinthe again*
**(3)** *I suspect (that) John has been visiting the fortune teller*

(The *that* complementiser may optionally be omitted when it immediately follows a transitive verb, as in (2) and (3).)

Now there is another construction type which shows some similarities to—but also important differences from—the THAT complement construction:

**(4a)** *'John, I suspect, has been visiting the fortune teller*
**(4b)** *John 'has, I suspect, been visiting the fortune teller*
**(4c)** *John has been visiting the fortune teller, I suspect*

There are exactly parallel sentences relating to (2): *Mary remarked* could be inserted after *John,* or after *John had,* or after the whole of *John had been drinking absinthe again.*

In (4a–c) the complement clause, from (3), has become the main clause and the original subject-plus-main-verb, *I suspect,* becomes a parenthetical insert which can come at any of the positions normally open to a clause introducing direct speech, as in (1a–c)—after the subject, or after the first auxiliary verb (or perhaps after a later auxiliary verb, or after the entire auxiliary constituent and before the main verb), or at the end of the sentence. The parenthetical insertion must be set off from the rest of the sentence—by commas in writing, or by appositional intonation when speaking; and, as for a direct speech introducer, the preceding word is stressed for a clause-internal parenthetical. The positional possibilities are similar to those for a contrastive linker such as *however* or *moreover*; see §2.12. There is a significant difference between parentheticals and contrastive linkers, on the one hand, and sentential adverbs; see §12.3.1.

A parenthetical may not normally come at the beginning of the sentence and remain parenthetical. If it occurs initially then it becomes the main clause and what was the main clause in (4a–c) becomes a complement clause, as in (3); the whole sentence is now a single intonation unit. (The verb *reckon*—in the sense 'think', not the sense 'calculate'—may for many speakers only occur in a parenthetical. In this case the parenthetical can occur sentence-initially, e.g. *I reckon he's crazy*; note that *that* may not be included before *he's crazy* here.)

A parenthetical construction can parallel any kind of sentence which includes a THAT complement clause coming after the verb. It could be one in object function, as in (4a–c), or one in post-object function, as in:

**(5a)**   *He promised me (that) the building will be ready on time*
**(5b)**   *The building 'will, he promised me, be ready on time*

Or a THAT complement clause which has been extraposed from subject function, as in (6a–b), or even from derived passive subject function, as in (7b–c) (a corresponding active is given in (7a)):

**(6a)**   *It is correct that Mary is a genius*
**(6b)**   *Mary 'is, it is correct, a genius*
**(7a)**   *People suspect (that) John has visited the fortune teller*
**(7b)**   *It is suspected (that) John has visited the fortune teller*
**(7c)**   *John 'has, it is suspected, visited the fortune teller*

There is a difference in meaning between sentences like (3) and (4a–c). Sentence (3) asserts a suspicion and details what it is (through a complement clause). Sentences (4a–c) assert that John has been visiting the fortune teller and then qualify the assertion by *I suspect*, which has a similar function to an adverb such as *allegedly*, *presumably* or *probably*.

The difference in meaning can be shown by a specific example. Suppose that a lady customer storms into the manager's outer office and tells his secretary that she has been short-changed. The secretary listens, and forms her own judgement. Then she takes the customer into the manager, and might say either (8a) or (8b):

(**8a**)   *This lady complains* (*that*) *she has been short-changed*

(**8b**)   *This lady 'has, she complains, been short-changed*

By uttering (8b) the secretary would be asserting that the customer had been short-changed, i.e. the manager would gather that the secretary was convinced that the complaint was a valid one. But if (8a) were uttered the secretary would be making no judgement at all, merely reporting the complaint.

A parenthetical is most often short, consisting of subject and verb or, just occasionally, of subject, verb and object (as in (5b) and in *The last person to leave 'must, the boss has instructed Fred, turn out the lights*). Subject and object are likely to be short—consisting just of a pronoun, or proper name, or article plus common noun. This is simply because a long parenthetical would be likely to provide too severe a disruption of the main clause, and make the listener lose track of what is happening. (Thus, one is most unlikely to encounter a parenthetical of the length of *The apartment 'will, our absentee landlord who lives in Florida and usually only communicates with us through his agent told my absent-minded but well-meaning room-mate, be sold after Christmas*.)

A parenthetical generally provides a simple statement, and is very unlikely to have a negative predicate; in (4a–c) *I suspect* could not be replaced by *I didn't suspect*. The most common situation is for the verb in a parenthetical to be in generic tense. But past tense is also possible (as in the parenthetical versions of (2), with *Mary remarked*), as are previous and/or imperfective aspect (for, example, *She 'is, we have been assuming, available on those dates*). We also find imperative parentheticals, e.g. *Tomorrow 'is, don't forget, a public holiday*, corresponding to the THAT complement construction *Don't forget* (*that*) *tomorrow is a public holiday!*; and interrogative parentheticals, e.g. *Has 'he, I wonder, enough stamina for the task?*

Every verb that occurs in parentheticals takes a THAT complement clause, but not vice versa. Thus, a syntactic analysis that derived parentheticals, like (4a–c), from complement clause constructions, such as (3), would be perfectly valid so long as due account was taken of the semantic differences involved.

We can now turn to the question of which verbs occur in parentheticals, dealing first with Primary and then with Secondary types. It appears that almost every verb in a Primary type—other than LIKING and ANNOYING—which takes a THAT complement clause can be used parenthetically. There is one qualification—the verb must have a positive meaning. Thus, just as we cannot have an overt negative in a parenthetical (*I didn't suspect) so we cannot have a verb that is inherently negative, such as forget or doubt. We can, however, get a 'double negative', in the form of not plus a negative verb, e.g. don't forget, exemplified in the last paragraph but one, and don't doubt, in Mary 'is, I don't doubt, a good doctor.

Primary verbs that are used in parentheticals include all those from ATTEN-TION which take a THAT complement (except watch and listen, which have a special sense of the THAT construction—see §8.4.1), e.g. see, hear, notice, discover, witness; from THINKING, e.g. think, imagine, suppose, speculate, dream, remember, know, learn, understand, conclude, argue, believe; from DECIDING, e.g. decide, resolve, choose; and from SPEAKING, e.g. shout, read, say, joke, report, regret, explain, suggest, undertake, promise, instruct, warn.

It appears that very few verbs from the ANNOYING type may felicitously be used in parentheticals, e.g. not *He 'is, it annoys/delights me, going to France on vacation corresponding to It annoys/delights me that he is going to France on vacation; however, we do get He 'is, it might interest you to know, going to France on vacation. LIKING verbs which take a THAT complement generally include the impersonal pronoun it before this constituent. Two verbs that do not are fear and rejoice, and they appear to be the only members of the type to occur in parentheticals.

Turning now to the Secondary type WANTING, parentheticals are possible with hope, expect, pretend and perhaps with plan and intend (and with wish only when there is an impersonal subject, e.g. one might wish) but not with other members of this type such as desire and require. Consider:

(9a)   I hope (that) he will come today
(9b)   He 'will, I hope, come today

Sentence (9a) simply conveys a hope, and the addressee has no way of knowing what chance there is of it becoming realised. But on hearing (9b) one would infer that there is a very good chance of his coming—this is an assertion that he will come, quantified by the parenthetical I hope.

Now compare (9a) with sentences that show no corresponding parenthetical construction:

(10)   I desire (that) he should come today
(11)   I require that they (should) report at the office on arrival

Hope describes the Principal's thought that something may happen, and they may also have a good idea that it is likely to happen (as in (9b)). In contrast, desire simply comments on the Principal's eagerness that something should happen, and *require* on their opinion that something should be done—in neither case is there likely to be any degree of expectation that the something will eventuate. It is this expectation which is necessary for a WANTING verb to be used in a parenthetical, as in (9b).

Only *ensure* from the MAKING type accepts a THAT complement clause and this may be used as a parenthetical, e.g. *The property 'will, the contract ensures, revert to its original owner.* The Secondary-D verb *matter* can never be in a parenthetical.

Of the adjectives that may take a THAT complement, the VALUE and HUMAN PROPENSITY types (many of whose members have a similar meaning to LIKING and ANNOYING verbs) are not found in parentheticals. Most QUALIFICATION adjectives which take THAT complements may be used in parentheticals, e.g. *The King 'will, it is definite/probable/true/likely/certain/ correct/right, visit this province in the spring.* (As before, negative forms such as *improbable, untrue* and *wrong* are excluded from parentheticals.)

Both *probable* and *possible* may occur in a parenthetical, e.g. *He 'will, it is probable, announce an election for next month* and *He 'may, it is possible, announce an election for next month.* Note that *probable*, implying a high chance, is compatible with modal *will* in the main clause, whereas *possible*, implying a much smaller chance, is more compatible with *may.*

Verbs of the SEEM type may appear in a parenthetical with an appropriate adjective (those exemplified in the last paragraph but one), e.g. *The King 'will, it seems definite/likely/etc., visit this province in the spring. Seem, happen* and *appear* may also appear alone in a parenthetical, e.g. *John 'is, it seems/appears/happens, a very polite person.*

Parentheticals may occur at the same syntactic positions as sentential adverbs (see §12.3.1) and often have a similar semantic effect. Thus, *definitely* may be substituted for *it is definite* with very little change in meaning, and also *probably, certainly, hopefully.* Some adverbs are roughly equivalent to parentheticals with first person subject, or with subject coreferential with main clause subject, e.g. *She will, regrettably, have to sell her car* could relate to *She 'will, I regret, have to sell her car* or to *She 'will, she regrets, have to sell her car* but scarcely to *She 'will, Fred regrets, have to sell her car.* Some are roughly equivalent to parentheticals with third person subject, e.g. *reportedly* to *he/she reports* but not to *I report* or *You report.*

Many verbs and adjectives used in parentheticals do not have a corresponding adverb. And for some which do have, the adverb has a quite different meaning. Compare *The King 'will, it is correct, enter by the front door* (i.e. this is a correct statement of what he will do) with *The King will, correctly, enter by the front door* (he will act in a correct manner).

## 8.2. Meanings of complement clauses

Each of the seven varieties of complement clause has a meaning—and range of use—relative to the other choices from the system. It is thus especially profitable to contrast their meanings, taking them two or three at a time.

### 8.2.1. THAT *and* WH-

A THAT complement refers to some definite event or state. Thus:

**(12)**   *I know that John is on duty today*

WH- complements involve either (i) *whether* or *if*, which enquires about a complement event or state; or (ii) another *wh-* word (*who, what, which, why*, etc.), which enquires about some aspect of an event or state. They may be the indirect speech correspondents of questions, e.g. *They asked whether he is sick, She enquired who was sick.* WH- complements also occur with many verbs not concerned with speaking, then referring to something about which clarification is needed, e.g.

**(13)**   *I (don't) know whether/if John is on duty today*
**(14)**   *I (don't) know who is on duty today/when John is on duty*

The most typical pattern—with verbs like *know, hear, understand, remember, decide* and *remark*—is for a THAT complement to occur in a positive sentence and a WH- one in a negative one. Thus *I know that John is on duty today* and *I don't know whether John is on duty today*. But all WH-complements can be used without a negative, e.g. *I know whether John is on duty today*. And THAT clauses may be used with a negative, as in:

**(15a)**   *I don't know that John is on duty today*
**(15b)**   *I didn't know that John was on duty today*

Both (15a) and (15b) would be likely to be used when someone else had made an assertion that John is on duty today. By using (15a), in present tense, the speaker declines to agree with the assertion—(15a) has a meaning not very different from *I don't believe that John is on duty today*. Sentence (15b), in past tense, indicates not so much disagreement as surprise—the speaker thought that they knew John's duty days, and hadn't realised today was one of them.

Verbs like *ponder*, *speculate*, *wonder* and *guess* tend to relate to some matter that requires clarification, and typically take a WH- complement without also including *not* (although they can also accept *not*), e.g. *I wondered whether/when I would get released, She guessed what he would be wearing/who would come*.

*Doubt* has an inherently negative meaning and commonly takes a *whether* complement in a positive clause; it also takes a THAT complement. There is a subtle difference in meaning—*I doubt that he is sick* is most likely to imply disagreement with an assertion which has been made that he is sick, whereas *I doubt whether he is sick* could be used when no one has seriously suggested that he was sick, but the idea has just been floated as one possible explanation for his absence. A negative sentence with *doubt* may take a THAT complement, e.g. *I don't doubt that he is sick*, and is very close in meaning to the positive assertion *I believe that he is sick*. A negative statement with *doubt* does not permit a *whether* complement, *\*I don't doubt whether he is sick* (it is as if a double negation does not make sense in connection with an appeal for clarification); but note that a negative question with *doubt* may take a *whether* complement, e.g. *Don't you doubt whether he ever intended to do it?*

Verbs *ask*, *request*, and *enquire* can refer to an act of questioning and are then restricted to a WH- complement clause. *Ask*—but not *enquire*—has a second sense of 'ordering' and then takes a THAT complement, which will generally include a modal, e.g. *I asked that he (should) clean the stables*.

Almost all verbs that take WH- complements also take THAT clauses. The few exceptions include *enquire* (mentioned in the last paragraph) and *discuss*, which must refer to some ongoing activity (through an ING complement) or to something about which clarification is sought (through a WH- clause). There are a fair number of verbs that take a THAT but not a WH- complement, e.g. *believe*, *assume*, *suppose*, which make unequivocal assertions, and *order*, *urge*, which issue instructions.

The LIKING and ANNOYING types describe an Experiencer's feelings about a Stimulus, something which is not compatible with a clause that indicates a need for clarification; most verbs from these types take THAT clauses but none accept WH- complements. A number of Secondary verbs take THAT complements but these essentially provide semantic qualification of the verb of the complement clause, and again it would not be appropriate to have a WH- clause in this function. We can thus say both *I didn't know (that) it was you* (sc. coming) and *I hoped (that) it was you* (sc. coming) but only *I didn't know who it was*, with the Primary verb *know*, not *I hoped who it was*, since *hope* is a Secondary verb. (A WH- clause is possible with the Secondary-D verb *matter*, e.g. *Whether he wins matters to me*.)

Of the adjectives that take complement clauses, WH- complements are found in subject function with a handful that have negative meanings, e.g. *be unsure*, *be uncertain*, and with others when there is a negative in the sentence, e.g. *not be certain*, as in *It is not certain whether he will come*. WH-complements may also occur after some HUMAN PROPENSITY adjectives, e.g. *He is curious (about) where we'll sleep tonight*, *She is interested (in) whether we'll be allowed in*.

(In any investigation of WH- complement clauses one must take special care to distinguish these from fused relatives, such as *I like who my daughter married*, i.e. I like the person who my daughter married, and *I like what you have*, i.e. I like that which you have. See §§2.6–7.)

In §2.7 we mentioned a group of verbs which commonly take the obligation modal *should* in a THAT complement; in fact, the meanings of the verbs imply obligation and they may freely omit the *should*, e.g. *He suggests that we (should) go tomorrow*. These verbs include *order*, *urge*, *recommend* and others from the ORDER subtype of SPEAKING; *propose*, *suggest* and *insist*; and a very limited sense of *want* (as in *I want that you (should) be satisfied*).

## 8.2.2. THAT and ING

A THAT complement essentially refers to some activity or state as a single unit, without any reference to its inherent constitution or time duration. In contrast, an ING complement refers to an activity or state as extended in time, perhaps noting the way in which it unfolds. Compare:

(**16a**)  *I heard that John had slapped his sister*
(**16b**)  *I heard John('s) slapping his sister*
(**17a**)  *He thought that Mary would apply for the job*
(**17b**)  *He thought of Mary('s) applying for the job*

Sentence (16a) states that I heard a piece of news, whereas (16b) implies that I overheard what actually happened—the noise of palm hitting arm, the girl's screams, etc. And (17a) states an opinion that the application would be made, where (17b) may be taken to relate to how she would go about it—searching for pencil and paper, wondering how to frame the letter, then buying a stamp.

Some verbs are, by virtue of their meaning, restricted to only one of these complement constructions. *Suppose*, which relates to whether or not something might happen or have happened, may only take THAT. The meaning of *describe* implies reference to the unfolding of an activity, and this verb is restricted to an ING complement.

For many verbs THAT and ING complements show considerable overlap in meaning and use. But there is always an implicit—or potential—semantic contrast, along the lines we have described. Consider *propose*, in

(**18a**)   *I propose (our) walking from John o' Groats to Land's End to raise money for charity*
(**18b**)   *I propose that we (should) do the walk in the spring*
(**18c**)   *I propose that we (should) forget the whole thing*

Each of (18a–c) could have a THAT or an ING complement. The ING alternative sounds fine in (18a), since it introduces the idea of a continuous activity. For (18b) a THAT construction is preferred—the walk is now being referred to as an 'event' and a time suggested for it. Sentence (18c) again refers to the walk as a 'unit'; the ING alternative to (18c), *\*I propose (our) forgetting the whole idea*, sounds particularly infelicitous.

There is another factor which motivates the choice between THAT and ING complement clauses: only an ING construction allows the complement clause subject to be omitted when it is coreferential with an appropriate main clause constituent. There is, in most styles of English, a preference to omit a repeated constituent and—all else being equal, or nearly equal—an ING complement may be preferred to a THAT one for this reason. Thus, if I were the only person planning to walk the length of Britain, then *I propose doing the walk in the spring* might be preferred to *I propose that I (should) do the walk in the spring*. Or, consider *regret*, which can take a THAT or ING complement, as in:

(**19a**)   *I regret that they didn't walk out of that film when the violence started*
(**19b**)   *I regret their not walking out of that film when the violence started*

Native speakers find (19a) and (19b) about equally acceptable. However, when the complement clause subject is coreferential with main clause subject they exhibit a preference for the ING construction, *I regret not walking out ...*, over the THAT one, *I regret that I didn't walk out ...* (although the latter is still considered grammatical).

The predicate of a THAT complement clause must involve a tense inflection, and can include any of: a Modal, previous aspect *have*, imperfective aspect *be*. An ING clause may not include tense or a Modal. The time reference of an ING clause can often be inferred from the lexical meaning of the main verb, e.g. in (18a) it is taken to refer to something projected for the future because *propose* has an inherently future meaning, and in (19b) to something which took place in the past, because of the meaning of *regret*. Note that past time can be shown in an ING or TO complement clause by the *have* auxiliary (see §2.7). An alternative to (19b) is *I regret their not having walked out ...* But to include *have* here would be a little pedantic, since the past tense reference of the ING clause in (19b) can adequately be inferred from the meaning of the main verb *regret*.

### 8.2.3. Modal (FOR) TO, Judgement TO, and THAT

There is, at first blush, syntactic similarity between constructions like (20)–(21) and those like (22)–(23).

(**20**)  *I want Mary to be a doctor*
(**21**)  *She forced him to recite a poem*
(**22**)  *I discovered him to be quite stupid*
(**23**)  *We had assumed Mary to be a doctor*

In fact (20)–(21) are examples of Modal (FOR) TO complement constructions, while (22)–(23) are Judgement TO constructions. There are considerable semantic and syntactic differences, which fully justify the recognition of two varieties of complement clause both involving *to*.

Modal (FOR) TO complements relate to the subject of the complement clause becoming involved in the activity or state referred to by that clause, or to the potentiality of such involvement. Thus: *I am hoping for John to go tomorrow*, *I wish ( for) Mary to accompany me*. The *for* may optionally be omitted after certain main verbs (with a semantic effect), the complement clause subject then becoming surface object to the main verb; this is discussed in §8.2.4. Note that some verbs must retain *for*, e.g. *hope*, whereas some must omit it, e.g. *force*.

It is always possible—and often obligatory—for the subject to be omitted from a Modal (FOR) TO clause when it is coreferential with an NP in the main clause; *for* is then also omitted. If the complement clause is in subject function then its subject is omitted under coreferentiality with main clause object, e.g. *(For Mary) to have to travel so much annoys John.* If the complement clause is in object function then its subject may be omitted under coreferentiality with main clause subject, e.g. *I don't want (Mary) to travel so much.* If the complement clause is in post-object slot with verbs of the ORDER subtype then its subject is omitted under coreferentiality with main clause object, e.g. *I asked (the matron for) Mary to nurse me.*

Many verbs that take a Modal (FOR) TO complement also accept a THAT complement clause. The meaning of the (FOR) TO construction is often similar to the meaning of the THAT construction when a Modal is included. Compare:

(24a)  *I wish that John would go*
(24b)  *I wish ( for) John to go*
(25a)  *I decided that Mary should give the vote of thanks*
(25b)  *I decided for Mary to give the vote of thanks*
(26a)  *I decided that I would give the vote of thanks*
(26b)  *I decided to give the vote of thanks*
(27a)  *I expect that Mary will be appointed*
(27b)  *I expect Mary to be appointed*
(28a)  *I ordered that the flag should be raised*
(28b)  *I ordered the flag to be raised*

It seems here as if the complementiser *to* carries the same sort of semantic load as a Modal does in a THAT clause; this is why we refer to this variety of complement as 'Modal' (FOR) TO.

Some verbs which take both Modal (FOR) TO and THAT complements are seldom found without a Modal in the THAT clause. But others may freely include or omit a Modal. Alongside (25a) and (26a) we get:

(29)  *I decided that I was sick*

There is no (FOR) TO correspondent of (29). We do get *I decided to be sick*, but this is most similar in meaning to *I decided that I would be sick*, which does include a Modal.

Although a Modal (FOR) TO construction will frequently have a similar meaning to a THAT construction with a Modal, they will never be exactly synonymous. Compare:

(30a)  *I remembered that I should lock the door* (but then decided not to, as a way of asserting my distaste for authority)

(30b)  *I remembered to lock the door* (but then Mary took the key and pushed it down a grating, so I couldn't)

The THAT clause in (30a) simply records a fact, what my obligation was; it says nothing about my attitude to that obligation. A (FOR) TO complement, as in (30b), refers to the involvement in an activity of the subject of the complement clause (which is here coreferential with the subject of the main clause). The unmarked situation is that the subject would if at all possible become so involved, i.e. on hearing just *I remembered to lock the door* one would infer that the speaker did lock it. The subject would only not become involved if something outside their control intervened, as in the parenthesis added onto (30b).

A further pair of sentences exhibiting the delicate semantic contrast between THAT (with a Modal) and Modal (FOR) TO is:

(31a)  *John and Mary have decided that they will get married* (e.g. when both have completed their professional qualifications)

(31b)  *John and Mary have decided to get married* (e.g. next month)

Sentence (31a) announces an intention to get married; no date need yet have been mooted. But (31b) carries an implication that they have definite plans to marry in the foreseeable future.

Judgement TO complements have a rather different meaning. The subject of the main clause verb ventures a judgement or opinion about the subject of the complement clause predicate (this semantic characterisation will be expanded in §8.4.3). Most often the judgement is about some state or property which is either transitory, e.g. *I noticed John to be asleep*, or else a matter of opinion, e.g. *They declared Fred to be insane*. A Judgement TO construction is unlikely to be used to describe some permanent, objective property; thus, one would be unlikely to hear ?*He noticed her to be Chinese* (only *He noticed that she was Chinese*). And most often the subject of the Judgement TO clause is human—?*I believe that glass to be unbreakable* sounds rather odd.

Whereas a Modal (FOR) TO complement can fill subject, object or post-object slot, a Judgement TO clause must immediately follow a transitive verb, effectively in object function. There is never any *for*, and the under-lying complement clause subject is surface syntactic object of the main verb. This constituent is seldom coreferential with main clause subject (since it is relatively unusual to make judgements about oneself); when it is, it can never be omitted. Compare the Modal (FOR) TO construction *I want Mary to win* and, with optional coreferential omission, *I want (myself) to win*, with the Judgement TO constructions *I consider Mary (to be) cleverer than Fred* and *I consider myself to be cleverer than Fred*. *Myself* cannot be omitted from the last example.

A Judgement TO construction is frequently found with the main clause passivised, often so as to avoid specifying who is responsible for the judgement, e.g. *He was declared to be insane*. In fact, the verb *say* only takes a Judgement TO complement in the passive, e.g. *Mary is said to be a good cook* (but not *\*They say Mary to be a good cook*).

The predicate of a Judgement TO clause most often begins with *be*. This can be the copula *be*, as in *I reported John to be absent today*; or passive *be*, as in *I believed John to be beaten*; or imperfective *be*, as in *I suspect him to be hiding in the shrubbery, eavesdropping on what we are saying*. Past tense can be shown—as in ING and Modal (FOR) TO complements—by the inclusion of *have*, e.g. *I believed John to have been beaten*. It is possible to have Judgement TO complements without *be*, as in (33b), but they are relatively rare. (There is a special kind of Judgement TO construction with the SEEM type, and here complements without *be* are commoner—see §§6.4.1, 8.3.5.)

All verbs which take Judgement TO also accept a THAT complement clause, sometimes with a very similar meaning. Compare:

(32a)  *I know that Mary is clever*
(32b)  *I know Mary to be clever*
(33a)  *I know that Mary raced giraffes in Kenya*
(33b)  *I know Mary to have raced giraffes in Kenya*

Note that a Judgement TO complement corresponds semantically to a THAT clause without a Modal. It is of course possible to include a Modal in a THAT clause after *know*:

(34)   *I know that Mary may/must/should be clever*

But there is then no corresponding Judgement TO construction. A TO clause cannot include a Modal and there is no means of coding the information shown by the Modal in (34) into a Judgement TO construction. (It is also

relevant to note that a Judgement TO clause puts forward a specific assertion, and the inclusion of a Modal would be semantically incompatible with
this.)

This is a major difference between the two varieties of TO complement. A
Modal (FOR) TO clause frequently corresponds semantically to a THAT
clause with a Modal, as in (24)–(28). If a Modal is not included in the
THAT clause, as in (29), then there is no corresponding Modal (FOR) TO
construction. In contrast, a Judgement TO clause corresponds to a THAT
clause without a Modal, as in (32)–(33). Once a Modal is included in the
THAT clause, as in (34), there is no corresponding Judgement TO construction.

Many verbs take a Modal (FOR) TO complement in object slot and a fair
number take a Judgement TO clause, but only a handful may occur with
both. Those which do—*remember*, *know* and *learn*—never omit the *for*
from a Modal (FOR) TO clause when the complement clause subject is
included, so that there could be no difficulty in the listener spotting which
type of complement is being used. In fact these verbs most often have the
subject of a Modal (FOR) TO clause coreferential with main clause subject
and then omitted, as in (37b).

(35a)   *I remembered that Mary was very smart*
(35b)   *I remembered Mary to be very smart* (Judgement TO)
(36a)   *I remembered that Mary should sign the visitors' book*
(36b)   *I remembered for Mary to sign the visitors' book* (Modal (FOR) TO)
(37a)   *I remembered that I should sign the visitors' book*
(37b)   *I remembered to sign the visitors' book* (Reduced Modal (FOR) TO)

There is a further, rather special, kind of Modal (FOR) TO construction.
For some, but not all, verbs that take a (FOR) TO clause in object or post-
object slot there is a noun derived from the verb that can be head of the
subject NP, with the original subject becoming the possessor within this
NP; the main clause then has as its predicate head the copula *be*. Compare:

(38a)   *I had intended ( for) us to have lunch on top of the mountain*
(38b)   *My intention was for us to have lunch on top of the mountain*

Such a post-copula Modal (FOR) TO clause cannot omit the *for* if the
complement clause subject is retained. However, the complement clause
subject frequently is coreferential with the original main clause subject
(now possessor within the subject NP) and is then omitted, together with
*for*. Thus:

(39a)   *I hope to be chosen as captain*
(39b)   *My hope is to be chosen as captain*
(40a)   *She prefers to go in the evening*
(40b)   *Her preference is to go in the evening*

This construction is available to some verbs from the WANTING type—
*wish, desire, crave/craving, long/longing, hope, need, intend/intention, plan,
aim* (but not *want, mean, prepare*)—and to at least *prefer/preference* from
the LIKING type. Note that some of these verbs are unchanged in form when
used as a noun, while others have a derived form. (The forms and functions
of nominalisations are discussed in Chapter 10.)

*Warn* and *instruct* from the ORDER subtype take a post-object Modal
(FOR) TO complement. They enter into a similar construction (with nouns
*warning* and *instruction*) and here the original direct object is marked by
preposition *to*, within the subject NP, e.g.

(41a)   *I instructed the hired hands to keep out of the paddock*
(41b)   *My instruction to the hired hands was to keep out of the paddock*

In English there are wider possibilities for adjectival modification of a
noun than there are for adverbial modification of a verb. The (b) alternatives in (38)–(41) are likely to be used when such modification is desired.
We might find *my unwavering intention* in (38b), *my fondest hope* in (39b),
*her firm preference* in (40b) and *my strict instruction* in (41b). The corresponding adverbs either seem a little clumsy (*strictly*) or else have a different meaning (*fondly, firmly*), or are not really acceptable at all
(**unwaveringly*).

§§8.2.4–6 continue this discussion of kinds of TO complement, dealing
with the omission of *for*, the omission of *to* from Modal (FOR) TO, and the
omission of *to be* from both Judgement TO and Modal (FOR) TO.


## 8.2.4. The role of for in Modal (FOR) TO complements

A Modal (FOR) TO complement clause can be in subject, object or post-
object function in the main clause. When in object function it is open to
passivisation (although in fact Modal (FOR) TO complements seldom are
passivised, for semantic reasons—see Chapter 11). A Modal (FOR) TO clause
in subject—including derived passive subject—function is most often extraposed, as in (42b).

**(42a)**   *They had intended for Mary to lead the parade*
**(42b)**   *It had been intended for Mary to lead the parade*

A Modal complement clause can include *for* before its subject. Or it can omit the *for* while still retaining this underlying subject NP, which then becomes surface direct object of the main verb, as in (43a). It is this NP which is then subject to passivisation, as in (43b).

**(43a)**   *They had intended Mary to lead the parade*
**(43b)**   *Mary had been intended to lead the parade*

In §2.7 we stated that *for* can only be omitted when the complement clause immediately follows a transitive main verb (and gave a list of the other possible positions for a Modal (FOR) TO clause, when *for* must be retained). This is because the complement clause subject then becomes main clause object, and an object NP must immediately follow its verb.

In §2.5 we mentioned that an adverb cannot intrude between a verb and an NP object; however, it may come between verb and complement clause object. An adverbial phrase like *quite seriously* could in (42a) be placed after *had* or after *intended*; in (43a) it could only come after *had*, since here *intended* has an NP object.

What is the semantic consequence of omitting *for*? This can best be inferred from study of those verbs which do allow it to be either included or omitted. A pair of sentences with *choose* was given at (44)–(45) in §2.7. Consider also:

**(44a)**   *I had wished for Mary to win the prize*
**(44b)**   *I wish Mary to stand up*
**(45a)**   *I'd like it for you to kiss Auntie Daphne every time she calls*
**(45b)**   *I'd like you to kiss Auntie Daphne now* (she's just arrived)

(With LIKING an *it* is generally included before a Modal (FOR) TO clause; *it* drops when the *for* drops.)

A construction without *for* and with the underlying subject of the Modal (FOR) TO clause as main clause object is used when the sentence relates directly to the referent of that NP: (44b) might be used in addressing a class of children that included Mary; (45b) is an instruction to the addressee to kiss Auntie Daphne at once. In contrast, a construction with the *for* retained is likely to be used for a more general statement, without the same pragmatic pressure directed towards the complement clause subject. Sentence (44a) could be a wistful thought, which Mary wasn't even aware of; (45a) is a general request concerning what the addressee should do whenever an appropriate occasion arises, i.e. when Auntie Daphne calls. (Note that *it for* could be omitted from (45a), giving this sentence more pragmatic force; but *it for* could not be included in (45b).)

Similar semantic considerations apply to complement clauses—with and without *for*—following *intend*. Little difference may be discernible between (42a) and (43a) but when different NPs are chosen the contrast becomes plainer. Suppose I had understood that I was to lead the parade and then saw someone else in position. I would be more likely to say to the organiser *You said (that) you intended me to lead the parade*, rather than *You said (that) you intended for me to lead the parade*. Omitting *for* and making *me* (rather than the whole clause *for me to lead the parade*) the object of *intended* adds force to my complaint about how the organiser had wronged me in this instance.

In summary, when the activity referred to by the main clause relates directly to the subject of a Modal (FOR) TO complement clause, in object function, then the *for* will be omitted and the complement clause subject becomes surface direct object of the main verb.

Some verbs that take a Modal (FOR) TO complement never omit the *for* when the complement clause subject is retained, e.g. *hope, long, decide, undertake, remember*. The meanings of these verbs are incompatible with the pragmatic implications of having complement clause subject become main clause object. There is a second set of verbs that may either retain or omit the *for*—besides *intend, choose, wish, like* (and other LIKING verbs), this set includes *desire, propose, recommend, urge*.

A third class of verbs—including *want, need, require, order*—may have the verb followed by an adverb and then a complement beginning with *for*, but when there is no adverb the *for* will be omitted. Thus *I need most urgently for Mary to give me an injection* but only *I need Mary to give me an injection*, not (in most dialects) *\*I need for Mary to give me an injection*. It seems that the pragmatic force of these verbs is such that the complement clause subject should normally also be main clause object. But verbs of this class do not readily take an adverb between subject and verb (*?I most urgently need ...* sounds odd, although not totally impossible). Because of this there is a preference for the adverb to follow the verb and in such circumstances a *for* must be included.

A final class comprises Secondary-C verbs of the MAKING and HELPING types. The meanings of these verbs require complement clause subject to become main clause object, and *for* must be omitted. It is not permissible to include an adverb after a verb from these types, e.g. we can only say *He stupidly forced her to sign the paper*, not *\*He forced stupidly for her to sign the paper*.

The question as to whether *for* can be, or may be, or may not be included in a Modal (FOR) TO clause is largely determined by the semantic nature of the main verb. The meaning of the Modal (FOR) TO complement—relating to its subject getting involved in the activity referred to—is basically the same in each instance. Consider:

**(46a)**   *The boss decided for Dr Jane Smith to examine Mary Brown (but she refused)*
**(46b)**   *The boss decided for Mary Brown to be examined by Dr Jane Smith (but she refused)*
**(47a)**   *The boss expected Dr Jane Smith to examine Mary Brown (but she refused)*
**(47b)**   *The boss expected Mary Brown to be examined by Dr Jane Smith (but she refused)*
**(48a)**   *The boss tried to force Dr Jane Smith to examine Mary Brown (but she refused)*
**(48b)**   *The boss tried to force Mary Brown to be examined by Dr Jane Smith (but she refused)*

It has been suggested that *force* differs syntactically from verbs like *decide* and *expect*. The reason given is that active and passive complement constructions with *force*—as in (48a/b)—show a striking difference in meaning, which is not the case for active and passive constructions with verbs like *expect* and *decide* (as in (47a/b), (46a/b)).

In fact (46a/b), (47a/b) and (48a/b) are syntactically parallel. They involve the same syntactic and also semantic differences; it is just that the semantic differences are more evident with *force*, because of the meaning of that verb. The semantic congruence of (46a/b), (47a/b) and (48a/b) can be seen with the addition of *but she refused*. In each of the six sentences the *she* is taken to refer to the complement clause subject—to *Dr Jane Smith* in (46a), (47a) and (48a), and to *Mary Brown* in (46b), (47b) and (48b). Active and passive versions of a Modal (FOR) TO clause show the same basic semantic difference for every main verb, because a different NP is in the crucial complement clause subject slot in the two alternatives; the meaning of the Modal (FOR) TO construction relates to this complement clause subject becoming involved in the activity (or state) referred to by that clause.

This provides a further point of difference from Judgement TO complements, where the substitution of passive for active in the complement clause provides no more overall difference in meaning than this substitution produces in a main clause, e.g. *I believed Dr Jane Smith to have examined Mary Brown* and *I believed Mary Brown to have been examined by Dr Jane Smith*. One could add *but she denied it* to these two sentences and in each case the reference of *she* is unclear—it could be to *Dr Jane Smith* or to *Mary Brown*. A Judgement TO construction does not provide the semantic means to resolve this ambiguity, as a Modal (FOR) TO construction does.

### 8.2.5. Omitting to from Modal (FOR) TO complements

As already mentioned, verbs from the MAKING and HELPING subtypes must omit *for* from a Modal (FOR) TO complement. Most of them do retain *to*, e.g. *force, cause, get, tempt, permit, allow, assist*. However, *make, have* and *let* must omit the *to* in an active sentence:

(**49**) *Mary made/had/let John drive the car*

*Make* may be used in the passive and *to* is then retained, e.g. *John was made to drive the car*. *Let* is only used in the passive in a few idiomatic combinations and no *to* is included, e.g. *The balloons/pigeons/prisoners were let go*. The causative sense of *have* is (like the other senses of this word) not used in the passive.

We were able to focus on the semantic role of *for* by considering those verbs that allow it optionally to be omitted and seeing what semantic effect this has. There is one verb for which *to* may be either included or omitted; this is *help*. The pair of sentences *John helped Mary eat the pudding* and *John helped Mary to eat the pudding* were mentioned in §6.3.2 (see also Erades 1950a and Bolinger 1974: 75). Now consider:

(**50a**)   *John helped me to write the letter*
(**50b**)   *John helped me write the letter*

Sentence (50a) might be used to describe John facilitating my writing the letter—suppose that he provided pen and ink, suggested some appropriate phrases and told me how one should address a bishop. But, in this scenario, I actually wrote the letter myself. Sentence (50b), on the other hand, might be used to describe a cooperative effort where John and I did the letter together, perhaps writing alternate paragraphs.

Sentence (50b)—without *to*—is likely to imply that John gave direct help; there is here a direct link between the referents of main and complement clause verbs. In contrast, (50a) is more likely to be used if he gave indirect assistance. This semantic principle explains, at least in part, the inclusion or omission of *to* with MAKING verbs. As outlined in §6.3.1, *cause* can be used of indirect action which brings about a certain result; it naturally takes *to*. *Make*, in contrast, relates to something done—on purpose or accidentally—to bring something about directly. *Let* focuses on the main clause subject, and the effect it has on the subject of the complement clause. These two verbs naturally exclude *to*. (This does not, however, explain why *force*, which often relates to coercion, takes *to*; and why the causative sense of *have*, which may involve some indirect means, omits *to*.)

There is a small group of ATTENTION verbs which (together with *know*) take what appears to be a variety of Modal (FOR) TO complement; *to* is omitted in the active but included in the passive:

(**51a**)   *They saw/heard/noticed John kick Mary*
(**51b**)   *John was seen/heard/noticed to kick Mary*

These do demonstrate the semantic characteristics of a Modal (FOR) TO complement—they describe John becoming involved in the activity of kicking Mary. (Note that if the complement clause is passivised we get an unacceptable sentence *\*They saw/heard/noticed Mary (to) be kicked by John*, simply because Mary—who is now complement clause subject—is not the participant who initiates the activity.) *See*, *hear* and *notice* do, in this construction, imply direct and often spontaneous perception of some activity (without the additional semantic overtones carried by verbs such as *recognise*, *discover* and *witness*, which do not occur in the construction). It may be because of this that the *to* is omitted.

But why is it that *to* must be included when *make*, *see*, *hear* and *notice* are used in the passive? Putting (49) (with *make*) or (51a) in the passive, in the context of a Modal (FOR) TO complement clause, loses the pragmatic immediacy of (49) and (51a). The passive verges towards being the description of a state, and that is why *to* is included. (*Help* may include or omit *to* in the passive, as in the active, but—for the same reason—it does seem more likely to include it in the passive.) Interestingly, *watch* and *listen to* occur in a construction like (51a) (*They watched John kick Mary, I listened to him sing*), but there is no corresponding passive, either with or without *to* (*\*John was watched (to) kick Mary*, *\*John was listened (to) sing*). One must instead employ what could be analysed as a reduced relative clause with imperfective aspect (*John was watched kicking Mary*). The meanings of *watch* and *listen to* imply perception over a period of time, which is highly compatible with a reduced relative in imperfective aspect. A Modal (FOR) TO construction is allowed in the active, but its passive equivalent ('in a state of being watched/listened to') is rejected in favour of a construction more in keeping with the meanings of *watch* and *listen to*.

## 8.2.6. *Omitting* to be *from* TO *complements*

As mentioned briefly in §2.8, the sequence *to be* can be omitted from some Judgement TO and from some Modal (FOR) TO complements. The conditions for this omission are quite different in the two cases.

For Judgement TO, a limited number of verbs may omit both the *to* and a copula *be* which begins the predicate when the predicate is a typical semantic accompaniment for the verb.

Most ATTENTION and SPEAKING verbs must retain the *to be*, e.g. nothing can be dropped from *She saw/reported/acknowledged him to be stupid/wrong/the decision-maker*. *Declare* and *proclaim* may omit *to be* when they are used in a performative sense, with a predicate that is prototypical for that verb, e.g. *The Council of Barons proclaimed Alfred (to be) King*, *The doctor declared him (to be) dead on arrival*, *The judge declared Mary (to be) the winner*. Note, though, that *to be* could scarcely be omitted from non-prototypical sentences involving these verbs, e.g. not from *They proclaimed/declared him to be clever*.

The verbs *think*, *consider* and *imagine*, from the THINKING type, may omit *to be* from a Judgement TO complement that makes a straightforward assertion concerning a quality or state, where this is shown by an adjective or by a participial form of a verb, e.g. *I thought him (to be) stupid/wrong/healthy/dead/vanquished*. *To be* may not be omitted from other kinds of Judgement TO complement with these verbs, e.g. not from *I thought him to be getting healthier each day*.

*Find* and *prove* may omit *to be* when the Judgement TO complement relates to some official or objective judgement, e.g. *find guilty*, *prove wrong*; but *to be* would be likely to be retained in a sentence like *We found him to be very unsure of himself*. (See also §6.4.1.) *To be* can be omitted after *believe* with the adjective *dead* (e.g. *He was believed (to be) dead*), a common collocation; nothing is likely to be omitted from *He is believed to be clever/the fastest gun in the West*. Verbs like *know* and *assume* appear never to omit *to be* from a Judgement TO complement, perhaps because there is no particular kind of predicate that could be considered prototypical for these verbs.

Turning now to Modal (FOR) TO complements, in §6.3.1 we discussed how *make* and *let* can omit *be* or *to be*, and the causative sense of *have* must omit *be*; the *be* here can be copula or passive or imperfective. A sentence with no (*to*) *be*, such as *I made John interested in the puzzle*, implies that I did something as a result of which he became spontaneously interested. In contrast, *I made John be interested in the puzzle* carries a more direct meaning—I influenced John to force himself to be interested in it.

*To be* may also be omitted from a Modal (FOR) TO complement after a small group of verbs which includes *order*, *wish*, *want*, *need* and *require*. This happens when the complement clause subject is not the controller of the activity (and so it would not be appropriate for *to* to be included). Typically, the complement clause will be in the passive, with an inanimate NP as derived passive subject, e.g. *He ordered the floors* (*to be*) *cleaned, I want this picture* (*to be*) *restored, I need my bandages* (*to be*) *changed*. Note that *to be* must be included when the main clause is passivised, e.g. *The floors were ordered to be cleaned*.

There is surface similarity to a construction where an object NP is followed by a 'resulting state' adjective, e.g. *She shot him dead, I swept it clean* (see §4.2). As pointed out in §2.8, the two constructions are in fact quite different. *Shoot dead* is simply a verb-plus-adjective construction—no *to be* enters in the passive, for instance (*He was shot dead*, not *\*He was shot to be dead*), whereas *cleaned* in *I ordered it cleaned* is a reduced clause—other clause constituents can be included with it (e.g. *I ordered it* (*to be*) *cleaned by an expert*).

In summary, *to be* can be omitted from a Judgement TO clause when the main clause verb and the adjective from the predicate of the complement clause typically belong together (e.g. *declare X dead, proclaim X King, find X guilty*). With Modal (FOR) TO clauses a (*to*) *be* can be omitted if the main clause subject does not directly 'control' the complement clause subject in doing something. And whereas only copula *be* may be omitted from a Judgement TO clause, any of the three varieties of *be*—copula, passive and imperfective—may be omitted from a Modal (FOR) TO clause, as shown in (69)–(71) of §2.8.

### 8.2.7. ING and Modal (FOR) TO

An ING construction describes the complement clause subject taking part in some activity which is extended in time. A Modal (FOR) TO clause refers to (the potentiality of) the subject's getting involved in some activity. Compare:

(**52a**)   *John tried to drive the Honda*
(**52b**)   *John tried driving the Honda*

Sentence (52b) states that he did drive the Honda for a while, perhaps for long enough to know whether he liked the car; (52a) suggests that he wasn't able actually to drive it (perhaps he is only used to automatics and this is a manual, or perhaps the owner of the car wouldn't let him drive it).

ING, Modal (FOR) TO and THAT complements all occur after *remember*, with significant semantic differences:

(**53a**)   *The doctor remembered that he had examined Mary Brown*
(**53b**)   *The doctor remembered examining Mary Brown*
(**53c**)   *The doctor remembered to examine Mary Brown*

Sentence (53a) might be used when he remembered that the consultation had taken place but couldn't recall any of the details—he just remembers the 'fact' of the examination; (53b) implies that he had a clear recollection of what happened—Mary Brown's giggles when he asked her to put out her tongue, the high blood pressure reading, and so on. Both (53a) and (53b) refer to some actual event, in the past. In contrast, (53c) has a prospective meaning, stating that he knew he had to involve himself in an activity. Unless something is stated to the contrary we would infer from (53c) that he did examine her. However, the sentence could be continued: *but when he looked in the waiting room he found she'd grown tired of waiting and gone off home.*

Another contrastive illustration of the three complement types is given in §8.4.5, with the verb *like*.

### 8.2.8. WH- TO

A WH- TO complement is like a Modal (FOR) TO clause with a *wh-* word (as in a WH- complement) at the beginning, in place of *for*. The complement clause subject must be coreferential with either main clause subject or object, and omitted. The *wh-* word refers to any constituent of the main clause except its subject.

A WH- TO clause combines the meanings of Modal (FOR) TO and of WH-complements. It refers to some activity in which the subject has the potential for getting involved, and it is an activity about which some clarification is required. Compare the THAT construction in (54a), the Modal (FOR) TO one in (54b), the plain WH- in (54c), and the WH- TO complement in (54d).

(54a)   *He knew (that) he should stand up when the judge entered*
(54b)   *He knew to stand up when the judge entered*
(54c)   *He didn't know whether he should stand up when the judge entered*
(54d)   *He didn't know whether to stand up when the judge entered*

Any verb which permits both a WH- and a Modal (FOR) TO clause will also take a WH- TO complement. Besides *know*, these include *remember* and *decide*, e.g. *He couldn't remember whether to close the window or leave it open*, and *I'll decide tomorrow who to fire, when to fire them, and how to appease the union*. It appears that no verb which does not take a plain WH-complement may take WH- TO. But there are verbs which take WH- and not Modal (FOR) TO and do accept WH- TO, e.g. *report*, *think* (*about*) and *understand*, as in *She's thinking about whether to accept the offer*, and *I don't understand how to behave*.

A plain WH- complement, such as (54c), may include *whether* or *if*, with a subtle difference in meaning (see Bolinger 1978); only *whether* is allowed in a WH- TO clause such as (54d). All other *wh-* words may begin a WH- TO complement excepting *why*. There appears to be a semantic reason for this. Consider first

(55)   *I don't know why I should go*

This sentence is acceptable, with a meaning something like 'I don't know what my obligation is supposed to be that would make me go'. Now recall that there is always a semantic difference between a THAT construction including *should* and a Modal (FOR) TO construction; this was exemplified at (30a/b) in §8.2.3 with *remember*. Whereas a THAT-plus-*should* clause refers to some extraneous obligation, a Modal (FOR) TO construction refers to the potentiality of the subject's getting involved in the activity. *\*I don't know why to go* is ungrammatical since *why*, demanding clarification of the reason for entering into an activity, is semantically incompatible with

Modal (FOR) TO, stating that the subject does volitionally become involved in the activity. But Modal (FOR) TO is perfectly compatible with all other *wh-* words, e.g. *I don't know how to open the door/when to arrive/who to blame.*

### 8.2.9. *(FROM) ING*

The (FROM) ING variety of complement clause occurs with negative verbs from the ORDER subtype of SPEAKING and with negative verbs from the MAKING type. It relates to the subject of the main clause doing something so that the subject of the complement clause does not become involved in the activity described by that clause.

We can first compare *persuade* and *dissuade*, positive and negative members of ORDER:

**(56a)**   *I persuaded John that Mary/he should go*
**(56b)**   *I persuaded Mary to go*
**(57)**    *I dissuaded Mary from going*

Sentence (56a) has a THAT complement in post-object slot. Example (56b) has an underlying Modal (FOR) TO clause in post-object function; the complement clause subject must be coreferential with main clause object, and then omitted (together with *for*). Sentence (57) is exactly parallel to (56b); the difference is that with *dissuade* there is no corresponding THAT construction. The object NP may be passivised in (57) as in (56b), e.g. *Mary was persuaded to go, Mary was dissuaded from going.* The other ORDER verbs that occur in a (FROM) ING construction include *discourage* and *prohibit. Forbid* was originally used with a Modal (FOR) TO complement but nowadays an increasing number of speakers prefer a (FROM) ING complement, which accords better with the negative meaning of this verb. One hears both *She forbade him to go* and *She forbade him from going*, with no difference in meaning.

Looking now at positive and negative members of the MAKING type:

**(58)**   *I made her go*
**(59)**   *I forced her to go*
**(60)**   *I prevented her ( from) going*

Sentences (58)–(59) involve a Modal (FOR) TO complement clause in object function; the *for* must be omitted with verbs of this type, and complement clause subject becomes surface object of the main clause. Sentence (60) is a construction exactly parallel to (58)–(59), in the same way that (57) parallels (56b). The other MAKING verbs which take a (FROM) ING construction include *stop, save, spare* and special senses of *check (oneself), rescue* and *release.*

The interesting point here is that *from* can be omitted from a (FROM) ING complement following some negative MAKING verbs, and its omission carries a semantic difference. *I prevented her going* would be likely to be used when I employed some direct means, e.g. I blocked her path. In contrast, *I prevented her from going* would be the appropriate thing to say if I employed indirect means, e.g. I used my influence to make sure she didn't get her passport renewed. ORDER verbs, such as *dissuade*, must include *from*, and this is at least partly because such verbs refer to the use of speech to bring about some result, which is necessarily an indirect means. (The other part of the reason may be syntactic—the fact that (57) relates to a post-object complement clause, and (60) to a complement clause in object function.)

The semantic effect of omitting *from* is very similar to that of omitting *to* from Modal (FOR) TO clauses, discussed in §8.2.5. In each case the loss of a preposition implies a direct link between the referents of main clause and complement clause verbs. Note that, like *to, from* may be omitted from an active clause but is always likely to be retained in the passive, e.g. *She was prevented from going*, but scarcely *\*She was prevented going.*

## 8.2.10. Summary

The main points from our discussion of the meanings of kinds of complement clauses are:

- THAT complements refer to some assertable activity or state as a single unit, without any reference to its inherent constitution or time duration.
- WH- complements relate to some aspect of an assertable activity or state (again, treated as a single unit), about which clarification is needed.
- ING complements refer to some activity or state as extended in time, perhaps noting the way in which it unfolds.
- Modal (FOR) TO complements relate to (the potentiality of) the subject of the complement clause becoming involved in the state or activity referred to by that clause.

- Judgement TO complements refer to a judgement or opinion which the main clause subject makes, through the complement clause, generally relating to a state or property of the subject of that clause.
- WH- TO complements effectively combine the meanings of WH- and Modal (FOR) TO, referring to some activity in which the subject will get involved, and about some aspect of which clarification is required. (All verbs that take WH- TO also take WH- complements.)
- (FROM) ING complements relate to the subject of the main clause doing something so that the subject of the complement clause does not become involved in the activity or state referred to by that clause.

THAT or WH- complements must show tense inflection and may include a Modal. The other five varieties of complement clause do not take a Modal or tense inflection, although past time can be coded through the *have* auxiliary. With certain verbs, the time reference of an ING complement is not stated, but can often be inferred from the meaning of the verb (e.g. future with *propose*, past with *regret*). Many verbs which take a Modal (FOR) TO complement also accept a THAT clause, and then the meaning of the Modal (FOR) TO construction is generally similar—though not identical—to a THAT construction where the complement clause includes a Modal. All verbs that take Judgement TO also accept a THAT complement, and the meaning of the Judgement TO construction is similar to the meaning of a THAT construction which does not include a Modal.

THAT and WH- complements must contain an overt subject. For Judgement TO and (FROM) ING the underlying complement clause subject must be included, but is coded as surface object of the main verb. A WH- TO complement must have its subject coreferential with main clause subject or object, and then omitted. ING and Modal (FOR) TO complements may omit their subject NP when it is coreferential with an NP in appropriate function in the main clause (*for* then also drops). With some main verbs this omission is obligatory, with some it is optional, and with others it is not allowed.

A Modal (FOR) TO complement may, when it directly follows a transitive main verb, drop the *for*; complement clause subject then becomes surface direct object of the main verb. *For* is omitted when the subject of the complement clause is directly affected by the activity referred to by the main verb. *To* from a Modal (FOR) TO and *from* from a (FROM) ING complement may be omitted after some verbs (and *to* must be after others) when there is a direct link between the activity referred to by the main verb and that referred to by the complement clause verb.

## 8.3. Complement clauses with Secondary verbs

Leaving aside MODALS, Secondary verb constructions in English show a non-alignment between syntax and semantics. The Secondary verb is syntactically the main verb but from a semantic point of view it modifies the verb of the complement clause, which is the semantic focus of the sentence.

The kinds of semantic relation between a Secondary verb and the verb in the subordinate clause can be coded—in semantically appropriate ways— by THAT, ING, Modal (FOR) TO and (FROM) ING complement constructions. Secondary verbs of types A, B and C do not allow WH- or WH- TO complements since they provide semantic qualification of another verb, which is incompatible with seeking clarification; and they do not occur in Judgement TO constructions since they do not delineate opinion or judgement. The Secondary-D types have somewhat different properties—SEEM may occur in a special kind of Judgement TO construction, and MATTER may occur with a WH- complement.

### 8.3.1. MODALS and SEMI-MODALS

The SEMI-MODALS—*be going to, have to, have got to, be able to, be about to, get to* and *be bound to*—could on syntactic grounds be regarded as main verbs taking a Modal (FOR) TO complement clause (with subject that is coreferential with the main clause subject and thus omitted), similar to *attempt* or *fail*. The main reason for our linking them with MODALS lies in the semantic parallels between *will* and *be going to, must* and *have (got) to, can* and *be able to*.

But we did demonstrate a recurrent semantic difference, in examples (1a/b), (2a/b) and (3a/b) of §6.1.1. MODALS tend to indicate prediction, ability, necessity, etc. under specific circumstances, while SEMI-MODALS are more likely to have an 'unconditional' sense and relate to the subject's involvement in an activity. Compare (61a), with MODAL *must*, and (61b), with SEMI-MODAL *have to*:

(61a)   *You mustn't mind what he says when he's drunk*
(61b)   *You have to watch out for muggers after dark in the town centre*

It is thus entirely appropriate for all SEMI-MODALS to include *to*, in terms of the meaning of the Modal (FOR) TO complement discussed in §8.2.

In §§6.1.5 and 6.2.1, we illustrated the two uses of *dare* and of *need*. When used to refer to some general circumstance (almost always in questions and negatives) they may behave syntactically like MODALS, e.g.

(**62**)   *No one dare question my credentials*

But when *need* and *dare* refer to a definite subject becoming involved in some activity, then they behave like a non-MODAL and take complementiser *to* (although this may sometimes be omitted), e.g.

(**63**)   *That man dares* (*to*) *question my credentials*

Just three of the fifteen MODALS include *to*. This is semantically appropriate with *be to*, a verb which most often has a human subject who is scheduled to become involved in an activity, e.g. *I am to call on the Vice-Chancellor tomorrow*. However, it is hard to discern any semantic reason for the *to* of *ought to* and *used to*; we should perhaps search for a historical explanation in these instances.

### 8.3.2. BEGINNING, TRYING, HURRYING *and* DARING

A Secondary-A verb shares all the semantic roles of the verb it modifies. It is thus, on a priori syntactic grounds, restricted to a choice from ING and Modal (FOR) TO, the only complement types that may omit the complement clause subject when it is coreferential with main clause subject. In fact, these two complement constructions reflect the semantic possibilities of a Secondary-A verb: an ING clause is used when the Secondary verb construction refers to an activity taking place over a period of time, and a reduced Modal (FOR) TO complement is used in a construction that refers to the subject's getting involved in an activity.

The semantic contrast between ING and Modal (FOR) TO complements with Secondary-A verbs is illustrated at (52a/b) in §8.2.7, (1a/b) and (2a/b) in §6.1.3, and in:

(**64a**)   *Mary tried telling that joke about nuns* (but no one laughed)
(**64b**)   *Mary tried to tell that joke about nuns* (but forgot how it went)
(**65a**)   *Fred started hitting Mary* (but she cried so much he stopped)
(**65b**)   *Fred started to hit Mary* (but checked himself before actually delivering the blow)
(**66a**)   *John continued painting the wall* (despite all the distractions)
(**66b**)   *John continued to paint the wall* (after that interruption)

Sentence (64a) implies that Mary did tell the joke (or a good part of it); hearing (64b) one might infer that, despite her best efforts, Mary wasn't able properly to become involved in telling it. Sentence (65a) implies that Fred hit Mary for a period; (65b) could be used if he raised his stick, ready to bring it down on her head—if nothing else were said one would assume that he did hit her at least once, but the sentence could be continued as in the parenthesis of (65b). Sentence (66a) states that John carried on with an established activity, rather than stopping it, whereas (66b) might be used when he becomes involved again after having stopped.

All BEGINNING verbs can take an ING complement. Members of this type refer to the inception, continuation or ending of some continuous activity referred to by the verb of the complement clause. *Begin, start, continue, go on* and *cease* also occur with TO complements, whereas *commence, keep (on), finish, stop, complete* and *discontinue* do not. For most (perhaps all) of these verbs there is a semantic explanation as to why they do not take TO.

As discussed in §6.1.2, *finish* has 'object orientation'; in *John has finished peeling the potatoes* the activity terminates because the potatoes are all peeled. It would not be appropriate to use a Modal (FOR) TO construction, since this must relate to the subject's involvement in (here, finishing) an activity. *Cease*, in contrast, relates to an activity terminating because of something to do with the subject—they withdraw involvement; so we could, conceivably, say *He ceased to shell the peas*.

*Commence* and *complete* are also object-oriented, referring to some definite and significant piece of work, and must take an ING clause referring to the durative activity needed to achieve the work. *Keep (on (with))* implies uninterrupted pursuit of some task, and is restricted to ING. *Continue (with)* and *go on (with)* can refer to an activity continuing without a break and then take ING, as in (66a). Or they can—unlike *keep (on (with))*—refer to something being restarted, and may then take Modal (FOR) TO, as in (66b).

*Cease, stop* and *discontinue* have rather similar meanings, but there are also crucial differences. As discussed in §6.1.2, *cease* can imply 'gradually falling away', e.g. *My faith gradually faded during those adolescent years and I finally ceased to believe in God on my sixteenth birthday*. *Stop* tends to refer to something terminating rather abruptly, e.g. *I stopped believing anything Bush said when no weapons of mass destruction were found in Iraq*. But this does not explain why *stop* should not take a TO complement. The crucial factor here may be syntactic interference from the intransitive REST verb *stop*, which typically takes an *(in order)* to construction; thus *stop* in *I stopped to eat* is always identified as the REST verb, not the BEGINNING one.

*Discontinue* has subject orientation, like *cease* and *continue*, and on these grounds would be expected to take a Modal (FOR) TO complement. Interestingly, most verbs commencing with the negative prefix *dis-* may not take any kind of TO complement clause, even though the corresponding positive verb does—compare *agree/disagree, believe/disbelieve, claim/disclaim, like/ dislike, prove/disprove, allow/disallow* and *persuade/dissuade, encourage/discourage*. This lack may be in some way connected with the meanings of *dis-* and of TO complement constructions.

Turning now to the TRYING type, we mentioned in §6.1.3 that *try* itself has two different senses. The first, which correlates with a Modal (FOR) TO complement, relates to the subject making efforts to get involved in some activity (but not necessarily being able to). The second, which takes an ING complement, relates to them engaging in it for a sample period.

As their meanings were described in §6.1.3, *attempt, manage*—and *fail*, in many contexts—all imply considerable effort on the part of the subject, which is why they are found most often with a Modal (FOR) TO complement (although *attempt* and *manage* are, occasionally, used in an ING construction). *Succeed* and *miss* have a wider, more general meaning—it is possible to succeed with scarcely any effort, and one can miss (e.g. seeing someone) entirely by chance; only the ING complement is compatible with these meanings. The semantic difference between *fail* and *miss* is brought out in *He just failed to run her over* (i.e. he tried to kill her, but didn't manage it), where a Modal (FOR) TO clause indicates volition, and *He just missed running her over* (he didn't intend to hit her, but she seemed just to step in front of the car and he had to swerve), where the choice of an ING clause shows that the subject did not attempt to get involved in the deed.

*Practise* refers to a continuous activity, which must be described by an ING clause. *Repeat* refers to a complete activity being done again; once more ING is, on semantic grounds, the appropriate choice.

Looking now at the HURRYING type, *hurry* (*over/with*) takes both ING and Modal (FOR) TO complement clauses:

(**67a**)   *Tom hurried over eating his dinner*
(**67b**)   *Tom hurried to eat up his dinner*

Sentence (67a) would be used appropriately to describe Tom eating quickly right through the meal, whereas (67b) might describe him hurrying only towards the end, perhaps when he realised that it would be taken away if he didn't eat everything before the bell sounded. (The inclusion of *up* adds a completive sense; (67b) has a very similar meaning to *Tom hurried to finish eating his dinner*.) An ING clause is likely to describe the subject doing something fast over the whole duration of an activity, whereas a Modal (FOR) TO clause is likely to describe the subject doing something fast to reach a particular goal. *Hasten* (*over/with*) has a similar meaning to *hurry* (*over/with*) (see §6.1.4) but is more often used to describe an action directed towards a goal, and is thus more often found with a Modal (FOR) TO complement (although ING is also possible). *Dawdle* (*over*) refers to doing something slowly over the whole duration of the activity, and is restricted to an ING construction.

*Hesitate* (*over/with*) relates to uncertainty on the part of the subject over whether to engage in some activity, referred to by the complement clause. When an ING complement is used the unmarked implication is that the subject did undertake the activity, e.g. *She hesitated over writing the letter* (*but eventually she did write it*). When a Modal (FOR) TO complement is used a listener might understand—if nothing else were said—that the subject did not in the end get involved in the activity, e.g. *She hesitated to write the letter herself* (*and finally prevailed upon her mother to write it for her*).

*Dare*, and *venture*, from the DARING type, indicate that the subject has sufficient courage to become involved in some activity; they are thus naturally restricted to a Modal (FOR) TO complement construction. (And *dare* can also be used like a MODAL, with no *to*, to describe some general circumstance—see §8.3.1.)

## 8.3.3. *WANTING and POSTPONING*

These two Secondary-B types both introduce one role (the subject of the Secondary verb) in addition to the roles of the verb in the complement clause: this is the Principal role for WANTING, and the Timer role for POSTPONING.

A WANTING verb describes the Principal's attitude towards the event or state described by the complement clause. This can be expressed through a THAT complement clause (usually including a Modal), or through a Modal (FOR) TO clause. Compare:

**(68a)**   *I'm hoping (that) John won't fight the bully*
**(68b)**   *I'm hoping for John to beat up the bully*

The Modal (FOR) TO construction, in (68b), is appropriate when the Principal would like to see the subject of the complement clause get involved in the activity described by that clause. The THAT construction, in (68a), is more neutral, and might be preferred when the Principal just wished for a certain result.

A WANTING verb frequently deals with the Principal's attitude towards something that they are involved in. The complement subject can be omitted (together with *for*) from a Modal (FOR) TO clause when it is coreferential with main clause subject. A THAT clause, of course, can never omit the subject. Thus:

**(69a)**   *I'm hoping that I will be allowed to visit him in jail*
**(69b)**   *I'm hoping to be allowed to visit him in jail*

The Modal (FOR) TO alternative is frequently preferred in such circumstances, simply because it does allow subject omission. Indeed, if a verb like *hope* or *wish* has coreferential subjects and the subject controls the activity referred to by the complement clause—which it does not in (69a/b)—then only a Modal (FOR) TO complement may be allowed—(70a), but not (70b):

**(70a)**   *I hope to visit him in jail*
**(70b)**   *\*I hope that I will visit him in jail*

Note that although a coreferential complement clause subject is generally omitted after a WANTING verb, it can be included, usually in a situation of special emphasis, e.g. *I didn't want John to be chosen, I wanted MYSELF* (or *ME*) *to be chosen.*

Some WANTING verbs allow *for* to be retained; the complement clause subject then does not become surface object of the Secondary verb. We mentioned in §8.2.4 that *for* tends to be omitted when the Principal is communicating their attitude directly to the complement clause subject, and to be retained when the attitude is expressed more indirectly. Compare (42a/43a), (44a/b) in §8.2.4, and also:

**(71a)**   *I hadn't intended for you to find out about the party until your actual birthday*
**(71b)**   *I had intended you to overhear what we were saying*

Sentences (72a–c) contrast three constructions with *wish*: (72a), a Modal (FOR) TO with the *for* retained, relates to the Principal's (lack of need for any) desire that John should make an effort to behave better; (72b), with the *for* omitted after *wish*, is used to describe the Principal telling John this, quite directly; (72c), with a THAT clause, expresses a general wish concerning John's behaviour.

**(72a)**   *I couldn't have wished for John to behave any better*
**(72b)**   *I told John that I wished him to improve his manners*
**(72c)**   *I wish that John would improve his manners*

The meanings of some verbs from the WANTING type are such that they can only be used in an indirect manner, as in (68b). These verbs—*hope, long, pine, wait, plan, aim, prepare, crave, deserve, dread*—always include *for* before the subject of a Modal (FOR) TO clause. *Demand* behaves in a similar way—we can say *I demand that you (should) resign*, but only *I demand for you to resign*; for a direct, pragmatic communication to the complement clause subject a verb like *order* is preferred, e.g. *I order you to resign*, rather than *\*I demand you to resign*.

A second set of verbs from this type can either include or omit *for*; it includes *wish, desire, intend, mean, pretend*. A final set has meanings which imply a direct communication of the attitude, and these verbs—*want, need, require, expect*—omit *for* from a Modal (FOR) TO complement when it immediately follows the main verb. They can, however, retain the *for* when an adverb intervenes, e.g. *I want very much for Mary to win* (but only *I want Mary to win*, not—in most dialects—*\*I want for Mary to win*). And when the complement clause is syntactically 'dislocated' from its main verb, the *for* may optionally be included, e.g. *I need Mary to help me, not (for) John to help me*.

We can now discuss the meanings of some of the individual verbs in the type, as they relate to the choice of complementiser. *Want* is directly pragmatic, relating to the Principal's attitude towards the complement clause subject getting involved in some activity regarded as achievable, e.g. *I want Mary to sing*. Because of this, *want* is restricted to a Modal (FOR) TO construction; it is one of the few WANTING verbs not to take a THAT clause. *Wish* may have a wistful sense, relating to something that is not possible, and then takes a THAT complement (usually with past tense, previous aspect or a modal such as *would* or *could*), e.g. *I wish (that) Mary could sing (but I know that she can't, after the throat operation)*. Interestingly, when *wish* is used with a Modal (FOR) TO clause it takes on a quite different sense, becoming more peremptory and authoritarian than *want*, e.g. *The Queen wishes you to sing.* This may be because Modal (FOR) TO is the 'marked' complement choice for *wish*, and thus has a 'marked' meaning. *Long (for)* and *crave (for)* describe emotional attitudes of great intensity, and in view of this they are almost restricted to Modal (FOR) TO complements.

*Need* also has a strongly pragmatic meaning, being typically used to say what should be done, to a person who could be expected to do it; like *want*, it cannot take a THAT complement but is restricted to Modal (FOR) TO, e.g. *I need you to wash up for me (since I've got a rash on my hands)*. *Require* tends to be used for an impersonal or institutional obligation on the subject of the complement clause to become involved in an activity, and is often used in the passive with a Modal (FOR) TO complement, e.g. *You are required to sign here.* It may also refer to some general instruction, through a THAT clause, e.g. *The duchess requires that her sheets be changed each day*.

*Aim (for)* differs semantically from *intend* in implying a single-mind-edness of purpose—this is why it is typically used in a Modal (FOR) TO construction with coreferential subjects (and thus omission of complement clause subject), e.g. *I aim to win*, as against *I intended Mary to win*. *Prepare* relates to the complement clause subject becoming involved in an activity and is—like *want* and *need*—restricted to a Modal (FOR) TO construction, e.g. *I am preparing for John to bring his new bride home to meet me*.

All WANTING verbs take a Modal (FOR) TO complement. All save *want*, *need* and *prepare* take a THAT complement. An ING complement clause (whose subject must be coreferential with main clause subject, and then omitted) is possible with those verbs which relate to the Principal's thought that they will do a certain thing in the future—*intend*, *plan*, and also *prepare for*, *aim at*. Compare:

(**73a**)   *He is planning to build a rockery*
(**73b**)   *He is planning building a rockery*

Sentence (73a), with a Modal (FOR) TO complement, just states that he has the idea of 'getting involved' in putting in a rockery; (73b), with an ING complement, suggests that he is thinking of the details of the activity—where it will go, how to build the stones up, and so on.

Verbs in the POSTPONING type generally refer to some activity with temporal extent, and thus naturally take ING complements, e.g. *I delayed writing the letter*, *The Prime Minister put off meeting the union leaders*. Alternatively, an ACTIVITY or SPEECH ACT noun may fill the O slot, e.g. *He put off the meeting.* Verbs from this type do not take a THAT complement, simply because they refer to a projected event, not to the fact of an event, e.g. we do not say *\*He delayed that he would write the letter.*

### 8.3.4. *MAKING and* HELPING

Positive verbs from the MAKING type refer to the Causer (main clause subject) doing something so that the complement clause subject becomes involved in the activity referred to by that clause. For verbs from the HELPING type the Helper (again, main clause subject) joins in with the complement clause subject to bring about some event. Both of these semantic specifications are compatible only with a Modal (FOR) TO construction, and one where the *for* is omitted.

Both main and complement clause subjects are typically human, although either can be inanimate, e.g. *The flooded river forced/caused me to change my plans,* and *He made/let the marble roll into the hole.* The Causer or Helper is unlikely to be coreferential with complement clause subject; when it is, the latter cannot be omitted, e.g. *I made/let myself eat the chocolates,* not *\*I made/let eat the chocolates.*

*Help* may omit *to,* implying a direct link between the referents of main and complement clause verbs, or retain it, in the case of an indirect link (§§8.2.5, 6.3.2). *Make* and *let* imply a direct link and must omit *to* in an active sentence. As an illustration, compare *let* with *permit* and *allow,* which do take *to* since they can both refer to indirect sanction, e.g. *Standing orders don't allow/permit you to enter the hangars.* One could scarcely say *\*Standing orders don't let you enter the hangars,* although *The Squadron Leader won't let you enter the hangars* is fine since it relates to direct interaction between Causer and complement clause subject.

As mentioned in §8.2.5 we would—on semantic grounds—expect *force* to omit the *to,* whereas it always retains it; and we would expect the causative sense of *have* to retain the *to,* whereas it always omits it.

Negative verbs from the MAKING type take a (FROM) ING complement, in keeping with their meaning. As described in §8.2.9, the *from* can be omitted—in much the same way that *to* can be omitted after *help*—when direct means of coercion are employed.

*Ensure* stands out from other MAKING verbs in that it can simply refer to the 'Causer' checking the fact of something being in a certain state; it may not matter who put it in that state. This meaning of *ensure* demands a THAT complement, referring to an 'assertable event or state', e.g. *She ensured that all the windows were open.*

### 8.3.5. *SEEM and* MATTER

A verb from the SEEM type may function like a copula, being followed by an adjective and with a complement clause in subject function. As mentioned in §6.4.1, the complement clause possibilities are determined by the adjective. The semantic profiles of complement clauses described in the present chapter still apply. Thus, a Modal (FOR) TO clause is appropriate when the complement clause subject is to get involved in some activity, e.g. *It appears to be normal for the captain to lead his team onto the field.* A THAT clause is likely for describing some state of affairs, e.g. *It seems curious that Mary went.* And an ING clause may be chosen to describe a durational activity, e.g. *John's walking to work this morning seems strangely out of character.*

SEEM verbs can also occur without an adjective, followed by a THAT clause and with impersonal *it* in subject slot, as in (74a) and (75a). There is a corresponding Judgement TO construction in which the complement clause subject replaces *it* as surface subject of the SEEM verb, as in (74b) and (75b).

(**74a**)   *It seems that Fred wants to go*
(**74b**)   *Fred seems to want to go*
(**75a**)   *It seems that Tom is stupid*
(**75b**)   *Tom seems (to be) stupid*

Note that, as is normal with Judgement TO constructions, (74b) and (75b) correspond to THAT constructions with no Modals, in (74a) and (75a). If a Modal were inserted in a sentence like (75a), e.g. *It seems that Tom may/ must/could be stupid*, then there is no corresponding TO construction.

There is an important difference between a Judgement TO construction with a SEEM verb, as in (74b) and (75b), and a Modal (FOR) TO clause in subject relation (and extraposable) before a SEEM verb, acting as copula, and an adjective, e.g. *It seems unusual for him to come home so late.* If such a Modal (FOR) TO clause could be replaced by a THAT complement—with similar meaning—then the latter would often include a MODAL, e.g. *It seems unusual that he should come home so late.*

*Matter*, and *count*, from the MATTER type, relate to the fact of some event, not to any potentiality of involvement, or to the durational detail of an activity. They are in view of this restricted to a THAT or WH- complement clause, e.g. *That John cheated matters a lot to his mother*, and *It matters to me who gets to deliver that speech*.

## 8.4. Complement clauses with Primary-B verbs, and with adjectives

Complement clauses can function as subject for verbs from the ANNOYING type, as object for LIKING, ATTENTION, THINKING and DECIDING, and in either object or post-object slot for SPEAKING. Some adjectives can take a complement clause in subject and others in post-predicate position. Only some verbs from the COMPARING and RELATING types may (like some verbs from MAKING and HELPING) have complement clauses in both subject and object relations.

### 8.4.1. ATTENTION

Verbs in the ATTENTION type have a number of special properties that set them off—semantically and syntactically—from other types. Firstly, they are generally used to describe the Perceiver seeing or hearing something outside themself. The subject of a complement clause will normally be different from the main clause subject. And in the rare instances when it is the same it must still be stated; that is, ATTENTION verbs do not permit omission of a coreferential subject from ING or Modal (FOR) TO complement clauses, e.g. *I heard myself telling a story on the radio*, not *\*I heard telling a story on the radio*.

Secondly, one may become aware of some activity—using sight or hearing—either directly or indirectly. With ATTENTION verbs, THAT complements are used to refer to indirect knowledge. Compare *I heard that John let off the fireworks* (i.e. I heard someone recounting this piece of news) with *I heard John letting off the fireworks* (i.e. I heard it happening). And also *I noticed that Mary had hit Jane* (I may have seen Mary grasping a blood-stained stick, and Jane holding her head and weeping, and thus drawn this conclusion) with *I noticed Mary hitting Jane* (I saw the actual blows).

Some ATTENTION verbs take a Modal (FOR) TO complement, which of course relates to direct perception of the complement clause subject becoming involved in the activity. Since, for this type, THAT clauses refer only to indirect perception we do not get the meaning similarity between a Modal (FOR) TO and a THAT-including-Modal complement, which was noted in §8.2.3 for verbs from other types.

Modal (FOR) TO complements with ATTENTION verbs must omit the *for* and also—in an active sentence—the *to*. Compare the Modal (FOR) TO construction in (76a) with the ING construction in (76b):

**(76a)**    *I saw John jump across the stream*
**(76b)**    *I saw John('s) jumping across the stream*

(The *'s* on the subject of an ING complement clause after an ATTENTION verb is often omitted; it cannot generally be included after an inanimate subject e.g. *I saw it(*s) raining*. See §2.7 (and §5.1).)

An ING complement refers to some durative activity; (76b) might be used when John was seen crossing the stream by jumping from one stepping-stone to the next. Sentence (76a) states that I saw John get involved in the act of jumping across the stream; the details are immaterial—(76a) could relate to a single jump that took him clear across, or to a series of jumps.

We described (in §8.2.4) how, when the activity referred to by the main clause relates directly to the subject of a Modal (FOR) TO complement clause in object function, then *for* should drop, with the complement clause subject becoming surface object of the main verb. This semantic condition plainly prevails with ATTENTION verbs; hence, *for* cannot be included. In §8.2.5 we saw that the *to* is omitted when there is a direct connection between the referents of main clause and complement clause verbs. This connection holds in (76a)—which describes direct perception— and so *to* must be omitted. Note though that *to* has to be included in the passive version of (76a), i.e. *John was seen to jump across the stream*. A passive provides an adjective-like description which lacks the pragmatic immediacy of the active (it is almost 'John was in a state of being seen ...') so that *to* is not omitted.

In §5.1 we distinguished seven subtypes of ATTENTION. The LOOK class— with *look (at)*, *stare (at)*, *hunt (for)* and so on—refers to the Perceiver directing their attention onto some Impression, which will be an NP, not a complement clause; some verbs in this subtype (*investigate, examine, check, explore*) may relate to the Perceiver directing their attention to uncovering some information that can be realised through a WH- clause, e.g. *He investigated whether she was dead/who had killed her.*

The SEE subtype involves straightforward description of an act of perception. SHOW describes how one person assists another to see or hear something. RECOGNISE relates to perceiving something and knowing what it is, and DISCOVER to perceiving something that was not apparent before. Verbs from these four subtypes take THAT and WH- complements, and also Judgement TO clauses, e.g.

(77a)   *I saw/recognised/discovered that he was their leader/who was their leader*

(77b)   *I saw/recognised/discovered him to be their leader*

Only SEE and SHOW may relate to a durative activity and thus only verbs from these subtypes accept ING clauses. The Modal (FOR) TO complement construction (with both *for* and *to* omitted in the active) occurs most commonly with the SEE subtype, dealing with a straightforward act of perception.

*Witness*, making up a subtype on its own, must describe some activity, rather than a state. It takes THAT, WH- and ING clauses, but not Judgement TO. *Watch* refers to deliberate perception over a period of time. It is generally found with an ING clause (e.g. *I watched John building the wall*), although a Modal (FOR) TO is also possible in the active (*I watched John build the wall*) but not in the passive (**John was watched (to) build the wall*).

*Watch*, and the sense of *listen* (*to*) that belongs to the WATCH subtype, may also take a THAT (or WH-) complement, but with a quite different meaning from the 'indirect knowledge' sense of THAT with SEE, SHOW, RECOGNISE and DISCOVER. A THAT clause with *watch* or *listen* (*to*) simply relates to the fact of some event, with an instruction to ensure that it does or doesn't take place; compare the THAT complement in *You watch that the soup doesn't boil* with the ING clause in *You watch the soup boiling*. (Significantly, *watch* and *listen* are perhaps the only verbs from the ATTENTION, THINKING and DECIDING types which take a THAT construction but may not be used in a parenthetical—see §8.1.)

## 8.4.2. *THINKING*

This type includes verbs of thinking, knowing, believing and the like. They typically refer to some unit of information, which can be realised as a THAT, WH-, WH- TO or Judgement TO complement. Thus, *I thought that it would rain today, She forgot whether she had turned the stove off, We pondered over who to appoint, She believed him to be handsome.*

The ASSUME subtype and positive members of the BELIEVE class must refer to something quite definite, and thus cannot take WH- or WH- TO complements. Compare with verbs from CONCLUDE, which can indicate that a conclusion has been reached without necessarily revealing what it is; thus *We believe that John did it*, but not *\*We believe who did it*, as against *We have inferred that John did it* and *We have inferred who did it*. *Doubt*, a negative member of BELIEVE, takes *whether* (and also THAT) clauses—see §8.2.1.

Verbs from the PONDER subtype refer to modes of thinking; they typically take WH- complements, e.g. *We speculated over who might have killed him, They brooded over whether to go or not*. Most of these verbs will seldom (or never) occur with THAT complements—referring to some definite fact—or with Judgement TO clauses. *Forget* and *doubt*, because of their inherently negative meanings, are seldom found with Judgement TO—thus *I remembered/believed her to be polite* but not *\*I forgot/doubted her to be polite* (although some speakers can say *I'd forgotten him to be so tall*).

Verbs in the THINK, PONDER and REMEMBER subtypes, and *understand* from KNOW—but not ASSUME, CONCLUDE, SOLVE, BELIEVE and the remainder of KNOW—may relate to some continuous activity, by means of an ING complement, e.g. *I thought of/pondered over/remembered her building that wall all by herself*. If the complement clause subject is coreferential with main clause subject it will be omitted, e.g. *I thought of/remembered building that wall all by myself*. The potential semantic contrast between THAT (referring to some specific event or state) and ING (referring to something extended in time) is brought out in:

(78a)  *I can understand that Mary was upset* (when her spectacles broke)
(78b)  *I can understand Mary('s) being upset* (all this year, because of the legal fuss over her divorce)

*Remember, forget, know* and *learn* may relate to the complement clause subject getting involved in some activity, described by a Modal (FOR) TO complement, e.g. *I remembered/knew for Mary to take a pill after breakfast yesterday*. One most commonly remembers etc. something that one should do oneself; complement clause subject will then be coreferential with main clause subject and will be omitted (together with *for*), in the same way that the coreferential subject of an ING clause is omitted—thus

*I remembered/knew to take a pill after breakfast yesterday*. For *teach*, a lexical causative related to *know* (see §5.2), the subject of the complement clause—which is in post-object slot—is omitted when coreferential with main clause object, e.g. *I taught Mary to take a pill after breakfast each day*. *Think* can also be used with a Modal (FOR) TO complement in marked circumstances (typically, in a question or a negative clause), e.g. *Did you think to lock the door?* or *I didn't think to lock the door* (but scarcely *\*I thought to lock the door*).

### 8.4.3. DECIDING

*Decide* (*on*) and related verbs have two senses: (*a*) a reasoned judgement about the present or past, e.g. *I decided that it was too cold to cycle to work today*; and (*b*) an intention regarding the future, e.g. *I decided that I would drive instead*. They may take THAT or WH- complement clauses in both senses. Corresponding to sense (*b*) there can be a Modal (FOR) TO or a WH-TO construction, e.g. *I decided to drive today, I'll decide when to drive*. The Decision-Maker most frequently thinks about something that concerns themself; complement clause subject (plus *for*) is omitted when it is coreferential with the main clause subject, as in the example just given. But it is possible for the subjects to differ, e.g. *I decided for Mary to make the sandwiches and John the scones*. The *for* may not then be omitted, after *decide, determine* or *resolve*, since the main verb relates to the complete activity referred to by the complement clause, not specifically to its subject. *Choose* can, however, be used to address the complement clause subject, as when addressing a class of children: *I choose Mary to carry the banner*; the *for* is then omitted (see also (44)–(45) in §2.7).

   *Decide* (*on*) and *determine* (*on*)—but not *resolve* or *choose*—can relate to some durational activity, and may then take an ING complement, e.g. *I decided/determined on re-laying the lawn while Mary is away on vacation in Florida*.

   As mentioned in §8.4.2, most THINKING verbs may take a Judgement TO complement—compare *I think/know/believe that John is stupid* with *I think/know/believe John to be stupid*. The Judgement TO construction is only marginally acceptable with verbs from the CONCLUDE subtype of THINKING, e.g. *?I concluded/inferred/argued John to be stupid*. It is quite unacceptable with DECIDING verbs, e.g. *I decided that John is stupid*, but not *\*I decided*

*John to be stupid.* It seems that Judgement TO can only be related to some straightforward impression or opinion, not to the result of a process of reasoning.


### 8.4.4. SPEAKING

Verbs of this type cover a wide semantic spectrum, and take a corresponding diversity of complement clauses. It will be useful to deal with the subtypes one at a time. Note that all those verbs which may introduce direct speech can also show reported speech (in the Message role) through a THAT and/or a WH- complement clause.

TALK verbs—such as *talk, speak, chat, joke*—refer to the activity of social communication. They can introduce an ING or WH- clause by a preposition and this clause omits its subject when coreferential with main clause subject, e.g. *John spoke about (Mary('s)) leaving home.*

Verbs from the DISCUSS subtype are transitive, with the Message in O function. They report some activity (which is likely to be extended in time), or something about which clarification is required—coded by an ING or WH- TO clause, e.g. *They described the police rescuing the trapped child, We discussed whether to invite Mary.*

The SHOUT subtype refers to manner of vocal production. These verbs may be used intransitively, without any mention of the Message (or Addressee or Medium). But they can also introduce direct speech, or a THAT clause, or a Message consisting of Label-NP-plus-preposition-plus-Content, which may be an ING or WH- complement clause. The Label can be omitted but the preposition must then be retained; this contrasts with verbs from the DISCUSS subtype where the preposition will drop with the Message-Label. Thus:

(79a)   *They discussed/referred to (the news about) John('s) being arrested*
(79b)   *He shouted/read (the news) about John('s) being arrested*

The meanings of DISCUSS verbs relate to a specific Message (which must be stated); it can be a complement clause in O function. But the Message is an optional accompaniment of a SHOUT verb, and it is thus appropriate that any complement clause (as Message-Content) be introduced by a preposition. There is an important difference between *refer to* (in (79a)), which is a strictly transitive verb including an inherent preposition, and *shout* (in

(79b)), which can optionally take an appropriate preposition plus complement clause or NP.

The REPORT subtype contains a fair number of verbs, which in §5.4 we divided into eight sets. Leaving aside for the time being set (viii) (with *promise* and *threaten*), REPORT verbs are transitive with the Message in O slot. This may always be a THAT or WH- clause, corresponding to direct speech.

Verbs *say, declare, state, affirm* (in sets (i) and (ii)) necessarily make an assertion, and are restricted to THAT or WH- complements. Other REPORT verbs may relate to some fact, or to a durational activity, and then accept an ING complement, e.g. *She reported/commented on/boasted about/admitted (John's) having spent the past year in jail.* (With *confess (to)* the complement clause subject must be coreferential with main clause subject and thus omitted, simply because one can only confess to something one has done oneself, e.g. *He confessed to taking the gold.*)

A Judgement TO construction is possible with *declare, state, report, announce, claim, admit* and other verbs that can provide straightforward introduction to an opinion about someone's state, e.g. *They declared/admitted him to be insane.* (*Say*, from this subtype, may only take a Judgement TO construction in the passive, e.g. *He is said to be insane.*) The Judgement TO construction is not possible with verbs that include an inherent preposition, such as *remark (on), boast (about/of), complain (about/of)*—one must say *She boasted that he was clever* or *She boasted about him/his being clever*, not *\*She boasted (about) him to be clever.* (The prohibition may essentially relate to the meanings of verbs like *boast* and *complain*, which include an emotional component that would not accord well with the 'judgement' meaning of this TO construction.) *Explain* is another verb which is not allowed in a Judgement TO sentence (*She explained that he was ill*, not *\*She explained him to be ill*); the meaning of *explain*, 'give reasons for something', is incompatible with the meaning of the Judgement TO complement, 'give a judgement about something'.

*Promise* and *threaten* have the Addressee in O slot; this can be followed by *with* plus Message-Content, or a THAT clause, or direct speech. These verbs, plus *undertake, offer* and *propose* (which have the Message in O slot), may relate to the subject of the complement clause getting involved in the activity referred to by that clause, and this can be expressed through a Modal (FOR) TO complement. Since one generally promises/threatens/offers to do something oneself, the complement clause subject is most often coreferential with main clause subject and is then omitted, together with *for*, e.g. *I offered to clean the house*. All dialects allow a similar construction with *promise* and *threaten* when the Addressee NP is not stated, e.g. *I promised to clean the house*. Only some dialects permit this construction with *promise* when the Addressee is stated, e.g. *I promised John to clean the house* (dialects which exclude this are here restricted to a THAT construction, e.g. *I promised John that I would clean the house*). *Promise* is perhaps the only verb which—in some dialects—can freely omit the subject of a post-object Modal (FOR) TO clause when it is coreferential with main clause subject, i.e. in *I promised John to clean the house* it is I who will do the cleaning. All other verbs—e.g. *order, persuade, urge*—omit this NP when it is coreferential with main clause object, i.e. in *I ordered John to clean the house* it is John who should do the cleaning. It may be this surface similarity with *I ordered John to clean the house*—and the danger of semantic confusion—which has unconsciously motivated speakers of some dialects to consider *I promised John to clean the house* an ungrammatical sentence. (There are a couple of verbs which can omit the subject NP from a post-object Modal (FOR) TO complement when it is coreferential with the main clause subject only if the complement clause is passive, e.g. *I asked/begged John to be allowed to clean his house*.)

*Undertake* and *offer* may, exceptionally, have a Modal (FOR) TO clause with subject different from that of the main clause; *for* must then be retained—e.g. *I offered for my charwoman to clean the house*. Such a construction is infelicitous with *promise* and *threaten*, a THAT clause being used instead—thus *I promised (John) that my charwoman would clean the house*, not *\*I promised (John) for my charwoman to clean the house*.

The INFORM subtype has Addressee in O slot. The Message is introduced by *of* or *on* or *about* (the preposition must drop before a THAT and may drop before a WH- complement). These verbs may relate to some fact (THAT), clarification (WH- or WH- TO), or durational activity (ING complement), e.g. *Remind me that I have to set the alarm, She'll inform us (about) whether (we have) to dress for dinner, Fred informed Mary about John's having been waiting outside her door all afternoon*. The basic construction for verbs from the TELL type is with Addressee as O, followed by preposition *or* or *about* plus Message, which can be a THAT, WH- or ING complement, very much as for INFORM.

Verbs from the ORDER subtype relate to a Message directed at the Addressee. The Addressee is in O slot, and is followed by the Message, which can be a THAT clause (generally including a Modal) or a Modal (FOR) TO or WH- TO complement. Alternatively, the Message may be direct speech. The Addressee may be omitted in the presence of direct speech or a THAT clause. The complement clause subject is sometimes not coreferential with main clause object. If this is so then *for* must be retained in a Modal (FOR) TO clause (recall that it may only be omitted when the complement clause immediately follows the main clause verb), e.g. *The general ordered all officers for their men to parade at dawn.* (A fair number of speakers find this ungrammatical, and might instead use a THAT construction, i.e. *The general ordered all officers that their men should parade at dawn.*) Typically, someone is ordered or instructed or recommended to do something themself (rather than for someone else to do something); the expectation with ORDER verbs is for the subject of a Modal (FOR) TO complement clause to be coreferential with main clause object and then the complement clause subject and *for* are omitted, e.g. *The general ordered all officers to parade at dawn.* Recommend, from this subtype, offers advice rather than instructions, and may then take an ING complement (see §5.4).

There is a certain parallel between the Secondary verb type MAKING and the ORDER subtype of SPEAKING, with Causer corresponding to Speaker and the complement clause with the MAKING verb corresponding to the Message of the ORDER verb. Thus, *I forced John to go* and *I ordered/persuaded John to go.* There are, however, significant differences. MAKING verbs involve action to bring about some event and are restricted to Modal (FOR) TO complements; ORDER verbs merely use speech to influence the Addressee and may also take THAT complements. Note also that there is an additional role with ORDER, the Addressee, which may be included before the complement clause, e.g. *I ordered/persuaded John that his wife should sign the declaration herself.*

Some ORDER verbs may have a passive complement clause with inanimate subject, e.g. *General Vasey ordered the barracks to be cleaned.* In fact he must have ordered the appropriate people to perform the task; the use of this construction focuses on what was done to the barracks, ignoring the insignificant matter of which particular minions did it. (From the MAKING type only *cause* behaves in this way, e.g. *He caused it to be destroyed.*)

Just like negative MAKING verbs, so negative ORDER verbs such as *prohibit, dissuade, discourage* (and, nowadays, *forbid*) take a (FROM) ING complement. Here the main clause object must be identical to complement clause subject—thus *John dissuaded Mary from going* is a close syntactic analogue of *John prevented Mary (from) going.*

The FORGIVE type conveys the speaker's emotional attitude towards the Addressee, which is often realised through speech. As discussed in §5.4, some verbs from this type may have an ING clause, introduced by a preposition, giving additional information about the attitude or the reason for it. Like TALK and DISCUSS, this subtype does not usually introduce direct speech (some minor exceptions were mentioned in §5.4), and cannot take a THAT or WH- complement clause.

## 8.4.5. *LIKING, ANNOYING and adjectives*

Verbs from the LIKING and ANNOYING types describe the feelings an Experiencer (who must be human or a higher animal) has about a Stimulus. For LIKING the Experiencer may control the activity, and is mapped onto subject function (e.g. *John tried to like Mary*). For ANNOYING the Experiencer has no possibility of control but in some circumstances control may lie with the Stimulus if it is human, and Stimulus is thus in subject relation (e.g. *Mary tried to please/annoy John*).

The Stimulus may be some object, referred to by an NP (e.g. *Mary hates horses*), or some habitual or durative activity, shown by an ING clause (*Mary hates riding horses*). Or it can involve Label-plus-preposition-plus-Content. The Label can be an NP with an abstract noun as head, or else just *it*; the Content can be an NP or a THAT, ING or Modal (FOR) TO complement clause.

A LIKING verb can relate just to the Experiencer's feelings about the fact of a certain thing happening (they may not be at all interested in the internal details of the event). A THAT complement is then appropriate, as in:

(80a)   *I like it that Mary sings the blues each Friday evening* (because she goes out, and I get peace to work out my betting system for Saturday's races)

Or the LIKING verb may relate to the Experiencer's feelings about some activity as it unfolds; ING is then the appropriate complement choice:

(80b)   *I like Mary('s) singing the blues* (and could listen to her all night)

Or, the Experiencer might have good (or bad) feelings about the complement clause subject's getting involved in an activity (without necessarily enjoying the activity per se); a Modal (FOR) TO complement would then be used:

**(80c)**   *I like (it for) Mary to sing the blues* (because she makes a lot of money doing it)

**(80d)**   *I would like Mary to sing the blues* (because I think her voice is just right for that style—although in fact my own preference is for opera)

In §8.2.4 we described how the *for* should be omitted when the emotional feeling described by the LIKING verb is directed particularly at the complement clause subject, rather than at the whole clause; *it* must then also drop, and the complement clause subject becomes surface object of the main verb. See examples (45a/b) in §8.2.4.

It is perfectly normal for the complement clause subject to be different from the main clause subject, or equally for them to be coreferential. In the latter case the complement clause subject drops from an ING or Modal (FOR) TO clause (and then *for* and *it* also drop), e.g. *I like singing the blues, I like to sing the blues*.

Only some LIKING verbs have the width of meaning that allows all three complement choices; they include *like, love, hate, prefer*. Other verbs—such as *loathe, admire, value, regret, (don't) care about*—can relate to feelings about the fact of some event or about a durational activity, but less readily to a potentiality of involvement; these are unlikely to be found with Modal (FOR) TO complements. A third set of LIKING verbs are pretty well restricted by their meanings to reference to durational activity and thus to an ING complement, e.g. *enjoy* 'get pleasure from something happening', *object to* 'take exception to something happening' (see the fuller list in §5.5). Finally, there are *worship* and *fall for*, which must have an entity (i.e. an NP, and not a complement clause) as Stimulus, e.g. *He worships Allah/money, She fell for him*.

Subject and object possibilities are effectively reversed between the LIKING and ANNOYING types. THAT, ING and Modal (FOR) TO complements may, as Stimulus, fill the subject slot for ANNOYING verbs. Complement clause subject can be omitted when it is coreferential with main clause subject, from an ING or a Modal (FOR) TO clause (the *for* also drops). THAT and Modal (FOR) TO complements can be extraposed to the end of the main clause with *it* then filling subject slot. Note that *for* can never be omitted when complement clause subject is retained (even under extraposition)—see the discussion of syntactic and semantic conditions on *for* omission in §§2.7 and 8.2.4.

The same semantic principles apply as with LIKING. An ANNOYING verb can relate to the Experiencer's feelings about the fact of some event, referred to by a THAT clause:

**(81a)**  *That Phil is now dating Ann surprises me/It surprises me that Phil is now dating Ann*

Or it can refer to an ongoing activity, referred to by an ING clause:

**(81b)**  *Fred('s) telling jokes all evening entertained us greatly*

Or to the potentiality of someone's getting involved in some activity:

**(81c)**  *It would please me for John to marry Mary*
**(81d)**  *It might confuse you to try to learn three new languages all at the same time*

When there is a Modal (FOR) TO clause as Stimulus—with an ANNOYING or a LIKING verb—the main clause predicate often includes a MODAL, as in (80d), (81c), (81d). Indeed, there is often also a SEMI-MODAL in the Modal (FOR) TO clause (which, of course, cannot include a MODAL), as in:

**(82)**  *To have to carry a fifty-kilo pack on my back would exhaust me*

The ANNOYING type carries a wide semantic range (far broader than LIKING), e.g. *scare, surprise, offend, delight, amuse, worry, annoy, anger, puzzle, interest, disgust, tire*. It seems that all these verbs have the potential for taking all three kinds of subject complement; but most do have preferences that are determined by their individual meanings, e.g. *surprise* is perhaps most used with a THAT clause, *satisfy* with an ING complement.

Turning now to Adjectives, we find that the VALUE type and a number of subtypes of HUMAN PROPENSITY have similar meanings and complement possibilities to ANNOYING and LIKING verbs (see §3.2). *Fond (of )*, from HUMAN PROPENSITY, refers to a durational activity and thus takes an ING clause, similar to *enjoy*, e.g. *She's fond of listening to Bach, She enjoys listening to Bach.*

Adjectives from the ANGRY, HAPPY and UNSURE subtypes have similar meanings to the past participles of ANNOYING verbs. The UNSURE set involves the speaker's assessment about some potential event and is confined to THAT or WH- complements, e.g. *I'm certain that a crime was committed but I'm unsure (about) who to blame*. The ANGRY subtype—including *angry (about), jealous (of ), mad (about)*—describes an emotional reaction to some definite happening (either the fact of an event, or some durational activity), and may take a THAT or ING complement, e.g. *Fred was angry that Mary resigned, I'm sad about John's digging up the flower garden*. Verbs from the HAPPY subtype—including *anxious (about), happy (about), afraid (of )*—deal with an emotional response to some actual or potential happen-

ing; besides THAT and ING they may also take a Modal (FOR) TO complement, relating to the potentiality of complement clause subject becoming
involved in an event, e.g. *I'd be happy/afraid (for Mary) to cross the desert
alone.*

VALUE adjectives provide a judgement about some unit event or durational activity and may take a THAT or ING clause in subject function, e.g.
*It is good that Mary plays hockey, Flying kites is amusing*; subset (*b*) (see
§3.2) may also have a Modal (FOR) TO subject complement, e.g. *It was
strange for Mary to resign like that.* Some VALUE adjectives are similar in
meaning and syntax to ANNOYING verbs, except that the latter relate the
emotional judgement to a specific Experiencer (in object slot), whereas
VALUE adjectives purport to give an objective, impersonal judgement—
compare the examples just given with *It pleases her uncle that Mary plays
hockey, Flying kites amuses some people, It puzzled me for Mary to resign
like that.* Compare also *That John likes Bach is curious/surprising* with *That
John likes Bach interests/surprises me.*

Adjectives from the EAGER subtype of HUMAN PROPENSITY are similar in
meaning and syntax to WANTING verbs, expressing the Principal's attitude
towards some event or state that is not (yet) real. Like WANTING verbs,
EAGER adjectives can take a THAT or a Modal (FOR) TO complement, e.g. *I'm
eager (for Mary) to enter the race, I want (Mary) to enter the race.* *Ready*
focuses on the subject's involvement in some activity and is restricted to a
Modal (FOR) TO complement; it is thus like *want, need* and *prepare* from the
WANTING type—see the discussion in §8.3.3.

Those adjectives which are most different in meaning from verbs are the
DIFFICULTY and QUANTIFICATION types, and the CLEVER and HONEST subtypes of HUMAN PROPENSITY. Some QUANTIFICATION adjectives—such as
*definite, probable, true*—provide a factual qualification regarding a definite
event, and are restricted to THAT subject complements, e.g. *It is true that
John forged Mary's signature.* Others describe the speaker's opinion about
some actual or potential happening and may take THAT or Modal (FOR) TO
subject complements, e.g. *It is normal/sensible for a policeman to carry a
gun.* One group of QUALIFICATION adjectives relates to the potentiality of
the complement subject behaving in a certain way; this subject may then be
raised from an extraposed Modal (FOR) TO complement to replace *it* in main
clause subject slot—compare *It is likely that al-Qaeda will bomb New York*
(the event is likely) with *Al-Qaeda is likely to bomb New York* (it is likely
that the al-Qaeda terrorist organisation will act in this way).

Adjectives in the CLEVER and HONEST subtypes of HUMAN PROPENSITY have similar properties. They can relate to a unit event, through THAT, or to someone's involvement in an activity, through Modal (FOR) TO, e.g. *It was stupid that no one answered the door*, *It would be stupid for John to ignore those rumours* (see §3.2). These adjectives may also directly describe some person, who is in subject slot, with a preposition introducing a clause that gives the reason for this description, e.g. *John is stupid in the way that he is always trying to buck authority*.

Adjectives from the DIFFICULTY class may relate to some specific involvement in an event, through a Modal (FOR) TO subject complement, e.g. *It is hard for young children to sit still during a long sermon*. Or they can refer to some very general mode of behaviour, then taking as subject an ING complement with subject omitted, e.g. *Cooking scones is easy (for some people)*.

The difficulty or value of an activity may be a function of the object of the complement clause, and there is an alternative construction with this NP as subject of the adjective, e.g. *Scones are easy to cook*.

The BUSY subtype of HUMAN PROPENSITY relates to continuing activity, and is thus restricted to an ING complement clause, as in *She is currently preoccupied with marking the exam papers*.

## 8.4.6. Other Primary-B types

Verbs from the COMPARING type—e.g. *resemble, differ from*—and Adjectives from the SIMILARITY type—e.g. *like, unlike, similar (to), different (from)*—must have subject and post-predicate (direct object or prepositional object) constituents with comparable meanings. Both may refer to people, things or places, e.g. *Adelaide resembles Auckland in some ways*. Or both may relate to kinds of activity, which can be referred to through subjectless ING complements, e.g. *Trying to get John to smile is like getting blood out of a stone*.

Verbs from the RELATING type refer to some natural or logical relationship. The possibilities for both subject and object slots are: (i) an NP, often with a SPEECH ACT noun as head; (ii) an NP of this kind followed by a THAT clause which is referred to by the head noun of the NP, e.g. *the report that John is lost* or *the verdict that he is guilty*; (iii) a plain THAT clause; (iv) an ING complement; or (v) a WH- complement clause. A THAT complement in subject slot with a verb from this type is most unlikely to be extraposed to the end of the main clause, e.g. *That John was found innocent indicates that the jury was made up of fools*, not **It indicates that the jury was made up of fools that John was found innocent.*

*Indicate, show, demonstrate* and *suggest* (in their meanings that fall within the RELATING type) take any of (i)–(iv) as subject. They may describe how the situation referred to by a THAT clause in object slot follows from that referred to by the subject, e.g. *The fact that John didn't turn up suggests that he may be sick, Mary's having slept through the concert shows that she doesn't care for Mozart.* Or the referent of the subject may help resolve some point of clarification posed by a WH- clause as object, e.g. *The fact that John had flecks of cream in his beard suggests (to me) who it was that stole the trifle. Imply* is limited to the first sense, with a THAT object clause; it does not take a WH- clause in object slot.

*Relate* (and *is related to*) simply state that two things are connected. The subject may be any of (i)–(v) and the object any of these save a plain THAT clause, e.g. *Mrs Smith's being so rude to you relates to the fact that she was friendly with my first wife. Depend on* will typically link two hypotheticals, both expressed by WH- clauses, e.g. *How we climb the mountain depends on what equipment John brings. Result from* deals with a connection between two actual states or activities; it must take NP or NP-plus-THAT-clause or ING clause in subject and object slots, e.g. *The fact that John was found innocent results from the jury('s) being totally incompetent.* None of *relate to, depend on* and *result from* may take a plain THAT clause in object slot; this may be at least in part because the preposition, which is an important component of each verb, would then have to drop before *that.* Compare *That Arwon won the Melbourne Cup demonstrates (the fact) that he is a horse of quality*, with *That Arwon won the Melbourne Cup relates to the fact that he is a horse of quality*, where *the fact* could not be omitted.

Some verbs from the ACTING type may relate either to an entity (shown by an NP), e.g. *She copied the poem on the board*, or to some activity (shown by an ING complement clause), e.g. *She copied John's eating his cake with a fork.*

Verbs such as *experience* and *undergo*, from the HAPPENING type, have in O slot a description of something that happens to the subject. This can be expressed through an ACTIVITY or STATE noun or through an ING complement clause (often in the passive, as is appropriate for something that befalls the subject), e.g. *She underwent an operation for appendicitis, She underwent having her belly cut open and the appendix taken out.*

## Notes to Chapter 8

§8.1. The classic paper on parentheticals is Urmson (1952). He gives an example which is similar to my (8a/b). Suppose John knows that the trains are on strike and sees Mary rush to the station. John could then use a THAT complement construction, *Mary believes that the trains are running*. But he could not, in these circumstances, use the parenthetical construction *The trains, Mary believes, are running* since by so doing he would be implying that the trains are running. Another paper dealing with parentheticals is Hooper (1975).

§8.2–4. A large number of books and papers have been published in recent years on the syntax (and sometimes also the semantics) of complement clauses in English, all of them containing useful information and ideas but none making the full set of distinctions revealed in this chapter. These include Akmajian (1977); Bolinger (1968, 1972, 1977a); Bresnan (1979); Duffley (1992); Huddleston (1984); Huddleston and Pullum (2002); Kiparsky and Kiparsky (1970); Menzel (1975); Ney (1981); Noonan (1985); Ransom (1986); Riddle (1975); Stockwell, Schachter and Partee (1973); Thompson (1973); Vendler (1967, 1972); Wierzbicka (1988).

§8.2.2. The omission or inclusion of *'s* in an ING complement clause is not an automatic matter, and may sometimes carry a meaning difference. This is a topic that will repay further research.

§8.2.3–4. Rosenbaum (1967) drew a distinction between 'noun phrase complements' and 'verb phrase complements'. Verbs like *force*, *help* and *order* were said to take VP complements while *believe*, *expect*, *remember* and others were said to take NP complements. This categorisation has been repeated in many works since, e.g. Perlmutter and Soames (1979). As shown in §8.2.4, there is no essential syntactic or semantic difference between the Modal (FOR) TO complements with *force*, *help*, *order*, *expect* and *remember*. *Believe* takes a quite different variety of complement construction, Judgement TO. Other differences that have been quoted in the literature between verbs like *force* and *help*, on the one hand, and verbs like *believe* and *expect*, on the other hand, are a consequence of differences in meaning, and carry no syntactic implications. The Rosenbaum distinction is simply incorrect. (For a line of argument similar to that followed here, see Schmerling 1978.)

§8.2.4. Henry (1992) describes the inclusion of *for* in Belfast English, where one can say things like *I want for to meet him* and *It is difficult for to see that*. Henry's paper includes references to publications on other dialects which include *for* in places where Standard English would not have it.

§8.2.6. Borkin (1973, 1984) discuss conditions for the omission of *to be*.

# 9

## I kicked at the bomb, which exploded, and wakened you up
## Transitivity and causatives

Some languages have a strict division of verbs into transitive—those that take A (transitive subject) and O (transitive object) core syntactic relations—and intransitive—those that have just one core syntactic relation, S (intransitive subject). A few languages even employ morphological marking so that there can never be any doubt as to whether a verb is transitive or intransitive, e.g. if a verb in Fijian shows a transitive suffix then it must have an object; if it lacks this suffix there will be no direct object.

Transitivity is a much more fluid matter in English. There are, it is true, a number of verbs that are strictly transitive, e.g. *like, promote, recognise, inform*, and a few that are strictly intransitive, e.g. *arrive, chat, matter*. But many verbs in English may be used either transitively or intransitively.

There are two kinds of correspondence between the syntactic relations of intransitive and transitive constructions:

(i)  those for which S = A, e.g. *She's following (us), Have you eaten (lunch)?, He's knitting (a jumper), I won (the game)*;
(ii) those for which S = O, e.g. *The ice melted/Ivan melted the ice, Mary's arm hurts/John hurt Mary's arm, Fred tripped up/Jane tripped up Fred, Tim is working hard/Tim's boss is working him hard.*

If the transitive version is taken as prior for (i), then we can say that the intransitive version is obtained by omitting the object, and that this is possible for some—but not all—transitive verbs in English. If the intransitive construction is taken as prior for (ii), then we can say that the transitive is a causative version of the intransitive, with the original S becoming O and a 'Causer' introduced in A relation. A full discussion of dual transitivity is in §9.3.

There is also the matter of prepositions. Some transitive verbs may optionally insert a preposition before the direct object, e.g. *He kicked (at) the door, She bit (on) the strap.* Is the original object NP still an object when it is now preceded by a preposition? Some verbs may omit the preposition before a peripheral constituent, either before a 'measure phrase', e.g. *run (for) a mile, stand (for) two hours in the rain*, or before a non-measure phrase, e.g. *jump (over) the ravine, speak (in) French.* Are measure phrases like *a mile* and *two hours*, or non-measure phrases like *the ravine* and *French*, now in direct object function? (Note that in each instance the inclusion or omission of a preposition has a definite semantic effect.)

There are a number of verbs that must take a preposition, and this behaves in some ways as if it were an 'inherent' part of the verb; a following NP will have many of the characteristics of a direct object, e.g. *rely on, hope for.* Related to this are 'phrasal verbs', combinations of verb and preposition that have meaning (and syntax) not inferrable from those of the two components, e.g. *take after, put off.* §9.2 discusses the question of prepositions and transitivity.

## 9.1. The semantic basis of syntactic relations

A verb has—according to its semantic type—one or two or three semantic roles; each of these must be mapped onto a core or peripheral syntactic relation.

If there is only one role then it is mapped onto S. As mentioned in §3.3.1, S has a wide semantic range, relating both to roles that control an activity (e.g. *He ran, They chatted, She winked*) and those that cannot—or are unlikely to—exercise control (e.g. *The stone rolled down the hill, The old man died, My bubble burst*).

If there are two or more core roles then one will be mapped onto A and the other onto O syntactic relation. That role which is most likely to be relevant to the success of the activity will be A, e.g. *the wind* in *The wind blew down my house*, and *the thunder* in *The thunder frightened the child*. Most often, the role mapped onto A will be human and 'most relevant to the success of the activity' then equates with 'could initiate or control the activity'.

For most semantic types one particular role will always be mapped onto A (i.e. there is no choice involved)—this is the Perceiver for ATTENTION, the Cogitator for THINKING, the Speaker for SPEAKING, the Human for CORPOREAL, the Causer for MAKING, the Principal for WANTING, and so on. The GIVING type uses different lexemes depending on whether Donor or Recipient is exercising control, and is thus in A relation, e.g. *Mary* (Donor: A) *tried to lend the blue hat* (Gift: O) *to me* (Recipient) and *I* (Recipient: A) *tried to borrow the blue hat* (Gift: O) *from Mary* (Donor). The LIKING and ANNOYING types involve the same two roles; for LIKING the Experiencer may be in a position to exercise control, and so is in A relation, whereas for ANNOYING the success of the activity may be due to the Stimulus, and this is A—compare John (Experiencer: A) *tried to like/dislike Mary* (Stimulus: O) and *Mary* (Stimulus: A) *tried to please/annoy John* (Experiencer: O).

The only verbs that may allow either of two roles to be mapped onto A relation are some from AFFECT. Normally the agent is A, e.g. *John* (Agent: A) *hit Mary* (Target: O) *with his stick* (Manip), but there is another construction in which Manip is A, e.g. *The stick* (Manip: A) *hit Mary* (Target: O) (e.g. as John swung it). Use of this construction may effectively deny that the Agent was responsible for the action, suggesting that it was, perhaps, an accident.

If a verb has just two core roles then that which is not coded into A is placed in O syntactic relation—the Impression for ATTENTION, the Thought for THINKING, the Substance for CORPOREAL, the Stimulus for LIKING, the Experiencer for ANNOYING.

But verbs from some types have three core roles. There is no question about which role should be in A syntactic relation—that which is most relevant to the success of the activity. Of the remaining roles, that which is most salient to the activity (often, that which is affected by the activity) is mapped onto O; the roles which do not correspond to A or to O are marked by an appropriate preposition. For instance, some subtypes of SPEAKING focus on the Addressee (which goes into O relation) while others focus on the Message (which is then O)—compare *He* (Speaker: A) *informed Mary* (Addressee: O) *of the floods in Queensland* (Message) and *He* (Speaker: A) *mentioned the floods in Queensland* (Message: O) *to Mary* (Addressee).

The O relation does in fact show much more variation than A in connection with which roles may be mapped onto it. There are a number of verbs from types that involve three roles—AFFECT, GIVING and SPEAKING—which allow two construction types, with different roles in O relation (that is, with different roles being focused on, as particularly salient in that instance of the activity). One would be likely to use *John* (Agent: A) *hit the vase* (Target: O) *with his stick* (Manip) if the vase broke, but to use *John* (Agent: A) *hit his stick* (Manip: O) *against the concrete post* (Target) if the stick broke.

## 9.2. Prepositions and transitivity

The primary use of prepositions in English is to introduce a peripheral noun phrase, providing locational or temporal specification (e.g. *in the house, at three o'clock*) or marking an instrument (*with a stone*), a beneficiary (*for Mary*), a recipient (*to John*), etc. Each type of prepositional NP can occur with a wide variety of verbs.

Prepositions have two further uses—within 'inherent preposition' verbs and within phrasal verbs. It is important to distinguish these two kinds of verb. The root of an inherent preposition verb is not normally used alone—*refer* only occurs in *refer to*, with an object NP, e.g. *She referred to my book*. *Refer to* is syntactically parallel to *mention*, as in *She mentioned my book*, suggesting that *refer to* should be treated as a single, transitive-verb, lexeme.

The root of a phrasal verb is used alone, but its meaning in a phrasal verb is quite different from its meaning when used alone. Thus we have the simple transitive root *take*, and also phrasal verbs such as *take after* 'resemble' (e.g. one's mother), *take up* 'practise' (e.g. medicine), *take on* 'accept' (e.g. new responsibilities). The meaning of a phrasal verb cannot be inferred from the meanings of its constituent root and preposition; it must be regarded as a separate lexeme.

We thus distinguish (i) verbs that consist just of a root, e.g. *take, mention*; (ii) those that consist of root plus preposition, where the root cannot be used alone, e.g. *refer to*; and (iii) those that consist of root plus preposition, where the root can be used alone, but with a different meaning, e.g. *take after, take up, take on*. §9.2.1 deals with type (ii), with an inherent preposition. We show that the inclusion of a preposition, and the choice of which preposition, is semantically motivated. §9.2.2 deals with type (iii), phrasal verbs; there are six syntactic types, exemplified by *set in*, *take after* NP, *put* NP *off*, *see* NP *through* NP, *take up with* NP and *put* NP *down to* NP. §§9.2.3–5 then consider the semantic and syntactic effects of the insertion of a preposition, e.g. *kick* (*at*) *the door*, and of the omission of a preposition, e.g. *swim* (*across*) *the river*.

## 9.2.1. Verbs with an inherent preposition

There are two ways of treating verbs like *refer* and *rely* within a grammar of English: either (i) as part of two-word lexemes *refer to* and *rely on*, which behave as transitive verbs; or (ii) as intransitive verbs, which must obligatorily be followed by a prepositional NP. Under (ii) they would be treated as similar to verbs like *travel* and *float*, which may optionally take prepositional NPs, e.g. *refer to Jespersen*, *travel* (*to Japan*), *rely on his sense of propriety*, *float* (*on the pool*).

There are two difficulties with alternative (ii). One is that an NP which follows *refer to* or *rely on* behaves like a transitive object in that it can freely become passive subject, quite unlike an NP which follows *travel to* or *float on*. Thus, *Jespersen was referred to by everyone attending the symposium*, but not *\*Japan was travelled to by everyone attending the symposium*, and *John's sense of propriety can be relied on*, but not *\*That pool has been floated on*. The second point to note is that *travel*, *float* and other intransitive verbs can be followed by any one of a number of prepositions (e.g. *travel to/towards/around/in Japan*, *float in/on/across the pool*) whereas *refer* must take *to* and *rely* is confined to *on*.

We thus opt for (i), treating *refer to*, *rely on*, *decide on*, *wish for*, *approve of* and other 'inherent preposition' combinations each as a single, transitive verb. These are often semantically and syntactically similar to a simple transitive verb, e.g. *approve of* and *like*, *wish for* and *want*, *decide on* and *choose*, *refer to* and *mention*, *rely on* and *trust*.

Note that there is one way in which inherent preposition verbs differ from simple verbs. An adverb scarcely ever intervenes between a verb and its direct object, but may come between verb and preposition of an inherent preposition item (see §12.3.2). One can say *He relies on his mother totally* or *He relies totally on his mother* but only *He trusts his mother totally*, not *\*He trusts totally his mother*. Thus, an inherent preposition verb functions like a transitive verb in most respects, but with regard to adverb placement is more akin to intransitive verb plus prepositional NP.

As already mentioned, some inherent preposition verbs can take a complement clause in object relation; following a general rule of English syntax (§2.13B), the preposition drops before complementisers *that*, *for* and *to*. Compare:

(1)   *We decided on/chose Spain for a holiday this year*
(2)   *We decided/chose that we would go to Spain*
(3)   *We decided/chose to go to Spain*

Many transitive verbs in English may omit the object NP in appropriate circumstances (see §9.3.1 and the discussion throughout Chapters 4–6). Not surprisingly, some inherent preposition verbs fall into this category; and when the object NP is omitted the preposition also drops—thus, *listen* (*to*), *confess* (*to*), *approve* (*of*). Note that, as with *refer to* and *rely on*, the prepositional choice is fixed, and the object is readily passivisable, e.g. *That recording which I handed in with my essay last week hasn't been listened to yet.*

Having suggested that *decide on*, *refer to* and similar combinations should be treated as a type of transitive verb, we must now hasten to add that it is not an arbitrary matter that some verbal lexemes consist of just a root, while others involve root plus preposition. The inclusion of a preposition—and which preposition is included—is, without doubt, semantically motivated. Inherent preposition verbs have a meaning which is subtly but significantly different from corresponding simple verbs.

Each preposition in English has a fair semantic range. There is generally a fairly concrete sense—for *at* this is demonstrated by *stay at the seaside*—but in addition a set of more abstract senses—as in *at a rough estimate*, *jump at the chance*, *laugh at John*, *be dismayed at the news*. I plan within the next few years to conduct a full study of the function and meaning of English prepositions, and should then be in a position to explain the semantic rationale for the inclusion of *on* with *rely*, *of* with *approve*, and so on. Meanwhile, just a few informal remarks can be offered on why certain verbs include a preposition, but related verbs do not.

(i) *Wish for* and *want*. With *wish* the preposition *for* introduces an object that may not be attainable, e.g. *For more than forty years Rudolf Hess wished for his freedom*, whereas *want* most often relates to something that can readily be achieved, e.g. *I want my dinner now*. (One can say *John often wants the unobtainable*, and this implies that John is unrealistic, treating the unobtainable as if it were something that he could get.)

(ii) *Confess to* and *admit*. One is likely to confess after a lengthy inner struggle (or after extended questioning by the police); the details of the crime may already be known. The verb *confess* thus focuses on the fact that the subject now says that they did do it, with preposition *to* marking the event that the confession is orientated towards. With *admit* the main interest is likely to be on the object constituent (what the subject did), which may be new information. (*Admit* may, for some speakers, optionally include *to* before the object; it is likely to include *to* when the possibility of the subject's having committed the crime etc. has already been mooted, i.e. in similar circumstances to that in which *confess to* is used.)

(iii) *Refer to* and *mention*. The verb *mention* has casual overtones—in conversation I might just 'mention' Jespersen's grammar. But in writing a paper I would be likely to 'refer to' it; *refer to* carries a sense of purpose and directionality, which is brought out by the inclusion of *to*.

(iv) *Decide on* and *choose*. The verb *choose* can be employed where there was little mental effort involved, and it may be used in a way that relates pragmatically to the object role, e.g. *'I'd have chosen you', he told her, 'if it had been up to me'. Decide* is likely to refer to an act that involved considerable thought, and focuses on the mental act; the preposition *on* introduces the object that the decision finally rested on. (Cf. the remarks in §8.4.3 on the possible omission of *for* from a Modal (FOR) TO complement clause after *choose*, but not after *decide*.)

There is one limited context in which *decide* can be used without *on* preceding an object NP. Compare:

(**4**)   *The President decided on the order of precedence*
(**5**)   *The President decided the order of precedence*

Sentence (4) could be used when the President sat down, thought out the order of precedence, and announced it (no one else need be involved). But (5) might be used when there was a dispute over the order of precedence and he settled it; this sentence focuses on the matter of the order. (Note that *on* could not be omitted after *decide* before other kinds of NPs, referring to things that are not crucially affected by the act of deciding, e.g. not from (1) above or from *The Duke decided on Eton for his son's education*.)

(v) *Look at* and *see*, *listen to* and *hear*. *See* and *hear* refer to acts of attention that need not be volitional but must have a positive result; it is in view of this that they are simple transitive verbs, e.g. *I saw the car go by*. *Look* and *listen* refer to the Perceiver directing their attention in a certain way; they may not necessarily achieve a desired goal. These verbs can be used intransitively, e.g. with an adverb (*He looked up, She listened carefully*); or else an object can be included after a preposition. But why should *look* take *at* and *listen* take *to*? Well, one directs one's gaze 'at' a thing, and may see nothing else. But our ears pick up every sound around; it is necessary to concentrate one's mind and direct it towards one particular type of sound. (It is possible to use *listen* with *at*, e.g. *He listened at the door*, when he put his ear against the door, but here *at the door* is a locative expression, whereas in *He looked at the door*, the *at* is part of the verbal expression *look at*.)

Other inherent preposition verbs are listed under the various semantic types (see Appendix). They include *object to* (compare with *dislike*), *approve of*, and *consist in/of*.

Overall, it seems that an inherent preposition verb is more likely to imply directed volition than a single word semi-synonym; compare *refer to* and *mention*, *look at* and *see*, *decide on* and *choose*.

## 9.2.2. Phrasal verbs

English has some hundreds of phrasal verbs, each a combination of verb plus preposition(s) that has a meaning not inferrable from the individual meanings of verb and preposition(s), so that it must be regarded as an independent lexical item, and accorded a dictionary entry of its own.

There are six varieties of phrasal verb. Their structures can be abbreviated, using 'p' for preposition and 'N' for a noun phrase or functionally equivalent constituent:

(i)    verb-plus-p, e.g. *set in, come to, pass out*
(ii)   verb-plus-pN, e.g. *set about X, come by X, pick on X*
(iii)  verb-plus-Np, e.g. *put X off, take X on, bring X down*
(iv)   verb-plus-NpN, e.g. *see X through Y, hold X against Y*
(v)    verb-plus-ppN, e.g. *take up with X, go in for X, scrape by on X*
(vi)   verb-plus-NppN, e.g. *put X down to Y, let X in for Y, take X up on Y*

The difference between (ii) and (iii) is particularly important. A p can move to the left over a noun (but not over an unstressed personal pronoun) in (iii), e.g. *put the meeting off, put off the meeting* and *put it off* but not *\*put off it*.

The p cannot move in (ii), e.g. *pick on Mary*, not *\*pick Mary on*. Some verbs of set (vi) may also move the first p to the left over a preceding noun (but not over a pronoun), e.g. *He played John off against Mary*, *He played off John against Mary*.

There is an explanation for why a preposition can move to the left over a full NP but not over a pronoun. As mentioned in §1.5, object pronouns are clitics, phonologically attached to the preceding verb. And a preposition cannot be moved to intrude into the middle of a verb-plus-clitic-pronoun sequence. The phonological form of *put the meeting off* is /pút ðə=mí:tiŋ ɔ́f/ and this can be rearranged, by leftwards movement of the preposition, to be /pút ɔ́:f ðə=mí:tiŋ/. The phonological form of *put it off* is /pút=it ɔ́:f/ (where '=' indicates a clitic boundary) and here the /ɔ́:f/ cannot be moved into the middle of /pút=it/.

The vast majority of phrasal verbs are based on monosyllabic roots of Germanic origin, almost all belonging to the types MOTION (e.g. *bring*, *carry*), REST (*sit*, *stand*), AFFECT (*cut*, *kick*, *scrape*), GIVE (*give*, *get*, *have*), MAKING (*make*, *let*), or the grammatical verbs *be* and *do*. The resulting phrasal verbs are distributed over a wider range of types; some of them have quite abstract and specialised meanings, for which there is no mono-morphemic synonym, e.g. *let X in for Y*, *see X through Y*, *take up with X*. Nevertheless, only a small proportion of them allow a complement clause in one of the slots designated 'N' in the formulas above.

The transitivity of phrasal verbs is a fascinating and not altogether easy question. Firstly, an N which immediately follows the verbal element, as in (iii), (iv) and (vi), is clearly a direct object; it may become passive subject, e.g. *The meeting was put off*, *John's political opinions were held against him*, *Her failure was put down to nerves*. In these phrasal verb types the lexical unit is effectively discontinuous—we should write *put—off*, *hold—against*, and *put—down to*, the dash showing that a direct object intervenes between the elements of what is in each case a single semantic unit.

It would be reasonable to expect the N in a phrasal verb of type (ii) to behave like the NP following an inherent preposition verb such as *refer to* or *decide on*. In fact, it does not do so. Whereas the object constituent after *refer to*, *decide on* and similar verbs may freely passivise, the N in a phrasal verb of type (ii) may only occasionally become subject of a passive con-struction—it may for *pick on* (e.g. *Mary is always being picked on by the new teacher*), but it does not for *set about* and it does not very easily for *come by*, for instance. The N in type (ii) behaves syntactically like a prepositional object (as in *He sat on the river bank*), although it follows a verb-plus-preposition that makes up a single semantic unit. The N in type (v) shows even less tendency to passivise—a passive is barely possible with just a few phrasal verbs from this set, e.g. *put up with, look down on, make up for* (but not with *rub off on, come round to, pull out of* or many others).

We noted that the 'inherent preposition' from a verb like *hope for, decide on* or *think about* is dropped before a *that, for* or *to* complementiser. How do prepositions from phrasal verbs behave in these circumstances? In answering this question it will be useful to discuss the varieties one or two at a time.

*Structure (ii), verb-plus-pN*. Out of a sample of about a hundred phrasal verbs of this kind I have found none that may take a THAT clause in the N slot. There are a few that allow ING clauses (e.g. *He set about picking the grapes, She couldn't deal with her husband's making passes at all the maids*) and one or two that may take an NP which includes a THAT clause, but not a THAT complement alone (e.g. *She played upon the fact that he was frightened of the dark, He fell for the suggestion that he should nominate Mary*). It seems as if a THAT clause is never used with a phrasal verb of this type because *that* cannot normally follow a preposition with which its clause has a close syntactic connection, and to omit the preposition would destroy the phrasal verb (either changing the meaning of the sentence, or rendering it unintelligible).

The same argument should apply in the case of (FOR) TO complements; the preposition of a phrasal verb would have to drop before *for* or *to*, destroying the lexical form of the phrasal verb. In fact, (FOR) TO complements do not generally occur with phrasal verbs of type (ii). But there is an exception: *press for*, as in *She pressed for a recount*. Since this verb ends in *for* it can perfectly well be followed by a Modal (FOR) TO complement clause, e.g. *She pressed for the returning officer to recount the votes* or *She pressed for the votes to be recounted*. (In underlying structure there are two occurrences of *for*, and one is omitted.) If the complement clause subject is coreferential with main clause subject then it should be omitted, together with complementiser *for*. Here the *for* of the phrasal verb would immediately precede complementiser *to* and must be omitted; this is why a sentence like ?*She pressed to recount the votes* is at best dubiously acceptable.

*Structure (iii), verb-plus-Np* (where the p may be moved to the left over a preceding non-pronominal constituent). There are a small number of phrasal verbs of this type where the N may be (i) an NP, or (ii) an NP in apposition with a THAT clause:

**(6a)**   *He put the news about*
**(6b)**   *He put about the news*
**(7a)**   *He put the news that I had resigned about*
**(7b)**   *He put about the news that I had resigned*

There are further possibilities:

**(7c)**   *He put the news about that I had resigned*
**(7d)**   *He put it about that I had resigned*

We could say that in (7c) the THAT clause from the complex appositional constituent *the news that I had resigned* has been extraposed to the end of the sentence (parallel to the extraposition in *The news angered me that we are to have a new secretary*). In (7d) there must be—for most speakers—an *it* between *put* and *about*, effectively marking the fact that this is a phrasal verb of type 'verb-plus-Np'. (We cannot have *\*He put that I had resigned about*, and scarcely *?He put about that I had resigned*, where *the news* has been omitted without trace.)

It appears that an extraposed THAT clause can follow the 'p' element of a phrasal verb of type 'verb-plus-Np' only when there is some constituent filling the N slot.

Other phrasal verbs of type (iii) which occur in constructions (6a)–(7d) include *bring—about*, *give—out*, *put—across*. There are also just a few for which—at least in some dialects—the *it* may be omitted from a construction like (7d), e.g. *let—out* 'disclose', *work—out* 'deduce', *lay—down* 'stipulate'.

Since a preposition does not drop before an ING complement, it is possible to have an ING clause in the N slot for phrasal verbs of type (iii), e.g. *She'll never live down her husband's being sent to jail*. Note that here leftward movement of the preposition is almost obligatory, both to put the 'heavy constituent' at the end of its clause (§2.13A) and to ensure that the two words making up the phrasal verb are not too far apart.

*Structures (iv), verb-plus-NpN, and (vi), verb-plus-NppN.* There are relatively few phrasal verbs with these structures. A handful of them may take a complex NP including a THAT clause in the first N slot (i.e. as direct object) and then behave exactly like type (iii), with an *it* following the verbal root, and the THAT clause coming at the end of the main clause, e.g. *He held it against me that I didn't vote for him, I took it up with Mary that she didn't vote at all* and *I put it down to laziness that he never writes.*

The second N slot in structure (vi) may take NP-including-THAT-clause, e.g. *I played the fact that he can't cook off against the fact that I hate washing up,* but not a complement clause alone.

*Structure (v), verb-plus-ppN.* Here, the first preposition is like that in a phrasal verb of types (i)–(iv) and the second resembles an 'inherent preposition' (as in *decide on, hope for*). That is, the second preposition is omitted before a THAT clause in N slot—compare *He didn't let on about the accident* and *He didn't let on about Mary's being injured* with *He didn't let on (\*about) that Mary had been injured.* Another phrasal verb that omits the second preposition before *that* is *catch on to.*

In conclusion, we can state firstly that an N which comes immediately after the verbal part of a phrasal verb (syntactically intruding into the middle of a single semantic unit) in types (iii), (iv) and (vi) is clearly a direct object, and those phrasal verbs are transitive. The final N in types (iv) and (vi) is a core semantic role, but it is not in object syntactic relation.

The N in type (ii) has weak object status, since it may occasionally become passive subject; this object status is weaker than that of an NP which follows an inherent preposition, as in *hope for, refer to.* The N in type (v) has similar syntactic status—there are limited passivisation possibilities, and when N is a THAT complement clause the second of the two prepositions will drop before it.

Only phrasal verbs of structure (i) are fully intransitive.

### 9.2.3. Inserting a preposition

In §9.1 we said that a role may be assigned to O syntactic relation if it is saliently affected by the activity. Recall also the discussion in §3.3.1 showing that an O NP will generally have specific reference (which explains the unacceptability of \**John gave good causes all his money*). Related to this, we can note that a prototypical transitive sentence will refer to a complete unit of activity, involving a specific O (e.g. *She baked a cake, He broke the plate*).

If the activity referred to by a transitive verb does not achieve a definite result, or does not relate to some specific object, then a preposition may be inserted between verb and O NP, to mark the deviation from an 'ideal' transitive event.

A semantically canonical sentence with *kick* is something like *He kicked the ball*; one assumes that he aimed his foot at the ball, it made contact, and the ball flew off. On hearing *He kicked at the ball* one might infer that the aim was not achieved, i.e. he missed making contact. Similarly, *He kicked the door* implies that he intended to deliver a kick to the door, and did so, with the required result. One also hears *He kicked at the door*; here—unlike in the case of *He kicked at the ball*—contact is likely to have been made between foot and door. Inclusion of *at* could imply that the purpose was not achieved—he might have tried to open the door with a kick or two, but it didn't budge. (Suppose that eventually he did succeed. One might say, *He kicked at the door for twenty minutes and eventually he did kick it down*, where use of the phrasal verb *kick down* here signals success.) Or, *He kicked at the door* could be used to focus on the fact that he was angry and just kicking out in fury, with what the kicks made contact with being of secondary importance.

When *bite* has a non-animate object it generally refers to separating a portion of something with one's teeth, and eating it. On hearing *She bit the apple* one would infer that a piece was bitten out of the fruit, and then chewed and swallowed. But someone can also bite to relieve tension, e.g. if being operated on without an anaesthetic. In this instance a preposition would be inserted, e.g. *She bit on the leather strap*. Nothing really happens to the strap (a piece wasn't taken out of it) and this is marked by *on* since it is peripheral to the main focus of the sentence—the fact that she is biting.

*Hold* behaves in a similar way. The canonical sense focuses on the effect the activity has on an object, e.g. *John held the pig* (*then it couldn't run away*). If the subject clutches something so as to affect themself—e.g. *John held onto the post* (*so that he wouldn't be blown off his feet by the gale*)—then a preposition is inserted, marking the fact that the actual identity of the object is of peripheral interest, and that it is not affected by the action.

The verb *pull* implies that a Causer exerts pressure on an object so that it should move. If it does move then a plain transitive construction is appropriate, e.g. *John pulled the rope*. If he cannot get it to move then *pull* may still be used but with a preposition inserted to signal this non-achievement, e.g. *John pulled on the rope*.

A quite different kind of example involves *win*. When there is a specific object NP the plain transitive verb will be used, e.g. *Vladimir won that game of chess last night*. But if the object is generic and non-specific the preposition *at* must be inserted, e.g. *Vladimir usually wins at chess*.

In fact only a handful of transitive verbs may insert a preposition before an object to mark that it lacks some of the salient properties associated with the syntactic relation 'object'. They include a number of AFFECT items such as *hit, strike, hammer, cut, saw, punch, kick, scrape, rub, tear* (all taking *at*), a few MOTION and REST verbs such as *pull* (*on*) and *hold* (*onto*), a number of CORPOREAL verbs such as *bite, chew, nibble, suck* (taking *on* or *at*), *smell, sniff* (taking *at*) (but not *eat* or *drink*), perhaps just *win* (*at*) from COMPETITION, and some from the TELL subtype of SPEAKING (§5.4(*f*)).

Many of these verbs may not (except in some marked context) be used intransitively—we cannot say just *\*He hit* or *\*She cut*. Some object must be specified, but the fact that it is not an 'ideal' object in this instance of the activity can be shown by the insertion of a preposition.

*Hunt* is particularly interesting. There is a semantic link between *hunt* and *hunt for*—both being associated with killing game—but the plain transitive is most similar to AFFECT verbs, whereas *hunt for* is more like *look for* and *search for* from the ATTENTION type. The sentence *He is hunting lions* suggests that there may be a known group of lions that the hunter is attempting to kill. But *He is hunting for lions* implies only that he is directing his attention towards finding lions (which he would then kill). The NP *lions* refers to something that may not be attainable, and it is naturally introduced by *for* (cf. the *for* in *wish for*).

In summary, a preposition can be inserted before the object NP of a transitive verb to indicate that the emphasis is not on the effect of the activity on some specific object (the normal situation) but rather on the subject's engaging in the activity.

## 9.2.4. Omitting a preposition before non-measure phrases

In the last subsection we described how a preposition can be inserted before an O NP which is not saliently affected by the activity, or when it does not have specific reference.

There are also instances of what could be called the opposite kind of circumstance. If the referent of a peripheral NP, marked by a preposition, is particularly salient in some instance of an activity, then it may drop its preposition and move to a position immediately after the verb, becoming direct object. As we shall show, this can happen with both intransitive and transitive verbs.

A Locus description can—but need not—be included with a verb from the RUN subtype of MOTION, e.g. *jump* (*over the log*), *climb* (*up the mountain*), *swim* (*across the stream*). If the activity could be considered a significant achievement, with regard to the nature of the Locus, then the preposition can be omitted and the Locus NP moved to a position immediately after the (now transitive) verb, as its direct object. *They climbed up the mountain* leaves open whether they got to the top, but *They climbed the mountain* indicates that the pinnacle was reached. The preposition-less construction would be likely to be used when it was a difficult mountain to climb—one would surely always say *They climbed Everest*, with no *up*, but *We climbed up the little hill in the south-east corner of Regent's Park*, with *up* included. Similar considerations apply to *swim*—*She swam the English Channel*, a considerable achievement which is marked by having *the English Channel* as direct object, as opposed to *She swam across the millstream*, which anyone who can swim at all can do, and here the Locus is marked by preposition *across*.

*Jump* may be used for motion up (*jump up onto the ledge*) or down (*jump down off/from the ledge*) or over some vertical obstacle (*jump over the fence*) or over a discontinuity in the ground (*jump over the brook*) or it can just refer to a mode of locomotion (*jump around the garden*). Only the preposition *over* can be omitted, and then just when the vertical obstruction or the discontinuity in the ground poses a definite challenge (which not everyone could meet). Thus, *She jumped the six-foot fence/the wide ravine* but not, because of the piffling nature of the obstruction, *\*She jumped the snail/the ten-inch gap in the path* (these sentences require *over*). A best-selling Australian autobiography was called *I Can Jump Puddles*; the author, Alan Marshall, had been crippled by polio and for him jumping a puddle represented a significant achievement, thus he omitted the preposition before *puddles*.

Any verb from the RUN subtype may have the Locus promoted from a prepositional NP to be direct object, if that Locus is in some way significant for the activity; for many verbs there is no such Locus, e.g. *crawl, stroll, roll*. With other RUN verbs a degree of contextualisation is necessary. A professional golfer, on the day before a big tournament at an unfamiliar location, is likely to *walk* (*over*) *the course*. Here the preposition may be dropped, not because this is any sort of achievement (in the way that swimming the

Channel is) but because the salient fact here is not just his walking, but his walking-the-course, looking at the lie of the land from every angle.

Intransitive verbs from other subtypes may occasionally drop a preposition in appropriate circumstances. The CORPOREAL verb *pee* can take a prepositional NP indicating where the stream of urine was directed, e.g. *He peed into the potty*. But in *He peed (into) his pants* the preposition can be omitted, since the pants are saliently affected by the activity. (This construction is similar to *He wet his pants*.)

In §5.4 we described how *speak* and *talk* may omit the preposition before a Medium NP, e.g. *speak (in) French*. This is likely to happen when the Medium itself is being focused on—compare *The President spoke some harsh words in French to his secretary* (the harsh words are the focus of this sentence) with *They speak French in that bank*, or *French is spoken in that bank* (the fact of that language being spoken there is focused upon). Another example is *Can you really speak Fijian?*, where being able to converse in that language is being highlighted, as an unusual feat.

The basic syntactic frame for GIVING verbs is with the Gift as O and with the Recipient marked by preposition *to*. But when the Recipient is the most salient non-A role it can drop its preposition and move into direct object slot, immediately after the verb. Compare:

(8)   *I've lent all my phonetics books to different people*
(9)   *I've lent my favourite student a bunch of different sorts of books*

Sentence (8) focuses on the specific NP *all my phonetics books* whereas (9) directs attention onto *my favourite student*. In a construction like (9) the original O NP (the Gift) is still retained, as a sort of 'second object'. (There are similar syntactic possibilities with verbs from the TELL subtype of SPEAKING—see §5.4(*f*).)

As mentioned in §4.3, *borrow* is the converse of *lend*. But here the Gift must be O, e.g. *John borrowed a book from Mary*. *Borrow* and related verbs (e.g. *buy, purchase*) focus on what is given, and this cannot be displaced from the object slot by the Donor.

In §4.6 we mentioned the construction *That free kick won/lost the match for us*, with *win* and *lose* from the COMPETITION type. Here the NP marked by *for* can be focused on, and moved into direct object slot, e.g. *That free kick won/lost us the match*.

*Search for* can be considered an inherent preposition verb, similar to *refer to*. A location can be specified, by a prepositional NP, e.g. *He searched for his wallet in the field.* This verb allows a location NP to drop its preposition and move into direct object slot if the location is somehow significant and worth focusing on, e.g. *He searched (in) forty-three different places for his wallet (before eventually finding it).*

We have thus far examined instances of 'prepositional omission' with intransitive verbs (*jump, climb, swim, walk, pee, speak*), with transitive verbs (GIVING, the TELL subtype of SPEAKING, *win* and *lose* from COMPETITION), and with an inherent preposition transitive verb (*search for* from ATTEN-TION). In each case the omission takes place in circumstances particular to the type or subtype.

There is one general circumstance in which a preposition can be omitted (with the NP it governed becoming direct object). This involves *for* + NP (or, sometimes, *to* + NP) with the benefactive sense 'for NP to get'. Thus:

(10a)   *I cut a slice of bread for Mary*
(10b)   *I cut Mary a slice of bread*
(11a)   *I brought an apple for Mary*
(11b)   *I brought Mary an apple*
(12a)   *I knitted a jumper for Mary*
(12b)   *I knitted Mary a jumper*
(13a)   *I threw an apple to Mary*
(13b)   *I threw Mary an apple*
(14a)   *I chose a book for Mary*
(14b)   *I chose Mary a book*
(15a)   *I recommended a good thriller to Mary*
(15b)   *I recommended Mary a good thriller*

A benefactive NP of this kind may omit the *for* or *to* and become direct object (displacing the original direct object to become 'second object'), with a variety of verbs from at least MOTION, AFFECT, DECIDING and SPEAKING. The 'beneficiary' can, in appropriate circumstances, be regarded as the most salient non-A role with these verbs.

Note that each of the (a) sentences quoted has two senses: (i) for Mary to get the slice of bread/apple/jumper/etc.; and (ii) the activity being done on behalf of Mary—suppose Mary was meant to slice the bread but I did it instead. The NP governed by *for* can be promoted to direct object only in sense (i), not (ii).

Now consider verbs of GIVING. We can have

(16a)   *John* (Donor) *sold a book* (Gift) *to Fred* (Recipient) *for Mary* (Beneficiary) (i.e. for Fred to give it to Mary)
(16b)   *John* (Donor) *sold Fred* (Recipient) *a book* (Gift) *for Mary* (Beneficiary)

**(17a)**   *Fred* (Recipient) *bought a book* (Gift) (*from John* (Donor)) *for Mary* (Beneficiary)

As described above, we have the possibility in (16a) of promoting the Recipient to O slot, if it is sufficiently salient—as in (16b). It is perhaps in view of this that with verbs like *sell*, *lend* and *give*, the Beneficiary may not become object. (On hearing *\*John sold Mary a book to Fred*—derived from (16a) by promotion of *Mary*—one would interpret the first five words as implying that Mary was the Recipient, and then be confused by the final *to Fred*.) But, as noted above, the Donor cannot be promoted to object in (17). Here the beneficiary may be promoted, in the same way that it can be with *cut*, *bring*, *knit*, etc., i.e.

**(17b)**   *Fred* (Recipient) *bought Mary* (Beneficiary) *a book* (Gift) (*from John* (Donor))

But note that while construction (17b) is fully acceptable with *buy*, it is more marginal with the syntactically and semantically related verb *borrow*, *?Fred borrowed Mary a book* (*from John*). This may be because people often buy things to give them to someone else, whereas it is rare to borrow something from someone and then pass it on to a third person.

In summary, a non-measure NP that is normally marked by a preposition (and is a peripheral part of the activity) may lose its preposition and be moved into object slot if it is being focused on, as a particularly salient element, in some instance of the activity.

## 9.2.5. Omitting a preposition before measure phrases

Any verb of MOTION, and some from other types such as ATTENTION, can take a peripheral NP that contains a numeral (or *a*) and a noun that refers to a unit of spatial measure. This NP is normally marked by a preposition (generally, *for*) but this can be omitted, e.g. *He runs* (*for*) *three miles before breakfast every day*, *She carried the parcel* (*for*) *twenty-five miles*, *From the top of that mountain you can see* (*for*) *thirty miles on a clear day*.

Analogously, an NP referring to temporal measure can occur with a wider range of verbs, including MOTION, REST, AFFECT, CORPOREAL and TALK. The preposition may again be omitted, e.g. *I like to run* (*for*) *an hour and then walk* (*for*) *an hour*, *She stood* (*for*) *twenty minutes in the pouring rain, He whipped the dog (for) two hours yesterday, You've been talking (for) twenty minutes without stopping.*

In the last subsection we explained how non-measure phrases that lose a preposition move into direct object slot, immediately after the verb. As always, an adverb may not intervene between verb and object—compare *He walked (purposefully) over the course (purposefully)* with *He walked (\*purposefully) the course (purposefully)*.

A prepositionless measure phrase behaves quite differently. It is not in direct object slot and does not have to come immediately after the verb, e.g. *She stood in the pouring rain twenty minutes*. Even if a prepositionless measure phrase does occur next to the verb, an adverb can still come between them, e.g. *She stood (pathetically) twenty minutes in the pouring rain*. A non-measure phrase promoted into direct object slot can often be passivised, e.g. *That mountain has not yet been climbed*, but a preposition-less measure phrase can only very exceptionally become passive subject, e.g. we cannot have *\*Three miles is run by John before breakfast every day.* (It should be noted that *the mile*, as in *The mile was first run in four minutes by Roger Bannister*, is effectively functioning here as a non-measure phrase; note that it is 'the mile' rather than 'a mile').

Although omitting the preposition from a measure phrase does not make it an object NP there is still a semantic effect that bears some relation to the omission of a preposition from a non-measure phrase: attention is directed towards the measure, as a particularly significant aspect of the activity— the *length* of time or distance will often be significant. Thus, I might offer the accusation *You whipped the dog two hours solid* (with no preposition, emphasising the enormity of doing it for so long) and you could reply *I only whipped it for about three seconds* (including the preposition).

A measure phrase may be used without a preposition when that particular measure carries implications about the completion of the activity. *She followed the thief seven miles into the forest* might be used when the thief travelled seven miles to his hide-out and she followed him all the way, whereas *She followed the thief for seven miles into the forest* could be appropriate when he travelled further, but she only followed him for the first seven miles.

There is not always a choice involved. If a distance phrase is included with *throw* it is normally a significant result of the activity and a preposition is seldom or never included, e.g. *He threw the javelin (?for) eight yards*. With *fall* a preposition is likely to be omitted in a sentence that refers to a 'completed' event, e.g. *She fell* (*through*) *thirty feet to her death.* However, a preposition may be included when there is an incompletive overtone, e.g. *She fell* (*through*) *thirty feet until her fall was arrested by the branches of a tree.*

In summary, a non-measure phrase may omit its preposition if the temporal or spatial distance is particularly significant; but this NP does not have to come immediately after the verb, and it does not become a direct object.


## 9.3. Dual transitivity

Many verbs in English may be used either with an object (transitively) or without any object (intransitively); these are called ambitransitives (or 'labile' verbs). They divide into two classes according to whether the intransitive subject is identical with the transitive subject (S = A) or with the transitive object (S = O).


### 9.3.1. S = A: transitive verbs that can omit an object

For almost all verbs that are used both transitively and intransitively with the same subject, the transitive form can be taken as basic (there is a minor exception, mentioned at the end of this subsection); we simply have to say that the object can be omitted, under certain circumstances.

First, a note about two kinds of exception. There are some basically intransitive verbs such as *climb, jump, swim, speak* (discussed in §9.2.4) which may omit the preposition before a non-measure NP and make this into a direct object. Occurrence in a transitive frame is a secondary property for such verbs.

Then there are a number of CORPOREAL and WEATHER verbs that are basically intransitive but may be followed by a cognate NP, e.g. *He laughed a really dirty laugh, It thundered the most ear-splitting crack of thunder.* A cognate NP is always likely to include some modifiers (*He laughed a laugh* sounds infelicitous) and is likely to be used because there are much greater possibilities for adjectival etc. modification of a noun than there are for adverbial modification of a verb. We suggested in §§4.4 and 4.5 that these cognate NPs have at best very weak object properties, e.g. they do not readily become passive subject (although, exceptionally, one could say something like *A happy smile is smiled by a happy person*). Other CORPOREAL verbs are clearly transitive. Thus, alongside *yawn*, *laugh*, *sleep*, *wink*, which can only be followed by a cognate NP (not by a full direct object), there are verbs like *swallow*, *bite*, *taste* and *pee*, which can take a direct object or a cognate NP.

It was suggested, in §§4.4 and 5.2, that *think* and *dream* belong to both the CORPOREAL and THINKING types. In the former sense they can be followed by a cognate NP (with no preposition), which is rather unlikely to become passive subject, e.g. *I thought the most horrid evil thoughts* (*which I'm now ashamed of*). And in the latter sense they take an inherent preposition plus a direct object, which can freely passivise, e.g. *People have been thinking about your idea an awful lot*, *Your idea has been thought about an awful lot*.

Verbs in the SHOUT subtype of SPEAKING may have a Message NP—with a speech act noun as head—in object relation, e.g. *recite a poem*, *narrate a story*. There are speech act nouns cognate with some of the verbs from this subtype (e.g. *recitation*, *narration*) but—as with CORPOREAL and WEATHER items—there is a tendency not to use verb and noun together unless there is some significant modification of the noun, e.g. *He prayed a really beautiful prayer*, *She prayed a prayer about redemption*. (There is the common collocation *sing a song*, with no modifier, but here the cognate object is not a regular derivation from the verb.) A SPEECH ACT NP can become passive subject (although it may be less likely to be if it has as head a noun cognate with the verb, e.g. *The sermon should be preached before the benediction is given*, but scarcely ?*A really beautiful prayer was prayed at this morning's service*). It thus seems that such a SPEECH ACT NP should be accorded full object status, unlike the cognate NPs that can follow CORPOREAL and WEATHER verbs, whose object status is at best weak. In summary, verbs from the SHOUT subtype appear to be basically transitive, but the Message role in O slot can be omitted.

Turning now to the main body of transitive verbs, we can enquire in what circumstances an object may be omitted. How is it, for instance, that an object need not be stated after *saw*, *knit*, *notice*, *remember*, *know*, *choose*, but should be (save in exceptional circumstances) after *hit*, *wrap*, *discover*, *realise*, *take*? It appears that the conditions for object omission vary across different semantic types.

An AFFECT verb will generally describe some unit of activity that involves a specific Target or Product, e.g. *He sawed the log*, *She knitted a jumper*. But an Agent may pursue a certain type of activity for a longish period, and/or on a variety of Targets or Products. It is then possible to use the appropriate verb without a stated object. The fact that the activity was extended is then generally marked by imperfective aspect *be . . . -ing*, or by a time phrase like *all day*, or a time adverb such as *always*, e.g. *She is knitting, He has been sawing all morning*. If past tense were used, with no time adverbial, then *\*She knitted*, *\*He has sawn* would be incomplete—an object should be added to obtain a grammatical sentence. (But note that an object may be omitted from such verbs when they are linked together, e.g. *First she knitted, then she sewed*; or where a reason clause is included, e.g. *She knitted to pass away the time*.)

Verbs like *saw*, *knit*—and others such as *sweep*, *rake*, *polish*—refer to activities that often are done over an extended period. Other AFFECT verbs—*hit* and *wrap*, for instance—generally refer to discrete actions. These may (unusually) be done over an extended period or habitually, but an object NP can never be omitted (although it may have a very general noun as head, e.g. *He's always hitting people*, *She's been wrapping things all morning*).

Some transitive CORPOREAL verbs omit an object under similar conditions to AFFECT verbs like *saw* and *knit*; that is, in the presence of imperfective *be . . . -ing* or an appropriate adverb—*He's eating/drinking*, *He's always eating/drinking!* *Eat* may also omit an object NP in quite different circumstances—where the identity of the object could be inferred from social context. If a guest calls at 1 p.m. you might politely ask *Have you eaten?*; this would be understood as an abbreviation of *Have you eaten lunch yet?* But if a friend knocks on the door at 1 a.m. it would be distinctly odd just to enquire *Have you eaten?* Suppose that they did look thin and hungry and you thought of offering food, the appropriate thing to say would be something like: *Have you eaten anything recently?*, including an object NP.

Transitive verbs of MOTION, REST and GIVING must generally specify an object—one could say *He often throws things*, but scarcely *\*He often throws*. In §4.1 we mentioned an exception: *follow* and *lead* have converse meanings and if they are used together either or both objects may be omitted, e.g. *I'll lead* (sc. you) *and you follow* (sc. me). There are other instances of a pair of semantically related verbs being used together and both omitting the object (which would, in normal circumstances, have to be stated). Thus, in chapter 7 of *Through the Looking Glass* the White King explains to Alice about his messengers: 'I must have *two*—to fetch and carry. One to fetch, and one to carry.' And people say *It is better to give than to take.*

A number of basically intransitive verbs from MOTION, AFFECT and COR-POREAL may be used in causative form, e.g. *The officer marched the soldiers, The nurse sat the patient up, John wakened Mary.* The object NP could never be omitted from any transitive sentence for which there was a corresponding intransitive with S = O. If the O NP were omitted from *John wakened Mary*, then *John wakened* would be understood to imply that it was John who came out of a sleep, not that he caused someone else to. (We noted in §4.1 that *ride* and *drive* appear to belong to the RUN subtype of MOTION, but may only be used transitively, e.g. *He drove his car here.* Since there is no corresponding S = O intransitive (\**The car drove here*) these verbs do allow the O NP to be omitted, e.g. *He drove here.*)

Quite different circumstances attend the omission of an object constituent after some of the most common verbs from Primary-B and Secondary types. If the identity of the object could be inferred by a listener from what has gone before in the discourse, or from what can be observed of the situation, or from shared knowledge, then it may be omitted. This applies to *see*, *hear* and *notice* from ATTENTION (§5.1); *remember, forget, know, realise* and *understand* from THINKING (§5.2); *decide* and *choose* from DE-CIDING (§5.3); but not to other verbs—which have a more specialised meaning—from these types. It also applies to a few Secondary verbs such as *help* and *try*. Suppose I see that John is attempting, without success, to unscrew a bottle top. I might say *Can I help?* (sc. to unscrew it), and he might reply *OK, you try!* (sc. to unscrew it).

Some verbs from these types may—like some from MOTION and GIVING—omit an object when used contrastively, e.g. *He theorises* (sc. about languages) *but I describe* (sc. languages).

There are many transitive verbs which can never be used without a specified object (which may be an NP or a complement clause). They include all those in the LIKING type, all in ANNOYING (save *worry, grieve* and *delight*; §9.3.2), as well as many from other types, e.g. *want, attempt, force, let, recognise, inform, mention, put, appoint, imply* and *resemble.*

In summary, an object NP may be omitted in varying circumstances: when an activity is extended in time and/or may relate to a variety of objects, rather than one specific object; when the identity of the object can be inferred from the situation; and when two verbs are used contrastively, with the same implied object, e.g. *You should think* (sc. about the question) *before you answer* (sc. the question). Object omission is more likely with frequently used verbs which have a wide, general meaning.

There is one minor construction type which appears to involve an intransitive/transitive pair where the intransitive sense is primary. For example, *They laughed him off the stage, She cried herself to sleep, We talked him into staying*. The verb-plus-object requires a post-object constituent introduced by a preposition which specifies what resulted from the action of the verb—for example, we talked to him until he said he would stay. This construction type appears to be limited to *talk* and a small number of basically intransitive CORPOREAL verbs including *laugh* and *cry*.

## 9.3.2. S = O pairs: which is basic?

For almost all verbs that show dual transitivity on the S = A pattern, native speakers have a clear intuition that the transitive use is prior, i.e. they consider *knit, saw, eat, remember, know* and *help* to be basically transitive verbs, which may also be used intransitively.

For most verbs with dual transitivity on the S = O pattern, native speakers consider the intransitive sense to be prior (e.g. *The horse trotted around the park, My leg hurt*) and the transitive to be a secondary, causative sense (e.g. *I trotted the horse around the park, John hurt my leg*). This applies to:

(i)   *march, run, walk, fly, swim, shake* from the RUN subtype, and *return* from the ARRIVE subtype, of MOTION;

(ii)  *sit, stand, lie, float, lean* from the SIT subtype, and *settle* from the STAY subtype, of REST;

(iii) *wake(n), grow, hurt, bleed* from CORPOREAL;

(iv)  *work* from SOCIAL CONTRACT;

(v)   *race* from COMPETITION.

(It appears that the only true transitive verbs which may be used causatively are the Secondary-A forms *start, stop, keep, begin, hurry* and *hasten*, e.g. *The workmen started laying the tiles this morning, I started the workmen laying the tiles this morning*; see §9.3.3. Native speakers regard the non-causative use of these verbs as basic.)

There are a number of verbs from the DROP subtype of MOTION and from the BREAK and STRETCH subtypes of AFFECT which have dual transitivity on the S = O pattern:

| DROP | BREAK | STRETCH |
|---|---|---|
| (a) *drop, spill, upset, overturn* | (a) *break, crush, smash* | (a) *extend, stretch, coil* |
| | (a-b) *tear, chip* | (b) *bend, curl; freeze, cool, melt, dissolve, burn* |
| (b) *trip* | (b) *burst, explode* | |

Native speakers consider certain of these verbs to be basically intransitive, and certain of them to be basically transitive; for others it is difficult to assign priority to either transitivity value.

Thus, from the BREAK subtype, *break*, *crush* and *smash* are considered basically transitive, *burst* and *explode* basically intransitive, with *tear* and *chip* some way in between. Similarly, *drop*, *spill*, *upset* and *overturn* are considered basically transitive but *trip* basically intransitive; and *extend, stretch, coil* basically transitive but *bend, curl* and *freeze, cool, melt, dissolve* and *burn* basically intransitive. (Note that native speaker intuitions vary a little from person to person, and some are stronger than others.)

The principle in operation here appears to be: if the S/O role often gets into the state described by the activity on its own, without outside assistance, then the verb is thought to be basically intransitive. But if one would normally expect there to be a Causer (even if one might not know who or what it is) then the verb is thought to be basically transitive. A person can trip without anyone else being around—so *trip* is regarded as an intransitive verb, with derived causative sense. But if a liquid spills it is normally someone's fault—the basic construction for this verb is transitive, although it may also be used intransitively. (*The liquid spilled* is normally used to disclaim responsibility, in a rather disingenuous way; cf. construction type III for AFFECT verbs, e.g. *Oh, did my stick hit you?* in §4.2. In each case the Causer/Agent is omitted.) Similarly, things may readily burst (a bubble or a balloon) or explode (a nut that falls into the fire) without any human intervention. Something *may* break by itself (e.g. the bough of a tree, as it becomes old and dry) but for most instances of breaking a human agent is involved.

Some verbs pose additional problems due to special syntactic or semantic features. *Open* and *close* are used as transitive verbs, but in nontransitive constructions one most frequently finds the related adjectives *open* and *closed* (e.g. *The door is open*), although intransitive use of the verbs is also possible (*The door opened silently*). The verb *return* is regarded as basically intransitive, and the S NP is likely to be a human (e.g. *The librarian returned to work today*); when it is used transitively the O NP is likely to be inanimate (e.g. *John returned the book to the library*). *Settle* is another verb described as basically intransitive; the S NP can be any human or animal. But it may also be used transitively, and then the A NP is likely to be someone in a position of authority, e.g. *The nurse settled all the sick children down for the night*, and *The Israeli government has now settled Jewish farmers in the Gaza Strip*.

*Worry*, *grieve* and *delight* are transitive verbs in the ANNOYING type, e.g. *Mary's staying out late every night worries Granny*. They can be used in the passive, e.g. *Granny is/gets worried by Mary's staying out late every night*. But they may also—unlike most other ANNOYING verbs—be used intransitively, e.g. *Granny worries a lot* (*over/about Mary's staying out late every night*). When asked about *worry*, native speakers do not have any strong intuition that either of the transitive and intransitive senses is more basic than the other.

Finally, we can note that the set of verbs which have dual transitivity of type S = A and the set which have dual transitivity of type S = O are not mutually exclusive. At least some verbs from the RUN subtype of MOTION enter into pairs of both kinds, e.g. *That horse* (S) *jumped over the gate*, *That horse* (A) *jumped the gate* (O), and *John* (A) *jumped the horse* (O) *over the gate* (but notice that the preposition *over* cannot be omitted from the causative, even if it is a significant piece of jumping—one can say *John jumped the gate*, but not \**John jumped the horse the gate*). A sentence like *M jumped the N* is potentially ambiguous between (i) M being the Causer and N the Moving role; and (ii) M being the Moving and N the Locus role. In fact the choice of NPs is likely to provide disambiguation, e.g. the Causer is generally HUMAN and an inanimate NP can only be Locus, so that *The horse jumped the gate* must be (ii) and *John jumped the horse* is most likely to be (i).

## 9.3.3. Causatives

All verbs with dual transitivity on the S = O pattern can be considered to be underlyingly intransitive, with a causative version that involves S becoming O and a new role, the Causer (which is most frequently human), entering as A. (For some AFFECT verbs the Causer coincides with Agent.)

This applies both to (i) those verbs that native speakers think of as basically intransitive, e.g. *walk, bleed, work, trip, burst, curl, burn*, and to (ii) those that native speakers think of as basically transitive, e.g. *drop, spill, break, extend, coil*. The difference lies in the fact that verbs of set (ii) are thought of as generally involving a Causer, and those of set (i) as just occasionally involving a Causer.

Only a limited number of intransitive verbs can be used in a simple causative (i.e. S = O transitive) construction. But virtually all verbs—both intransitive and transitive—can occur in a periphrastic causative construction with Secondary verbs from the MAKING type, i.e. *make, force, cause, get, have*. Although 'causative' is the traditional label for these constructions (which I retain here), in fact a periphrastic construction with the verb *cause*—often referring to action which brings about a result by indirect means—is far removed in meaning from a simple causative (see §6.3.1). The verb *cause* in English has a limited range of use—one could scarcely say *\*He caused the dog to walk in the park*, and if one could it would mean something quite different from *He walked the dog in the park*.

It is instructive to compare *make* (the most commonly used verb from the MAKING type) with a simple causative:

(**18a**)   *John walked the dog in the park*
(**18b**)   *John made the dog walk in the park*
(**19a**)   *Mary opened the door*
(**19b**)   *Mary made the door open*
(**20a**)   *Fred dissolved the sugar in the liquid*
(**20b**)   *Fred made the sugar dissolve in the liquid*

There is considerable semantic difference between the sentences in each pair. The (b) alternatives imply that some difficulty was encountered, that the event did not happen naturally. Hearing (18b) one might infer that the dog did not want to walk in the park, (19b) that the door could have been stuck and needed a hard shove, (20b) that Fred had perhaps to heat the liquid to get the sugar to dissolve. In contrast, the (a) sentences imply a natural activity—the dog was eager to walk, the door opened easily, and the sugar began to dissolve as soon as it was put in the liquid.

The differences between the (a/b) pairs relate to the fact that in (b) *the dog/door/sugar* is subject of the complement clause verb (it is also coded as surface direct object of *make*, but this is a secondary matter). It has the semantic properties of a subject, the role which is most relevant to the success of the activity. It is generally only appropriate to use a *make* construction when the subject of the complement clause is—by its character or nature—impeding the success of the activity; *make* refers to overcoming this impedance. In contrast, *the dog/door/sugar* is in the (a) sentences simply the object of the complement clause verb; it has the semantic characteristics of an object, i.e. the role which is most saliently affected by the activity described by the verb (there is here no hint of an impedance which has to be overcome).

Other MAKING verbs enter into constructions with a meaning similar to the (b) sentences. *He got the dog to walk in the park* and *He forced the dog to walk in the park* also imply that there was an element of impedance which had to be overcome.

Verbs from the MAKING type also occur freely with HUMAN PROPENSITY adjectives, e.g. *She made me (be) angry*, *She got me (to be) angry*. Adjectives from other types can also be used with *make*, in appropriate circumstances. We mentioned, in §3.2, that many adjectives from the DIMENSION, PHYSICAL PROPERTY, SPEED, AGE and COLOUR types may be used as both intransitive and transitive verbs, either in root form (e.g. *narrow*, *warm*) or by the addition of a derivational suffix *-en* (e.g. *deepen*, *sweeten*). There is a semantic contrast between a lexical causative such as *deepen*, *sweeten*, and a periphrastic one such as *make deep*, *make sweet*. The lexical form is most often used when the quality referred to by the adjective was already present to some extent and has now been intensified, i.e. *deepen*, 'make deeper', *sweeten* 'make sweeter'. The periphrastic causative states that the quality has been engendered (it may or may not have been present to some degree before), e.g. *Mary made the tea very sweet (in my opinion) but John complained and she had to sweeten it some more*. (See also the discussion, in §5.6, of periphrastic causatives involving the past participles of ANNOYING verbs, e.g. *make frightened*, and the meaning contrast between this and *frighten*.)

The simple causative construction (as in (18a), (19a), (20a)) is available for those intransitive verbs for which it is plausible that a Causer could be responsible for the event happening in a natural manner.

Almost all transitive verbs in English lack a simple causative use. This appears to be due to a syntactic constraint. Transitive verbs already have a direct object and any putative causative construction would be likely to be confused with the straightforward transitive. If corresponding to the periphrastic causative *Mary made John cut the cake* we were to have a simple causative, then *Mary*—as Causer—would become subject of *cut*. We could get either *Mary cut John* PREPOSITION *the cake* or else *Mary cut the cake* PREPOSITION *John*. Each of these would be understood to imply that Mary did the cutting, whereas what we are trying to describe is John doing the cutting and Mary making him do it. (There is an 'inherent preposition' transitive verb that does form a causative, *refer to*, e.g. *Noam referred me to Mithun's new book*, alongside *I referred to Mithun's new book*. Here the presence of the preposition avoids any possibility of confusion.)

However, Secondary-A verbs involve no roles beyond those of the complement clause verb—nothing comes between the two verbs in *John started running* or *Nanny started washing the baby*. *Start*—and also *stop, keep, begin, hurry, hasten*—can be used causatively (see §6.1.2). The new Causer comes in before *start* with the original subject now moving to a position between the two verbs, e.g. *The official started John running* (i.e. gave the signal for him to start) or *Mother started Nanny washing the baby* (told her it was now bath-time). Note the difference in meaning from *The official made John start running*, which carries the implication that he didn't want to run.

There are two points to note about simple causatives of Secondary-A verbs. The first is that only an ING complement clause may be involved, not a Modal (FOR) TO complement—we can say *John started to run*, but not *\*The official started John to run*. This is because Modal (FOR) TO relates to the subject getting involved in the activity normally on their own volition, not at a signal from someone else. The second is that there is no simple causative construction with *finish*; that is, there is no causative corresponding to *John finished making the beds*. A putative causative, *\*Mother finished John making the beds*, would imply that she gave a signal for the activity to terminate, and this would be incompatible with the 'object orientation' meaning of *finish*—the activity terminates when all the beds are made. (But note that we can have *Mother made John finish making the beds*, demonstrating once again the considerable semantic difference between simple causatives and periphrastic causatives in English.)

The verb *marry* has wide syntactic possibilities. In §2.11.6 we classed it as an 'inherent reciprocal' verb that may omit an O NP if it is *each other*, e.g. *John and Mary married* (*each other*), corresponding to *John married Mary* and *Mary married John*. There is a causative corresponding to this, e.g. *Father O'Leary married John and Mary*. There is also a causative corresponding to the simple transitive (non-reciprocal) use of *marry*, e.g. *Father O'Leary married John and Bill to Mary and Jane respectively*—here *to* introduces what is direct object in the non-causative *John and Bill married Mary and Jane respectively*.

In summary, a periphrastic causative construction, with a verb from the MAKING type, can, potentially, involve any transitive or intransitive verb or any adjective. It most often involves getting someone to do something that they did not want to do, or getting something into a new state. Simple causatives are available for some Secondary-A verbs, for some intransitive Primary-A verbs (the verb is used in a transitive frame, with the original S becoming O) and for adjectives from certain types (either the adjectival root is used as a transitive verb, or *-en* is added). A simple causative implies that the Causer is responsible for an event happening in a natural manner, or for a property being intensified.

## Notes to Chapter 9

There are some minor exceptions to the general statement in the first paragraph of this chapter about transitivity in Fijian—for full details see Dixon (1988: §18.1).

§9.2.2.   See Dixon (1982a) for a fuller discussion of phrasal verbs in English, and further references therein (including Bolinger 1971). Note that other terms are sometimes used for what are here called 'phrasal verbs', e.g. 'verb-particle combination' (Lipka 1972; Fraser 1974). Quirk and Greenbaum (1973: 347ff.) use 'phrasal verb' for my p and Np varieties and 'prepositional verb' for my pN; ppN is then called a 'phrasal-prepositional verb'.

§9.2.3. The criteria given by Hopper and Thompson (1980) for transitivity correlate well with the evidence presented here, e.g. if an O NP is not fully affected this 'lowering of transitivity' may be marked by inserting a preposition before it.

§9.2.4.   See also Green (1974) for discussion of benefactive constructions.

§9.2.5.   See also McCawley (1988a) for discussion of prepositionless measure phrases.

§9.3. The terms 'unaccusative' and 'unergative', introduced by Perlmutter (1978), are sometimes used for S = O and S = A ambitransitives respectively. But they have also been used with different meanings. For example, a number of languages have one set of intransitive verbs which mark S like A (these are often called 'actives') and another set which mark S like O ('statives'). Active verbs have been called 'unergative' and statives 'unaccusative'. Then there are some languages with no ambitransitive verbs and with all S marked in the same way; those verbs which typically take an antipassive or applicative derivation are called 'unergative' while those which typically take a passive or causative derivation are called 'unaccusative'. This plethora of different meanings for 'unaccusative' and 'unergative' suggests that the terms are best avoided (see Dixon 1999), with the clear and unambiguous labels S = A and S = O ambitransitive being used instead.

§9.3.1. Some intransitive verbs referring to continuous activities may be followed by a time adverbial from which the preposition can be omitted; for example, *John slept (for) the whole afternoon, Mary danced (for) the entire night*. When the preposition is omitted, adverb *away* may be added, giving *John slept the whole afternoon away, Mary danced the entire night away*; the *away* implies that the subject squandered this period of time. Interestingly, if the quantifier *whole* or *entire* is not included, then the preposition may only be omitted if *away* is included; one can say *John slept the afternoon away* and *John slept for the afternoon* but not *\*John slept the afternoon*. In these sentences, *the whole afternoon* and *the entire night* do not have the criterial properties of objects (pace Jackendoff 1997) with respect to passivisation, etc.; they are simply reduced time adverbs, with intransitive verbs.

§9.3.3. There is another rather special transitive construction in English. Alongside *Nine people can sleep in this inn*, we can have *This inn can sleep (or sleeps) nine people*. It might be thought that what was a prepositional NP (*this inn*) goes into A function while the original S NP (*nine people*) becomes O. However, this is not a valid derivational description, as can be seen from *This bus can seat (or seats) forty people*. We can say *Forty people can sit on this bus*, but here the verb is different. The intransitive sentence corresponding to *This bus seats forty people* is *There are seats for forty people on this bus*. There is plainly a correspondence between intransitive (or copula) and transitive sentences, but it is not a matter of straightforward syntactic derivation.

# 10

## *Our manager's annoyance at thoughts of residence rearrangement bears no relation to his assistant's criticism of building restrictions*
## Nominalisations and possession

## 10.1. Possession

I was once conducting a class on the Aboriginal languages of Australia and, for every grammatical topic, I'd enquire of each participant 'How is this shown in your language?', referring to the language they were investigating. One student came to me after class and requested: 'Could you please not refer to "our languages". They don't belong to us but to the Aboriginal community.'

The student assumed that the use of a possessive form (a possessive pronoun or a noun phrase marked by *'s*) is equivalent to a claim of ownership. In fact it extends far beyond. In brief, a possessive form is used for:

(a)  An alienable possession, something that the possessor does own—*John's car, Mary's ring, my dog.*

(b)  A kin relation (whether consanguineal or affinal)—*my mother, Mary's husband.*

(c)  An inalienable part of the possessor—*John's foot, the tree's blossom, my name.*

(d)  An attribute of the possessor—*Mary's age, your jealousy, John's good character, Bill's idea.*

(e)  Something typically associated with the possessor—*Mary's hometown, my dentist, your boss.* Note that *John's firm* is ambiguous. It could refer to the firm John works for or invests in (something associated with John), or it could be a firm which John owns, being then possession of type (a).

It will be seen that only (a) implies ownership. You could *not* be said to own your mother or your foot or your age or your dentist. There is in fact wide latitude for using a possessive form in sense (e). A colleague once said to me that she'd read something in, as she put it, '*your New Yorker*'. Now I don't own this magazine, and didn't even have a copy of (or have seen) the issue being quoted from. But I did, at that time, often read *The New Yorker* and set high credence upon it. The colleague was, effectively, saying 'I read this in *The New Yorker*, a magazine which I associate with you.'

When a possessor is a noun phrase (which can be just a noun) there are, in fact, two ways of marking it—by suffix *'s* on the possessor (which precedes the possessed) or by the preposition *of* before the possessor (which follows the possessed). One can say:

(1)  EITHER                                              OR

(a) *the president's private plane*        *the private plane of the president*
(b) *my friend's sister*                          *the sister of my friend*
(c) *the table's leg*                               *the leg of the table*
(d) *the jumbo jet's length*                  *the length of the jumbo jet*
(e) *the Tsotsi tribe's homeland*           *the homeland of the Tsotsi tribe*

However, there is only sometimes a choice between *'s* and *of*. For instance, it is in most circumstances infelicitous to say *the car of John, the husband of Mary, the foot of Bill, the anger of Jane, the dentist of Fred*. (And one could never use *of* in place of a possessive pronoun; for example, *my car* could not be rephrased as \**the car of me*.)

In essence, the *'s* alternative is preferred (and the *of* alternative dispreferred) according as:

(i)   The possessor is human (or at least animate), specific and singular. A proper name always takes 's. And whereas *the boy's leg* is preferred over *the leg of the boy* (singular human possessor), *the legs of the boys* (plural human possessor) is more acceptable, with *the legs of the antique tables* (plural inanimate possessor) sounding better still.

(ii)  The possessed is specific and singular. For example, *my friend's sister* is preferred over *the sister of my friend* (singular possessed) but *the sisters of my friend* (plural possessed) sounds considerably better.

(iii) The possessor has few words. The 's alternative is not liked on a long possessor, and here *of* may be preferred. For example, *the gun of that evil character who lives in the tumbledown shack down the road*, rather than *that evil character who lives in the tumbledown shack down the road's gun*.

(iv)  The possessor is familiar information. For instance, in a discussion about my wife I might say *my wife's jewels*, since my wife is familiar information and this is the first mention of the jewels. But if in a discussion about jewels I suddenly mention those belonging to my wife, I would be more likely to say *the jewels of my wife*, since this is the first mention of my wife (it is not familiar information).

Thus, for some instances of possession only 's is considered felicitous. For others—such as those in (1)—either 's or *of* is acceptable. And for others only *of* is likely to be used in normal circumstances; for example, one hears *the names of mountains, the virulence of the mosquitoes, the haunts of evil spirits*. (There are just a few idiomatic phrases which transgress principles (i) and (ii); for example, one generally says *a summer's day* rather than *a day of summer*.)

A possessive modifier (noun plus 's, or a possessive pronoun) is mutually exclusive with the article *a* and demonstratives, *this, that, these, those*. But one might want to include both *a* or a demonstrative and a possessive modifier in the same noun phrase. This is achieved by placing the possessive modifier after the head of the noun phrase, linked to it by *of*. Thus *John's picture* but *a picture of John's*; *my picture* but *that picture of mine*. Here the possessive relation *of* is shown by 's or *mine*, with the *of* simply a linker. One can also say *a picture of John*, but this has a quite different meaning. Whereas *a picture of John's* is a picture belonging to John, *a picture of John* is a picture for which John was the subject (it may well belong to someone else).

The preposition *of* shows a wide range of uses beyond that of marking possession. It can introduce a predicate argument, as in *jealous of his rival, fond of golf, dream of Dinah*. It is used to indicate quantity or material—*all of the boys, six kilos of potatoes, eight years of war, the value of these artefacts, a cup of tea, a skirt of grass.* It takes part in other grammatical constructions, as in *a giant of a man, less of a fool.* And it is a constituent of a number of complex grammatical markers, such as *out of, in terms of* and *in view of.*

In the remainder of this chapter 'possessive construction' will be used in a narrow sense to refer only to possession marked by *'s* (or by a possessive pronoun).

English has a rich range of derivational processes which form a nominal from a verb—these are nominalisations, and they have a close link with possession. A noun phrase which is in S, A, O or indirect object function to a verb may become possessor of a nominalisation based on that verb. For example:

|  | {UNDERLYING ROLE OF POSSESSOR}'S {UNDERLYING ROLE OF <NOMINALISATION>} |
|---|---|
| **(2)** *John resides at 10 Apple Avenue* <br> *John's residence* (that is, 10 Apple Avenue) | S's <underlying locative argument> |
| **(3)** *Kennedy discovered the Hull River* <br> *Kennedy's discovery* (that is, the Hull River) | A's <underlying O argument> |
| **(4)** *John laughed noisily* <br> *John's noisy laugh* | S's <unit of activity> |

There may be nominalisations relating to both A and O, linked by possessive marker to O and A respectively:

**(5)** (a)  *John employs Bill*
     (b)  *Bill's employer* (i.e. John)   O's <A>
     (c)  *John's employee* (i.e. Bill)   A's <O>

There are a number of instances where a possessive construction involving a nominalisation is ambiguous. Consider:

UNDERLYING ROLE OF<br>POSSESSOR

**(6)**  *The teacher whipped the boy*
    (a)  *[The teacher's whipping (of the boy)] set*      A
       *a precedent*
    (b)  *[The boy's whipping (by the teacher)] caused*   O
       *him shame*
**(7)**  *John nominated Bill (for the committee)*
    (a)  *John's nomination (of Bill) (for the committee)*  A
       *was seconded*
    (b)  *Bill's nomination (by John) (for the committee)*  O
       *was accepted*
**(8)**  *Mary gave a book to Kate*
    (a)  *Mary's gift (of a book) (to Kate) was much*   A
       *appreciated by Kate*
    (b)  *Kate's gift (of a book) (from Mary) helped*   indirect object
       *her pass the exam*

The ambiguity can extend further; for example, *John's painting* could be something done by John (*John painted X*) or something done of John (*X painted John*). Or it could be neither of these, but instead a painting owned by John (painted by someone other than John, and of someone or something other than John).

It will be seen that a nominalisation can refer to one of a number of aspects of the basic sentences it is associated with—*employer* in (5b) is a volitional agent; *discovery* in (3), *employee* in (5c) and *gift* in (8) are all underlying objects; and *residence* in (2) is a locus. In contrast, *whipping* in (6) refers to an activity, while *laugh* in (4) and *nomination* in (7) refer to a unit of activity.

There are a multitude of morphological processes for nominalisation. In the case of verbs of Germanic origin (henceforth called Germanic verbs), the plain root may be used (zero derivation), as with *laugh* in (4). Verbs of Romance origin (from Latin or early stages of French; henceforth, Romance verbs) typically take a suffix—*residence* in (2), *discovery* in (3), *nomination* in (7). Agentive nominalisations are typically marked by *-er* on both Germanic and Romance verbs, as *employer* in (5b), while some object nominalisations are shown by *-ee*, as *employee* in (5c). We find *-ing* on many Germanic and some Romance verbs, as *whipping* in (6). Finally, there are a number of irregular derivations of ancient origin, such as *gift* in (8).

§10.2 outlines the nine major types of deverbal nominalisation, their meanings, criteria for recognising and distinguishing them, and whether they automatically enter into a possessive construction with an argument from the underlying clause. §10.3 surveys the morphological processes involved, their phonological forms, and the types of nominalisation each relates to. The fascinating question of how phrasal verbs form nominalisations is explored in §10.4. Then, §10.5 deals in turn with the verbal semantic types, indicating which varieties of nominalisation (and which realisations) are associated with each.

## 10.2. Varieties of deverbal nominalisation

There are a number of ways of forming, from an adjective, an abstract noun which describes the property associated with the adjective. Most typically these use the suffix *-ness*—as in *happiness, brightness*—but they can involve other morphological processes, illustrated by *merriment, falsehood, length* and *heat*. There are also a number of ways of deriving a noun from another noun with a different meaning. For example, *X-ist* describes a person associated with X, which could be a person, a thing or an idea; for example, *Platonist, clarinettist, motorist, humorist* and *leftist*. There are many other processes—*childhood* is the state or period of being a child, *spoonful* is the measure of what will fill a spoon. These types of nominalisation are not dealt with in the present volume (they can be followed up in Marchand 1969).

What we focus on here are the nine varieties of nominals derived from verbs. These will be briefly listed, and then each discussed in detail.

(I)   Nominalisation describing a unit of activity, Unit-nom, as *shout* in *Mary's loud shout frightened the sheep.*

(II)  Nominalisation just describing an activity, Activity-nom, as *shouting* in *Mary's loud shouting wakened me up.*

(III) Nominalisation describing a state, State-nom, as *dislike* in *John's active dislike of porridge puzzled Aunt Maud.*

(IV)  Nominalisation describing a property, Property-nom, as *resemblance* in *Mary's close resemblance to her grandmother was commented on.*

(V) Nominalisation describing a result, Result-nom, as *arrangement* in *The arrangement of flowers adorned the coffee table.*

(VI) Nominalisation describing an object, Object-nom; for example, *converts* (those who are converted), *payment* (that which is paid).

(VII) Nominalisation describing the locus of an activity, Locus-nom; for example, *trap, entry.*

(VIII) Nominalisation describing a volitional agent, Agent-nom, as *killer, organiser.*

(IX) Nominalisation describing an instrument or material used in the activity, Inst-nom; for example, *mower* (machine used to mow with), *swimmers* (garment to wear when swimming).

## 10.2.1. Nominalisations denoting unit of activity and activity itself

Verbs referring to an activity may have one nominalisation referring to a unit of activity and another to the activity itself. For example:

| (9) Verb | *joke* | *speak* | *apologise* | *run* |
|---|---|---|---|---|
| Unit-nom | *joke* | *speech* | *apology* | *run* |
| Activity-nom | *joking* | *speaking* | *apologising* | *running* |
| Verb | *prick* | *smile* | *think* | *throw* |
| Unit-nom | *prick* | *smile* | *thought* | *throw* |
| Activity-nom | *pricking* | *smiling* | *thinking* | *throwing* |

It will be seen that a Unit-nom can have the same form as the verb, or a different form (as in *speech, apology,* and *thought*). Activity-nom's typically end in *-ing*, although there are other possibilities (for example, *resistance, recovery*).

Now, as mentioned in §2.7—see the discussion of (37)–(38) there—the verb in an ING complement clause and an Activity-nom can have the same form, ending in *-ing*. There is, however, a considerable grammatical difference. Consider:

(10) (a) *I criticised [John's throwing of the dice]*$_{NP:O}$

(b) *I criticised [John's throwing the dice]*$_{COMPLEMENT CLAUSE:O}$

The object argument of (10a) is a noun phrase with the nominalisation *throwing* as head, whereas the object of (10b) is the complement clause

*John's throwing the dice*. There is a difference in meaning, with (10b) stating that I criticised the fact that he threw the dice, while (10a) states that I criticised the way in which he threw them.

There are three grammatical criteria for distinguishing between an ING complement clause and a noun phrase with an Activity-nom as head:

(i)   In a noun phrase the nominal head can be modified by an adjective (not an adverb); the noun phrase in (10a) could be expanded to *John's lazy throwing of the dice*. A complement clause can include an adverb (not an adjective); the complement clause in (10b) could be expanded to *John's lazily throwing the dice* or *John's throwing the dice lazily*.

(ii)  If the verb in a complement clause is transitive, it may be directly followed by an object noun phrase, as *throwing the dice* in (10b). In contrast, an Activity-nom must include *of* before the noun phrase which was object of the underlying verb, as *throwing of the dice* in (10a).

(iii) In a noun phrase a possessive modifier can be replaced by the definite article, *the*—in (10a) we could have *the throwing of the dice* in place of *John's throwing of the dice*. Such a substitution is not possible in a complement clause.

It is important to keep in mind, throughout the discussion which follows, that each *-ing* form being discussed is a nominalisation and not the verb of a complement clause. This can easily be checked by the adjective/adverb test, or the zero/*of* test, or by the possibility of using an article.

The Unit-nom corresponding to (10a) is:

(11)   *I criticised [John's (lazy) throw of the dice]*~NP:O~

This again includes *of* and an adjective rather than an adverb; in addition, *the* can be substituted for *John's*.

There is a semantic difference here; (11) states that John had a single throw of the dice, whereas (10a) implies that he threw the dice more than once, over a period of time. Similar differences apply for each of the nominalisation pairs in (9). There can be a Unit-nom *run* (such as running a race) or an Activity-nom *running*, referring to a period of activity; just one *prick* of a pin, or a period of *pricking*; a single flashing *smile*, or a continuous period of *smiling*. And so on.

One must, of course, have a grammatical criterion to justify the decision to recognise distinct varieties of nominalisation. A Unit-nom is countable—that is, it can be modified by a number adjective and may take the plural suffix *-s*. One may say:

**(12)**   (a)   *There was only one joke/\*joking in the whole meeting*
      (b)   *John told several jokes/\*jokings*

Activity-nom's are not countable. A typical environment for them is after *a period of*, as in:

**(13)**   *There was a period of joking/\*joke, then the meeting relapsed into seriousness*

But, whereas no Activity-nom is countable, there are a few Unit-nom's that refer to a unit of activity which is extended in time and can thus occur in the frame 'a period of—'. Consider Unit-nom *conversation* and Activity-nom *conversing* in:

**(14)**   *The delegates were conversing seriously*
      (a)   *There were [several serious conversations/\*conversings] going on at the same time*
      (b)   *There was [a period of [serious conversation]]*
      (c)   *There was [a period of [serious conversing]]*

Sentence (14b) implies that there was a unit of conversation (with a beginning and an end) extending over a fair period of time, whereas (14c) states that the delegates conversed for a while, with this perhaps gradually blending into some other activity (maybe drinking or sleeping).

Leaving aside LIKING, ANNOYING, COMPARING and RELATING (discussed in §10.2.2), and the Secondary-D types, every semantic type includes some verbs which form a Unit-nom or an Activity-nom. The subject argument of the verb can generally be a pronoun or a human (or animate) noun with specific, singular reference, and may then function as possessor to the nominalisation, marked by *'s* (or by the possessive form of a pronoun). Examples include:

- Primary-A, AFFECT type. *John cold-bloodedly shot the dog*, giving nominalisation [*John's cold-blooded shooting of the dog*] *amazed the priest.*
- Primary-B, ATTENTION type. *Little Johnny cheekily tasted the brandy*, giving nominalisation [*Little Johnny's cheeky tasting of the brandy*] *got him into trouble.*
- Secondary-A, TRYING type. *Bill eagerly attempted to solve the problem*, giving nominalisation [*Bill's eager attempt to solve the problem*] *proved fruitless.*
- Secondary-B, WANTING type. *Matilda desperately wished to get married*, giving nominalisation [*Matilda's desperate wish to get married*] *was satisfied.*
- Secondary-C, HELPING type. *Mary supported John unstintingly*, giving nominalisation [*Mary's unstinting support of John*] *helped him through the crisis.*

It is possible to have a subject argument which does not satisfy (or scarcely satisfies) the criterion for attachment of possessive marker *'s*, so that *of* may be preferred (although *'s* and *of* are likely both to be possible). For example:

POSSESSED NOMINALISATION

| | | BASIC SENTENCE | PREFERRED | LESS PREFERRED |
|---|---|---|---|---|
| **(15)** | (a) | *John arrived* | *John's arrival* | *the arrival of John* |
| | (b) | *The letter arrived* | *the arrival of the letter* | *the letter's arrival* |
| **(16)** | (a) | *Rommel surrendered* | *Rommel's surrender* | *the surrender of Rommel* |
| | (b) | *The enemy surrendered* | *the surrender of the enemy* | *the enemy's surrender* |

If an O argument satisfies the conditions to take *'s*, then it too may be marked as possessor to a Unit-nom or Activity-nom, as an alternative to the A argument being so marked. This is illustrated in (6) and (7). In many cases the O argument is not a pronoun or a noun with human (or animate), specific, singular reference, and is thus not eligible to take *'s*. As stated before, the alternative in such cases is *of*. Example (6), repeated here as (17), describes the teacher's whipping the boy. One can also whip cream. Compare:

**(17)**   *The teacher whipped the boy*
    (a)   *[The teacher's whipping (of the boy)] set a precedent*
    (b)   *[The boy's whipping (by the teacher)] caused him shame*
**(18)**   *The cook whipped the cream*
    (a)   *[The cook's whipping (of the cream)] was noisy*
    (b)   *[The whipping of the cream (by the cook)] was noisy*

Should we consider *the whipping of the cream* in (18b) as the equivalent of *the boy's whipping* in (17b)? There is an alternative. One of the criteria for distinguishing between a complement clause and an Activity-nom or a Unit-nom is that, in the nominalisation, the erstwhile O is preceded by *of* and a possessive modifier may be replaced by *the*. In (18a) we have *the cook's whipping of the cream*. Substituting *the* for *the cook's* gives *the whipping of the cream*, as in (18b). That is, *the cook's whipping of the cream* can be analysed in either of two ways:

- (i)   As an O-possessed Activity-nom, corresponding to *the boy's whipping* in (6b) but with *of* in place of *'s* due to the nature of the referent of the O argument.
- (ii)   As a reduction of the A-possessed Activity-nom, *The cook's whipping of the cream*, in (18a), with *the* replacing *the cook's*.

The alternative analyses carry the same meaning, and there seems no reason to prefer one over the other.

## 10.2.2. Nominalisations denoting a state or a property

Verbs in the LIKING and ANNOYING semantic types describe states, not activities. They share the same semantic roles, but for LIKING verbs the Experiencer is the A and the Stimulus is the O argument, with this being reversed for ANNOYING verbs. Most verbs in these types form nominalisations, State-nom's, which describe the state referred to by the verb. Some verbs use the same form for State-nom (zero derivation) while others employ a derivation. A sample is:

| (19) | State-nom's | PLAIN VERB ROOT USED | | DERIVATION USED | |
|---|---|---|---|---|---|
| | LIKING type | *love* | *dislike* | *liking* | *hatred* |
| | | *dread* | *fear* | *loathing* | *admiration* |
| | | *envy* | *pity* | *favouring* | *enjoyment* |
| | ANNOYING type | *surprise* | *scare* | *pleasure* | *satisfaction* |
| | | *delight* | *concern* | *annoyance* | *amusement* |
| | | *disgust* | *interest* | *grief* | *exhaustion* |

A State-nom can be possessed by the noun phrase which is in the Experiencer role—in A function for LIKING and in O function for ANNOYING verbs. For example:

| (20) | (a) | *John dislikes clergymen* | [*John's dislike*] *of clergymen* |
|---|---|---|---|
| | (b) | *Mary admires athletes* | [*Mary's admiration*] *for athletes* |
| (21) | (a) | *The news surprised Mary* | [*Mary's surprise*] *at the news* |
| | (b) | *Fred's promotion pleased Bill* | [*Bill's pleasure*] *at Fred's promotion* |

With a nominalisation based on a LIKING verb, the stimulus role (the original O) is marked by a preposition, generally *of*, sometimes *for*, sometimes either (*love for a family member* or *for a lover*, but *love of life, of one's country* or *of God*). For State-nom's based on verbs from the ANNOYING type, the stimulus role (the erstwhile A) can be included, marked by a preposition; this is typically *at*, as in (21), but we also find, for example, *interest in, worry about, inspiration from.*

It is interesting to compare State-nom's for verbs with similar (and opposite) meanings and to see the difference in forms. Quoting verb/State-nom:

*love/love*          *like/liking*          *dislike/dislike*          *hate/hatred*

There is also what could be called 'unit' nominalisations of state—*hate, love* and *like.* Besides *John's hatred of/love for spinach*, we get *Bill's three pet hates/loves are dogs, clergymen and children.*

A few verbs from the ANNOYING type form a State-nom which can be used with a 'counting token' such as *a fit of*, to engender a 'unit' effect; for instance:

(22)   (a)   *The war news depressed John*
               *John had* [*a fit of depression*] (*when he heard the war news*)
       (b)   *The loss of the document angered Mary*
               *Mary had* [*a fit of anger*] (*when she heard of the loss of the document*)

Verbs in the COMPARING and RELATING types refer to neither an activity nor a state, but rather to a kind of property. Here the underlying subject may function as possessor to a nominalisation (Property-nom), as in:

(23)   (a)   *Mark differs from his twin*
               [*Mark's difference from his twin*] *is significant*
       (b)   *Jane depends on her mother*
               [*Jane's dependence on her mother*] *is worrying*

## *10.2.3. Nominalisations describing a result*

A nominalisation may describe the result of an activity, a Result-nom. This is generally formed from a transitive verb. A Result-nom relates to the original O of the verb by means of a preposition—most often *of*, sometimes *to* or *on* or *out of.* For example:

(24)   (a)   *X imitated Van Gogh*                    *imitation of Van Gogh*
       (b)   *X arranged some flowers*            *arrangement of flowers*
       (c)   *X declared war*                            *declaration of war*
       (d)   *X extended the house*                *extension of the house*
       (e)   *X lost a diamond ring*                *loss of a diamond ring*

| | | |
|---|---|---|
| (f) | *X solved the problem* | *solution to/of the problem* |
| (g) | *X bit the apple* | *bite out of the apple* |
| (h) | *X wounded John* | *wound on John* |
| (i) | *X injured Mary* | *injury to Mary* |

All of the nominalisations could be preceded by *the* or *a(n)*. For (24a–g), the possessor *X's* could be added before the Result-nom: *X's imitation of Van Gogh*, *X's arrangement of flowers*, and so on. This shows that the forms *imitation*, *arrangement*, etc.—in (24a–g)—function both as Result-nom and as Unit-nom. From this list, just *wound* and *injury* are restricted to a Result-nom sense.

The question now arises as to whether a possessive relation should be recognised between a Result-nom and the erstwhile O. Generally, the original O does not have human reference and would be expected to be marked by *of* rather than *'s*. We do get *of* in (24a–f); but *to* may be used as an alternative to *of* in (24f) and different prepositions are required in (24g–i). It seems that the use of *of* in (24a–f) is coincidental, and that it would not be useful or appropriate to consider any of (24a–i) as a kind of possessive construction. One can, of course, say *John's wound* and *Mary's injury* (as an alternative to *the wound on John* or *the injury to Mary*); however, these are possessive constructions of type (c) from §10.1—where *wound* and *injury* are inalienable aspects of the possessor, on a par with *mouth* and *pimple*—rather than being related to the nominalisation.

### 10.2.4. Object nominalisations

One variety of nominalisation, Object-nom, can function as object for the verb from which it is derived—*dream a dream* (where the Object-nom has the same form as the verb) or *pay a payment* (where the forms differ). Note that these are not 'patient' nominalisations (*dream* and *payment* are not patients); they relate to the syntactic function of object, rather than to a semantic role.

As mentioned in §§4.4–5, such 'cognate objects' are in fact seldom used as is, but generally require one or more modifiers which provide significant extra information in the object noun phrase (over and above that conveyed by the verb). For example, *I dreamed the horrible and frightening dream* (or the first line of a well-known song, *To dream the impossible dream*) rather than just *I dreamt a dream*, and *He paid the rather steep but unavoidable down-payment on the house* rather than just *He paid the payment.* Here are some examples of Object-nom's, with sample modifiers:

**(25)**

| Semantic type | SAME FORM AS VERB | DERIVED FORM |
|---|---|---|
| MOTION | *spray a nauseous spray* | *bear a heavy burden* |
| AFFECT | *fry up a big fish fry* | *build the biggest building in the world* |
| GIVING | *supply sufficient supplies to last them for a long voyage* | *possess more bulky and useless possessions than you could imagine* |
| CORPOREAL | *drink the strongest drink on offer* | *spit out a huge, wet and revolting blob of spittle* |
| THINKING | *suspect the usual suspects* | *think the most beautiful thoughts* |

Other Object-nom's of this type include *plant, smoke, sell, taste, feed/ food, favour/favourite*, and derivations ending in *-ee*, such as *employee, nominee, appointee*. Some nominalisations are used in plural form; for example, *supplies* in (25) and *nibbles*, as in *I nibbled the most delicious oriental nibbles at that cocktail party.* And there are also nominalisations which may be used as peripheral arguments: for example, *The American tourist tipped the taxi driver with a most generous tip* (and similarly for *reward* and *bribe*, among others).

The verbs mentioned so far are fully transitive, with the nominalisation available for object (or indirect object) slot as alternative to a non-cognate form; for example, one can say either *He drank a malt whisky* or *He drank the strongest drink on offer.* As discusssed in §9.3.1, there are also a number of verbs, most from the CORPOREAL (and a few from the WEATHER) type, which are basically intransitive, and can only be followed by a noun phrase (in apparent object function) when this has an Object-nom as head. For example:

**(26)**   *John smiled happily*
      *John smiled the happiest smile we've ever seen*

Other verbs of this type include *laugh, cough, sneeze, yawn* and *wink*.

Using a verb with an Object-nom, even with heavy modification in the object noun phrase, is not common in formal style. It is probably most acceptable when the nominalisation has a derived form, as different as possible from the verb (for example, *bear* and *burden*, where the derivation goes back to Old English). But collocations such as those in (25)–(26) are common in colloquial speech and in spoken rhetoric.

An Object-nom is most frequently found with a verb other than that from which it is derived, but with a similar meaning; for example, *apply a spray*, *carry a burden*, *cook up a fish fry*, *erect a building*.

There are a number of further Object-nom's which are scarcely likely to function as object of the verb on which they are based, even in the most colloquial speech (although, with ingenuity, contexts could well be devised for them). However, they can be equated (by copula *be*) with the object of the verb. For example:

(27)    *X assumed Y*            implies    *Y was the (/X's) assumption*

                                           as in:

    *John assumed that Mary*                    *That Mary will be on time was the*
    *will be on time*                              *(/John's) assumption*

Object-nom's of this type include those formed with -(*t*)*ion* (others are *selection*, *proposal* and *supposition*) and *convert*, *discovery*, *choice*. And also *view*—*We viewed the forest from the window* implies that *The view from the window is the forest*.

Some derived forms may function both as a Unit-nom, as in (28a), and as an Object-nom, as in (28b):

(28)    *John most generously gave a dictionary to Mary*
    (a)    *[John's most generous gift (of a dictionary) to Mary] surprised everyone*
    (b)    *John gave [a most generous gift] to Mary*

However, one cannot have both simultaneously. That is, *\*John's gift of [a most generous gift] to Mary ...* is quite unacceptable.

And *building*, for example, can be an Activity-nom, as in (29a), or an Object-nom, as in (29b):

(29)    *Robin built the skyscraper*
    (a)    *[Robin's building (of the skyscraper)] took a long time*
    (b)    *Robin built [a tremendously high building]*

Again, we cannot have both at once—*\*John's building of [a tremendously high building] took a long time* is scarcely acceptable.

An Object-nom can generally be in possessive relation with the erstwhile A argument of the verb, if this satisfies the conditions for taking 's (or if it is a pronoun with animate reference). Besides the examples given in (3) and (5) there are *my burden, the rich tourist's tip, Mary's thoughts, John's assumption.*

## 10.2.5. Locus nominalisations

There are three kinds of nominalisation relating to the locus of the underlying verb, Locus-nom.

(i)   Several verbs from the REST-b subtype form a nominalisation such that 'X Verb at/on Y' implies 'X's Locus-nom is (at/on) Y'. *Residence* was illustrated in (2); there is also *encampment* and *settlement*:

(30)   *The refugees settled on Pie Island*
       *The refugees' settlement is (on) Pie Island*

(ii)   A number of verbs from the MOTION-b and MOTION-d subtypes form nominalisations such that 'X Verb the Y' can imply 'X is on/in the Locus-nom to/of the Y'. These include:

(31)   (a)   *John is approaching the airfield*   *John is on the approach to the airfield*
       (b)   *Mary is entering the hall*   *Mary is in the entrance to the hall*
       (c)   *Bill is tracking the thief*   *Bill is on the track of the thief*

(iii)   A number of verbs from the REST-c, REST-d and REST-e subtypes form a nominalisation for which 'X Verb the Y' implies 'The Y is in/on the/a Locus-nom'. For example:

(32)   (a)   *They beached the boat*   *The boat is on the beach*
       (b)   *We trapped the monkey*   *The monkey is in the/a trap*
       (c)   *He packed the sandwiches*   *The sandwiches are in a pack*
       (d)   *We enclosed the fruit trees*   *The fruit trees are in an enclosure*

Other verbs in this set include *land, ground* and *shelve.*

All of the Locus-nom's of type (iii)—except for *enclose/enclosure*—involve a zero derivation. Each of these forms originally entered the language as a noun, the same form being used as verb at a later stage. Diachronically we have a process of verbalisation; nevertheless, within a synchronic grammar of modern English, it is useful to regard these as Locus-nom's. The three Locus-nom's of type (i) involve the addition of *-ence* and *-ment*, while for type (ii) we have *enter/entrance* but the same form for others—*approach*, *track* (and *exit*).

In type (i) there is possessive relation between the underlying S argument of the verb and the Locus-nom, as in *John's residence*. For type (ii), it is just possible to have the erstwhile O as possessor, as in *the hall's entrance* (an alternative to *the entrance of/to the hall*). No relation of possession pertains to type (iii).

Some of the nominalisations of type (ii) have double function. Besides its Locus-nom sense, *entrance* can also be a Unit-nom, as in:

(33)    *The queen slowly entered the cathedral*
        [*The queen's slow entrance into the cathedral*] *was wonderful to behold*

*Approach* behaves in a similar way. And besides the Locus-nom *track*, there is also an Activity-nom *tracking*, as in [*The policeman's careful tracking of the criminal*] *earned him a medal*.

A further type of nominalisation relating to a place is included under (f) of Inst-nom's in §10.2.7. It is marked by suffix *-er*; for example, *sleeper*.

## 10.2.6. Agentive nominalisations

The most pervasive suffix which forms a nominalisation relating to the subject of an activity is *-er*. This generally refers to an habitual, volitional agent, and will be called Agent-nom.

Suffix *-er* is of Germanic origin. Alongside it are two suffixes of Romance origin, generally used with Romance verbs: *-or* (as in *inspector*, *possessor*, *actor*, *competitor*) and *-ar* (as in *bursar*). The three suffixes have merged in pronunciation, all being just /-ə/ (a linking /r/ can be inserted before a following word commencing with a vowel, such as *of*). Spellings vary and in fact some Germanic Agent-nom's are written with *-ar*, including *liar* and *beggar*.

Almost all semantic types include some or many verbs forming Agent-nom's with *-er* (or *-or* or *-ar*). There are rather few in the Secondary types (except for the HELPING subtype); see §10.5.3. And there are virtually none in the LIKING and ANNOYING types, since one cannot have an agentive nominalisation of a state. We do find *worshipper*, but this implies undertaking something physical as an act of worship (for example, kneeling and praying before a cross or other idol, or making a sacrifice), and not just worshipping in the non-physical sense of 'like a lot'.

The conditions for use of *-er* can be seen by examining verbs from the subtype MOTION-a. One often hears *runner, dancer, diver, jogger* and *swimmer* since these are all volitional activities that people indulge in habitually. Less common are *waver* and *wriggler* since these actions are generally not done habitually; but if they were to be, the Agent-nom's are available.

An Agent-nom is typically used with a modifying adjective which describes how the agent characteristically performs the activity. For example:

(34)   *a good tipper   a heavy/light sleeper       a deep thinker*
       *a fast runner   a heavy smoker/drinker*

All of these Agent-nom's describe a habitual activity. One can say *He is the winner of the 3.20 race*, but to describe a horse just as *a winner* will generally imply that he has won a number of races.

However, there are a few verbs that describe an action which if performed at all is highly significant. For these, an Agent-nom may be used to describe the action being done just once, not habitually—for example, *killer, murderer, deserter* (from an army or similar force).

Note that *-er* is not possible with verbs which are unlikely to be agentive, such as *fall, spill, upset, capsize* (and others from the MOTION-g subtype) and *die*. And it is not used with verbs referring to an activity which is unlikely to be performed habitually, such as *assume, suspect, consider, imagine, ponder, reward, bequeath, insult*.

In some situations (in a courtroom, and in formal writing), words of Romance origin are considered to be of a higher class and more acceptable than those of Germanic origin. Certain nominalisations are most used in such situations. This has led to a number of instances where there are two verbs, of similar meaning, and an Agent-nom is generally formed just from the Romance verb, not from that of Germanic origin. For example:

(35)   ONE PREFERS      RATHER THAN           ONE PREFERS      RATHER THAN
       *demonstrator*   *show-er* or *prov-er*   *selector*      *choos-er*
       *enquirer*       *ask-er*                *observer*       *look-er* or *see-er*
       *admirer of*     *lik-er of*

There was at one time an Agent-nom based on *see*, but this has now taken on a specialised meaning, *seer* 'prophet', and is no longer associated with *see*. There was originally an Agent-nom *looker*; it was only as this dropped out of use that a new word *looker* evolved, with a quite different meaning—

'look good', as in *She's a (good) looker*. (But note that one can still say *a looker on*.)

In times gone by, a feminine suffix *-ess* (of Romance origin) could be added after agentive *-er* (with phonological shortening), as in *manageress, actress*. This is now frowned on; a female film star generally prefers to be called just an *actor*. (Although it has proved useful to retain the *-ess* form for certain purposes, as when Oscars are awarded for 'best actor' and for 'best actress'.) Note that, although lost from Agent-nom's, *-ess* is still retained for referring to animals and the aristocracy—*lioness, duchess, princess*.

There is a less pervasive affix which can be an alternative to (sometimes an addition to) *-er*. Suffix *-ant/-ent* is of Romance origin and is generally added to Romance verbs. In some cases, both verb and nominalisation were borrowed into Middle English from Old French; for example, *appeal* and *appellant, defend* and *defendant*. The affix has been extended to some words of Germanic origin; for example, *coolant* (from 1930) by analogy with *lubricant* (attested from 1822).

The partial equivalence of *-er* and *-ant/-ent* can be seen by their occurrence on pairs of Germanic/Romance words which have a similar meaning; for example:

(36)  *helper/assistant*          *learner/student*

In these and in some other nominalisations, *-ant/-ent* has an habitual, volitional agentive meaning, like *-er*; I group it with *-er* in forming Agent-nom's. However, the agentive component is sometimes minimal, as in *defendant, resident*.

For a fair number of *-ant/-ent* Agent-nom's, there is the sense of 'one of a group involved in the activity', for example:

(37)  *student*      *discussant*      *participant*      *resident*
      *assistant*    *contestant*      *inhabitant*

However, this does not apply to others, such as *claimant, defendant*, and *president*.

There are a few verbs which form both *-er* and *-ant/-ent* Agent-nom's, with a difference in meaning:

(38)  (a)  *defender*—of a castle, of one's reputation, of political ideals
          *defendant*—nowadays mostly confined to legal matters
    (b)  *opposer*—of a motion, by analogy with proposer
          *opponent*—in battle, in sporting contests, in argument

(c)  *proposer*—of a motion (in debate)
     *proponent*—of an idea or course of action
(d)  *informer*—this has acquired the rather specific meaning of someone
     who tells the authorities that someone else has done something they
     shouldn't (and may be punished for)
     *informant*—used since the late nineteenth century for a person who
     supplies information to a linguist or anthropologist concerning their
     language and culture (this has recently been hounded out of use by
     'politically correct' people who lack sufficient intelligence to perceive
     the difference in form and meaning between *informant* and *informer*)

There is a further suffix forming Agent-nom's, *-ard/-art*. This typically
carries an opprobrious meaning; for example, *drunkard, braggart, laggard*
(and note *dullard*, from adjective *dull*). There are no examples of a verb
which forms Agent-nom's with both *-ard/-art* and *-er*.

There are some nouns which have the same form as a verb and which
refer to an agent; these include *cook* and *guide*. However, they do not
qualify as Agent-nom's. Whereas *John baked this loaf* gives *John is the
baker of the loaf*, corresponding to *John cooked this meal*, one cannot say
\**John is the cook of this meal*. (For each of these, the nominal form is the
older, having been later extended to use as a verb.)

An Agent-nom formed from a transitive verb can be possessed by the
object of the underlying verb if this fulfils the conditions to take *'s* (or is a
pronoun with animate reference). Thus: *My cousin's murderer, Fred's
employer, Kate's lecturer, our leader, the professor's assistant*. When the
underlying O argument only partially satisfies the criteria, we may get
either *'s* or *of*—*the governor of the province, the province's governor*, and
*the operator of the machine, the machine's operator*. For others, just *of* may
be used—*wrecker of cars, worshipper of idols, eater of chocolate, framer of
pictures, bearer of gifts, explorer of the rain forest*.

## 10.2.7. Instrumental nominalisations

The suffix *-er* also derives an Inst-nom; that is, a nominalisation which
describes an instrument (including a machine or vehicle) or some other
material object involved in the activity. The main possibilities are:

(a) Instrument, typically derived from AFFECT verbs, including *mower, shaver,
    curler, mixer*. The meaning is sometimes restricted by a modifier; for example,

(*baby*) *feeder*, (*tin*) *opener*, (*post hole*) *digger*. Some Inst-nom's have a special-ised function—a (*door*) *knocker* is fixed to the door, a *bumper* (*bar*) is on a car, a (*door*) *closer* automatically closes a door, a *shutter* is a specific contraption to shut a window. A *scraper* can be something fixed to the ground near a front door, for visitors to scrape mud off their boots on, or a hand-held device to scrape old paint off a surface.

**(b)**  Machine, which can function as A argument to the verb. A *heater* or a *freezer* or *starter* (motor in a car) does not require any human intervention, but can perform an activity on its own—*Turn the ignition on and the starter* (*motor*) *starts the engine*, and *The heater will soon warm up the room*.

**(c)**  Vehicle involved in an activity—*transporter*, *loader*.

**(d)**  Clothing or footwear typically donned by Agent undertaking the activity—*swimmers* (bathing costume), *runners* (shoes), *joggers* (shoes to jog in, and some-times also trousers to wear while jogging). Note that all these require plural -*s*.

**(e)**  A body part used in the activity; for example, *feeler* 'tentacles' and, colloqui-ally, *smeller* 'nose'.

**(f)**  The location at which an activity takes place; for example *sleeper* (where one sleeps, on a train), *diner* (in a train or otherwise), *kneeler* (a cushion to kneel on), *locker* (cupboard in which things can be locked up).

Many of these Inst-nom forms are ambiguous, and can also have an Agent-nom sense. A man who manually mixes cement with sand and water to make concrete could be called a *mixer*; alternatively, a *cement mixer* (a machine) could be used. A person who mows a lawn using a *motor mower* could be called a *mower*. Anyone who knocks on doors (using the attached *door knocker*), collecting money for charity, can be called a *door knocker*. *Diner* can refer to someone who dines, whether at a high-class restaurant or in a cheap *diner*. Someone who operates a large *transporter* truck can be called a *transporter*.

There is generally no automatic relation of possession between an Inst-nom and an argument of the underlying verb. When one hears *Mary mixed the ingredients with an electric mixer*, the mixer may or may not be Mary's. However, if Simon books a sleeper on a train from Amsterdam to Milan then—for that night only—the berth is *Simon's sleeper*.

## 10.2.8. Possession of a nominalisation: summary

We have seen that all but two of the nine varieties of deverbal nominalisa-tion take part in a possessive construction—marked by *'s* or a possessive pronoun—with an argument of the underlying verb. The exceptions are

Result-nom's (§10.2.3) and Inst-nom's (§10.2.7). A possessive relation is also lacking for Locus-nom's of type (iii).

That is, we have:

- Unit-nom's and Activity-nom's. Possessor can be in S, A or O relation, if these arguments satisfy the conditions for use of *'s*, set out in §10.1. Examples are at (4), (6) and (7).
- State-nom's. The Experiencer role can be possessor—this is the underlying A argument for a LIKING verb (for example, *Mary's fear of the dark*) and the underlying O argument for an ANNOYING verb (*John's surprise at the news*).
- Property-nom's. If underlying S or A argument has an appropriate referent, it can be a possessor; for example, [*John's exact measurement of the artefact*] *was appreciated*.
- Object-nom's. If the referent of the A argument is human (or animate), singular and specific then it may be a possessor—*Santa Claus' gifts, the missionary's converts*.
- Locus-nom's. For type (i) the underlying S argument can be possessor (*my residence*). For type (ii) it is just possible to have the underlying O as possessor (*the church's entrance*).
- Agent-nom. The O of the underlying verb can be possessor, if it has an appropriate referent—*our leader, Goliath's opponent, (I am) mother's washer upper*.

Type (e) of possession, in §10.1, involves 'something typically associated with the possessor'. This covers *my general* (said by a soldier), *my men* (said by a general), *my doctor* (said by a patient) and *my patients* (said by a doctor). That is, we have:

(39)   *Dr Pill treated Mrs Malingerer*
      (a)   *Dr Pill is Mrs Malingerer's doctor*
      (b)   *Mrs Malingerer is Dr Pill's patient*

This is iconic with (5) in §10.1. If *John employs Bill*, then *John is Bill's employer* and *Bill is John's employee*.

This shows the intertwining of strands within the grammar. A grammar is not like a machine with wheels and pulleys and shuttles; neither is it like a building with bricks and doors and roof. The aptest metaphor is of a tree with branches and leaves, threaded through by vines and ferns which compete for movement and light. Indeed, a grammar—an inalienable attribute of a community of humans—is a living organism, constantly shifting and adapting.

## 10.3. Derivational processes

We can now examine the range of morphological processes which can be utilised to derive a nominal from a verb.

Using the verb root unchanged (zero derivation) is attested for eight of the nine varieties of nominalisation (the exception is Property-nom):

- Unit-nom—many, including *jump, throw, chat, offer, laugh, cough, cheer*
- Activity-nom—a few, including *use*
- State-nom—a fair few, including *love, envy, delight, interest*; see (19)
- Result-nom—a few, including *wound, bite, plan*
- Object-nom—quite a few, including *plant, taste, smell*, and those in (25)
- Locus-nom—a few, including *track, exit, trap* and those in (32)
- Agent-nom—a few, including *witness*
- Inst-nom—a few, including *cart, plaster, veil*

Just as a nominalisation ending in *-ing* must be distinguished from the verb in an ING complement clause, so a zero derivation nominalisation must be distinguished from the use of the base form of a verb in a GIVE A VERB, HAVE A VERB or TAKE A VERB construction (these are discussed, with their defining criteria, in Chapter 14). For instance, the verb *borrow* does not have a zero derivation nominalisation, but it can be used after *have a*, as in *Can I have a borrow of your car for the weekend please?* And *track* is used both as a verb and as a Locus-nom, but not after *give a, have a* or *take a*.

Other derivational processes involve the addition of a suffix. Some suffixes do not engender any changes in a root to which they are added; for example, *-er, -ing, -ment, -al, -ee*. Others are to some degree fused with the root and may involve stress shift and/or phonological changes; these include *-ant/-ent, -(t)ion, -ance/-ence, -ure*. Deverbal nominalising suffixes will now be briefly discussed, one at a time.

(i)    *-er* (or *-or* or *-ar*), pronounced as /ə(r)/. Used only for Agent-nom and Inst-nom. (We find verb *pray* and Object-nom *prayer* but these are loans from Old French *preier* and *preiere* respectively; the final *-er* in *prayer* is not an instance of the nominalising suffix *-er*.)

The suffix *-er* also attaches to some nouns, such as *footballer, New Yorker*. It is highly productive and is frequently added to a multi-word sequence, as *Pacific Islander, clock-watcher* and *do-gooder*.

(ii)    *-ant* (and *-ent*), pronounced as /-ənt/ (or just as /nt/). Can involve change in root vowel and in stress; for example, *preside* /prizáid/, *president* /prézidənt/, and *reside/resident*. The root-final diphthong is dropped from *occupy* /ɔ́kjupai/, *occupant* /ɔ́kupənt/; see also *study/student* and *supplicate/supplicant*. Used for Agent-nom's (see §10.2.6) and for some Inst-nom's (including *lubricant*).

**(iii)   *-ard*** (or *-art*), pronounced as /-əd/ or /-ət/. In most cases, simply added to the root. Restricted to Agent-nom; see §10.2.6.

**(iv)   *-ing***, pronounced as /-iŋ/. Forms five varieties of nominalisation:

- Unit-nom—just a few, including *happening*
- Activity-nom—very many, including *running*, *drowning*, *trapping*, *understanding*, *urging*
- State-nom—a few, including *liking*, *rejoicing*, *craving*, *longing*
- Result-nom—many, which also function as Unit-nom's, including *weaving*, *wrapping*, *building*, *knitting*
- Object-nom doubling as Activity-nom—*building*

**(v)   *-ation, -ition, -tion, -ion***, pronounced as /-eiʃən/, /-iʃən/ or /-ʃən/. Of Romance origin, mostly used on Romance verbs. There is considerable allomorphic variation, of which just the basic outline is sketched here. First, with verbs ending in *-ate*, *-ise/-ize* and *-ify* we get:

— (a)   Ending in *-ate*, /-eit/. Replace final /t/ by /ʃən/, shift stress to penultimate vowel. For example:

      *nominate*, /nɔ́mineit/              *nomination*, /nɔminéiʃən/

— (b)   Ending in *-ise/-ize*, /aiz/. Add /-éiʃən/, with stress shift. For example:

      *organise*, /ɔ́:gənaiz/           *organisation*, /ɔ:gənaizéiʃən/

— (c)   Ending in *-ify* /-ifai/. Replace final /ai/ by /ikéiʃən/ with stress shift. For example:

      *qualify*, /kwɔ́lifai/           *qualification*, /kwɔlifikéiʃən/

Looking now at other verbs, we find:

— (d)   Ending in /t/, /d/ or /s/. One of two possibilities.

(d$_1$) /ʃən/ replaces final *t*, *d* or *s*. For example:

      *extend*, /eksténd/           *extension*, /eksténʃən/

This is shown in various ways in spelling. Final *t* is sometimes retained, as in *desert/desertion*, and sometimes replaced by *ss* or *s*, as in *permit/permission*, *convert/conversion*. Final *d* is sometimes changed to *t*, as in *intend/intention*, but more often replaced by *s*, as in *extend/extension*. Final *ss* or *s* (before *e*) is generally retained, as in *discuss/discussion*, *confuse/confusion*.

(d$_2$)   Add /íʃən/ or /éiʃən/, with vowel change and stress shift. For example:

      *suppose*, /səpóuz/           *supposition*, /sʌpəzíʃən/
      *converse*, /kɔ́nvə:s/          *conversation*, /kɔvəséiʃən/

And *compete/competition*, *oppose/opposition*, *recite/recitation*, *accuse/accusation*. Note that different processes apply for *convert/conversion* and *converse/conversation*; if they did not, the two nominalisations might coincide.

—(e)   Ending in /m/, /b/ or /v/; add /pʃən/ with vowel change, retaining /m/ but replacing /b/ or /v/. For example:

*assume*, /əsjúːm/                    *assumption*, /əsʌmpʃən/

And *describe/description, perceive/perception*. But note that *observe/observation* is an exception, being of type (f).

Some verbs ending in /v/ replace this by /úːʃən/, with vowel change and stress shift. For example:

*solve*, /sɔ́lv/                    *solution*, /səlúːʃən/

and *resolve/resolution* (which comes from the same Romance root).

— (f)   Ending in /l/ or /n/. Generally add /-éiʃən/, with stress shift:

*install*, /instɔ́ːl/          *installation*, /instəléiʃən/

And *imagine/imagination, resign/resignation, explain/explanation, console/consolation*.

Verbs which used to end in /r/, but have now lost this in most dialects, include it before /éiʃən/ (as before other suffixes commencing with a vowel). For example:

*declare*, /dikléə/                    *declaration*, /dekləréiʃən/

and *consider/consideration, admire/admiration, prepare/preparation*.

The suffix derives five varieties of nomination:

- Unit-nom—very, very many, including *installation, extension, donation, assassination, promotion, imagination, continuation*, and a considerable number from the SPEAKING type, such as *declaration, narration, explanation*
- State-nom—quite a few, including *admiration, inspiration*
- Property-nom—a few, including *indication, distinction, inclusion*
- Result-nom—a few, such as *information*; and a fair few which also function as Unit-nom, including *imitation, solution, decision*
- Object-nom—a few, including *assumption, supposition, selection, possession*

**(vi)** *-ment*, pronounced /-mənt/ (or sometimes just /-mnt/). Another suffix of Romance origin, found mostly with Romance verbs but also with some Germanic verbs, such as *amazement, settlement*. Used with many verbs which include prefix *em-/en-* or *be-*, including *embarrassment, endorsement, belittlement*. Forms six varieties of nominalisation (no more than a few instances of each). Examples include:

- Unit-nom—*statement, argument, commencement, postponement*
- State-nom—*enjoyment, bewilderment, excitement, entertainment*
- Property-nom—*measurement*
- Result-nom—*arrangement* (also functions as Unit-nom)
- Object-nom—*payment*
- Locus-nom—*settlement, encampment*

**(vii)** *-ance/-ence*, pronounced /-əns/. A further suffix of Romance origin used with many Romance and just a few Germanic verbs (for example, *utterance*). It can also nominalise adjectives ending in *-ent* through replacing this with *-ence*; for example, *violent/violence*.

Some verbs simply add /-ens/; for example, *guide, attend, resist, perform, appear, depend, avoid, assist*. Others involve stress shift and vowel change, for example:

*reside*, /rizáid/              *residence*, /rézidəns/

A number, ending in *-er*, /ə/, replace this by /rəns/, for example:

*remember*, /rimémbə/          *remembrance*, /rimémbrəns/

Others, ending in *-er* /ə:/, replace this with /(ə)rəns/ plus vowel change and stress shift:

*refer*, /rifə:/                *reference*, /réfrəns/
*prefer*, /prifə:/              *preference*, /préfərəns/

Note also *utter/utterance, differ/difference, hinder/hindrance, infer/inference*. And there is *enter/entrance*.

This suffix forms six varieties of nominalisation; again, there are no more than a few instances of each. Examples include:

- Activity-nom—*avoidance, assistance, guidance, attendance, resistance, performance, appearance, remembrance*
- State-nom—*annoyance, preference*
- Property-nom—*resemblance, dependence*
- Result-nom, and also Unit-nom—*utterance*
- Locus-nom—*residence*
- Locus-nom doubling as Unit-nom—*entrance*

**(viii)** *-y*, pronounced as /i/. This is an old Germanic suffix, basically used to form adjectives from nouns; for example *leaf-y, risk-y*. It also derives a number of nominals from verbs. Most of the verbs end in orthographic *-re* or *-er*, phonological /ə/; the suffix adds /ri/ and sometimes omits the preceding /ə/; for example:

*injure*, /índjə/            *injury*, /índj(ə)ri/
*enter*, /éntə/              *entry*, /éntri/

With *apologise*, suffix /i/ substitutes for /aiz/. There are five varieties of nominalisation involving *-y*, each with just a few members. They include:

- Unit-nom—*apology, enquiry, delivery*
- Activity-nom—*recovery*
- Result-nom—*injury*
- Object-nom—*discovery*
- Locus-nom—*entry*

**(ix)**   *-al*, pronounced /əl/, almost exclusively with Romance verbs. This is simply added to the root. *Approval* is a State-nom, and there are a number of Unit-nom's, including *arrival, dismissal, refusal, proposal, deferral, recital* and *revival*.

**(x)**   *-ee*, pronounced /iː/. Also a Romance suffix, simply added to the root. Almost all examples are Object-nom's—*nominee, employee, lessee, assignee, grantee*. Fairly recently, this suffix has been generalised from applying just to an underlying O argument to also describing an underlying S (a special intransitive agentive nominal). *Standee* ('someone who stands') dates from about 1830, *escapee* from about 1860, and *attendee* and *retiree* from about 1940. It appears that all four words were introduced in the USA and have now spread to other English-speaking communities.

**(xi)**   *-ure*. This suffix, also of Romance origin, has a number of different forms. We find /-ʃə/ added to *depart*, /-tjə/ to *mix* and /-jə/ to *fail*. Final /z/ is replaced by /-ʒə/ with *enclose* and *please* (the latter also involves a vowel change). This suffix derives four varieties of nominalisation:

- Unit-nom—*failure, departure*
- State-nom—*pleasure*
- Object-nom—*mixture*
- Locus-nom—*enclosure*

**(xii)**   *-t*. There are old Germanic verb/Object-nom-plus-Unit-nom pairs *give/gift* and *bequeath/bequest*, each with the addition of *-t* plus considerable phonological change. A phonologically similar but etymologically unrelated pair is *complain/complaint*, both forms being loans from Old French.

There are just one or two examples of other morphological processes which form nominalisations from verbs. They can usefully be listed according to type of nominalisation. (This is not an exhaustive list.)

Unit-nom—*analyse/analysis, speak/speech, believe/belief*
Activity-nom—*grieve/grief, behave/behaviour, pretend/pretence*
State-nom—*hate/hatred*
Result-nom and Unit-nom—*lose/loss*
Object-nom—*know/knowledge, lend/loan, bear/burden, choose/choice, favour/favourite, spit/spittle*
Object-nom and Unit-nom—*think/thought, feed/food*

## 10.4. Nominalisation of phrasal verbs

The question of which nominalisations may apply to phrasal verbs is a fascinating one. Of the thirty-seven verbs which function as first element in the great majority of phrasal verbs, only two (*carry* and *round*) are of Romance origin. As we have seen, most nominalising suffixes are of Romance origin, used predominantly on Romance verbs. And a phrasal verb consists of two or three elements—a verb and one or two prepositions. Where would a nominalising suffix attach—to the verb, or to the preposition(s), or to both?

This is not an easy topic to study. Phrasal verbs are most used in colloquial speech, and nominalisations based on them even more so. The nominalisations are generally not included in dictionaries. The linguist simply has to examine colloquial speech, augmented by their own judgements (if a native speaker).

Just two nominalising suffixes (both of Germanic origin) are used with phrasal verbs. Agent-nom's derived with *-er* are the topic of §10.4.1. There are also a number of Unit-nom's involving the bare form of the phrasal verb (with no suffix) and a few Activity-Nom's involving *-ing*; these are dealt with in §10.4.2.

### 10.4.1. Agentive nominalisations

The six varieties of phrasal verb were discussed in §9.2.2. The possibilities for agentive nominalisation, with examples, are summarised in Table 10.1, using 'p' for preposition and 'N' for a noun phrase or functionally equivalent constituent.

**Table 10.1.** *Agentive nominalisation of varieties of phrasal verbs*

| | PHRASAL VERBS | | AGENTIVE NOMINALISATIONS | | |
|---|---|---|---|---|---|
| | VARIETY | EXAMPLE | FORM | NUMBER | EXAMPLE |
| (i) | verb + p | *sleep in* | verb-*er* p | very few | *sleep-er in* |
| (ii) | verb + pN | *look after* N | verb-*er* p | very few | *look-er after* |
| (iii) | verb + Np | *pick N up* | verb-*er* p-*er* | quite a few | *pick-er upp-er* |
| (iv) | verb + NpN | *see N through N* | | | |
| (v) | verb + ppN | *fall out with N* | | none | |
| (vi) | verb + NppN | *put N down to N* | | | |

I have not been able to find any Agent-nom's based on phrasal verbs of varieties (iv–vi). (However, there is a suffix *-able*, which forms adjectives from verbs. While discussing how a rather difficult student, S, had fallen out with his adviser, A, I indicated that in my opinion it was S's fault by saying that A was *not really very fall-able out-able with*. Here, an adjective is derived from a type (v) phrasal verb, *fall out with* N, by adding *-able* to both *fall* and *out*. It may be that a more prolonged search would uncover occasional nominalisations based on variety (v) phrasal verbs.)

We can now discuss varieties (i–iii).

**Variety (i).** Most phrasal verbs of this type are not amenable to nominalisation with *-er*. Just a few are, for example: *looker on*, *sleeper in*, and possibly *chopper about*. Note that *-er* just goes onto the verb.

Most phrasal verbs (made up of two Germanic elements) have a single-word synonym or semi-synonym (often a Romance verb), and it is this which forms an Agent-nom. Compare:

| SINGLE VERB/AGENT-NOM | PHRASAL VERB WITH NO AGENT-NOM |
|---|---|
| *survive/survivor* | *get by* |
| *leave/leaver* | *clear out* |
| *escape/escaper* | *get away* |

**Variety (ii).** *Looker after* is a rare instance of an Agent-nom:

(40)   *Jane looks after children from many families*
        *Jane is* [*a looker after of children from many families*]

As with variety (i), the *-er* goes just on the verb. There are again one-word synonyms or semi-synonyms (often Romance verbs) which form Agent-nom's. For example:

| SINGLE VERB/AGENT-NOM | PHRASAL VERB WITH NO AGENT-NOM |
|---|---|
| *pursue/pursuer* | *run after* |
| *investigate/investigator* | *look into* |
| *attack/attacker* | *turn on* |
| *kill/killer* | *do in* |

**Variety (iii).** There are several hundred phrasal verbs with structure 'verb plus N p' (with the N being moveable to the position after the p if it is not a pronoun). Quite a few of them (although only a minority overall) do form an Agent-nom, indicating a habitual, volitional agent. For example:

(41)   *Tom usually washes up the dishes very well/washes the dishes up very well*
       *Tom is a very good washer upper (of dishes)*

Note that the agentive suffix *-er* generally goes onto both verb and preposition. Other examples include:

| | |
|---|---|
| *picker upper* (of rubbish) | *filler outer* (of forms) |
| *putter offer* (of meetings) | *eater upper* (of leftovers) |
| *puller offer* (of publishing scoops) | *turner upper* (of beds in a hotel) |
| *fixer upper* (of gadgets) | *cleaner upper* (of rooms) |

As with varieties (i) and (ii), there is often a single word (often of Romance origin) as synonym or semi-synonym, and an Agent-nom is more likely to be formed on this than on the phrasal verb (although, in the right context, it may be possible to place *-er* on the elements of the phrasal verb). For example:

| | PHRASAL VERB UNLIKELY |
|---|---|
| SINGLE VERB/AGENT-NOM | TO FORM AN AGENT-NOM |
| *calculate/calculator* | *figure out* |
| *store/storer* | *put away* |
| *remove/remover* | *take away* |
| *gather/gatherer* | *get in* |
| *save/saver* | *put by* |

Whether or not Agentive nominalisation *-er* may go onto a phrasal verb of variety (iii)—which attaches *-er* to both verb and preposition—appears to depend in part on the identity of the preposition. Prepositions which accept *-er* most readily are *up*, *out* and *off*—these are in fact the most commonly occurring prepositions in phrasal verbs. Others are *down*, *in* and *on*, which are the next most common prepositional components; for example, *runner downer* (of someone's reputation), *filler inner* (of forms), *taker onner* (of challenges). (*Over* and *back* are somewhat marginal.) It seems rather unlikely that *-er* could ever be added to *about, across, away, by* or *round*, all of which do occur in phrasal verbs of variety (iii). That is, one would not normally say *\*bring-er about-er*, *\*gett-er across-er*, *\*putt-er away-er*, *\*putt-er by-er* or *\*hav-er round-er*.

In summary, *-er* may go onto just the verb of a phrasal verb of variety (i)—verb plus p—or (ii)—verb plus p N—or onto both verb and preposition for variety (iii)—verb plus N p. No example is attested of it just going at the end of the phrasal verb, on the preposition (we do not get, for example, *\*sleep-in-er*, *\*look-after-er* or *\*pick-upp-er*).

## 10.4.2. Unit and activity nominalisations

Unit-nom's generally involve the plain form of a Germanic verb but a derived form (often with -*tion*) for a Romance verb. Most often, there is a Unit-nom for the single-word synonym of a phrasal verb, but not for the phrasal verb itself. With phrasal verb of variety (ii) *go over* and its semi-synonym *examine* we get:

(**42**)  (a)  *John examined the accounts*
               *John's examination of the accounts was thorough*
         (b)  *John went over the accounts*
               *\*John's go over of the accounts was thorough*

(We can have *John's going over the accounts* but this is a complement clause, not a nominalisation.)

And with *cut in on*, a phrasal verb of type (v), and its semi-synonym *interrupt*, we get:

(**43**)  (a)  *Ralph interrupted the president*
               *Ralph's interruption of the president was rather rude*
         (b)  *Ralph cut in on the president*
               *\*Ralph's cut in on of the president was rather rude*

Other examples involve phrasal verbs of variety (iii):

| SEMI-SYNONYM/UNIT-NOM | PHRASAL VERB (NOT USED AS UNIT-NOM) |
|---|---|
| *discover/discovery* | *find out* |
| *postpone/postponement* | *put off* |
| *invent/invention* | *make up* |

There are, however, a number of phrasal verbs of variety (iii) which can be used (with zero derivation) as a Unit-nom. For example:

(**44**)  (a)  *John summarised the discussion*
               *John's summary of the discussion was most helpful*
         (b)  *John summed up the discussion*
               *John's sum up of the discussion was most helpful*

Other examples are:

| SEMI-SYNONYM/UNIT-NOM | PHRASAL VERBS (ALSO USED AS UNIT-NOM) |
|---|---|
| *support/support* | *back up* |

| | |
|---|---|
| *swindle/swindle* | *rip off* |
| *calculate/calculation* | *figure out* |

The suffix *-ing* is Germanic and can be used on some phrasal verbs, generally occurring just on the verb. It most frequently creates an Activity-nom; for example, *cleaning up, putting off, talking into, making up*. In the case of *telling off* we have a Unit-nom (this is countable; for example, *I had four tellings off from the teacher last week*).

And matters can be much more complex. One day recently, a parks attendant in Melbourne explained to me: *I'm just doing a bit of rubbish pick-ing upp-er-ing*. This includes *-ing* on *pick*, plus both *-er* and *-ing* on *up*. Why? (Well, it sounds pretty good.)

## 10.5. Nominalisation by semantic type

It is instructive to survey briefly the semantic types belonging to the word class verb, and see which varieties of nominalisation are associated with each.

### 10.5.1. Primary-A types

- MOTION type. Agent-nom's are available for most verbs; exceptions being the non-volitionals in MOTION-g (*fall, capsize*, etc.) and verbs denoting an activity which is scarcely likely to be habitual (*approach, cross, pass*). There are a few Inst-nom's—garments associated with MOTION-a verbs (*swimmers*) and vehicles associated with MOTION-c (*transporter, cart*).

  Many verbs have both Unit-nom (*run, throw*) and Activity-nom (*running, throwing*). Some have just a Unit-nom (*arrival*) and some just an Activity-nom (*carrying*). There are scarcely any Result-nom's or Object-nom's (*spray* and *burden* are two). As described in §10.2.5, there are Locus-nom's based on some verbs in MOTION-b and MOTION-d.

- REST type. Agent-nom's are largely confined to REST-b (*resident, settler*), REST-c (*arranger, installer*) and REST-e (*handler, catcher*). There are just a few Inst-nom's, including *kneeler, planter, opener* and *closer*.

  There are a fair number of Unit-nom's, across all subtypes—*attendance, desertion, grab*, and so on—but rather few Activity-nom's—*opening, closing* (and one often sees signs saying *The dumping of rubbish is prohibited*). Verbs in REST-c form Result-nom's which also function as Unit-nom's (*arrangement, installation*), and there is *plant*, an Object-nom. As described in §10.2.5, Locus-nom's are formed from verbs in REST-b/c/d/e.

- AFFECT type. Virtually all verbs may form Agent-nom's (*killer, pruner, roofer, destroyer*) and many also have an Inst-nom (*polisher, freezer, (nut)cracker*). There is a set of Inst-nom's with the same form as the verb. For *plaster, grease, roof, veil* and *butter*, the noun is older, having been later extended to function as a verb (but for *paint* and *cover* the verb is older).

  Many AFFECT verbs have a Unit-nom (*cut, pinch*) and a good many have an Activity-nom (*cutting, pinching*). Many also have a Result-nom (*slice, mark, break, wreckage*) or a Result-nom which is also a Unit-nom (*extension*). There are also some forms which double as Object-nom and as Unit-nom (*try*) or as Object-nom and Activity-nom (*building*).

- GIVING type. Many have an Agent-nom (*donor, lender, receiver, owner*); I know of just one Inst-nom (*feeder*). There are many nominalisations which function both as Object-nom and Unit-nom (*payment, possession, contribution, delivery*) and some as Result-nom and Unit-nom (*loss*). *Servery*, a place where food or drink is served, is an unusual Locus-nom.

- CORPOREAL type. Virtually all verbs have (or could have) an Agent-nom (for example, *smoker, drunkard, murderer*), and there are a few Inst-nom's (*sleeper, diner*). A number of verbs have a nominalisation which functions as Object-nom and as Unit-nom (*drink, smell, laugh*), while others just have an Object-nom (*spittle*). Some couple Result-nom with Unit-nom (*vomit, growth, cure, wound*). And there are many Activity-nom's (*sucking, comforting*).

- WEATHER type. Generally, Activity-nom's involve the addition of *-storm* (for example, *thunderstorm, hailstorm*). There are Result-nom's *snow* and *rain*; for example, *It snowed all yesterday and now the snow is thick on the ground.*

- COMPETITION type. All verbs describe an activity which can be habitual and all form an Agent-nom (even *lose*, which in normal circumstances is not volitional). Some also have Unit-nom's (*race, fight, win, loss, competition*).

- SOCIAL CONTRACT type. There are some Agent-nom's (*employer, prosecutor, applicant*) and a handful of Object-nom's (*employee, convert*), together with many Unit-nom's (*appointment, employment, dismissal*).

- USING type. All refer to volitional actions, which can be performed habitually, and almost all form Agent-nom's (for example, *user, operator*). There are also some Activity-nom's, such as *manipulation, operation, use.*

- OBEYING type. There are some Agent-nom's (*executor, processor, performer*) and also some Unit-nom's (*refusal, performance, processing*).

## 10.5.2. Primary-B types

- ATTENTION type. Many have Agent-nom's, including *observer*, *demonstrator*, *discoverer*, *witness*, *student*, *investigator*, *watcher*, *listener*. There are a fair number of Activity-nom's, such as *observation*, *perception*, *notice*. The few Unit-nom's include *demonstration* and *appearance*, while *discovery* doubles as Object-nom and Unit-nom.

- THINKING type. There are just a few Agent-nom's (*thinker*, *brooder*, *dreamer*) but many Activity-Nom's (*consideration*, *imagination*, *reflection*, *realisation*) and also a scattering of Object-nom's, such as *suspect*, *knowledge*, *assumption*, *supposition*. Some nominalisations can function as Object-nom and Unit-nom (*thought*, *dream*), while others can be Result-nom and Unit-nom (*solution*, *belief*).

- DECIDING type. All can, potentially, form Agent-nom's although only some are in common use, including *planner*, *selector*. (*Decider* generally has a quite different sense, referring to the final match in a sporting context where each side has won an equal number of the lead-up games.) There are a number of Unit-nom's—*decision*, *selection*, *election*, *appointment*.

- SPEAKING type. Agent-nom's are largely concentrated in subtypes SPEAKING-a/b/c (*speaker*, *communicator*, *discussant*, *narrator*) although we also find *claimant*, *braggart*, *informer* (and *informant*), *lecturer*, and *nominator*, among others. There are many Unit-nom's, including *speech*, *argument*, *quarrel*, *chat*, *joke*, *talk*, *narration*, *utterance*, and some which can also double as Object-nom—*assertion*, *suggestion*, *offer*. Some SPEAKING verbs have a Result-nom, as in *His joke was published*, *Her offer was refused*. For some, a Result-nom can also function as Unit-nom—*declaration*, *proclamation*. And some form an Activity-nom; one can talk of *fierce quarrelling*, *extravagant boasting*, *loud applauding*.

- LIKING and ANNOYING types. All verbs from these types form a State-nom— *liking*, *preference*, *amusement*, *distraction*, and so on. As mentioned in §10.2.2, there are also 'unit' type State-nom's—*hate*, *love*, *like*. Agent-nom's only exist when some physical action is involved—*worshipper*, *entertainer*. And there is the Object-nom *favourite*.

- ACTING type. We find some Agent-nom's (*actor*, *imitator*), many Unit-nom's (*action*, *behaviour*) and some which can be Result-nom and Unit-nom (*imitation*).

- HAPPENING type. There are Agent-nom's for some of the transitive members— *organiser*, *arranger*—and for some intransitive verbs even though there is no volition involved—*undergoer* and *experiencer*. A number of the verbs form Unit-nom's, including *happening*, while *arrangement* and *change* function as both Unit-nom and Result-nom.

- COMPARING and RELATING types. Some of these verbs form Property-nom's, described in §10.2.2—*resemblance, inclusion, dependence*, and so on. There are just a few Agent-nom's, often for specialised occupations, such as *weigher* and *timer*.

## 10.5.3. Secondary verbs

**Secondary-a**. Some derivations have the form of an Agent-nom but a specialised meaning. A *beginner* is not someone who habitually begins things but rather someone who is new and inexperienced at a particular task. *Finisher* can refer to a workman who performs the final task in a production process. A *starter*, based on the transitive sense of the verb, is someone who gives the signal for a race to start; this is a kind of Agent-nom. There is also *starter* (motor) in a car, which is an Inst-nom (and the quite different word *starters*, which describes the first course in a meal, and has had its meaning extended to refer to the first part of any reasonably complex activity). To describe someone as a *trier* implies that they don't often succeed, but refuse to give up. Perhaps the only straightforward Agent-nom's of Secondary-a verbs, maintaining the same focus of meaning as the verb, are *manager, dawdler* and *venturer*.

Most Secondary-a verbs do have a Unit-nom (which is countable). In the BEGINNING type we find *beginning, start, finish, commencement, continuation, cessation, completion*. In the TRYING type there are *try, attempt, practice, repetition. Failure* functions both as a Unit-nom and as a special kind of Agent-nom (someone who habitually, although not volitionally, fails). In the HURRYING type there is Unit-nom *hesitation* and Activity-nom's *hurrying, hastening, dawdling* and *hesitating*. In the DARING type there is the noun *dare*, relating to the causative sense of the verb—*He dared me to enter the lion's den and I responded to his dare*. There is also the Unit-nom *venture*.

**Secondary-b**. Only a couple of verbs in the WANTING type form an Agent-nom—*planner* and *pretender*. However, most of them have Unit-nom's—*wish, desire, hope, dread, craving, expectation*, and so on. *Needs* and *requirement* are Object-nom's, while *plan* and *aim* are Result-nom's. Verbs in the POSTPONING type form Unit-nom's—*postponement, deferral, delay*.

**Secondary-c**. Just a few verbs in the MAKING type form an Agent-nom—*rescuer, tempter*. The Agent-nom *causer* tends nowadays to be restricted to technical usage. (For example, in this book I use it for the semantic role associated with the MAKING type.) This was not always so; in Act 1, Scene 2 of Shakespeare's *Richard III* we find *Is not the causer of the timeless death ... As blameful as the executioner?* Here *causer*, like *cause*, refers to an indirect action to bring something about.

Verbs in the HELPING type readily form Agent-nom's—*helper, assistant, collaborator, supporter, opposer* and *opponent*. They also form Activity-nom's—*help, aid, assistance, cooperation, collaboration, hindrance, support, opposition*.

**Secondary-d**. There are basically no nominalisations of these verbs. There are the nouns *appearance, look, sound, feeling* and *matter*, but these do not show any of the relationships to the underlying verbs which have been taken to be characteristic of the nine varieties of nominalisation dealt with here.

## Notes to Chapter 10

The many useful discussions of factors motivating the choice between *'s* and *of* in English include Deane (1987), Anschutz (1997) and Johansson and Oksefjell (1998); and see further references therein.

Marchand (1969) is an invaluable source of information concerning the history and application of derivational suffixes in English. There is also useful discussion in Huddleston and Pullum (2002: 1696–706).

Details of phrasal verbs, including a list of the thirty-seven most common verb components, is in Dixon (1982a).

# 11

## *The plate, which had been eaten off, was owned by my aunt*
## Passives

A passive sentence in English is not an automatic transformation of an active one. It is an alternative realisation of the relation between a transitive verb and its object, and involves an intransitive construction with a subject (corresponding to the transitive object), a copula-like verb *be* or *get*, and a participial form of the verb. Thus, corresponding to *A man took away the mad dog* we get the passive *The mad dog was taken away*. A passive clause may include an NP, introduced with *by*, corresponding to the transitive subject (e.g. *by a man*), but it does so only relatively seldom (in formal, written English, more than 80 per cent of passives are agentless, and the figure is undoubtedly higher for colloquial, spoken styles).

There is always a meaning difference between active and passive constructions. There are some transitive verbs which—for semantic or other reasons —never occur in the passive (§§11.2–3) and, for many verbs, ability to passivise depends on the nature of the object. As Bolinger (1977a: 10) puts it:

We can say *George turned the pages* or *The pages were turned by George*; something happens to the pages in the process. But when we say *George turned the corner* we cannot say \**The corner was turned by George*—the corner is not affected, it is only where George was at the time. On the other hand, if one were speaking of some kind of marathon or race or game in which a particular corner is thought of as an objective to be taken, then one might say *That corner hasn't been turned yet.* I can say *The stranger approached me* or *I was approached by the stranger* because I am thinking of how his approach may affect me—perhaps he is a panhandler. But if a train approaches me I do not say \**I was approached by the train*, because all I am talking about is the geometry of two positions.

The passive is a marked construction, used according to one or more of a number of factors that are mentioned in §11.1. A passive should ideally be quoted together with its discourse and socio-cultural context; sometimes, a putative passive which sounds odd when spoken in isolation is immediately acceptable when placed in an appropriate context. When judging the examples quoted in this chapter, the reader is asked to keep their imagination on a loose rein, adding a bit of prior discourse and attributing to the speaker a motive for using a passive construction.

## 11.1. The nature of passive

Everything else being equal, a speaker of English will prefer to use a verb with two or more core roles (a transitive verb) in an active construction, with subject and object stated. A passive construction may be employed in one of the following circumstances:

**1.** To avoid mentioning the subject
A surface subject is obligatory in each non-imperative English sentence. It is always possible to put *someone* or *something* in the subject slot, but such an indefinite form serves to draw attention to the fact that the subject is not being specified as fully as it might be. The passive may be used (*a*) if the speaker does not know who the subject was, e.g. *Mary was attacked last night*; or (*b*) if the speaker does not wish to reveal the identity of the subject, e.g. *It has been reported to me that some students have been collaborating on their assignments*; or (*c*) the identity of the subject is obvious to the addressees and does not need to be expressed, e.g. *I've been promoted*; or (*d*) the identity of the subject is not considered important.

Heavy use of the passive is a feature of certain styles; in scientific English it avoids bringing in the first person pronoun, e.g. *An experiment was devised to investigate* ... rather than *I devised an experiment to investigate* ... This is presumably to give an illusion of total objectivity, whereas in fact the particular personal skills and ideas of a scientist do play a role in his work, which would be honestly acknowledged by using active constructions with first person subject.

**2.** To focus on the transitive object, rather than on the subject
In §3.3 we enunciated the semantic principles that underlie the assignment of semantic roles to syntactic relations, and stated that the role which is likely to be most relevant to the success of the activity will be placed in A (transitive subject) relation.

We can construct a referential hierarchy, going from first person pronoun, through second person, proper names of people, human common nouns with determiner or modifier indicating specific reference (e.g. *that old man, my friend*), human common nouns with indefinite reference, to inanimate nouns. It is certainly the case that a transitive subject is likely to be nearer the beginning of the hierarchy than its co-occurring object, e.g. *I chose the blue cardigan, You should promote John, My teacher often canes boys, The fat girl is eating an ice cream.*

However, the object can—in some particular instance of the activity—be nearer the beginning of the hierarchy than the subject. In such a circumstance the passive construction may be used, putting the role which is in underlying O relation into the surface S slot. Thus, in place of *A boy kicked Mary at the picnic*, the passive *Mary was kicked (by a boy) at the picnic* might be preferred. Similar examples are: *Guess what, you have been chosen (by the team) as captain, I got promoted, My best friend often gets caned.* Compare these with prototypical transitive sentences (subject above object on the hierarchy), for which a passive sounds most odd, e.g. *The blue cardigan was chosen by me, An ice cream is being eaten by the fat girl.*

We mentioned in §3.3 that if there are several non-A roles, any of which could potentially be coded onto O relation, then one which has specific reference is likely to be preferred over others which have non-specific reference (e.g. *John told the good news* (O: Message) *to everyone he met*, but *John told Mary* (O: Addressee) *something or other*). In the same spirit, an O NP which has specific reference is more likely to be amenable to passivisation than one which is non-specific. For example, *Our pet dog was shot by that new policeman* sounds much more felicitous than *A dog was shot by that new policeman* (here the active would surely be preferred—*That new policeman shot a dog*).

**3.** To place a topic in subject relation

A discourse is normally organised around a 'topic', which is likely to recur in most sentences of the discourse, in a variety of semantic roles. There is always a preference for a topic to be subject, the one obligatory syntactic relation in an English sentence (and the pivot for various syntactic operations—see **4**). If a topic occurs in underlying O relation then a passive construction may be employed, to put it in surface S slot, e.g. *The hold-up man hid in the woods for five days, living on berries, and then he* (underlying O, passive S) *was caught and put in jail*. (A topic NP is of course likely to have specific reference, demonstrating a correlation between criteria **2** and **3**.)

**4.** To satisfy syntactic constraints

Every language has some syntactic mechanism for cohering together consecutive sentences in an utterance, identifying common elements and eliminating repetitions. English has a straightforward syntactic rule whereby, if two consecutive clauses have the same subject, this may be omitted from the second clause, e.g. *John took off his coat and then* (*John*) *scolded Mary*. However, if two coordinated clauses share an NP which is in subject relation in one and in object relation in another, then omission is not possible—from *John took off his coat and then Mary scolded John*, the final *John* cannot be omitted. In such circumstances a passive construction may be used; the NP which would be in O relation in an active transitive becomes subject of the passive and, in terms of the syntactic convention, can now be omitted, e.g. *John took off his coat and was then scolded by Mary*. (In English a pronoun may substitute for a repeated noun between coordinated clauses whatever the syntactic relations involved, and pronominalisation would of course be used when omission of the NP is not permissible.)

Conditions **4** and **3** for using a passive are interrelated. If an object NP in one clause has been subject in a previous clause then it is functioning as topic for at least a small segment of the discourse, and will almost certainly have specific and individuated reference. On these grounds, quite apart from the speaker's wanting to meet the syntactic condition on omission, it would be a prime target for passivisation.

A reflexive clause—one in which subject and object are identical—is very unlikely to be cast into passive form, since none of the conditions just listed for using a passive can be satisfied: (1) it is impossible to avoid mentioning the subject, since it is identical with the object; (2) it is not meaningful to focus on object rather than on subject, since they are identical; and (3)–(4) there is no advantage in moving O into surface subject slot, since it is already identical with the subject. If a reflexive passive is ever used it is likely to be an 'echo' of a preceding sentence in the discourse that was in passive form, e.g. *My brother was taught linguistics by Kenneth Pike*, followed by *Oh really! Well my brother's a better linguist than yours and he was taught by himself*.

**5.** To focus on the result of the activity
The passive construction involves a participial form of the verb which functions very much like an adjective; it forms a predicate together with copula *be* or *get*. This participle is also used to describe the result of the activity (if it does have a definite result). A passive construction may be used in order to focus on this result, e.g. *My neighbour was appointed to the board (by the managing director)*, *The goalkeeper is being rested from next week's game*, *That cup was chipped by Mary when she washed the dishes*.

There are two possibilities for the first element in a passive VP—*be* and *get*. *Be* is the unmarked form and—as discussed in §11.2–3—may be used with a wider range of verbs than *get*. It seems that *get* is often used when the speaker wishes to imply that the state which the passive subject (deep O) is in is not due just to the transitive subject, or to the result of chance, but may in some way be due to the behaviour of this passive subject. Consider *John was fired*—this could be used if there was a general redundancy in the firm. But *John got fired* implies that he did something foolish, such as being rude to his supervisor, which would be expected to lead to this result.

The verb *get* has a wide range of senses: (i) it is a member of the OWN subtype of GIVING, e.g. *Mary got a new coat*; (ii) *get to* has an achievement sense, as a member of the SEMI-MODAL type, e.g. *John got to know how to operate the machine*; (iii) it is a member of the MAKING type, e.g. *I got John to write that letter to you*; (iv) it can be a copula before an adjective or it can begin a passive VP, in both cases generally implying that the surface subject was at least partly responsible for being in a certain state, e.g. *Johnny got dirty, Mary got promoted*.

In fact the copula/passive sense, (iv), can plausibly be related to the causative sense, (iii). We can recall that, as a member of the MAKING type, *get* takes a Modal (FOR) TO complement clause, and the *for* must be omitted (§8.3.4), e.g. *The boss got Mary to fire John.* The complement clause can be passive and *to be* may then be omitted under certain semantic conditions (discussed in relation to (2a/b) in §6.3.1); thus, *The boss got John fired.*

Now the object of a MAKING verb (which is underlying subject of the complement clause) is not normally coreferential with the main clause subject; if it is it cannot, as a rule, be omitted (§8.3.4); that is, we may say *John forced himself to be examined by a specialist*, but not *\*John forced to be examined by a specialist.*

Thus, a normal MAKING complement construction would be *John got himself fired.* I suggest that the *get* passive is related to this, through the omission of *himself.* The point is that this omission—of main clause object (= complement clause subject) when it is coreferential with main clause subject—is not allowed for other MAKING verbs, but is put forward as a special syntactic rule which effectively derives a *get* passive from a MAKING construction involving *get.* This formulation states that an underlying *get* (MAKING verb) plus reflexive pronoun plus *to* (complementiser) plus *be* (unmarked passive introducer) plus passive verb can omit both the *to be* and the reflexive pronoun, and *get* then appears to be the marker of a variety of passive, parallel to *be.* (In fact, this explanation mirrors the historical development of the *get* passive in English; see Givón and Yang 1994.)

This analysis explains the distinctive meaning of *get* passives. Syntactic support is provided by the possible positionings of a sentential adverb such as *recently* (see Chapter 12). This can occur at the places marked by '(A)' in:

(1)  (A) *John was* (A) *fired* (A)
(2)  (A) *John* (A) *got* (A?) *fired* (A)

Some speakers will accept *John got* (A) *fired* but it is much less acceptable than *John* (A) *got fired.* *\*John* (A) *was fired* is judged as ungrammatical.

With an active predicate a sentential adverb can come after the first word of the auxiliary; if there is no auxiliary, it will immediately follow a copula but immediately precede a non-copula verb (§12.3). Thus, with a canonical passive, involving *be*, an adverb may come between the passive auxiliary *be* and the passive verb (as in (1)) but not between the subject and *be.* In a causative construction with a passive complement clause the adverb placement is as shown in: (A) *Mary* (A) *got John to be* (A) *fired* (A). When the *to be* is omitted, with causative *get*, the adverb position which immediately followed *to be* becomes less acceptable, e.g. (A) *Mary* (A) *got John* (A?) *fired* (A). We suggested that the *get* passive is essentially a reflexive version of this construction, i.e. (A) *John* (A) *got (himself)* (A?) *fired* (A). This precisely explains the adverb possibilities in (2). (Note that when the *himself* is dropped, the adverb position immediately before *fired* becomes even more marginal than it was before.)

Although the *get* passive thus appears to be syntactically related to the MAKING verb *get*, it has now taken on a wider range of meaning, and does not always imply that the passive subject is partly responsible for being in the described state. *That meeting got postponed*, for instance, could not felicitously be expanded to *That meeting got itself postponed*, although it does carry a certain overtone that the meeting seems fated never to be held. The *get* passive is certainly more used in colloquial than in formal styles. I have the feeling that a *by* phrase is less likely to be included with a *get* passive than with a *be* passive (even in the same, colloquial style); this is something that would need to be confirmed by a text count. *Get* passives may also carry an implication that something happened rather recently— one might hear *He got run over* concerning something that occurred last week, but for something that took place ten years ago *He was run over* would be a more likely description.

Returning now to our general discussion of the nature of the passive, we can conclude that almost anything can be stated through an active construction but that only rather special things are suitable for description through a passive construction. For instance, there may be some special significance to the object NP, as it is used with a particular verb, or with a particular verb and a certain subject.

Consider *John's mother saw a brick in the bar*. The passive correspondent of this, *A brick was seen by John's mother in the bar*, sounds ridiculous, something that is most unlikely to be said. But if the event reported were *John's mother saw him in the bar*, then the passive, *John was seen (by his mother) in the bar*, is perfectly feasible. If the passive were used one might guess that he shouldn't have been there, and may now get into trouble. 'John' is a definite, individual human, a prime candidate to be in the subject relation. Casting the sentence into passive form implies that the concatenation of John's being in the bar and his mother's seeing him there has a particular significance.

## 11.2. Which verbs from Primary types may passivise

For the great majority of transitive verbs it is possible to find some O NP (or some particular combination of O and A NPs) which has the right sort of semantic significance—in conjunction with the meaning of the verb—for a passive construction to be a felicitous alternative to the unmarked active. But very few (if any) verbs may passivise with equal facility on *any* kind of O. Consider *leave*, for instance. This verb can have as object a person, place or thing. A person or thing can be affected or potentially affected by being left—a person may refuse to be left, may run after the person who is trying to leave them somewhere; a thing might become liable to be stolen if left in a certain place. Corresponding to *Fred left Mary at the station* and *Fred left your bicycle at the station* we can have passives *Mary was left at the station (by Fred)* and *Your bicycle was left at the station (by Fred)*. However, if *leave* has a place description as object there is not likely to be a corresponding passive, simply because the place is not affected in any way by someone departing from it—one could say *Fred left the office at five o'clock*, but scarcely *\*The office was left (by Fred) at five o'clock*.

Verbs which are particularly open to passivisation are those whose object is likely to be human, or else something with specific reference that is being particularly focused on. ANNOYING verbs, for instance, have the Experiencer in O relation and this is generally human. Verbs from this type are very frequently used in passive form, e.g. *John was pleased (by that concert)*. (See §5.6 for the semantic and syntactic contrast between passive and past participle (derived adjective) use of ANNOYING verbs.) Most ANNOYING verbs may take either *be* or *get*, e.g. *He was annoyed (by her behaviour)*, or *He got annoyed*, which could be used when he worked himself up into a state of being annoyed. Those which would seldom be used with *get* include *delight, please, satisfy, amuse* and *astonish*, verbs referring to feelings that tend to be experienced naturally, with the Experiencer having little or no role in bringing them about.

In §9.2.4 we described how, with certain verbs, if the referent of a peripheral NP marked by a preposition is particularly salient in that instance of the activity, it may drop its preposition and move into direct object slot, e.g. *They climbed up a little hill* (preposition included) but *I climbed a high mountain* (preposition omitted). Such an NP is, by virtue of its salience, a good candidate for passivisation, and this is particularly likely when it is nearer the beginning of the referential hierarchy described under condition **2** in §11.1 than is the A NP, e.g. *That tall mountain hasn't yet been climbed (by anyone)* alongside the active *No one has yet climbed that tall mountain.* Note how negation appears in the A NP of the active; this becomes an optional *by-* phrase in the passive, so that the negator must transfer to an obligatory constituent, here the predicate; see §12.11.7.

When there is already an object NP, as in example (3), this remains when a peripheral NP is promoted into the first object slot, as in (4):

(3)   *John gave a single red rose to Mary*
(4)   *John gave Mary a single red rose*

Only the object NP *a single red rose* may be passivised from (3), but—for most speakers—either of the objects from (4) can become passive subject:

(3a)   *A single red rose was given to Mary (by John)*
(3b)   *\*Mary was given a single red rose to (by John)*
(4a)   *Mary was given a single red rose (by John)*
(4b)   *A single red rose was given Mary (by John)*

(As mentioned in §9.2.5, when the preposition is omitted from a measure phrase this does not become direct object and is not open to passivisation. In §§4.4–5 and §9.3.1 we discussed cognate NPs which can follow CORPOR-EAL and WEATHER verbs and decided that these have only weak object properties, largely because they can only become passive subject in rather special circumstances.)

We can now consider those transitive verbs from Primary types in English which do not allow a passive, or else have one in very limited circumstances. There appear to be three main reasons for this: a verb may be symmetrical, it may refer to a static relation, or it may inherently focus on the subject. Taking these one at a time:

**(*a*)   Symmetric verbs**
These are verbs referring to a state or activity that relates equally to two entities—either could be subject and the other will then be object. Thus, if it is the case that *Mary resembles John* it must also be the case that *John resembles Mary*. Alternatively, we can use a reciprocal construction, *John and Mary resemble each other* or *Mary and John resemble each other*. Either of the roles may be placed in subject slot, and so there is no possible need for a passive construction.

Some verbs, such as *resemble* and *look like*, must be symmetrical. Others have two senses, one with a symmetrical meaning and one without. *John met Mary at the station* is, for instance, ambiguous between (i) he went to the station to meet her off a train, and (ii) they just happened to meet each other there. Sense (ii), but not (i), could be paraphrased *Mary met John at the station*. The passive *Mary was met (by John) at the station* is not ambiguous; it can only relate to the non-symmetrical sense, (i). Similarly, *fight* may be symmetrical, with a human as O, e.g. *John fought Tom in 1979/ Tom fought John in 1979*, or non-symmetrical with an activity noun as O, e.g. *Tom fought a fierce battle*. Only the second sense is open to passivisation (and even this would need considerable contextualisation, since *a fierce battle* is below *John* on the referential hierarchy).

**(b)**   Verbs that refer to a static relationship
Verbs such as *contain, cost, weigh* and *last*—as in *The carton contains milk, This book costs ten dollars, My son weighs a hundred and fifty pounds, The meeting lasted all morning*—indicate a static relationship between two things. Nothing 'happens' and so a passive construction, which normally describes the result of an activity, could not be used. (Note also that in a passive construction the *by* phrase is always omissible, and for these verbs both poles of the relationship must be stated.) Other verbs of this kind include *fit, suit, comprise, depend on, result from, relate to*. Some symmetric verbs, like *resemble*, specify a relationship, and their lack of a passive is due to (*b*) as well as to (*a*).

Verbs in the OWN subtype of GIVING refer to the relationship between Owner and Possession roles. The verb *own* can form a passive, e.g. *John owns that car, That car is owned by John*. Why is it that *have* does not form a corresponding passive, **That car is had by John*? In fact the corresponding active is inadmissible, at least in the present tense—we would not say *John has that car* (where *have* has a meaning similar to *own*; there is another sense of have, 'be using', and in this sense we can say *John has that car today*). *Have* refers to a general property of the Owner, e.g. *John has a car. Own*, in contrast, focuses on the Possession and implies that the Owner has legal or some other official right to it; the Possession can be foregrounded as passive subject (but note that the Owner is invariably included, through a *by* phrase). *Belong to* is effectively the converse of *own* and *have*, with Owner in object slot, after *to*; if a speaker wishes to focus on the Owner, putting it in subject slot, they will use *own* or *have*, rather than a passive of *belong to*. *Lack* is never used as a passive participle since it does not refer to the result of an activity (contrast with *is owned by*, which could be used to describe the result of a purchase or bequest, say); the present participle is used instead, e.g. *Brains are sorely lacking in that family*, alongside the active *That family sorely lack brains*.

The verb *equal* generally describes a static relationship, e.g. *Two and two equals four*, and cannot then be used in a passive construction. But it can also be used with a more dynamic sense, to describe something getting into a relationship of equality with something else. Suppose Tom runs a mile in three and a half minutes and then Fred repeats the feat the following month; we can say *Fred equalled Tom's time*—Tom's time existed first, and then Fred came along and clocked a time that was equal to it. In this circumstance it is permissible to use a passive, especially if the O of *equal* is an established topic: *Tom set a new world record, but it was equalled by Fred the next month*.

**(c)** Verbs that inherently focus on the subject
The LIKING type is the converse of ANNOYING in terms of role-relation correspondence. LIKING verbs have the Experiencer (which is normally human) in A relation and the Stimulus as O; they express a feeling that the Experiencer has about a Stimulus. It is thus scarcely plausible to avoid stating A, or to focus more on the identity of O than of A. The object of a LIKING verb will seldom be passivised—it is most likely to be when continuing an established topic, e.g. *That concert, which was put on by the sixth-grade pupils, was thoroughly enjoyed*.

*Possess*, from the OWN subtype, differs from *own* in that it implies a strong emotional or mental connection between Owner and Possession, e.g. *She possesses a fine sense of loyalty/a good brain*. It is because of this focus on the Owner that *possess*—unlike *own*—is seldom used in the passive. (The verb *be possessed by* (e.g. *the devil*) is best considered a separate lexeme.)

*Know* and *believe* are further verbs that focus on the subject and are only occasionally found in the passive—generally, when the original A NP has non-individual or indefinite reference, e.g. *His testimony was believed by every person in court that day*. For *know*, the past participle is used, with an NP introduced by *to*, and this is often preferred over a passive construction, especially when the underlying A is human, e.g. *John is known to/?*by everyone in the room*.

The verb *join*, in the sense 'become a member of', has as subject an NP referring to a person (or perhaps a few people) and as object the name of an organisation, e.g. *John joined the Catholic Church, Mary joined our film society*. The object refers to a group of people; the important point is not that the group became slightly enlarged (what does it matter if the film society has fifty members or fifty-one?), but that Mary joined it. For this activity, the subject must be more important than the object, and that is why a passive construction would not be appropriate.

In summary, those Primary verbs which are seldom or never found in the passive fall into three classes, *(a)–(c)*, which can be accounted for in terms of conditions **1–5** from §11.1.

## 11.3. How verbs from Secondary types passivise

Overall, Secondary verbs passivise much less readily than do Primary verbs. There are a number which occur in a *be* passive construction, but rather few that take a *get* passive.

Secondary-D verbs, the SEEM and MATTER types, are essentially intransitive and thus not open to passivisation. Secondary-C verbs, from the MAKING and HELPING types, can take a direct object (which is underlying complement clause subject). Some of these may passivise on this object NP, e.g. *John was made/permitted/allowed/helped to fill in the form, Mary was prevented from seeing the doctor*. A passive is scarcely possible, however, with *let* (save of the idiomatic *let X go*), since this verb focuses on the main clause subject (§6.3.1), or with the causative sense of *get*, and quite impossible with the causative sense of *have*. *Force* may have a normal passive, e.g. *The guerrillas forced John to walk home (by holding a gun to his back)* and *John was forced to walk home (by the guerrillas, holding a gun to his back)*. There is also a special passive of *force* that cannot have a *by* phrase but which may include a subordinate clause stating a reason, e.g. *John was forced to walk home, because his car has broken down* (the corresponding active, something like *John's car breaking down forced him to walk home*, feels somewhat strained).

With the Secondary type WANTING, the subject of a Modal (FOR) TO complement clause is often identical with the subject of the WANTING verb, and is then omitted. But they can be different, and with some WANTING verbs *for* may be or must be omitted, so that the complement clause subject becomes surface object of the main verb. It should then theoretically be available for passivisation. A passive construction is used with some verbs from this type, e.g. *expect* and *intend*—we can say *Mary was expected/intended to drive the bus today*. Passive is much less plausible with *want, wish* and *deserve* simply because the meanings of these verbs inherently focus on the subject, expressing the subject's attitude towards something—this is (*c*) from §11.2.

Some WANTING verbs, and a few Primary-B verbs such as *choose* and *order*, may have both main and complement clauses in passive form, the original complement clause object first becoming derived passive subject of that clause, simultaneously—in the absence of *for*—surface object of the main clause, and then derived passive subject of the main clause. For example, from *They intended someone to murder Hitler* we can get *They intended Hitler to be murdered* and finally *Hitler was intended to be murdered*. Such a double-passive construction becomes rather less acceptable if any *by* phrase is included, e.g. ?*Hitler was intended by the Russians to be murdered by their crack marksman*.

The BEGINNING type of Secondary-A verbs is particularly interesting from the point of view of passivisation. We can recall that these verbs have no independent role, sharing with the verb for which they provide semantic modification its subject (and, if it is transitive, its object), e.g.

(5)   *The warders began to count the prisoners*
(6)   *The warders began counting the prisoners*

Now (5) and (6) each contain two verbs, *begin* and *count*. We can enquire whether it is possible (*a*) to have a passive form of *begin*, but not of *count*; (*b*) to have a passive form of *count*, but not of *begin*; (*c*) to have both verbs in passive form. Consider:

(5a)   *\*The prisoners were begun to count*
(6a)   *\*The prisoners were begun counting*
(5b)   *The prisoners began to be counted*
(6b)   *The prisoners began being counted*
(5c)   *The prisoners were begun to be counted*
(6c)   *The prisoners were begun being counted*

Sentences (5a) and (6a), where just *begin* is in passive form, are totally ungrammatical. However, (5b) and (6b), where just *count* is in passive form, are quite acceptable to all native speakers. Sentences (5c) and (6c), with both verbs in passive form, are rejected by perhaps the majority of native speakers, but judged as perfectly acceptable by a significant minority.

There appears to be a potential difference in meaning between the (b) and (c) alternatives for those speakers who can accept either. Suppose that the prisoners began to file past the head warder in order to be counted—(5b) or (6b) might be an appropriate description for this. But (5c) or (6c) could just refer to a much-postponed counting of the prisoners finally being undertaken by the warders, and maybe the prisoners themselves weren't even aware of it, e.g. *The prisoners were finally begun to be counted at four o'clock.*

These passive possibilities support our proposal that a BEGINNING verb forms a single semantic unit with the verb it modifies. We can suggest that in (5b) and (6b) *begin* modifies a passive verb, whereas in (5c) and (6c) the whole complex of *begin*-plus-active-transitive-verb is passivised. A sentence like *The warders began to count the prisoners*, with a secondary verb in the main clause, is syntactically similar to *John likes/decided/remembered to kiss Aunt Mary*, with a primary verb in the main clause (and both clauses having the same subject, this being omitted from the complement clause). Note that we can here get a construction that looks like (5b), e.g. *Aunt Mary likes/decided/remembered to be kissed*, but nothing at all that resembles (5c) (i.e. not *\*Aunt Mary is liked/was decided/was remembered to be kissed*). This again emphasises the secondary nature of verbs from the BEGINNING type, that they effectively form a semantic unit with the following verb (although this is syntactically in a complement clause).

*Finish, start* and *continue* have basically the same passive possibilities as *begin*. Of the other verbs in the type, *cease, stop* and *keep on* are restricted to the (b) passive, while *commence, complete* and *discontinue* are scarcely plausible in any variety of passive.

When a complement clause verb is omitted (§6.1.2), BEGINNING verbs passivise like any other transitive verb, e.g. *They finished the house on Tuesday, The house was finished on Tuesday.*

In §6.1.2 we mentioned intransitive uses of BEGINNING verbs, with an activity noun as subject. Corresponding to *They began (fighting) the battle on Tuesday* there is *The battle began on Tuesday*. There is a contrast between the intransitive and the passive of the transitive, i.e. *The battle was begun on Tuesday*. The passive implies a deliberate decision to begin fighting on that day, whereas the plain intransitive could be used if it just happened—if fighting broke out spontaneously.

TRYING is another Secondary-A type. Most TRYING verbs are similar to *want, wish, possess* and the LIKING type in that they focus semantically on the subject, and are thus not appropriate in a passive construction; there are no *try* sentences parallel to (5c) and (6c). TRYING verbs can, of course, modify either an active or a passive verb in the complement clause, e.g. *John failed to invite Mary, Mary failed to get invited.* HURRYING verbs also occur in constructions parallel to (5b) and (6b) but not (5c) and (6c). MODALS and SEMI-MODALS have no passive form, although they can of course modify a passive verb, e.g. *Mary ought to be punished.*

All the examples we have given of the passive of secondary verbs have involved *be*. The *get* variety is far rarer—*get allowed* or *get needed* or *get intended* or *get expected* are at best marginal, while *get begun* is almost impossible. *Get* passives may be used with some members of the Secondary-B type POSTPONING and also, to a limited extent, with Secondary-C verbs such as *force* and *prevent*.

## 11.4. Complement clauses as passive subjects

An ING complement clause in O relation can almost always become passive subject. This applies whether the verb of the main clause is primary—*Mary's having been passed over was mentioned at the party*—or secondary—*Counting the prisoners was begun/tried on Tuesday.* It also applies to ING clauses that are the object of a verb with an inherent preposition, e.g. *Jane's having been promoted was pondered over.* As mentioned in §11.2, the NP object of a LIKING verb is not very frequently passivised, and this applies also to an ING clause, although it is just possible to say, for instance, *Mary's singing the blues was preferred to John's warbling Verdi.*

A THAT or WH- clause in O relation passivises much like an ING clause, except that here the complement clause is most often extraposed to the end of the main clause, with *it* filling the subject slot, e.g. with primary verbs, *It was reported that war had broken out, It was recognised that we would all die,* and with secondary verbs, *It was expected/hoped that it would all be over quickly.* Exceptions include *ensure*, the only verb from the MAKING type to take a THAT complement, which is scarcely acceptable in the passive; and LIKING verbs, which must include *it* before a THAT complement (*They like it that Mary plays the fiddle*), do not allow the THAT clause to become passive subject (*\*It is liked that Mary plays the fiddle*).

Verbs from the ORDER subtype of SPEAKING have an Addressee NP in O slot, and this can be followed by a THAT clause. Most ORDER verbs may omit the Addressee, and the THAT clause may then be passivised, e.g. *It is requested that empty cans be placed in the litter bin, It has been ordered that all prisoners should be shot at dawn*. However, if an Addressee NP is included only this may become passive subject, not the THAT clause, e.g. *The firing squad have been ordered that all prisoners should be shot at dawn*, not \**It has been ordered the firing squad that all prisoners should be shot at dawn*.

A Modal (FOR) TO complement clause has three variant forms: (i) the full form with *for* retained, e.g. *I chose for Mary to go*—here *for Mary to go* fills the O slot; (ii) a reduced form in which *for* is omitted but the complement clause subject retained, e.g. *I chose Mary to go*—here *Mary* is surface object of the main verb, with *to go* being a post-object constituent; (iii) a further reduced form where the complement clause subject is omitted under co-referentiality with the subject NP in the main clause, e.g. *I chose to go*—here *to go* fills object slot. As discussed above, the only possible passive of type (ii) is on the surface object NP (which is also underlying subject of the complement clause), e.g. *Mary was chosen to go*. We can now enquire whether the *for* clause in (i) and the *to* clause in (iii) may become passive subject.

They may be in principle, but seldom are in practice. A Modal (FOR) TO complement describes the complement clause subject getting involved in an activity, but also carries a sense that the subject of the main clause wanted it to happen; in view of this, the transitive subject is seldom open to demotion in a passive. It is just possible for a full Modal (FOR) TO clause to be passivised with some verbs from DECIDING, WANTING and LIKING, e.g. *For John to receive the house and Mary the money was finally decided on* or *It was finally decided for John to receive the house and Mary the money*; *It had been intended for Mary to go*; and *It was preferred for the sermon to come last*. A reduced form of Modal (FOR) TO, as in (iii) of the last paragraph, may also become passive subject with some verbs from DECIDING and WANTING (but not, it seems, from LIKING), e.g. *It was decided to eliminate wastage, It is hoped/planned/intended to complete these tasks today*.

For a Judgement TO complement the complement clause subject is always the surface object of the main verb. This kind of complement construction is very frequently passivised, often so as to avoid specifying who is responsible for the judgement, e.g. *They know John to be stupid, John is known to be stupid*. The verb *say* only takes a Judgement TO complement in the passive, e.g. *He is said to be stupid* but not \**They say him to be stupid*.

The verb *rumour* may take a THAT or a Judgement TO complement clause but is seldom (or never) found in anything but the passive, e.g. *It was rumoured that John had died, John was rumoured to be dead* (but scarcely *\*They rumoured that John had died, \*They rumoured John to be dead*). Similar remarks apply to *repute*, which is generally used in the passive, with a Judgement TO complement, e.g. *Mary is reputed to be a secret drinker*, but not *\*They repute Mary to be a secret drinker*.

The subject of a FROM ING complement clause is always also identified as surface object of the main verb, and may be passivised, e.g. *John was stopped from going* (see §8.2.9). WH- TO complements seldom or never passivise, partly because, as with Modal (FOR) TO, the semantic orientation of the main clause subject demands that it be kept in that syntactic slot (e.g. *They didn't understand how to behave*, but scarcely *\*How to behave was not understood*).

In summary, the possibilities of a complement clause, in underlying object function, becoming passive subject are again determined by conditions **1–5** from §11.1.

## 11.5. Prepositional NPs becoming passive subjects

In §9.2.1 we discussed verbs that must take an inherent preposition before an NP. This NP has many of the characteristics of a direct object, and can almost always passivise. Quite a range of prepositions are involved and the verbs come from a fair array of types, e.g. *deal with, rely on, decide on, think about, listen to, look at, wonder at, dawdle over, search for*. The object of the inherent preposition verb *confess to* does not readily become a passive subject but this is because *confess to* focuses semantically on the subject, similar to LIKING verbs, and *want* and *possess*—see (*c*) in §11.2—and it is not appropriate to demote this subject. (Similar remarks apply to *boast of/ about* and *brag of/about*, but to a lesser extent—a passive here, although not common, is possible.)

Phrasal verbs, discussed in §9.2.2, are combinations of verb plus preposition(s) which have an independent meaning, not predictable from the meanings of the component elements. An NP which immediately follows the verbal element has direct object status and may always passivise, e.g.

Np type: *They put the wedding off until next week, The wedding was put off until next week*

NpN type: *They took me for a preacher, I was taken for a preacher*
NppN type: *They tied the conference in with the school holidays, The conference was tied in with the school holidays*

An NP which follows the preposition(s) of a phrasal verb (with no other NP preceding it) has weak object status, and shows limited passivisation possibilities, e.g.

pN type: *The teachers are always picking on John, John is always being picked on (by the teachers)*
ppN type: *They did away with the position of Assistant Secretary, The position of Assistant Secretary was done away with*

If there is a direct object NP, coming immediately after the verbal component, and a second NP following the preposition(s), as in NpN and NppN types of phrasal verb, then the later NP can never be passivised. For example, *a preacher* and *the school holidays* from the examples above could not become passive subject.

Leaving aside the special cases of inherent preposition verbs and phrasal verbs, we can now consider the question of passivisation of an NP that is straightforwardly governed by a preposition. This is plainly possible in English—as in *Oh dear, my new hat has been sat on* and *This bed was slept in by Queen Elizabeth*—but in quite limited circumstances. What are these circumstances?

Recall that a direct object NP may only become passive subject when it is sufficiently special—in that semantic-syntactic context—to merit being focused on, perhaps in contrast to something else. At a party, someone could wander into another room and exclaim: *Hey, whiskey is being drunk in here*; one would infer that something less strong was being consumed in the room the speaker has just left. A peripheral NP, marked by a preposition, may also be passivised when it refers to something that is the most significant element in an activity. If you were handed a glass and noticed someone else's dregs at the bottom, or lipstick on the rim, you could use a construction with an adjectival predicate—*This glass is dirty*; or a construction with the underlying direct object passivised—*This glass has been used*; or a sentence that involves passivisation on a peripheral NP to the verb *drink* (which is the activity being alluded to)—*This glass has been drunk out of.*

There are two syntactic restrictions on a peripheral NP becoming passive subject:

(*a*)    There must be no direct object present. If there is, it is only the direct object that can be passivised, not the prepositional object. Consider *Someone has drunk whiskey out of this glass*; it is quite unacceptable to say *\*This glass has been drunk whiskey out of*. It is only when the object NP is omitted that passivisation on a prepositional NP becomes possible. As further examples we can quote *This spoon has been eaten with* but not *\*This spoon has been eaten beans with*, and *My new cushion has been sat on by a dog* but not *\*My new cushion has been sat a dog on* (corresponding to the causative *Someone has sat a dog on my new cushion*).

This restriction relates to our earlier observation that an NP which follows the preposition(s) of a phrasal verb may sometimes be passivised but only if there is no preceding direct object NP which comes between verbal and prepositional components, i.e. $N_2$ may sometimes be passivised from $pN_2$ and $ppN_2$ but never from $N_1pN_2$ or $N_1ppN_2$.

It is not the case that a passive verb may not be followed by a direct object. Where a prepositional NP with a transitive verb is promoted into object slot (§9.2.4) the original object remains, e.g. *give Mary a book, tell Mary a story*. Either of the two objects may be passivised, with the other remaining after the verb in the passive clause, e.g. *Mary was told a story, A story was told Mary*. The rule appears to be that if there are two objects then either may passivise, but if there is an object and a prepositional NP then passivisation is restricted to the object. Only when there is no object present may the prepositional NP become passive subject.

(Quasi-exceptions to this rule involve idioms such as *shake hands with, find fault with, make an honest woman of*. It is possible to say things like *Have you been shaken hands with yet?*)

(*b*)    The prepositional NP must not be alternatively codable as direct object. We often have available two possible syntactic frames for a given concatenation of verb and semantic roles; a certain role may be mapped onto O relation in one frame and marked by a preposition in another frame. In such a case, it will generally be passivisable only from the frame in which it is object, and not from that in which it appears with a preposition. There are several kinds of instance of this restriction:

(i)    In §9.2.3 we discussed a group of transitive verbs that may insert a preposition before a direct object NP, e.g. *He kicked the box, He kicked at the box*. This NP may be passivised from simple direct object position, but not as a rule when there is a preceding preposition. We could say *That box was kicked (and dented )*, *This sheet has been torn* but scarcely *\*That box has* *been kicked at (and dented), *This sheet has been torn at.* Inserting the preposition indicates that the activity did not relate to some specific object, or did not achieve a specific result, and in such semantic circumstances we would not expect passivisation to be possible.

There is one notable exception: one can say *Mary was shot* (implying that the bullet or arrow hit her) or *Mary was shot at* (suggesting that the projectile missed her). In the second sentence the Target is not physically affected but she is likely to be mentally disturbed by the incident—she will have had a scare, and may realise that she is at risk of a further attack. It is here possible to passivise on an NP governed by a preposition (even though there is an alternative construction in which it is direct object); but this appears only to be possible when the NP has animate reference since only animates are affected by being shot at.

(ii)   In §9.2.4 we discussed verbs that may promote a peripheral NP—normally marked by a preposition—into direct object slot, if it is particularly significant in this instance of the activity. It was remarked, in §11.2, that the salience of such an NP is such that it may readily be passivised (especially if the transitive subject is non-specific), e.g. *The English Channel was first swum in 1875, That peak has never been climbed, French is spoken throughout my chain of boutiques.* Such an NP—which can be promoted to object and passivised from that slot—may never be passivised from its original post-prepositional position. That is, we could not say *\*The English Channel was first swum across in 1875, \*That peak has never been climbed up,* or *\*French is spoken in throughout my chain of boutiques.*

Promotion to object is also possible in transitive sentences, e.g. *John gave an apple to Mary, John gave Mary an apple; Granny knitted a jumper for Mary, Granny knitted Mary a jumper.* The NP *Mary* may only be passivised from the second sentence of each pair—*Mary was given an apple (by John), Mary was knitted a jumper (by Granny).* Passivisation of *Mary* from the first sentence of each pair, where this NP is marked by a preposition, is blocked on two grounds: (i) it is preceded by a direct object, and (ii) there is an alternative construction available in which it is direct object. Thus, we do not get *\*Mary was given an apple to,* or *\*Mary was knitted a jumper for.*

In §4.2 we described, for AFFECT verbs, frame I, which has Target role as O and Manip role marked by a preposition, e.g. *John hit the vase with that stick,* and frame II, which has Manip as O and Target marked by a preposition, e.g. *John hit that stick on the vase.* The Target may only be passivised from frame I, in which it is object (*The vase was hit with that stick*), and the Manip may only be passivised from frame II, in which it is object (*That stick was hit on the vase*). There are again two reasons why we cannot passivise the Manip when it is preceded by *with*, in frame I, or the Target when it is preceded by a preposition like *on*, in frame II: (i) they are preceded by a direct object NP; and (ii) there is an alternative construction in which this role is in direct object relation. This explains the unacceptability of \**That stick was hit the vase with* and \**The vase was hit that stick on*.

In summary, English may allow a prepositional NP to become passive subject (the preposition remaining after the verb) only if there is no direct object and if there is no alternative construction type in which the NP could be coded as direct object.

Passivisation of a peripheral NP seldom happens in English. We can mention three of the kinds of circumstance in which it is permitted:

(*a*)   When the referent of the NP has been (or may be) affected, to its detriment, by the activity; a *by* phrase, marking passive agent, is unlikely to be included, e.g. *That window shouldn't be leaned against* (it might break); *My new hat has been sat on*.

(*b*)   Where it is a particular feature of some object that it was involved in a certain activity with a particularly important subject. Here the significant factor is concatenation of object and verb with that subject, which must be included, in a *by* phrase. Imagine an auctioneer describing a four-poster: *The next item is an antique bed which is reputed to have been slept in by Queen Elizabeth I*.

(*c*)   Where the NP is discourse topic and is brought into passive subject slot for this reason, e.g. *Those stairs were built by John, then they were run up by Mary and promptly collapsed* (cf. Bolinger 1977b: 69). (On its own *Those stairs were run up by Mary* is much less acceptable.)

Note the contrast between (*a*) and (*b*). If you are shown to an hotel room and notice that the sheets on the bed are all mussed up you might exclaim in annoyance: *This bed has been slept in!* (It doesn't matter who by; the fact you are drawing attention to is that it's not clean.) But in a higher-quality establishment the manager might conduct you to his finest suite and announce with pride: *This bed was slept in by Winston Churchill*. In the first utterance a *by* phrase would not normally be included; in the second it must be.

Circumstance (*a*) invariably deals with something that is regarded as undesirable. It does in fact shed interesting light on our cultural norms—the acceptability of *This plate has been eaten off, This spoon has been eaten with, This cup has been drunk out of, This bed has been slept in* illustrates the phobia English-speakers have about certain kinds of cleanliness. *This knife has been cut with* should be just as natural a sentence on syntactic grounds, but in fact we don't usually care so much whether a knife has been used previously. For that reason—and that reason alone—this sentence sounds less felicitous than the others.

A wide range of prepositions may be involved in this kind of passivisation, similar to those which occur as 'inherent prepositions'—*in, on, against, with, to* (*I've never been written to by Maria*), *at* (*That hat is always getting laughed at*), *over* (*The bewitched diamond is being fought over again*), *for* (*John was sent for*), *about* (*The accident is being talked about a lot*), and *from* (*Aikhenvald's book on classifiers is always being quoted from*).

## Notes to Chapter 11

Useful general discussions of passives—in English and other languages—include Jespersen (1909–49: part iii, pp. 299–319), Hasegawa (1968), Huddleston (1971: 93–108), R. Lakoff (1971), Sinha (1974), Bolinger (1975), Barker (1975), Davison (1980), Keenan (1980, 1985), Chappell (1980), Rice (1987), Thompson (1987), Givón and Yang (1994). Langacker and Munro (1975) discuss passives in Uto-Aztecan and Mojave, and treat them in a way similar to that followed here for English. Figures on the percentages of passives for which no agent is given are quoted in Svartvik (1966), Givón (1979) and Thompson (1987).

§11.2. Kruisinga (1927) has an interesting discussion of the passivisability of both objects with verbs such as *ask*. Lists of verbs that do not passivise are included in Quirk and Greenbaum (1973: 359), G. Lakoff (1970: 19), Svartvik (1966: 115).

§11.4. The passivisation of prepositional NPs is discussed in Bolinger (1977b), Van der Gaaf (1930) and Givón (1984).

# 12

## *Yesterday, even the rather clever bishops could not very easily have sensibly organised a moderately unusual exorcism here*
## Adverbs and negation

This chapter outlines the grammatical behaviour of adverbs in English. There is brief mention of the forms of adverbs, and then detailed analysis of their five functional roles—modifying a clause or a sentence (sentential function), a verb-plus-object (manner function), an NP, an adjective, or another adverb. Subclasses of adverbs are outlined, together with the functional possibilities for each. There is also discussion of how adverbs can be combined within a single clause. The final section, §12.11, examines the functional roles of negation, comparing these with the functional possibilities for adverbs.

Adverbs form a large class in English, with wide possibilities. I have made no attempt to deal exhaustively with every adverb and every possible use. Rather, the focus has been on the basic grammatical patterns and parameters of the class of adverbs, and the canonical properties of its main members.

## 12.1. Adverbs

Whereas an adjective can modify a noun (or occur as copula complement), an adverb has the potential for a wide range of functions. These are, in outline:

(a)   Modifying a complete clause or sentence—sentential function.
(b)   Modifying a verb (plus object, if it has one)—manner function.
(c)   Modifying a complete noun phrase—NP (modifying) function.
(d)   Modifying an adjective—adjectival (modifying) function.
(e)   Modifying another adverb—adverbial modifying function.

These can be illustrated in the following monoclausal sentence (chosen because it has a two-word auxiliary and an object NP):

(1)   *She had been arranging the beautiful flowers*

   **(a)**   We can add *also* in sentential function, following the first word of the auxiliary (throughout this chapter, adverbs quoted within a sentence or phrase are underlined):

(2a)   *She had <u>also</u> been arranging the beautiful flowers*

Adverbs which modify a complete sentence have a wide range of meanings, including reference to time (for instance, *yesterday*), place (*outside*), the appropriateness or mode or likelihood of an activity (*correctly*, *deliberately*, *regretfully*, *probably*), in addition to *also*, *almost*, *even* and others. See Tables 12.4, 12.5 and 12.7.

   **(b)**   Or we can add a manner adverb, such as *attractively*. This may immediately precede (or it may follow) the verb-plus-object:

(2b)   *She had been <u>attractively</u> arranging the beautiful flowers*

A manner adverb may typically provide a response to a question with *how*. For example, (2b) could answer *How has she been arranging the beautiful flowers?* Manner adverbs describe the way in which the activity is performed (for example, *easily*, *well*), or the degree to which it was done (*quite*, *precisely*). See Tables 12.6 and 12.7.

**(c)**   An adverb such as *only* may modify an NP, preceding an article at the beginning of the NP, as in:

**(2c)**   *She had been arranging [only the beautiful flowers]*

NP-modifying adverbs provide a sort of qualification (for example, *just*, *even*). See Table 12.3.

**(d)**   The fourth possibility is for an adverb to modify an adjective, as *truly* does in:

**(2d)**   *She had been arranging the truly beautiful flowers*

Adverbs which modify an adjective typically indicate the degree or status of a property (for example, *rather*, *slightly*, *very*, *appropriately*). See Tables 12.4–7.

**(e)**   Finally, there are a number of adverbs which may modify another adverb, as *quite* modifies *attractively* in:

**(2e)**   *She had been quite attractively arranging the beautiful flowers*

A wide range of adjectives can modify another adverb, including specifying degree (for example, *somewhat*, *almost*). See Tables 12.4 and 12.6–7.

There may be an adverb in more than one of these five functions. Indeed, the sentence

**(2f)**   *She had also been quite attractively arranging only the truly beautiful flowers*

is perfectly acceptable (if a trifle florid).

A clause may generally include only one adverb in manner function— although there can be a complex manner adverb involving a coordination of simple manner adverbs, as in *He did it easily and expertly* (see §12.6)— but there can be a string of adverbs in sentential function; for example:

**(3)**   *She had also deliberately just been arranging the beautiful flowers*

Some adverbs have a single function. For example, *again* may only modify a clause or a sentence. Others can have two or more. *Attractively* may have manner function, or it can modify an adjective, as in *an attractively slim woman*. And *only* has functions (a) and (c–e):

**(4a)**   *She had only been arranging the beautiful flowers* (she hadn't been doing anything else)

**(4c)**  *She had been arranging only the beautiful flowers* (not the windblown ones)

**(4d)**  *She had been arranging the only beautiful flowers* (there were just a few of them)

**(4e)**  *She had been only attractively arranging the beautiful flowers* (she hadn't done anything that was not highly aesthetic)

*Really* may be the only adverb to show all five functions (but note that modifying an NP, (c), is possible only when the NP is in copula complement function):

**(5a)**  *She had really been arranging the beautiful flowers* (we thought she was just saying she had done it, but she actually had arranged them)

**(5b)**  *She had been really arranging the beautiful flowers* (not just popping them into vases any old how)

**(5c)**  *She had been [really a great beauty] in her day*

**(5d)**  *She had been arranging the really beautiful flowers* (but not the less beautiful ones)

**(5e)**  *She had been really attractively arranging the beautiful flowers* (no one can deny that she has great skill at this task)

(*Truly* has similar properties to *really*, but is much less felicitous in a number of contexts which are natural with *really*.)

This is an outline of the functional possibilities for adverbs in English. Some other functions are simply variants of one of the basic ones. For example, an adverb can precede a preposition followed by an NP; but the possibilities are the same as for an NP with no preposition. Compare:

|  |  |
|---|---|
| *only the beautiful flowers* | *only in America* |
| *just the beautiful flowers* | *just in America* |
| *even the beautiful flowers* | *even in America* |

And an adverb may modify a complement clause. This again shows the same possibilities as for modification of an NP. Compare *only* modifying an NP (in O function) in

**(6a)**  *I want [only the top job]*

with *only* modifying a THAT complement clause, in (6b), or a (FOR) TO complement clause, in (6c) (both in O function) as in (see also (45)–(46) in §12.4):

**(6b)**  *I want [only that Mary should get the top job]*

**(6c)**  *I want [only for Mary to get the top job]*

Every adverb can function either as sentence modifier or in manner function (modifying verb-plus-object) or both; this is taken as the defining property for 'what is an adverb' in English. Some may also modify an NP and/or an adjective and/or an adverb.

§12.4 summarises the possibilities for NP modification. Then §§12.5–7 discuss, in turn, adverbs which have sentential but not manner function, those with manner but not sentential function, and those with both. For each set, possibilities for adjectival and adverbial modification are considered, and this is then summarised in §12.8. In §12.9 there is discussion of comparatives, and of adverbs as complete utterances. Then §12.10 examines combinations of adverbs.

But first we need, in §12.2, to examine the forms of adverbs—whether simple or derived, and what they are derived from—and, in §12.3, to enumerate the possibilities for positioning within a clause corresponding to the five functions of adverbs.

## 12.2. Forms and types

An adverb can be a word or a phrase or a clause. Dealing first with words, we can recognise two basic forms:

I.   Those which are derived from an adjective by adding -*ly*, and which maintain the meaning (or a major part of the meaning) of the adjective; for example, *quickly, rudely, narrowly, humbly, simply, probably, sensibly*.
II.  The rest, which further divide into two sub-kinds:
     IIa. Those which end in -*ly*, but have a quite different meaning from the form obtained by deleting the -*ly*. They include *hardly, fairly, really, terribly*.
     IIb. Those which do not end in -*ly*. Most of these are not morphologically analysable; for example, *quite, just, even, also*, plus time adverbs such as *still, now, soon, then*, and spatial adverbs such as *here* and *out*. Others have an historical analysis but are perceived as unanalysable forms in the modern language. They include *almost, somewhat*, and time adverbs such as *always, today, tomorrow* and *yesterday*.

In fact, the division between I and IIa is not clear-cut. Some adverbs ending in -*ly* have a degree of semantic similarity to the corresponding adjective, but not so much as prototypical members of I; for example, *truly, scarcely, surely, simply*.

Speakers of some dialects of English may in certain circumstances omit the -*ly* so that adjective and adverb have the same form; for example, *I want it <u>real bad</u>* (in place of *I want it <u>really badly</u>*). Note that this applies not only for adverbs of type I (*badly*) but also for some of type IIa (*really*).

Just a few adjectives function in Standard English as adverbs without the addition of *-ly*; for example, *hard* as in *He's a hard* (adjective) *worker and he also plays <u>hard</u>* (adverb).

Adverbs can be derived from adjectives which are themselves derived from nouns; for example, noun *geography* giving adjective *geographical* giving adverb *geographically*. And a few adverbs are directly derived from nouns by adding *-ly*; for example, *partly* and *purposely* (there is also adverb *purposefully*, derived from adjective *purposeful*, which is in turn derived from noun *purpose*).

A number of the most frequently used adverbs are traditionally written as two words but in fact function as a single (phonological and grammatical) word in present-day English. These include:

| *kind-of* | [kaindəv] | *sort-of* | [sɔːtəv] |
|---|---|---|---|
| *a-bit, a-bit-of* | [əbit], [əbitəv] | *of-course* | [əvkɔːs] |

Most of the discussion in this chapter concerns single-word adverbs. There are also adverbial phrases (often called adjuncts). Many—but by no means all—manner adverbs which are derived from adjectives by adding *-ly* can be replaced by a phrase *in a* [adjective] *manner/way*; for example, *in a rude manner* has very similar meaning to *rudely* (but exhibits more formal overtones). Many phrases function as time adverbs (with there being no single-word equivalent); for example, *in the morning, at night*—which include a preposition—and *last night, every night*—which don't.

Spatial adverbs generally consist of a preposition with local meaning followed by an NP—*in the house, up the tree, around the garden*. The NP can often be omitted, leaving just the preposition, as in *I've put the cake in* (sc. the oven) and *The lodger went up* (sc. the stairs). Grammarians have long been disputing whether *up* in *The lodger went up* is a preposition implicitly followed by an NP which has in this instance been omitted, or an adverb which is homonymous with the preposition. Arguments can be put forward in favour of both positions; which is followed remains a matter of personal choice.

Adverbial clauses typically have time or spatial reference; for example, *We'll stop work <u>when the sun sets</u>*, and *I'll plant the fuchsias <u>where you planted the rhubarb</u>*. Some grammars describe subordinate clauses introduced by links such as *although* or *if* as adverbial clauses; these are briefly mentioned in §2.12.

## 12.2.1. Adjective types and derived adverbs

Adjectives do not all behave alike with respect to the derivation of adverbs by suffix *-ly*. There is a principled basis, which is determined by the semantic type of the adjective. Table 12.1 provides an outline summary of the possibilities for each adjectival semantic type forming adverbs in (a) sentential function, (b) manner function, and (d) adjectival modifying function. Note that no adverbs derived from adjectives (with maintained meaning) may felicitously modify an NP (function (c)). Only adverbs derived from VALUE adjectives and *similarly* and *deliberately* may readily modify adverbs (function (e)). §§12.5–7 discuss the details of sentential and manner functions. Here I mention a few of the semantic characteristics of de-adjectival adverbs.

There is one restriction which should be mentioned. An adjective which is derived from a noun by the addition of *-ly* cannot, in Standard English, form an adverb by the addition of a further *-ly*. That is, there is no adverb corresponding to adjectives such as *friendly* and *cowardly*; one simply has to say *in a friendly/cowardly way/manner/fashion*.

Adverbs derived from the HUMAN PROPENSITY, SPEED and SIMILARITY types score 'yes' for the manner and sentential columns in Table 12.1. The contrasting semantic effects of the functions are illustrated and explained in §12.3 and §12.7. All QUALIFICATION items have sentential function (and many also adjectival function) but most lack manner function. The remaining semantic types occur in manner (and some also in adjectival function) but generally not in sentential function.

Almost all members of the PHYSICAL PROPERTY type, and some from COLOUR, have derived adverbs but the adverb most often corresponds to a secondary, metaphorical sense of the adjective. Thus, *hotly* refers not to temperature (as in *hot tea*) but to temperament (as in *hot temper*) and *bitterly* not to taste (as in *bitter chocolate*) but to attitude (as in *bitter dispute*). Many of these adverbs are mainly used with SPEAKING and THINK-ING verbs—*hotly* deny, *coldly* assert, *dryly* remark, *warmly* invite, *coolly* consider, *sweetly* request, *sourly* reject, *bitterly* complain, and—with a COL-OUR item—*darkly* frown.

A number of DIMENSION adjectives—such as *big, small, little*—do not form adverbs. For some others, the adverb relates to the result of an action: *He sliced the bread thinly* indicates that he produced *thin slices*. Adverbs *narrowly* and *broadly* relate to a metaphorical sense of the adjective, like

**Table 12.1.** *Functions of adverbs derived from adjectival semantic types*

| | (a) SENTENTIAL FUNCTION | (b) MANNER FUNCTION | (d) ADJECTIVAL MODIFYING FUNCTION |
|---|---|---|---|
| DIMENSION | no | some—relating to the meanings of adjectives in semantically diverse ways | no |
| COLOUR | no | some | some |
| PHYSICAL PROPERTY | no | generally relate only to secondary sense of the adjective | yes |
| SPEED | yes (similar meaning to manner function) | yes | no |
| AGE | no (but *newly* is a time adverb modifying participles—see §12.8) | no | no |
| VALUE | no | yes | yes (except for *well*, *badly*) |
| VOLITION | no | yes | yes |
| DIFFICULTY | no | yes | yes |
| QUALIFICATION | | | |
|   DEFINITE | yes | no | yes |
|   POSSIBLE | yes | no | yes |
|   USUAL | yes | no | yes |
|   LIKELY | yes | no | no |
|   SURE | yes | no | no |
|   CORRECT | yes | some | yes |
| HUMAN PROPENSITY | yes | yes | limited |
| SIMILARITY | yes | yes | yes |

PHYSICAL PROPERTY items, as in *narrowly conceived* and *broadly intended*. *Deeply* has both a concrete sense (*dive deeply*) and a metaphorical one (*think deeply*). The adjectives *short* and *long* have a secondary sense relating to time (*short meeting*, *long interval*); adverbs *shortly* and *lengthily* (the latter being based on the adjective *lengthy*, from noun *length*, from adjective *long*) are time adverbs.

In essence, an adjective (or the sense of an adjective) which relates to an objective or (semi-)permanent property is unlikely to form an adverb. An adjective (or the sense of an adjective) referring to people's skill and ability, and to types and degrees of success, is a good candidate for adverbialisation.

A fascinating property of English is that a manner adverb derived from an adjective is used with an underived verb, but the underlying adjective is used with a nominal derived from the verb (an action nominalisation). A small sample of examples is in Table 12.2. In the middle column, the adjective must precede the noun. For the right-hand column, the adverb has generally been placed before the verb but it could, equally acceptably, follow—*deeply* embed or embed *deeply*, *warmly* recommend or recommend *warmly*. Only for the main VALUE terms, and for SIMILARITY, do we find that the adverb must follow the verb.

It will be seen that either the modifier is derived and the head non-derived (in the right-hand column of Table 12.2) or the modifier is underived and the head derived (in the middle column). All of the adverbs are derived by means of suffix *-ly*, save for the suppletive *well*. The derived nouns involve a variety of processes: suffixes *-(at)ion*, *-ing*, *-ment* and *-our*,

**Table 12.2.** *Interaction of adverb and nominal derivation*

| SEMANTIC TYPE | ADJECTIVE PLUS DERIVED NOUN | DERIVED MANNER ADVERB PLUS VERB |
|---|---|---|
| DIMENSION | *deep embedding* | *deeply embed* |
| PHYSICAL PROPERTY | *warm recommendation* | *warmly recommend* |
| SPEED | *quick consideration* | *quickly consider* |
| COLOUR | *clear enunciation* | *clearly enunciate* |
| VALUE | *good organisation* | *organise well* |
| DIFFICULTY | *easy ascent* | *easily ascend* |
| QUALIFICATION | *definite decision* | *definitely decide* |
| | *possible resignation* | *possibly resign* |
| | *usual response* | *usually respond* |
| | *correct judgement* | *correctly judge* |
| HUMAN PROPENSITY | *loyal greeting* | *loyally greet* |
| | *clever solution* | *cleverly solve* |
| SIMILARITY | *similar behaviour* | *behave similarly* |

besides changes *ascend* to *ascent* and *respond* to *response*. There are, in addition, some items which have the same form for noun and verb; for example, *a generous laugh*/*laugh generously*, *a rough copy*/*roughly copy*.

A smallish set of English adjectives can or must, when used in copula complement function, govern a following NP (or, sometimes, a subordinate clause) which is marked by a preposition. For adjectives from the HUMAN PROPENSITY type, a following preposition-plus-NP is optional, as in:

(**7a**)   *She is angry (at the customs official)*
(**7b**)   *He is jealous (of his rival)*
(**7c**)   *She is curious (over/about what is happening next door)*

The *-ly* manner adverbs derived from these adjectives do not govern a preposition-plus-NP. Consider:

(**8a**)   *She behaved angrily (*at the customs official)*
(**8b**)   *He acted jealously (*of his rival)*
(**8c**)   *She looked curiously (*over what is happening next door)*

These clauses can be followed by preposition-plus-NP, but the nature of the preposition is determined by the verb used, not by the adverb. That is, one can say *She behaved angrily towards the customs official* (but not, with the corresponding adjective, *\*She is angry towards the customs official*), or *He acted jealously towards his rival* (but not *\*He is jealous towards his rival*), or *She looked curiously at what is happening next door* (but not *\*She is curious at what is happening next door*).

There are other adjectives for which a following preposition-plus-NP is obligatory. These belong to the SIMILARITY type. Examples include:

(**9a**)   *Jane is similar to her mother*
(**9b**)   *Tom is different from his father*
(**9c**)   *Michael is independent of his parents*
(**9d**)   *This question is separate from that one*

When a governed argument is obligatory for an adjective, it is also obligatory for a manner adverb derived from that adjective. For example:

(**10a**)   *Jane behaves similarly to her mother*
(**10b**)   *Tom reacts differently from his father*
(**10c**)   *Michael lives independently from his parents*
(**10d**)   *This question must be debated separately from that question*

It is of course possible to omit the preposition-plus-NP from any of (10a–d) as it is for any of (9a–d) in an appropriate discourse context. Thus, if in a discussion about Jane's mother and her behaviour, someone then mentions Jane, it could be permissible to say either *Jane is similar* or *Jane behaves similarly*, with the other participants in the conversation understanding from the context that *to her mother* is implied. That is, a governed preposition-plus-NP must be explicitly stated or implicitly understood for (10a–d) in the same way as for (9a–d). In contrast, the adjectives in (7a–c) may optionally govern a preposition-plus-NP, but this is not available for adverbs based on them in (8a–c).

## 12.3. Positioning

Adverbs show considerable freedom of positioning so that it might appear, at first blush, that no definite rules for placement within a clause or sentence could be given. However, detailed study of the different functions of adverbs indicates that for each function there are one or more preferred positions.

English sentences show a canonical ordering of their constituent clauses, phrases and words. Variations from the template are possible but are generally marked by distinctive stress or intonation. For example, a DIMENSION adjective will generally precede a COLOUR adjective, so that one says *little white 'houses* (where ' indicates that major stress goes just on the head noun, *houses*, in this NP). It is permissible to say *'white little 'houses* (for instance, when comparing them with *'black little 'houses*), but such a non-prototypical word order is marked by stressing the COLOUR adjective. However, in written English there is no device generally accepted available to mark this special contrastive stress.

Another technique used to indicate that a constituent is in a non-prototypical position is appositional intonation; this is sometimes (but not always) indicated in writing by the inclusion of a comma before and/or after the constituent. Some sentential adverbs may freely occur after the first word of the auxiliary or at the end or beginning of the clause; for example, *He'll soon come*, or *He'll come soon*, or *Soon he'll come*. However, the sentential adverb *again* is prototypically restricted to just the first two of these positions: *She's again coming*, or *She's coming again*. It can be placed in initial position, but then makes up a separate intonation unit from the rest of the sentence, marked in writing by a comma: _Again_, _she's coming_. This is called 'appositional intonation' or 'comma intonation'.

One of these devices—contrastive stress or comma intonation—is typically used to indicate deviation from the placement preferences to be explained.

There are three prototypical positions in which a sentential adverb can occur, and two for a manner adverb. A single letter is assigned to each; these will be used throughout the remainder of this chapter.

**(a)**   Sentential adverbs

- 'A' position. After the first word of the auxiliary, if there is one, as in (11a–b); this is independent of the identity of the verb. If there is no auxiliary then the adverb comes immediately before the verb, as in (11c), unless the verb is copula _be_, in which case it follows it, as in (11d).

**(11a)**   _He [might now be hoping] to stand for Parliament_
**(11b)**   _He [might now be] a candidate_
**(11c)**   _He [now hopes] to stand for Parliament_
**(11d)**   _He [is now] a candidate_

Some other positions are possible, but are marked and require contrastive stress: for example, _He now 'is a candidate_ in place of (11d), where the word following the adverb is specially stressed.

- 'F' position. As final element in the clause. For example, _now_ could be moved to the end of each of (11a–d): _He might be hoping to stand for Parliament now_, _He is a candidate now_, and so on.
- 'I' position. As initial element in the clause. For example, _now_ could be moved to the beginning of each of (11a–d): _Now he might be a candidate_, _Now he hopes to stand for Parliament_, and so on.

§12.5 and §12.7 survey the positional possibilities for individual sentential adverbs. Some may be used in all three slots, others in only one or two of them.

**(b)** Manner adverbs

- 'V' position. Immediately before the verb, as in (12a).
- 'O' position. Immediately after the verb, or verb-plus-object if there is an object as in (12b) (an adverb may not normally intrude between verb and object).

**(12a)**   _She might have [slightly underestimated the difficulties]_
**(12b)**   _She might have [underestimated the difficulties slightly]_

(A manner adverb may alternatively follow a prepositional NP, which then falls within its scope. See the discussion of (30c) in §12.3.2.)

Most manner adverbs may occur in positions V and O but some are restricted to O (these include *well*, *badly*, *simply* and *a-bit*) while others are confined to V (including *really*, *truly*, and *quite*). There is a full discussion in §§12.6–7.

There are a number of adverbs which can have both sentential and manner functions, including HUMAN PROPENSITY items such as *generously*, *angrily*, *cleverly* and *stupidly*. They do, of course, have different semantic effects in the two functions. Consider a situation where a soldier is standing on parade and an inspecting officer asks a question of him. Trouble ensues. Later, someone suggests a reason, using the basic sentence *The soldier must have answered the officer's question* with the addition of adverb *stupidly*. The adverb could be used in sentential function, in position A (after the first word of the auxiliary), or F (clause-finally) or I (clause-initially). That is:

(13a)   SENTENTIAL   A   *The soldier must stupidly have answered the officer's question*
(13b)   SENTENTIAL   F   *The soldier must have answered the officer's question, stupidly*
(13c)   SENTENTIAL   I   *Stupidly, the soldier must have answered the officer's question*

The sentential use of *stupidly* implies that the solder was stupid to provide an answer to the question. It was perhaps a rhetorical question, and any attempt to answer it smacked of insubordination. (There is no significant difference in meaning between these three sentences.)

Now consider *stupidly* used as a manner adverb, which can be in position V (immediately before the verb) or O (following the object NP):

(14a)   MANNER   V   *The soldier must have [stupidly answered the officer's question]*
(14b)   MANNER   O   *The soldier must have [answered the officer's question stupidly]*

The manner use of *stupidly* carries a quite different meaning. One infers that the question was not rhetorical but did require an answer, and that the answer which the soldier provided was a stupid answer. (There is no significant difference in meaning between these two sentences.)

Note that (13b) and (14b) are identical except that in (13b) the sentential adverb is set off by comma intonation. In (13a) the adverb is in position A, following the first word of the auxiliary, and in (14a) it is in position V, immediately before the verb. But if there were no auxiliary, then positions A and V would coincide. That is, *The soldier stupidly answered the officer's question* is ambiguous between a sentential meaning (position A) and a manner meaning (position V). The ambiguity could be resolved by rephrasing the sentence; say, *The soldier was stupid to answer the officer's question* (sentential meaning) or *The soldier answered the officer's question in a stupid way* (manner meaning). In negation, the difference is always clear—*The soldier stupidly (A) didn't answer the officer's question* for the sentential adverb, and *The soldier didn't stupidly (V) answer the officer's question* for the manner adverb.

Table 12.2 showed the correspondence between adjective-plus-derived-noun and derived-manner-adverb-plus-verb. For the manner function in (14a–b) we get:

(15)   *stupid answer   —   stupidly* (V) *answer*      (manner function)

(Here, noun and verb have the same form.) For the sentential function in (13a–b) we get the underlying adjective modifying the subject of the sentence (here *soldier*); that is:

(16)   *stupid soldier   —   stupidly* (A) ... *answer*      (sentential function)

A third function of *stupidly* is to modify an adjective, as in *He was stupidly loyal*. The corresponding NP would be *stupid loyalty*:

(17)   *stupid loyalty   —   stupidly loyal*   (adjectival function)

Note the congruence between (15) and (17)—corresponding to a manner adverb, the adjective modifies a deverbal noun, and corresponding to an adjectival adverb, the adjective modifies a de-adjectival noun.

*Stupidly* (and *cleverly*) maintain the same meaning when used in sentential or manner function; they just modify in different ways. However, some adverbs show a difference of meaning in the two functions. Consider *quietly* in:

(18a)  SENTENTIAL   A   *He might quietly have closed the door*
(18b)  MANNER       O   *He might have [closed the door quietly]*

Sentence (18a) could refer to the action being performed surreptitiously, so that no one noticed, whereas (18b) would be appropriate when it was done quietly, so as not to disturb anyone (but perhaps done ostentatiously, so that everyone saw him doing it).

The difference is greater with *honestly*:

(19a)  SENTENTIAL   A   *I honestly thought that I had marked the exam*
(19b)  MANNER       O   *I thought that I had [marked the exam honestly]*

In (19a), the question to be resolved is whether or not I had marked the exam, and the adverb *honestly* here carries the meaning 'really, truly'. In contrast, the manner function of *honestly* in (19b) implies 'in an honest way'. There is a similar division of meanings for *frankly*; when used in sentential function the speaker implies 'in my candid opinion', and when used in manner function it implies that the subject of the clause is doing something 'in an open and unrestrained manner'.

Positions I, clause-initially, and V, immediately before the verb, are unambiguous. However, the other positions do require a measure of clarification and discussion. §12.3.1 deals with A position for sentential adverbs, comparing these adverbs with contrastive linkers such as *however, moreover, nevertheless* and *therefore*. Then §12.3.2 examines the possibilities for positions F, for sentential adverbs, and O, for manner adverbs.

## 12.3.1. Position 'A' and other medial positions

The placement of sentential adverbs in a position other than clause-final (F) or clause-initial (I) can best be illustrated in terms of clauses that include a long auxiliary, such as:

(20)   *The petitioners* **0** *would* **1** *have* **2** *been* **3** *dealt with in strict sequence*
(21)   *John* **0** *must* **1** *have* **2** *been* **3** *weeding the garden* (and so he didn't hear when you rang the front doorbell)

If a sentential adverb such as *normally* were included in (20), its preferred position would be **1**, after the first word of the auxiliary: *The petitioners would* <u>normally</u> *have been dealt with in strict sequence*. As the language is used in informal conversation, one sometimes hears a sentential adverb located later—after the second word of the auxiliary, position **2**, or even after the third word, position **3**; these sound progressively less good to native-speaker ears. Similarly, if sentential adverb *also* were inserted into (21), the sentence would be judged as most felicitous with the adverb at position **1**, less so at position **2**, and still less so at **3**. Note that none of these variant positions is likely to involve any difference in stress or in meaning.

There is a further possibility, which is to place a sentential adverb at position **0**, before the first word of the auxiliary. This generally involves contrastive stress on the first word of the auxiliary:

**(20a)**   *The petitioners <u>normally</u> 'would have been dealt with in strict sequence*

**(21a)**   *John <u>also</u> 'must have been weeding the garden*

That is, placing of a sentential adverb before the auxiliary entails contrastive focus on *would* in (20a), and on *must* in (21a).

It is instructive to compare the clause-internal placement of sentential adverbs with the placement of contrastive clausal linkers—sometimes also called 'adverbs' but with quite different properties from adverbs as discussed here—such as *however, moreover, nevertheless, therefore, accordingly, on the other hand, at all events*, and *still* (a different item from sentential adverb *still*); see §2.12. These serve to link two clauses and can be placed at the end or—more typically—at the beginning of the second clause, as in:

**(22a)**   *John had voted Labour; however, his brother had voted Conservative*

Now a contrastive linker such as *however* can alternatively be placed between the subject NP and the auxiliary, as in (22b), or after the first word of the auxiliary, as in (22c). Note that in each instance the linker has comma intonation:

**(22b)**   *John had voted Labour; his 'brother, however, had voted Conservative*

**(22c)**   *John had voted Labour; his brother 'had, however, voted Conservative*

When a contrastive linker is placed within the clause, the constituent immediately preceding it is accorded contrastive stress—*(his) brother* in (22b) and *had* in (22c). (This is similar to the behaviour of parentheticals, described in §8.1.) In (22b) there is focus on what the brother did on this occasion, in contrast to what John did; in (22c) there is focus on the 'previous' aspect of the clause, realised through *had*.

We can note that the positioning of a contrastive linker after the subject is only possible if the two clauses have different subjects, which can be contrasted. Consider:

**(23a)**   *John had said he was going to vote Labour; he 'had, however, voted Conservative*

It is not possible to move the contrastive linker *however* to the position after *he*, since *he* is coreferential with the subject of the first clause, *John*, and cannot be contrasted with it. That is, it is not permissible to say (with *he* referring back to *John*):

**(23b)**   *\*John had said he was going to vote Labour; 'he, however, had voted Conservative*

Sentential adverbs and contrastive clause linkers can both be placed either between subject and the first word of the auxiliary or after the first word of the auxiliary. There are, however, clear differences between them:

**(i)**  Sentential adverbs are prototypically placed after the first word of the auxiliary, position A; there is then no contrastive stress within the clause. Alternatively, they can occur between subject and auxiliary but then the FOLLOWING word (the first word of the auxiliary) bears contrastive stress. When a contrastive clause linker is placed within the clause there must always be contrastive stress on the PRECEDING word. Compare (24a–b), involving a sentential adverb, with (25a–b), which include a clause linker.

**(24a)**  *Her brother had <u>definitely</u> voted Conservative*
**(24b)**  *Her brother <u>definitely</u> 'had voted Conservative*
**(25a)**  *Her 'brother, however, had voted Conservative*
**(25b)**  *Her brother 'had, however, voted Conservative*

**(ii)**  A contrastive clause linker always has comma intonation, setting it off from the remainder of the clause. Most sentential adverbs never take comma intonation when in position A; some may optionally do so when positioned between subject and auxiliary, as in (24b).

There is a variant on the basic positioning of a sentential adverb, which applies in the presence of ellipsis. Consider a clause with normal placement of sentential adverbs *never* and *always* at position A within its clauses:

**(26a)**  *Mary has <u>never</u> voted Labour but I have <u>always</u> voted Labour*

The repeated *voted Labour* can be omitted from the second clause. However, we cannot have a sentence ending \* ... *but I have <u>always</u>*. There are two alternatives. One is to include *do so* in place of *voted Labour*, giving:

**(26b)**  *Mary has <u>never</u> voted Labour but I have <u>always</u> done so*

The other is to simply move *always* to a position before the first word of the auxiliary, giving:

**(26c)**  *Mary has <u>never</u> voted Labour but I <u>always</u> have*

We can now add a rider to the description of position A given near the beginning of §12.3: when everything after the first word of the auxiliary is ellipsed, a sentential adverb may precede the first word of the auxiliary.

When an English sentence which lacks an auxiliary is made into a polar question, the dummy element *do* (which takes the tense inflection) is included before the subject, as in *John ran* and *Did John run?* Interestingly, no adverb or contrastive clause linker can intervene between *do* and the following subject. Neither can the unreduced negator *not* intervene; one may say *Did John not come?* but not \**Did not John come?* However, when *not* is reduced to be clitic *-n't*, then it attaches to the initial *do* form; for example, *Didn't John come?* (Further discussion is in §12.11.1.)

Sentences involving a contrastive clause linker often also include *do*, but this is simply a consequence of the fact that such a linker has contrastive function, and this *do* has a contrastive role. For example, in *His brother 'did, however, vote Conservative*, the linker *however* follows *do*, which takes stress (as it always does when used in contrastive function). This is a rather different matter from the inclusion of *do* in a polar question or with *not*, mentioned in the last paragraph.

## 12.3.2. Positions 'F' and 'O'

Time and spatial adverbs typically come at the end of a clause. And many non-time, non-spatial sentential adverbs may occur in what I call the clause-final position, F. A single-word sentential adverb (not referring to space or time) can be placed immediately after verb (plus object, if there is one) or in between or after time and/or spatial specifications. For example, *sensibly* in its sentential function can be at position A or at any of $F_1$, $F_2$, or $F_3$ in (27).

(**27**)   *Mary* [A] *completed her tax return* [,$F_1$,] (*in April*) [,$F_2$,] (*in New York*) [,$F_3$]

The scope of *sensibly* in one of the F positions extends over all that precedes. For example, if *sensibly* is placed at $F_1$, we get *Mary completed her tax return, sensibly, in April in New York*; this states that in completing her tax return Mary behaved sensibly, and that it was done in April in New York, these two additional pieces of information being irrelevant for the judgement of sensibleness. However *Mary completed her tax return in April in New York, sensibly* implies that it was sensible for her to do it in April (when her accountant was available) and in New York (where she keeps all her financial records). Note that comma intonation is usual for any of the three F positions.

Turning now to manner adverbs, these can occur in position V, which is immediately before the verb, or in position O, which is immediately after verb-plus-object, as in:

| (28a) | MANNER | V | *They most carefully chose a new chairperson* |
| (28b) | MANNER | O | *They chose a new chairperson most carefully* |

Now in §1.4, I mentioned that English has a number of transitive verbs which include an inherent preposition; these include *rely on, hope for, refer to* and *decide on*; a two-word unit such as *decide on* behaves in many ways like a one-word lexeme such as *choose* (see §9.2.1). Now consider where the complex manner adverb *most carefully* can occur in the sentence *They decided on a new chairperson*:

| (29a) | MANNER | V | *They most carefully decided on a new chairperson* |
| (29b) | MANNER | $O_1$ | *They decided most carefully on a new chairperson* |
| (29c) | MANNER | $O_2$ | *They decided on a new chairperson most carefully* |

The manner adverb can felicitously be placed between *decide* and *on a new chairperson*. The less preferred—but still perfectly acceptable—position is after *a new chairperson*. That is, with a two-word verb, the adverb can come between the components or it can follow the whole-verb-plus-object, as variants of position O.

Whereas an adverb is scarcely ever found between a verb and a following NP in O function, it may come between a verb and a complement clause in O function; see the discussion of (42)–(43) in §8.2.4. Indeed, the *for* from a FOR TO complement clause must be retained after an adverb (although it could—or must—be omitted when there is no adverb present); for example, *I want (very much for) Mary to give me an apple*. See the discussion in §6.2.1, §8.2.4 and §8.3.3.

We can examine the O position of a manner adverb with respect to a spatial adverb. Consider the placement of adverb *proudly* in *My uncle marched in the ex-servicemen's procession*:

| (30a) | MANNER | V | *My uncle proudly marched in the ex-servicemen's procession* |
| (30b) | MANNER | $O_1$ | *My uncle marched proudly in the ex-servicemen's procession* |
| (30c) | MANNER | $O_2$ | *My uncle marched in the ex-servicemen's procession proudly* |

There is a subtle difference between (30b) and (30c). Using *proudly* in position $O_1$, in (30b), simply states that my uncle marched proudly (maybe he always does). On the other hand, (30c), with the adverb in position $O_2$, implies that what he did in a proud way was march-

in-the-ex-servicemen's-procession, probably because he greatly values being
an ex-serviceman. That is, the adverb has scope over all that precedes.

A verb-plus-adverb can give rise to an adjectival derivation; from *organise* plus *well* we get *well-organised*, as in *a well-organised event*. It is important to distinguish between such a derived expression and a passive
construction. Consider:

**(31a)**   *John *V organised the event* O

Manner adverbs such as *well, badly* and *differently* only occur at position O,
never at V. Now let us look at the passive of (31a):

**(31b)**   *The event was organised* O *(by John)*

Sentence (31b) is a derived intransitive construction, with *was organised* as
the predicate, involving *was* (*be* plus past tense) as marker of the passive
construction. A manner adverb such as *well* may only occur at position O,
after the verb.

This is quite different from:

**(32)**   *The event was* [*well organised*]

This is a copula construction with *was* as the copula verb and the adjectival
phrase *well organised* as copula complement.

## 12.4. Adverbs modifying NPs

A relatively small number of adverbs may modify a full NP, coming at the
very beginning (before any article or preposition) and/or at the very end.
Some are restricted to NPs in copula complement function, some to NPs in
non-copula-complement function, while some can be in NPs in any function.

It is important to distinguish between an adverb modifying an NP in
copula complement (CC) function, and the same adverb with sentential
function in A position. Consider:

**(33)**   *John is* <u>*certainly*</u> *an appropriate candidate*

Now this could conceivably be parsed as *John is* [<u>*certainly*</u> *an appropriate
candidate*]$_{CC}$ with the adverb as a modifier to the NP. Or *certainly* could be
a sentential adverb in A position—that is, after the first word of the

auxiliary if there is one, otherwise immediately before a verb other than copula *be*, or immediately after *be*. Which analysis is appropriate may be decided by adding an auxiliary. One can say:

(34a)   *John should certainly be an appropriate candidate*

but scarcely:

(34b)   *\*John should be [certainly an appropriate candidate]*

That is, *certainly* functions as a sentential adverb in A position, as in (34a). It cannot modify an NP, as shown by the unacceptability of (34b). (Note that *certainly an appropriate candidate* also cannot occur in any other function in a clause; for example, one cannot say *\*[Certainly an appropriate candidate] applied for the position.*) We infer that *certainly* must be in sentential function, at position A, in (33).

Other adverbs are unlike *certainly* in that they may have sentential function, at position A, and also modify an NP which is in copula complement function. Consider *just* in a copula clause with an auxiliary:

(35a)   SENTENTIAL, A           *It might just be a speck of dust in the carburettor*
(35b)   MODIFIER to CC NP   *It might be [just a speck of dust in the carburettor]*cc

There is a meaning difference. (35a) suggests that what was wrong with the car might be simply a speck of dust in the carburettor, rather than something more serious (such as a cracked cylinder), while (35b) suggests that it may be simply a speck of dust (not any bigger lump of dust) in the carburettor. Note that when there is no auxiliary, just a copula verb, both (35a) and (35b) reduce to:

(36)   *It is just a speck of dust in the carburettor*

This is ambiguous between the two parsings (with distinct meanings)—one having *just* as sentential adverb in A position, and the other having *just* as modifier within the NP in copula complement function. In spoken language, the two senses of (36) may be distinguishable by stress going on *just* for the sentential meaning, as in (35a), and on *dust* in the modifier-to-CC sense, as in (35b). (Note that an NP modified by *just* may have other functions besides copula complement; for example, [*Just a speck of dust in the carburettor] caused all that trouble.*)

Quite often, an adverb modifier within an NP is a syntactic alternative (with very similar meaning) to the same adverb used in sentential function, in A position, with the NP stressed to show that it is in focus. Consider *only*; this can be a sentential adverb in position A, as in *Children may only play soccer on the back lawn*. This sentence can be accorded contrastive stress on either the object NP or the spatial NP:

**(37a)**   *Children may only play 'soccer on the back lawn*
**(37b)**   *Children may only play soccer on the 'back lawn*

An alternative way of saying (37a) is to place *only* at the beginning of the object NP, *soccer*, as in (38a); and an alternative way of expressing (37b) is to place *only* at the beginning of the spatial NP *on the back lawn*, as in (38b).

**(38a)**   *Children may play [only soccer] on the back lawn*
**(38b)**   *Children may play soccer [only on the back lawn]*

That is, placing *only* in an object NP or in a prepositional NP produces a similar effect to having *only* in A position with contrastive stress on the appropriate NP. *Only* may, of course, also modify a subject NP, as in *[Only children] may play soccer on the back lawn*, meaning that people other than children may not play soccer on the back lawn. There is then no equivalent construction with *only* as sentential adverb in A position. (*'Children may only play soccer on the back lawn* has a quite different meaning, perhaps implying that adults may play soccer on both back and front lawns).

Table 12.3 summarises properties of the main adverbs which may modify an NP. Commenting first on the columns, we find that *alone*, *only* and *even* may follow an NP while all items except for *alone* may precede. It will be seen that some adverbs are restricted to an NP in copula complement function while for others the NP may be in any function. In addition, an NP modified by *alone* or *even* may be in any function other than copula complement, while one modified by *almost* or *hardly* or *also* may only be in O function. (We can, however, have an adjective—as opposed to an NP—modified by any of these adverbs (except for *alone*) in copula complement function; for example, *She is even beautiful*, *It is almost new*.)

In the last two columns, most items may also directly modify an adjective or an adverb (those in set (m) then omit the *much*). *Alone* and *also* appear to have neither of these properties, while items in set (l) may scarcely modify an adverb. Forms in sets (h–m) also have manner function, in position V or O or both. Those in sets (a–h) also have sentential function—*really*, *truly* and *also* in positions A, F and I, *alone* in F and I, the remainder just in A. An adverb in sentential function, in A position, and the same adverb

Table **12.3.** *Adverbs which modify an NP, and their other properties*

| | AS MODIFIER TO NP | | FUNCTIONS AVAILABLE TO NP | | OTHER FUNCTIONS AVAILABLE TO ADVERB | | | |
|---|---|---|---|---|---|---|---|---|
| | FOLLOWS NP | PRECEDES NP | NOT COPULA COMPLEMENT | COPULA COMPLEMENT | SENTENTIAL POSITIONS | MANNER POSITIONS | ADJECTIVAL MODIFYING | ADVERB MODIFYING |
| a *alone* | ✓ | — | ✓ | — | F, I | — | — | — |
| b *only* | ✓ | ✓ | ✓ | ✓ | A | — | ✓ | ✓ |
| c *even* | ✓ | ✓ | ✓ | — | A | — | ✓ | ✓ |
| d *just* | — | ✓ | ✓ | ✓ | A | — | ✓ | ✓ |
| e *almost, hardly* | — | ✓ | only O | — | A | — | ✓ | ✓ |
| f *also* | — | ✓ | only O | — | A, F, I | — | — | — |
| g *simply,* etc. | — | ✓ | — | ✓ | A | — | ✓ | ✓ |
| h *really, truly* | — | ✓ | — | ✓ | A, F, I | V | ✓ | ✓ |
| i *rather, quite* | — | ✓ | ✓ | ✓ | — | V (O) | ✓ | ✓ |
| j *a-bit(-of)* | — | ✓ | — | ✓ | — | O | ✓ | ✓ |
| k *kind-of, absolutely, fully* | — | ✓ | — | ✓ | — | V, O | ✓ | ✓ |
| l *exactly, precisely* | — | ✓ | ✓ | ✓ | — | V, O | ✓ | — |
| m *very much, terribly much,* etc. | — | ✓ | — | ✓ | — | O (V) | ✔ (omit *much*) | ✓ |

modifying an NP in O or oblique function, have very similar meanings. *Even, just, almost* and *hardly*, in sets (c–e), behave like *only*, set (b), in this property, as exemplified by (37)–(38).

The forms in (a–d) also occur as adjectives, with a difference of meaning from the corresponding adverb; for example, *John is alone, This is the only way to go, The surface is even, The judge was just*. Those in (g), and (l), and all in (m) except for *very* (*much*), are productively derived from an adjective by the addition of *-ly*.

Looking now at the rows, in turn:

**(a)**   *Alone* may only follow (not precede) an NP, as in [*The manager alone*] *is permitted to take an extra-long lunch break* (meaning, no one but the manager is allowed this privilege). It has a slightly different meaning when used as a sentential adverb, as in *John did the job alone*, or *Alone, John did the job*, here indicating that there was no one with John, assisting him. When used as a sentential adverb, *alone* may be modified by *all*, as in *John did the job all alone*.

**(b–c)**   *Only* and *even* can either precede or follow an NP which they modify, as in:

**(39a)**   [*Only* initiated men] *may view the sacred stones*
**(39b)**   [*Initiated men only*] *may view the sacred stones*
**(40a)**   [*Even John*] *couldn't understand it*
**(40b)**   [*John even*] *couldn't understand it*

The properties of *only* were discussed above; *even* differs just in that an NP it modifies may not be in copula complement function.

**(d)**   There are two homonymous adverbs *just*, one with a time and the other with a non-time meaning. For example, *Mary just smiled* could mean (i) that she smiled a few moments ago; or (ii) that all she did was smile (for example, she did not also laugh). We deal here with the non-time adverb, which has very similar properties to *only*, save that it must precede (never follow) an NP it modifies, as in [*Just a cheap hat*] *will suffice*, or *He is* [*just a boy*]. (A further use of *just* is as a strengthener, similar to *really* and *very*, as in *She was just beautiful*.)

**(e)**   This row in Table 12.3 relates to *almost* when not followed by *all* or *every*, and to *hardly* when not followed by *any*. These can function as sentential adverbs, in position A—as in (41a) and (42a)—or (with similar meaning) as pre-modifier to an NP, but probably only when that NP is in O function—as in (41b) and (42b). For example:

(**41a**)  *He had hardly written a word*
(**41b**)  *He had written [hardly a word]*
(**42a**)  *He had almost lost a thousand dollars at the Casino*
(**42b**)  *He had lost [almost a thousand dollars] at the Casino*

*Almost all*, *almost every* and *hardly any* can modify an NP in any function. They are best treated as complex adjectives (lacking sentential or manner or other adverbial functions).

(**f**)  *Also* can modify an NP in O function, as in *See [also the examples in the appendix]*, and can have sentential function, as in *He might also have stolen the spoons*. In addition, it functions as a clause linker.

(**g**)  This set involves a number of de-adjectival forms such as *simply*, *mainly*, *merely*, *mostly* and *chiefly*. They can modify an NP in copula complement function, as in *The proposal must have been [simply a mess]*, or function as sentential adverb in A position, as in *He must simply have wanted to succeed*.

(**h**)  *Really* has a wide set of properties. It can be a sentential adverb in all three positions (for example, *He had really not expected that*, or *He had not expected that, really* or *Really, he had not expected that*). It can be an manner adverb in V position (*He had not really enjoyed it*) or a modifier to an NP in copula complement function (*He could have been [really a hero]*); see also (5) in §12.1. *Truly* has similar properties to *really*, but is used far less often.

Whereas the sentential function of an adverb generally has similar meaning to its NP-modifying function, a manner function will typically have rather different semantic effect from an NP-modifying function. This applies to sets (h–m).

(**i**)  An NP modified by *rather* or *quite* may be in any function; for example, *[Rather an odd man] called on me today*, *I saw [quite a peculiar happening]* and *He is [rather a funny fellow]*. When used as manner adverb, the meaning is rather different (if not quite different), as in *I rather like it*

(V position) or *I like it rather* (O position), indicating 'to a certain degree'. These adverbs may also modify an adjective or another adverb, as in *a rather odd fellow* and *quite stupidly*.

(**j–k**) We find *a-bit-of* and *kind-of* as modifier to an NP in copula complement function, as in *She's [a-bit-of a joker]* and *He's [kind-of a sissy]*. They may also modify an adjective or an adverb, *a-bit-of* then omitting its *of*; as in *kind-of jealous*, *a-bit cleverly*. When in manner function, *kind-of* generally precedes the verb-plus-object but may follow it:

(**43a**)   *I had been [kind-of expecting it]*
(**43b**)   *I had been [expecting it kind-of]*

In contrast, *a-bit* (again omitting the *of*) can only be in O position, following verb-plus-object:

(**44**)   *I had been [enjoying it a-bit]*

*Absolutely* and *fully* have very similar properties to *kind-of*.

(**l**)   This set comprises a group of de-adjectival adverbs including *exactly* and *precisely*. They can modify an NP which is in copula complement function. For example, in *That is [precisely the same thing]*, the adverb *precisely* means 'identical to'. When used as a manner adverb—for example, *He might have [precisely positioned it]* or *He might have [positioned it precisely]*—the meaning is 'in a precise (or accurate) way'.

(**m**)   The final set comprises *very much* and many de-adjectival adverbs followed by *much*, such as *terribly much, awfully much, dreadfully much, incredibly much* (this is just a small sample of the possibilities). They may modify an NP in copula complement function, as in *He is [very much the master of the house]*. Retaining the *much*, they may function as manner adverb, typically in O position; for example, *I [like it very much]*. V position is possible with *very much* and *terribly much* (for example, *I very much like it*) but is less felicitous with some of the other items. Discarding the *much*, they may modify an adjective or an adverb, with intensifying meaning— *very clear, very clearly, terribly clever, terribly cleverly*.

*Very* is unusual in that it may also directly modify a noun, as in *You are [the very man (for the job)]*. In this function, *very* could be classed as an adjective, and has a meaning something like 'appropriate' (reminiscent of its original meaning when borrowed from French *vrai*, 'true').

The head of an NP may be followed by a prepositional phrase, typically referring to time or place; for example, *the meeting on Monday* or *the bench in the garden*. Alternatively, an NP head may be followed by a single-word time or spatial adverb; for example, *the meeting yesterday* or *the bench outside/there*.

There are other items which may modify an NP, with adverb-like function: for example, *such* and *what* (as in *It was [such a sad story]* and *[What a clever girl] she is*); they have no other adverbial functions. *Enough* can function as an adjective and may then either precede or follow the noun it modifies (*enough money* or *money enough*). It may follow an adjective or adverb with what appears to be adverbial function (*He is [loyal enough]*, *She spoke [clearly enough]*). And we do also get *enough* plus *of* (rather like *a-bit-of* and *kind-of*) as adverbial modifier to a complete NP in copula complement function, as in *He isn't [enough of a man]* (*to defend the honour of his wife*). Although Table 12.3 presents the main features of adverbs which may modify an NP, it does not pretend to comprise an exhaustive account.

Adverbial modification may apply in a similar way for NPs in all functions (save copula complement). The NP may be in subject or object function, or it may be in a peripheral function, marked by a preposition. As pointed out in §12.1, the same adverbial possibilities apply to an NP whether or not it is marked by a preposition—for example, *I saw [exactly/precisely five owls] [exactly/precisely at ten o'clock]*. And, as shown in (6b–c), an adverb may modify a complement clause just as it may an NP. Examples require semantic compatibility between adverb and complement clause, giving a fair range of possibilities. *Even*, which can precede or follow a noun, as in (45a–b), may also precede or follow a complement clause, as in (46a–b).

**(45a)**  *I regret [even my marriage]*
**(45b)**  *I regret [my marriage even]*
**(46a)**  *I regret [even that I married Mary]*
**(46b)**  *I regret [that I married Mary even]*

SPEED adverbs, such as *quickly* and *slowly*, cannot modify an NP in a core syntactic function. It might be thought that *quickly* and *slowly* modify prepositional NPs in a sentence like:

**(47)**  *John ran quickly around the garden and slowly along the road*

Isn't it the case that *quickly around the garden* and *slowly along the road* are each a constituent here? In fact they are not. *Quickly* and *slowly* are manner adverbs in position O (they could alternatively occur in position V, immediately before *ran*). The underlying sentence here is:

(47a)   *John [ran quickly] [around the garden] and John [ran slowly] [along the road]*

The repeated words *John ran* are omitted, giving (47).

## 12.5. Adverbs with sentential but not manner function

A survey of the main adverbs with sentential but not manner function is in Table 12.4. There is a fair degree of fluidity in the placement of these items, in position A and/or I and/or F. The most common positions are given in the table; others may very well occur, in appropriate discourse and pragmatic contexts. These adverbs fall into six sets.

**(1)**   Those forms—mostly monosyllabic—which can also modify a full NP, from rows (a–g) in Table 12.3. *Alone* occurs in position F and I, *also* in positions A, F and I, while for the remainder A is the favoured position—*only, even, just, almost, hardly, simply, mainly, merely, chiefly*, etc.

**(2)**   Other monomorphemic forms, plus *of course*. *Indeed* typically occurs in position I, otherwise in A, generally with comma intonation. The meaning of *indeed* naturally correlates with the inclusion of emphatic *do*; for example, *Indeed, John did sign the document* or *John did, indeed, sign the document*. *Of course* may occur in all three positions, always expecting comma intonation. Adverb *too* is unusual in that it is normally found in F position, as in *John laughed too*; less often it may be in A position, with comma intonation, as in *John, too, laughed*.

All the items in set (1), except for *alone* and *also*, may also modify an adjective or an adverb. From set (2), *indeed* and *of course* lack these functions. *Too* may be restricted to modification of an adjective which is in copula complement function. When modifying an adjective or an adverb, it generally expects a following qualification; for example, *John is too stupid (to be entrusted with this task)*, and *Mary talks too quickly (for foreigners to understand)*. The items in sets (3)–(6) may all—except, perhaps, for *certainly*—modify some adjectives. Some of those in sets (4)–(5) may also modify an adverb.

**Table 12.4.** *Adverbs with sentential but not manner function (and not referring to time or space)*

| | MOST COMMON SENTENTIAL POSITIONS | MAY ALSO MODIFY | | |
|---|---|---|---|---|
| | | NP | ADJECTIVE | ADVERB |
| 1 *alone* | F, I | ✓ | — | — |
| *only, even, just, almost, hardly, simply*, etc. | A | ✓ | ✓ | ✓ |
| *also* | A, I, F | ✓ | — | — |
| 2 *indeed* | I, A | — | — | — |
| *of course* | A, I, F | — | — | — |
| *too* | F, A | — | only CC | — |
| 3 *definitely, probably* | A | — | ✓ | — |
| *possibly* | A, I, F | — | ✓ | — |
| *commonly* | A | — | ✓ | — |
| *usually, normally* | A, I, F | — | ✓ | — |
| *certainly* | A, I | — | — | — |
| *obviously* | A, I, F | — | ✓ | — |
| (from QUALIFICATION adjectives) | | | | |
| 4 *deliberately* | F, A, I | — | ✓ | ✓ |
| (from VOLITION adjective) | | | | |
| 5 *accidentally* (from VOLITION adjective) | F, I, A | — | ✓ | — |
| *architecturally, procedurally* | F, I | — | ✓ | — |
| *suicidally* | F | — | ✓ | — |
| *geographically* | F, I, A | — | ✓ | ✓ |
| *poetically, geologically, historically* | F, I | — | ✓ | — |
| *archaeologically, pedagogically*, etc. | F | — | ✓ | — |
| *economically, politically, linguistically, phonetically, mathematically* | F, I | — | ✓ | — |
| *basically* | F, I, A | — | ✓ | ✓ |
| 6 *forgetfully, resentfully, regretfully, doubtfully, mournfully*, etc. | F, I, A | — | ✓ | — |

**(3)** Adverbs derived by the addition of *-ly* to monomorphemic QUALIFI-CATION adjectives (save for the CORRECT subtype, whose adverbs have both sentential and manner functions; see Table 12.7). These always occur in position A and—as tentatively shown in Table 12.4—have varying possibilities for positions I, or for I and F. The peripheral positions generally carry a contrastive meaning; compare *He's <u>obviously</u> forgotten* (simple statement of inference) with *He's forgotten, obviously* (sardonic overtone, 'what would you expect of him?').

Note that the adverb *truly* has a rather different meaning from the adjective *true* (which is placed in the same adjectival subtype as *definite* and *probable*); *truly* patterns with *really*—see Tables 12.3 and 12.7. The adjective *likely* (in the same subtype as *certain*) does not form an adverb, no doubt due at least in part to the fact that it already ends in *-ly*.

Negative congeners of these items tend to have somewhat different meanings and syntactic possibilities. *Impossibly* cannot be substituted for *possibly* in *He may possibly come*, nor *uncertainly* for *certainly* in *He will certainly come*. And one cannot substitute *possibly* or *certainly* into *He behaved impossibly/uncertainly*. *Indefinitely* has limited use (as in *postpone indefinitely*), rather different from that of *definitely*. *Uncommonly* and *commonly* have some shared possibilities, as in *These plants occur commonly/ uncommonly in the savannah*. But they also show differences; one cannot substitute *commonly* into *He did uncommonly/well*.

(4) *Deliberately*, from the VOLITION type. This is most at home in position F, but is also found in I and A. Its antonym, *accidentally*, in set (5), has the same placements, as does *purposefully* (which could be from either noun *purpose* or verb *purpose*, plus *-ful* to derive an adjective, plus *-ly*).

(5) Adverbs which are derived (by the addition of *-ly*) from already derived adjectives. The first group involves adjectives derived from nouns by the addition of *-al*. For example:

| NOUN | ADJECTIVE | ADVERB |
|---|---|---|
| *accident* | *accident-al* | *accident-al-ly* |
| *architecture* | *architectur-al* | *architectur-al-ly* |
| *procedure* | *procedur-al* | *procedur-al-ly* |
| *suicide* | *suicid-al* | *suicid-al-ly* |

The second group is based in adjectives ending in *-ical*, also formed on nouns. For some, but not for others, an intermediate stage of derivation is represented by an adjective ending in *-ic*. For example:

| NOUN | ADJECTIVE | ADJECTIVE | ADVERB |
|---|---|---|---|
| *geography* | *geograph-ic* | *geograph-ic-al* | *geograph-ic-al-ly* |
| *poetry* | *poet-ic* | *poet-ic-al* | *poet-ic-al-ly* |
| *geology* | — | *geolog-ical* | *geolog-ical-ly* |
| *history* | *histor-ic* | *histor-ic-al* | *histor-ic-al-ly* |
| *archaeology* | — | *archaeolog-ical* | *archaeolog-ical-ly* |
| *pedagogy* | *pedagog-ic* | *pedagog-ic-al* | *pedagog-ic-al-ly* |

We also find nouns ending in *-ics*, which drop the *-s* to form an adjective, add *-al* to form another adjective and then *-ly* to derive an adverb; however, for some of them either the *-ic* form or the *-ical* form is missing. Examples include:

| NOUN | ADJECTIVE | ADJECTIVE | ADVERB |
|---|---|---|---|
| *economic-s* | *economic* | *economic-al* | *economic-al-ly* |
| *politic-s* | *politic* | *politic-al* | *politic-al-ly* |
| *linguistic-s* | *linguistic* | — | *linguistic-ally* |
| *phonetic-s* | *phonetic* | — | *phonetic-ally* |
| *mathematic-s* | — | *mathematic-al* | *mathematic-al-ly* |
| *basic-s* | *basic* | — | *basic-ally* |

Whereas *geographic* and *geographical*, *poetic* and *poetical*, and *pedagogic* and *pedagogical* have pretty much the same meaning, there is a difference between *historic* and *historical*, *economic* and *economical*, and *politic* and *political* (see any good dictionary). There is a further adverb which involves *-ly* being added to *politic*, without the intervening *-al*. For most speakers today, *politically* and *politicly* are variants with the same meaning.

All the items in set (5) typically occur in position F. Their predispositions towards placement at I and A vary; a first impression is provided in Table 12.4. There is also the adverb *drastically*, derived from adjective *drastic* (there is no noun *drastics*); however, this functions as a manner adverb—see set (9) in Table 12.6.

**(6)**   Adverbs derived (by *-ly*) from adjectives which are themselves derived from verbs by the addition of *-ful*; for example, verb *forget*, adjective *forget-ful*, adverb *forget-ful-ly*. Other base verbs include *resent*, *regret*, *doubt* and *mourn*. These may occur in all of the three positions, F, I and A.

Whereas adverbs from sets (1)–(4) may, potentially, occur with any type of verb, those in sets (5) and (6) are limited to verbs (and adjectives) with a related meaning; for example, *Suicidally, she drove the car at two hundred kilometres an hour*, *The proposal is not economically viable*, and *He regretfully declined the invitation*.

## 12.5.1. Time adverbs

English has a profusion of single-word time adverbs and also many ways of creating phrasal and clausal adverbs. The main placement possibilities are shown in Table 12.5, together with an indication of whether the adverbs may also modify an adjective; none of them—except perhaps *always*—can easily modify an adverb. Phrasal and clausal time adverbs may modify an NP, following the head noun; for example, *I dread [the hour before dawn]* and *I remember [the day when you got married]*. And, as mentioned in §12.4, some single-word time adverbs—predominantly from set (2)—may follow a noun, as in *the conference tomorrow*.

Some phrasal adverbs involve no preposition, for example, *last week, this morning, all night long, next summer*. Others are marked by a preposition; for example, *in the morning, at three o'clock, for a week, on Monday*. Clausal adverbs may be introduced by a *wh-* word; for example, *when the sun sets, while you were away*. Or they may take a preposition; for example, *after the sun sets, since Churchill died*. As shown in row (1) of Table 12.5, phrasal and clausal time adverbs may be felicitously placed in position F. They may also be in position I, but this generally requires contrastive intonation and often special semantic conditioning. Consider, for example:

(48a)   *The exhibition will be opened at three o'clock this afternoon*
(48b)   *The exhibition was opened at three o'clock this afternoon*
(49a)   *At three o'clock this afternoon, the exhibition will be opened*
(49b)   *\*At three o'clock this afternoon, the exhibition was opened*

**Table 12.5.** *Time adverbs*

|  |  | MOST COMMON SENTENTIAL POSITIONS | MAY ALSO MODIFY ADJECTIVE |
|---|---|---|---|
| 1 | phrasal and clausal adverbs | F (I) | — |
| 2 | *today, tomorrow, yesterday* | F, I, A | — |
| 3 | *hourly, weekly, monthly*, etc. | F | — |
| 4 | *just* | A | — |
| 5 | *always* | A (F, I) | ✓ |
| 6 | *still, already, often, permanently* | A, F | ✓ |
| 7 | *presently* | I, F, A | ✓ |
| 8 | *again, once, once more* | A, F (I) | — |
| 9 | *now, sometimes, recently, generally, originally, temporarily, subsequently* | A, F, I | ✓ |
| 10 | *soon, later, eventually, as usual* | F, A, I | — |
| 11 | *then* | F, A | — |

Either future or past time reference is acceptable in (48a–b) when *at three o'clock this afternoon* is in the unmarked position, F. Position I, together with comma intonation, is fine in (49a) with future time reference. However, (49b), with the time adverb in position I and past time reference, would only be accepted in a highly marked, declamatory speech style. It seems that this adverb may felicitously precede the clause only when the event referred to has not yet taken place.

It is possible to place some phrasal time adverbs after the first word of an auxiliary, with contrastive intonation, as in *He will, by tomorrow, have completed it*. If there is no auxiliary then the dummy element *do* is required—one can say *John did, in the middle of the night, jump out of bed*. This is a variant on position A, which specifies placement after the first word of the auxiliary, if there is one, otherwise immediately before the verb. In this instance an auxiliary should normally be supplied (one can scarcely say *\*John, in the middle of the night, jumped out of bed*).

Set (2) in Table 12.5 consists of forms that are in modern English a single word but derive historically from a phrase—*today, tomorrow* and *yesterday*. They behave like phrasal adverbs in being always acceptable in position F and often possible in position I, within a contrastive context. For example, *Yesterday it rained but today it will be fine* is felicitous, because of the contrast between the different state of the weather yesterday and today. However, if the weather were the same on both days, one is more likely to hear *It rained yesterday and it'll rain again today*, with time adverbs in position F, rather than *Yesterday it rained and today it'll rain again*, with *yesterday* and *today* in the contrastive position, I.

Words in set (2) may occasionally occur in position A; for example, *The King will today issue a pardon*. And set (2) items do also function as nouns (as in *Tomorrow promises to be a fine day*).

Phrasal time adverbs, clausal adverbs, and the items in set (2) may be clefted. For example, *It was yesterday/in the middle of the night/after his outburst/while he was on vacation that John got the sack*. This may also apply to just a few items in other sets, such as *recently*.

Set (3) consists of adverbs formed by adding *-ly* to nouns referring to units of time—*hour, day, night, week, month, season, year* (but not *second, minute, decade* or *century*). They can be combined with number words; for example, *six-monthly, half-hourly*. These adverbs are basically restricted to position F, as in *He gets paid weekly*. They do not modify an adjective but do have adjective-like function, directly modifying a noun, as in *on a (six)-monthly basis*.

Set (4) consists of *just* in its time sense of 'happened very recently'. It is restricted to position A, as in *He has just entered the room*. This adverb does not modify an adjective.

Set (5) also consists of a single item, *always*. This can refer to a continuous activity or to a repeated event, depending on the meaning of the verb; for example, *She has always been on time* (that is, on every single occasion) and *She has always lived in Cardwell* (that is, for all her life). It is generally in position A, although it can be used, contrastively, in F or I. *Always* may modify an adjective, as in *An always cheerful receptionist brightens up the office*.

Set (6) consists of *still, already, often* and the derived adverb *permanently*. These occur in positions A and F and may also modify an adjective (for example, *a still cheerful colleague* or *a permanently cruel master*). There is a homonymous form *still* which functions as a contrastive linker (like *however* and *although*). Compare the adverb *still* in (50) with the contrastive linker *still* in (51).

**(50)**   *John is (still) living with Mary (still)*
**(51)**   *Still, I don't believe it*

Set (7) involves just *presently*; this may also modify an adjective, as in *the presently jealous husband*. *Presently* is derived from adjective *present* but has a wider range of meaning. When in position F it can relate to future time and requires a clause with future reference; for example, *I'll do it presently* (*I'm doing it presently* is not acceptable). When used in position I, either present or future reference is acceptable—*Presently, I'm weeding the garden* or *Presently, I'll weed the garden*. Position A is restricted to present time reference, as in *She is presently weeding the garden*.

Set (8) consists of *again, once* and the phrasal adverb *once more*. These occur in all three positions, but do not modify adjectives. A is effectively the default position, while positions I and F indicate a contrastive sense. Compare:

(52a)   *I once got drunk* (routine report; implying that anyone is likely to get drunk on one occasion)

(52b)   *Once, I got drunk* (you may not believe it but this is what happened)

(52c)   *I got drunk once* (but never again)

(53a)   *He again arrived late* (routine report; it may be only the second time it has happened)

(53b)   *Again, he arrived late* (his doing so is getting to be a habit, and is not acceptable)

(53c)   *He arrived late again* (this may be the third or fourth time it has happened)

Set (9) consists of a fair number of time adverbs which may appear in all three positions and may also modify an adjective. They include *now*, *sometimes* and the derived forms *recently, generally, originally, temporarily* and *subsequently*. For items in set (9)—and also those in set (10)—position F generally carries a contrastive overtone. Examples of this are: *He's out of work temporarily* (but he'll soon get a job) and *He's praying now* (he's never done that before). A typical example of adjectival modification is *his generally generous nature*.

It should be noted that the division between time and non-time adverbs is not clear-cut. *Normally* and *usually*, included in set (3) of Table 12.4, could equally appropriately have been placed in set (9) here.

Set (10) covers a number of adverbs which may again function in all three positions but, unlike set (9), do not modify an adjective. It includes *soon*, the derived form *eventually* and the phrasal form *as usual*. Interestingly, *soon* appears to be most at home later in the clause; *He'll weed the garden soon* sounds more felicitous than *He'll soon weed the garden*. The time adverb *late* is generally used in F position; however, comparative form *later* can be used with a non-comparative meaning, in place of *late*, and may then occur in any of the three positions (although F is most favoured).

Set (11) consists just of the time adverb *then* 'at that time', which is restricted to F and A positions, as in:

(54)   *Mary was (then) baking a cake (then)*

Here *then* has anaphoric function, referring back to some explicit or implicit time specification in the text; for example, *John arrived at four o'clock and Mary was then baking a cake* or *John suddenly collapsed; Mary was then baking a cake*.

The adverb *then* must be distinguished from coordinator (*and*) *then*, meaning 'the next thing was'. This typically occurs in clause-initial position; for example, (*And*) *then Mary made a cake*. It can follow the first word of the auxiliary, as in *Mary was then jolted into action*. The two forms *then* occur in quite different syntactic and discourse contexts and there is little or no chance of their being confused. (There is a third *then*, a discourse marker which only occurs in non-formal speech, as in *It's going to be a fine day today then*.)

A sentence can include a variety of time adverbs, either in different positions (for example, *In the summer* Mary *always* gets up *at six a.m.*) or in the same position (for example, *Now, in the spring, the flowers are blooming*). There may be a sequence of adverbs each of which has a time reference included within that of the adverb which follows. Consider:

(55)   *John married Mary* [*at ten o'clock*]₁ [*on Saturday*]₂ [*last week*]₃

Here 1 is referentially within 2 which is within 3. The most natural order is, as in (55), 1 2 3. One could have 3 1 2 or 2 3 1 or 3 2 1 but there would then be comma intonation after each adverb which is out of sequence; for example, *John married Mary on Saturday last week, at ten o'clock*. Or one could have 2 3 or just 3 in position I (with 1 or 1 2 in position F), as in *On Saturday last week, John married Mary at ten o'clock*. But it would be infelicitous to have 1 or 1 2 in position I, and 2 3 or 3 in F (one would not say \**At ten o'clock John married Mary on Saturday last week*). That is, a time adverb at position I can include in its reference one at position F but not vice versa.

## 12.5.2. Spatial adverbs

Spatial adverbs never modify an adjective or an adverb. A spatial adverb occurs in sentential function, generally in position F. Some may be placed in position I and are then generally used deictically (with topicalisation and stress), with a verb in present tense form: for example, *Here* John *comes* and *Down the hill* Mary *runs*. Interestingly, in this construction, subject and following intransitive verb may swap positions—*Here comes John* and *Down the hill runs Mary*. (This is not possible with a transitive verb.) Only in exceptional circumstances does a spatial adverb occur in a non-peripheral position.

All spatial adverbs may be clefted. For example, *It was here/upstairs/in the bedroom/where he saw the bull that John lost his wallet.*

As mentioned in §2.5, spatial adverbials fulfil two rather different roles, depending on the semantics of the verb they occur with. For verbs from the REST and MOTION types and from the LOOK subtype of ATTENTION, a spatial adverb may be an intrinsic part of the description of the activity—*He stood on the pavement, She brought John to the house, I gazed into her eyes.* A handful of verbs actually require such an 'inner adverbial'—*put, set* and *live*. One can say *I live in Melbourne* but scarcely just *I live* (except with a quite different sense of the verb). We also have 'outer adverbials', which can be used with any verb, there being no intrinsic semantic link between verb and adverbial; for example, *He yawned in the garden.*

Inner adverbials are almost confined to position F, although they may be fronted, for emphasis, as in *On the ground he put it and on the ground it stays.* An inner adverbial is always placed closer to the verb than an outer adverbial; for example, *He put it [on the ground]$_{INNER}$ [early in the morning]$_{OUTER}$.* (Note that although inner adverbials are predominantly spatial, there are a number which are required by a time verb; for example, *The concert lasted (for) two hours.*)

Spatial adverbs divide into four types:

1. Clauses introduced by a *wh-* form, as in *You'll find it where you left it.*
2. Phrases introduced by any of the several score prepositions in English. In an appropriate context, the NP following a preposition may be omitted, leaving just the preposition, which effectively functions as an adverb all by itself; for example, *He ran down (the hill), She came behind (her father).*
3. A number of single-word adverbs which are either (i) derived from a preposition or a noun—for example, *upwards, heavenwards*; or (ii) a reduced form of an NP—for example, *upstairs, downhill, overboard.*
4. The demonstratives *here* and *there*, and related forms such as *hereabouts, therein.*

As with time adverbs, a clause can include a number of spatial adverbs, which may be distributed between I and F or else all appear in the one position. Also like time items, the reference of one spatial adverb may be included in the reference of the spatial adverb which follows in sequence, as in:

(56)    *John married Mary [on the lawn]$_1$ [in the garden]$_2$ [behind Jane's house]$_3$*

It is possible to get other orders (3 1 2 or 2 3 1 or 3 2 1), but comma intonation is required when an adverb occurs out of numerical order (for example, *John married Mary behind Jane's house, on the lawn in the garden*). And, once more like time adverbs, one can place one or two higher-numbered adverbs in position I (for example, *In the garden behind Jane's house, John married Mary on the lawn*) but one cannot have 1 or 1 2 in position I and 2 3 or 3 in position F (that is, not *On the lawn, John married Mary in the garden behind Jane's house*). Exactly as with time adverbs, an item at position I can include in its reference one at position F but not vice versa.

Spatial adverbs may modify an NP and then follow the head noun, as in [*That picture there*] *appeals to me*, and *I like* [*houses in the country*]. However, in this function a spatial adverb consisting of preposition plus NP cannot be reduced to just the preposition. One can say *He put the cake in the oven* or *He put the cake in* but only *He took a look at* [*the cake in the oven*], not *He took a look at* [*the cake in*].

In written English, there may arise confusion between a spatial adverb within an O NP, and the same adverb with sentential function in F position, as in:

(57)   *I saw the man from across the street*

However, in speech the two interpretations are accorded different stress. When *across the street* is a constituent of the NP, stress will go onto the head noun, as in:

(57a)   *I saw* [*the 'man from across the street*] (the man lives across the street from me, but I may have seen him somewhere else)

When *across the street* is a direct constituent of the clause, stress is likely to go on the preposition:

(57b)   *I saw* [*the man*] [*'from across the street*] (I looked across the street and saw the man you had been talking about)

A clause may include a spatial adverb and a time adverb; these may occur in either order (although there appears to be a tendency for a spatial adverb to come first). Or it may include several of each variety of adverb; the only constraint is that the two varieties of adverb should not be intermingled. Example (55) has three time adverbs and (56) has three spatial adverbs; these can be combined with either all the spatial adverbs coming first or all the time adverbs coming first. Or the time adverbs may all be in position I and the spatial items in position F; or vice versa. Just one or two of one kind of adverb can be in position I and the other(s) in F (for example, *On Saturday last week* John married Mary *at ten o'clock on the lawn in the garden behind Jane's house*). However it would be scarcely felicitous to divide both time and spatial adverbs between positions I and F.

As discussed in §12.3.2, a manner adverb in position O may precede or follow time and/or spatial adverbs; it has scope over all that precedes. Only relatively rarely would one encounter a non-time non-spatial sentential adverb (from Table 12.4) with a time or spatial adverb, all in position F. When this does happen, it appears that there are no preferences for relative ordering (and no significant meaning differences between different orderings). For example, one can say either *John sat alone in the garden* or *John sat in the garden alone*, and *He spilt ink deliberately on the carpet* or *He spilt ink on the carpet deliberately*.

## 12.6. Adverbs with manner but not sentential function

A clause can include several adverbs in sentential function, either in different positions or all in the same position—see example (3) in §12.1. In contrast, there can only be one manner adverb in a clause. Manner adverbs *carefully* and *successfully* can both be in either position V or position O; one can say either *He carefully constructed the model* or *He constructed the model carefully*, and *He successfully constructed the model* or *He constructed the model successfully*. It is not possible to include both *carefully* and *successfully* as separate adverbs; one cannot say *\*He carefully constructed the model successfully* or *\*He successfully constructed the model carefully* or *\*He carefully successfully constructed the model* or *\*He constructed the model carefully successfully*. What has to be done is form a complex manner adverb by conjoining two simple manner adverbs—*carefully and successfully* (or *successfully and carefully*), then saying *He carefully and successfully constructed the model* or *He constructed the model carefully and successfully*.

Adverbs with manner but not sentential function can be conveniently divided into nine sets, as in Table 12.6. These will be discussed in turn.

**(1)** This set repeats rows (i–l) from Table 12.3, adverbs which also modify a full NP or an adjective or (save for the derived forms *exactly* and *precisely*) an adverb. *Quite* appears to be pretty well restricted to position V (as in *I quite like it*) and *a-bit* to O (*I like it a-bit*). *Rather* is preferred in V

**Table 12.6.** *Adverbs with manner but not sentential function*

| | MOST COMMON MANNER POSITIONS | MAY ALSO MODIFY | | |
|---|---|---|---|---|
| | | NP | ADJECTIVE | ADVERB |
| 1   *rather* | V, O | ✓ | ✓ | ✓ |
|     *quite* | V | ✓ | ✓ | ✓ |
|     *a-bit(-of)* | O | ✓ | ✓ | ✓ |
|     *kind-of, absolutely, fully* | V, O | ✓ | ✓ | ✓ |
|     *exactly, precisely* | V, O | ✓ | ✓ | — |
| 2   *very much, terribly much, awfully much, dreadfully much, amazingly much, incredibly much*, etc. | O (V) | ✓ | ✓ (omit much) | ✓ (omit much) |
| 3   *slightly, somewhat, especially, fairly* | V, O | — | ✓ | ✓ |
| 4   *narrowly, thickly, deeply*, etc. (from DIMENSION adjectives) | V, O | — | — | — |
| 5   *dryly, sweetly, warmly, darkly*, etc. (from PHYSICAL PROPERTY and COLOUR adjectives) | V, O | — | ✓ | — |
| 6   *easily* | V, O | — | — | — |
|     *simply* (from DIFFICULTY adjectives) | O | — | — | — |
| 7   *well, badly* | O | — | — | — |
|     *atrociously, beautifully* (from VALUE adjectives) | O | — | ✓ | ✓ |
| 8   *carefully, sorrowfully, successfully, skilfully*, etc. | V, O | — | ✓ | — |
| 9   *drastically, expertly* | V, O | — | — | — |

(*I <u>rather</u> like it*) but possible in O (*I like it <u>rather</u>*). The other adverbs may appear in either position.

These adverbs may be used in manner function, mostly with verbs from the LIKING and ANNOYING semantic types. However, their prime role lies in modifying adjectives and adverbs, providing a nuance of augmentation or diminution of the property described by the item they modify. They occur with adjectives of all semantic types, and their derived adverbs (if these exist). For example:

| | | | |
|---|---|---|---|
| *rather wide(ly)* | *a-bit slow(ly)* | *quite black(ly)* | *absolutely stupid(ly)* |
| *exactly correct(ly)* | *kind-of old* | *rather good/well* | *quite heavy/heavily* |
| *fully certain(ly)* | *a-bit angry/angrily* | | |

It is important to distinguish the manner adverb *rather* from the comparative marker *would rather — (than —)*, as in *I would rather walk (than run)*. Whereas the manner adverb *rather* may not occur with another manner adverb, the comparative marker may, as in *I would rather Mary do it carefully (than sloppily)*.

**(2)**    The items in this set come from row (m) of Table 12.3—*very much, terribly much, awfully much, dreadfully much, incredibly much*, among many others. The *much* is retained when used in manner function (*I like it terribly much* or *I terribly much like it*) and when modifying an NP (*She is very much a professor*), but omitted when modifying an adjective or an adverb. Like the items in set (1), these adverbs are in fact typically used to modify an adjective or an adverb and can occur with all semantic types. A few examples are:

| | | |
|---|---|---|
| *very narrow(ly)* | *terribly bad(ly)* | *awfully clever(ly)* |
| *dreadfully jealous(ly)* | *very strong(ly)* | *terribly easy/easily* |

These adverbs may be repeated—for added emphasis—when modifying an adjective or adverb. One can say *terribly terribly easy/easily* or *very very good/well*. Or *terribly terribly terribly easy/easily* or *very very very good/well*; there is no definite upper limit to the number of repetitions.

In fact, the items in set (2) comprise the main adverbs which may be repeated. Others are *quite*, from set (1) (as in *the new ball gown is quite quite beautiful*), *too* from set (2) of Table 12.4 (as in *You are too too kind*) and *really* and *truly* from set (1) of Table 12.7 (see §12.7).

**(3)**    This set consists of adverbs which also play a major role in modifying adjectives and adverbs—*slightly, somewhat, especially, fairly*. For example, *slightly warm(ly), somewhat anxious(ly), especially eager(ly), fairly stupid(ly)*. Unlike the items in sets (1) and (2), they appear not to modify a full NP. In manner function, these adverbs may occur in V or in O position; for example, *I somewhat disliked him* or *I disliked him somewhat*. *Fairly* is used much more in position V (for example, *I fairly asked for that, didn't I?*) than in position O.

**(4)**    This set consists of a number of adverbs derived from adjectives of the semantic type DIMENSION, occurring at positions V and O. They do not modify an NP, an adverb or a simple adjective (as opposed to a participial form; for example, *a narrowly conceived endeavour*). In manner function, they sometimes retain the central meaning of the adjective; for example, *She (thickly) sliced the bread (thickly)* and *He (thinly) spread the margarine (thinly)* and *He (deeply) dug the hole (deeply)*. Often, the adverbs take on a metaphorical sense, as in *I (deeply) dislike 'fashion linguistics' (deeply)* and *They have (widely) recognised his talent (widely)*. (The last sentence would more often be in passive form, *His talent has been (widely) recognised (widely)*, with the *widely* doing away with any need to state the underlying agent.)

*Shortly* and *lengthily*—from the DIMENSION adjectives *short* and *long*—function only as time adverbs in sentential function. They typically occur with speaking verbs; for example, *He spoke lengthily on the topic*. *Shortly* also has the sense 'soon' as in *He will shortly be announcing his resignation*.

(5)  This set involves a number of adverbs derived from PHYSICAL PROP-ERTY and COLOUR adjectives. As mentioned in §12.2.1, they typically occur, in V or O slot, with speaking verbs. For example:

| | | |
|---|---|---|
| *dryly mention* | *lightly accept* | *coldly assert* |
| *warmly recommend* | *coolly reject* | *sweetly agree* |
| *sourly refute* | *bitterly protest* | *softly whisper* |
| *darkly denounce* | | |

Each adverb occurs with a limited range of verbs—for example, one can *hotly deny*, *hotly accuse*, *hotly assert*, *hotly interpose*—so that these verge on being idiomatic collocations. There are also some uses with other types of verb; for example, *hotly pursue*. And there are some examples of an adverb retaining the central meaning of the PHYSICAL PROPERTY adjective; for example, *fall heavily*, *lightly rub*, *handle roughly*.

These items appear not to modify NPs or adverbs, but they have limited occurrence as modifiers of adjectives; for example, *bitterly jealous*.

(6)  Adjectives in the semantic type DIFFICULTY behave in a variety of ways with respect to the derivation of adverbs and their properties. *Easily* has manner function in V and O positions; for example, *She (easily) solved the puzzle (easily)*. There is an adverb *difficultly* which can be used in a similar manner, but it sounds awkward (perhaps because of the consonant cluster *-ltl-*) and *with difficulty* is generally preferred. There is an adverb *toughly*, but with a low frequency of usage. *Hard* does not form an adverb since there is a form *hardly* with a quite different meaning; see set (1) in

Table 12.4. Corresponding to adjective *simple*, there is the adverb *simply* 'in a simple manner', which has manner function, as in *He explained it simply*. This appears to be restricted to O position, probably to avoid confusion with the quite different sentential adverb *simply* 'just this and nothing else', as *I was simply asking* and *He simply can't do it*; this is in row (g) of Table 12.3 and set (1) of Table 12.4.

**(7)** There are a number of adverbs derived from VALUE adjectives. The main value terms, *good* and *bad*, form adverbs *well* and *badly*. These may function as manner adverbs but generally only in position O—*He wrote the report well/badly* but not *\*He well/badly wrote the report*. They may not modify an NP, an adjective, or an adverb. (Note the quite different form *badly*, meaning 'a lot' as in *I badly want to go*.)

*Well* (but not *badly*) may also function as a sentential adverb but with a quite different meaning, 'most certainly', as in *I well remember that day*. Inversion is possible here, similar to that found with some negators (see §12.11.6)—for example, *Well might he pretend* (carrying an ironic overtone) and *Well do I remember that day* (note the necessary inclusion of *do* in this inversion, in the absence of an auxiliary).

Other VALUE adverbs appear also to be restricted to position O; for example, *He built it atrociously*, *She sang it beautifully*. They may modify an adjective or an adverb—for example, *atrociously unlucky/unluckily*—but not an NP. Note that there is some overlap here with set (2); *terribly* and *awfully*, for example, are derived from VALUE adjectives.

**(8)** This set consists of adverbs derived (by *-ly*) from adjectives which are themselves derived from abstract nouns by the addition of *-ful*; the nouns include *care*, *sorrow*, *success* and *skill*. They may function as manner adverbs in positions V or O; for example, *He (skilfully) navigated the channel (skilfully)*. These adverbs do not modify an NP or an adverb but they may sometimes modify an adjective; for example, *skilfully adept*.

**(9)** The final set consists of a residue of manner-only adverbs such as *drastically* (from the adjective *drastic*) and *expertly* (from noun *expert*). These may occur in both V and O positions; for example, *The numbers were (drastically) reduced (drastically)*; and *He will be (expertly) overseeing the work (expertly)*.

Manner adverbs relate to the way in which some action (described by a verb) is performed. There is thus a close semantic association between manner adverb and verb. As a consequence, there is rather limited occurrence of manner adverbs with secondary verbs, which do not directly relate to an activity. For example, a speaker would prefer to say *He started to hotly deny it*, rather than *\*He hotly started to deny it*, and *He wanted to narrowly miss the target*, rather than *\*He narrowly wanted to miss the target*.

It was pointed out in §6.1 that the verb in a complement clause following a secondary verb may be omitted, if the nature of the action referred to is clear to the addressee. When describing a bookbinder at work, one could reduce *He began binding the grammar of Tariana* to *He began the grammar of Tariana*.

Now a manner adverb such as *carefully* can be associated with the verb *bind*:

(58)   *John began (carefully) binding the grammar of Tariana (carefully)*

It is possible in this instance to move the adverb *carefully* to precede *began*:

(58a)   *John carefully began binding the grammar of Tariana*

However, in (58a) the adverb *carefully* is still related to complement clause verb *binding*. Note that it is not felicitous to omit *binding* from (58a); one would not—except in a very specific context—say *\*John carefully began the grammar of Tariana*. If a manner adverb is included then the verb to which it relates should be retained (even if the nature of the activity is clear from the context).

Just a few manner adverbs from sets (1) and (2) have the potential to modify directly a secondary verb: for example, *I rather/terribly much want to go*, and *John kind-of made Mary kind-of mess things up*.

## 12.7. Adverbs with both sentential and manner function

Table 12.7 summarises the properties of adverbs with both sentential and manner function, divided into five sets.

Set (1) involves *really* and *truly*, which were in row (h) of Table 12.3. These are the most omni-functional of adverbs. As illustrated for *really* at

**Table 12.7.** *Adverbs with both sentential and manner function*

| | MOST COMMON SENTENTIAL POSITIONS | MOST COMMON MANNER POSITIONS | MAY ALSO MODIFY | | |
| --- | --- | --- | --- | --- | --- |
| | | | NP | ADJECTIVE | ADVERB |
| 1  *really, truly* | A, F, I | V | only ✔ CC | ✔ | ✔ |
| 2  *stupidly, cleverly, angrily, happily, eagerly, honestly, frankly, generously*, etc. (from HUMAN PROPENSITY adjective type) | A, F, I | V, O | — | ✔ | — |
| 3  *correctly, rightly, wrongly, appropriately, sensibly*, etc. (from CORRECT subtype of QUALIFICATION type) | A, F, I | V, O | — | ✔ | — |
| 4  *similarly* (from SIMILARITY type) | A, F, I | O | — | ✔ | ✔ |
| 5  *slowly, quickly, rapidly, speedily, fast* (from SPEED type) | A, F, I | V, O | — — | | — |

(5a–e) in §12.1, they have all five functions. In addition, they may modify an adverb-plus-adjective, or an adverb-plus-adverb. For example:

| | |
| --- | --- |
| *truly architecturally beautiful* | *really hardly competent(ly)* |
| *really rather wide(ly)* | *really permanently sick* |
| *truly quite jealous(ly)* | *really beautifully cool* |
| *really very good/well* | |

We frequently find these two adverbs coordinated, as one complex adverb; they are always in the order *really and truly*. For example, *He really and truly believed me*, and *She is really and truly the most beautiful person I have ever seen.*

*Really* and *truly* often modify an adverb from set (2) in Table 12.6, which may be repeated. *Really* or *truly* may then also be repeated. That is, one can say any of:

| | | |
| --- | --- | --- |
| *very good* | *very very good* | |
| *really very good* | *really very very good* | *really really very very good* |

However, *really* (or *truly*) is not likely to be repeated unless the following adverb is; that is one would not expect to hear \**really really very good*. For *very* could be substituted *terribly*, *awfully*, etc.

All of the remaining sets in Table 12.7 involve adverbs derived from adjectives by the addition of *-ly*. The way in which *stupidly* occurs in sentential function at positions A, I and F and in manner function at positions V and O was illustrated in §12.3. Using *stupidly* in sentential function, as in (13a–c), implies that the soldier was stupid to answer the officer's question, whereas using the adverb in manner function, as in (14a–b), implies that he answered the question in a stupid manner.

Set (2) covers adverbs derived from HUMAN PROPENSITY adjectives. Alongside *stupidly* we have *cleverly*, *angrily*, *happily*, *eagerly* and many others. In some contexts it is not easy to identify the different meanings these adverbs have in their sentential and manner functions. However, there always is an implied meaning difference, which can be brought out in an appropriate context. Consider *happily*, for instance. It is used in sentential function in (59a–c):

**(59a)** SENTENTIAL  I  *Happily, John has been studying for the examination*
**(59b)** SENTENTIAL  A  *John has, happily, been studying for the examination*
**(59c)** SENTENTIAL  F  *John has been studying for the examination, happily*

These sentences imply that the speaker is happy about John's studying for the examination, without any implication that John is happy about doing this (he might be or he might not be). Now consider *happily* used as a manner adverb, in (60a–b).

**(60a)** MANNER  V  *John has been [happily studying for the examination]*
**(60b)** MANNER  O  *John has been [studying for the examination happily]*

These sentences state that John is studying in a happy mode.

Most adverbs in Table 12.7 retain the same meaning but just provide different kinds of modification when used in sentential and in manner functions. For example, *sensibly* means 'it is sensible to do it' in sentential and 'it is done in a sensible way' in manner function. But for some adverbs there is a slight meaning difference between the two functions. In §12.3, this was illustrated for *quietly* at (18a–b) and for *honestly* at (19a–b); it was there noted that *frankly* shows a similar difference.

Set (3) consists of adverbs from the CORRECT subset of the QUALIFICATION type of adjectives—*correctly*, *rightly*, *wrongly*, *appropriately*, and *sensibly* (mentioned in the preceding paragraph). These behave in a similar way to adverbs in set (2). For example, *correctly* could be substituted for *stupidly* in (13a–c)—stating that the soldier was correct to offer an answer to the question—and in (14a–b)—stating that he provided the correct answer. Adverbs from sets (2) and (3) may also modify an adjective (for example, *stupidly anxious*, *appropriately diligent*).

Set (4) consists just of *similarly*. This generally relates to something preceding in discourse. Suppose one person says *Mary has been making a model*. Someone else could reply, using any of:

(61a)   SENTENTIAL   I   *Similarly, John has been making a model*
(61b)   SENTENTIAL   A   *John, similarly, has been making a model*
(61c)   SENTENTIAL   F   *John has been making a model, similarly*
(62)    MANNER       V   *John has been making a model similarly to Mary*

Sentences (61a–c) state that John has been doing a similar thing to Mary, making a model. In contrast, (62) says that he has been making a model in a similar manner to Mary. It appears that, in manner function, *similarly* is restricted to position O. *Similarly* may also modify an adjective or an adverb; for example, *similarly clever(ly)*.

The other items in the SIMILARITY semantic type do not pattern in this way. *Differently* simply functions as manner adverb in position O. *Separately* and *independently* function as manner adverbs in positions V and O. Adjectives *like* and *unlike* do not form adverbs since in modern English there already exist forms *likely* and *unlikely* with quite different meanings.

Set (5) involves adverbs derived from adjectives of the SPEED semantic type—*slowly*, *quickly*, *rapidly*, *speedily* and also *fast* (where adjective and adverb have the same form). These may occur in the three sentential and two manner positions. Of all the adverbs in Table 12.7, these pose the most difficulty for perceiving distinct sentential and manner function senses. It seems that the manner positions are used to describe the speed of a volitional action; for example, *She has been* [(*slowly*) *writing her memoirs* (*slowly*)]. And the sentential positions may be preferred to describe the speed at which something happens; for example, (*Slowly*) *she has* (*slowly*) *been gaining in confidence* (*slowly*). These adverbs are unlikely to occur with LIKING verbs; and they do not easily modify adjectives or adverbs.

## 12.8. Adverbs modifying adjectives and adverbs

As mentioned before, the primary function of some adverbs is to modify an adjective, or an adverb derived from it. This applies to *very, terribly, awfully*, etc., which are set (2) in Table 12.6 and row (m) in Table 12.3. Beyond this, we find:

**(i)** All monomorphemic adverbs may modify adjectives and adverbs except for *alone* and *also* (Tables 12.3 and 12.4), *indeed* and *of course* (Table 12.4), and time adverbs *just, again, once, soon, later, then, today, tomorrow, yesterday*, etc. (Table 12.5).

**(ii)** Of the adverbs derived by the addition of *-ly*, we find:

- Those that can easily modify adjectives: adverbs derived from adjectives in types PHYSICAL PROPERTY, COLOUR and VALUE, excluding *well* and *badly* (see Table 12.6), HUMAN PROPENSITY and SIMILARITY (Table 12.7), and QUALIFICATION and VOLITION (Tables 12.4 and 12.7); those ending in *-ally* (Table 12.4); those ending in *-fully*, whether derived from a verb (Table 12.4) or a noun (Table 12.6); *slightly, somewhat, especially, fairly* (Table 12.6); and *really, truly* (Tables 12.3 and 12.7).
- Those that can scarcely or never modify an adjective: *badly, well*, those based on DIMENSION and DIFFICULTY adjectives, plus *drastically, expertly* (Table 12.6); those derived from SPEED adjectives (Table 12.7), *certainly* (Table 12.4), and time adverbs such as *weekly* (Table 12.5).

In addition, no phrasal or clausal adverb, nor any place adverb, may modify an adjective.

There are a few forms which just modify an adjective (or an adverb). They are thus not classified as adverbs, according to the definition followed here—a word which may occur in sentential or in manner function or both. These include:

- *Extremely*; for example, *extremely clever(ly)*. Note that *extremely* would be a marginal member of set (2) in Table 12.6.
- *Far*, used only with *too* (from set (2) of Table 12.4) and with comparatives (see §12.9.1); for example, *far too long* and *far more attractive*. *Far* may be repeated, as in *far, far, far too long*.
- *Newly*, derived from the AGE adjective *new*, has a restricted function, almost exclusively (or exclusively) with participles—for example, *a newly hatched chicken* and *a newly discovered river*—not with monomorphemic adjectives. (These follow a pattern similar to that in Table 12.2 of §12.2.1—*new discovery* and *newly discovered, new hatching* and *newly hatched*.)

*However* is a fascinating word, with a wide range of meaning. It is historically based on the interrogative *how* and can have a similar meaning, as in *Do it how(ever) you want!* It can occur with *much* to indicate an indefinite meaning, as in *However much it costs, I'll buy it*. It may function as a clause linker, as in *He is attractive, however he doesn't have a cent to his name*. And it may modify an adjective in a two-clause construction such as *However big yours is, I'll bet mine is bigger*. The first clause here has the structure *however*-plus-adjective (as copula complement), copula subject, copula verb. A similar use of *however*, this time modifying an adverb, is *However strongly you pull, you'll never dislodge it*. In this function, *however* can modify virtually any adjective or derived adverb.

Adjectives which may modify adverbs are a subset of those which may modify adjectives. An indication of the possibilities is set out in the tables, although judgements here are—even more than usual—of a 'more/less' rather than a 'yes/no' nature.

The most common adverb-modifying adverbs are the monomorphemic items and *kind-of*, as in *almost stupidly*, *rather cleverly*, *kind-of badly*, *very angrily*. Also those adverbs ending in *-ly* which do not in the modern language directly relate to an adjective. They include those in set (2) of Table 12.6—for example, *terribly easily*, *awfully strongly*—those in row (g) of Table 12.3—as in *simply stupidly*, *mostly sensibly*—and *really*, *truly*, *hardly*, *fully*, *slightly*, *especially*, *fairly*. Some adverbs derived from VALUE adjectives may also modify other adverbs; for example, *atrociously jealously*.

Generally, an adverb derived from an adjective by adding *-ly* is unlikely to modify another adverb derived from an adjective by adding *-ly*, where in each instance adverb and adjective have the same basic meaning. Alongside *sweetly cool*, *appropriately angry* and *obviously proud* one would be unlikely to hear *sweetly coolly*, *appropriately angrily* or *obviously proudly*. It seems that there is a preference for avoiding a sequence of adverbs ending in *-ly*, if the *-ly* is morphologically segmentable.

## 12.9. Other properties

### 12.9.1. Comparatives

Forming comparatives is a property of adjectives which they may pass on to adverbs derived from them. Basically, adverbs have a comparative form if:

(i)    They are derived from an adjective by the addition of -*ly*, with no significant change of meaning being involved.
(ii)   They are used in manner function, generally in position O.

Comparatives are thus formed from adjectives in sets (4)–(9) of Table 12.6 (those that occur in manner but not in sentential function), and in sets (2)–(3) and (5) of Table 12.7 (those that occur in both manner and sentential function). *Similarly*, in set (4) of Table 12.7, is an exception; because of its meaning, this is unlikely to be used in a comparative. Note that there are no comparatives of monomorphemic adverbs (such as *rather*, *quite*) nor of forms ending in -*ly* where there is a significant meaning difference from the corresponding adjective (such as *really*, *slightly*).

There are just a few adverbs (ending in -*ly*) that generally occur only in sentential function, which may form comparatives. The comparative is then used in manner function, generally in position O. This applies to *usually*, *normally*, *obviously* and *deliberately*, from sets (3)–(4) of Table 12.4, and to *permanently* from set (6) of Table 12.5: for example, *They flirted <u>more obviously</u> on the second occasion*. It also applies to the monomorphemic time adverb *often*, also in set (6) of Table 12.5: for example, *He now arrives late <u>more often</u> (than he did before)*; and also the idiomatic adverb *more often than not*. And it applies to *soon* and *later* in (10) of Table 12.5.

We saw in §3.2.1 how some adjectives form the comparative by adding -*er*, some by preposing *more*, and some by either means. However, English does not permit a sequence of -*er* plus -*ly*, and as a consequence the regular comparative of adverbs always uses *more*. Alongside *ruder* we get *more rudely*, alongside *more careful* there is *more carefully*, and corresponding to both *cleverer* and *more clever* there is just *more cleverly*.

There are just a few exceptions:

* *Fast, hard, early* and *late* have the same form for adjective and adverb, and the comparatives *faster, harder, earlier* and *later* also function as adjective and as adverb; for example, *A faster car goes <u>faster</u> (than a slower one)*.
* The adjectives *quick, slow* and *long* form regular comparatives, *quicker, slower* and *longer*. However, there are alternative forms for the corresponding adverbs—*quick* or *quickly*, *slow* or *slowly*, and *long* or *lengthily*. Each of these adverbs has its own comparative— one can say *quicker* or *more quickly*, *slower* or *more slowly*, and *longer* or *more lengthily*.
* And for *good* and *bad* we have suppletive forms:

| | PLAIN | COMPARATIVE | SUPERLATIVE |
|---|---|---|---|
| ADJECTIVE | *good* ⎱ | | |
| ADVERB | *well* ⎰ | *better* | *best* |
| ADJECTIVE | *bad* ⎱ | | |
| ADVERB | *badly* ⎰ | *worse* | *worst* |

One interesting property of comparatives is the behaviour of forms like *very (much)*, *terribly (much)* and *awfully (much)* from row (m) of Table 12.3 and set (2) of Table 12.6. We can recall that their forms and functions are as follows (illustrating here for *very (much)*):

The form *very much* is used
—when modifying an NP, as in *She is very much a professor*
—when in manner function, as in *She very much likes it* or *She likes it very much*
Form *very* is used
—when modifying an adjective, as in *I saw a very strange sight*
—when modifying an adverb, such as *He behaved very strangely*

Now when *very (much)* modifies a comparative adjective or a comparative adverb, both forms—*very* and *very much*—can be used, as in:

(63a)  *Mary is much more beautiful (than Jane)*
(63b)  *Mary is very much more beautiful (than Jane)*
(64a)  *Jane did it much more cleverly (than Mary)*
(64b)  *Jane did it very much more cleverly (than Mary)*

*Very much* (or *terribly much*, *awfully much*, etc.) implies a higher degree of the quality than plain *much*.

With a verb such as *like*, one can use *very much* but not *much* as manner modifier (\**She much likes it* and \**She likes it much* are not acceptable). However, with *prefer* both *much* and *very much* are possible, as in:

(65a)  *I much prefer Bach (to Beethoven)*
(65b)  *I very much prefer Bach (to Beethoven)*

This shows that the verb *prefer* has an inherently comparative meaning.

An adjective which forms a comparative with *-er* or *more* forms a superlative by suffixing *-est* or preposing *most*. Basically, this carries over into adverbs (employing *most*), although the superlative of an adverb is not very common. It may be most frequent with adverbs from set (3) of Table 12.7: for example, *Most sensibly, she dressed up warmly in the winter cold* and *It is most appropriately regarded as a nonce form*. One can also say *She did it best/very cleverely/most cleverly*.

## 12.9.2. An adverb as a complete utterance

Most adverbs can make up a complete utterance, either in reply to a question or in response to a statement. The main adverbs which are unlikely to have this function are:

- from Table 12.4—*only, even, just* (non-time sense), *also, too, simply*, etc.

Discourse contexts in which an adverb may make up a full reply or response include:

**(a)**   An answer to a *wh-* question with

*where* or *in which direction*, etc.—spatial adverbs; for example, *'Where is he?'* *'Downstairs.'*

*when* or *for how long*, etc.—all phrasal and clausal time adverbs and most mono-morphemic time adverbs (in Table 12.5); for example, *'When will it be ready?'* *'Presently.'*

*how*—adverbs derived from adjectives, including sets (4)–(6) in Table 12.4, sets (4)–(9) in Table 12.6, and sets (2)–(5) in Table 12.7; for example, *'How did he react?'* *'Jealously.'*

*how much*—set (2) in Table 12.6; for example, *'How much do you like him?' 'Awfully much.'*

**(b)**   An answer to a polar question can be an adverb which here functions as an interjection; for example, *'Has he finished it?' 'Almost'*, and *'Is she the best candidate?' 'Obviously.'* These include:

from Table 12.4, set (1): *almost, hardly*
    set (2): *indeed, of course*
    set (3): *definitely, usually, obviously*, etc.
from Table 12.6, set (1): *rather, quite, a-bit, kind-of, absolutely*
    set (3): *slightly, somewhat*

**(c)**   A questioning response to a statement; for example, *'Mary did it.' 'Really?'* and *'John has finished it.' 'Already?'* These include:

from set (1) of Table 12.4: *alone?*
from Table 12.5: *always?, still?, already?, again?* (and perhaps others)
from set (1) of Table 12.7: *really? truly?*

## 12.10. Combinations of adverbs

A clause can include a wide range of adverbs, as illustrated in the title of this chapter:

(66)  *Yesterday, [even the rather clever bishops] could not very easily have sensibly organised [a moderately unusual exorcism] here*

Besides the negator *not* (discussed in §12.11), this sentence features eight adverbs:

- *Yesterday*, a sentential time adverb in initial position, I
- *Even*, modifying the following NP, *the rather clever bishops*
- *Rather*, modifying adjective *clever*
- *Very*, modifying adverb *easily*
- *Very easily*, sentential adverb in position A, following the first word (*could*) of the auxiliary (*could have*)
- *Sensibly*, manner adverb in position V, immediately preceding the verb *organised*
- *Moderately*, modifying adjective *unusual*
- *Here*, sentential spatial adverb, in final position, F

We can now look, in turn, at the overall possibilities for an adverb modifying an adverb, and for the inclusion of more than one adverb in a clause. Firstly, we consider which adverbs may modify an adverb which is (a) modifying an NP; or (b) in some other function. Secondly, we examine the multitudinous possibilities for combination of adverbs in sentential function.

**(a)**  Modifying an NP

Adverbs following an NP (*alone, only, even*) may not receive any modification. For those that precede, it is generally possible for them to be modified by *really* or *truly*, as in *She's going to be [truly kind-of an intermediate boss]* and *He has been [really very much the person in charge]*.

**(b)**  In another function

The right-hand columns of Tables 12.4–7 indicated whether a given adverb may modify an adjective or an adverb. We can now look at things the other way round, and investigate which adverbs may be modified by another adverb.

First, it is generally not possible for time and spatial adverbs to be modified by a further adverb, although there is a modifier *right* used with some of these items; for example, *right there, right down, right now*. And a small number of single-word time adverbs may be modified by *rather, truly, very, terribly*, etc.; for example, *very recently, terribly often, rather soon*.

Monomorphemic adverbs, and those ending in *-ly* but with a different meaning from the corresponding adjective, may be modified by *really* or *truly* (for example, *really rather jealously*). This covers set (1) in Table 12.4 and sets (1)–(3) in Table 12.6. Adverbs formed from an adjective by the addition of *-ly*, where the meaning is preserved, have wider possibilities. This covers sets (3)–(6) in Table 12.4, sets (4)–(8) in Table 12.6, and sets (2)–(5) in Table 12.7. They may be pre-modified by:

- Adverbs such as *slightly* and *somewhat*, from set (3) of Table 12.6; for example, *somewhat easily, slightly angrily*.
- Adverbs such as *rather, quite, kind-of* from set (1) of Table 12.6; for example, *rather cleverly, quite narrowly, kind-of obviously, quite poetically*. There is an exception; because of its meaning, *similarly*—set (4) of Table 12.7—can scarcely be modified by these adverbs.
- *Very, terribly, awfully*, and other adverbs from set (2) of Table 12.6; for example, *awfully carefully, terribly slowly*. The exception here is that adverbs ending in *-ally*, in set (5) of Table 12.4 (which are formed on derived adjectives), may not easily be modified by *very, terribly, awfully*, etc.

Adverbs such as *very* and *terribly* may themselves by modified by some items from set (1) of Table 12.4, such as *just, only* and *even*; for example, *only very rarely, just terribly cleverly*. *Really* and *truly* may modify other adverbs, and they may even modify an adverb which is modifying a second adverb which is modifying a third adverb, as in *She behaved really rather stupidly jealously*. No other adverbs may modify *really* or *truly*.

An adverb in manner or sentential function may be modified in the ways just outlined. We now examine how a clause may include more than one adverb in manner and/or in sentential function.

As pointed out in §12.6, there can be only one manner adverb in a clause. Two positions are available for a manner adverb—V, immediately before the verb, and O, following verb plus object, etc.—but only one of these may be filled. In contrast, a clause can include a number of sentential adverbs;

these may all be in position A (following the first word of the auxiliary, or preceding a non-copula verb but following the copula when there is no auxiliary), or all in position F (clause-final), or distributed between positions I (clause-initial), A and F.

There can be one manner adverb and one or more sentential adverbs. When there is no auxiliary, positions A (for sentential adverbs) and V (for manner adverbs) will coincide. And positions O (for manner adverbs) and F (for sentential adverbs) will often coincide. The general rule is that a manner adverb should occur nearer to the verb than a sentential adverb. For example, one can say *He again* (A) [*warmly* (V) *recommended her*] or *He* [*recommended her warmly* (O)] *again* (F); the order of adverbs cannot be reversed in these examples.

Adverbs in Table 12.7 can occur in manner or in sentential function. We may have two of these in a clause, but only one can be in manner function, the other taking on sentential function: for example, *He had stupidly* (A) *been* [*slowly* (V) *embezzling the funds*].

When a clause includes more than one sentential adverb, there is generally a preferred order of occurrence. For example, *also* will most often precede *deliberately*. They can both occur in position A, or in I  A, or A  F, or I  F, as in:

**(67a)**   *He had also* (A) *deliberately* (A) *been taking the money*
**(67b)**   *Also* (I) *he had deliberately* (A) *been taking the money*
**(67c)**   *He had also* (A) *been taking the money deliberately* (F)
**(67d)**   *Also* (I) *he had been taking the money deliberately* (F)

However, there can be complications. A clause may involve *really* and *deliberately* as sentential adverbs in positions I  A or A  F or I  F, as in:

**(68a)**   *Really* (I) *he had deliberately* (A) *been taking the money*
**(68b)**   *He had really* (A) *been taking the money deliberately* (F)
**(68c)**   *Really* (I) *he had been taking the money deliberately* (F)

One can place *really* and *deliberately* after the first word of the auxiliary, as in:

**(69)**   *He had* [*really deliberately* (A)] *been taking the money*

However, since *really*—unlike *also*—may modify an adverb, (69) is taken to include a complex sentential adverb *really deliberately*, rather than two independent sentential adverbs, *really* and *deliberately*. Note that the wide possibilities illustrated by (68a–c) do provide ample opportunity for including *really* and *deliberately* as distinct sentential adverbs.

In essence, there can be a sequence of sentential adverbs at position A. Or the first of them may be put into position I and the final one (or perhaps more than one) into position F. It is not normally possible to have more than one in position I, and the possibilities for position F are more limited than those for position A. Thus, for a sequence such as *also possibly deliberately*, the possibilities are A A A, or I A A, or A A F, or I A F.

Sequencing preferences may be contravened by restriction on the occurrence of a particular sentential adverb. In §12.1, a sequence of three sentential adverbs in slot A was illustrated by:

(3)   She had *also* (A) *deliberately* (A) *just* (A) been arranging the beautiful flowers

However, although *also* and *deliberately* can occur in all three positions (A, I and F), *just* (here the non-time adverb) is confined to position A. We may thus get:

(3a)   *Also* (I) she had *deliberately* (A) *just* (A) been arranging the beautiful flowers
(3b)   *Also* (I), she had *just* (A) been arranging the beautiful flowers *deliberately* (F)
(3c)   She had *also* (A) *just* (A) been arranging the beautiful flowers *deliberately* (F)

Since *just* may not go into position F, *deliberately* does so in (3b-c), even though this reverses the preferred order at position A. (If we were to encounter *just deliberately* at position A, this would probably be taken to be one complex sentential adverb, with *just* modifying *deliberately*, rather than two distinct sentential adverbs.)

There are many adverbs which can occur in sentential function and there are very many combinations of them. Each adverb sequence has its own personality, as it were, so that no absolute algorithm can be provided for preferred sequencing. However, a general template may be perceived, which accounts for most ordering preferences within A position (or across I, A and F positions). The canonical ordering is as follows:

   I. Phrasal adverbs—such as *of course, once again, as usual*—generally come first; and also *indeed* which, like the phrasal adverbs, demands comma intonation. For example, *John was, of course* (I), *always* (V) *almost* (VII) *top of the class*, and *Mary's work had, indeed* (I), *hardly* (VII) *been noticed*.
  II. *Also*, from row (f) of Table 12.3 and set (l) of Table 12.4; see (67) and (3). (But note that there are instances where *also* comes later in sequence, at VI.)
 III. *Really* and *truly*, set (1) of Table 12.7. For example, *She also* (II) *really* (III) *again* (V) *prevaricated*.

IV. Adverbs derived from adjectives by *-ly*, with meaning retained in set (3) of Table 12.4 and sets (2)–(5) of Table 12.7. For example, *He* <u>*also*</u> (II) *stupidly* (IV) <u>*still*</u> (V) *retained his stock options*.

V. Those time adverbs which may appear in position A—sets (4)–(11) in Table 12.5. For example, *He* <u>*cleverly*</u> (IV) <u>*again*</u> (V) <u>*deliberately*</u> (VI) *avoided answering the question*.

VI. *Deliberately*, and adverbs ending in *-ally* or *-fully*, sets (4)–(6) of Table 12.4. For example, *He* <u>*stupidly*</u> (IV) <u>*later*</u> (V) <u>*accidentally*</u> (VI) *extinguished the flame*, and *The land claim* <u>*correctly*</u> (IV) <u>*now*</u> (V) <u>*geographically*</u> (VI) <u>*almost*</u> (VII) *extends to the state border*.

VII. Monomorphemic adverbs from rows (b)–(e) and (g) of Table 12.3—and set (1) of Table 12.4—such as *only, even, just, almost, hardly, simply*, etc. For example, *They* <u>*also*</u> (II) <u>*now*</u> (V) <u>*simply*</u> (VII) *disregarded the instructions*.

It was noted under (d) in §12.4 that there are two homonymous adverbs *just*. These feature at different places in the preferred ordering. The time adverb *just* 'happened a few moments ago' is in V; for example, *He* <u>*just*</u> (V) <u>*deliberately*</u> (VI) *erased it from the board*. The non-time adverb *just* 'this and nothing more' is in VII; for example, *He* <u>*deliberately*</u> (VI) <u>*just*</u> (VII) *outlined the main points* (but refused to go into any detail).

There are also a number of adverb combinations, each of which effectively functions as a single complex adverb. These include *only just, just about, just now, only now, even now* and *once again*.

It was mentioned in §12.5.2 that spatial adverbs generally do not occur in A position. At the end of a clause we may get one (sometimes more) non-time non-spatial sentential adverbs and/or a sequence of time adverbs and/or a sequence of spatial adverbs. As stated in §12.5.2, time and spatial adverbs in F position may occur in either order, so long as they are not intermingled. And, as noted in the discussion of (27), in §12.3.2, a non-time non-spatial adverb—such as *sensibly*—may occur in position F, before or after time adverbs and before or after spatial adverbs; its semantic scope is everything that precedes in the clause.

It must once more be emphasised that the adverb orderings just described are simply preferences. There can be deviations from the canonical pattern in particular pragmatic and discourse circumstances, and in view of the relation between meanings of the adverbs involved.

## 12.11. Negation

The negator *not* in English is very like a multi-functional adverb in some respects, while different in others. We can first examine its main functions.

### 12.11.1. Sentential and manner-type negation

The only negator found in all languages is that with scope over a whole sentence. Although English has many other negator functions, the sentential one is the most common. This is similar to a sentential adverb save that it must appear in a modified A position, never in I or F.

The positioning in a main clause of sentential *not*—which is typically reduced to enclitic /=nt/ or even just /=n/ (see §1.5)—is:

- after the first word of the auxiliary if there is one, whether or not there is a copula, as in (70a–b);
- if there is no auxiliary and the verb is the copula *be*, after the copula, as in (70c);
- if there is no auxiliary and the verb is not a copula, then a dummy element *do* (a surrogate auxiliary) must be included, and *not* follows this, as in (70d).

(**70a**)   *John mightn't have been in love*
(**70b**)   *John mightn't have laughed*
(**70c**)   *John wasn't in love*
(**70d**)   *John didn't laugh*

Comparing these with (11a–d), the difference is that when there is no auxiliary, a sentential adverb simply precedes a non-copula verb (for example, *He <u>now</u> hopes to stand for Parliament*) whereas the negator requires *do* (for example, *He doesn't hope to stand for Parliament*). Tense goes onto *do*, as it goes onto the first word of an auxiliary.

The possessive verb *have* behaves in an interesting way; it can be followed by *not*, like the copula *be*, or it can be preceded by *do* plus *not*, like a non-copula verb. Thus, corresponding to *She has courage/a new car/a sore foot*, we can have—with no significant difference in meaning—either of:

(**71a**)   *She doesn't have courage/a new car/a sore foot*
(**71b**)   *She hasn't courage/a new car/a sore foot*

A negative imperative always requires *do*, even if there is a copula or auxiliary; for example, *Don't be silly!* and *Don't have drunk all the wine before the main course arrives!*

There is a historical reason for the *do*-requirement on the negator. In Middle English, *not* would generally follow a non-copula verb, as in *I say not*. The Elizabethans used *do* a good deal, for all sorts of purposes, and the negator naturally followed it, as in *I did not say*. Gradually, *do* became restricted to marking emphasis (*I did say that*) and to use in polar questions (*Did he say that?*). It was also retained in sentential negation with a non-copula verb when there was no auxiliary (see Jespersen 1917/1933: 9–10).

The negator *not* can also be used in a manner-type function, modifying verb, plus object (if there is one) and sometimes other following constituents. The negator must be in position V, immediately preceding the verb (never in position O). Furthermore, if there is no auxiliary or copula then a preceding *do* must be included, just as with sentential negation.

The contrast between sentential negation (modified A position) and manner-type negation (V position) can be seen in (72a–b).

(72a)   *The honest cricket captain might not* (A) *have won this time* (but he always tries to win)

(72b)   *The crooked cricket captain might have* [*not* (V) *won*] *this time* (on purpose, since the bookmakers paid him to lose)

When in sentential function, *not* can almost always reduce to *n't*, an enclitic to the preceding auxiliary or copula or *have* or *do*; this is shown in (70a–d) and (71a–b). And in (72a) *might not* may be reduced to *mightn't*. In contrast, a manner-type *not* will not normally be reduced after an auxiliary. For example, *have not* in (72b) may not be reduced to *haven't*; contrast this with *have not* alternating with *haven't* in *I have not seen him/I haven't seen him*.

As mentioned at the end of §12.3.1, if *n't* is cliticised to the preceding item, it is fronted with it in a question, as in *Hasn't he come?*, *Didn't he come?* However, when the full form *not* is used, this is retained after the subject, so that one says *Has he not come?*, *Did he not come?* (rather than \**Has not he come?*, \**Did not he come?*).

When there is a single-word auxiliary or no auxiliary at all, A and V functions coincide, as in:

(73a)   *The honest cricket captain did not* (A) *win yesterday*

(73b)   *The crooked cricket captain did* [*not* (V) *win*] *yesterday*

The sequence *did* (A) *not* in (73a) may be freely reduced to *didn't*. In (73b) the manner-type function of *not* may be made clear by pronouncing *not win* as if it were a compound with a single stress: *The crooked captain did 'not-win yesterday*. In this circumstance, *did* and *not* will not be reduced to *didn't*. If, however, there is some other clue to the manner-type function of *not*—for example, if *on purpose* were added—then *did not* in (73b) could well be reduced to *didn't*.

A further pair of examples contrasting the two functions of *not* is:

**(74a)**   *John could not* (A) *have written the review* (he doesn't have the competence to have done so)

**(74b)**   *John could have* [*not* (V) *written the review*] (if he didn't wish to risk offending a friend, John had the option of declining the offer to review the friend's book)

The existence of these two distinct functions of *not* is confirmed by their co-occurrence in a single clause, such as:

**(75)**   *I didn't* (A) *dare not* (V) *buy the diamond ring*

With respect to (75), my wife might have told me to buy a diamond ring for her. I didn't want to since I know we can't really afford it, but I'm so scared of my wife that I had not the courage to disobey her.

Note that if two *not*'s are included, one in sentential and one in manner-type function—as in (75)—only the first *not* requires a preceding auxiliary or *do*.

The positioning of the negator with respect to an adverb can also indicate its function. Compare the placements of *not* and of sentential adverb *also* in:

**(76a)**   *John had not* (A) *also* (A) *resigned*

**(76b)**   *John had also* (A) [*not* (V) *resigned*]

Sentence (76a) implies that many people had resigned but that John didn't; he was unusual in not having resigned. In contrast, (76b) implies that quite a few people didn't resign, and John joined this group.

Another illustration involves *correctly*, which can have manner or sentential function:

**(77a)**   *He didn't* (A) [*correctly* (V) *position it*] (he should have positioned it properly and didn't)

**(77b)**   *He correctly* (A) [*didn't* (V) *position it*] (what he had been told to do was not position it, and he obeyed this instruction)

An alternative to (77a) is *He didn't* (A) [*position it correctly* (O)].

Often, the sentential and manner-type functions of *not* have different tense-aspect expectations. Compare:

**(78a)**   *John did not* (A) *accept the job* (he declined it)
**(78b)**   *John has* [*not* (V) *accepted the job*] (he's still thinking about it)

That is, past tense in (78a) refers to something which has definitely happened, whereas the *have* form in (78b) refers to a decision which is still pending. In (78b) *not* might be augmented by *yet*, creating the complex negator *not yet*— *John has not yet accepted the job* or *John has not accepted the job yet*.

When the negator and an adverb occur together, in the same functional slot, they may potentially occur in either order; *not* has scope over all that follows. Compare—with *easily* and *not* both in A position—*He could not easily have done it* (it would have been too difficult for him) and *He could easily not have done it* (he had the option to neglect doing it).

## 12.11.2. Negative attraction

The preferred position for the negator *not* is after the first word of the auxiliary or after a copula, in a main clause. Under various circumstances, a negator that should properly be placed elsewhere is attracted into this position.

Firstly, note that what is here called sentential negation can apply either to a main clause, as in (79), or to a complement clause, as in (80).

**(79)**   *I didn't say* [*that he lied*] (I said nothing)
**(80)**   *I said* [*that he didn't lie*] (I said that he told the truth)

Here the difference in meaning is significant, and the negator *n't* is likely to be maintained in its proper place. But consider:

**(81)**   *I don't think* [*that he came*] (I don't know what he did)
**(82)**   *I think* [*that he didn't come*] (I think that he stayed away)

The sentiment expressed in (81) is not likely to be often expressed, whereas that in (82) is much used. As Jespersen (1909–49, pt.V: 444) mentions, people often say *I don't think that he came* when they actually mean (82), that he stayed away. This can be accounted for by attraction of *n't* from the complement clause into the preferred position, after the first word of the auxiliary in the main clause. As another example, Jespersen (1940–49, pt.V: 440) points out that a sentence such as *We aren't here to talk nonsense but to act* is used when *We are here [not to talk nonsense but to act]* is intended; the *not* has once more been attracted into the preferred position.

One reads in prescriptive works that two negatives in a clause should generally be interpreted as indicating a positive; that is, for example, *I couldn't do nothing about it* should be taken to have the same meaning as *I could do something about it*. However, the people who insist on this rule would scarcely be likely to use a repeated negative of this kind. Other people often do use a double negative of this type, and then intend it to emphasise the negation; *I couldn't do nothing about it* means something like *I really could do nothing about it*. Double (or triple) realisation of a single negation most often includes *not* in the preferred position, as well as modifying a constituent; for example, *You'd never heard nothing*, and *I don't want nobody to get hurt*. This could be described as the negation on a constituent being also copied into the preferred position. (It is, of course, possible to have two independent negations in a clause, as shown in (75).)

## 12.11.3. Constituent negation

Examples (37)–(38) in §12.4 illustrate the two ways in which an adverb may modify an NP which follows the verb. It can either immediately precede the NP (as in *Children may play [only soccer] on the back lawn*) or occur in position A, with the appropriate NP bearing stress (as in *Children may only play 'soccer on the back lawn*).

Potentially the same possibilities are available for the negation of an NP. However the 'sentential *not* plus stress on the NP' alternative is preferred. Thus:

(83a)   *Children may not* (A) *play 'soccer on the back lawn* (but they may play cricket there)

(83b)   *Children may not* (A) *play soccer on the 'back lawn* (but they may play it on the front lawn)

In fact, one cannot say *\*Children may play [not soccer] on the back lawn* or *\*Children may play soccer [not on the back lawn]*.

It was pointed out in §12.4 that an adverb in position A may modify a following NP but not a preceding one; that is, not one in subject position. Similar remarks apply for the negator. As a consequence, we can get a subject NP modified by *not*, as in:

**(84)**   [*Not a guest*] *arrived before nine o'clock* (although they were all invited for eight-thirty)

The language must allow *not* to directly modify the subject NP in (84), since if *not* is included in position A and the subject NP is stressed, we get a sentence with an entirely different meaning:

**(85)**   [*'A guest*] *didn't* (A) *arrive before nine o'clock*

Sentence (84) implies that all the guests arrived after nine o'clock whereas (85) states that only one did.

An adverb... Although a post-verbal NP may not be simply modified by *not*, it can involve two components, one of which is modified by *not*. For example:

**(86a)**   *Children may play* [*not soccer but cricket*] *on the back lawn*
**(86b)**   *Children may play soccer* [*not on the back lawn but on the front lawn*]

It is possible to have a complex NP in which both parts are negated, as in:

**(87a)**   *Children may play* [*neither soccer nor cricket*] *on the back lawn*

In this instance there is an alternative, with the same meaning, where the negator is in position A:

**(87b)**   *Children may not* (A) *play* [*either soccer or cricket*] *on the back lawn*

We have [*neither* NP *nor* NP] in (87a) and *not* (A) [*either* NP *or* NP] in (87b), and similarly *Children may play soccer* [*neither on the back lawn nor on the front lawn*] or *Children may not* (A) *play soccer* [*either on the back lawn or on the front lawn*].

An adjective or a manner adverb may also be negated, and similar remarks apply as for NP negation in (83)–(87). To negate a manner adverb, *not* may be placed in position A with the adverb (in position O) being stressed, as in:

**(88)**   *He didn't* (A) *write the report* '<u>carefully</u>

It is not acceptable to say *\*He wrote the report not <u>carefully</u>*. However, one can say:

**(89)**   *He wrote the report* [*not <u>carefully</u> but <u>sloppily</u>*]

And one can say either *He wrote the report* [*neither <u>carefully</u> nor <u>cleverly</u>*] (with the negator on both parts of the complex adverb) or *He didn't write the report* [*either <u>carefully</u> or <u>cleverly</u>*] (with the negator in position A).

Similar remarks apply for adjectives in copula complement function. Alongside *He might not* (A) *have been 'generous*, one cannot normally say \**He might have been* [*not generous*], although it is possible to say either *He might have been* [*not generous to some people but generous to others*]. And *He is* [*neither generous nor kind*] is an alternative to *He is not* (A) [*either generous or kind*].

It will be seen that *neither* and *nor* are blends of *not* plus *either* and *not* plus *or*. It is when such a blend exists that we may negate an NP (or an adverb or adjective) either by sentential *not* in position A—with the appropriate constituent often being stressed—or by negating the constituent itself. This also applies for forms like *nobody* and *nowhere*. Compare these positive sentences, labelled (p), with their two possible negations, labelled (n).

**(90p)**   *It is somewhere to be found*
**(90n)**   *It isn't anywhere to be found* or *It is nowhere to be found*
**(91p)**   *I saw somebody*
**(91n)**   *I didn't see anybody* or *I saw nobody*

There is an interesting alternation between *some* in positive and *any* in the corresponding negative clauses, as illustrated in (90)–(91). However, it should be noted that there are two items *some*, with rather different meanings:

* *some₁* is a qualifier (like *all*) and refers to a selection of several items from a group, as in *some₁* (*of the*) *boys*; this belongs in slot (b) of NP structure in §2.3
* *some₂* has an adjective-like function (like numbers), referring to an unspecified but definite individual, as in *some₂ boy* or *some₂ boys*; this belongs in slot (d) of NP structure in §2.3

Consider a positive sentence in which *some₁* occurs in a post-verbal NP:

**(92p)**   *He might have seen some₁ of the boys* (that is, just a few of them)

There are two ways of negating this:

**(92n-s)**   *He might not* (A) *have seen any of the boys* (he saw not a single one of them)
**(92n-m)**   *He might have* [*not* (V) *seen some₁ of the boys*] (he saw almost all of them but may have missed a few)

In (92n-s) *not* is used as a sentential negator and *some*$_1$ is here replaced by *any*. In (92n-m), *not* is in manner-type function and here *some*$_1$ is retained, rather than being replaced by *any*. The contrasting functions of *not* in these two sentences can be seen from their placements—position A, after the first word of the auxiliary, in (92n-s), and position V, immediately before the verb, in (92n-m). Note that if there were no auxiliary, the sentences would reduce to *He didn't see any of the boys* and *He didn't see some*$_1$*of the boys* respectively, now being distinguished only by *any* and *some*$_1$. However, when a multi-word auxiliary is included, the position of *not* indicates its distinct functions in the two sentences.

Now consider a positive sentence with *some*$_2$:

(**93p**)  *He might have seen some*$_2$ *boys*

There is only one way of negating this, with *not* in sentential function and position A:

(**93n-s**)  *He might not have seen any boys*

Note that *\*He might have [not seen some*$_2$ *boys]*, with *not* in manner-type function and V position, is not acceptable.

We have seen that *any* is here the automatic alternant of *some* (of *some*$_1$ or of *some*$_2$) under sentential negation, but never under manner-type negation. It is, however, possible to include *any* in a positive sentence. There are, in fact, two distinct forms *any*:

- *any*$_1$, indicates an open possibility of choice from a group, as in *I can climb (absolutely) any tree in the garden*; this belongs in slot (b) of NP structure in §2.3
- *any*$_2$, the automatic alternant of *some* under sentential negation; this belongs in slot (d) of NP structure in §2.3

Suppose people are being asked about their colour recognition. It has been observed that Mary is pretty good at this task. She is asked:

(**94**)  *Can you distinguish (absolutely) any*$_1$*colours?*

Mary might reply with a negative sentence:

(**95**)  *No, I can't distinguish (absolutely) any*$_1$*colours (only the great majority of them)*

Suppose that John is known to have great difficulty in colour discrimination. The investigators wonder whether he might be completely colour blind and enquire:

**(96)**   *Can you distinguish some$_2$ colours?*

The reply might be in the negative:

**(97)**   *No, I can't distinguish any$_2$ colours (at all)*

Both (95) and (97) can be just *No, I can't distinguish any colours*, which is ambiguous between the *any$_1$* and *any$_2$* readings. The difference can be brought out by additions to the basic sentence. *Absolutely* is virtually always possible with *any$_1$*—as in (94)–(95)—but not with *any$_2$*. And *at all* may generally be added after an NP with *any$_2$*—as in (97) and also (90n), (91n), (92n-s) and (93n-s)—but not after an NP with *any$_1$*.

The composite form *anything* has special properties. To appreciate this it is useful first to examine positive and negative sentences with *some/any$_2$* and with *any$_1$*, where the head of object NP is *task* or *tasks*.

**(98p)**   *He does some$_1$ tasks (but not all)*
**(98n-s)**   *He doesn't (A) do any$_2$ tasks (at all)*
**(99p)**   *He does (absolutely) any$_1$ task (whatever he is asked to do)*
**(99n-s)**   *He does not (A) do (absolutely) any$_1$ task (he's selective about which ones he does)*

We can substitute *thing* for *task*, and then get:

**(100p)**   *He does some$_1$ things (but not all)*
**(100n-s)**   *He doesn't (A) do any$_2$ thing (at all)*
**(101p)**   *He does (absolutely) any$_1$ thing (whatever he is asked to do)*
**(101n-s)**   *He does not (A) do (absolutely) any$_1$ thing (he's selective about which things he does)*

When the bits in parentheses are omitted, (98n-s) and (99n-s) are distinguished by *any$_2$ tasks* in the first and *any$_1$ task* in the second. But when the bits in parentheses are omitted from (100n-s) and (101n-s), the sentences are identical. For (100n-s) we would expect *He doesn't do any$_2$ things (at all)*. However, this sounds distinctly odd; speakers naturally use *anything* (rather than *any things*) here. As a result, *He doesn't do anything* is ambiguous between the *any$_2$* sense (he does nothing at all) and the *any$_1$* sense (he is selective in what he does). However, in speech it can be disambiguated by stress, which is likely to be placed on *any$_1$ thing* for the *any$_1$* reading but on *do* for the *any$_2$* reading.

## 12.11.4. Inherently negative verbs

There are a number of English verbs which are inherently negative, as can be seen by their requirement for *any* rather than *some* in certain environments. These verbs divide into two types.

Firstly, there are verbs like *forbid* which involve inherent negation of the complement clause. Compare:

(102a)   *I ordered Mary to eat some apples*
(102b)   *I ordered Mary not to eat any apples*
(102c)   *I forbade Mary to eat any apples*

Here, *forbade* (*to*) takes *any*, as does *order not* (*to*). Other inherently negative verbs of this type include *deny that* (equivalent to *say/state that not*), *doubt that* (equivalent to *think that not*), and *dissuade from* (equivalent to *persuade not to*). There are also adjectives which show inherent negation of a following complement clause; for example, *reluctant to* (equivalent to *eager not to*). (It will be seen from (102a–b) that *not* with a TO complement clause does not require a preceding *do*.)

The other type involves inherent negation of the main clause verb. Compare:

(103a)   *I accepted the idea that Mary had eaten some cakes*
(103b)   *I didn't accept the idea that Mary had eaten any cakes*
(103c)   *I rejected the idea that Mary had eaten any cakes*

Here *reject* is like *not accept* in taking *any* within the appositional complement clause, whereas *accept* takes *some*. Further examples of this type include *forget* (equivalent to *not remember*).

It must be borne in mind that the use of the *some/any* alternation here applies only to sentential negation with *some*, involving *any₂*. It is perfectly possible to say, for example, *I ordered Mary to do* (*absolutely*) *anything* (*she was asked to do*), or *I ordered Mary not to do* (*absolutely*) *anything* (*she was asked to do*), or *I forbade Mary to do* (*absolutely*) *anything* (*she was asked to do*), all involving *any₁*.

## 12.11.5. Negation and sentential adverbs

When a clause includes both a sentential adverb and *not* in sentential function, then *not* will generally precede the adverb, as in (66). With some sentential adverbs, *not* must come first, as in *not slowly* and *not geographically*. There is, however, contrastive positioning with a meaning difference for certain adverbs. Compare:

(**104a**)   *He <u>definitely</u> hadn't been working* (it is clear that he did no work at all)
(**104b**)   *He hadn't <u>definitely</u> been working* (it is unclear whether or not he had been working)
(**105a**)   *He <u>once</u> didn't come* (he came on every occasion but one)
(**105b**)   *He didn't <u>once</u> come* (he never came)

Here *not* has scope over all that follows in the clause. Such alternative orderings are found with items from sets 3 and 4 of Table 12.4 (*deliberately, definitely, probably, usually, obviously*, etc.) and with some time adverbs from Table 12.5 (including *always, often, once, again*).

If a clause includes an auxiliary, a sentential adverb, and *not*, then *not* must come after the auxiliary, but the adverb either precedes auxiliary-plus-*not* or comes between them; in the latter case, the *not* is stressed. Thus:

(**106a**)   *He <u>probably</u> won't come*
(**106b**)   *He will <u>probably</u> 'not come*

These two sentences have similar meanings; they differ just in that the negation is emphasised in (106b). (A sequence with the adverb last—as in *\*He won't <u>probably</u> come*—is scarcely acceptable.)

*Not* can occur either before or after some adverbs from Table 12.7, which have both sentential and manner functions. When one of these adverbs precedes *not* it is generally in sentential function, and when it follows *not* it is generally in manner function. This is exemplified in (77) and:

(**107a**)   *He really* (A) *[didn't* (V*) do it]* (although he had meant to do so)
(**107b**)   *He didn't* (A) *[really* (V) *do it]* (he only pretended to)

An alternative to (107b) is *He didn't* (A) *[do it really* (O)], with the manner adverb following verb plus object.

Note that *not* in a main clause may have scope over just that clause, as in (108a), or over the whole sentence, as in (108b).

(**108a**)   *Mary [didn't beat John], because she loves him* (she didn't beat him, and the reason she didn't is that she loves him)
(**108b**)   *Mary [didn't beat John because she loves him]* (she did beat him, but for some other reason)

In speech, these sentences would be distinguished by intonation.

### 12.11.6. Complex negators

There are a number of sequences of sentential adverb plus *not* which function as a complex negator. They include:

> *not only*        *not just*        *not even*        *never* (from *not ever*)

A number of other complex forms, such as *no sooner*, behave in a similar way.

These complex negators have two special properties. Firstly, they are unlike simple *not* in not requiring a preceding auxiliary or *do*: for example, *He not only resigned his job,* ... Indeed, if there is an auxiliary, a complex negator may precede it, as in *She never had liked her father-in-law*.

Secondly, the complex negator may come at the beginning of a sentence. There must be an auxiliary—or the surrogate auxiliary *do*—as the immediately following word, between complex negator and subject. For example, *Not only did he resign,* ... and *Never had she hated anyone more*.

A number of sequences of *not* plus time adverb also show this second property—*not always, not often, not once*. For example, *Not always was he fully honest* and *Not often did she cheat*. However, these sequences do not show the first property of complex negators. That is, when in medial position they require a preceding auxiliary or *do*. One can say *She doesn't often cheat* but not *\*She not often cheats*. And note that such sequences can follow another sentential adverb; for example, *He had <u>stupidly</u> [not always] been attending*.

There are a number of sentential adverbs which may occur initially followed by an auxiliary or *do*—*hardly, scarcely, barely, seldom, rarely*. For example, *<u>Hardly</u> had she reached the door,* ... and *<u>Seldom</u> does he listen carefully*. Since this is a characteristic of negative adverbs—complex negators like *not just* and negative time adverbs like *not always*—we can suggest that *hardly, seldom* and the others have an inherent negative meaning, and it is by virtue of this that they may be used initially. Another criterion is that these adverbs take a positive tag, which is symptomatic for a negative clause; compare *John <u>hardly</u> swears, does he?* with *John <u>often</u> swears, doesn't he?*

There are limited possibilities in English for a normally non-initial element to be placed at the front of a sentence. Near the beginning of §2.12, we mentioned *Were Mary to come* ... as an alternative to *If Mary were to come*... Note that the fronted auxiliary (here, *were*) cannot take with it a following clitic negator. One can say *If Mary had not come* ... and

*If Mary hadn't come* ... but only *Had Mary not come* ... , not (with this sense) *\*Hadn't Mary come* ...

## 12.11.7. Negative modifier to a noun

There is one other negator in English. The form *no* may directly modify a noun, in place of a number or qualifier. One can say *no houses*, in paradigmatic array with *one house*, *two houses*, *many houses*, *some houses*, *all houses*, etc.

In §12.11.3 it was pointed out that when *some* is negated by sentential *not* we get *not* (A) ... *any₂*. An alternative is to replace the NP modifier *any₂* (*of the*) by *no* and omit the *not* from position A. Thus, in place of *He might not have seen any₂* (*of the*) *boys*, in (93n-s), one could say *He might have seen no boys*. And similarly *I can distinguish no colours* (*at all*), as an alterative to (97), *I can't distinguish any₂ colours* (*at all*). Instead of *He doesn't do any₂thing* (*at all*), in (100n-s), one can say *He does nothing* (*at all*). Note, though, that *nothing* may only substitute for *any₂thing*, not for *any₁thing*, in a sentence like (101n-s).

It is interesting to investigate the acceptability of the *not* ... *any₂* and *no* alternations with different verbs. Compare:

| | | | |
|---|---|---|---|
| **(109a)** | *He didn't ask for anything* | **(109b)** | *He asked for nothing* |
| **(110a)** | *He didn't request anything* | **(110b)** | *(\*)He requested nothing* |
| **(111a)** | *He didn't give anything to the appeal* | **(111b)** | *He gave nothing to the appeal* |
| **(112a)** | *He didn't donate anything to the hospital* | **(111b)** | *(\*)He donated nothing to the hospital* |

The *not* ... *any₂* construction, in (a), is acceptable with all verbs. But whereas the *no* construction, in (b), is fine with *ask for* and *give*, it is less felicitous with *request* and *donate*. The generalisation—based on these and other examples—is that the *no* construction, in (b), is more acceptable for a commonly occurring verb with a wide general meaning (such as *ask for* and *give*) and less acceptable for a less common verb with a more specialised meaning (such as *request* and *donate*).

Just as *nothing* relates to *something*, so does *no one* to *someone*, *nobody* to *somebody*—as in (91)—and *nowhere* to *somewhere*—as in (90). And *none of* is the negation for *some of*. One can say *He might have seen none of the boys*, instead of *He might not have seen any of the boys*, in (92n-s).

In §11.2, we noted that the active sentence *No one has yet climbed that tall mountain* has as its passive *That tall mountain hasn't yet been climbed (by anyone)*. For the active, the negator is in the (obligatory) subject NP *no one* (which is underlyingly *not* plus *anyone*); in the passive, this goes into a *by*-phrase, which can be omitted. As a consequence the negator moves onto an obligatory constituent, the predicate.

There are additional negative elements in English grammar. For example, the preposition *without* is equivalent to *with no*. Instead of *languages without a consecutive tense* one can say *languages with no consecutive tense*.

The remarks in §12.11 are simply an outline of some of the major properties of negation in English, a full study of which would fill a hefty volume. My aim has been to compare the functions of negator *not* with those of the various varieties of adverbs.

## Notes to Chapter 12

There are good discussions of adverbs in Declerck (1991: 214–35) and Zandvoort (1966: 247–51, 320–2), and much good material in Huddleston and Pullum (2002) and in Quirk and Greenbaum (1973) and Quirk et al. (1985); also see Dik (1973) and Kjellmer (1984). In addition, Greenbaum (1969) and Hasselgård (1996) include interesting empirical data. Discussions within the transformational/generative formalism include Jackendoff (1972: 47 ff.) and McCawley (1988b: 631 ff.).

§12.11. There is a wealth of material on negation in Huddleston and Pullum (2002: ch. 9), in Jespersen (1909–49: part IV, part v ch. 23), and in Jespersen (1917); see also Tottie (1991).

§12.11.2. Anderwald (2002: ch. 5) examines multiple realisation of a single negation ('negative concord') in non-standard British English, and shows (tables 5.2 and 5.3) that in about 97% of instances, one of the negators is *not*, *n't* or *never*, in position A.

§12.11.3. Among the many discussions of the *some/any* alternation, those by R. Lakoff (1969), Bolinger (1977a: 1–21) and Declerck (1991: 299–305) are particularly useful.

# 13

# *What sells slowly, but wears well?* Promotion to subject

## 13.1. General characteristics

We have said, several times, that the semantic role which is most likely to be relevant for the success of an activity is placed in syntactic subject relation; this is *Mary* in *Mary sells sports cars*, *Mary cut the veal with the new knife*, *Mary poured the custard* (*onto the pie*) *with the new jug*. If an adverb like *quickly*, *easily*, *properly* or *well* is added to these sentences it will be taken to describe the way in which the subject performed the activity—*Mary certainly sells sports cars quickly*, *Mary cut the veal easily with the new knife*, *Mary didn't pour the custard properly* (*onto the pie*) *with the new jug* (*but spilt some on the cloth*).

It is possible, in some particular instance of an activity, for the success or lack of success to be due not to the subject (which is usually the responsible role) but to some role in non-subject relation. If this is so, then that role may be promoted into subject slot (and the original subject is omitted from the sentence). For example, *Sports cars sell quickly* (this implies that it is inherent in the nature of the vehicle that people want to buy them), *The veal cuts easily* (it isn't tough or sinewy), *The new knife cuts veal easily* (it is nice and sharp), *The custard doesn't pour properly* (it has too many lumps in it),

*The new jug doesn't pour properly* (it may have a crooked spout), *The new jug doesn't pour custard properly* (but it might be all right for water or milk, which have a thinner consistency).

Some linguists have labelled constructions like *Sports cars sell quickly* as 'ergative'. They say that a transitive object (O) becomes intransitive subject (S) and point out that 'ergative' is the term used to demonstrate a link between O and S. This terminology is misconceived, for at least three reasons. Firstly, promotion to subject is available for some O NPs (as with *Sports cars sell quickly, The veal cuts easily, The custard won't pour properly*) but it is also possible from a peripheral NP (as with *The new knife cuts the veal easily, The new jug doesn't pour the custard properly*). Secondly, promotion to subject does not alter the transitivity of a sentence; if an NP other than object is promoted to subject then the object may be retained (as *the veal* and *the custard* are in examples just given). An O NP or a peripheral NP from a transitive clause is promoted into A relation, not S. Thirdly, even if it were only O that could be promoted, and even if it were promoted to S, 'ergative' would still not be an appropriate label. 'Ergative' is normally used of a linguistic system where A is marked in a distinctive way (by ergative case), differently from S and O which are marked in the same way (by absolutive case); see Dixon (1994). It is not an apt label for describing an S derived from O. (In fact, passive S does correspond to transitive O. People who label *Sports cars sell quickly* as 'ergative' should, if they were consistent, apply the same label to a passive like *Sports cars are sold quickly*, where there is a definite link between O and S.)

It is possible to find sentences describing some complex activity where any one of four roles may be held to be responsible for the success of the activity—see the examples given in §2.11.4 and:

(1)    *Mary washed the woollens* (*with Softly*) (*in the Hoovermatic*)

*Mary*, in subject slot, refers to the person who does the washing. She may do it well:

(1a)    *Mary washed the woollens well* (*with Softly*) (*in the Hoovermatic*)

But the garments may be manufactured in such a way that they respond well to washing (to any sort of washing, or to washing with that brand of soap mixture and/or washing in that make of washing machine):

(1b)    *The woollens washed well* (*with Softly*) (*in the Hoovermatic*)

Washday success could alternatively be attributed to the type of soap used:

(1c)   *Softly washed the woollens well (in the Hoovermatic)*

or to the machine employed:

(1d)   *The Hoovermatic washed the woollens well (with Softly)*

Note that when a non-subject role is promoted to subject the original subject is lost. It cannot be included as a peripheral constituent (in the way that a transitive subject can be included, as a *by* phrase, in a passive). Non-subject roles that are not promoted to subject may be retained in their original post-verbal position. And—also unlike passive, which has an explicit marker *be . . . -en*—nothing is added to the verb in a promotion-to-subject construction.

The fact that the direct object may be retained (as *the woollens* is in (1c) and (1d)) when a non-object NP is promoted to subject shows that constructions (1b–d) are still transitive sentences. What we have in (1b–d) is a single semantic role effectively functioning in two syntactic relations simultaneously. *The Hoovermatic* in (1d) is still in locative relation to the verb, as it is in (1a–c), but it is also in subject relation, as a means of showing that the success of this particular instance of washing activity is due to the machine in which the clothes were placed. In (1b) *the woollens* is still understood to be in object relation to the verb (this NP refers to the things that are affected by the activity, i.e. they get washed) but it is also in surface subject slot, to mark that the success of the activity is due to the nature of this instance of the role. Subject relation takes precedence over other syntactic relations in determining where the NP comes in the sentence, but anyone who hears (1b) will understand that *the woollens*, although in surface subject slot, is also the object of the verb; and so on.

Most examples of promotion to subject involve transitive clauses, but there are some intransitive instances. Consider *John jumped with the pogo stick*. This could have a satisfactory outcome either because John is something of an expert, e.g. *John jumped well with the pogo stick*, or because the pogo stick has a good spring in it, e.g. *That pogo stick jumps well*. Potentially, any non-subject NP from a transitive or intransitive clause may be promoted into subject slot; the transitivity of the clause is not affected.

There is a clear difference between promotion-to-subject clauses and passives (which are intransitive). Recall from Chapter 11 that a prepositional object can only become passive subject if there is no direct object, that it leaves its preposition behind it, and that the original transitive subject can be retained in a *by* phrase, e.g. *This knife has been cut with by John.* A prepositional NP can be promoted to subject even if there is a direct object (which may be retained), its preposition is omitted, and the original subject is omitted, e.g. *This knife cuts (veal) easily.*

There is also a clear semantic difference between passive and promotion to subject. Passivisation does not change or add to the relation between object and verb—it merely focuses on the object, or on the effect the activity has on it. In *The woollens were washed well* the *well* is taken to refer to the skill of the transitive subject—even though this is not identified here—exactly as it is in (1a). Compare this with *The woollens washed well*, where *well* refers to the washable qualities of the clothes. We can also compare *The custard wasn't poured properly* (the person holding the jug didn't look to see what they were doing) with *The custard doesn't pour properly* (it is too thick, and will have to be spooned onto the pie).

Although an object can be retained when a peripheral NP is promoted to subject, it is not then available for passivisation. If it were, confusion could arise. If corresponding to *The Hoovermatic washed the woollens well* we could have *The woollens were washed well (by the Hoovermatic)*, this could be confused with a passive corresponding to sentence (1a), *The woollens were washed well (by Mary) (in the Hoovermatic)*. Since a *by* phrase may always be omitted, *The woollens were washed well* would then be irretrievably ambiguous, and a listener would not know whether *well* referred to the Agent, the machine, the soap mixture, or what.

## 13.2. The circumstances in which promotion is possible

Promotion to subject is possible when there is some marker of the success of the activity. This marker can be an adverb, the negative particle, a modal, or emphatic *do*.

(**a**)  Adverb. Only a small set of adverbs occur in promotion-to-subject constructions. They are based on adjectives from three semantic types: (i) SPEED—*slowly, fast, quickly, rapidly*, as in *The bucket rapidly filled*; (ii) VALUE—*well, badly, properly, oddly, strangely* (but not most other members of this type), e.g. *I am afraid that this scene does not photograph well*; (iii) DIFFICULTY—*easily* and the adverbial phrases *with/without difficulty* (there is no adverb *difficultly), e.g. *These mandarins peel easily but those oranges peel only with great difficulty.* All of these adverbs may also be used as comparatives, e.g. *Datsuns sell quicker than Toyotas, Those tiles lay better if you wet them first.*

(b) Negation. This can be used when the lack of success of some activity is imputed to the qualities of the referent of a non-subject role, e.g. *That book didn't sell. Not* often co-occurs with the modal *will*, e.g. *The middle house won't let.*

(c) Modal. Most modals may be the marker in a promotion-to-subject construction, e.g. *Do you think this material will make up into a nice-looking dress? Yes, it must/should/ought to/might make up into a really stunning gown.*

(d) Emphatic *do*. The semantic effect of *do* can be similar to that of an adverb like *well*, e.g. *These red sports models do sell, don't they?*

The most common tense choice for promotion to subject is generic, e.g. *That type of garment wears well.* But past tense is also possible, as in (1b–d). Sometimes an adverb like *well* may be omitted when the construction is in generic tense, perhaps reinforced by an adverb such as *always*, e.g. *I find that Easter eggs always sell* (sc. well).

It must be emphasised that some marker from (*a*)–(*d*) is almost always obligatory if a non-subject role is to be promoted into subject slot, with the transitivity value of the sentence maintained. Sentences like *The new jug pours*, *Sports cars sell*, *The woollens washed* are ungrammatical; but if something like *well* or *don't* or *won't* is added, then they become acceptable English sentences. *Sell* is one of the verbs most frequently used in promotion-to-subject constructions, and one does hear, with a definite subject, a sentence like *Did those sports cars sell?*; but most verbs always require a marker.

In §3.2 we mentioned that VALUE and DIFFICULTY adjectives—i.e. two of those types whose adverbs may assist promotion to subject—are used in a special construction in which what would be object of a complement clause functions as subject of the adjective. Alongside a regular Modal (FOR) TO construction such as *It is easy (for anyone) to shock John* we can have:

(2)   *John is easy to shock*

Recall that although we may say *That picture is good to look at*—a construction parallel to (2) but involving a VALUE adjective—there are no corresponding sentences, with a closely similar meaning, that have a

Modal (FOR) TO clause in subject relation. We can say *It is good to look at that picture* but this has a different meaning from *That picture is good to look at*.

Now compare (2) with the promotion-to-subject construction:

(3)   *John shocks easily*

The two sentences have similar, but not identical, meanings: (2) would be preferred when someone deliberately sets out to shock John, and succeeds without any real difficulty (the someone could be mentioned by using the related construction, *It was easy for Mary to shock John*); (3) would be preferred if John just gets shocked at the mildest swear-word without anyone meaning to shock him (an 'agent' NP could not be included in (3)). The contrast between these construction types is less clear when the subject is inanimate, e.g. *Porcelain sinks are easy to clean*, and *Porcelain sinks clean easily*, but still the first sentence implies that some effort is required (although not so much as with other kinds of sink) while the second sentence suggests that one just has to wipe a cloth over and the job is done. With other adjective/adverb pairs the difference between constructions like (2) and those like (3) is even more obvious; *These clothes are good to wash* seems to imply that it's fun washing them, a quite different meaning from *These clothes wash well*.

Promotion to subject is an even more marked construction than passive, and is used only when the nature of the referent of a non-subject NP is the major factor in the success of some instance of an activity. There has to be a contrast involved—some models of car sell quickly and others slowly, some types of woollens wash easily but others don't.

## 13.3.  Which roles may be promoted

At the beginning of Chapter 11 we noted that a passive should really be quoted together with the full context in which it might be used. This applies at least as much in the case of promotion-to-subject constructions. Instead of doing this, we rely on the reader's imagination, on their being able to invest the referent of a non-subject NP with the particular properties that make or mar some instance of an activity, and justify its promotion into subject slot.

For those verbs which exist in both transitive and intransitive forms, with S = O, it can be hard to distinguish between promotion-to-subject of an O NP and a plain intransitive. Consider *waken*—this can be intransitive, as in *Mary wakened at seven o'clock*, or transitive, as in *John wakened Mary at seven o'clock*. A sentence such as *Mary wakens easily* is ambiguous between (i) a simple intransitive construction, in which the adverb *easily* implies that Mary is able to waken spontaneously, at any time she sets her mind to; and (ii) a promotion-to-subject construction from a transitive clause with the meaning that she is able to be wakened easily—one only has to whisper 'It's seven o'clock' and Mary is immediately wide awake and ready to get up. For some S = O verbs there is no ambiguity—*The dog walks slowly* would be taken to be a plain intransitive and not a promotion-to-subject version of a causative (such as *Mary walks the dog slowly*). But many verbs from the DROP, STRETCH and BREAK subtypes, and some such as *hurt*, *bleed* and *drown* from CORPOREAL, show the same sort of syntactic ambiguity as *waken*. Because of this, we will omit S = O verbs from the brief survey that follows.

It must be noted that promotion to subject is not a very common phenomenon. It applies only for certain kinds of NP filling non-subject relations, for just a handful of verbs from any one type. But it does occur with a fair spread of verbs, from quite a number of semantic types.

The discussion below deals mainly with the promotion to subject of core roles. But, as exemplified above and in §2.11.4, promotion is also possible for some peripheral roles—instruments like *with the Beyer microphone* and *with Softly* or, in very special circumstances, locational descriptions such as *in Studio B* and *in a Hoovermatic*.

We will first consider Primary-A types, i.e. those for which every role must be realised by an NP (not by a complement clause).

MOTION and REST. There are some examples of the Moving and Resting roles being promotable to subject, with verbs for which they are not the natural subject. Besides *The custard doesn't pour easily* we can have *This boomerang throws well*, *That box lifts easily*, *The new design of ball catches well*, *Your case carries easily*, *The boxes will not transport easily*, *A good tent puts up in five minutes*, *Evonne's racket handles well*, *That pram pushes easily*, *Your trailer pulls easily*, *Mushrooms store best in a brown-paper bag*.

AFFECT. There are quite a number of examples of Manip and Target being promoted to subject (from frames I and II in §4.2). Examples involving Manip are *That knife cuts well*, *This string won't tie properly*, *My new steel-tipped boots kick well*. Those with Target promoted are *That cheese cuts easily*, *Stainless-steel pans clean easily*, *That shape of box doesn't wrap* up *very easily*, *Clothes iron better when damp*. We can also get *This dirt won't brush off my coat* and *That flour cooks well*, *This oven cooks well*.

GIVING. The Gift NP may be promoted to subject, as in *Those cars sell quickly*, *These Mills and Boon novels lend rather rapidly* (said by a librarian), *Top-floor apartments tend not to rent so easily as ground-floor ones*, and *Milk won't keep in hot weather (but it does keep if you put it in a fridge)*. The Recipient may also be promoted, as in *The Kingsland police bribe easily*.

CORPOREAL. The Substance role may be promoted to subject with just a few verbs, e.g. *These pills swallow easily*, *This meat chews rather easily*, *Beancurd digests easily*, and, of a wine, *forty years old and still drinking beautifully* (Harris 2003: 61). In 1697 the English explorer William Dampier said of the turtles on the Galapagos Islands: *they are extraordinarily large and fat; and so sweet, that no pullet eats more pleasantly* (Norris 1994: 51). An instrumental NP is promoted in *This straw sucks well*.

From the other Primary-A types, listed in §4.6, we may get *This new board game plays well* for a COMPETITION verb, *That machine operates easily* and *Those clothes wear well* from the USING type, and perhaps *That kingdom governs easily* from SOCIAL CONTRACT.

In summary, there are *some* examples of promotion to subject for every role (that is not canonically mapped onto subject) with Primary-A verbs.

We now turn to Primary-B, those types which have one role that may be realised either through a complement clause or through an NP. This role is in transitive subject relation for ANNOYING and in object or a post-object slot for the other Primary-B types.

ATTENTION. The Impression, in O slot, cannot be promoted to subject. Alongside *John watched that film* and *Mary heard thunder* it is not possible to say *\*That film watches well* or *\*Thunder hears easily*. (One could instead use the derived adjective *watchable*, as in *That film is very watchable*, and the alternative construction with *easy*, illustrated by example (2) above, i.e. *Thunder is easy to hear*.)

THINKING. Again the role (here, Thought) in O slot may not be promoted. Alongside *John learnt Swahili*, *Fred remembers the Kennedy years*, *I believe his story*, *I believe in God*, we cannot say *\*Swahili learns easily* (only *Swahili is easy to learn*), *\*The Kennedy years remember well* (here one could say *The Kennedy years were memorable*) or *\*His story/God believes well* (*His story is believable* is acceptable, but *God is believable* much less so).

DECIDING. The Course role, in O slot, may not be promoted to subject. Corresponding to *Mary chose the Persian kitten* we cannot have *\*The Persian kitten chose easily*. However, some verbs of the DECIDING type show a special kind of reflexive construction, with a meaning not dissimilar from promotion to subject with verbs from other types, e.g. *That cute little Persian kitten really chose/picked itself* (i.e. it was so appealing that I couldn't help but buy it). *That cute little Persian kitten* is properly the object of the DECIDING verb but also functions simultaneously as subject, in this unusual kind of reflexive construction. (There are several points of difference between this reflexive and promotion to subject; for instance, the reflexive does not require an adverb, modal or negation.)

SPEAKING. This type has four roles (one with two components). The Speaker is always underlying subject. There are just a few instances of an Addressee being promotable to subject, e.g. *She persuades easily* (as an alternative to *She is easy to persuade*) and *He insults easily*. The Medium role may just occasionally be promotable to subject slot, as in *Pica type reads more easily than Elite*. The Message role may have two components: Message-Label, which can only be an NP, and Message-Content, which can be an NP or a complement clause. There are some examples of Message-Label (but none of Message-Content) being promoted to subject, e.g. *That joke tells well, doesn't it?*, *Your new story/book/poem reads well*, *That sermon, from the old book I found, preaches well*.

LIKING. The Stimulus role, which is mapped into O relation, can be a plain NP, or NP plus complement clause, or a complement clause. It may not be promoted to subject. That is, we cannot say *\*Ballet likes well*, *\*Insincerity hates easily*, or even *\*John pities easily* (meaning that people are always pitying him).

ANNOYING. Here the Experiencer, which is in O slot, must be an NP (normally with Human reference). This may be promoted to subject—in the presence of an appropriate marker—with a number of ANNOYING verbs, e.g. *Mary scares/excites/annoys/angers/shocks easily*, *Granpa tires quickly these days* or (heard on the radio) *I don't think this government embarrasses very easily*.

COMPARING. The object of *compare* may be an NP with plural reference, or several coordinated NPs, e.g. *The travel agent compared those two countries/Greece and Italy in terms of cuisine*. Such an O can be promoted to subject—when there is an adverb or negation etc. present—*Those two countries compare favourably in terms of cuisine, Greece and Italy don't compare in terms of cuisine.* Alternatively, we can have an NP as O and post-object constituent introduced by *with*; the O NP can be promoted to subject and the *with* phrase remains in post-verbal position, e.g. *The travel agent compared Greece with Rome in terms of cuisine, Greece doesn't compare with Rome in terms of cuisine.* Less frequently, the O and the following *with* constituent for *compare* can be coordinated ING clauses, e.g. *John compared lying in the sun with going to a garden party at the Governor's.* Here the ING clause can be promoted to subject, in the right circumstances, e.g. *Lying in the sun compares quite favourably with going to a garden party at the Governor's.* (Other verbs from the COMPARING type, discussed in §5.7, appear not to occur in promotion-to-subject constructions.)

If we leave aside, for the moment, the single verb *compare*, this survey of which roles may be promoted to subject yields an intriguing generalisation:

those non-subject roles that may be realised by an NP or a complement clause are not promotable to subject; but those which must be realised through an NP (not a complement clause) are potentially promotable.

We saw that all non-subject roles with Primary-A verbs may be promoted. For Primary-B types those roles that can be realised by a complement clause may not be promoted—Impression for ATTENTION, Thought for THINKING, Course for DECIDING, Message-Content for SPEAKING and Stimulus for LIKING. But those roles that can only be filled by NPs are promotable—Addressee, Medium and Message-Label for SPEAKING, Experiencer for ANNOYING.

The only serious counter-example is *compare*, where the 'object of comparison', in O relation, may be NPs or ING clauses, and either of these may be promoted to subject. Note that all other roles (mentioned in the last paragraph) which are not open to promotion may involve several different kinds of complement clause. It may be that *compare* is simply an exception—note that it is the only verb which allows a complement clause (rather than just an NP) to be promoted. Or the generalisation should perhaps be amended: roles which may be realised by a complement clause other than ING may not be promoted to subject. (We noted in §2.7 that ING clauses are the closest of all complements to an NP in their syntactic function.)

There is a single, quite minor exception to the generalisation: we might expect that Stimulus-Label for LIKING should be promotable, parallel to Message-Label for SPEAKING, but in fact it appears not to be.

The force of this generalisation should be emphasised. If a certain role can be realised by a complement clause (other than ING) for *some* verbs from a type then that role may not be promoted to subject for *any* verb from the type. We related all ATTENTION verbs to the Perceiver and Impression roles. Impression may be either an NP or a complement clause for some subtypes, e.g. SEE and DISCOVER, but it may only be an NP for some verbs from the LOOK subtype such as *scrutinise*, *survey*, *explore* and *visit*. The Impression role may not be promoted to subject with LOOK verbs, any more than it can be for SEE and DISCOVER (that is, we cannot say *\*This document scrutinises easily*, or *\*That terrain explores easily*). This provides justification for the category 'role', which is a critical component of my semantically oriented approach to syntactic study. Each role has a certain semantic character, and only those roles which relate to entities, described by NPs (or activities, described by ING clauses)—not those which may relate to THAT or Modal (FOR) TO complements, etc.—can contribute to the success of an activity in such a way that they may be promoted into subject slot.

Secondary verbs take a syntactic complement clause, containing a verb which they modify semantically. The only possible promotion to subject is with BEGINNING, and then only where promotion is possible for an underlying complement clause verb. When this verb is omitted, the promotion may still be possible, now to the subject of the BEGINNING verb. Thus, *John read that novel*, *That novel reads well*; *John began* (*reading*) *that novel*, *That novel begins well* (but not *\*That novel begins reading well*). And *Mary told that joke about nuns*, *That joke about nuns tells well*; *Mary began* (*telling*) *that joke about nuns*, *That joke about nuns begins well* (but not *\*That joke about nuns begins telling well*). (We mentioned in §6.1.2 that some BEGINNING verbs may occur in an intransitive frame with an activity noun as subject, e.g. *The sale began at three o'clock*. Such sentences can involve an adverb, e.g. *That sale began slowly*, but this is not an instance of promotion to subject, parallel to those discussed above.)

There is one circumstance in which a promotion-to-subject construction might be ambiguous. Consider a transitive verb where the object may be omitted (a dual transitivity verb of type S = A; §9.3.1). If we get a construction consisting only of SUBJECT, TRANSITIVE VERB, ADVERB, how do we know whether this is the original subject, with the object omitted, or whether this construction involves promotion to subject of the transitive object, with the original subject having been omitted?

There will be no danger of ambiguity if the various roles have different referential possibilities. Only a human can pour, only a liquid can be poured, and only a container can be poured out of. We know that *John pours well* is a transitive clause with object omitted, but that *The custard pours well* and *The jug pours well* involve promotion to subject.

There are verbs for which subject and object can be human, and which do allow the object to be promoted to subject. But these are all strictly transitive, i.e. the object cannot be omitted. If such a verb occurs with just a subject and no stated object, we know that the subject must be a promoted object, e.g. *bribe*, *persuade*, and verbs from the ANNOYING type.

There is a verb which can involve ambiguity—*translate* (and *interpret* might provide similar examples). This can omit its object, and does also permit promotion of object into subject slot. *John translates well*, where the O NP is omitted, is an acceptable sentence (the speaker will probably assume that the listener already knows what sort of thing John translates, and between what languages). With a stated object NP we get *Many people have translated Shakespeare's works into Greek* and then, with the O promoted into A slot, *Shakespeare's works translate well into Greek*. The subject of *translate* will have human reference, with the object generally referring to some piece of written or spoken language. But a set of literary works is sometimes abbreviated to just the name of the author—instead of *Shakespeare's works* people will often say just *Shakespeare*. With this particular object NP there will be no ambiguity. *Shakespeare translates well into Greek* will be understood as a promotion-to-subject construction, not as a transitive clause with object omitted, simply because people know that Shakespeare is dead and that he didn't do any translating. However, if we were talking about some living author (call him Adam Dawkins) whose works do get translated and who also undertakes translation himself, then *Adam Dawkins translates well into Greek* would be ambiguous. If Dawkins were equally well known for his original works, which are translated into many languages, and for the translations he does, then the unmarked interpretation of this sentence would surely be that it was a transitive construction with the object omitted (that is, *Adam Dawkins* would be taken as underlying subject, not object, of *translate*).

This underlies the point we made earlier, that promotion-to-subject is a marked construction, and is only permitted where there is space left by the rest of the grammar.

## Notes to Chapter 13

There are useful discussions of 'promotion to subject' in Jespersen (1909–49: part iii, pp. 347–52) and especially in Erades (1950b). They include examples gathered from written English texts and I have freely drawn on their examples in this chapter. Many other sources each give just a few examples, including G. Lakoff (1977), van Oosten (1977) and Keyser and Roeper (1984).

§13.1. For a general account of the misuse of the term 'ergative' see Dixon (1994: 18–22; 1987: 5–6, 13). Scholars who deal with what is here referred to as 'promotion to subject' within a discussion of 'ergative in English' include Halliday (1967) and J. M. Anderson (1968). The term 'middle' was originally used for the form of a verb in Ancient Greek. In recent times it has been employed for a variety of quite diverse grammatical constructions, one being the 'promotion to subject' described here (see, among others, Kemmer 1993). This simply serves further to muddy the waters. (For a certain construction type to be termed 'ergative' by some people and 'middle' by others beggars belief.)

# 14

## *She gave him a look, they both had a laugh and then took a stroll* GIVE A VERB, HAVE A VERB and TAKE A VERB constructions

Parallel to *Mary walked in the garden* we can say *Mary had a walk in the garden*. Here the verb *have* substitutes for *walk*, and takes tense inflection. The original verb base *walk* now functions as head of an NP which follows *have*, with the singular indefinite article *a*. The locational phrase *in the garden* is carried over unaltered. These two sentences, *Mary walked in the garden* and *Mary had a walk in the garden*, have a similar meaning; there is, however, a definite and predictable semantic difference, which we discuss in §14.3.

There is also the TAKE A VERB construction, built on similar principles—compare *John kicked at the ball* and *John took a kick at the ball*. TAKE A VERB, like HAVE A VERB, is most frequently used with intransitive verbs (there are exceptions, discussed in §14.2). The GIVE A VERB construction differs in that it most often involves a transitive verb, e.g. *Mary punched John* and *Mary gave John a punch*. Here *give* substitutes for the original verb, which becomes (in base form) the head of a 'second object' NP, again preceded by the indefinite article *a*.

Many verbs occur with HAVE A, TAKE A and GIVE A, but there are many others which resist use in such constructions. Compare the following samples:

| Possible | Impossible |
|---|---|
| *have a walk in the garden* | *\*have an arrive at the gate* |
| *have a swim in the river* | *\*have a cross over the bridge* |
| *have a sit-down on the sofa* | *\*have a settle-down in the country* |
| *have a look at the baby* | *\*have a see of the baby* |
| *have a think about the solution* | *\*have a know of the solution* |
| *have a talk with Mary* | *\*have a speak with Mary* |

In British English, the verbs which occur with TAKE A appear to be a subset of those which occur with HAVE A. One can *take a walk*, *take a swim* or *take a look* but not *\*take a sit-down*, *\*take a think* or *\*take a talk*. Parallel to *have a kick* and *have a bite* there are *take a kick* and *take a bite*; but although it is possible to say *have a shave* or *have a laugh*, it is not permissible to say *\*take a shave* or *\*take a laugh*.

Turning now to GIVE A, we can contrast:

| Possible | Impossible |
|---|---|
| *give the rope a pull* | *\*give the rope a tie* |
| *give the lamp a rub* | *\*give the bottle a break* |
| *give the child a carry* | *\*give the child a take* |
| *give the pudding a stir* | *\*give the pudding a bake* |
| *give Mary a smile* | *\*give Mary a laugh* |

I have examined about 700 of the most common English verbs and find that about one-quarter of them can occur in at least one of the constructions HAVE A VERB, TAKE A VERB and GIVE A VERB. Whether or not a verb can occur in one or more of these constructions is largely semantically based, as we shall show in this chapter.

Most grammars of English scarcely mention the HAVE A, GIVE A and TAKE A construction types. The linguist Edward Sapir did mention them, putting *give him a kick* alongside *kick him*, and *take a ride* with *ride*. He commented (Sapir 1949: 114): 'at first blush this looks like a most engaging rule but ... anyone who takes the trouble to examine these examples carefully will soon see that behind a superficial appearance of simplicity there is concealed a perfect hornet's nest of bizarre and arbitrary usages....We can "give a person a shove" or "a push," but we cannot "give them a move" nor "a drop" (in the sense of causing them to drop).' The aim of the discussion below will be to show that the occurrence of verbs with HAVE A, TAKE A and GIVE A is not at all arbitrary.

These constructions tend to carry an overtone of friendliness and intimacy, and are found far more frequently in colloquial than in formal styles of English. Some examples are found in the older literature, e.g. *give a cry* from 1300, *have a run* from 1450, but these are comparatively rare. Note, though, that very little of premodern literature reflected colloquial usage.

It does seem likely that the use of the constructions has increased over the past 200 years, and that it has done so in different ways in different dialects. In British (and Australian) English HAVE A VERB has increased in popularity while TAKE A VERB may actually have dropped in frequency; in American English the TAKE A construction has become more common and HAVE A appears to have contracted. This would account for the fact that Americans prefer to say *take a run/kick/swim/look* where an Englishman would use *have a run/kick/swim/look* (although the TAKE A construction is also possible in British English and differs in meaning from HAVE A, as will be discussed below). GIVE A appears also to occur with a more limited range of verbs in American English, e.g. *give the child a carry* is generally accepted by speakers of British English but rejected by Americans.

There are also periphrastic constructions with *make, do* and *pay* that show some similarity to HAVE A/GIVE A/TAKE A VERB. *Pay* is very restricted—the main verbs it occurs with are *visit* and *compliment*, as in *visit Mary, pay Mary a visit; compliment Mary, pay Mary a compliment. Do* occurs with a slightly larger set of verbs, e.g. *do a dance/mime/dive/jump/pee* (and in 'The Stockbroker's Clerk', a client tells Sherlock Holmes that he was *sitting doing a smoke*). *Make* occurs with quite a number of verbs from the THINKING, DECIDING, SPEAKING, ATTENTION and COMPARING types. Sometimes the plain verb base becomes head of an NP following *make* (with the indefinite article *a*), e.g. *make a remark/claim/comment/report/mention/request*, but in most cases it is a derived nominal, e.g. *make a statement/suggestion/complaint/confession/enquiry/decision/assumption/inspection/comparison.* MAKE/DO/PAY A VERB constructions fall outside the scope of our discussion in this chapter. (Under REST-c in §4.1 we mentioned the periphrastic use of *put*, as in *put the blame on, put trust in, put a question to*; these also fall outside the present discussion.)

The next section presents criteria for distinguishing between the HAVE A, GIVE A and TAKE A constructions which are the topic of this chapter, and other constructions involving these verbs. §14.2 deals with the syntax of the constructions, and then §14.3 discusses their meanings. Finally, §14.4 explains which verbs may occur in the constructions; this relates to the meaning of a given verb and the meanings of the construction types.

## 14.1. Criteria adopted

The large *Oxford English Dictionary* lists twenty-seven senses of *have*, sixty-four of *give* and ninety-four of *take*. Each of these verbs shows a very varied set of syntactic usages. In view of this, it is important that I should give explicit criteria to define the constructions I am describing, which will serve to distinguish them from other constructions involving *have*, *give* and *take*.

The criteria I adopt relate to: (*a*) form; (*b*) meaning; (*c*) adverb/adjective correspondence; and (*d*) preservation of peripheral constituents. In discussing these it will be useful to refer to a 'basic sentence' and then to a peripheral HAVE A, GIVE A or TAKE A correspondent of this, e.g. *Mary walked in the garden* is a basic sentence, and *Mary had a walk in the garden* is a periphrastic HAVE A version of it.

(*a*)  Form
A periphrastic construction should show (i) the same subject as the basic sentence; (ii) *have*, *take* or *give* as the main verb; (iii) the base form of the verb of the basic sentence as head of a postpredicate NP, preceded by the indefinite article *a* or *an*.

*I had a kick of the ball* is a bona fide HAVE A construction, as can be seen by comparison with *I kicked the ball*. But *I had a kick from the horse* is not a HAVE A correspondent of *The horse kicked me* since the two sentences have different subjects.

I am here adopting the quite restrictive condition that a plain verb base (not a derived form) must occur, with *a*, in an NP following *have*, *give* or *take*. *John and Mary had a chat about the accident* is an instance of the HAVE A construction, since it relates to the basic sentence *John and Mary chatted about the accident*. But *John and Mary had a discussion about the accident* is not, since the NP involves a derived noun, *discussion*, and not the verb root *discuss*. Relating to *John regretted that he had to leave early* there is *John had regrets about leaving early*, but this does not satisfy the criterion since the post-verbal NP is *regrets* rather than *a regret*. (It also fails criterion (*d*) concerning peripheral constituents, since the basic sentence involves a THAT complement clause and the *have* construction shows preposition *about* plus an ING clause.)

Nominalisations, derived from verbs, are discussed in Chapter 10. Most nominalisations involve a morphological process, which is generally a suffix such as *-ing*, *-tion* or *-ment*. But some use zero derivation (§10.3), where the nominalisation has the same form as the verb, e.g. *wound*, *cart*, *offer*. There are just a few instances where a Unit-nom or State-nom, involving zero derivation, could conceivably be confused with the base form of the verb in a HAVE A, TAKE A or GIVE A construction. These include *run, throw, smile, shout* and *dread*. Compare:

| example of nominalised verb | basic sentence<br>GIVE A or HAVE A construction |
|---|---|
| *Her smile brightened his day* | *She smiled at him*<br>*She gave him a smile* |
| *That run tired me out* | *I ran in the park*<br>*I had a run in the park* |
| *She thought with dread of the*<br>    *hot summer ahead* | *She dreaded the hot summer*<br>*She had a dread of the hot summer* |

**(b)**   Meaning

We will show in §14.3 that each of HAVE A, GIVE A and TAKE A adds a special semantic element to the basic sentence. Leaving this aside, criterion (b) demands that the periphrastic sentence should have essentially the same meaning as the basic sentence. *I looked in the suitcase* and *I had/took a look in the suitcase* satisfy this criterion. But *I chanced to see Mary* and *I had a chance to see Mary* have quite different meanings—the first can mean 'I saw Mary accidentally' and the second 'I had the opportunity to see Mary but didn't avail myself of it'. By criterion (b), *I had a chance to see Mary* is not an instance of the HAVE A construction that is the topic of this chapter. (Note also that *the* can be used in place of *a*, e.g. *I had the chance to see Mary*. This is never possible in a HAVE A, TAKE A or GIVE A construction, e.g. not *\*I had/took the look in the suitcase.*)

Criteria (a) and (b) interrelate to give similar results. In *John had a talk with Mary*, it is the base form of the verb that has become head of the NP, and this sentence does have a similar meaning to *John talked with Mary*. But in *John gave a speech to Mary* the NP involves a derived noun (not the verb base *speak*), and this sentence does have a quite different meaning from *John spoke to Mary*, confirming that *give a speech* is not an example of our GIVE A construction.

Corresponding to *Mary thought about the party* we get the HAVE A sentence *Mary had a think about the party*, where the NP does involve the base form of the verb. These two sentences have similar meanings—the thinking went on for a period of time (and need not necessarily have yielded any conclusive ideas). Contrast these with *Mary had a (sudden) thought about the party*, which has a quite different meaning (referring to a flash of inspiration) and also involves the derived noun *thought*; this sentence is thus not an instance of the HAVE A construction.

*(c)*   Adverb/adjective correspondence
The way in which an adjective provides semantic modification to the head of an NP is similar to the way in which an adverb modifies a verb. Corresponding to an adverb in a basic sentence we would expect an adjective in a corresponding periphrastic HAVE A, TAKE A or GIVE A construction, e.g.

*John climbed easily up the rocks/John had an easy climb up the rocks*
*Mary kissed him passionately/Mary gave him a passionate kiss*
*Fred looked more closely at the hole in the fence/Fred took a closer look at the hole in the fence*

An adverbial phrase describing time or distance in a basic sentence may correspond to an adjective in a periphrastic construction.

*I sat down briefly/I had a brief sit-down*
*I sat down for a long while/I had a long sit-down*
*I walked (for) a long distance* ⎫
*I walked for a long while* ⎭   *I had a long walk*

And the adverb *again* may correspond to adjective *another*:

*She looked again at the ring/She had another look at the ring*

The condition that there should be adverb/adjective correspondence often helps to distinguish a true HAVE A, TAKE A or GIVE A construction from one of the verbs *have*, *take* or *give* used with an independent noun that has the same form as the verb. In

**(1a)**   *She scratched her mosquito bites savagely/for a long time*
**(1b)**   *She gave her mosquito bite a savage/long scratch*

the adverb/adjective condition is satisfied. But now consider:

**(2)** *She gave him a long scratch on the leg*

This does not relate to *She scratched him on the leg for a long time*. It is not the action of scratching which is long; rather, a long wound has been inflicted on him by the scratching. This indicates that *scratch* is an independent noun in (2), and that this is not an instance of the GIVE A construction.

*Drink*, as an independent noun, may be the object of a verb like *consume*, or of *have*, e.g. *He consumed a* (or *the*) *drink/a* (or *the*) *drink of whiskey/a* (or *the*) *whiskey* and *He had a* (or *the*) *drink/a* (or *the*) *drink of whiskey/a* (or *the*) *whiskey*. Also, corresponding to a basic sentence such as *Go on, you drink my new Californian wine* we can get the HAVE A construction *Go on, you have a drink of my new Californian wine*.

The sentence *Have a drink* is thus ambiguous between these two readings. However, the inclusion of an adverb may help to resolve this ambiguity. Corresponding to *Have a sneaky/quick drink of the whiskey* there is *Drink the whiskey sneakily/quickly*, the adjective/adverb correspondence showing that this is a true HAVE A construction. On the other hand, corresponding to *Have an ice-cold drink* it is not possible to say *\*Drink ice-coldly*, showing that *drink* is here an independent noun.

The dividing lines between similar construction types are seldom water-tight in any language. People do say *Have a quick whiskey*, which is a blend of *Have a quick drink* (the HAVE A construction based on *Drink quickly*) and *Have a whiskey/drink of whiskey/drink*, which is a different *have* construction, involving an independent noun as NP head. Still, blends like this are unusual; in the vast majority of cases the adverb/adjective correspondence condition does enable us to distinguish between HAVE A, GIVE A, TAKE A and other constructions involving these verbs.

It will be seen that a number of roots, like *scratch* and *drink*, may be used (i) as a verb, whose base form is extended to occurrence in HAVE A, TAKE A or GIVE A constructions; and (ii) as a noun. But there are other roots which may only be used as a verb, not as an independent noun. *Carry*, for instance, only occurs in an NP within a HAVE A or GIVE A construction, e.g. *John gave the baby a carry*.

**(d)** Preservation of peripheral constituents

In the next section we discuss the syntax of HAVE A, GIVE A and TAKE A constructions. To anticipate: if HAVE A or TAKE A relates to a basic sentence that is transitive, the preposition *of* is likely to be inserted before the erstwhile direct object, e.g. *I smelt the pudding* and its periphrastic correspondent *I had a smell of the pudding.* GIVE A may relate to an intransitive basic sentence including a prepositional NP, with the preposition being omitted in the GIVE A construction, e.g. *Mary winked at John, Mary gave John a wink.*

Leaving aside these differences, which involve core constituents, all peripheral constituents of the basic sentence should be exactly preserved in the periphrastic construction. Thus, *I always swim in the pool before breakfast on weekdays* and *I always have a swim in the pool before breakfast on weekdays*—here the correspondence of *in the pool*, *before breakfast* and *on weekdays* between the two sentences shows that we are dealing with a bona fide HAVE A construction.

Now consider:

(**3a**)   *John painted the wall with Dulux*
(**3b**)   *John gave the wall a paint with Dulux*
(**4a**)   *Mary coated the table with wax*
(**4b**)   *Mary gave the table a coat of wax*

Sentence (3b) is a GIVE A construction since the peripheral NP *with Dulux* has the same form as in the basic sentence. Sentence (4b), in contrast, is a different kind of construction, since it includes the NP *a coat of wax* where (4a) has *coat ... with wax.*

It may be useful at this stage briefly to mention one of the many other constructions involving *give*, and one of those involving *have*, that we are excluding from consideration here:

(i)   The 'Permissive' *give* construction, e.g. *I gave Mary a lick of my lollipop*, which is similar in meaning to *I let Mary lick my lollipop*. Compare this with the GIVE A construction *I gave my lollipop a lick*, corresponding to the basic sentence *I licked my lollipop.*

(ii)   The 'Experiencer' *have* construction, e.g. *I had/experienced a heart attack/a stab in the back/the misfortune to be dropped from the side/a brainwave/a move to head office.*

A fair number of forms that function as verbs and enter into the HAVE A construction also function as an independent noun in the Experiencer *have* construction. A doctor might say: *Go on, cough gently* or else they could use the HAVE A sentence: *Go on, have a gentle cough*. But *cough* may also be used as a noun, as in *I had a bad cough* (parallel to *I had a headache*).

Other Experiencer *have* sentences are *I had/got/received a kick from Mary/a kiss from Mary*; these relate to sentences with a different subject,

*Mary kicked/kissed me.* Notice the contrast with the HAVE A verb sentences *I had a kick at the ball* (basic sentence *I kicked at the ball*) and, with plural subject, *John and Mary had a kiss* (corresponding to *John and Mary kissed*).

*Walk* enters into HAVE A constructions (e.g. *Why don't we have a little walk before breakfast?*). But it is also an independent noun, as in *That walk tired me* and *I had a tiring walk*; the fact that the last sentence is Experiencer *have* and not the HAVE A construction is seen from the failure of the adverb/ adjective criterion (*\*I walked tiringly* is scarcely felicitous). *He had a fall* is also an instance of Experiencer *have*; any one of an array of adjectives may be included in the NP (e.g. *nasty, awful, serious*), but for most of these there is no corresponding adverb that could be used with *I fell*.

*Take* also occurs in an 'Experiencer' construction, e.g. *He took a (bad) tumble, She took a punch in the stomach* (relating to *Someone punched her in the stomach*), *She took offence at John's behaviour* (relating to *John's behaviour offended her*).

## 14.2. Syntax

More than two-thirds of the verbs from my sample occurring in HAVE A or TAKE A constructions are intransitive. This is a very natural syntactic correlation. The verbs *have* and *take* involve two core NPs—the original subject remains as subject and an NP consisting of *a* plus the original verb base goes into post-verbal position, e.g. *I rode (on the elephant), I had/took a ride (on the elephant)*.

There are, however, a fair number of instances of HAVE A and TAKE A with transitive verbs. Here a new syntactic slot has to be created in the periphrastic construction for the original transitive object. It is generally introduced by the preposition *of*. Thus *John bit/smelt the cake* and *John had a bite/smell of the cake*. Similarly, *Can I borrow your ruler?* and *Can I have a borrow of your ruler?*; also *Can I ride your bike for a little while?* and *Can I have a little ride of your bike?*

About 90 per cent of the verbs occurring in the GIVE A construction are transitive. This is again a natural syntactic correlation—a transitive clause will have two core NPs and *give* has three, with *a*-plus-verb-base making up the third. Subject remains as is, the original object remains as first object of *give*, and *a* plus the original verb fills the second object slot, e.g. *John pushed Mary, John gave Mary a push.*

For the lexical verb *give*, referring to transfer of possession, the most basic syntactic frame is with Gift in O slot and Recipient introduced by preposition *to*, e.g. *John gave the book to someone*. In §9.2.4 we described how a prepositional NP—such as the Recipient here—can drop its preposition and move into direct object slot when it is particularly salient to some instance of an activity, e.g. *John gave Tom a book*. GIVE A constructions invariably employ the latter syntactic frame—one would say *give Mary a push*, scarcely *\*give a push to Mary*. In fact, GIVE A constructions tend only to be used when the original transitive object has a specific, individuated reference, and thus fits naturally into object slot; the NP consisting of *a* plus verb base does not have reference to an entity, and it is not plausible for an NP like *a push* to be first object, with an NP like *Mary* relegated to a prepositional phrase.

Note also that although the lexical verb *take* may passivise on its object, and *give* may potentially passivise on both first and second objects (§11.2), the *a*-plus-verb-base NP in a HAVE A, TAKE A or GIVE A construction may never become passive subject—we would never hear *\*A swim (in the pool) was had/ taken* or *\*A push was given Mary*. The HAVE A, TAKE A and GIVE A constructions satisfy none of the criteria for passivisation that were presented in §11.1.

Some intransitive verbs—and also some inherent preposition verbs—do occur in the GIVE A construction. They divide into two sets. With one set *give* has a single NP following it, consisting of *a* plus the intransitive verb base, e.g. *John laughed, John gave a laugh*. With the other set there are two NPs following *give*, the second being *a* plus verb root while the first corresponds to a prepositional NP (generally marked by *at* or *to*) from the basic sentence, e.g. *John looked/smiled/winked at Mary, John gave Mary a look/smile/wink*; and *Mary waved to/at John, Mary gave John a wave*.

There are rare instances of the GIVE A construction occurring with a ditransitive verb, such as *lend* in *Will you give me a lend of your ruler?* This is most appropriately related to the basic sentence *Will you lend me your ruler?* (itself derived from *Will you lend your ruler to me?* by reassignment of the prepositional NP into direct object slot). The original first object remains as first object, *a* plus verb base is the new second object, and the original second object becomes marked by *of* in the GIVE A construction (as a constituent within the NP *a lend of your ruler*). *Of* here plays a similar role to that described above for HAVE A and TAKE A constructions involving a transitive verb—compare with the basic sentence *Can I borrow your ruler?* and periphrastic *Can I have a borrow of your ruler?*

## 14.3. Meaning

*(a)*  HAVE A VERB

We can say *I walked in the garden after lunch yesterday* or *I walked in the garden from dawn until dusk yesterday*. The periphrastic construction *have a walk* is possible in the first instance, *I had a walk in the garden after lunch yesterday*, but not in the second; one would not use *have a walk* with *from dawn until dusk*. Similarly, one can say *We ran around the oval until the rain began* but scarcely *\*We had a run around the oval until the rain began.*

Looking now at locational specification, we can say *walk in the park* or *walk from Oxford to Reading*. The first is fine for *have a walk* but not the second; *have a walk* would not be used with a definite statement of journey or destination, such as *from Oxford to Reading*. Similarly, one could say *have a swim in the river* but scarcely *\*have a swim across the river.*

It appears that there is no periphrastic HAVE A construction corresponding to a basic sentence describing some activity that is related to a time or space limitation, or that is being used to achieve some goal. The HAVE A construction emphasises the activity, and the fact that the subject indulges in it for a certain period. The subject is not trying to walk or swim to get anywhere, they are just 'having a walk' or 'having a swim'. One could say that an element of the meaning of the HAVE A construction is 'do it a bit'. Indeed, it is common to insert *a bit of* between *a* and the verb, e.g. *We had a bit of a walk/talk/think.*

It is possible to *have a long walk* or *have a long laugh* or *have a short swim*. The adjective indicates that the subject indulged in the activity for a long or short time (or over a long or short distance)—but they are still just walking or whatever because they want to, rather than to get anywhere or for any other purpose.

The verb *stroll* refers to 'slow, leisurely walking, with no desire to arrive somewhere'. This accords well with the meaning of HAVE A. In fact, *stroll* is one of the verbs most frequently used in the HAVE A construction.

HAVE A always describes some volitional act and the subject must be human (or perhaps a higher animal). We can say *That child had a roll down the grassy bank* (when they were doing it on purpose, for fun) but not *\*That stone had a roll down the grassy bank*. The volitional element is brought out by comparison between *slip*, which refers to an unwanted, uncontrolled activity, and *slide*, which can refer to something done voluntarily, for pleasure. One may say *She had a slide on the ice* but not *\*She had a slip* *on the ice* (or, if the latter is possible, it must be an instance of the Experiencer *have* construction—§14.1).

HAVE A describes something done 'a bit', done voluntarily. And we have said that it is an activity the subject indulges themself in—if not for pleasure, then for relief. Suppose someone is upset, and holding back tears. We might encourage them: *Go on, you have a cry*. That is: you indulge in the activity of crying, for a period, for the relief it will provide. Similarly *have a grumble* (you'll feel better after it) or *have a sit-down* (after all, you've been standing up all morning).

It is interesting that one often hears *Have a sit-down* or *Have a lie-down* but seldom *Have a stand-up*. The last example is perfectly possible; it is just that the circumstances for its use do not readily arise. It can, however, easily be contextualised. Suppose a lot of people are sitting or squatting in a restricted space, some getting cramps, and there is room for just one person at a time to stand up. The leader might say: *Go on Tom, you have a stand-up now* (that is, indulge yourself for a while in the activity of standing up).

In summary, the HAVE A construction carries meaning elements: (i) something done voluntarily, by the subject; (ii) to indulge themself in something they enjoy doing, or which provides relief; (iii) the activity being done 'for a bit', at the subject's whim (rather than to achieve any transcendental goal).

### (*b*)   GIVE A VERB

We can distinguish two subtypes of the GIVE A VERB construction: (I) involving an NP (with noun or pronoun as head) as first object, before the NP consisting of *a* plus verb base, e.g. *She gave me a punch/push/kiss/ smile/look*; (II) where the only NP following *give* is *a* plus verb base—this occurs with some verbs from the CORPOREAL type and from the SHOUT subtype of SPEAKING, e.g. *He gave a laugh/cry/sob/sigh/cough/shout*.

Some of the restrictions on the GIVE A construction are similar to those on HAVE A. We can say *She looked at him all day* but not \**She gave him a look all day*, and *I pushed the car all the way home* but not \**I gave the car a push all the way home*. It is acceptable to say *I gave the child a carry while going up that hill on the way to town* but scarcely \**I gave the child a carry to town*. From these and similar data we can infer that the GIVE A construction refers to the subject doing something at their own whim, for a certain period, and not to satisfy any external goal (as expressed by *all day, to town*, etc.).

There is a subtle difference between the HAVE A and GIVE A constructions. We have already said that HAVE A implies 'do it for a bit'. If a certain verb refers to some activity that can be done in incremental units, then GIVE A plus that verb is likely to refer to just one unit of the activity. *Give a laugh* most often relates to a single 'ha', whereas *have a laugh* could describe someone laughing for a minute or two at something they found excruciatingly funny. *Give a cry* (or *sob*) is likely to be a single sob, whereas *have a cry* could be someone crying their heart out, for as long as it took to relieve some condition of distress. A trainer might say to a boxer: *Go on, you have a punch of the punchball now*; this invites them to rain punches on it for a reasonable period of time. But if the trainer said: *Go on, you give it a punch*, just a single hit might be expected. The difference is apparent even with *pull* and *push*, which describe activities that are most often continuous. *You have a pull of the rope* could be realised by the addressee pulling for a few minutes, whereas *You give the rope a pull* might relate to a single tug. The verb *jerk* generally refers to a single unit of pulling; note that we can say *Give it a jerk* but not *\*Have a jerk of it*. (It is sometimes possible to use *a bit of* with *give*, if the underlying verb can refer to a continuous activity—*Give it a bit of a pull* has a meaning very similar to *Have a bit of a pull of it*. The important point is that when *a bit of* is not included, the GIVE A construction is likely to refer to a single unit of activity.)

Like HAVE A, the GIVE A construction of type (I) is limited to human subjects acting with volition. If Mary were walking past John then *He bumped her* could describe either a purposeful or an accidental bump but *He gave her a bump* must refer to something done on purpose.

Let us turn now to a critical semantic difference between HAVE A and GIVE A constructions. Consider:

(5a)  *Mary looked at John* (*through the window*)
(5b)  *Mary had a look at John* (*through the window*)
(5c)  *Mary gave John a look* (*through the window*)

Sentence (5b) describes Mary indulging herself in looking at John, for a period; it is immaterial whether or not John realises that he is being observed. Sentence (5c), in contrast, describes Mary communicating with John—she gives him a look and he notices it. It could be a look of warning, of invitation, of loathing, or of love.

The GIVE A construction of type (I) describes something being 'transferred' from subject to object (a metaphorical extension of the 'transfer of possession' in lexical use of *give*)—that is, the object must be affected by the activity.

*Give a carry* can have a human object as in *I gave the child a carry*; the child is affected by this beneficial gesture (it does not now have the effort of walking on its own). But it would be quite infelicitous to say *\*I gave the suitcase a carry*, since the suitcase would not be affected by being carried. The GIVE A construction can involve a verb with an inanimate object, but there is always an implication that the object is affected in some way, e.g. *give the table a wipe* (it was dirty before and is now clean), *give the door a kick* (say, to break it down), *give the pudding a warm* (to make it more palatable), *give the car a push* (to get it to start), *give the rope a pull* (to try to dislodge the end from where it is trapped).

The verb *smile* has two senses: (i) showing amusement at something, e.g. *smile at Zelig's antics*; (ii) using the gesture to communicate with someone, e.g. *smile at Mary*. The first sense is similar to *laugh* in *laugh at Zelig's antics*, the second to *wink* in *wink at Mary*. Now *smile* can occur in both HAVE A and GIVE A constructions. But it is the first sense that is involved with HAVE A, e.g. *Tom had a smile at Zelig's antics*, where Tom is indulging himself in smiling, for a period, at something he finds funny (whether Zelig knows that his antics have evinced a smile is immaterial). And it is the second sense of *smile* that is involved in a GIVE A construction of type (I), e.g. *Tom gave Mary a smile*; use of this sentence implies that Mary did notice the smile. *Laugh*, parallel to the first sense of *smile*, occurs just with HAVE A but not with the GIVE A construction of type (I), e.g. *Tom had a laugh at Zelig's antics* but not *\*Tom gave Mary a laugh*. And *wink*, parallel to the second sense of *smile*, takes just GIVE A, e.g. *Tom gave Mary a wink* but not *\*Tom had a wink at Zelig's antics*. The two senses of *smile* are, in fact, parallel to the two senses of *look* (one contemplative, one communicative) illustrated in (5b) and (5c).

It may be useful to give one further example of the semantic difference between HAVE A and GIVE A. The verb *stroke* can occur in

(6a)  *Go on, you have a stroke of it!*
(6b)  *Go on, you give it a stroke!*

Now consider two scenarios. In the first a friend has bought a new fur coat, which you admire. She invites you to stroke it. Would she be more likely to use sentence (6a) or (6b)? In the second scenario a friend's cat brushes against you. The friend knows that you like cats and encourages you to stroke it. Again, would she use (6a) or (6b)?

Native speakers prefer sentence (6b) for stroking a cat and (6a) for stroking a fur coat. The GIVE A construction is used when the object is likely to be affected by the action—the cat will probably enjoy being stroked, and may purr in response. The HAVE A construction is appropriate for stroking a coat; the garment is unaffected and in this instance it is simply the stroker who is indulging themself.

In summary, the GIVE A construction, type (I), carries the following meaning elements: (i) something done voluntarily by the subject; (ii) to 'transfer' something to an object, either affecting the object in some physical way, or communicating with another person; (iii) the activity being 'done a bit', at the subject's whim—and often, if the verb refers to an activity that can be incremental, just one unit of the activity is performed. (Note that the 'one unit' interpretation does not always apply, e.g. *give the cat a stroke* could refer to as long or longer a period of stroking as *have a stroke of the fur coat*.)

We can now look at GIVE A construction type (II), where there is no object NP of the underlying verb. Semantic characteristic (iii) certainly applies: *give a laugh/cry/cough/shout/roar* is likely to refer to a single corporeal gesture in contrast to *have a laugh/cry/cough/shout/roar*, which is likely to refer to someone indulging in the activity for as long as they need.

Semantic characteristic (ii) applies in an indirect way in that an act of communication may be involved (as it never could be with HAVE A). Someone may *give a cough* to warn a friend to be careful in what they say, or *give a hollow laugh* to show that they don't think much of what has just been said; and similarly with *give a sigh*, *give a whistle*. In these circumstances the activity is voluntary, according with (i). It is, however, possible for someone to *give a cough* (or *a laugh*) spontaneously, without planning to do so; and we can also have a non-human subject, as in *The machine gave a long hiss/a loud bang and suddenly stopped*. It appears that the second type of GIVE A construction does not necessarily carry meaning element (i), that the subject acts in a volitional manner.

## (c)  TAKE A VERB

The lexical verb 'take' refers to a unit of activity that is volitional and premeditated; it involves physical effort, e.g. *She took the bottle out of the fridge*, *He took his shirt off*.

The periphrastic TAKE A VERB construction has relatively limited use in British English, being restricted to a subset of those verbs that occur in the

HAVE A construction. We will show that there are definite semantic differences between TAKE A and the HAVE A and GIVE A constructions. We will also show that the meaning of TAKE A shows some similarities to the lexical meaning of *take*.

Like HAVE A and type (I) of GIVE A, TAKE A refers to some volitional activity, done for its own sake (rather than to meet some external goal). Like HAVE A there is no overtone of a 'transfer', with the object being affected by the activity, which we identified for GIVE A.

TAKE A is like GIVE A—and contrasts with HAVE A—in often referring to a 'single unit' of activity. Both HAVE A and TAKE A can be used with *smell* and *sniff* but *take a sniff of it* seems a little more felicitous than *have a sniff of it* (because the verb *sniff* generally refers to a single inhalation) whereas *have a smell of it* is preferred over *take a smell of it* (since *smell* is likely to refer to an action extended in time, with many inhalations). TAKE A is particularly at home with *bite* and *swallow*—activities that have to be performed incrementally—and generally refers to a single unit of activity. But with verbs like *taste* and *suck*—referring to non-segmented activities—TAKE A sounds odd; *have a taste* and *have a suck* would be preferred. The 'unit' interpretation of TAKE A is most noticeable with CORPOREAL verbs but can also appear with verbs from other types. One may *take a walk around the lake*—the perimeter of the lake is a 'unit' walking course—in contrast to *have a walk in the park*—where the subject just walks 'for a bit'.

One important aspect of the meaning of TAKE A is that there is often physical effort involved on the part of the subject. Suppose Maggie is a small child playing off to one side; all you have to do is turn your head to look at her. I might suggest *Have a look at Maggie!*, if she is doing something cute. But if Maggie were asleep in her cot in another room and I wanted you to make sure she was all right, I would be likely to use the TAKE A construction (since you will have to move in order to check up on her), e.g. *Could you go and take a look at Maggie?* Indeed, it is normal to say *Have a look at this* but *Take a look at that*, since more exertion is likely to be involved in looking at 'that' than at 'this'.

The 'physical effort' component explains why one can use TAKE A with *walk* or *swim* but not with *sit down*; with *kick* or *bite* but not with *think*, *talk*, *laugh*, *cry* or *cough* (HAVE A can be used with all these verbs).

TAKE A often refers to a premeditated action, whereas HAVE A may be used for something done on the spur of the moment. One is likely to plan to *take a stroll* (e.g. *We always take a stroll after lunch on Sundays*) but one could just *have a stroll* at whim (e.g. *We had a stroll around the garden while we were waiting for you to get ready*).

In summary, the TAKE A VERB construction carries the meaning elements: (i) something done voluntarily, by the subject; (ii) often a definite premeditated activity; (iii) generally involving some physical effort on the part of the subject; (iv) just one unit of the activity being completed.

It was noted in §14.2 that there is a strong correlation (but not a coincidence) between transitivity and the use of HAVE A/TAKE A versus GIVE A. This has a semantic basis.

Type (I) of the GIVE A VERB construction refers to something being 'transferred' to an object. Plainly, transitive verbs, which refer to activities that link subject and object, are prototypical fillers of the 'VERB' slot. We also find that GIVE A occurs with a few inherent preposition verbs like *look at*, and with a few others like *smile* and *wink* where there is an 'addressee' marked with a preposition.

HAVE A and TAKE A just refer to the subject indulging in or taking part in some activity, for their own sake. It is natural that they should occur mostly with intransitive verbs. There are also a fair number of occurrences with transitive verbs, describing the subject indulging in doing something with respect to a particular object. With some of these verbs a preposition can intrude before the O NP in the basic sentence, and carries over into the periphrastic construction (e.g. *kick at the door, have a kick at the door*). With others *of* is inserted before the transitive object just in the HAVE A or TAKE A construction (e.g. *have a lick of the ice-cream*).

In §§2.11.5–6 we mentioned transitive verbs that may omit a reflexive or reciprocal pronoun, e.g. transitive *shave* (*someone*) and the inherently reflexive intransitive *shave* (sc. oneself); transitive *kiss* (*someone*) and the inherently reciprocal intransitive *kiss* (sc. each other). As might be predicted, the transitives occur with GIVE A and the intransitives with HAVE A. Thus, *John gave Fred/himself a shave* and *John had a shave* (this is in fact ambiguous between the HAVE A construction, where John does the shaving, and the Experiencer *have* construction, when it is related to *The barber shaved John, John had a shave at the barber's*). With *Mary gave John a kiss* we see that John is affected by the activity, which would be expected to be a single kiss. This contrasts with *John and Mary had a kiss*—they are indulging themselves in the activity of kissing, for a period of time.

In final summary, the semantic conditions for the GIVE A construction, involving 'transfer' from one participant to another, are similar to the characterisation of a transitive verb (i.e. that there be two core semantic roles). This is why the great majority of verbs taking GIVE A are transitive. The semantic conditions for HAVE A and TAKE A are that the activity be focused on, not its effect on any object; this is why most verbs occurring in these construction types are intransitive.

## 14.4. Occurrence

The semantic characteristics of the HAVE A, GIVE A and TAKE A constructions determine the verbs that occur in these syntactic frames. They are only compatible with verbs that describe volitional activities, and where the subject can just do it for a short period, without necessarily reaching any final result. GIVE A normally involves 'transfer' to some object which must be concrete (preferably human), never abstract.

It will be useful quickly to run through the semantic types, examining those verbs which have a semantic characterisation compatible with one or more of the HAVE A, GIVE A and TAKE A constructions.

MOTION and REST. Verbs in the RUN subtype describe a mode of motion (but no end-point) and may take HAVE A and TAKE A if it is plausible that the subject should want to indulge in that sort of activity, e.g. *run, walk, crawl, slide, roll, climb, dive, stroll, jump, swim*. Note that these verbs only occur in periphrastic constructions when they describe the activity done for its own sake, not when it has some definite goal—we can say *He had a jump down the path* parallel to *He jumped down the path*, but not *\*He had a jump over the fence* alongside *He jumped over the fence*.

Similar comments apply to the SIT subtype, which includes *sit (down), stand (up), lie (down), crouch (down), lean, float*; here HAVE A is possible but not TAKE A (possibly because there is no physical effort involved). If some SIT verbs seem uneasy with HAVE A, this is simply because people do not often indulge themselves in that activity, e.g. *?Have a crouch*. But such usages can be contextualised, as we demonstrated in §14.3 for *have a stand-up*.

Some RUN verbs can be used as causatives. These may occur with GIVE A, parallel to the corresponding intransitive with HAVE A, e.g. *I walked for a while after lunch, I walked the dog for a while after lunch, I had a bit of a walk after lunch, I gave the dog a bit of a walk after lunch.*

SIT verbs may also be used causatively, e.g. *I sat down after lunch, I sat the child down after lunch.* Yet we can say *I had a bit of a sit-down after lunch* but not *\*I gave the child a bit of a sit-down after lunch.* There is a straightforward explanation. The intransitive verb *sit* (*down*) has two senses: (i) get into a sitting position, e.g. *He sat down rather suddenly*, and (ii) be in a sitting position, e.g. *He sat (down) on the sofa all afternoon.* HAVE A can only apply to sense (ii), a continuous activity with no end-point, whereas the causative is based on sense (i), 'put into a sitting position' (this cannot be 'done a bit' and so is incompatible with the GIVE A construction).

Verbs in the ARRIVE, TAKE, STAY and PUT subtypes describe motion or rest with respect to a definite Locus, e.g. *arrive, return, go, cross, take, send, move, stay, put.* One either arrives at a place or one doesn't, crosses a bridge or doesn't, puts a thing in a place or doesn't—it is not possible to indulge in arriving or crossing or putting for a short while. Because of their meanings, these verbs cannot be used with HAVE A, TAKE A and GIVE A.

Sapir's example *move* is particularly interesting. The way this verb is generally used—both intransitively and transitively—it implies shifting position from one definite Locus to another, e.g. *They've moved (from London to Bristol)* or *She moved it (from the mantelpiece to the coffee table).* There is an end-point implied, which is why *move* is not used with HAVE A, GIVE A or TAKE A. Note that HAVE A is quite acceptable with a verb such as *wriggle*—from the RUN subtype—which does just refer to a mode of motion, with no end-points.

The FOLLOW subtype refers to motion with respect to something that is moving, e.g. *follow, lead, track*, and the CONTAIN subtype refers to position with respect to something that is at rest, e.g. *surround.* The meanings of these types are incompatible with the HAVE A, TAKE A and GIVE A constructions.

The CARRY subtype refers to motion in juxtaposition with some moving object. Here HAVE A is possible when the subject just wants to indulge in the activity for a little while, e.g. *Let me have a carry of that new suitcase you designed*, and GIVE A when the thing carried is affected (it may be saved from exertion by the carrying), e.g. *Give the sick dog a carry.* Handle and *catch*, from the HOLD subtype, may also be used to refer to the subject indulging themself in something for a bit and may occur with HAVE A, e.g. *Let me have a handle of that new racket/catch of that new ball.*

Verbs from the THROW subtype describe causing something to be in motion. Such an activity can be done 'a bit', at the subject's whim, and these verbs may occur with HAVE A and GIVE A, e.g. *Can I have a throw of that new Frisbee?* and *Give the bed a push, will you, then I can sweep around this side*. Once again, the activity must be potentially continuous—we can *pull the rope* or *give the rope a pull* but, parallel to *pull/draw the sword from the scabbard* it is not possible to say *\*give the sword a pull/draw from the scabbard*, since this activity does have an end-point.

*Open, close* and *shut*, from the OPEN subtype, refer to an end-point and are not semantically compatible with HAVE A, TAKE A or GIVE A. Most verbs in the DROP subtype describe involuntary motion, e.g. *fall, spill*. There is *drop*, referring to something that may be done deliberately, but it is in- stantaneous—one either drops a vase or one doesn't; it would not be plausible to indulge in 'having a drop of the vase' or 'giving the vase a drop'.

AFFECT. Many verbs of straightforward affect, from the HIT, STAB, RUB and TOUCH subtypes, may occur with HAVE A or GIVE A. There is a tendency to use GIVE A with a basic sentence in straightforward transitive form, but HAVE A with a basic sentence that has a preposition inserted before the object (§9.2.3), e.g. *give the door a kick* (here the kick affects the door) and *have a kick at the door* (here the subject indulges in kicking, with where the kick is aimed being quite secondary). Similarly with *stroke, punch, rub, wipe, brush*. Note that one can *have a shoot at* (e.g. *the rabbits*) but not *\*give the rabbits a shoot* (this could only be interpreted as the Permissive *give* construction; §14.1). Shooting something implies a definite result, and it cannot be 'done a bit'.

Whether a periphrastic construction is possible may depend on the semantic nature not only of the verb but also of the object NP. For instance, one could say *have a kick of the ball* (with a meaning difference from *have a kick at the ball*), but scarcely *\*have a kick of the door*.

A number of nouns describing weapons or implements may also be used as AFFECT verbs, e.g. *stone, spear, knife, whip, belt, brush*. They would generally not be used with GIVE A if the object is human because of the possibility of confusion with the lexical verb *give*, e.g. we can say *They stoned the Christians* but scarcely, with similar meaning, *They gave the Christians a stone*—this would imply handing them a stone, rather than throwing stones at them. (Note that the lexical verb is likely to be accorded precedence, if there is a conflict between lexical use of *give* and the periphrastic GIVE A construction.) However, GIVE A constructions with such verbs are acceptable if the object is inanimate, and could not be Recipient of the lexical verb *give*, e.g. *give the overcoat a brush* (note that GIVE A is allowed here since the overcoat is affected by the activity, being made clean).

HAVE A and GIVE A are most common in colloquial styles and often refer to something done quite casually, for fun. A professional painter, for instance, would scarcely be likely to say that he was *having a paint*—he just paints, because that's his job. But if a group of friends had organised a painting party, doing up someone's house, then someone could well extend an invitation: *Come on, John, you have a paint now!* or *Why don't you give the banisters a paint, Mary?*

Verbs from the AFFECT type that refer to an end-product are unlikely to be found with HAVE A or GIVE A, e.g. *clothe, cover, bake, melt, break, chip, crash*. However, a verb like *tear* refers to an activity that may be done to varying degrees—one can *tear it a little bit*, or *give it a little tear* (whereas one cannot, because of the meaning of *smash*, \**smash it a little bit* or \**give it a little smash*).

TAKE A is found with only a handful of AFFECT verbs—*take a kick at the ball, take a punch at Tom*, and very few others.

GIVING. Some verbs from this type refer to temporary transfer of possession, which can be for a short while; these verbs may occur with HAVE A or GIVE A. The interesting point is that the focus appears always to be on the Recipient. Thus *lend* has Recipient as object and here GIVE A is used (e.g. *I'll give you a lend of my boat for the weekend if you like*) whereas *borrow* has Recipient as subject and this verb occurs with HAVE A (e.g. *Can I have a borrow of your boat for the weekend, please?*). *Rent* can be used in either syntactic frame and so we get both *I'll give you a rent of my boat* and *Can I have a rent of your boat?* (*Can I have the/a loan of your boat for the weekend?* involves the derived form *loan*, plus either definite or indefinite article. There appears to be little meaning difference between this and the HAVE A construction, *Can I have a lend of your boat for the weekend?* The latter may just be more colloquial.)

Other GIVING verbs refer to some definite action which could not be done 'for a bit'; i.e. something is either given, sold, bought, bequeathed, presented, exchanged or not, with no half-measures possible. These verbs are thus not found in HAVE A, GIVE A or TAKE A constructions.

CORPOREAL. HAVE A is possible with many verbs of this type, whether describing something that is taken into or expelled from the body, or just referring to a bodily gesture or state, e.g. *drink, chew, suck, smoke, bite, taste, sniff, fart, pee, yawn, sneeze, sleep, hug, kiss, fuck.* HAVE A is plainly not possible with an end-point verb like *die*, nor with something that describes an inevitable process and could not normally be indulged in just a bit, such as *breathe* (although one might conceivably say to a sick person: *Have a breathe of this oxygen*). TAKE A is possible with verbs describing things being taken into the body, particularly if this is likely to be performed incrementally, e.g. *bite, swallow, sniff.*

It is interesting to consider why we can *have a drink/bite/chew/nibble/taste* but not *\*have an eat*. There may in fact be a number of contributory reasons. One could be that there is an independent noun *drink*, cognate with the verb *drink*, but corresponding to *eat* there are only the non-cognate nouns *feed* and *meal*. It may be because we can say *Have a* (e.g. *ice-cold*) *drink*, where *drink* is a noun, that the HAVE A construction is also used with *drink*, e.g. *Have a sneaky drink*, where *drink* is a verb. I must confess to being slightly mystified as to why *\*have an eat* is unacceptable; we are not, however, unduly impoverished by this lack since the activity of consuming food 'just a bit' may be expressed by *have a bite/nibble/taste* (e.g. *of this pie*), parallel with *have a drink/sip/taste* for the consumption of a liquid.

Transitive verbs from the CORPOREAL type that refer to something which affects another person may take the GIVE A construction type (I), e.g. *smile, wink, kiss, hug, fuck, wake*. And a number of verbs describing bodily gestures take GIVE A sense (II), where there is no independent object, e.g. *laugh, cry, sob, cough.*

The other Primary-A types do not occur with HAVE A, GIVE A or TAKE A. WEATHER verbs lack a human subject. And verbs in COMPETITION, SOCIAL CONTRACT, USING, and OBEYING are not amenable to a 'do it a bit' interpretation. The verb *use*, for instance, implies using something for a purpose, and not just indulging in using it for the sake of doing so.

Turning now to Primary-B verbs, the LOOK and WATCH subtypes of ATTENTION refer to the Perceiver directing their attention, and this may be done 'just a bit'. Thus, HAVE A may be used with *look (at), listen (to), search, hunt* and *watch*, e.g. *Have a look at this photo, Have a listen to my new record, if you like. Look* may also occur with TAKE A, when the subject has to move to see, and with GIVE A, referring to a mode of communication. The other subtypes of ATTENTION—with verbs such as *see, hear, notice, show, recognise, discover, witness*—refer to some definite act of perception, which could not be done 'a bit'; they are not found in HAVE A, TAKE A or GIVE A constructions.

HAVE A can be used with those verbs from the THINKING type that can refer to a general, undifferentiated chain of thought—*think, ponder* and perhaps also *meditate*. Verbs like *remember, assume, suppose, know, believe* (as well as all in the DECIDING type) refer to some definite act, while *consider* implies that all aspects of some topic are carefully thought over; for none of these is an 'indulge' or 'do a bit' meaning possible. *Guess* can also refer to a definite act but *have a guess* is said, often with strongly jocular overtones—*'How old am I?' 'Oh, I don't know.' 'Go on, have a guess!'*

Many SPEAKING verbs have a derived nominal which may be used with *make a*, and sometimes with *have a* or *give a*, e.g. *suggestion, declaration, explanation, proposal*. Some occur in their base form, e.g. *make a promise/ offer, give a promise*. None of these satisfy the criteria set out in §14.1 (peripheral constituents in the basic sentence may not all be retained when *give* or *have* is added). HAVE A VERB constructions of the kind dealt with in this chapter occur just with some verbs from the TALK subtype, referring to the activity of vocal communication (e.g. *have a talk/chat/joke*), and with some from the SHOUT subtype, referring to the manner of vocal production (e.g. *have a shout/swear/pray/whistle*). *Shout* itself also occurs with GIVE A. The occurrence of *shout* in peripheral constructions is very similar to that of *laugh*—compare *give a shout* (a single cry, which may be involuntary) and *have a shout* (the subject indulges in the activity, perhaps to let off steam).

*Speak* just refers to the fact that someone uses a language; *talk*, in contrast, describes the use they make of it (recall the discussion in §5.4). The activity referred to by *talk* can be done 'for a bit'—alongside *John and Mary talked in the lounge* there is *John and Mary had a talk in the lounge*. With *speak*, on the other hand, one either does it or one doesn't; this is why it is not felicitous to say *\*John and Mary had a speak in the corridor*, corresponding to *John and Mary spoke in the corridor*. Note that *give a talk* is not an instance of GIVE A, since it fails the semantic criterion—*John talked to the children* can be quite casual but *John gave the children a talk* (or *John gave a talk to the children*) implies a formal address. *Talk* is here an independent noun, just like *speech* in *John gave a speech*.

*Argue* is an interesting verb. There is the derived noun *argument*—one can *have an argument*. But there is also the HAVE A construction *have (a bit of) an argue*. This would only be said in colloquial speech, and it could only refer to a mild, friendly altercation, in contrast to *have an argument*, which implies a more deeply felt disagreement. (If two people were having an argument about something then it might lead to blows, but if they were having (a bit of) an argue it never would.)

Some verbs in the ANNOYING type can occur with *give* and *a*, e.g. *He gave me a shock/scare/surprise*, but this is not the GIVE A construction. It fails criterion (*a*) in §14.1 since the subject of an ANNOYING verb can be an NP or a complement clause but the subject of *give a* plus ANNOYING verb can only be an NP—we can say *That John has been released from prison scares me* but not *\*That John has been released from prison gives me a scare* (only *John gave me a scare*). Note that the verb *frighten*, with similar meaning to *shock*, *scare* and *surprise*, takes on a different form after *give*, i.e. *give a fright*. LIKING verbs also have derived nominals (e.g. *take a liking to*) but—save for *dread* in *have a (bit of a) dread of*—they do not occur with HAVE A, TAKE A or GIVE A. The ACTING, HAPPENING, COMPARING and RELATING types are not amenable to a 'do it a bit' interpretation and so are not used with HAVE A, TAKE A or GIVE A.

No secondary verbs are found in HAVE A, TAKE A or GIVE A constructions. There are collocations *have a try (at)*, *have a (further) attempt (at)*, *give it a try*, *(don't) have a hope (of)* but these do not satisfy the criteria set out in §14.1. HAVE A and GIVE A constructions may not productively be based on sentences with *try*, *attempt* or *hope*—that is, corresponding to *Try to eat the spinach*, *Try eating the breadfruit*, *I don't hope to win*, we cannot say *\*Have a try to eat the spinach*, *\*Have a try eating the breadfruit*, *\*I don't have a hope to win*. There are of course many idioms involving *have*, *give* and *take*—e.g. *have a go*, *give (someone) a hand (with)*, *take hold (of)*—which must be carefully distinguished from the constructions discussed in this chapter.

We have seen, in this section, that the occurrence of a verb in the HAVE A, GIVE A and TAKE A construction is determined by whether the meaning of the verb is compatible with the meaning components of the constructions, as they were described in §14.3.

The fact that HAVE A, GIVE A and TAKE A are most used in colloquial speech may impose another restriction—only colloquial-sounding verbs are likely to be found in this construction. One may talk about *having a pee* but not *\*having a urinate*, and *having a think* but not *\*having a contemplate*.

It would surely be instructive to study the occurrence of HAVE A, TAKE A and GIVE A across a variety of speech styles. Indeed, these constructions might well prove to be an indexical feature for the sociolinguistic classification of different formal and informal speech styles.

## Notes to Chapter 14

My criterion (*c*) in §14.1, concerning adverb/adjective correspondence, is based on Cattell (1969: 278ff.). Other useful discussions of these constructions include Strang (1970: 101), Vissler (1963: 138–41), Curme (1931: 22–3), Poutsma (1914–29: part II, sect. ii, pp. 397–400), Olsson (1961), Green (1974), Prince (1972, 1974), Nickel (1968), Cattell (1984) and especially Wierzbicka (1982). Stein (1991) combines useful discussion with a thorough survey of the literature.

Research on this topic was assisted by consulting materials in the Survey of English Usage at University College London. In 1980 Professor Randolph Quirk allowed me to riff through drawers of slips, and in 1987 Professor Sidney Greenbaum let me search the computerised corpus. Judith L. Klavans was generous in printing out instances of *give* from an electronic corpus she had assembled at IBM. Calvert Watkins and Steve Johnson provided most insightful comments during seminar presentations of an earlier version of this chapter, in 1980, at Harvard and at University College London respectively.

The topic of this chapter is a major source of dialect variation between American and British/Australian varieties. In his generous review of the first edition of this book, Charles W. Kreidler (1991: 200–1) says, 'Dixon is aware that dialect differences can interfere with the reader's understanding and acceptance of what he presents … He suggests that such differences "should not affect the broad sweep of conclusions reached in this book, only their detailed articulation." Actually, it is only in Chapter 11 [now the present chapter, 14] that Canadian and American readers are likely to find any great differences of usage. In the first ten chapters an occasional example or interpretation may seem slightly awry or unfamiliar, but only slightly. With Chapter 11 [now 14], on periphrastic verb expressions, North Americans may feel that they have stepped through a looking glass into a surreal world'.

# Appendix
## List of adjective and verb types,
## with sample members

The lists below recapitulate the adjective types given in §3.2 and the verb types from Chapters 4–6, and their semantic roles and subtypes, with the sample members quoted there.

## Adjective types

DIMENSION type, e.g. *big, great, short, thin, round, narrow, deep*

PHYSICAL PROPERTY type, e.g. *hard, strong, clean, cool, heavy, sweet, fresh, cheap, quiet, noisy*
  CORPOREAL subtype, e.g. *well, sick, ill, dead; absent; beautiful, ugly*

SPEED type—*quick (at), fast (at), slow (at), rapid, sudden*

AGE type—*new, old, young, modern*

COLOUR type, e.g. *white, black, red, crimson, mottled, golden*

VALUE type, e.g. (*a*) *good, bad, lovely, atrocious, perfect;* (*b*) *odd, strange, curious; necessary, crucial; important; lucky*

DIFFICULTY type, e.g. *easy, difficult, tough, hard, simple*

VOLITION type, e.g. *deliberate, accidental, purposeful*

QUALIFICATION type
  DEFINITE subtype, e.g. *definite, probable, true, obvious*
  POSSIBLE subtype, e.g. *possible, impossible*
  USUAL subtype, e.g. *usual, normal, common*
  LIKELY subtype, e.g. *likely, certain*
  SURE subtype, e.g. *sure*
  CORRECT subtype, e.g. *correct, right, wrong, appropriate, sensible*

HUMAN PROPENSITY type

FOND subtype, e.g. *fond* (*of*)

ANGRY subtype, e.g. *angry* (*with/at/about*), *jealous* (*of*), *mad* (*about*), *sad* (*about*)

HAPPY subtype, e.g. *anxious, keen, happy, thankful, careful, sorry, glad* (all taking *about*); *proud, ashamed, afraid* (all taking *of*)

UNSURE subtype, e.g. *certain, sure, unsure* (all taking *of* or *about*), *curious* (*about*)

EAGER subtype, e.g. *eager, ready, prepared* (all taking *for*), *willing*

CLEVER subtype, e.g. *clever, adept, stupid; lucky; kind, cruel; generous* (all taking *at*)

HONEST subtype, e.g. *honest* (*about/in/at*), *frank* (*in/about*)

BUSY subtype, e.g. *busy* (*at/with*), *occupied* (*with*), *preoccupied* (*with*), *lazy* (*over*)

SIMILARITY type, e.g. *like, unlike, similar to, different from, equal to/with, identical to, analogous to, separate from, independent of, consistent with*

## Primary-A verb types

MOTION type (Roles: Moving, Locus)

MOTION-a, the RUN subtype, e.g. *run, walk, crawl, slide, spin, roll, turn, wriggle, swing, wave, rock, shake, climb, dive, stroll, trot, gallop, jog, dance, march, jump, bounce, swim, fly, play; ride, drive*

MOTION-b, the ARRIVE subtype, e.g. (i) *arrive, return, go, come*; (ii) *enter, exit, cross, depart, travel, pass, escape; come in, go out*; (iii) *reach, approach, visit*

MOTION-c, the TAKE subtype, e.g. (i) *take, bring, fetch*; (ii) *send*; (iii) *move, raise, lift, steal*

MOTION-d, the FOLLOW subtype, e.g. (i) *follow, track, lead, guide, precede, accompany*; (ii) *meet*

MOTION-e, the CARRY subtype, e.g. *carry, bear, transport, cart*

MOTION-f, the THROW subtype, e.g. *throw, chuck, fling, pour, spray, water; push, press; pull, jerk, drag, tug, draw*

MOTION-g, the DROP subtype, e.g. *fall, drop, spill, tip* (*over*), *upset, overturn, capsize, trip, slip*

REST type (Roles: Resting, Locus)

REST-a, the SIT subtype, e.g. *sit* (*down*), *stand* (*up*), *lie* (*down*), *kneel*, *crouch, squat, lean, hang* (*down*), *float*

REST-b, the STAY subtype, e.g. *stay, settle* (*down*), *live, stop, remain, reside; attend*

REST-c, the PUT subtype, e.g. (i) *put, place, set, arrange, install, put* NP *on, sow, plant, fill, load, pack; hide; beach, land, shelve, dump;* (ii) *leave, desert, abandon, ground, take* NP *off*

REST-d, the CONTAIN subtype, e.g. *contain, enclose, encircle, adjoin; surround*

REST-e, the HOLD subtype, e.g. (i) *hold, handle;* (ii) *grab; grasp, clutch, catch, gather, pick up; capture, trap*

REST-f, the OPEN subtype, e.g. *open, close, shut; lock*

AFFECT type (Roles: Agent, Target, Manip)

AFFECT-a, the TOUCH subtype, e.g. *touch, stroke*

AFFECT-b, the HIT subtype, e.g. *hit, strike, punch, bump, kick, knock, tap, bash, slap, spank; whip, belt, stone, cane, hammer; shoot*

AFFECT-c, the STAB subtype, e.g. *pierce, prick, stab, dig, sting, knife, spear; cut, prune, mow, saw, slice, chop, hack*

AFFECT-d, the RUB subtype, e.g. *rub, wipe, scrape, scratch, mark; sweep, brush, shave, rake; polish, lick; wash*

AFFECT-e, the WRAP subtype, e.g. *wrap; cover; butter, roof, veil, clothe, dress, grease; plaster, paint, coat; surround, frame; put* NP *on; unwrap, uncover, unroof, undress; take* NP *off, peel, shell*

AFFECT-f, the STRETCH subtype, e.g. *stretch, extend, compress, bend, curl, fold, coil; twist, pinch, squeeze; vaporise, liquefy, solidify, melt; dissolve; freeze, cool* (*down*), *warm* (*up*), *heat* (*up*), *burn, singe*

AFFECT-g, the BUILD subtype (Product role), e.g. *build, knit, tie, make, weave, sew, shape, form, stir, mix, knead; fry, bake, cook; mend, repair; draw, write, sign, forge*

AFFECT-h, the BREAK subtype (Breaking role), e.g. *break, crush, squash, destroy, damage, wreck, collapse; tear, split, chip, crack, smash, crash; burst, explode, blow* NP *up, let* NP *off, erupt*

GIVING type (Roles: Donor, Gift, Recipient), e.g. *give, hand* (*over*), *lend, sell, rent, hire, pay, owe, bequeath; serve, feed, supply; present; donate, contribute, deliver, let; tip; reward, bribe; market; exchange, trade; borrow, buy, purchase, accept, receive*

OWN subtype (Roles: Owner, Possession), e.g. *have, lack, get, obtain, come by, gain, own, possess; belong to; lose*

CORPOREAL type (Roles: Human, Substance), e.g. *eat, dine (on), chew, suck, drink, smoke; bite, nibble, sip; smell, feel, taste, sniff, swallow, breathe, smile, fart, burp, cough, spit, shit, pee, vomit; live; yawn, sneeze, laugh, leer, wink, blink, sob, sleep, dream, think, die; weep, cry, shiver, faint, pass out, wheeze, sweat, rest, ache, suffer, come to, recover, be born; wake, waken, grow, swell, hurt, bleed, heal, drown; bring* NP *to, comfort, console, cure, soothe, ease, nurse, doctor; kill, murder, assassinate, beat up, injure, wound, poison, give birth to; kiss, embrace, hug, cuddle, fuck*

WEATHER type (no roles), e.g. *rain, snow, hail, thunder*

COMPETITION type (Competitor role), e.g. *conquer, beat, overcome, race (against); resist, fight, play; win, lose; attack, guard, shield, surrender; defend; compete (with), struggle (against)*

SOCIAL CONTRACT type, e.g. *appoint, employ, dismiss, sack, fire; promote, nominate, convert, arrest, prosecute, impeach, punish; govern, rule, civilise, missionise, join; manage; apply for; qualify for, resign from; withdraw (from), work (at); marry*

USING type, e.g. *use, operate, manipulate, work, employ, wear, waste, fiddle with*

OBEYING type, e.g. *obey, execute, process, deal with, grant, refuse; perform*

## Primary-B verb types

ATTENTION type (Roles: Perceiver, Impression)

ATTENTION-a, the SEE subtype, e.g. *see, hear, smell, taste, feel; observe, notice, perceive*

ATTENTION-b, the SHOW subtype, e.g. *show; demonstrate*

ATTENTION-c, the RECOGNISE subtype, e.g. *recognise, spot*

ATTENTION-d, the DISCOVER subtype, e.g. *discover, find*

ATTENTION-e, the WITNESS subtype—*witness*

ATTENTION-f, the LOOK subtype, e.g. *look (at), listen (to); stare (at), glare (at), peep (at), peer (at), squint (at), eavesdrop (on); search (for), look* (*for*), *hunt* (*for*); *inspect, study, investigate, scan, scrutinise, examine, check, view; explore, survey; visit*

ATTENTION-g, the WATCH subtype, e.g. *watch, listen* (*to*)

Also: (i) *ignore, disregard, overlook, pass* NP *over*; (ii) *appear, disappear*; (iii) *look, sound; smell, taste, feel*

THINKING type (Roles: Cogitator, Thought)

THINKING-a, the THINK subtype, e.g. *think* (*of/about/over*), *consider, imagine*

THINKING-b, the ASSUME subtype, e.g. *assume, suppose*

THINKING-c, the PONDER subtype, e.g. *ponder* (*on/over*), *meditate* (*on/about*), *brood* (*on/over*), *speculate* (*on/about*), *wonder* (*at/about*), *reflect* (*on/about*), *dream* (*of/about*), *contemplate*

THINKING-d, the REMEMBER subtype, e.g. *remember, forget*

THINKING-e, the KNOW subtype, e.g. *know, sense, feel, realise, learn, understand; teach*

THINKING-f, the CONCLUDE subtype, e.g. *conclude, infer, reason, argue, prove, demonstrate, show, guess*

THINKING-g, the SOLVE subtype, e.g. *solve, work* NP *out, devise, make* NP *up; analyse*

THINKING-h, the BELIEVE subtype, e.g. *believe, suspect, doubt*

DECIDING type (Roles: Decision-maker, Course)

DECIDING-a, the RESOLVE subtype, e.g. *decide* (*on*), *determine* (*on*), *resolve, plan, settle*

DECIDING-b, the CHOOSE subtype, e.g. *choose, select, pick* (*out*), *appoint, elect, vote* (*for/on*)

SPEAKING type (Roles: Speaker, Addressee(s), Medium, Message—with components Message-Label and Message-Content)

SPEAKING-a, the TALK subtype, e.g. *speak, talk, chat, gossip, converse, communicate, quarrel, argue, joke; write*

SPEAKING-b, the DISCUSS subtype, e.g. *discuss, refer to, describe*

SPEAKING-c, the SHOUT subtype, e.g. *shout, call, cry, roar, swear, pray, preach, narrate, recite, intone, read, sing; whistle, warble; translate, pronounce, mispronounce, utter; name*

SPEAKING-d, the REPORT subtype

set (i), e.g. *say, declare, assert, observe, joke, put* NP *about, give* NP *out, let* NP *out, put* NP *across, let on about*

set (ii), e.g. *state, affirm, rumour*

set (iii), e.g. *announce, proclaim, mention, note, report, regret*

set (iv), e.g. *remark (on), comment (on); explain*

set (v), e.g. *boast (about/of), brag (about/of), complain (about/of), grumble (about)*

set (vi), e.g. *suggest, claim, acknowledge, admit, confess (to), repute*

set (vii), e.g. *undertake, offer, propose, agree (with)*

set (viii), e.g. *promise, threaten*

SPEAKING-e, the INFORM subtype, e.g. *inform, lecture, agree (with); remind*

SPEAKING-f, the TELL subtype, e.g. *tell, ask, request, beg, enquire, demand; answer, reply (to)*

SPEAKING-g, the ORDER subtype, e.g. (i) *order, command, urge, instruct, encourage; warn, caution, persuade, invite, recommend (to); tell, remind, ask, request, beg;* (ii) *forbid, discourage, dissuade, prohibit*

SPEAKING-h, the FORGIVE subtype, e.g. (i) *insult, slander, curse, abuse, scold, blame, rebuke, forgive, pardon, praise, thank, congratulate, compliment, tell* NP *off, pick on;* (ii) *accuse, excuse;* (iii) *greet, welcome, introduce;* (iv) *cheer, applaud, apologise*

LIKING type (Roles: Experiencer, Stimulus—with components Stimulus-Label and Stimulus-Content), e.g. (i) *like, love, hate, prefer, fear; dread;* (ii) *dislike, loathe, abhor, admire, value; regret; rejoice in/at; (don't) mind (about), (don't) care (about);* (iii) *enjoy, favour, object to, approve of;* (iv) *worship, fall for;* also: *envy, pity*

ANNOYING type (same roles as LIKING), e.g. *frighten, terrify, scare, shock, upset, surprise; offend; delight, please, satisfy, entertain, amuse, excite, inspire; impress, concern, trouble, worry, grieve, dismay, depress, sadden; madden, infuriate, annoy, anger, disappoint; confuse, bewilder, deceive, trick, perplex, puzzle; interest, distract, bore; attract; embarrass, disgust; tire, exhaust, bother*

ACTING type, e.g. *act, behave; adopt, copy, imitate, mimic, mime, reproduce*

HAPPENING type, e.g. *happen, take place; organise, arrange, bring* NP *about; commit, attend to, neglect, put* NP *on, take* NP *on, do, tie* NP *in with, change, devise; experience, undergo; transpire*

COMPARING type, e.g. *resemble, differ (from); take after; distinguish (between), compare; class, group, cost, grade; match, balance, measure, weigh, time, count; fit, suit; equal; include, comprise, consist in/of, be made up of*

RELATING type, e.g. *depend* (*on*), *result* (*from*), *indicate*; *relate* (*to*), *imply, be due* (*to*); *show, demonstrate, suggest*

## Secondary-A verb types (no independent roles)

MODAL type—*will, would, shall, should, ought to, must, can, could, be to, may, might*; *used to*; *had better*; *need, dare*

SEMI-MODAL type—*be going to, have to, have got to, be able to, be about to, get to, be bound to*

BEGINNING type, e.g. (i) *begin, start, commence*; (ii) *continue* (*with*), *keep* (*on* (*with*)), *go on* (*with*); (iii) *finish, cease, stop, complete, discontinue*; also: *set in, break out*

TRYING type, e.g. (i) *try*; *attempt*; (ii) *succeed* (*in/at*), *manage*; (iii) *miss, fail*; (iv) *practise, repeat*

HURRYING type, e.g. *hurry* (*over/with*), *hasten* (*over/with*); *dawdle* (*over*); *hesitate* (*over/with*)

DARING type, e.g. *dare, venture*

## Secondary-B verb types

WANTING type (Role: Principal), e.g. (i) *want, wish* (*for*), *desire, crave, long* (*for*), *pine* (*for*); (ii) *hope* (*for*); (iii) *demand*; (iv) *need, require, deserve*; (v) *expect, wait* (*for*), *dread*; (vi) *intend, plan* (*for*), *aim* (*for*), *mean, prepare* (*for*); (vii) *pretend*

POSTPONING type (Role: Timer), e.g. *postpone, defer, put off, delay*; *avoid*

## Secondary-C verb types

MAKING type (Role: Causer), e.g. (i) *make, force, cause, drive, get, have*; *tempt*; (ii) *let, permit, allow*; (iii) *prevent, stop, spare, save, check* (*oneself*), *rescue, release*; (iv) *ensure*

HELPING type (Role: Helper), e.g. *help, aid, assist; cooperate (with), collaborate (with); hinder; support, oppose*

## Secondary-D verb types (Role: Arbiter)

SEEM type, e.g. *seem, appear, look, sound, feel; happen, come about*

MATTER type, e.g. *matter, count*

# References

AARTS, B. 1995. 'Secondary predicates in English', pp. 75–101 of *The verb in contemporary English: theory and description*, edited by B. Aarts and C. F. Meyer. Cambridge: Cambridge University Press.

ADAMS, V. 1973. *An introduction to Modern English word-formation*. London: Longman.

AIKHENVALD, A. Y. 2003. *A grammar of Tariana, from northwest Amazonia*. Cambridge: Cambridge University Press.

AKMAIJAN, A. 1977. 'The complement structure of perception verbs in an autonomous syntax framework', pp. 427–81 of *Formal syntax*, edited by P. W. Culicover, T. Wascow and A. Akmajian. New York: Academic Press.

ANDERSON, J. M. 1968. 'Ergative and nominative in English', *Journal of Linguistics*, 4: 1–32.

ANDERSON, S. R. 1971. 'On the role of deep structure in semantic interpretation', *Foundations of Language*, 7: 387–96.

ANDERWALD, L. 2002. *Negation in non-standard British English: gaps, regularizations and asymmetries*. London: Routledge.

ANSCHUTZ, A. 1997. 'How to choose a possessive noun phrase construction in four easy steps', *Studies in Language*, 21: 1–35.

BARKER, E. J. W. 1975. 'Voice—beyond the passive', *Proceedings of the Annual Meeting of the Berkeley Linguistics Society*, 1: 16–24.

BINNICK, R. I. 1971. '*Will* and *be going to*', *Papers from the Regional Meeting of the Chicago Linguistic Society*, 7: 40–51.

—— 1972. '*Will* and *be going to* II', *Papers from the Regional Meeting of the Chicago Linguistic Society*, 8: 3–9.

BOLINGER, D. L. 1942. '*Need*, auxiliary', *College English*, 4: 62–5.

—— 1968. 'Entailment and the meaning of structures', *Glossa*, 2: 119–27.

—— 1971. *The phrasal verb in English*. Cambridge, MA: Harvard University Press.

—— 1972. *That's that*. The Hague: Mouton.

—— 1974. 'Concept and percept: two infinitive constructions and their vicissitudes', pp. 65–91 of *World papers in phonetics: Festschrift for Dr Onishi's Kiju*. Tokyo: Phonetic Society of Japan.

—— 1975. 'On the passive in English', pp. 57–80 of *The first LACUS forum, 1974*, edited by A. Makkai and V. B. Makkai. Columbia, SC: Hornbeam Press.

—— 1977a. *Meaning and form*. London: Longman.

BOLINGER, D. L. 1977b. 'Transitivity and spatiality: the passive of prepositional verbs', pp. 57–78 of *Linguistics at the crossroads*, edited by A. Makkai, V. B. Makkai and L. Heilmann. Padua: Liviana Editrice; Lake Bluffs, IL: Jupiter Press.

—— 1978. 'Yes–no questions are not alternative questions', pp. 87–105 of *Questions*, edited by H. Hiz. Dordrecht: Reidel.

—— 1979. 'The jingle theory of double *-ing*', pp. 41–56 of *Function and context in linguistic analysis, a festschrift for William Haas*, edited by D. J. Allerton, E. Carney and D. Holdcroft. Cambridge: Cambridge University Press.

BORKIN, A. 1973. '*To be* and not *to be*', *Papers from the Regional Meeting of the Chicago Linguistic Society*, 9: 44–56.

—— 1984. *Problems in form and function*. Norwood, NJ: Ablex.

BRESNAN, J. W. 1979. *Theory of complementation in English syntax*. New York: Garland.

BROWN, K. 1991. 'Double modals in Hawick Scots', pp. 75–103 of *Dialects of English: studies in grammatical variation*, edited by P. Trudgill and J. K. Chambers. London: Longman.

CATTELL, N. R. 1969. 'The role of give and some related verbs in English Syntax', Ph.D. thesis, University of Newcastle, NSW.

—— 1984. *Composite predicates in English* (Syntax and semantics, 17). Sydney: Academic Press.

CHAPPELL, H. M. 1980. 'Is the *get*-passive adversative?', *Papers in Linguistics*, 13: 411–52.

COATES, J. 1983. *The semantics of the modal auxiliaries*. London: Croom Helm.

CURME, G. O. 1931. *A grammar of the English language*, vol. 3, *Syntax*. Boston: Heath.

—— 1935. *Parts of speech and accidence*. Boston: Heath.

—— 1947. *English grammar*. New York: Barnes and Noble.

DAVISON, A. 1980. 'Peculiar passives', *Language*, 56: 42–66.

DEANE, P. 1987. 'English possessives, topicality, and the Silverstein hierarchy', *Proceedings of the Annual Meeting of the Berkeley Linguistics Society*, 13: 65–76.

DECLERCK, R. 1991. A *comprehensive descriptive grammar of English*. Tokyo: Kaitakuska.

DIK, S. 1973. 'The semantic representation of manner adverbials', pp. 96–121 of *Linguistics in the Netherlands, 1972–73*, edited by A. Kraak. Assen: Van Gorcum.

DIXON, R. M. W. 1972. *The Dyirbal language of North Queensland*. Cambridge: Cambridge University Press.

—— 1977a. 'Where have all the adjectives gone?', *Studies in Language*, 1: 19–80. [Reprinted in Dixon 1982b: 1–62.]

—— 1977b. *A grammar of Yidiɲ*. Cambridge: Cambridge University Press.

—— 1979. 'Ergativity', *Language*, 55: 59–138.

DIXON, R. M. W. 1982a. 'The grammar of English phrasal verbs', *Australian Journal of Linguistics*, 2: 1–42.

—— 1982b. *Where have all the adjectives gone? and other essays in semantics and syntax*. Berlin: Mouton.

—— 1987. 'Studies in ergativity: introduction', *Lingua*, 71: 1–16. [This volume of *Lingua* was also issued as a monograph: *Studies in ergativity*, edited by R. M. W. Dixon. Amsterdam: North-Holland, 1987.]

—— 1988. *A grammar of Boumaa Fijian*. Chicago: University of Chicago Press.

—— 1991. *A new approach to English grammar, on semantic principles*. Oxford: Clarendon Press.

—— 1994. *Ergativity*. Cambridge: Cambridge University Press.

—— 1999. 'Semantic roles and syntactic functions: the semantic base for a typology', *Proceedings of the 35th Annual Meeting of the Chicago Linguistic Society, Part 2: Papers from the Panels*, 323–41.

—— 2002. 'Copula clauses in Australian languages: a typological perspective', *Anthropological Linguistics*, 44: 1–36.

—— 2004a. *The Jarawara language of southern Amazonia*. Oxford: Oxford University Press.

—— 2004b. 'Adjective classes in typological perspective', pp. 1–49 of *Adjective classes: a cross-linguistic typology*, edited by R. M. W. Dixon and A. Y. Aikhenvald. Oxford: Oxford University Press.

—— Forthcoming. 'Clitics in English'.

DUFFLEY, P. J. 1992. *The English infinitive*. London: Longman.

ENGLAND, N. C. 1983. *A grammar of Mam, a Mayan language*. Austin: University of Texas Press.

ERADES, P. A. 1950a. 'Points of Modern English syntax, X', *English Studies*, 31: 121–4.

—— 1950b. 'Points of Modern English syntax, XII', *English Studies*, 31: 153–7.

—— 1959/60. 'Points of Modern English syntax, XXXVIII', *English Studies*, 40: 462–3, 41: 58–61.

EVANS, N. D. 1995. *A grammar of Kayardild: with historical-comparative notes on Tangkic*. Berlin: Mouton de Gruyter.

FILLMORE, C. J. 1968. 'The case for case', pp. 1–88 of *Universals in linguistic theory*, edited by E. Bach and R. T. Harms. New York: Holt, Rinehart and Winston.

FOLEY, W. A. 1991. *The Yimas language of New Guinea*. Stanford: Stanford University Press.

—— and Van Valin, R. D. 1984. *Functional syntax and universal grammar*. Cambridge: Cambridge University Press.

FRASER, B. 1974. *The verb-particle combination in English*. Tokyo: Taishukan. Reprinted, with corrections, New York: Academic Press, 1976.

FREED, A. F. 1979. *The semantics of English aspectual complementation*. Dordrecht: Reidel.

GIVÓN, T. 1979. *On understanding grammar*. New York: Academic Press.

—— 1984. 'Direct object and dative shifting: semantic and pragmatic case', pp. 151–82 of *Objects: towards a theory of grammatical relations*, edited by F. Plank. London: Academic Press.

—— and Yang, L. 1994. 'The rise of the English GET-passive', pp. 119–49 of *Voice, form and function*, edited by B. Fox and P. J. Hopper. Amsterdam: John Benjamins.

GREEN, G. 1974. *Semantics and syntactic regularity*. Bloomington: Indiana University Press.

GREENBAUM, S. 1969. *Studies in English adverbial usage*. London: Longmans.

—— and Quirk, R. 1990. *A student's grammar of the English language*. Harlow: Longman.

HAAS, M. 1940. *Tunica*. New York: J. J. Augustin.

HALL, R. M. R. 1970. 'A note on *Will* vs. *Going to*', *Linguistic Inquiry*, 1: 138–9.

HALLIDAY, M. A. K. 1967. *Grammar, society and the noun*. London: University College London.

HALPERN, A. M. 1942. 'Yuman kinship terms', *American Anthropologist*, 44: 425–41.

HARRIS, R. 2003. *Pompeii*. London: Hutchinson.

HASEGAWA, K. 1968. 'The passive construction in English', *Language*, 44: 230–43.

HASSELGÅRD, H. 1996. *Where and when? Positional and functional conventions for sequences of time and space adverbials in present-day English*. Oslo: Scandinavian University Press.

HENRY, A, 1992. 'Infinitives in a for-to dialect', *Natural Language and Linguistic Theory*, 10: 270–301.

HOOPER, J. B. 1975. 'On assertive predicates', pp. 91–124 of *Syntax and semantics*, 4, edited by J. B. Kimball. New York: Academic Press.

HOPPER, P. J., and Thompson, S. A. 1980. 'Transitivity in grammar and discourse', *Language*, 56: 251–99.

HOUSEHOLDER, F. W. 1981. *The syntax of Apollonius Dyscolus*. Amsterdam: John Benjamins.

HUDDLESTON, R. D. 1971. *The sentence in written English*. Cambridge: Cambridge University Press.

—— 1984. *Introduction to the grammar of English*. Cambridge: Cambridge University Press.

—— and Pullum, G. K. 2002. *The Cambridge grammar of the English language*. Cambridge: Cambridge University Press.

JACKENDOFF, R. 1972. *Semantic interpretation in generative grammar*. Cambridge, MA: MIT Press.

—— 1997. 'Twistin' the night away', *Language*, 73: 534–59.

JACOBSON, P. 1982. 'Comments on "Subcategorization and grammatical relations" by Jane Grimshaw', pp. 57–66 of *Subjects and other subjects* (Proceedings of the

Harvard Conference on the Representation of Grammatical Relations), edited by A. Zaenen. Bloomington: Indiana University Linguistics Club.

JESPERSEN, O. 1909–49. *A Modern English grammar on historical principles*. Copenhagen: Munksgaard; London: Allen and Unwin.

—— 1917. *Negation in English and other languages*. Copenhagen: Det. Kgl. Danske Videnskabernes Selskab. Historisk-filologiske Meddelelser. [Reprinted as pp. 3–151 of *Selected writings of Otto Jespersen*. London: Allen and Unwin; Tokyo: Senjo, 1933.]

JOHANSSON, S., and OKSEFJELL, S. 1998. '*A friend of my mother('s)*: on the use of genitive vs. common case in postmodifying *of*-phrases', *Studia Anglica Posnaniensia*, 33: 153–64.

KEENAN, E. L. 1980. 'Passive is phrasal (not sentential or lexical)', pp. 181–213 of *Lexical grammar*, edited by T. Hoekstra, H. van der Hulst and M. Moortgat. Dordrecht: Foris.

—— 1985. 'Passive in the world's languages', pp. 243–81 of *Language typology and syntactic description*, vol. 1, *Clause structure*, edited by T. Shopen. Cambridge: Cambridge University Press.

KEMMER, S. 1993. *The middle voice*. Amsterdam: John Benjamins.

KEYSER, S. J., and ROEPER, T. 1984. 'On the middle and ergative constructions in English', *Linguistic Inquiry*, 15: 381–416.

KIM, YUN KUNG. 1995. *Tiksŭn yŏngmunpŏp*. Seoul: Han'guk Munhwa-sa (Korean Cultural Company). [Translation into Korean of the first eight chapters of Dixon 1991.]

KIPARSKY, P., and KIPARSKY, C. 1970. 'Fact', pp. 143–73 of *Progress in linguistics*, edited by M. Bierwisch and K. Heidolph. The Hague: Mouton. [Reprinted as pp. 345–69 of *Semantics: an interdisciplinary reader in philosophy, linguistics and psychology*, edited by D. D. Steinberg and L. A. Jakobovits. Cambridge: Cambridge University Press, 1971.]

KJELLMER, G. 1984. 'Why *great: greatly* but not *big: bigly*? On the formation of English adverbs in *-ly*', *Studia Linguistica*, 38: 1–19.

KREIDLER, C. W. 1991. Review of Dixon 1991. *Georgetown Journal of Languages and Linguistics*, 2: 195–202.

KRUISINGA, E. 1927. 'Contributions to English syntax XVI: retained accusative in passive sentences', *English Studies*, 9: 38–40.

LAKOFF, G. 1970. *Irregularity in syntax*. New York: Holt.

—— 1977. 'Linguistic gestalts', *Papers from the Regional Meeting of the Chicago Linguistic Society*, 13: 236–87.

LAKOFF, R. 1969. 'Some reasons why there can't be any some-any rule', *Language* 45: 608–15.

—— 1971. 'Passive resistance', *Papers from the Regional Meeting of the Chicago Linguistic Society*, 7: 149–61.

LANGACKER, R. W. 1972. *Fundamentals of linguistic analysis*. New York: Harcourt, Brace, Jovanovich.

—— and MUNRO, P. 1975. 'Passives and their meaning', *Language*, 51: 789–830.

LEECH, G. N. 1971. *Meaning and the English verb*. London: Longman.

—— and SVARTVIK, J. 1975. *A communicative grammar of English*. London: Longman.

LEVIN, B. 1993. *English verb classes and alternations: a preliminary investigation*. Chicago: University of Chicago Press.

LIPKA, L. 1972. *Semantic structure and word-formation: verb particle constructions in Contemporary English*. Munich: Fink.

MCCAWLEY, J. D. 1979. 'On identifying the remains of deceased clauses', pp. 84–95 of his *Adverbs, vowels and other objects of wonder*. Chicago: University of Chicago Press.

—— 1988a. 'Adverbial NPs: bare or clad in see-through garb?', *Language*, 64: 583–90.

—— 1988b. *The syntactic phenomena of English*, vol. 2. Chicago: University of Chicago Press.

MCDAVID, V. 1964. 'The alternation of "that" and zero in noun clauses', *American Speech*, 39: 102–13.

MCINTOSH, A. 1966. 'Predictive statements', pp. 303–20 of *In memory of J. R. Firth*, edited by C. E. Bazell, J. C. Catford, M. A. K. Halliday and R. H. Robins. London: Longmans.

MAKEBA, M. 1988. *Makeba, my story*. London: Bloomsbury.

MARCHAND, H. 1969. *The categories and types of present-day English word-formation*. Munich: Beck.

MATISOFF, J. A. 1973. *The grammar of Lahu* (University of California Publications in Linguistics 75). Berkeley and Los Angeles: University of California Press.

MATTHEWS, P. H. 1997. *The concise Oxford dictionary of linguistics*. Oxford: Oxford University Press.

MENZEL, P. 1975. *Semantics and syntax in complementation*. The Hague: Mouton.

NEWMEYER, F. J. 1970. 'On the alleged boundary between syntax and semantics', *Foundations of Language*, 6: 178–86.

—— 1975. *English aspectual verbs*. The Hague: Mouton.

NEY, J. W. 1981. *Semantic structure for the syntax of complements and auxiliaries in English*. The Hague: Mouton.

NICHOLS, J. 1978. 'Secondary predicates', *Proceedings of the Annual Meeting of the Berkeley Linguistics Society*, 4: 114–27.

NICKEL, G. 1968. 'Complex verb structures in English', *International Review of Applied Linguistics*, 6: 1–21.

NOONAN, M. 1985. 'Complementation', pp. 42–140 of *Language typology and syntactic description*, vol. 2, *Complex constructions*, edited by T. Shopen. Cambridge: Cambridge University Press.

NORRIS, G. 1994. *William Dampier, Buccaneer explorer*. London: Folio Society.

OLSSON, Y. 1961. *On the syntax of the English verb, with special reference to* HAVE A LOOK *and similar complex structures*. Gothenburg: Elanders Boktryckeri Aktiebolag.

OOSTEN, J. Van. 1977. 'Subjects and agenthood in English', *Papers from the Regional Meeting of the Chicago Linguistic Society*, 13: 459–71.

OSBORN, H. A., Jr. 1967. 'Warao III: verbs and suffixes', *International Journal of American Linguistics*, 33: 46–64.

PALMER, F. R. 1979. *Modality and the English modals*. London: Longman.

PERLMUTTER, D. M. 1970. 'The two verbs *begin*', pp. 107–19 of *Readings in English transformational grammar*, edited by R. A. Jacobs and P. S. Rosenbaum. Waltham, MA: Ginn.

——— 1978. 'Impersonal passives and the unaccusative hypothesis', *Proceedings of the Annual Meeting of the Berkeley Linguistics Society*, 4: 157–89.

——— and SOAMES, S. 1979. *Syntactic argumentation and the structure of English*. Berkeley and Los Angeles: University of California Press.

PINKER, S. 1989. *Learnability and cognition, the acquisition of argument structure*. Cambridge, MA: MIT Press.

POUTSMA, H. 1914–29. *A grammar of Late Modern English*. Groningen: Noordhoff.

PRINCE, E. 1972. 'A note on aspect in English: the *take a walk* construction', pp. 409–20 of *Transformationelle analyse*, edited by S. Plötz. Berlin: Athenäum.

——— 1974. 'English aspectual constructions', Ph.D. dissertation, University of Pennsylvania.

——— 1982. 'The simple futurate: not simply progressive futurate minus progressive', *Papers from the Regional Meeting of the Chicago Linguistic Society*, 18: 453–65.

PULLUM, G. K. 1974. 'Restating doubl-ing', *Glossa*, 8: 109–20.

QUIRK, R. 1957. 'Relative clauses in educated spoken English', *English Studies*, 38: 97–109.

——— and GREENBAUM, S. 1973. *A university grammar of English*. London: Longman. [Published in USA as *A concise grammar of contemporary English*. New York: Harcourt, Brace, Jovanovich, 1973.]

——— ——— LEECH, G., and SVARTVIK, J. 1985. *A comprehensive grammar of the English language*. London: Longman.

RADFORD, A. 1988. *Transformational grammar: a first course*. Cambridge: Cambridge University Press.

RANSOM, E. N. 1986. *Complementation, its meanings and forms*. Amsterdam: John Benjamins.

RICE, S. 1987. 'Towards a transitive prototype: evidence for some atypical English passives', *Proceedings of the Annual Meeting of the Berkeley Linguistics Society*, 13: 422–34.

RIDDLE, E. 1975. 'Some pragmatic conditions on complementiser choice', *Papers from the Regional Meeting of the Chicago Linguistic Society*, 11: 467–74.

ROSENBAUM, P. S. 1967. *The grammar of English predicate complement constructions*. Cambridge, MA: MIT Press.

ROSS, J. R. 1972. 'Doubl-ing', *Linguistic Inquiry*, 3: 61–86.

SAPIR, E. 1922. 'The Takelma language of south-western Oregon', pp. 1–296 of *Handbook of American Indian languages*, vol. 2, edited by F. Boas (Bulletin 40, Bureau of American Ethnology, Smithsonian Institution, Washington, DC).

—— 1930. 'Southern Paiute: a Shoshonean language', *Proceedings of the American Academy for Arts and Sciences*, 65: 1–296.

—— 1949. *Selected writings of Edward Sapir in language, culture and personality*, edited by D. G. Mandelbaum. Berkeley and Los Angeles: University of California Press.

SCHMERLING, S. F. 1978. 'Synonymy judgments as syntactic evidence', pp. 299–313 of *Pragmatics* edited by P. Cole (Syntax and Semantics, 9). New York: Academic Press.

SINHA, A. K. 1974. 'How passive are passives?', *Papers from the Regional Meeting of the Chicago Linguistic Society*, 10: 631–42.

STEIN, G. 1991. 'The phrasal verb type "to have a look" in Modern English'. *International Review of Applied Linguistics in Language Teaching*, 29: 1–29.

STOCKWELL, R. P., SCHACHTER, P., and PARTEE, B. H. 1973. *The major syntactic structures of English*. New York: Holt.

STRANG, B. M. H. 1970. *A history of English*. London: Methuen.

SVARTVIK, J. 1966. *On voice in the English verb*. The Hague: Mouton.

SWEET, H. 1891–8. *A new English grammar, logical and historical*. Oxford: Clarendon Press.

THOMPSON, S. 1973. 'On subjectless gerunds in English', *Foundations of Language*, 9: 374–83.

—— 1987. 'The passive in English, a discourse perspective', pp. 497–511 of *In Honor of Ilse Lehiste: Ilse Lehiste Pühendusteos*, edited by R. Channen and L. Shockey. Dordrecht: Foris.

TOTTIE, G. 1991. *Negation in English speech and writing: a study in variation*. San Diego: Academic Press.

TRUDGILL, P., and HANNAH, J. 1982. *International English: a guide to varieties of Standard English*. London: Edward Arnold.

URMSON, J. O. 1952. 'Parenthetical verbs', *Mind*, 61: 480–96. [Reprinted as pp. 220–40 of *Philosophy and ordinary language*, edited by C. E. Caton. Urbana: University of Illinois Press, 1963.]

VAN DER GAAF, W. 1930. 'The passive of a verb accompanied by a preposition', *English Studies*, 12: 1–24.

van Ek, J. A. 1966. *Four complementary studies of predication in contemporary British English*. Groningen: Wolters.

Vendler, Z. 1967. *Linguistics in philosophy*. Ithaca, NY: Cornell University Press.

—— 1972. *Res cogitans: an essay in rational psychology*. Ithaca, NY: Cornell University Press.

Vissler, Th. 1963. *An historical syntax of the English language*, part 1, *Syntactical units with one verb*. Leiden: E. J. Brill.

West, M. 1953. *A general service list of English words*. Revised and enlarged edition. London: Longmans.

Wierzbicka, A. 1982. 'Why can you *have a drink* when you can't *\*have an eat?*', *Language*, 58: 753–99.

—— 1988. *The semantics of grammar*. Amsterdam: John Benjamins.

Zandvoort, R. W. 1966. *A handbook of English grammar*, fourth edition. London: Longmans.

# Books by R. M. W. Dixon

## On linguistics

Linguistic science and logic
What *is* language? A new approach to linguistic description
The Dyirbal language of North Queensland
A grammar of Yidiɲ
The languages of Australia
Where have all the adjectives gone? and other essays in semantics and
  syntax
Searching for Aboriginal languages: memoirs of a field worker
A grammar of Boumaa Fijian
Words of our country: stories, place names and vocabulary in Yidiny, the
  Aboriginal language of the Cairns-Yarrabah region
Ergativity
The rise and fall of languages
Australian languages: their nature and development
The Jarawara language of southern Amazonia

## with W. S. Ransom and Mandy Thomas

Australian Aboriginal words in English: their origin and meaning

## with Grace Koch

Dyirbal song poetry: the oral literature of an Australian rainforest people

## On music

## with John Godrich

Recording the blues

## with John Godrich and Howard Rye

Blues and gospel records, 1890–1943

## Novels (under the name Hosanna Brown)

I spy, you die
Death upon a spear

## Editor of books on linguistics

Grammatical categories in Australian languages
Studies in ergativity

## with Barry J. Blake

Handbook of Australian languages, volumes 1–5

## with Martin Duwell

The honey ant men's long song, and other Aboriginal song poems
Little Eva at Moonlight Creek: further Aboriginal song poems

## with Alexandra Y. Aikhenvald

The Amazonian languages
Changing valency: case studies in transitivity
Areal diffusion and genetic inheritance: problems in comparative linguistics
Word, a cross-linguistic typology
Studies in evidentiality
Adjective classes: a cross-linguistic typology
Serial verb constructions: a cross-linguistic typology

## with Alexandra Y. Aikhenvald and Masayuki Onishi

Non-canonical marking of subjects and objects

# Index

Sample members of Verb and Adjective classes have their TYPE or TYPE/SUBTYPE indicated in parentheses. Note that occurrences in the Preface, Appendix and References are not indexed.